William Cronon

Historians and economists will here find what their fields have in common – the movement since the 1950s known variously as "cliometrics," "econometric history," or "historical economics." A leading figure in the movement, Donald McCloskey, has compiled with the help of George Hersh and a panel of distinguished advisers the only full bibliography of historical economics. The many thousands of items cover all countries for all periods in which historical economics has been written. The book will be useful to all economic historians, as well as to quantitative historians, applied economists, historical demographers, business historians, national income accountants, and social historians.

A Bibliography of Historical Economics to 1980

A Bibliography of Historical Economics to 1980

DONALD N. McCLOSKEY AND GEORGE K. HERSH, JR.

With the assistance of
John Coatsworth, Stefano Fenoaltea, John Komlos,
Michelle McAlpin, Pedro de Mello, Richard Roehl,
Lars Sandberg, Gary Saxenhouse, and Steven Webb
and
Nejat Anbarci, Metin Cosgel, Kevin O'Meara

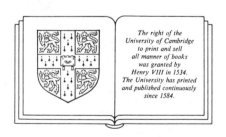

*The right of the
University of Cambridge
to print and sell
all manner of books
was granted by
Henry VIII in 1534.
The University has printed
and published continuously
since 1584.*

CAMBRIDGE UNIVERSITY PRESS
Cambridge
New York   Port Chester   Melbourne   Sydney

Published by the Press Syndicate of the University of Cambridge
The Pitt Building, Trumpington Street, Cambridge CB2 1RP
40 West 20th Street, New York, NY 10011, USA
10 Stamford Road, Oakleigh, Melbourne 3166, Australia

© Cambridge University Press 1990

First published 1990

Printed in the United States of America

Library of Congress Cataloging-in-Publication Data
McCloskey, Donald N.
A bibliography of historical economics to 1980 / Donald N.
McCloskey and George K. Hersh, Jr.; with the assistance of John Coatsworth . . . [et al.].
p. cm.
ISBN 0-521-40327-8
1. Historical school of economics – Bibliography. I. Hersh,
George K. II. Title.
Z7164.E2M43 1991
[HB97]
016.33015'42 – dc20   90-45767
                                    CIP

British Library Cataloging in Publication applied for

ISBN 0-521-40327-8 hardback

Contents

Contents

Introduction

by Donald N. McCloskey

A historical economist applies economic methods (usually simple) to historical facts (not always quantitative). Before 1958 little of this was done. In that year two assistant professors at Harvard, Alfred Conrad and John Meyer, published "The Economics of Slavery in the Antebellum South" and two assistant professors at Purdue, Jonathan Hughes and Stanley Reiter, published "The First 1,945 British Steamships." Historical economics since then has widened into a river. The present bibliography begins with the thin, bright stream before the assistant professors and ends with 1980, as the river reached full flow. By now most serious departments of economics have one or two historical economists, members of a group now numbered in the hundreds, with its own Society, an unusually productive annual conference, and cascading generations of youth and grayheads. The movement begun in the United States is spreading to other countries (many foreign scholars also had contributed to the stream before 1958). Important pieces of history have been decisively reinterpreted. And even economics, after a long run of present-mindedness, has begun to think of olden times.

The bibliography contains about 4,300 items. To use a favorite word of Alexander Gerschenkron's, the number flummoxed me. At the project's beginning, in a footnote to a 1978 application to the National Science Foundation (NSF) for its annual conference on historical economics, I reckoned that a complete bibliography would contain at most 500 items. As someone who earns his living making estimates of upper bounds, I am embarrassed by this one. For most purposes a factor of eight is not a very good degree of approximation.

The 4,300 are closely defined – not out of disdain for the other sorts of quantitative history and for the mildly past-conscious economics that the definition excludes, but merely to make the book usefully coherent, as a starting point for further research and as a reminder for reading lists. The bibliography includes almost no book reviews in book-review sections. It includes a few papers in progress (in progress in 1980, that is; most if not all have been published since then), which seems reasonable in the age of the copying machine and prepublication publication. Four thousand published books and articles over a couple of decades exhibit historical economics as a large supplement to economics and to history.

I have avoided the word "cliometrics." Despite its loony charm (it was coined by that same assistant professor, the mathematical economist Stanley Reiter), and its appearance in recent dictionaries (misdefined as "quantitative history" *tout court*), the word "cliometrics" has given the field more trouble than pleasure. If the late Simon Kuznets's work is not covered perfectly in this bibliography, for example, it is partly because he stoutly denied being a "cliometrician," and would not give us his *curriculum vitae* as a starting point for our search in his voluminous output. A few Europeans stayed away from the recent, successful Second International Congress of the Cliometric Society, held in Santander, Spain, under the mistaken impression that "cliometrics" means fancy work beyond their ken. On these grounds, too, Douglass North, one of the founders of the field, edges away from the word. Even my own pamphlet for the Economic History Society, which shows how simple is the economics in historical economics and how workaday are its statistical tools, carries forward the confusion, by its title: *Econometric History*. Historical economics, to repeat, is merely economics about history. National income analysis of past economies, loaded with economic thinking at every step, is well within the fence; so is political economy about the past.

The committee of scholars mentioned on the title page assisted us with languages other than English. George Hersh, Jr., was the administrative director of the project while it was in Chicago. Kevin O'Meara devised the computer program well before such programs became common; Professors Nejat Anbarci of the University of Buffalo and Metin Cosgel of the University of Connecticut saw the manuscript into print. I am to blame for the delays, omissions, misconceptions, misspellings, and errors in classification. I am planning to spend a few centuries in purgatory on these counts.

The Economics Program of the National Science Foundation has played a special role in the field and in the bibliography. Much of the work catalogued here was in some way encouraged by the Foundation – in its series of unique conferences since 1961 highlighting new work (called, alas, the "Cliometrics Conferences") or in its research grants to historical economists. Historical economics would not have flourished without the NSF, and economics would have been the less.

It would have been the less in what it lacks the most, although recently it has shown signs of wider reform. Economics needs what historical economics has gotten from its association with history: seriousness about facts, an interest in the long run, and habits of scholarship that make for a cumulative science. Economics will not be as cumulative as its sister discipline evolutionary biology, say, or its cousin from the Scottish Enlightenment geology, until it takes over some of the practices of history. Historical economics, scientifically speaking, is one of the most advanced parts of economics. If other economists learn to read what has gone before, yet keep their foxy love of theory, they will build a science that makes progress.

At a congressional hearing in 1987, Senator William Proxmire, as was his practice, was torturing the man from the National Science Foundation about silly projects, perhaps worthy of the discoveted Golden Fleece. Someone on Proxmire's staff had caught sight of what was supposed to be such a project in the Economics Program, on the industrial revolution in England. (I forget who the alleged culprit was; I was not the one.) Why, asked the senator, would Americans want to know about such a dusty old subject as the British industrial revolution?

Proxmire had a reputation for being open to argument, so I wrote to him, arguing against the line he took. I tried to say why one would care about dusty old economies, even to the point of compiling bibliographies of what has been written about them:

> Nothing could be more practical for thinking about our present plight [I wrote him in defense of the study of the British industrial revolution], since Britain's is so similar to ours – seventy years on. The leading industrial power loses its market share and then its nerve and finally its principles: that's a story from today's headlines in America, and from yesterday's in Britain. The only way to get the wisdom our people and our leaders need to face relative decline is through historical example. You and I don't want America to repeat the sixty years of misery that Britain has just passed through....
>
> Whatever you think of the policy issue, I suppose you want economics to be good, because you think it useful. Well, good economics must be historical. The data of economics is necessarily historical, because there's no such thing as future data. And for most questions it doesn't matter how old the data is: economic behavior is economic behavior, whenever it occurs. If you think you can explain industrial growth, you had better be able to explain old industrial growth, too. Explaining the data in the few months before April 1987 is not much of a scientific test.
>
> Old data is often a lot better than new. For one thing, it's often a better experiment. Did you know that a good example of a country with a high ratio of government debt to national income is not the USA now but Britain long ago? How long ago? In 1815. If we want to know how debt affects economic growth, then a good, clean, simple experiment is Britain in the age of the industrial revolution.
>
> And old data is often better because the people with an interest in hiding it are dead. Only for a handful of recent cases can you get the intimate files of price fixers to see what devices they use and how to combat them. For the nineteenth century you can get them for any of the numerous companies whose records have survived.
>
> Dozens of other examples come to mind. Here's an instance close to your own heart. I know you are interested in uncovering waste in government. But we can learn more about waste in the First World War, and still better in the Civil War, than we can about waste in the Pentagon now, because there's no one around to protect the guilty. We don't even need whistleblowers: just step over to the archives of the War Department or the major arms manufacturers, and bring along an economic historian. The way waste develops is not some-

thing new. I would think that you in particular would want to find out why waste occurs, in order to do something about it, for good. To do it you need political, economic, and social historians, such as Robert Higgs, in his new book on the growth of public spending in America since 1900. If you don't look into waste during America's progressive age or Britain's Napoleonic Wars you're missing a scientific trick. It would be like confining astronomy to the nearer stars.

Anyway, the issue of Britain's industrial revolution is intrinsically important, because it was the granddaddy of... all [industrial revolutions]. The biggest question in economics, of course, is what explains modern economic growth, the growth which (we learn from historians) has increased our standard of living over the past two centuries by a factor of ten [or twenty]. It started in Britain. I think you'll agree that if we knew what explains modern economic growth we would have made a discovery more important than an awful lot of drugs that cure or machines that think. In fact, we'd have the money to pay for the drugs and the machines. If we could persuade senators to take the discovery seriously, we could eliminate poverty, worldwide.

A pipe dream? It's no more of a pipe dream than the dream of stable democracy that the people of the 1780s wrote and thought about; or of stable monetary and trade systems that the people of the 1880s wrote and thought about. These programs of research in social science worked (for 200 and 30 years, respectively). Nowadays it's the sober judgment of experts in economics and history that by studying economic growth hard we might be able to find a cure for poverty. We've already discovered many useful things about what does *not* explain modern economic growth, which is irritating but the way research on any tough problem tends to go. You probably agree with me that the case doesn't differ obviously from cancer research or fusion power or elementary particle physics. But on these tens of thousands of times more money has been spent than on explaining modern economic growth.

Sure, it's a longshot. We may discover in the end that modern economic growth is just too hard to understand. But we've made a lot of progress, with sums that would not pay for the spare parts for the latest no-go military tank.... It's not in anyone's short-term, practical, applied interest to show that security of contract (say) or elementary education caused economic growth and can cause it again....

So I think you ought to rethink your opposition to research on Britain's industrial revolution. I'd be interested in what you conclude.

Proxmire was a senator of quality. He replied, and agreed, although I do not believe he relented in his pursuit of the National Science Foundation. This bibliography shows that economists are willing to work furiously on the largest scientific problem of the age, the nature and causes of the wealth of nations, and to build a truly historical economics.

Chapter 1

COLLECTIONS, TEXTBOOKS, AND SOURCES

United States

Andreano, Ralph L., ed. *New Views on American Economic Development: A Selective Anthology of Recent Work.* Cambridge, Mass.: Schenkman, 1965.

Brady, Dorothy S., ed. *Output, Employment, and Productivity in the United States after 1800* (Studies in Income and Wealth, vol. 30). New York: Columbia University Press for the National Bureau of Economic Research, 1966.

David, Paul A. and Reder, M.W., eds. *Nations and Households in Economic Growth: Essays in Honor of Moses Abramovitz.* New York: Academic Press, 1974.

Davis, Lance E.; Hughes, Jonathan R.T. and McDougall, Duncan. *American Economic History: The Development of a National Economy.* Homewood, Ill.: Richard D. Irwin, 1961.

Davis, Lance E.; Easterlin, Richard A. and Parker, William N., eds. *American Economic Growth: An Economist's History of the United States.* New York: Harper & Row, 1972.

DeCanio, Stephen J.; Cooley, Thomas F. and Matthews, M. Scott. "ATICS: An Agricultural Time Series-Cross Section Dataset," National Bureau of Economic Research, no. 197, August 1977 [Working Paper].

Dodd, Donald B. and Dodd, Wynelle S. *Historical Statistics of the United States, 1790-1970* (2 vols; vol. 1: *The South, 1790-1970*; vol. 2: *The Midwest, 1790-1970*). University: University of Alabama Press, 1973.

Fishlow, Albert. "Trends in the American Economy in the Nineteenth Century: A Review Article," (Review of William N. Parker, ed. Studies in Income and Wealth. vol. 24. New York: Princeton University Press for the National Bureau of Economic Research, 1960) *Journal of Economic History*, 22(1), March 1962, pp. 71-80.

Fogel, Robert W. and Engerman, Stanley L., ed. *The Reinterpretation of American Economic History.* New York: Harper & Row, 1971.

Gray, Ralph and Peterson, John M. *Economic Development of the United States.* Homewood, Ill.: Richard D. Irwin, 1969.

Gunderson, Gerald A. *A New Economic History of America.* New York: McGraw-Hill, 1976.

Hughes, Jonathan R.T., ed. *Purdue Faculty Papers in Economic History, 1956-1966.* Homewood, Ill.: Richard D. Irwin, 1967.

Hutchinson, William K., ed. *American Economic History: An Annotated Bibliography.* Detroit: Gale Research, 1979.

Klingaman, David C. and Vedder, Richard K., ed. *Essays in Nineteenth Century Economic History: The Old Northwest*. Athens: Ohio University Press, 1975.

Lebergott, Stanley. *The American Economy*. Princeton: Princeton University Press, 1976.

Lee, Susan P. and Passell, Peter. *A New Economic View of American History*. New York: W.W. Norton, 1979.

Niemi, Jr., Albert W. *U.S. Economic History: A Survey of the Major Issues*. Chicago: Rand McNally, 1975.

North, Douglass C. and Thomas, Robert P. *A Documentary History of American Economic Growth, 1607-1860*. New York: Harper & Row, 1968.

Parker, William N., ed. *Trends in the American Economy in the Nineteenth Century* (Studies in Income and Wealth, vol. 24). Princeton: Princeton University Press for the National Bureau of Economic Research, 1960.

Parker, William N. *Commerce, Cotton, and Westward Expansion, 1820-1860*. Chicago: Scott, Foresman, 1964.

Porter, Glenn., ed. *Encyclopedia of American Economic History: Studies of the Principal Movements and Ideas* (3 vols). New York: Charles Scribner's Sons, 1980.

Ratner, Sidney; Soltow, James H. and Sylla, Richard E. *The Evolution of the American Economy: Growth, Welfare and Decision Making*. New York: Basic Books, 1979.

Shepherd, James F. and Walton, Gary M. *The Economic Rise of Early America*. London: Cambridge University Press, 1979.

Soltow, James H., ed. *Essays in Economic and Business History. Michigan State University Business Studies*. East Lansing: Michigan State University Press, 1979.

Temin, Peter., ed. *The New Economic History: Selected Readings*. Harmondsworth: Penguin Books, 1973.

Temin, Peter. *Causal Factors in American Economic Growth in the Nineteenth Century*. London: Macmillan, 1975.

U.S. Bureau of the Census., ed. *Historical Statistics of the United States, Colonial Times to 1970* (2 vols). Washington, D.C.: U.S. Government Printing Office, 1975.

Vedder, Richard K. *The American Economy in Historical Perspective*. Belmont, California: Wadsworth, 1976.

Walton, Gary M. and Miller, Roger Leroy. *Economic Issues in American History*. New York: Harper & Row, 1978.

Walton, Gary M. and Robertson, Ross M. *History of the American Economy* (Fourth Edition). New York: Harcourt, Brace, Jovanovich, 1978.

Rest of the World: Statistics

Bank of Japan, Statistics Department., ed. *Hundred Year Statistics of the Japanese Economy*. Tokyo: Bank of Japan, 1966.

Brockstedt, Jurgen. *Statistik der Schiffahrtsbeziehungen Schleswig-Holsteins nach Lateinamerika 1815-1848* [*Statistics of the Shipping Relationships of Schleswig-Holstein with Latin America, 1815-1848*]. Kiel, 1976.

Brockstedt, Jurgen. "Wirtschafts- und Sozialstatistik [Economic and

Social Statistics]," in Bracher, ed. *Die Krise Europas 1917-1975* [*Europe's Crisis, 1917-1975*], 1976, pp. 420-35.

Brockstedt, Jurgen. "Wirtschafts- und Sozialstatistik [Economic and Social Statistics]," in Schieder, ed. *Staatensystem als Vormacht der Welt: 1848-1918* [*National Systems as the Supreme Power of the World, 1848-1918*], 1977, pp. 430-7.

Brockstedt, Jurgen. "Wirtschafts- und Sozialstatistik [Economic and Social Statistics]," in Weis, ed. *Der Durchbruch des Burgertums 1776-1847* [*The Escape of the Middle Class, 1776-1847*], 1978, pp. 435-43.

De Brabander, G.L. "The 19th Century Belgian General Censuses as Sources for the Quantification of Regional Industrial Patterns of Specialization," Presented at the Workshop on Quantitative Economic History, Centrum voor Economische Studien, Paper #7502, 1975 [Working Paper].

Feinstein, Charles H. *Key Statistics of the British Economy, 1900-1962* (Second Edition). London: London and Cambridge Economic Service, 1965.

Floud, Roderick C. *Essays in Quantitative Economic History.* Oxford: Clarendon Press for the Economic History Society, 1974.

Hohorst, Gerd; Kocka, Jurgen and Ritter, Gerhard A. *Materialien zur Statistik des Kaiserreichs 1870-1914* [*Statistical Material on the German Empire, 1870-1914*]. (Sozialgeschichtliches Arbeitsbuch, vol. 2) Munchen: Verlag C.H. Beck, 1975.

Kahan, Arcadius. "Quantitative Data for the Study of Russian History," in Lorwin and Price, eds. *The Dimensions of the Past,* 1972, pp. 361-430.

Landes, David S. "Statistics as a Source for the History of Economic Development in Western Europe: The Protostatistical Era," in Lorwin and Price, eds. *The Dimensions of the Past,* 1972, pp. 53-91.

Lorwin, Val R. and Price, Jacob M. *The Dimensions of the Past: Materials, Problems, and Opportunities for Quantitative Work in History.* New Haven and London: Yale University Press, 1972.

Mamalakis, Markos J., ed. *Historical Statistics of Chile.* Westport, Conn.: Greenwood Press, 1978.

McAlpin, Michelle Burge. "Notes on Sources of Agricultural and Demographic Data for South Asia," Presented at the Workshop on the Generation of Quantifiable Historical Indicators for Asian History of the International Studies Association and the Social Science History Association, February 1976 [Working Paper].

McGreevey, William Paul. "Quantitative Research in Latin American History of the Nineteenth and Twentieth Centuries," in Lorwin and Price, eds. *The Dimensions of the Past,* 1972, pp. 477-501.

Mitchell, B.R., with the collaboration of Phyllis Deane., ed. *Abstract of British Historical Statistics* (Reprinted in a revised 2nd edition, 1970). Cambridge: Cambridge University Press, 1962.

Mitchell, B.R., Jones, H.G., ed. *Second Abstract of British Historical Statistics.* Cambridge University Press, 1971.

Mitchell, B.R. *European Historical Statistics, 1750-1970* (Abridged Edition, 1978). London and New York: Macmillan and Columbia University Press, 1975.

Morris, Morris D. "Quantitative Resources for the Study of Indian

History," in Lorwin and Price, eds. *The Dimensions of the Past* 1972, pp. 531-49.

Oden, Birgitta. "Historical Statistics in the Nordic Countries," in Lorwin and Price, eds. *The Dimensions of the Past,* 1972, pp. 263-99.

Ohkawa, Kazushi; Shinohara, Miyohei and Umemura, Mataji., eds. *Estimates of Long Term Economic Statistics of Japan since 1868.* Tokyo: Toyo Keizai Shinpo Sha, 1965.

Sweden Statistika centralbyran. *Historisk Statistik for Sverige,* Del. 1: *Befolkning, 1720-1967* [*Historical Statistics of Sweden,* part 1: *Population, 1720-1967*]. Stockholm: National Central Bureau of Statistics.

Sweden Statistika centralbyran. *Historisk statistik for Sverige,* Del. 2: *Vaderlek, lantmateri, jordbruk, skogsbruk, fiske tom ar* [*Historical Statistics of Sweden,* part 2: *Climate, Land Surveying, Agriculture, Forestry, Fisheries*]. Stockholm: National Central Bureau of Statistics, 1955.

Sweden Statistika centralbyran. *Historisk Statistik for Sverige,* Del. 3: *Utrikeshandel, 1732-1970* [*Historical Statistics of Sweden,* part 3: *Foreign Trade, 1732-1970*]. Stockholm: National Central Bureau of Statistics, 1972.

TePaske, John J. "Quantification in Latin American Colonial History," in Lorwin and Price, eds. *The Dimensions of the Past,* 1972, pp. 431-76.

Tilly, Louise A. and Tilly, Charles. "A Selected Bibliography of Quantitative Sources for French History and French Sources for Quantitative History since 1789," in Lorwin and Price, eds. *The Dimensions of the Past,* 1972, pp. 157-75.

Tilly, Louise A. "Materials of the Quantitative History of France since 1789," in Lorwin and Price, eds. *The Dimensions of the Past,* 1972, pp. 127-55.

Urquhart, M.C. and Buckley, K.A.H., ed. *Historical Statistics of Canada.* Toronto: Macmillan, 1965.

Van der Wee, Herman. "European Historical Statisics and Economic Growth," *Explorations in Economic History,* 13(3), July 1976, pp. 347-51.

Weiss, Thomas J.; Atack, Jeremy and Bateman, Fred. "The Manuscript Census as a Nineteenth Century Data Source," [Working Paper].

Wimmer, Larry T. and Pope, Clayne L. "The Genealogical Society of Salt Lake City: A Source of Data for Economic and Social Historians," *Historical Methods,* 8(2), March 1975, pp. 51-58.

Wright, Gavin. "Note on the Manuscript Census Samples," in Parker, ed. *The Structure of the Cotton Economy of the Antebellum South,* 1970, pp. 95-99.

Yamamura, Kozo and Hanley, Susan B. "Quantitative Data for Japanese Economic History," in Lorwin and Price, eds. *The Dimensions of the Past,* 1972, pp. 503-30.

Rest of the World:
Texts, Overviews, and Collections of Essays

Dick, Trevor J.O. *Economic History of Canada: A Guide to Information Sources.* Detroit: Gale Research, 1978.

Dick, Trevor J.O. "Growth and Canadian Welfare: A History of the Canadian Economy," [Working Paper].

Drummond, Ian M. *The Canadian Economy: Structure and Development.* [Translated into Japanese (1978)] Homewood, Ill.: Richard E. Irwin, 1972.

Floud, Roderick C. and McCloskey, Donald N., eds. *The Economic History of Britain since 1700.* (2 Vols; vol. 1: *1700-1860*; vol. 2: *1860 to the 1970s*). Cambridge: Cambridge University Press, 1981.

Hanley, Susan B. and Yamamura, Kozo. "A Quiet Transformation in Tokugawa Economic History," *Journal of Asian Studies*, 30(2), February 1971, pp. 373-84.

Hawke, Gary R. *The Development of the British Economy, 1870-1914.* Auckland: Heinemann, 1970.

Hawke, Gary R. *Evolution of the New Zealand Economy.* Auckland: Heinemann, 1977.

Herlihy, David. "Quantification and the Middle Ages," in Lorwin and Price, eds. *The Dimensions of the Past*, 1972, pp. 13-51.

Kumar, Dharma., ed. *A Cambridge Economic History of India*, vol. 2. Cambridge: Cambridge University Press, 1981.

Marr, William L. and Paterson, Donald G. *Canada, An Economic History.* Toronto: Macmillan of Canada, 1980.

McCloskey, Donald N., ed. *Essays on a Mature Economy: Britain after 1840.* (Proceedings of the MSSB Conference on the New Economic History of Britain, 1840-1930) London and Princeton: Methuen and Princeton University Press, 1971.

Morris, Morris D. "Trends and Tendencies in Indian Economic History," *Indian Economic and Social History Review*, 5(4), December 1968, pp. 319-88.

Morris, Morris D. and Stein, Burton. "The Economic History of India: A Bibliographic Essay," *Journal of Economic History*, 21(2), June 1961, pp. 179-207.

Neuhaus, Paulo., ed. *A Economia Brasileira: Uma Visao Historica* [*The Brazilian Economy: An Historical View*]. Rio de Janeiro: Editora Campus, 1979.

Pelaez, Carlos M. and Suzigan, Wilson. *Historia Economica do Brasil* [*Economic History of Brazil*]. Sao Paulo: Editora Atlas, 1979.

Rapp, Richard T. and Clough, Shepard B. *European Economic History: The Economic Development of Western Civilization.* New York: McGraw-Hill, 1975.

Rosovsky, Henry., ed. *Industrialization in Two Systems: Essays in Honor of Alexander Gerschenkron.* New York: John Wiley, 1966.

Rosovsky, Henry. "What Are the 'Lessons' of Japanese Economic History," in Youngson, ed. *Economic Development in the Long Run,* 1972, pp. 229-53.

Rostow, W.W. *How It All Began: Origins of the Modern Economy.* New York: McGraw-Hill, 1975.

Sayers, Richard S. and Ashton, T.S. *Papers in English Monetary History*. Oxford: Oxford University Press, 1953.

Toniolo, Gianni. "Alcune tendenze dello sviluppo economico italiano 1861-1940 [Some Tendencies of Italian Economic Development, 1861-1940]," (Reprinted in Toniolo, ed. *L'economia italiana 1861-1940*, 1978, pp. 3-46) in Toniolo, ed. *Lo sviluppo economico italiano, 1861-1940* [*Italian Economic Development, 1861-1940*], 1973, pp. 1-37.

Toniolo, Gianni. "Cause dello sviluppo economico europeo del dopoguerra: una riconsiderazione [Origins of Post-War European Economic Development: A Reconsideration]," *Quaderni storici*, (16), 1971, pp. 174-200.

Toniolo, Gianni. *L'economia dell'Italia Fascista* [*The Economy of Fascist Italy*]. Bari: Laterza, 1980.

Tortella Casares, Gabriel. "El desarrollo de la industria azucarera y la guerra de Cuba [The Development of the Sugar Industry and the Cuban War]," *Moneda y Credito*, (91), December 1964, pp. 131-63.

Tortella Casares, Gabriel. "El principio de responsabilidad limitada y el desarrollo industrial de Espana: 1829-1869 [The Principal of Limited Liability and the Industrial Development of Spain, 1829-1869]," *Moneda y Credito*, (104), March 1968, pp. 69-84.

Yamamura, Kozo. "Toward an Economic Analysis of the Sogoshosha," *Japan Business History Review (Keieishi)*, 10(1), Spring 1973.

Yamamura, Kozo. "Toward a Reexamination of the Economic History of Tokugawa Japan, 1600-1867," *Journal of Economic History*, 33(3), September 1973, pp. 509-46.

Yamamura, Kozo. "Recent Research in Japanese Economic History, 1600-1945," in Gallman, ed. *Recent Developments in the Study of Economic and Business History*, 1977, pp. 221-45.

Chapter 2

METHOD

Andreano, Ralph L. "Recent Research in Quantitative Economic History: Some Conceptual Implications," *Proceedings.* Indiana Academy of Science, 1963.

Andreano, Ralph L. "Editor's Introduction: The New Economic History/What is New?/An Appraisal," in Andreano, ed. *New Views on American Economic Development,* 1965, pp. 3-8.

Andreano, Ralph L. "Four Recent Studies in American Economic History: Some Conceptual Implications," in Andreano, ed. *New Views on American Economic Development,* 1965, pp. 13-26.

Andreano, Ralph L. *The New Economic History: Recent Papers on Methodology.* New York: John Wiley & Sons, 1970.

Basmann, R.L. "The Role of the Economic Historian in Predictive Testing of Proffered 'Economic Laws'," (Reprinted in Hughes, ed. *Purdue Faculty Papers in Economic History, 1956-1966,* 1967, p. 11-34) *Explorations in Entrepreneurial History,* Second Series, 2(3), Spring/Summer 1965, pp. 159-86.

Bateman, Fred. "Comments on Dissertations Presented to the 36th Annual Meeting of the Economic History Association," *Journal of Economic History,* 37(1), March 1977, pp. 276-80.

Benda, Gyula. "New Economic History," *Torteneti Statisztikai Kozlemenyek,* 1977, pp. 261-76.

Best, H. and Mann, R. *Quantitative Methoden in der Historisch-Sozialwissenschaftlichen Forschung* [*Quantitative Methods in Historical and Sociological Research*]. Stuttgart: Klett-Cotta, 1977.

Bruchey, Stuart. "Econometrics and Southern History: Comment on Conrad," Explorations in Entrepreneurial History, Second Series, 6(1), Fall 1968, pp. 59-65.

Cameron, Rondo E. "Has Economic History a Role in an Economist's Education?" *American Economic Review, Papers and Proceedings,* 55(2), May 1965, pp. 112-15.

Cameron, Rondo E. "Economic History, Pure and Applied," *Journal of Economic History,* 36(1), March 1976, pp. 3-27.

Chandler, Jr., Alfred D. "Econometrics and Southern History: Comment on Conrad," *Explorations in Entrepreneurial History,* Second Series, 6(1), Fall 1968, pp. 66-74.

Chandler, Jr., Alfred D. "Comment on Econometrics and Southern History," in Andreano, ed. *The New Economic History,* 1970, pp. 143-50.

Climo, T.A. and Howells, P.G. "Cause and Counterfactuals," *Economic History Review,* Second Series, 27(3), August 1974, pp. 461-68.

Coats, A.W. "The Historical Context of the 'New' Economic History," *Journal of European Economic History*, 9(1), Spring 1980, pp. 185-207.

Cochran, Thomas C. "Economic History, Old and New," *American Historical Review*, 74(5), June 1969, pp. 1561-72.

Coen, Robert M. "Labor Force and Unemployment in the 1920's and 1930's: A Re-examination based on Postwar Experience," *Review of Economics and Statistics*, 55(1), February 1973, pp. 46-55.

Coen, Robert M. "Labor Force and Unemployment in the 1920's and 1930's: A Reply to Lebergott," *Review of Economics and Statistics*, 55(4), November 1973, pp. 527-28.

Cohen, Jon S. "The Achievements of Economic History: The Marxist School," *Journal of Economic History*, 38(1), March 1978, pp. 29-57.

Cole, W.A. "Economic History as a Social Science," in Harte, ed. *The Study of Economic History*, 1971.

Coleman, D.C. "G.R. Hawke on -What? (Rejoinder on the New Draperies)," *Economic History Review*, Second Series, 24(2), May 1971, pp. 260-61.

Coleman, D.C. "The Model Game. Review Essay of 'Causal Explanation and Model Building in History, Economics, and the New Economic History' by Peter D. McClelland (Ithaca: Cornell University Press, 1975)," *Economic History Review*, Second Series, 30(2), May 1977, pp. 346-51.

Conrad, Alfred H. "Econometrics and Southern History," *Explorations in Entrepreneurial History*, Second Series, 6(1), Fall 1968, pp. 34-53.

Danhof, Clarence H. "Discussion of Papers by Lang, DeCanio, Ellsworth, and Lindley Presented to the 31st Annual Meeting of the Economic History Association," *Journal of Economic History*, 32(1), March 1972, pp. 421-22.

David, Paul A. "Economic History Through the Looking-Glass," (Summary of Paper Presented at the Meeting of the Econometric Society, Boston, December 1963) *Econometrica*, 32(4), October 1964, pp. 694-96.

David, Paul A. "The Future of Econometric History: Comments on Wright," in Intrilligator, ed. *Frontiers of Quantitative Economics* 1971, pp. 459-67.

Davis, Lance E.; Hughes, Jonathan R.T. and Reiter, Stanley. "Aspects of Quantitative Research in Economic History," (Reprinted in Hughes, ed. *Purdue Faculty Papers in Economic History, 1956-1966*, 1967, p. 3-10) *Journal of Economic History*, 20(4), December 1960, pp. 539-47.

Davis, Lance E. "Professor Fogel and the New Economic History," *Economic History Review*, Second Series, 19(3), December 1966, pp. 657-63.

Davis, Lance E. " 'And It Will Never Be Literature'- The New Economic History: A Critique," (Reprinted in Swierenga, ed. *Quantification in American History*, 1970, pp. 274-87) *Explorations in Entrepreneurial History*, Second Series, 6(1), Fall 1968, pp. 75-92.

Davis, Lance E. "Five Neophytes in Search of a Mentor: Discussion of Dissertations Presented at the 28th Annual Meeting of the Economic History Association," *Journal of Economic History*, 29(1), March 1969, pp. 183-88.

Davis, Lance E.   "Specification, Identification, and Analysis in Economic History," in Taylor and Ellsworth, eds.   *Approaches to American Economic History*, 1971, pp. 106-20.

Davis, Lance E.   "The New Economic History Re-examined," Presented at the Meetings of the Pacific Historical Association, Palo Alto, California, August 1967 [Working Paper].

De Vries, Jan.   "Comments on Dissertations Presented to the 35th Annual Meeting of the Economic History Association," *Journal of Economic History*, 36(1), March 1976, pp. 297-300.

Deane, Phyllis.   "The Relevance of New Trends in Economic History to the Information Needs of Research Workers," in Perlman, ed.   *The Organization and Retrieval of Economic Knowledge*, 1977.

Desai, Meghnad.   "Some Issues in Econometric History," *Economic History Review*, Second Series, 21(1), April 1968, pp. 1-16.

DeCanio, Stephen J.   "The Inadequacy of Economic Explanations of Major Historical Events," [Working Paper].

Diamond, Arthur M. Jr.   "Age and the Acceptance of Cliometrics: A Note," *Journal of Economic History*, 40(4), December 1980, pp. 838-41.

Dick, Trevor J.O.   "Frontiers in Canadian Economic History," (Summary of 1975 Research Workshop) *Journal of Economic History*, 36(1), March 1976, pp. 34-39.

Dowie, Jack A.   "As If or Not As If: The Economic Historian as Hamlet," *Australian Economic History Review*, (7), March 1967, pp. 69-85.

Easterlin, Richard A.   "Is There Need for Historical Research in Underdevelopment?" *American Economic Review, Papers and Proceedings*, 55(2), May 1965, pp. 104-8.

Easton, Stephen T.   "Continuing Themes in Economic History: A Report on the Meetings of the Economic History Association," *Journal of European Economic History*, 8(3), Winter 1979, pp. 761-72.

Edelstein, Michael and O'Grada, Cormac.   "Property Rights and History: A Report of the Meetings of the Economic History Association," *Journal of European Economic History*, 2(2), Fall 1973, pp. 439-46.

Engerman, Stanley L.   "Discussion: Papers in Economic History," *American Economic Review, Papers and Proceedings*, 57(2), May 1967, pp. 307-10.

Engerman, Stanley L.   "Comments on Dissertations Presented at the 30th Annual Meeting of the Economic History Association," *Journal of Economic History*, 31(1), March 1971, pp. 285-88.

Engerman, Stanley L.   "Recent Developments in American Economic History," *Social Science History*, 2(1), Fall 1977, pp. 72-89.

Engerman, Stanley L.   "Counterfactuals and the New Economic History," *Inquiry*, 23(2), June 1980, pp. 157-72.

Faucci, Riccardo.   "'Vecchia' e 'nuova' storia economica: quarant'anni di discussioni ['Old' and 'New' Economic History: Forty Years of Discussion]," in Toniolo, ed.   *Lo sviluppo economico italiano 1861-1940 [Italian Economic Development, 1861-1940]*, 1973, pp. 71-118.

Fenoaltea, Stefano.   "The Discipline and They: Notes on Counterfactual Methodology and the 'New' Economic History," *Journal of European Economic History*, 2(3), Winter 1973, pp. 729-46.

Field, Alexander J.   "Notes on the Use of Explanatory Models in

European Economic History," [Working Paper].

Fischer, Wolfram. "Some Recent Developments in the Study of Economic and Business History in Western Germany," in Gallman, ed. *Recent Developments in the Study of Economic and Business History,* 1977, pp. 247-85.

Fishlow, Albert and Fogel, Robert W. "Quantitative Economic History: An Interim Evaluation, Past Trends and Present Tendencies," *Journal of Economic History,* 31(1), March 1971, pp. 15-42.

Fishlow, Albert. "The New Economic History Revisited," *Journal of European Economic History,* 3(2), Fall 1974, pp. 453-68.

Floud, Roderick C. *An Introduction to Quantitative Methods for Historians.* London and Princeton: Methuen and Princeton University Press, 1973.

Floud, Roderick C. and McCloskey, Donald N. "The Economic History of Britain since 1700: Editor's Introduction," in Floud and McCloskey, eds. *The Economic History of Britain since 1700,* 1980.

Fogel, Robert W. "A Provisional View of the 'New Economic History'," (Reprinted in Andreano, ed. *New Views on American Economic Development,* 1965, pp. 201-208) *American Economic Review, Papers and Proceedings,* 54(3), May 1964, pp. 377-89.

Fogel, Robert W. "The Reunification of Economic History With Economic Theory," *American Economic Review, Papers and Proceedings,* 55(2), May 1965, pp. 92-98.

Fogel, Robert W. "The New Economic History: Its Findings and Methods," (Reprinted in Fogel and Engerman, eds. *The Reinterpretation of American Economic History,* 1971, pp. 1-12) *Economic History Review,* Second Series, 19(3), December 1966, pp. 642-56.

Fogel, Robert W. "The Specification Problem in Economic History," (A Correction for this article appears in this Journal, vol. 28(1), March 1968, p. 126) *Journal of Economic History,* 27(3), September 1967, pp. 283-308.

Fogel, Robert W. "Historiography and Retrospective Econometrics," *History and Theory,* 9(3), 1970, pp. 245-64.

Fogel, Robert W. "The Limits of Quantitative Methods in History," *American Historical Review,* 80(2), April 1975, pp. 329-51.

Fogel, Robert W. "From the Marxists to the Mormons: Thoughts on Cliometrics," *Times Literary Supplement,* (3823), June 13, 1975, pp. 667-70.

Fogel, Robert W. *Ten Lectures on the New Economic History* [in Japanese]. Tokyo: Nan-Un-Do, 1977.

Friedman, Philip. "Traditionele en Nieuwe Economische Geschiedenis: Een Vergelijking Van Methoden," Amsterdam: Streven, November 1977, pp. 112-17.

Furet, Francois. "L'Histoire Quantitative et la Construction du Fait Historique [Quantitative History and the Construction of Historical Fact]," *Annales: Economies, Societes, Civilisations,* 26(1), 1971, pp. 63-75.

Furet, Francois. "Quantitative History," in Gilbert and Graubard, eds. *Historical Studies Today,* 1974, pp. 45-61.

Gallman, Robert E. "The Role of Economic History in the Education of the Economist," *American Economic Review, Papers and Proceedings,* 50(2), May 1965, pp. 109-11.

Gallman, Robert E. "The Statistical Approach: Fundamental Concepts as Applied to History," in Taylor and Ellsworth, eds. *Approaches to American Economic History,* 1971, pp. 63-86.

Gallman, Robert E. "Comment on Papers by Anderson, Haeger, Kulikoff, and Lindstrom Presented to the 38th Annual Meeting of the Economic History Association," *Journal of Economic History,* 39(1), March 1979, pp. 311-12.

George, Peter J. and Oksanen, Ernest H. "Recent Methodological Developments in the Quantification of Economic History," *Histoire Sociale/Social History,* 2(3), April 1969, pp. 5-31.

George, Peter J. and Oksanen, Ernest H. "Recent Developments in the Quantification of Canadian Economic History," *Histoire Sociale/Social History,* 2(4), November 1969, pp. 76-95.

Goldin, Claudia D. "Comments on Dissertations by Alston and Shlomovitz Presented to the 38th Annual Meeting of the Economic History Association," *Journal of Economic History,* 39(1), March 1979, pp. 336-38.

Goodrich, Carter. "Recent Contributions to Economic History: The United States, 1789-1860," *Journal of Economic History,* 19(1), March 1959, pp. 25-43.

Goodrich, Carter. "Economic History: One Field or Two?" *Journal of Economic History,* 20(4), December 1960, pp. 531-38.

Gould, John D. "Hypothetical History," *Economic History Review,* Second Series, 22(2), August 1969, pp. 195-207.

Green, George D. "Potentialities and Pitfalls in Economic History: Comment on Redlich," *Explorations in Entrepreneurial History,* Second Series, 6(1), Fall 1968, pp. 109-15.

Habakkuk, H.J. "Economic History and Economic Theory," in Gilbert and Graubard, eds. *Historical Studies Today,* 1972, pp. 27-44.

Hacker, Louis H. "The New Revolution in Economic History. Review Essay of 'Railroads and Economic Growth: Essays in Econometric History' by Robert W. Fogel (Baltimore: Johns Hopkins University Press, 1964)," *Explorations in Entrepreneurial History,* 3(3), Spring 1966, pp. 159-75.

Harley, C. Knick. "Comments on Dissertations Presented at the 37th Annual Meeting of the Economic History Association," *Journal of Economic History,* 38(1), March 1978, pp. 297-300.

Hartwell, R.M. "Is the New Economic History an Export Product? A Comment on J.R.T. Hughes," in McCloskey, ed. *Essays on a Mature Economy.* 1971, pp. 413-22.

Hartwell, R.M. "Good Old Economic History," *Journal of Economic History,* 33(1), March 1973, pp. 28-40.

Hawke, Gary R. "Quantitative Economic History," in Social Science Research Council, ed. *Research in Economic and Social History,* 1971, pp. 19-25.

Hawke, Gary R. "D.C. Coleman on the Counterfactual History of the New Draperies," *Economic History Review,* Second Series, 24(2), May 1971, pp. 258-59.

Heckscher, Eli. "A Plea for Theory in Economic History," *Economic Journal,* 39, Supplement, January 1929, pp. 525-34.

Heckscher, Eli. "The Aspects of Economic History," in *Economic Essays in Honour of Gustav Cassel,* 1933, pp. 705-20.

11

Hohenberg, Paul M. "Comments on Dissertations Presented to the 33rd Annual Meeting of the Economic History Association," *Journal of Economic History*, 34(1), March 1974, pp. 308-12.

Hohorst, Gerd. "Historische Sozialstatistik und statistische Methoden in der Geschichtswissenschaft [Historical Social Statistics and Statistical Methods in the Science of History]," *Geschichte und Gesellschaft*, 3(1), 1977, pp. 109-24.

Hoselitz, Bert F. "Some Problems in the Quantitative Study of Industrialization," *Economic Development and Cultural Change*, 9(3), April 1961, pp. 537-50.

Hughes, Jonathan R.T. "A Note in Defense of Clio (A Reply to Burstein)," *Explorations in Entrepreneurial History*, Second Series, 2(2), Winter 1965, pp. 154.

Hughes, Jonathan R.T. "Fact and Theory in Economic History," (Reprinted in Hughes, ed. *Purdue Faculty Papers in Economic History, 1956-1966*, 1967, pp. 35-57) *Explorations in Entrepreneurial History*, Second Series, 3(2), Winter 1966, pp. 75-100.

Hughes, Jonathan R.T. "Is the New Economic History an Export Product?" in McCloskey, ed. *Essays on a Mature Economy*, 1971, pp. 401-12.

Hunt, E.H. "The New Economic History: Professor Fogel's Study of American Railways," *History*, 53(177), February 1968, pp. 3-18.

Itzcovich, Oscar. "I metodi matematici e statistici nella storiografia [Mathematical and Statistical Methods in Historiography]," Introduzione allo studio della storia, vol. 2 Milano: Marzorati Editore, 1974, pp. 351-428.

Itzcovitch, Oscar and Bulferetti, Luigi. *Orientamenti della storiografia quantitativa [Trends in Quantitative Historiography]*. Roma: Citta' nuova editrice.

Jaeger, Hans. "Nuovi metodi ed ipotesi nella storia economica tedesca [New Methods and Hypotheses in German Economic History]," *Quaderni storici*, (31), April 1976, pp. 409-21.

Jensen, Richard. "Quantitative American Studies: The State of the Art," *American Quarterly*, 26(3), August 1974, pp. 225-40.

Kelley, Allen C. and Williamson, Jeffrey G. "Modelling Economic Development and General Equilibrium Histories," *American Economic Review, Papers and Proceedings*, 63(2), May 1973, pp. 450-58.

Kowalska-Glikman, Stefania. "Quantitative Methods in History: A Conference Report," *Journal of European Economic History*, 3(1), Spring 1974, pp. 189-201.

Kuczynski, Thomas. "Mathematik und Gesellschaftswissenschaften [Mathematics and the Social Sciences]," *Jahrbuch fur Wirtschaftsgeschichte*, (2), 1969, pp. 379-82.

Kuczynski, Thomas. "Wirtschaftsgeschichte und Mathematik: Einige Methodologische Uberlegungen [Economic History and Mathematics: Some Methodological Considerations]," *Gesellscaft und Umwelt: Hans Mottek zum 65, Geburtstag*. Berlin: Akademie-Verlag, 1976, pp. 76-79.

Kuczynski, Thomas. "Wirtschaftsgeschichte und Mathematik (Gesellschaftswissenschaftler beantworten Fragen unserer Zeit) [Economic History and Mathematics (Scientists of History Answer Questions of Our Time)]," *Spektrum*, (5), 1976, pp. 13-14.

Kuczynski, Thomas. "Methodologische Uberlegungen zur Anwendbarkeit Mathematischer Methoden in der Wirtschaftsgeschichte [Methodological Considerations on the Applicability of Mathematical Methods in Economic History]," *Jahrbuch fur Wirtschaftsgeschichte*, (2), 1978, pp. 157-76.

Kuczynski, Thomas. "Burgerliche Gesellschaftsgeschichte und Mathematik: zumeist unnutze Theorie und nutzliche Empirie, aber auch 'verruckte Ideen' [Bourgeois Social History and Mathematics: Mostly Unused Theory and Useful Empirical Results, but also 'Crazy Ideas']," *Jahrbuch fur Wirtschaftsgeschichte*, (1), 1979, pp. 159-73.

Kuczynski, Thomas. *Zur Anwendbarkeit Mathematischer Methoden in der Wirtschaftsgeschichtsschreibung: Methodologische Uberlegungen und Praktische Versuche [On the Applicability of Mathematical Methods in Economic History: Methodological Considerations and Practical Tests]*. Berlin: Akademie Verlag, 1979.

Kuznets, Simon S. "Statistics and Economic History," *Journal of Economic History*, 1(1), May 1941, pp. 26-41.

Kuznets, Simon S. "The Integration of Economic Theory and History: Comments on Rostow and Meyer & Conrad," *Journal of Economic History*, 17(4), December 1957, pp. 545-53.

Landes, David S. "On Avoiding Babel," *Journal of Economic History*, 38(1), March 1978, pp. 3-12.

Lebergott, Stanley. "A New Technique for Time Series: A Comment on Coen," *Review of Economics and Statistics*, 55(4), February 1973, pp. 525-27.

Lee, Clive H. *The Quantitative Approach to Economic History*. London: Martin Robertson, 1977.

Leontief, Wassily. "When Should History Be Written Backwards?" *Economic History Review*, Second Series, 16(1), August 1963, pp. 1-8.

Levy-Leboyer, Maurice. "La New Economic History [The New Economic History]," *Annales*, 24(5), September/October 1969, pp. 1035-69.

Libecap, Gary D. "Aspects of Modern Growth: A Report of the Economic History Association Meetings," *Journal of European Economic History*, 5(1), Spring 1976, pp. 191-97.

Lindert, Peter H. "Discussion of Dissertations Presented to the 39th Annual Meeting of the Economic History Association," *Journal of Economic History*, 40(1), March 1980, pp. 181-83.

Loschky, David J. "Counterfactuals in Logically Formed Economic Analyses," *Journal of European Economic History*, 2(2), Fall 1973, pp. 421-37.

Loschky, David J. "What's Happening in the New Economic History," *Journal of European Economic History*, 3(3), Winter 1974, pp. 747-58.

Loschky, David J. "Are Counterfactuals Necessary to 'The Discipline and They'!" *Journal of European Economic History*, 4(2), Fall 1975, pp. 481-85.

Martin, David A. "Economics Is Not History: A Comment on the Current State of Economic History," *Agora*, 1(2), Spring 1970, pp. 67-85.

Matthews, R.C.O. "The New Economic History in Britain: A Comment on the Papers by Hughes, Hartwell and Supple," in McCloskey, ed.

Essays on a Mature Economy, 1971, pp. 431-34.

McClelland, Peter D. "Comments on Dissertations Presented at the 31st Annual Meeting of the Economic History Association," *Journal of Economic History,* 32(1), March 1972, pp. 423-27.

McClelland, Peter D. "Model Building in the New Economic History," *American Behavioral Scientist,* 16(5), May/June 1973, pp. 631-51.

McClelland, Peter D. *Causal Explanation and Model Building in History, Economics, and the New Economic History.* Ithaca: Cornell University Press, 1975.

McClelland, Peter D. "Cliometrics Versus Institutional History," in Uselding, ed. *Research in Economic History,* vol. 3, 1978, pp. 369-78.

McCloskey, Donald N. "The New Economic History: An Introduction," [in Spanish] *Revista Espanola de Economia,* May/August 1971.

McCloskey, Donald N. "La nuova storia economica nella Gran Bretagna [The New Economic History of Britain]," *Quaderni storici,* (31), April 1975, pp. 401-9.

McCloskey, Donald N. "Does the Past Have Useful Economics?" *Journal of Economic Literature,* 14(2), June 1976, pp. 434-61.

McCloskey, Donald N. "The Achievements of the Cliometric School," *Journal of Economic History,* 38(1), March 1978, pp. 13-28.

Meyer, John R. and Conrad, Alfred H. "Economic Theory, Statistical Inference, and Economic History," (Reprinted in Conrad and Meyer, *The Economics of Slavery,* 1964, pp. 3-30) *Journal of Economic History,* 17(4), December 1957, pp. 524-44.

Meyer, John R. and Conrad, Alfred H. "Statistical Inference and Historical Explanation," in Conrad and Meyer, *The Economics of Slavery,* 1964, pp. 31-40.

Mitch, David F. "Historical Dimensions of Social and Political Economy: A Report on the 1976 Meetings of the Economic History Association," *Journal of European Economic History,* 6(2), Fall 1977, pp. 481-86.

Moggridge, Donald E. "Comments on Papers by Friedman and Vandagna Presented to the 37th Annual Meeting of the Economic History Association," *Journal of Economic History,* 38(1), March 1978, pp. 202-4.

Morris, Morris D. "Some Comments on the State of Economic History," in Dasgupta, ed. *Methodology of Economic Research,* 1968, pp. 110-16.

Morris, Morris D. "The Economist as Economic Historian," in *Transactions, India Institute of Advanced Studies,* vol. 3, 1971.

Murphy, Earl F. "Comment on Papers by McCloskey, McManus, and Landes and Solmon Presented to the 31st Annual Meeting of the Economic History Association," *Journal of Economic History,* 32(1), March 1972, pp. 95-97.

Murphy, G.S. "On Counterfactual Propositions," *History and Theory,* 8, Beiheft 9, 1969.

Neuhaus, Paulo. "Trinta Anos de Historia Economica na Revista Brasileira de Economia [Thirty Years of Economic History in the Revista Brasileira de Economia]," *Revista Brasileira de Economia,* 31(4), October/December 1977, pp. 587-606.

North, Douglass C. "Quantitative Research in American Economic History," (Reprinted in Andreano, ed. *New Views of American*

Economic Development, 1965, pp. 9-12) *American Economic Review*, 53(1, Part 1), March 1963, pp. 128-30.

North, Douglass C. "The State of Economic History," *American Economic Review, Papers and Proceedings*, 55(2), May 1965, pp. 86-91.

North, Douglass C. "A New Economic History for Europe," in Giersch, ed. *Festschrift in Honor of Walther Hoffmann*, 1968, pp. 139-47.

North, Douglass C. "Economic History," in Sills, ed. *International Encyclopedia of the Social Sciences*, vol. 6, 1968, pp. 468-74.

North, Douglass C. "Beyond the New Economic History," *Journal of Economic History*, 34(1), March 1974, pp. 1-7.

North, Douglass C. "The Achievements of Economic History: Comments on Papers by McCloskey, Cohen, and Forster," *Journal of Economic History*, 38(1), March 1978, pp. 77-80.

Ohlin, G. "No Safety in Numbers: Some Pitfalls of Historical Statistics," in Floud, ed. *Essays in Quantitative Economic History*, 1974, pp. 59-78.

Olmstead, Alan L. "Discussion of Dissertations Presented at the 39th Annual Meeting of the Economic History Association," *Journal of Economic History*, 40(1), March 1980, pp. 183-86.

Parker, William N. "American Economic Growth: Its Historiography in the Twentieth Century," *Ventures*, 8(2), Fall 1968, pp. 71-82.

Parker, William N. "From Old to New to Old in Economic History," *Journal of Economic History*, 31(1), March 1971, pp. 3-14.

Parker, William N. "Comment on Papers by McAlpin, Libecap and Johnson, and Adelman and Morris Presented to the 38th Annual Meeting of the Economic History Association," *Journal of Economic History*, 39(1), March 1979, pp. 177-79.

Parker, William N. "Historiography of American Economic History," in Porter, ed. *Encyclopedia of American Economic History*, 1980, pp. 3-16.

Pope, David H. "Economic History and Scientific Inference," *Australian Economic History Review*, 13(1), March 1973, pp. 1-15.

Purdum, Jack J. "Ranking Graduate Schools in Economic History," [Working Paper].

Rapp, Richard T. and Edelstein, Michael. "Comparative Economic History: Promises and Problems. A Report of the Meetings of the Economic History Association," *Journal of European Economic History*, 4(1), Spring 1975, pp. 209-14.

Redlich, Fritz. "'New' and Traditional Approaches to Economic History and Their Interdependence," *Journal of Economic History*, 25(4), December 1965, pp. 480-95.

Redlich, Fritz. "Potentialities and Pitfalls in Economic History," (Reprinted in Andreano, ed. *The New Economic History*, 1970, pp. 85-99) *Explorations in Entrepreneurial History*, Second Series, 6(1), Fall 1968, pp. 93-108.

Redlich, Fritz. "American Banking and Growth in the Nineteenth Century: Epistemological Reflections (Comment on Sylla)," *Explorations in Economic History*, 10(3), Spring 1973, pp. 305-14.

Reid, Jr., Joseph D. "Understanding Political Events in the New Economic History," *Journal of Economic History*, 37(2), June 1977, pp. 302-28.

Roehl, Richard. "Comment on Papers by Reed and Bean Presented to the

32nd Annual Meeting of the Economic History Association," *Journal of Economic History*, 33(1), March 1973, pp. 228-31.

Roehl, Richard. "Comments on Dissertations Presented to the 36th Annual Meeting of the Economic History Association," *Journal of Economic History*, 37(1), March 1977, pp. 272-75.

Romano, R. "Conveniencias y peligros de aplicar los metodos de la 'nueva historia economica' [Opportunities and Dangers in Applying the 'New Economic History' Methods]," *La historia economica en America Latina*, vol. 1: *Situaciones y metodos*. Mexico City: Ed. SepSetentas, 1972, pp. 237-52.

Rostow, W.W. "The Interrelation of Theory and Economic History," *Journal of Economic History*, 17(4), December 1957, pp. 509-23.

Rostow, W.W. "The Strategic Role of Theory: A Commentary," *Journal of Economic History*, 31(1), March 1971, pp. 76-86.

Rothstein, Morton. "Comments on Dissertations Presented to the 32nd Annual Meeting of the Economic History Association," *Journal of Economic History*, 33(1), March 1973, pp. 333-35.

Rudolph, Richard L. "The New Versus the Old in Austrian Economic History," *Austrian History Yearbook*, 11), 1975, pp. 37-43.

Rutten, Andrew. "But It Will Never Be Science, Either," *Journal of Economic History*, 40(1), March 1980, pp. 137-42.

Salsbury, Stephen. "Comment on Papers by McCloskey, McManus, and Landes and Solmon Presented to the 31st Annual Meeting of the Economic History Association," *Journal of Economic History*, 32(1), March 1972, pp. 92-94.

Sandberg, Lars G. "La 'New Economic History' negli Stati Uniti: rassegna del risultati [The New Economic History in the United States: A Survey of Results]," *Quaderni storici*, (31), April 1976, pp. 382-401.

Saul, S.B. "Some Thoughts on the Papers and Discussion on the Performance of the Late Victorian Economy," in McCloskey, ed. *Essays on a Mature Economy*, 1971, pp. 393-400.

Saxonhouse, Gary R. "Concetti e metodi della scienza economica nelle ricerche di storia giapponese [Economic Concepts and Methods in Japanese Historical Research]," *Quaderni storici*, (31), April 1976, pp. 421-44.

Schaeffer, Donald F. and Weiss, Thomas J. "The Use of Simulation Techniques in Historical Analysis: Railroads Versus Canals," *Journal of Economic History*, 31(4), December 1971, pp. 854-84.

Scheiber, Harry N. "On the New Economic History--And Its Limitations: A Review Essay," *Agricultural History*, 41(4), October 1967, pp. 383-95.

Scheiber, Harry N. "Poetry, Proasism, and Analysis in American Agricultural History: A Review Article," *Journal of Economic History*, 36(4), December 1976, pp. 919-27.

Schremmer, Eckart. "Value-Judgement and Measurement in Quantitative History," *Studia Historiae Oeconomicae*, forthcoming.

Snooks, G.D. "Orthodox and Radical Interpretations of the Development of Australian Capitalism," *Labour History*, 28, May 1975, pp. 1-11.

Snooks, G.D. "The Radical View of Australian Capitalism: A Reply," *Labour History*, 28, May 1975, pp. 18-21.

Soltow, James H. "Recent Literature in American Economic History,"

American Studies International, 17(1), Autumn 1978, pp. 5-33.

Spree, Reinhard. "Zur Theoriebedurftigkeit Quantitativer Wirtschaftsgeschichte (am Beispiel der Historischen Konjunkturforschung und ihrer Validitatsprobleme) [On the Theoretical Shortcomings of Quantitative Economic History (as seen in the Historical Trade Cycle Research and its Validation Problems)]," in Kocka, ed. *Theorien in der Praxis des Historikers,* 1977.

Supple, Barry. "Can the New Economic History Become an Import Substitute?" in McCloskey, ed. *Essays on a Mature Economy, 1971,* pp. 423-30.

Sutch, Richard C. "The Frontiers of Quantitative Economic History, Circa 1975," in Intrilligator, ed. *Frontiers of Quantitative Economics*, vol. 3B, 1977, pp. 399-416.

Swanson, Joseph A. and Williamson, Jeffrey G. "Explanations and Issues: A Prospectus for Quantitative Economic History," *Journal of Economic History*, 31(1), March 1971, pp. 43-57.

Sylla, Richard E. and Toniolo, Gianni. "La 'New Economic History' -- metodi, obiettivi, limiti [The New Economic History: Methods, Objects, Limits]," (Reprinted in Toniolo, ed. *Lo sviluppo economico italiano 1861-1940,* 1973, pp. 41-70.) *Quaderni storici,* (11), 1969, pp. 229-64.

Sylla, Richard E. "Economic History "von unten nach oben" and "von oben nach unten": A Reply to Fritz Redlich," *Explorations in Economic History*, 10(3), Spring 1973, pp. 315-18.

Sylla, Richard E. "The Denigration of Cotton and Other Dissertations: A Discussion," *Journal of Economic History*, 35(1), March 1975, pp. 291-95.

Temin, Peter. "In Pursuit of the Exact," *Times Literary Supplement*, 65(3361), July 28, 1966, pp. 652-53.

Temin, Peter. "General Equilibrium Models in Economic History," *Journal of Economic History*, 31(1), March 1971, pp. 58-75.

Temin, Peter. "Methodology and Evidence in Economic History," *Economic Inquiry*, 12(3), September 1974, pp. 415-18.

Toniolo, Gianni. "La 'New Economic History'," *Quaderni storici*, (31), 1976, pp. 380-461.

Tuma, Elias H. "New Approaches in Economic History and Related Social Sciences," *Journal of European Economic History*, 3(1), Spring 1974, pp. 169-88.

Uselding, Paul J. and Pollack, Martin. "Data, 'Evidence' and Interpretation in Economic History," *Economic Inquiry*, 12(3), September 1974, pp. 406-14.

Von Tunzelmann, G. Nicholas. "The New Economic History: An Econometric Appraisal," *Explorations in Entrepreneurial History*, Second Series, 5(2), Winter 1968, pp. 175-200.

Von Tunzelmann, G. Nicholas. "The Cliometric Conference at Warwick (G.B.), 1978," *Journal of European Economic History*, 9(1), Spring 1980, pp. 219-32.

Von Tunzelmann, G. Nicholas. "Analytical Approaches and Interdisciplinarity in History," Paris: UNESCO, forthcoming.

Walton, Gary M. "Comments on Dissertations Presented to the 32nd Annual Meeting of the Economic History Association," *Journal of*

Economic History, 33(1), March 1973, pp. 326-32.

Weiss, Roger W.   "Comment on Papers by Jones, Shepherd and Walton, and McCusker Presented to the 31st Annual Meeting of the Economic History Association," *Journal of Economic History*, 32(1), March 1972, pp. 163-64.

White, Colin M.   "The Concept of Social Saving in Theory and Practice," *Economic History Review*, Second Series, 29(1), February 1976, pp. 82-100.

Williamson, Jeffrey G. and Kelley, Allen C.   "Modelling Economic Development and General Equilibrium Histories," *American Economic Review, Papers and Proceedings*, 63(2), May 1973, pp. 450-58.

Woodman, Harold D.   "Economic History and Economic Theory: The New Economic History in America," *Journal of Interdisciplinary History*, 3, Autumn 1972, pp. 323-50.

Woodman, Harold D.   "Economics and Scientific History," *Journal of Interdisciplinary History*, 5, Autumn 1974, pp. 295-301.

Woodman, Harold D.   "The Old South and the New History," Presented at the MSSB-University of Rochester Conference Time on the Cross: a First Appraisal, October 1974 [Working Paper].

Woodman, Harold D.   "A Cliometric Key for a Historical Lock," *Reviews in American History*, 4, June 1976, pp. 230-36.

Worland, Stephen T.   "The 'New' Economic History: Historical and Philosophical Antecedents," [Working Paper].

Wright, Gavin.   "Econometric Studies of History," in Intriligator, ed. *Frontiers of Quantitative Economics*, 1971.

Wright, Gavin.   "Comments on Dissertations Presented to the 33rd Annual Meeting of the Economic History Association," *Journal of Economic History*, 34(1), March 1974, pp. 304-7.

Yamamura, Kozo.   "Agenda for Asian Economic History," *Journal of Economic History*, 31(1), March 1971, pp. 199-207.

Yeager, Mary.   "Comment on Dissertations by Rotella and Easton Presented to the 38th Annual Meeting of the Economic History Association," *Journal of Economic History*, 39(1), March 1979, pp. 339-40.

Chapter 3

DEMOGRAPHY

International Migration

Bean, Richard N. "New Estimates of European Migration to British America in the Colonial Period," [Working Paper].

Dunlevy, James A. and Gemery, Henry A. "Some Additional Evidence on Settlements Patterns for Scandinavian Migrants to the United States: Dynamics and the Role of Family and Friends," *Scandinavian Economic History Review*, 24(2), 1976, pp. 143-52.

Dunlevy, James A. and Gemery, Henry A. "The Role of Migrant Stock and Lagged Migration in the Settlement Patterns of Nineteenth Century Immigrants," *Review of Economics and Statistics* , 59(2), May 1977, pp. 137-44.

Dunlevy, James A. and Gemery, Henry A. "British-Irish Settlement Patterns in the U.S.: The Role of Family and Friends," *Scottish Journal of Political Economy*, 24(3), November 1977, pp. 257-63.

Dunlevy, James A. and Gemery, Henry A. "Economic Opportunity and the Responses of 'Old' and 'New' Migrants to The United States," *Journal of Economic History*, 38(4), December 1978, pp. 901-17.

Easterlin, Richard A. "Influences in European Emigration Before World War I," (Reprinted in Fogel and Engerman, eds. *The Reinterpretation of American Economic History*, 1971, p. 384-395) *Economic Development and Cultural Change*, 9(3), April 1961, pp. 331-51.

Ellsworth, Robert A. "Migration of Native Americans: New Data of the Pre-1850 Period," *Inter-Mountain Economic Review*, 5(1), Spring 1974, pp. 13-57.

Farren, Michael A. "Regression Analysis of Factors Influencing Net Migration in the United States," Ohio University Economic History Research Paper no. G-1.

Gallaway, Lowell E. and Vedder, Richard K. "Settlement Patterns of Canadian Emigrants to the United States, 1850-1960," *Canadian Journal of Economics*, 3(3), August 1970, pp. 476-86.

Gallaway, Lowell E. and Vedder, Richard K. "The Increasing Urbanization Thesis: Did 'New Immigrants' to the United States Have a Particular Fondness for Urban Life?" *Explorations in Economic History*, 8(3), Spring 1971, pp. 305-19.

Gallaway, Lowell E. and Vedder, Richard K. "Emigration from the United Kingdom to the United States: 1860-1913," *Journal of Economic History*, 31(4), December 1971, pp. 885-97.

Gallaway, Lowell E. and Vedder, Richard K. "The Geographical Distribution of British and Irish Emigrants to the United States after 1800," *Scottish Journal of Political Economy*, 19(1), February

1972, pp. 19-36.

Gallaway, Lowell E.; Vedder, Richard K. and Shukla, Vishwa. "The Distribution of the Immigrant Population in the United States: An Economic Analysis," *Explorations in Economic History*, 11(3), Spring 1974, pp. 213-26.

Gallman, Robert E. "Human Capital in the First 80 Years of the Republic: How Much Did America Owe the Rest of the World?" *American Economic Review, Papers and Proceedings*, 67(1), February 1977, pp. 27-31.

Gemery, Henry A. and Dunlevy, James A. "Settlement Patterns of 'Old' and 'New' Migrants: A Dynamic Appraisal," *Proceedings: American Statistical Association, Business and Economics Statistics Section (1976)*. Washington, D.C.: American Statistical Association, 1976, pp. 282-85.

Gemery, Henry A. and Hogendorn, Jan S. "Editor's Introduction," in Gemery and Hogendorn, eds. *The Uncommon Market*, 1979, pp. 1-19.

Gemery, Henry A. "Emigration from the British Isles to the New World, 1630-1700: Inferences from Colonial Populations," in Uselding, ed. *Research in Economic History*, vol. 5, 1980, pp. 179-232.

Gjolberg, Ole. "Migration from Norway to the U.S., 1866-1914: A Comment," [Working Paper].

Gould, John D. "European Inter-Continental Emigration, 1815-1914: Patterns and Causes," *Journal of European Economic History*, 8(3), Winter 1979, pp. 593-680.

Gould, John D. "European Inter-Continental Emigration. The Road Home: Return Migration from the U.S.A.," *Journal of European Economic History*, 9(1), Spring 1980, pp. 41-112.

Gould, John D. "European International Emigration: The Role of 'Diffusion' and 'Feedback'," *Journal of European Economic History*, 9(2), Fall 1980, pp. 267-316.

Hamberg, Eva M. *Studier i Internationell Migration [Studies in International Migration]*. [Contains an English Summary] Stockholm: Almqvist & Wiksell, 1976.

Henriksson, Rolf G.H. "An Interpretation of the Significance of Emigration for the Growth of Economic Welfare in Sweden 1860-1910," Ph.D. Dissertation, Northwestern University, 1969.

Higgs, Robert. "Race, Skills, and Earnings: American Immigrants in 1909," *Journal of Economic History*, 31(2), June 1971, pp. 420-28.

Hill, Peter J. "The Economic Impact of Immigration into the United States," (Summary of Doctoral Dissertation) *Journal of Economic History*, 31(1), March 1971, pp. 260-63.

Hill, Peter J. *The Economic Impact of Immigration into the United States*. New York: Arno Press, 1975.

Hill, Peter J. "Relative Skill and Income Levels of Native and Foreign Born Workers in the United States," *Explorations in Economic History*, 12(1), January 1975, pp. 47-60.

Hogendorn, Jan S. and Gemery, Henry A. "Technological Change, Slavery, and the Slave Trade," in Dewey and Hopkins, eds. *The Imperial Impact*, 1978.

Jones, Donald W. "Emigration from the United Kingdom to the United States, 1875-1913," [Working Paper].

Kahan, Arcadius. "Economic Opportunities and Some Pilgrims' Progress:

Jewish Immigrants from Eastern Europe in the U.S., 1890-1914," *Journal of Economic History*, 38(1), March 1978, pp. 235-51.

Kelley, Allen C. "International Migration and Economic Growth: Australia, 1865-1935," *Journal of Economic History*, 25(3), September 1965, pp. 333-54.

Kikuchi, Shigeru. "The Settlement Patterns of Oriental Immigrants to the United States: An Economic Analysis of Immigrant Behavior," Ohio University Economic History Research Paper no. G-12 [Working Paper].

Kuznets, Simon S. and Rubin, Ernest. *Immigration and the Foreign Born* (National Bureau of Economic Research Occasional Paper, no. 46). New York: National Bureau of Economic Research, 1954.

Kuznets, Simon S. "The Contribution of Immigration to the Growth of the Labor Force," in Fogel and Engerman, eds. *The Reinterpretation of American Economic History*, 1971, pp. 396-401.

Marr, William L. "United Kingdom's International Migration in the Interwar Period: Theoretical Considerations and Empirical Testing," *Population Studies*, 31(3), November 1977, pp. 571-80.

McDougall, Duncan M. "Immigration into Canada, 1851-1920," (Reprinted in Hughes, ed. *Purdue Faculty Papers in Economic History, 1956-1966*, 1967, pp. 103-118) *Canadian Journal of Economics and Political Science*, 27, pp. 162-75.

Neal, Larry D. and Uselding, Paul J. "Immigration: A Neglected Source of American Economic Growth, 1790 to 1912," *Oxford Economic Papers*, New Series, 24(1), March 1972, pp. 68-88.

Neal, Larry D. "Cross Spectral Analysis of Atlantic Migration," in Uselding, ed. *Research in Economic History*, vol. 1, 1976, pp. 260-97.

Niemi, Jr., Albert W. "The Role of Immigration in United States Commodity Production, 1869-1929," *Social Science Quarterly*, 52(1), June 1971, pp. 190-96.

Ohlsson, Rolf. *Invandrarna pa Arbetsmarknadan* [*Immigrants on the Labour Market*]. [Contains an English Summary] Lund: University of Lund Press, 1975.

Ohlsson, Rolf. *Ekonomisk Strukturforendring och Invendring* [*Economic Structural Change and Immigration*]. [Contains an English Summary] Lund: University of Lund Press, 1978.

Percy, Michael B. "The Impact of American Immigration Legislation of the 1920's on the Rate of Canadian Emigration to the United States," [Working Paper].

Pope, David H. "Empire Migration to Canada, Australia and New Zealand, 1910-1929," *Australian Economic Papers*, 7(11), December 1968, pp. 167-88.

Pope, David H. "The Push-Pull Model of Australian Migration," *Australian Economic History Review*, 16(2), September 1976, pp. 144-52.

Pope, David H. "The Contribution of United Kingdom Migrants to Australia's Population, Employment and Economic Growth: Federation to the Depression," *Australian Economic Papers*, 16(29), December 1977, pp. 194-210.

Pope, David H. "The Peopling of Australia, 1900-1930," Presented at the Eighth Conference of Economists, La Trobe University, 1979

[Working Paper].

Pope, David H. "The Peopling of Australia: United Kingdom Immigration into Australia, Federation to the Depression," Ph.D. Dissertation, Australian National University, 1977 [Working Paper].

Poulson, Barry W. and Holyfield, Jr., James. "A Note on European Migration: A Cross Spectral Anaylsis," *Explorations in Economic History*, 11(3), Spring 1974, pp. 299-310.

Quigley, J.M. "An Economic Model of Swedish Emigration," *Quarterly Journal of Economics*, 86, February 1972, pp. 111-26.

Richardson, H.W. "British Emigration and Overseas Investment, 1870-1914," *Economic History Review*, Second Series, 25(1), February 1972, pp. 99-113.

Shergold, Peter R. "The Walker Thesis Revisited: Immigration and White American Fertility, 1800-60," *Australian Economic History Review*, 14(2), September 1974, pp. 168-89.

Swierenga, Robert P. and Stout, Harry S. "Dutch Immigration in the Nineteenth Century, 1820-1877: A Quantitative Overview," *Indiana Social Studies Quarterly*, 28(2), Autumn 1975, pp. 7-34.

Swierenga, Robert P. and Stout, Harry S. "Socio-Economic Patterns of Migration from the Netherlands to the U.S. in the Nineteenth Century," in Uselding, ed. *Research in Economic History*, vol. 1, 1976, pp. 298-333.

Swierenga, Robert P. "Dutch Immigrant Demography, 1820-1880," *Journal of Family History*, 5, Winter 1980, pp. 390-405.

Thomas, Brinley. "Migration and the Rhythm of Economic Growth, 1830-1913," *Manchester School of Economic and Social Studies*, 19(3), September 1951, pp. 215-71.

Thomas, Brinley. "The Changing Pattern of Internal Migration in the United Kingdom, 1920-50," in *World Population Congress, 1st, Rome, 1954: Proceedings*, 1955.

Thomas, Brinley. "Migration and International Investment," in Hall, ed. *The Export of Capital from Britain*, 1968, pp. 45-54.

Tomaske, John A. "International Migration and Economic Growth: The Swedish Experience," (Summary of Doctoral Dissertation) *Journal of Economic History*, 25(4), December 1965, pp. 696-99.

Tomaske, John A. "The Determinants of Intercountry Differences in European Emigration: 1881-1900," *Journal of Economic History*, 31(4), December 1971, pp. 840-53.

Uselding, Paul J. "Conjectural Estmates of Gross Human Capital Inflows to the American Economy: 1790-1860," *Explorations in Economic History*, 9(1), Fall 1971, pp. 49-61.

Vedder, Richard K. and Gallaway, Lowell E. "The Settlement Preferences of Scandinavian Emigrants to the United States, 1850-1960," *Scandinavian Economic History Review*, 18(2), 1970, pp. 159-76.

Vedder, Richard K. and Gallaway, Lowell E. "Settlement Patterns of Canadian Emigrants to the United States, 1850-1960," *Canadian Journal of Economics*, 3(3), August 1970, pp. 476-86.

Vedder, Richard K. and Gallaway, Lowell E. "The Geographic Distribution of British and Irish Emigrants to the United States after 1800," *Scottish Journal of Political Economy*, 19(1), February 1972, pp. 19-36.

Vedder, Richard K. and Gallaway, Lowell E. "Settlement Patterns of

American Immigrants, 1850-1968," in Van der Wee, Vinogradov, and Kotovsky, eds. *Fifth International Congress of Economic History,* Vol. 3, 1976, pp. 128-45.

Wilkinson, Maurice. "European Migration to the United States: An Econometric Analysis of Aggregate Labor Supply and Demand," *Review of Economics and Statistics,* 52(3), August 1970, pp. 272-79.

Williamson, Jeffrey G. "Migration to the New World: Long Term Influences and Impact," *Explorations in Economic History,* 11(4), Summer 1974, pp. 357-89.

Williamson, Jeffrey G. "Immigrant-Inequality Trade-Offs in the Promised Land: American Growth, Distribution and Immigration Prior to the Quotas," in Chiswick, ed. *The Gateway,* 1981.

Fertility: United States

Bolino, August C. "Population and Fertility in the Nineteenth Century: A Discussion of Papers by Vedder/Gallaway, Haines, and Mokyr Presented to the 39th Annual Meeting of the Economic History Association," *Journal of Economic History,* 40(1), March 1980, pp. 167-68.

David, Paul A. and Sanderson, Warren C. "The Effectiveness of Nineteenth Century Contraceptive Practices: An Application of Microdemographic Modelling Approaches," in International Economic History Association, ed. *Proceedings of the Seventh International Economic History Congress,* 1978, pp. 60-70.

Easterlin, Richard A. "Factors in the Decline of Farm Family Fertility in the United States: Some Preliminary Results," *Journal of American History,* 63(3), December 1976, pp. 600-614.

Engerman, Stanley L. "Black Fertility and Family Structure in the United States, 1880-1940," *Journal of Family History,* 2(2), Summer 1977, pp. 117-38.

Forster, Colin and Tucker, G.S.L. *Economic Opportunity and White American Fertility Ratios, 1800-1860.* New Haven: Yale University Press, 1972.

Haines, Michael R. "Fertility and Occupation: Coal Mining Populations in the Nineteenth and Early Twentieth Centuries in Europe and America," (Summary) *Population Index,* 40(3), 1974, pp. 417-18.

Haines, Michael R. "Fertility, Marriage and Occupation in the Pennsylvania Anthracite Region, 1850-1880," *Journal of Family History,* 2(1), Spring 1977, pp. 28-55.

Haines, Michael R. "Fertility Decline in Industrial America: An Analysis of the Pennsylvania Anthracite Region, 1850-1900, Using Own-Children Methods," *Population Studies,* 32(2), July 1978, pp. 327-54.

Haines, Michael R. "Fertility and Marriage in a Nineteenth-Century Industrial City: Philadelphia, 1850-1880," *Journal of Economic History,* 40(1), March 1980, pp. 151-58.

Haines, Michael R. "Why Were Nineteenth Century U.S. Urban Black Fertility Rates So Low? (Evidence from Philadelphia, 1850-1880)," Presented at the University of Chicago, Workshop in Economic History, no. 8081-4, October 1980 [Working Paper].

Leet, Don R. "Population Pressure and Human Fertility Response: Ohio, 1810-1860," (Summary of Doctoral Dissertation) *Journal of Economic History*, 34(1), March 1974, pp. 286-88.

Leet, Don R. "Human Fertility and Agricultural Opportunities in Ohio Counties: from Frontier to Maturity, 1810-60," in Klingaman and Vedder, eds. *Essays in Nineteenth Century Economic History*, 1975, pp. 138-58.

Leet, Don R. "The Determinants of the Fertility Transition in Antebellum Ohio," *Journal of Economic History*, 36(2), June 1976, pp. 359-78.

Leet, Don R. *Population Pressure and Human Fertility Response: Ohio, 1810-1860.* New York: Arno Press, 1978.

Lindert, Peter H. "American Fertility Patterns since the Civil War," in Lee, ed. *Population Patterns in the Past*, 1977, pp. 229-76.

Lindert, Peter H. *Fertility and Scarcity in America.* Princeton: Princeton University Press, 1978.

Lindert, Peter H. "Child Costs and Economic Development," in Easterlin, ed. *Population and Economic Change in Developing Countries*, 1980, pp. 5-69.

Mueller, Eva. "Child Costs and Economic Development: Comment on Lindert," in Easterlin, ed. *Population and Economic Change in Developing Countries*, 1980, pp. 69-74.

Sanderson, Warren C. "The Fertility of American Women since 1920," (Summary of Doctoral Dissertation) *Journal of Economic History*, 30(1), March 1970, pp. 271-72.

Sanderson, Warren C. "On Two Schools of the Economics of Fertility," *Population and Development Review*, 2(3-4), September/December 1976, pp. 469-78.

Sanderson, Warren C. "Quantitative Aspects of Marriage, Fertility and Family Limitation in Nineteenth Century America: Another Application of the Coale Specifications," *Demography*, 16(3), August 1979, pp. 339-58.

Sanderson, Warren C. *The Fertility of American Women, 1800-1975.* New York: Academic Press, 1980.

Sanderson, Warren C. and David, Paul A. "Contraceptive Technology and Family Limiting Behavior: Towards a Quantitative History of the Diffusion of Contraceptive Practices in America, 1850-1920," [Working Paper].

Sanderson, Warren C. and David, Paul A. "How Did They Do It?: Strategies of Marital Fertility Control among the Urban Middle Class in Victorian America," Stanford Project on the History of Fertility Control Working Paper no. 6, November 1979 [Working Paper].

Shergold, Peter R. "The Walker Thesis Revisited: Immigration and White American Fertility, 1800-60," *Australian Economic History Review*, 14(2), September 1974, pp. 168-89.

Steckel, Richard H. *The Economics of U.S. Slave and Southern White Fertility.* New York: Arno Press, 1977.

Steckel, Richard H. and Trussell, James. "The Age of Slaves at Menarche and Their First Birth," *Journal of Interdisciplinary History*, 8(3), Winter 1978, pp. 477-505.

Steckel, Richard H. "The Economics of U.S. Slave and Southern White

Fertility," (Summary of Doctoral Dissertation) *Journal of Economic History*, 38(1), March 1978, pp. 289-91.

Steckel, Richard H. "Antebellum Southern White Fertility: A Demographic and Economic Analysis," *Journal of Economic History*, 40(2), June 1980, pp. 331-50.

Sutch, Richard C. "The Breeding of Slaves for Sale and the Westward Expansion of Slavery, 1850-1860," in Engerman and Genovese, eds. *Race and Slavery in the Western Hemisphere*, 1975, pp. 173-210.

Vinovskis, Maris A. "The Demography of the Slave Population in Antebellum America: A Critique of 'Time on the Cross'," *Journal of Interdisciplinary History*, 5(3), Winter 1975, pp. 459-67.

Yasuba, Yasukichi. *Birth Rates of the White Population in the United States, 1800-1860: An Economic Study.* Baltimore: Johns Hopkins University Press, 1962.

Internal Migration: United States

Ball, Duane E. "The Process of Settlement in 18th Century Chester County, Pennsylvania: A Social and Economic History," [Working Paper].

Bogue, Allan G. "Population Change and Farm Settlement in the Northern United States: Comment on Easterlin," *Journal of Economic History*, 36(1), March 1976, pp. 76-81.

David, Paul A. "Fortune, Risk and the Microeconomics of Migration," in David and Reder, eds. *Households and Nations in Economic Growth*, 1974.

Easterlin, Richard A. "Population Change and Farm Settlement in the Northern United States," *Journal of Economic History*, 36(1), March 1976, pp. 45-75.

Easterlin, Richard A. "Population Change and Farm Settlement in the Northern United States: Reply to Bogue," *Journal of Economic History*, 36(1), March 1976, pp. 81-83.

Eldridge, Hope T. and Thomas, Dorothy Swaine. *Population Redistribution and Economic Growth, United States, 1870-1950*, vol. 3: *Demographic Analyses and Interrelations.* (Series edited by Simon S. Kuznets and Dorothy Swaine Thomas) Philadelphia: American Philosophical Society, 1964.

Gallaway, Lowell E. and Vedder, Richard K. "Internal Migration of Native-Born Ohioans: 1850-1960," *Bulletin of Business Research*, 15(6), June 1970, pp. 4-5.

Gallaway, Lowell E. and Vedder, Richard K. "Mobility of Native Americans," *Journal of Economic History*, 31(3), September 1971, pp. 613-49.

Lebergott, Stanley. "Migration in the United States, 1800-1960: Some New Estimates," *Journal of Economic History*, 30(4), December 1970, pp. 839-47.

Lebergott, Stanley. "Industrialization, Regional Change, and the Sectoral Distribution of the U.S. Labor Force, 1850-1880: A Reply (to Vatter)," *Economic Development and Cultural Change*, 23(4), July 1975, pp. 749-50.

Lee, Everett S.; Miller, Ann Ratner; Brainerd, Carol P. and Easterlin,

Richard A. *Population, Redistribution and Economic Growth: United States, 1870-1950*, vol. 1: *Methodological Considerations and Reference Tables*. (Series edited by Simon S. Kuznets and Dorothy Swaine Thomas) Philadelphia: American Philosophical Society, 1957.

Sokoloff, Kenneth and Villaflor, Georgia. "Colonial and Revolutionary Muster Rolls: Some New Evidence on Nutrition and Migration in Early America," National Bureau of Economic Research Working Paper No. 374, July 1979 [Working Paper].

Sutch, Richard C.; Roehl, Richard; Lyons, John and Boskins, Michael. "Urban Migration in the Process of Industrialization: Britain and the United States in the Nineteenth Century," University of California-Berkeley, Center for Research in Management Science, Working Papers in Economic Theory and Econometrics no. 162, August 1970 [Working Paper].

Vatter, Harold G. "Industrialization, Regional Change, and the Sectoral Distribution of the U.S. Labor Force, 1850-1880," *Economic Development and Cultural Change*, 23(3), April 1975, pp. 739-47.

Vatter, Harold G. "Industrialization, Regional Change, and the Sectoral Distribution of the U.S. Labor Force, 1850-1880: Comment on Lebergott," *Economic Development and Cultural Change*, 23(4), July 1975, pp. 739-47.

Vedder, Richard K. and Gallaway, Lowell E. "Internal Migration Patterns in the Midwest, 1850-1960," *Regional Science Perspectives*, 1(1), Spring 1971, pp. 65-82.

Vedder, Richard K. and Gallaway, Lowell E. "Population Transfers and the Postbellum Adjustments to Economic Dislocation, 1870-1920," *Journal of Economic History*, 40(1), March 1980, pp. 143-49.

Vedder, Richard K. and Gallaway, Lowell E. "A Nation of Movers: American Internal Migration in Historical Perspective," [Working Paper].

Vedder, Richard K. and Gallaway, Lowell E. "Migration and the Old Northwest," in Klingaman and Vedder, eds. *Essays in Nineteenth Century Economic History*, 1975, pp. 159-76.

Other Demography: United States

Ball, Duane E. "Dynamics of Population and Wealth in Eighteenth-Century Chester County, Pennsylvania," *Journal of Interdisciplinary History*, 6(4), Spring 1976, pp. 621-44.

Bateman, Fred and Foust, James D. "A Sample of Rural Households Selected from the 1860 Manuscript Censuses," *Agricultural History*, 48(1), January 1974, pp. 75-93.

Easterlin, Richard A. *Population, Labor Force, and Long Swings in Economic Growth: The American Experience* (General Series no. 86). New York: Columbia University Press for the National Bureau of Economic Research, 1968.

Easterlin, Richard A. "The American Population," in Davis, Easterlin, and Parker, eds. *American Economic Growth*, 1972, pp. 121-83.

Easterlin, Richard A. "Population Issues in American Economic History: A Survey and Critique," in Gallman, ed. *Recent Developments in the*

Study of Business and Economic History, 1977, pp. 131-58.

Easterlin, Richard A. "Population," in Porter, ed. *Encyclopedia of American Economic History*, vol. 1, 1980, pp. 167-82.

Engerman, Stanley L. "The Height of Slaves in the United States," *Local Population Studies*, (16), Spring 1976, pp. 45-50.

Fogel, Robert W.; Engerman, Stanley L.; Floud, Roderick C.; Wimmer, Larry T.; Trussell, James and Pope, Clayne L. "The Economics of Mortality in North America, 1650-1910: A Description of a Research Project," *Historical Methods*, 11(2), June 1978, pp. 75-108.

Fogel, Robert W. and Sokoloff, Kenneth. "The Economic and Demographic Significance of Secular Changes in Human Stature: The U.S., 1750-1960," [Working Paper].

Higgs, Robert and Stettler III, H. Louis. "Colonial New England Demography: A Sampling Approach," *William and Mary Quarterly*, Third Series, 27(2), April 1970, pp. 282-94.

Higgs, Robert. "Mortality in Rural America, 1870-1920: Estimates and Conjectures," *Explorations in Economic History*, 10(2), Winter 1973, pp. 177-95.

Higgs, Robert and Booth, David. "Mortality Differentials Within Large American Cities in 1890," *Human Ecology*, 7(4), December 1979, pp. 353-370.

Kelley, Allen C. "Demographic Cycles and Economic Growth: The Long Swing Reconsidered," *Journal of Economic History*, 29(4), December 1969, pp. 633-56.

Kelley, Allen C. "Demographic Changes and American Economic Development: Past, Present, and Future," in Morse and Reed, eds. *Economic Aspects of Population Change*, 1972, pp. 9-48.

Kelley, Allen C. "Scale Economies, Inventive Activity, and the Economics of American Population Growth," *Explorations in Economic History*, 10(1), Fall 1972, pp. 35-52.

Lee, Ronald D. "Causes and Consequences of Age Structure Fluctuations: The Easterlin Hypothesis," Presented at the IUSSP Economic Demography Conference, Helsinki, August 1978 [Working Paper].

Margo, Robert A.; Sokoloff, Kenneth and Villaflor, Georgia. "The Economic and Demographic Significance of Secular Changes in Human Stature: The U.S., 1750-1960," *NBER Reporter*, Winter 1979, pp. 6-8.

Margo, Robert A. and Steckel, Richard. "Height, Health, and Nutrition: Analysis of Evidence for U.S. Slaves," *Social Science History*, forthcoming.

McClelland, Peter D. "The Demographic Dimensions of the New Republic: American Interregional Migration, Vital Statistics, and Manumissions, 1800-1860," [Working Paper].

Meeker, Edward F. "Mortality Trends of Southern Blacks, 1850-1910: Some Preliminary Findings," *Explorations in Economic History*, 13(1), January 1976, pp. 13-42.

Miller, William L. "Slavery and the Population of the South," *Southern Economic Journal*, 28, July 1961, pp. 46-54.

Sutch, Richard C. "Comments on Papers by Smith and Vinovskis Presented to the 31st Annual Meeting of the Economic History Association," *Journal of Economic History*, 32(1), March 1972, pp. 216-18.

Demography: Rest of the World

Akerman, Sune; Johansen, Hans Chr. and Gaunt, David., ed. *Chance and Change: Social and Economic Studies in Historical Demography in the Baltic Area.* Odense: Odense University Press, 1978.

Baines, Dudley. "Birthplace Statistics and the Analysis of Internal Migration," in Lawton, ed. *The Census and Social Structure,* 1978, pp. 146-64.

Branson, William H. "Social Legislation and the Birth Rate in Nineteenth Century Britain," *Western Economic Journal,* 6(2), March 1968, pp. 134-44.

Branson, William H. "Social Legislation and the Demand for Children: Reply to West," *Western Economic Journal,* 6(5), December 1968, pp. 424.

Cole, W.A. "Deane and Cole on Industrialization and Population Change in the Eighteenth Century: A Rejoinder to Neal," *Economic History Review,* Second Series, 24(4), November 1971, pp. 648-52.

Crafts, N.F.R. "Some Aspects of Interactions between Population Growth and Economic Circumstances in the Eighteenth Century," in Minchinton, ed. *Exeter Papers in Economic History,* vol. 11, 1976, pp. 49-64.

Crafts, N.F.R. "English Economic Growth in the Eighteenth Century: A Re-examination of Deane and Cole's Estimates," *Economic History Review,* Second Series, 29(2), May 1976, pp. 226-35.

Crafts, N.F.R. and Ireland, N.J. "Family Limitation and the English Demographic Revolution: A Simulation Approach," *Journal of Economic History,* 36(3), September 1976, pp. 598-623.

Deane, Phyllis and Cole, W.A. *British Economic Growth, 1688-1959: Trends and Structure.* Second Edition, 1968 Cambridge: Cambridge University Press, 1962.

Desai, Meghnad. "Malthusian Crisis in Medieval England? A Critique of the Postan-Titow Hypothesis," Presented at the Social Science Research Council Cliometrics Conference, University of Warwick, January 1978 [Working Paper].

Dutta, Amita. "An Econometric Study of Indo-Ceylon Labor Migration, 1920-1938: A Critique," *Economic Development and Cultural Change,* 21(1), October 1972, pp. 142-56.

Easterlin, Richard A. *Population, Labor Force, and Long Swings in Economic Growth: The American Experience* (General Series no. 86). New York: Columbia University Press for the National Bureau of Economic Research, 1968.

Enke, S. "Economic Consequences of Rapid Population Growth," *Economic Journal,* 81(324), December 1971, pp. 800-811.

Enke, S. "Economic Consequences of Rapid Population Growth: A Reply to Mr. Hanson," *Economic Journal,* 83(329), March 1973, pp. 219-21.

Forster, Colin. "Aspects of Australian Fertility, 1861-1901," *Australian Economic History Review,* 14(2), September 1974, pp. 105-22.

Forster, Colin. "Aspects of Australian Fertility, 1861-1901," *Australian Economic History Review,* 14(2), September 1974, pp. 105-122.

Gemery, Henry A. "Absorption of Population Pressure in Nineteenth

Century Sweden," in Grebenik, ed. *Proceedings of the International Population Conference*, 1971, pp. 1688-702.

Greenwood, Michael J. and Thomas, Lloyd B. "Geographic Labor Mobility in Nineteenth Century England and Wales," *Annals of Regional Science*, 7(2), December 1973, pp. 90-105.

Haines, Michael R. "Fertility and Occupation: Coal Mining Populations in the Nineteenth and Early Twentieth Centuries in Europe and America," (Summary) *Population Index*, 40(3), 1974, pp. 417-18 [Working Paper].

Haines, Michael R. "Population and Economic Change in Nineteenth-Century Eastern Europe: Prussian Upper Silesia, 1840-1913," *Journal of Economic History*, 36(2), June 1976, pp. 334-58.

Haines, Michael R. "Fertility, Nuptiality, and Occupation: A Study of Coal Mining Populations and Regions in England and Wales in the Mid-Nineteenth Century," *Journal of Interdisciplinary History*, 8(2), Autumn 1977, pp. 245-80.

Haines, Michael R. *Economic-Demographic Interrelations in Developing Agricultural Regions: A Case Study of Prussian Upper Silesia, 1840-1914.* New York: Arno Press, 1978.

Haines, Michael R. *Fertility and Occupation: Population Patterns in Industrialization.* New York: Academic Press, 1979.

Haines, Michael R. "Industrial Work and the Family Life Cycle, 1889-1890," in Uselding, ed. *Research in Economic History*, vol. 4, 1979.

Hall, A.R. "Some Long Period Effects of the Kinked Age Distribution of the Population of Australia, 1861-1961," *Economic Record*, 39(85), March 1963, pp. 43-52.

Hanson, II, John R. "Economic Consequences of Rapid Population Growth: A Comment on Enke," *Economic Journal*, 83(329), March 1973, pp. 217-19.

Hicks, Neville. "Demographic Transition in the Antipodes: Australian Population Structure and Growth, 1891-1911," *Australian Economic History Review*, 14(2), September 1974, pp. 123-42.

Hoffman, Elizabeth. *The Sources of Mortality Changes in Italy since Unification.* Ann Arbor: University Microfilms, 1973.

Hohenberg, Paul M. "Migrations et fluctuations demographiques dans la France rurale, 1836-1901 [Migration and Natural Population Change in Rural France, 1836-1901]," *Annales: Economies, Societies, Civilisations*, 29(2), March/April 1974, pp. 461-97.

Hohorst, Gerd. "Bevolkerungsentwicklung und Wirtschaftswachstum als Historischer Entwicklungsprozess Demo-Okonomischer Systeme [Population Expansion and Economic Growth as an Historical Development Process of Demographic-Economic Systems]," in Mackensen and Wewer, eds. *Dynamik der Bevolkerungsentwicklung [The Dynamics of Population Expansion]*, 1972, pp. 91-118.

Hohorst, Gerd. *Wirtschaftswachstum und Bevolkerungsentwicklung in Preussen 1816 bis 1914 [Economic Growth and Population Expansion in Prussia, 1816 to 1914].* New York: Arno Press, 1977.

Hohorst, Gerd. "Demo-Okonomische Entwicklungsprozesse in Preussen im 19. Jahrhundert: Versuch eines Simulationstheoretischen Ansatzes [Demographic-Economic Development Processes in Prussia in the 19th

29

Century: A Hypothetical Simulation Experiment]," [Working Paper].
Johansen, Hans Chr. *Befolkningsudvikling og Familiestruktur I Det 18. Arhundrede* [*Population Development and Family Structure in the 19th Century*]. Odense: Odense University Press, 1975.
Johansen, Hans Chr., ed. *Studier I Dansk Befolkningshistorie 1750-1890* [*Studies in Danish Population History 1750-1890*]. Odense: Odense University Press, 1976.
Kammeyer, Kenneth C. W. and Skidmore, Arthur. "Demographic Transition: A Forcing Model?: Comment," Demography, 12(2), May 1975, pp. 343-50.
Kelley, Allen C. "Demographic Change and Economic Growth: Australia, 1861-1911," *Explorations in Entrepreneurial History*, Second Series, 5(3), Spring/Summer 1968, pp. 207-77.
Kelley, Allen C. "Demographic Cycles and Economic Growth: The Long Swing Reconsidered," *Journal of Economic History*, 29(4), December 1969, pp. 633-56.
Keyfitz, Nathan. "A Historical Perspective on Economic Aspects of the Population Explosion: Comment on Lee," in Easterlin, ed. *Population and Economic Change in Developing Countries*, 1980, pp. 557-59.
Kuznets, Simon S. *Growth, Population, and Income Distribution: Selected Essays.* New York: W.W. Norton, 1979.
Lee, Ronald D. "An Historical Perspective on Economic Aspects of the Population Explosion: The Case of Preindustrial England," in Easterlin, ed. *Population and Economic Change in Less Developed Countries*, 1980, pp. 517-57.
Lee, Ronald D. and Schofield, R.S. "British Population in the Eighteenth Century," in Floud and McCloskey, eds. *The Economic History of Britain since 1700*, vol. 1, 1980, pp. 17-35.
Loschky, David J. "The Usefulness of England's Parish Registers," *Review of Economics and Statistics*, 49(4), November 1967, pp. 471-79.
Loschky, David J. and Krier, Donald F. "Income and Family Size in Three Eighteenth Century Lancashire Parishes: A Reconstitution Study," *Journal of Economic History*, 29(3), September 1969, pp. 429-48.
Loschky, David J. "Urbanization and England's Eighteenth Century Crude Death and Birth Rates," *Journal of European Economic History*, 1(3), Winter 1972, pp. 697-712.
Loschky, David J. and Wilcox, William C. "Demographic Transition: A Forcing Model?" *Demography*, 11(2), May 1974, pp. 215-25.
Loschky, David J. and Wilcox, William C. "Demographic Transition: A Forcing Model?: Reply to Kammeyer and Skidmore," *Demography*, 12(2), May 1975, pp. 351-60.
McAlpin, Michelle Burge. "The Demographic Effects of Famines in Bombay Presidency, 1871-1931: Some Preliminary Findings," Presented at the Annual Cliometrics Conference, University of Wisconsin-Madison, April 1976 [Working Paper].
McInnis, R. Marvin. "Childbearing and Availability: Some Evidence from Individual Household Data," in Lee, ed. *Population Patterns in the Past*, 1977, pp. 201-27.
McInnis, R. Marvin. "The Demographic Focus in Economic History,"

(Summary of 1976 Research Workshop) *Journal of Economic History*, 37(1), March 1977, pp. 234-35.

McKenna, Edward E. "Age, Region, and Marriage in Post-Famine Ireland: An Empirical Examination," *Economic History Review*, Second Series, 31(2), May 1978, pp. 238-56.

Moe, Thorvald. "Some Economic Aspects of Norwegian Population Movements, 1740-1940: An Econometric Study," (Summary of Doctoral Dissertation) *Journal of Economic History*, 30(1), March 1970, pp. 267-70.

Mokyr, Joel. "The Deadly Fungus: An Econometric Investigation into the Short-Term Demographic Impact of the Irish Famine, 1846-1851," in Simon and Davanzo, eds. *Research in Population Economics*, vol. 2, 1980.

Mokyr, Joel. "Malthusian Models and Irish History," *Journal of Economic History*, 40(1), March 1980, pp. 159-66.

Morrow, Richard B. "Family Limitation in Pre-Industrial England: A Reappraisal of Wrigley," *Economic History Review*, Second Series, 31(3), August 1978, pp. 419-28.

Mosk, Carl A. "Demographic Transition in Japan," *Journal of Economic History*, 37(3), September 1977, pp. 655-74.

Mosk, Carl A. "Demographic Transition in Japan, 1920-1960," *Journal of Economic History*, 38(1), March 1978, pp. 285-86.

Mosk, Carl A. "Fecundity, Infanticide and Food Consumption in Japan," *Explorations in Economic History*, 15(3), July 1978, pp. 269-89.

Mosk, Carl A. "The Decline of Marital Fertility in Japan," *Population Studies*, 33(1), March 1979, pp. 19-38.

Neal, Larry D. "Deane and Cole on Industrialization and Population Change in the Eighteenth Century: Comment," *Economic History Review*, Second Series, 24(4), November 1971, pp. 643-47.

Nerlove, Mark. "A Historical Perspective on Economic Aspects of the Population Explosion: Comment on Lee," in Easterlin, ed. *Population and Economic Change in Developing Countries*, 1980, pp. 559-63.

Newell, William H. *Population Change and Agricultural Development in Nineteenth Century France*. New York: Arno Press, 1977.

O'Grada, Cormac. "Demographic Adjustment and Seasonal Migration in Nineteenth-Century Ireland," in Cullen and Furet, eds. *Ireland and France in the 17th-20th Centuries*, 1981, pp. 181-93.

Ohlin, G. "No Safety in Numbers: Some Pitfalls of Historical Statistics," in Floud, ed. *Essays in Quantitative Economic History*, 1974, pp. 59-78.

Ohlsson, Rolf and Bengtsson, Tommy. "Population and Economic Fluctuations in Sweden, 1749-1914," [Working Paper].

Paquet, Gilles. "L'emigration des Canadiens francais vers la Nouvelle-Angleterre, 1870-1910: prises de vue quantitatives," *Recherches Sociographiques*, 5(3), September/December 1964, pp. 319-70.

Paquet, Gilles. "La demographie historique au Canada," *Recherches Sociographiques*, 8(2), 1967, pp. 214-17.

Phelps Brown, E.H. and Hopkins, Sheila V. "Wage-Rates and Prices: Evidence for Population Pressure in the Sixteenth Century," *Economica*, 24(96), November 1957, pp. 289-306.

Phelps Brown, E.H. and Hopkins, Sheila V. "Builders' Wage-Rates, Prices and Population: Some Further Evidence," *Economica*, 26(101), February 1959, pp. 18-38.

Philpot, Gordon. "Enclosure and Population Growth in Eighteenth-Century England," *Explorations in Economic History*, 12(1), January 1975, pp. 29-46.

Philpot, Gordon. "Parliamentary Enclosure and Population Change in England, 1750-1830: A Reply to Turner," *Explorations in Economic History*, 13(4), October 1976, pp. 469-71.

Rudolph, Richard L. "Family Structure and Proto-Industrialization in Russia," *Journal of Economic History*, 40(1), March 1980, pp. 111-18.

Silber, Jacques. "Some Demographic Characteristics of the Jewish Population in Russia at the End of the Nineteenth Century," *Jewish Social Studies*, 42(3-4), Summer/Fall 1980, pp. 269-80.

Sinclair, Al. "Internal Migration in Canada, 1871-1951," Ph.D. Dissertation, Harvard University, 1966 [Working Paper].

Spencer, Barbara; Hum, Derek and Deprey, Paul. "Spectral Analysis and the Study of Seasonal Fluctuations in Historical Demography," *Journal of European Economic History*, 5(1), Spring 1976, pp. 171-90.

Sweden Statistika centralbyran. *Historisk Statistik for Sverige*, Del. 1: *Befolkning, 1720-1967* [*Historical Statistics of Sweden, part 1: Population, 1720-1967*]. Stockholm: National Central Bureau of Statistics.

Thomas, Brinley. "Demographic Determinants of British and American Building Cycles, 1870-1913," in McCloskey, ed. *Essays on a Mature Economy*, 1971, pp. 39-74.

Toutain, Jean Claude. "La population de la France de 1700 a 1959 [The Population of France, 1700-1959]," *Cahiers de L'Institut de Science Economique Appliquee*, 1963.

Tucker, G.S.L. "A Note on the Reliability of Fertility Ratios," Australian Economic History Review, 14(2), September 1974, pp. 160-67.

Turner, Michael. "Parliamentary Enclosure and Population Change in England, 1750-1830: A Comment on Philpot," *Explorations in Economic History*, 13(4), October 1976, pp. 463-68.

Vedder, Richard K. and Cooper, David C. "Nineteenth Century English and Welsh Geographic Labor Mobility: Some Further Evidence," *Annals of Regional Science*, 8(2), June 1974, pp. 131-39.

West, E.G. "Social Legislation and the Demand for Children: A Comment on Branson," *Western Economic Journal*, 6(5), December 1968, pp. 419-24.

Wilkinson, Maurice. "Evidences of Long Swings in the Growth of Swedish Population and Related Economic Variables, 1860-1965," *Journal of Economic History*, 27(1), March 1967, pp. 17-38.

Wrigley, E.A. "Family Limitation in Pre-Industrial England.," *Economic History Review*, Second Series, 19(1), April 1966, pp. 82-109.

Wrigley, E.A. "Marital Fertility in Seventeenth-Century Colyton: A Note on Morrow," *Economic History Review*, Second Series, 31(3), August 1978, pp. 429-36.

Yamamura, Kozo and Hanley, Susan B. "Population Trends and Economic

Growth in Preindustrial Japan," in Glass and Revelle, eds. *Population and Social Change*, 1972.

Chapter 4

NATIONAL ACCOUNTS

United States: National Income

Bean, Richard N. "Surrogate Price Indices for Several Countries in the Nineteenth Century," [Working Paper].

Brady, Dorothy S., ed. *Output, Employment, and Productivity in the United States after 1800* (Studies in Income and Wealth, vol. 30). New York: Columbia University Press for the National Bureau of Economic Research, 1966.

Brady, Dorothy S. "Price Deflators for Final Product Estimates," in Brady, ed. *Output, Employment, and Productivity in the United States after 1800* (Studies in Income and Wealth, vol. 30), 1966, pp. 91-115.

Brady, Dorothy S. "Consumption and the Style of Life," in Davis, Easterlin, and Parker, eds. *American Economic Growth*, 1972, pp. 61-91.

Buckley, Kenneth. "Development of Canada's Economy, 1850-1900: Comment on Firestone," in Parker, ed. *Trends in the American Economy in the Nineteenth Century* (Studies in Income and Wealth, vol. 24), 1960, pp. 246-48.

Cole, W.A. and Deane, Phyllis. "The Growth of National Incomes," in Habukkuk and Postan, eds. *The Cambridge Economic History of Europe*, vol. 6, 1965, pp. 1-55.

David, Paul A. "New Light on a Statistical Dark Age: U.S. Real Product Growth before 1840," *American Economic Review, Papers and Proceedings*, 57(2), May 1967, pp. 294-306.

David, Paul A. "The Growth of Real Product in the United States before 1840: New Evidence, Controlled Conjectures," *Journal of Economic History*, 27(2), June 1967, pp. 151-97.

Easterlin, Richard A. "Interregional Differences in Per Capita Income, Population, and Total Income, 1840-1950," in Parker, ed. *Trends in the American Economy in the Nineteenth Century* (Studies in Income and Wealth, vol. 24), 1960, pp. 73-140.

Easterlin, Richard A. "Regional Income Trends, 1840-1950," in Harris, ed. *American Economic History*, 1961, pp. 525-47.

Easterlin, Richard A. "Gross National Product in the United States, 1834-1909: Comment on Gallman," in Brady, ed. *Output, Employment, and Productivity in the United States after 1800* (Studies in Income and Wealth, vol. 30), 1966, pp. 76-90.

Firestone, O.J. *Canada's Economic Development, 1867-1953* (Income and Wealth Series, no. 7). London: Bowes & Bowes for the International Association for Research in Income and Wealth, 1958.

Firestone, O.J. "Development of Canada's Economy, 1850-1900," in ed. *Trends in the American Economy in the Nineteenth Century* (Studies in Income and Wealth, vol. 24), 1960, pp. 217-46.

Firestone, O.J. "Development of Canada's Economy, 1850-1900: Reply to Buckley and McDougall," in Parker, ed. *Trends in the American Economy in the Nineteenth Century* (Studies in Income and Wealth, vol. 24), 1960, pp. 249-52.

Friedman, Milton. "Monetary Data and National Income Estimates," *Economic Development and Cultural Change*, 9(3), April 1961, pp. 267-86.

Gallman, Robert E. "Commodity Output, 1839-1899," in Parker, ed. *Trends in the American Economy in the Nineteenth Century* (Studies in Income and Wealth, vol. 24), 1960, pp. 13-67.

Gallman, Robert E. "Commodity Output, 1839-1899: Reply to Potter," in Parker, ed. *Trends in the American Economy in the Nineteenth Century* (Studies in Income and Wealth, vol. 24), 1960, pp. 69-71.

Gallman, Robert E. "Estimates of American National Product Made before the Civil War," (Reprinted in Andreano, ed. *New Views on American Economic Development*, 1965, pp. 168-186) *Economic Development and Cultural Change*, 9(3), April 1961, pp. 397-412.

Gallman, Robert E. "Gross National Product in the United States, 1834-1909," in Brady, ed. *Output, Employment, and Productivity in the United States after 1800* (Studies in Income and Wealth, vol. 30), 1966, pp. 3-76.

George, Peter J. and Oksanen, Ernest H. "An Index of Aggregate Economic Activity in Canada, 1896-1939: A Factor Analytic Approach," (Reprinted in Flinn, ed. *Proceedings of the Seventh International Economic History Congress*, vol. 2, 1978, pp. 87-95) *Explorations in Economic History*, 17(2), April 1980, pp. 165-75.

Goldsmith, Raymond W. "National Balance Sheets and National Wealth Statements, 1896 to 1949," in Goldsmith et al. *A Study of Saving in the United States*, vol. 3, 1957, pp. 3-138.

Goldsmith, Raymond W. "Estimates of National Product, National Income, and Personal Income, 1897 to 1949," in Goldsmith et al, *A Study of Saving in the United States*, vol. 3, 1957, pp. 421-46.

Goldsmith, Raymond W. "Long Period Growth in Income and Product, 1839-1960," in Andreano, ed. *New Views on American Economic Development*, 1965, pp. 337-61.

Keller, Robert R. "Estimates of National Income and Product, 1919-1941: The Best of all Possible Worlds," *Explorations in Economic History*, 11(1), Fall 1973, pp. 87-94.

Kendrick, John W. "Productivity," in Porter, ed. *Encyclopedia of American Economic History*, vol. 1, 1980, pp. 157-66.

Kuznets, Simon S., assisted by Epstein, Lillian, and Jenks, Elizabeth. *National Product since 1869.* (Reprinted by Arno Press, New York, 1975) New York: National Bureau of Economic Research, 1946.

Kuznets, Simon S., ed. *Income and Wealth of the United States: Trends and Structure* (Income and Wealth, Series 2). London: Bowes & Bowes for the International Association for Research in Income and Wealth, 1952.

Kuznets, Simon S. "Long-Term Changes in the National Income of the United States of America Since 1870," in Kuznets, ed. *Income and*

Wealth of the United States: Trends and Structure (Income and Wealth, Series 2), 1952, pp. 29-241.

Kuznets, Simon S. "National Income Estimates for the Period prior to 1870," in Kuznets, ed. *Income and Wealth of the United States,* 1952, pp. 221-41.

Kuznets, Simon S. "National Income Estimates for the United States Prior to 1870," *Journal of Economic History,* 12(2), Spring 1952, pp. 115-30.

Lindley, Susan, Vedder, Richard K., Gallaway, Lowell E. "Some Quarterly Estimates of GNP, 1929-1940," Ohio University Economic History Research Paper no. F-48 [Working Paper].

McDougall, Duncan. "Development of Canada's Economy, 1850-1900: Comment on Firestone," in Parker, ed. *Trends in the American Economy in the Nineteenth Century* (Studies in Income and Wealth, vol. 24), 1960, pp. 248-49.

North, Douglass C. "Early National Income Estimates of the U.S.," *Economic Development and Cultural Change,* 9(3), April 1961, pp. 387-96.

Parker, William N. "Editor's Introduction," in Parker, ed. *Trends in the American Economy in the Nineteenth Century* (Studies in Income and Wealth, vol. 24), 1960, pp. 3-9.

Parker, William N., Whartenby, Franklee. "The Growth of Output Before 1840," in Parker, ed. *Trends in the American Economy in the Nineteenth Century* (Studies in Income and Wealth, vol. 24), 1960, pp. 191-212.

Parker, William N., ed. *Trends in the American Economy in the Nineteenth Century* (Studies in Income and Wealth, vol. 24). Princeton: Princeton University Press for the National Bureau of Economic Research, 1960.

Parker, William N. "Economic History Seen through the Income Accounts," *Zeitschrift fur die Gesamte Staatswissenschaft,* 124(1), February 1968, pp. 148-58.

Potter, Neal. "Commodity Output, 1839-1899: Comment on Gallman," in Parker, ed. *Trends in the American Economy in the Nineteenth Century* (Studies in Income and Wealth, vol. 24), 1960, pp. 67-69.

Rezneck, Samuel. "The Growth of Output Before 1840: Comment on Parker and Whartenby," in Parker, ed. *Trends in the American Economy in the Nineteenth Century* (Studies in Income and Wealth, vol. 24), 1960, pp. 212-16.

Swanson, Joseph A., Williamson, Samuel H. "Estimates of National Product and Income for the United States Economy, 1919-1941," *Explorations in Economic History,* 10(1), Fall 1972, pp. 53-74.

Taylor, George Rogers. "American Economic Growth Before 1840: An Exploratory Essay," in Andreano, ed. *New Views on American Economic Development,* 1965, pp. 57-72.

Thomas, Brinley. "Consumption, Investment and Employment: General Comment," in Brady, ed. *Output, Employment, and Productivity in the United States after 1800* (Studies in Income and Wealth, vol. 30), 1966, pp. 205-10.

Tice, Helen Stone. "Depreciation, Obsolescence, and the Measurement of the Aggregate Capital Stock of the United States, 1900-1962," *Review of Income and Wealth,* 13(2), June 1967, pp. 119-54.

United States: Capital Formation, Saving, and the Capital Stock

Adams, Jr., Donald R. "Earnings and Savings in the Early 19th Century," *Explorations in Economic History*, 17(2), April 1980, pp. 118-34.

Anderson, Terry L. "Wealth Estimates for the New England Colonies, 1650-1709," *Explorations in Economic History*, 12(2), April 1975, pp. 151-76.

Brady, Dorothy S. "Family Saving, 1888 to 1950," in Goldsmith et al. *A Study of Saving in the United States*, vol. 3, 1957, pp. 139-276.

Buckley, Kenneth. *Capital Formation in Canada, 1896-1930.* (Reprinted by Mclelland & Stewart, Toronto, 1974) Toronto: University of Toronto Press, 1955.

Creamer, Daniel; Dobrovolsky, Sergei and Borenstein, Israel. *Capital in Manufacturing and Mining: Its Formation and Financing.* Princeton: Princeton University Press for the National Bureau of Economic Research, 1960.

Creamer, Daniel. "Capital and Output Trends in Manufacturing Industries, 1880-1948," National Bureau of Economic Research, Occasional Paper no. 41, 1954 [Working Paper].

Davis, Lance E. "Capital Formation in the United States During the Early Period of Industrialization: Comment on North," in *Second International Conference of Economic History,* vol. 2, 1965, pp. 657-71.

Davis, Lance E. "The Capital Markets and Industrial Concentration: The U.S. and U.K., a Comparative Study," (Reprinted in Hughes, ed. *Purdue Faculty Papers in Economic History, 1956-1966,* 1967, pp. 663-682) *Economic History Review*, Second Series, 19(2), August 1966, pp. 255-72.

Davis, Lance E. "Capital Mobility and American Growth," in Fogel and Engerman eds. *The Reinterpretation of American Economic History,* 1971, pp. 285-300.

Davis, Lance E. "Capital and Growth," in Davis, Easterlin, and Parker, eds. *American Economic Growth,* 1972, pp. 280-310.

Davis, Lance E. "Savings Sources and Utilization," in Davis, Easterlin, and Parker, eds. *American Economic Growth,* 1972, pp. 311-39.

Davis, Lance E. and Gallman, Robert E. "The Share of Savings and Investment in Gross National Product during the Nineteenth Century in the United States of America," *Fourth International Conference of Economic History, Bloomington, 1968.* Paris and The Hague: Mouton, 1973, pp. 437-66.

Davis, Lance E. and Gallman, Robert E. "Capital Formation in the United States during the 19th Century," in Mathias and Postan, eds. *The Cambridge Economic History of Europe,* vol. 7, part 2, 1978, pp. 1-69.

Davis, Lance E. "Savings and Investment," in Porter, ed. *Encyclopedia of American Economic History: Studies of the Principal Movements and Ideas,* vol. 1, 1980, pp. 183-201.

Davis, Lance E. "Capital Immobilities and Economic Growth," Presented at the First International Economic History Conference, Rome, 1965 [Working Paper].

Deane, Phyllis. "Long-Term Trends in Capital Formation and Financing," (Review Essay of *Capital in the American Economy: Its Formation and Financing since 1870.* by Simon Kuznets, Princeton: Princeton University Press for the NBER, 1962) *Economic Journal*, 72(288), December 1962, pp. 926-30.

Denison, Edward F. *The Sources of Economic Growth in the United States and the Alternatives Before Us.* New York: Committee on Economic Development, 1962.

Fenichel, Allen H. "Growth and Diffusion of Power in Manufacturing, 1838-1919," in Brady, ed. *Output, Employment, and Productivity in the United States after 1800* (Studies in Income and Wealth, vol. 30), 1966, pp. 443-78.

Gallman, Robert E. "Capital Formation and Capital Allocation," [Working Paper].

Gallman, Robert E. and Howle, E.S. "The U. S. Capital Stock in the 19th Century," [Working Paper].

Goldsmith, Raymond W. "The Share of Financial Intermediaries in National Wealth and National Assets, 1900-1949," National Bureau of Economic Research, Occasional Paper no. 42, 1954 [Working Paper].

Goldsmith, Raymond W. *A Study of Saving in the United States*, vol. 1: *Introduction; Tables of Annual Estimates of Saving, 1897 to 1949.* Princeton: Princeton University Press, 1955.

Goldsmith, Raymond W. *A Study of Saving in the United States*, vol. 2: *Nature and Derivation of Annual Estimates of Saving, 1897 to 1949.* Princeton: Princeton University Press, 1955.

Goldsmith, Raymond W.; Brady, Dorothy S. and Menderhausen, Horst. *A Study of Saving in the United States*, vol. 3: *Special Studies.* Princeton: Princeton University Press, 1957.

Goldsmith, Raymond W. "National Balance Sheets and National Wealth Statements, 1896 to 1949," in Goldsmith et al. *A Study of Saving in the United States*, vol. 3, 1957, pp. 3-138.

Goldsmith, Raymond W. "Experiments with the Saving Function," in Goldsmith et al. *A Study of Saving in the United States*, vol. 3, 1957, pp. 385-420.

Grebler, Leo; Blank, David M. and Winnick, Louis. *Capital Formation in Residential Real Estate: Trends and Prospects.* Princeton: Princeton University Press for the National Bureau of Economic Research, 1956.

Jones, Alice Hanson., ed. *American Colonial Wealth: Documents and Methods.* New York: Arno Press, 1978.

Jones, Alice Hanson. *Wealth of a Nation to Be: The American Colonies on the Eve of the Revolution.* New York: Columbia University Press, 1980.

Juster, F. Thomas. *Household Capital Formation and Financing, 1897-1962* (General Series, no. 83). New York: Columbia University Press for the National Bureau of Economic Research, 1966.

Kendrick, John W., assisted by Lethem, Yvonne, and Rowley, Jennifer. *The Formation and Stocks of Total Capital* (National Bureau of Economic Research General Series, no. 100). New York: Columbia University Press for the National Bureau of Economic Research,

1976.

Kuznets, Simon S., assisted by Jenks, Elizabeth. *Capital in the American Economy: Its Formation and Financing Since 1870.* Princeton: Princeton University Press for the National Bureau of Economic Research, 1961.

Kuznets, Simon S. "Capital Formation in Modern Economic Growth (and some implications for the past)," *Third International Conference of Economic History, Munich, 1965, part 1.* Paris: Mouton, 1968, pp. 15-53.

La Tourette, J.E. "Potential Output and the Capital-Output Ratio in the United States Private Business Sector, 1909-1959," *Kyklos*, 18(2), 1965, pp. 316-31.

La Tourette, J.E. "Sources of Variation in the Capital-Output Ratio in the United States Private Business Sector, 1909-1959," *Kyklos*, 18(4), 1965, pp. 635-50.

North, Douglass C. "Capital Formation in the United States during the Early Period of Industrialization: A Reexamination of the Issues," *Second International Conference of Economic History, Aix-en-Provence, 1962,* vol. 2. Paris and The Hague: Mouton, 1965, pp. 643-56.

Peklar, Conrad. "Wealth in Colonial Connecticut, 1650-1760," Ohio University Economic History Research Paper no. G-10 [Working Paper].

Pomfret, Richard W.T. "Capital Formation in Canada 1870-1900," Concordia University Working Paper no. 77-1, January 1977 [Working Paper].

Stigler, George J. *Capital and Rates of Return in Manufacturing Industries* (General Series, no. 78). Princeton: Princeton University Press for the National Bureau of Economic Research, 1963.

Swierenga, Robert P. "The Tax Buyer as a Frontier Investor Type," *Explorations in Economic History,* 7(3), Spring 1970, pp. 257-92.

Tostlebe, Alvin S. *Capital in Agriculture: Its Formation and Financing since 1870.* Princeton: Princeton University Press for the National Bureau of Economic Research, 1957.

United States: Sectoral Contributions

Bowman, John D. and Danhof, Clarence H. "An Industrial Income Distribution for New York State, 1865," [Working Paper].

Bowman, John D. "Gross Agricultural Output, Value Added and Factor Shares in the Twelve Midwestern States, 1870 to 1900," [Working Paper].

Gallman, Robert E. "Commodity Output, 1839-1899," in Parker, ed. *Trends in the American Economy in the Nineteenth Century* (Studies in Income and Wealth, vol. 24), 1960, pp. 13-67.

Gallman, Robert E. "Commodity Output, 1839-1899: Reply to Potter," in Parker, ed. *Trends in the American Economy in the Nineteenth Century* (Studies in Income and Wealth, vol. 24), 1960, pp. 69-71.

Gallman, Robert E. and Howle, Edward S. "Trends in the Structure of the American Economy since 1840," in Fogel and Engerman, eds. *The*

Reinterpretation of American Economic History, 1971, pp. 25-37.

Kuznets, Simon S. "Quantitative Aspects of the Economic Growth of Nations (Part 3): Industrial Distribution of Income and Labor Force by States, United States, 1919-1921 to 1955," *Economic Development and Cultural Change*, 6(4, Part 2), July 1958, pp. 1-128.

Kuznets, Simon S. "Quantitative Aspects of the Economic Growth of Nations (Part 7): The Share and Structure of Consumption," *Economic Development and Cultural Change*, 10(2, Part 2), January 1962, pp. 1-92.

Lebergott, Stanley. "Estimates of PCE, by Detailed Item: U.S. Totals 1900-1928, Annually by State, 1970," [Working Paper].

Lewis, Frank D. "Explaining the Shift of Labor from Agriculture to Industry in the United States: 1869 to 1899," *Journal of Economic History*, 39(3), September 1979, pp. 681-98.

McInnis, R. Marvin. "Long-Term Changes in Industrial Composition with Particular Attention to Canada, 1911 and 1961," in Van der Wee, Vinogradov, and Kotovsky, eds. *Fifth International Congress of Economic History*, vol. 3, 1976, pp. 9-27.

Potter, Neal. "Commodity Output, 1839-1899: Comment on Gallman," in Parker, ed. *Trends in the American Economy in the Nineteenth Century* (Studies in Income and Wealth, vol. 24), 1960, pp. 67-69.

Poulson, Barry W. *Value Added in Manufacturing, Mining, and Agriculture in the American Economy 1809 to 1839*. New York: Arno Press, 1975.

Schwartz, Anna J. "Gross Dividend and Interest Payments by Corporations at Selected Dates in the 19th Century," in Parker, ed. *Trends in the American Economy in the Nineteenth Century* (Studies in Income and Wealth, vol. 24), 1960, pp. 407-45.

Whitney, W.G. "The Structure of the American Economy in the Late Nineteenth Century," Ph.D. Dissertation, Harvard University, 1968 [Working Paper].

United States: Distribution of Income

Andreano, Ralph L. "Reflections on the History of Poverty in America," *Earlham Review*, 1(2), Fall, 1966, pp. 51-60.

Bean, Richard N. "The Importance of Regional Cost of Living Differentials in Estimating Gini-Coefficients for U.S. Income Inequality," [Working Paper].

Brady, Dorothy S. "Consumption and the Style of Life," in Davis, Easterlin, and Parker, eds. *American Economic Growth*, 1972, pp. 61-91.

Budd, Edward C. "Factor Shares, 1850-1910," in Parker, ed. *Trends in the American Economy in the Nineteenth Century* (Studies in Income and Wealth, vol. 24), 1960, pp. 365-98.

Budd, Edward C. "Factor Shares, 1850-1910: Reply to Denison," in Parker, ed. *Trends in the American Economy in the Nineteenth Century* (Studies in Income and Wealth, vol. 24), 1960, pp. 403-6.

Daniels, Bruce C. "Long Range Trends of Wealth Distribution in 18th Century New England," *Explorations in Economic History*, 11(2), Winter 1974, pp. 123-36.

Denison, Edward F. "Factor Shares, 1850-1910: Comment on Budd," in Parker, ed. *Trends in the American Economy in the Nineteenth Century* (Studies in Income and Wealth, vol. 24), 1960, pp. 399-403.

DeCanio, Stephen J. "Productivity and Income Distribution in the Postbellum South," *Journal of Economic History*, 34(2), June 1974, pp. 422-46.

Gallman, Robert E. "The Social Distribution of Wealth in the United States of America," *Third International Conference of Economic History, Munich, 1965*, part 1. Paris and The Hague: Mouton, 1968, pp. 313-34.

Gallman, Robert E. "Trends in the Size Distribution of Wealth in the Nineteenth Century: Some Speculations," in Soltow, ed. *Six Papers on the Size Distribution of Wealth and Income* (Studies in Income and Wealth, vol. 33), 1969, pp. 1-25.

Gallman, Robert E. "Trends in the Size Distribution of Wealth in the Nineteenth Century: Reply to Soltow," in Soltow, ed. *Six Papers on the Size Distribution of Wealth and Income* (Studies in Income and Wealth, vol. 33), 1969, pp. 27-30.

Gallman, Robert E. "Professor Pessen on 'The Egalitarian Myth'," *Social Science History*, 2(2), Winter 1978, pp. 194-207.

Gallman, Robert E. "Equality in the United States at the Time of Tocqueville," [Working Paper].

Hartley, W.B. "Estimation of the Incidence of Poverty in the United States, 1870 to 1914," Ph.D. Dissertation, University of Wisconsin-Madison, 1969 [Working Paper].

Holt, Charles F. "Who Benefited from the Prosperity of the Twenties?" *Explorations in Economic History*, 14(3), July 1977, pp. 277-89.

Jones, Alice Hanson. "Wealth Distribution in the American Middle Colonies in the Third Quarter of the Eighteenth Century," [Working Paper].

Kearl, J.R.; Pope, Clayne L. and Wimmer, Larry T. "Household Wealth in a Settlement Economy: Utah, 1850-1870," *Journal of Economic History*, 40(3), September 1980, pp. 477-96.

Keller, Robert R. "Factor Income Distribution in the United States During the 1920's: A Reexamination of Fact and Theory," *Journal of Economic History*, 33(1), March 1973, pp. 252-73.

Keller, Robert R. "An Analysis of Relative Income Shares in the United States during the 1920's," Ph.D. Dissertation, University of Wisconsin-Madison, 1971 [Working Paper].

Klingaman, David C. "Individual Wealth in Ohio in 1860," in Klingaman and Vedder, eds. *Essays in Nineteenth Century Economic History*, 1975, pp. 177-90.

Kuznets, Simon S., ed. *Income and Wealth of the United States: Trends and Structure* (Income and Wealth, Series 2). London: Bowes & Bowes for the International Association for Research in Income and Wealth, 1952.

Kuznets, Simon S. "Quantitative Aspects of the Economic Growth of Nations (Part 4): Distribution of National Income by Factor Shares," *Economic Development and Cultural Change*, 7(3, Part 2), April 1959, pp. 1-106.

Kuznets, Simon S. "Quantitative Aspects of the Economic Growth of Nations (Part 8): Distribution of Income by Size," *Economic*

Development and Cultural Change, 11(2, Part 2), January 1963, pp. 1-80.

Kuznets, Simon S. *Growth, Population, and Income Distribution: Selected Essays.* New York: W.W. Norton, 1979.

Lampman, Robert J. "Changes in the Share of Wealth Held by Top Wealth-Holders, 1922-1956," *Review of Economics and Statistics,* 41(4), November 1959, pp. 379-92.

Lampman, Robert J. *The Share of Top Wealth-Holders in National Wealth, 1922-56* (General Series, no. 74) Princeton: Princeton University Press for the National Bureau of Economic Research, 1962.

Lebergott, Stanley. "Factor Shares in the Long Term: Some Theoretical and Statistical Aspects," in *The Behavior of Income Shares: Selected Theoretical and Empirical Issues* (Studies in Income and Wealth, vol. 27), 1964.

Lebergott, Stanley. *Wealth and Want.* Princeton: Princeton University Press, 1975.

Lebergott, Stanley. "Are the Rich Getting Richer? Trends in U.S. Wealth Concentration," *Journal of Economic History*, 36(1), March 1976, pp. 147-62.

Lindert, Peter H. and Williamson, Jeffrey G. "Three Centuries of American Inequality," in Uselding, ed. *Research in Economic History*, vol. 1, 1976, pp. 69-123.

Lindert, Peter H. and Williamson, Jeffrey G. *A Macroeconomic History of American Inequality.* New York: Academic Press, 1979.

Main, Gloria L. "Personal Wealth in Colonial America: Explorations in the Use of Probate Records from Maryland and Massachusetts, 1650 to 1720," (Summary of Doctoral Dissertation) *Journal of Economic History*, 34(1), March 1974, pp. 289-94.

Main, Gloria L. "Inequality in Early America: The Evidence from Probate Records of Massachusetts and Maryland," *Journal of Interdisciplinary History*, 7(4), Spring 1977, pp. 559-81.

Main, Jackson T. "Trends in Wealth Concentration Before 1860: A Note," *Journal of Economic History*, 31(2), June 1971, pp. 445-47.

National Bureau of Economic Research. *The Behavior of Income Shares: Selected Theoretical and Empirical Issues* (Studies in Income and Wealth, vol. 27). Princeton: Princeton University Press, 1964.

Peklar, Conrad. "Wealth in Colonial Connecticut, 1650-1760," Ohio University Economic History Research Paper no. G-10 [Working Paper].

Pope, Clayne L. "Measurement and Analysis of Distributions of Income and Wealth," (Summary of 1978 Research Workshop) *Journal of Economic History*, 39(1), March 1979, pp. 319-21.

Rees, Albert, assisted by Jacobs, Donald P. *Real Wages in Manufacturing, 1890-1914* (General Series, no. 70). Princeton: Princeton University Press for the National Bureau of Economic Research, 1961.

Schwartz, Anna J. "Gross Dividend and Interest Payments by Corporations at Selected Dates in the 19th Century," in Parker, ed. *Trends in the American Economy in the Nineteenth Century* (Studies in Income and Wealth, vol. 24), 1960, pp. 407-45.

Smolensky, Eugene. "The Past and Present Poor," in Fogel and Engerman, eds. *The Reinterpretation of American Economic History*, 1971, pp.

84-96.

Smolensky, Eugene and Weinstein, Michael M. "Poverty," in Porter, ed. *Encyclopedia of American Economic History*, vol. 3, 1978, pp. 1136-54.

Soltow, Lee C. "Income Equality in a Factory Payroll," *Southern Economic Journal*, 25(3), January 1959, pp. 343-48.

Soltow, Lee C., ed. *Six Papers on the Size Distribution of Wealth and Income* (Studies in Income and Wealth, vol. 33). New York: Columbia University Press for the National Bureau of Economic Research, 1969.

Soltow, Lee C. "Trends in the Size Distribution of Wealth in the Nineteenth Century: A Comment on Gallman," in Soltow, ed. *Six Papers on the Size Distribution of Wealth and Income* (Studies in Income and Wealth, vol. 33), 1969, pp. 25-27.

Soltow, Lee C. "Evidence on Income Inequality in the United States, 1866-1965," *Journal of Economic History*, 29(2), June 1969, pp. 279-86.

Soltow, Lee C. *Patterns of Wealthholding in Wisconsin since 1850.* Madison: University of Wisconsin Press, 1971.

Soltow, Lee C. "Economic Inequality in the United States in the Period from 1790 to 1860," *Journal of Economic History*, 31(4), December 1971, pp. 822-39.

Soltow, Lee C. "A Century of Personal Wealth Accumulation," in Vatter and Palm, eds. *The Economics of Black America*, 1972.

Soltow, Lee C. "The Censuses of Wealth of Men in Australia in 1915 and in the United States in 1860 and 1870," *Australian Economic History Review*, 12(2), September 1972, pp. 125-41.

Soltow, Lee C. *Men and Wealth in the United States, 1850-1870.* New Haven: Yale University Press, 1975.

Soltow, Lee C. "The Growth of Wealth in Ohio, 1800-1969," in Klingaman and Vedder, eds. *Essays in Nineteenth Century Economic History*, 1975, pp. 191-207.

Soltow, Lee C. and Smith, James D. "The Wealth, Income, and Social Class of Men in Large Nothern Cities of the United States in 1860," in Smith, ed. *The Personal Distribution of Income and Wealth* (Studies in Income and Wealth, vol. 39), 1975.

Soltow, Lee C. "Are the Rich Getting Richer? Trends in U.S. Wealth Concentration: Comment on Lebergott," *Journal of Economic History*, 36(1), March 1976, pp. 163-65.

Soltow, Lee C. "Distribution of Income and Wealth," in Porter, ed. *Encyclopedia of American Economic History*, vol. 3, 1980, pp. 1087-119.

Toda, Yasushi. "An Intercountry Comparison of the Consumption Levels of Industrial Workers' Families: Russia 1913-United States of America 1901," *Fourth International Conference of Economic History, Bloomington, 1968.* Paris: Mouton, 1973, pp. 477-84.

Williamson, Jeffrey G. and Lindert, Peter H. "Three Centuries of American Inequality," in Uselding, ed. *Research in Economic History*, vol. 1, 1976, pp. 69-123.

Williamson, Jeffrey G. "American Prices and Urban Inequality Since 1820," *Journal of Economic History*, 36(2), June 1976, pp. 303-33.

Williamson, Jeffrey G. "The Sources of American Inequality,

1896-1948," *Review of Economics and Statistics*, 58(4), November 1976, pp. 387-97.

Williamson, Jeffrey G. and Morley, S. "Class Pay Differentials, Wage Stretching and Early Capitalist Development," in Nash, ed. *Essays on Economic Development and Cultural Change*, 1977, pp. 407-27.

Williamson, Jeffrey G. "'Strategic' Wage Goods, Prices and Inequality," *American Economic Review*, 67(2), March 1977, pp. 29-41.

Williamson, Jeffrey G. "Inequality, Accumulation, and Technological Imbalance: A Growth-Equity Conflict in American History?" *Economic Development and Cultural Change*, 27(2), January 1979, pp. 231-54.

Williamson, Jeffrey G. and Lindert, Peter H.s *American Inequality: A Macroeconomic History*. New York: Academic Press, 1980.

Williamson, Jeffrey G. and Lindert, Peter H. "Long Term Trends in American Wealth Inequality," in Smith, ed. *Modeling the Distribution and Intergenerational Transmission of Wealth* (Studies in Income and Wealth, vol. 46), 1980, pp. 9-93.

Williamson, Jeffrey G. "Immigrant-Inequality Trade-Offs in the Promised Land: American Growth, Distribution and Immigration Prior to the Quotas," in Chiswick, ed. *The Gateway*, 1981.

Wimmer, Larry T. "Changing Economic Structure and the Rise of Inequality in Early Utah: 1850-1870," [Working Paper].

Wimmer, Larry T. "Income and Wealth in the Nineteenth Century: The Utah Experience," [Working Paper].

Wimmer, Larry T. "Relative Mobility through Nineteenth Century Wealth Distributions," [Working Paper].

Wimmer, Larry T. "Utah Heads of Households: Index of the 1850, 1860, and 1870 Censuses," [Working Paper].

Europe: National Income

Bairoch, Paul. "Europe's Gross National Product, 1800-1975," *Journal of European Economic History*, 5(2), Fall 1976, pp. 273-313.

Bergson, Abram. *The Real National Income of Soviet Russia Since 1928*. Cambridge: Harvard University Press, 1961.

Bjerke, Kjeld and Ussing, Niels. *Studier over Danmarks Nationalprodukt 1870-1950*. Kobenhavn: Universitits Okonomiske Institut, 1958.

Butlin, Noel G. and Tucker, G.S.L. "The Quantitative Study of British Economic Growth: A Review," (Review essay of *British Economic Growth, 1688-1959*. by Deane and Cole, 1968) *Economic Record*, 40(91), September 1964, pp. 455-60.

Butlin, Noel G. "Kaser on England and Wales Gross Product," *Bulletin of the Oxford University Institute of Economics and Statistics*, 30(1), February 1968, pp. 67-68.

Butlin, Noel G. "A New Plea for the Separation of Ireland," *Journal of Economic History*, 28(2), June 1968, pp. 274-91.

Cole, W.A. and Deane, Phyllis. "The Growth of National Incomes," in Habukkuk and Postan, eds. *The Cambridge Economic History of Europe*, vol. 6, Part 1, 1965, pp. 1-55.

Cole, W.A. "Deane and Cole on Industrialization and Population Change in the Eighteenth Century: A Rejoinder to Neal," *Economic History*

Review, Second Series, 24(4), November 1971, pp. 648-52.

Crafts, N.F.R. "English Economic Growth in the Eighteenth Century: A Re-examination of Deane and Cole's Estimates," *Economic History Review*, Second Series, 29(2), May 1976, pp. 226-35.

Deane, Phyllis. "The Implications of Early National Income Estimates for the Measurement of Long-Term Economic Growth in the United Kingdom," *Economic Development and Cultural Change*, 4(1), October 1955, pp. 3-38.

Deane, Phyllis. "Contemporary Estimates of National Income in the First Half of the Nineteenth Century," *Economic History Review*, Second Series, 8(3), 1956, pp. 339-54.

Deane, Phyllis. "The Industrial Revolution and Economic Growth: The Evidence of Early British National Income Estimates," *Economic Development and Cultural Change*, 5(2), January 1957, pp. 159-74.

Deane, Phyllis and Cole, W.A. *British Economic Growth, 1688-1959: Trends and Structure* Second Edition, 1968 Cambridge: Cambridge University Press, 1962.

Deane, Phyllis. "New Estimates of Gross National Product for the United Kingdom, 1830-1914," *Review of Income and Wealth*, 14(2), June 1968, pp. 95-112.

Falkus, Malcolm E. "Russia's National Income, 1913: A Reevaluation," *Economica*, 35(137), February 1968, pp. 52-73.

Feinstein, Charles H. *National Income, Expenditure and Output of the United Kingdom, 1855-1965.* Cambridge: Cambridge University Press, 1972.

Gregory, Paul R. "1913 Russian National Income: Some Insights into Russian Economic Development," *Quarterly Journal of Economics*, 90), August 1976, pp. 445-59.

Hoffmann, Walther G. *Das Deutsche Volkseinkommen 1811-1957.* Tubingen: J.C.B. Mohr, 1959.

Hoffmann, Walther G., with the collaboration of Grumbach, F., Hesse, H. *Das Wachstum der Deutschen Wirtschaft seit der Mitte des 19. Jahrhunderts.* Berlin and New York: Springer-Verlag, 1965.

Israelsen, L. Dwight. "The Determinants of Russian State Income, 1800-1914: An Econometric Analysis," Ph.D. Dissertation, Massachusetts Institute of Technology, 1979 [Working Paper].

Johansson, O. *The Gross Domestic Product of Sweden and Its Composition.* Stockholm: Almquist & Wicksell, 1967.

Jostock, Paul. "The Long-Term Growth of National Income in Germany," in Kuznets, ed. *Income and Wealth*, Series 5, 1955, pp. 79-122.

Larna, K. *The Money Supply, Money Flows, and Domestic Product in Finland, 1910-1956.* Helsinki: Finnish Economic Association, 1959.

Moliner, Jean-Claude. "Les calculs d'agregat en France anterieurement a 1850," *Revue d'economie politique*, 67(4), 1957, pp. 875-987.

Neal, Larry D. "Deane and Cole on Industrialization and Population Change in the Eighteenth Century: Comment," *Economic History Review*, Second Series, 24(4), November 1971, pp. 643-47.

O'Brien, Patrick K. "British Incomes and Property in the Early Nineteenth Century," *Economic History Review*, Second Series, 12(2), 1959, pp. 255-67.

Prest, A.R. "National Income of the United Kingdom, 1870-1946," *Economic Journal*, 58, March 1948, pp. 31-62.

Prest, A.R. and Adams, A.A. *Consumers' Expenditure in the United Kingdom, 1900-1919.* Cambridge: Cambridge University Press, 1954.

Pryor, Frederic L.; Pryor, Zora P.; Stadnik, Milos and Staller, George J. "Czechoslovak Aggregate Production in the Interwar Period," *Review of Income and Wealth,* 17(1), March 1971, pp. 35-60.

Stone, J.R.F. and Rowe, D.A. *The Measurement of Consumers' Expenditure and Behaviour in the United Kingdom, 1920-1938* (2 vols). Cambridge: Cambridge University Press, 1954 and.

Teijl, J. "National Inkomen van Nederland in de periode 1850-1900," *Economisch-en Sociaal-Historisch Jaarboek,* 34, 1971, pp. 232-62.

Thomas, Brinley. "The Dimensions of British Economic Growth, 1688-1959." (Review Essay of *British Economic Growth 1688-1959.* by Deane and Cole, 1964) *Journal of the Royal Statistical Society,* 127, Series A (General), Part 1, 1964, pp. 111-23.

Thornton, Judith G. "The Index Number Problem in the Measurement of Soviet National Income: A Review Article," (Review Essay of *The Real National Income of Soviet Russia Since 1928.* by Bergson, 1961) *Journal of Economic History,* 22(3), September 1962, pp. 379-89.

Toms, M. *Outline of National Income Development During 1937-1948 in Czechoslovakia.* Prague: Economic Institute of the Czechoslovak Academy of Sciences, 1966.

Toutain, Jean-Claude. *Le produit interieur brut de la France de 1889 a 1970.*

Vinski, Ivo. "National Product and Fixed Assets in the Territory of Yugoslavia, 1909-59," in Deane, ed. *Studies in Social and Financial Accounting* (Income and Wealth, Series 9), 1961, pp. 206-33.

Europe: Capital Formation, Saving, and Capital Stock

Aukrust, Odd and Bjerke, Juul. "Real Capital in Norway, 1900-56," in Goldsmith and Saunders, eds. *The Measurement of National Wealth* (Income and Wealth, Series 8), 1959, pp. 80-118.

Bos, Roeland W.J.M. "Kapitaal en industrialisatie in Nederland tijdens de negentiende eeuw [Capital and Industrialization in the Netherlands during the Nineteenth Century]," *Afdeling Agrarische Geschiedenis, Bijdragen,* 22), 1979, pp. 89-105.

Cairncross, Alec K. *Home and Foreign Investment, 1870-1913: Studies in Capital Accumulation.* Cambridge: Cambridge University Press, 1953.

Cole, W.A. "Deane and Cole on Industrialization and Population Change in the Eighteenth Century: A Rejoinder to Neal," *Economic History Review,* Second Series, 24(4), November 1971, pp. 648-52.

Crafts, N.F.R. "English Economic Growth in the Eighteenth Century: A Re-examination of Deane and Cole's Estimates," *Economic History Review,* Second Series, 29(2), May 1976, pp. 226-35.

Davis, Lance E. "The Capital Markets and Industrial Concentration: The U.S. and U.K., a Comparative Study," (Reprinted in Hughes, ed. *Purdue Faculty Papers in Economic History, 1956-1966,* 1967, pp. 663-682) *Economic History Review,* Second Series, 19(2), August 1966, pp. 255-72.

Deane, Phyllis. "Capital Formation in Britain Before the Railway Age," *Economic Development and Cultural Change*, 9(3), April 1961, pp. 352-68.

Deane, Phyllis and Cole, W.A. *British Economic Growth, 1688-1959: Trends and Structure.* (Second Edition, 1968) Cambridge: Cambridge University Press, 1962.

Edelstein, Michael. "United Kingdom Savings in the Age of High Imperialism and After," *American Economic Review, Papers and Proceedings*, 67(1), February 1977, pp. 288-94.

Feinstein, Charles H. "Income and Investment in the United Kingdom, 1856-1914," *Economic Journal*, 71(282), June 1961, pp. 367-85.

Feinstein, Charles H. "Income and Investment in the United Kingdom, 1856-1914: A Reply (to Maywald)," *Economic Journal*, 71(284), December 1961, pp. 857-59.

Feinstein, Charles H. *Domestic Capital Formation in the United Kingdom, 1920-1938.* Cambridge: Cambridge University Press, 1965.

Feinstein, Charles H. "The Compilation of Gross Domestic Fixed Capital Formation Statistics, 1856-1913," in Higgins and Pollard, eds. *Aspects of Capital Investment in Great Britain*, 1971.

Feinstein, Charles H. *National Income, Expenditure and Output of the United Kingdom, 1855-1965.* Cambridge: Cambridge University Press, 1972.

Feinstein, Charles H. "Capital Formation in Great Britain," in Mathias and Postan, eds. *The Cambridge Economic History of Europe*, vol. 7, Part 1, 1978, pp. 28-96.

Feinstein, Charles H. "Capital Accumulation and the Industrial Revolution," in Floud and McCloskey, eds. *The Economic History of Britain since 1700*, vol. 1, 1980, pp. 128-42.

Grunig, Ferdinand. "An Estimate of the National Capital Account of the Federal German Republic," in Goldsmith and Saunders, eds. *The Measurement of National Wealth* (Income and Wealth, Series 8), 1959.

Hart, P.E. "A Long-Run Analysis of the Rate of Return on Capital in Manufacturing Industry, United Kingdom, 1920-62," in Hart, ed. *Studies in Profit, Business Saving and Investment in the United Kingdom, 1920-1962* (vol. 2), 1968, pp. 220-83.

Hart, P.E. "A Macroeconometric Analysis of the Appropriation of Profit in Manufacturing," in Hart, ed. *Studies in Profit, Business Saving and Investment in the United Kingdom, 1920-1962* (vol. 2), 1968, pp. 109-43.

Hart, P.E., ed. *Studies in Profit, Business Saving and Investment in the United Kingdom 1920-1962* (2 vols; vol. 1, *1965*; vol. 2, *1968*). London: Allen & Unwin, 1965, 1968.

Hart, P.E. "The Factor Distribution of Income in the United Kingdom, 1870-1963," in Hart, ed. *Studies in Profit, Business Saving and Investment in the United Kingdom, 1920-1962* (vol. 2), 1968, pp. 17-72.

Higgins, J.P.P. and Pollard, Sidney., eds. *Aspects of Capital Investment in Great Britain, 1750-1850.* London: Methuen, 1971.

Hoffmann, Walther G., with the collaboration of Grumbach, F., Hesse, H. *Das Wachstum der Deutschen Wirtschaft seit der Mitte des 19. Jahrhunderts.* Berlin and New York: Springer-Verlag, 1965.

Kenwood, A.G. "Fixed Capital Formation on Merseyside, 1800-1913,"

Economic History Review, Second Series, 31(2), May 1978, pp. 214-37.

Kuznets, Simon S. "Quantitative Aspects of the Economic Growth of Nations (Part 6): Long-Term Trends in Capital Formation Proportions," *Economic Development and Cultural Change*, 9(4, Part 2), July 1961, pp. 1-124.

Kuznets, Simon S. "Capital Formation in Modern Economic Growth (and some implications for the past)," Third International Conference of Economic History, Munich, 1965, part 1 Paris: Mouton, 1968, pp. 15-53.

Levy-Leboyer, Maurice. "Capital Investment and Economic Growth in France, 1820-1930," in Mathias and Postan, eds. *The Cambridge Economic History of Europe*, vol. 7, part 1, 1978, pp. 231-95.

Lund, P.J., Holden, K. "Study of Private Sector Gross Fixed Capital Formation in the United Kingdom, 1923-1938," *Oxford Economic Papers*, 20(1), March 1968, pp. 56-73.

Maywald, K. "Income and Investment in the United Kingdom, 1856-1914: A Note (on Feinstein)," *Economic Journal*, 71(284), December 1961, pp. 856-57.

Neal, Larry D. "Deane and Cole on Industrialization and Population Change in the Eighteenth Century: Comment," *Economic History Review*, Second Series, 24(4), November 1971, pp. 643-47.

Pollard, Sidney. "The Growth and Distribution of Capital in Great Britain, c. 1770-1870," *Third International Conference of Economic History, Munich, 1965*, part 1. Paris and The Hague: Mouton, 1968, pp. 335-65.

Rapp, Richard T. "Real Estate and Rational Investment in Early Modern Venice," *Journal of European Economic History*, 8(2), Fall 1979, pp. 269-90.

Rostow, W.W. "Some Reflections on Capital Formation and Economic Growth," in *Universities-National Bureau Conference Series*, no. 6, 1955, pp. 635-67.

Tilly, Richard H. "Capital Formation in Germany in the Nineteenth Century," in Mathias and Postan. eds. *The Cambridge Economic History of Europe*, vol. 7, Part 1, 1978, pp. 382-441.

Uselding, Paul J. "Wages and Capital Consumption Levels in England and on the Continent in the 1830's," *Journal of European Economic History*, 4(2), Fall 1975, pp. 501-13.

Vinski, Ivo. "National Product and Fixed Assets in the Territory of Yugoslavia, 1909-59," in Deane, ed. *Studies in Social and Financial Accounting* (Income and Wealth, Series 9), 1961, pp. 206-33.

Europe: Sectoral Contributions

Alford, B.W.E. "New Industries for Old? British Industry between the Wars," in Floud and McCloskey, eds. *The Economic History of Britain since 1700*, vol. 2, 1980.

Cole, W.A. "Deane and Cole on Industrialization and Population Change in the Eighteenth Century: A Rejoinder to Neal," *Economic History Review*, Second Series, 24(4), November 1971, pp. 648-52.

Cole, W.A. "Changes in British Industrial Structure, 1850-1960," in Van der Wee, Vinogradov, and Kotovsky, eds. *Fifth International Congress of Economic History*, vol. 7, 1976, pp. 112-29.

Crouzet, Francois. "Essai de Construction d'un Indice Annuel de la Production Industrielle Francaise au XIXe Siecle [A Tentative Annual Index of French Industrial Production in the 19th Century]," (Reprinted in English in Cameron, ed. *Essays in French Economic History*, 1970, pp. 245-78) *Annales: Economies, Societes, Civilisation*, 25(1), January/February 1970, pp. 56-99.

Deane, Phyllis and Cole, W.A. *British Economic Growth, 1688-1959: Trends and Structure*. Second Edition, 1968 Cambridge: Cambridge University Press, 1962.

Feinstein, Charles H. "Production and Productivity in the United Kingdom, 1920-1962," (Reprinted in Aldcroft and Fearon, eds. *Economic Growth in Twentieth Century Britain*, 1969) *Times Review of Industry and Technology*, December 1963.

Feinstein, Charles H. *National Income, Expenditure and Output of the United Kingdom, 1855-1965*. Cambridge: Cambridge University Press, 1972.

Kuznets, Simon S. "Quantitative Aspects of the Economic Growth of Nations (Part 2): Industrial Distribution of National Product and Labor Force," *Economic Development and Cultural Change*, 5(4, Part 2), July 1957, pp. 3-110.

Kuznets, Simon S. "Quantitative Aspects of the Economic Growth of Nations (Part 7): The Share and Structure of Consumption," *Economic Development and Cultural Change*, 10(2, Part 2), January 1962, pp. 1-92.

Neal, Larry D. "Deane and Cole on Industrialization and Population Change in the Eighteenth Century: Comment," *Economic History Review*, Second Series, 24(4), November 1971, pp. 643-47.

Prest, A.R. and Adams, A.A. *Consumers' Expenditure in the United Kingdom, 1900-1919*. Cambridge: Cambridge University Press, 1954.

Singer, H.W. "Quantitative Aspects of the Economic Growth of Nations: A Footnote to Professor Kuznets," *Economic Development and Cultural Change*, 7(1), October 1958, pp. 73-74.

Stone, J.R.F. and Rowe, D.A. *The Measurement of Consumers' Expenditure and Behaviour in the United Kingdom, 1920-1938* (2 vols). Cambridge: Cambridge University Press, 1954.

Veverka, J. "The Growth of Government Expenditure in the United Kingdom since 1790," *Scottish Journal of Political Economy*, 10(1), February, 1963, pp. 111-27.

Europe: Distribution of Income

Blok, L. and De Meere, J.M.M. "Welstand, Ongelijkheid in Welstand en Censuskiesrecht in Nederland Omstreeks Het Midden van de 19de Eeuw [Prosperity, Wealth Inequality, and Franchise in the Netherlands in the Middle of the Nineteenth Century]," *Economisch- en Sociaal-Historisch Jaarboek*, 41, 1978, pp. 175-293.

Bry, Gerhard and Boschan, Charlotte. *Wages in Germany, 1871-1945* (National Bureau of Economic Research General Series, no. 68).

Princeton: Princeton University Press for the National Bureau of Economic Research, 1960.

Bry, Gerhard and Boschan, Charlotte. "Secular Trends and Recent Changes in Real Wages and Wage Differentials in Three Western Industrial Countries: The United States, Great Britain, and Germany," *Second International Conference on Economic History, Aix-en-Provence, 1962*, vol. 2. Paris: Mouton, 1965, pp. 175-208.

Chapman, A.L., assisted by Knight, R. *Wages and Salaries in the United Kingdom 1920-1938*. Cambridge: Cambridge University Press, 1953.

Cole, W.A. "Deane and Cole on Industrialization and Population Change in the Eighteenth Century: A Rejoinder to Neal," *Economic History Review*, Second Series, 24(4), November 1971, pp. 648-52.

Crafts, N.F.R. "English Economic Growth in the Eighteenth Century: A Re-examination of Deane and Cole's Estimates," *Economic History Review*, Second Series, 29(2), May 1976, pp. 226-35.

Crafts, N.F.R. "National Income Estimates and the British Standard of Living Debate: A Reappraisal of 1801-1831," *Explorations in Economic History*, 17(2), April 1980, pp. 176-88.

De Meere, J.M.M. "Inkomensgroei en -ongelijkheid te Amsterdam 1877-1940 [Growth and Inequality in Amsterdam, 1877-1940]," *Tijdschrift voor Sociale Geschiedenis*, 13, March 1979, pp. 3-47.

Deane, Phyllis and Cole, W.A. *British Economic Growth, 1688-1959: Trends and Structure*. Second Edition, 1968. Cambridge: Cambridge University Press, 1962.

Desai, Ashok V. *Real Wages in Germany, 1871-1913*. Oxford: Oxford University Press, 1968.

Engerman, Stanley L. and Hartwell, Ronald M. "Models of Immiseration: The Theoretical Basis of Pessimism," in Taylor, ed. *The Standard of Living in Britain in the Industrial Revolution*, 1975.

Feinstein, Charles H. "Evolution of the Distribution of the National Income in the U.K. Since 1860," in Marchal and Ducros, eds. *The Distribution of National Income*, 1968.

Feinstein, Charles H. *National Income, Expenditure and Output of the United Kingdom, 1855-1965*. Cambridge: Cambridge University Press, 1972.

Fua, Giorgio. *Formazione, distribuzione e impiego dal reddito del 1861: sintesi statistica [Origin, Distribution, and Destination of National Income (in Italy) since 1861: Statistical Synthesis]*. Roma: ISCO, 1972.

Hart, P.E. "A Long-Run Analysis of the Rate of Return on Capital in Manufacturing Industry, United Kingdom, 1920-62," in Hart, ed. *Studies in Profit, Business Saving and Investment in the United Kingdom, 1920-1962* (vol. 2), 1968, pp. 220-83.

Hart, P.E. "A Macroeconometric Analysis of the Appropriation of Profit in Manufacturing," in Hart, ed. *Studies in Profit, Business Saving and Investment in the United Kingdom, 1920-1962* (vol. 2), 1968, pp. 109-43.

Hart, P.E., ed. *Studies in Profit, Business Saving and Investment in the United Kingdom 1920-1962* (2 vols). (vol. 1, *1965*; vol. 2, *1968*). London: Allen & Unwin, 1965, 1968.

Hart, P.E. "The Factor Distribution of Income in the United Kingdom, 1870-1963," in Hart, ed. *Studies in Profit, Business Saving and*

Investment in the United Kingdom, 1920-1962 (vol. 2), 1968, pp. 17-72.

Jonung, Lars and Wadensjo, Eskil. "Wages and Prices in Sweden, 1912-1922: A Retrospective Test," *Scandinavian Journal of Economics*, 81(1), 1979, pp. 60-71.

Kuznets, Simon S. *Growth, Population, and Income Distribution: Selected Essays.* New York: W.W. Norton, 1979.

Loschky, David J. and Krier, Donald F. "Income and Family Size in Three Eighteenth Century Lancashire Parishes: A Reconstitution Study," *Journal of Economic History,* 29(3), September 1969, pp. 429-48.

Markovitch, Tihomir J. *Salaires et profits industriels en France* [*Wages and Industrial Profits in France*]. Cahiers de l'Institute de Science Economique Appliquee, 1967.

Neal, Larry D. "Deane and Cole on Industrialization and Population Change in the Eighteenth Century: Comment," Economic History Review, Second Series, 24(4), November 1971, pp. 643-47.

O'Brien, Patrick K. and Keyder, Caglar. "Niveles de vida en Gran Bretana y Francia entre 1780 y 1914 [The Standard of Living in Britain and France, 1780-1914]," *Investigaciones Economicas*, (6), August 1978, pp. 5-41.

O'Brien, Patrick K. and Engerman, Stanley L. "Changes in Income and Its Distribution during the Industrial Revolution," in Floud and McCloskey, eds. *The Economic History of Britain since 1700*, vol. 1, 1980, pp. 164-81.

Pettengill, John S. "The Impact of Military Technology on European Income Distribution," *Journal of Interdisciplinary History*, 10(2), Autumn 1979, pp. 201-25.

Phelps Brown, E.H. and Hart, P.E. "The Share of Wages in National Income," *Economic Journal*, 62(246), June 1952, pp. 253-77.

Phelps Brown, E.H. and Weber, Brian A. "Accumulation, Productivity and Distribution in the British Economy, 1870-1938," *Economic Journal*, 63(250), June 1953, pp. 263-88.

Rostow, W.W. "Some Reflections on Capital Formation and Economic Growth," *Universities-National Bureau Conference Series*, no. 6: *Capital Formation and Economic Growth.* New York: Arno Press, 1955, pp. 635-67.

Soltow, Lee C. "Long-Run Changes in British Income Inequality," (Reprinted in Floud, ed. *Essays in Quantitative Economic History,* 1974, pp. 152-165) *Economic History Review*, Second Series, 21(1), April 1968, pp. 17-29.

Soltow, Lee C. "An Index of the Poor and Rich of Scotland, 1861-1961," *Scottish Journal of Political Economy*, 18(1), February 1971, pp. 49-67.

Soltow, Lee C. "Wealth Distribution in Denmark in 1789," *Scandinavian Economic History Review*, 27(2), 1979, pp. 121-38.

Toda, Yasushi. "An Intercountry Comparison of the Consumption Levels of Industrial Workers' Families: Russia 1913-United States of America 1901," *Fourth International Conference of Economic History, Bloomington, 1968.* Paris: Mouton, 1973, pp. 477-84.

Van der Wee, Herman. "Real Wage Income during the Ancien Regime in the Light of Economic Growth," *Fourth International Conference of*

Economic History, Bloomington, 1968. Paris: Mouton, 1973, pp. 467-73.

Von Tunzelmann, G. Nicholas and Savin, N. Eugene. "The Standard of Living Debate and Optimal Economic Growth," [Working Paper].

Williams, J.E. "The British Standard of Living, 1750-1850," in Kellenbenz, Schneider, and Gommel, eds. *Wirtschaftliches Wachstum im Speigel der Wirtschaftsgeschichte*, 1978.

Williamson, Jeffrey G. "Earnings Inequality in Nineteenth-Century Britain," *Journal of Economic History*, 40(3), September 1980, pp. 457-75.

Williamson, Jeffrey G. "Urban Disamenities, Dark Satanic Mills and the British Standard of Living Debate," *Journal of Economic History*, 41(1), March 1981, pp. 75-84.

Williamson, Jeffrey G. and Lindert, Peter H. "English Experience with the Distribution of Wealth and Income Since the Late 17th Century and Their Determinants: A Companion Volume to 'A Macroeconomic History of American Inequality'," [Working Paper].

Zamagni, Vera. "The Rich in a Late Industrializer: The Case of Italy (1800-1945)," in Rubinstein, ed. *Wealth and the Wealthy in Modern Europe*, 1980.

Other: National Income

Ballestoros, Marto A. and Davis, Thomas E. "The Growth of Output and Employment in Basic Sectors of the Chilean Economy, 1908-1957," *Economic Development and Cultural Change*, 11(2), January 1963, pp. 152-76.

Buescu, Mircea. "Bresil, 1907: Un Exercice Macro-Economique [Brazil, 1907: A Macroeconomic Essay]," in Schneider, ed. *Festschrift fur Hermann Kellenbenz*, 1978, pp. 461-70.

Butlin, Noel G. "Long-Run Trends in Australia Per Capita Consumption," in Hancock, ed. *The National Income and Social Welfare*, 1965.

Cole, W.A. and Deane, Phyllis. "The Growth of National Incomes," in Habukkuk and Postan, eds. *The Cambridge Economic History of Europe*, vol. 6, Part1, 1965, pp. 1-55.

Deane, Phyllis. *The Measurement of Colonial National Incomes: An Experiment* (National Institute of Economic and Social Research Occasional Paper Series, no. 12). Cambridge: Cambridge University Press, 1948.

Deane, Phyllis. *Colonial Social Accounting* (National Institute of Economic and Social Research, Economic and Social Studies Series, no. 11). Cambridge: Cambridge University Press, 1953.

Friedman, Milton. "Monetary Data and National Income Estimates," *Economic Development and Cultural Change*, 9(3), April 1961, pp. 267-86.

Goldsmith, Raymond W. "A Synthetic Estimate of the National Wealth of Japan, 1885-1973," *Review of Income and Wealth*, 21(2), June 1975, pp. 125-52.

Haddad, Claudio L.S. "Crescimento do Produto Real Brasileiro, 1900-1947 [Growth of Brazilian Real Product, 1900-1947]," *Revista Brasileira de Economia*, 29(1), January/March 1975, pp. 3-26.

Haddad, Claudio L.S. and Contador, Claudio R. "Produto Real, Moeda e Precos: A Experiencia Brasileira no Periodo 1861-1970 [Real Product, Money and Prices: The Brazilian Experience in the Period 1861-1970]," *Revista Brasileira de Estatistica*, 36(143), July/September 1975, pp. 407-40.

Haddad, Claudio L.S.s "Crescimento do Produto Real no Brasil, 1900-1947 [Growth of Brazilian Real Output, 1900-1947]," Ph.D. Dissertation, University of Chicago, 1974 [Working Paper].

Haddad, Claudio L.S. "Crescimento Economico do Brasil, 1900-76 [Economic Growth of Brazil, 1900-76]," in Neuhaus, ed. *A Economia Brasileira [The Brazilian Economy]*, 1979.

Haig, Brian D. "1938/39 National Income Estimates," *Australian Economic History Review*, 7(2), September 1967, pp. 172-86.

Haig, Brian D. *Expenditure and Living Standards, Australia 1920-1950* (vol. 1: *Basic Estimates*; vol. 2: *Analysis and Sources*). Canberra: Australian National University, 1980.

Hawke, Gary R. "Income Estimation from Monetary Data: Further Explorations," *Review of Income and Wealth*, 21(3), September 1975, pp. 301-308.

Japanese Economic Planning Board. *National Income and National Economic Accounts of Japan, 1930-56*. Tokyo: Economic Planning Board, 1957.

Jefferys, James B. and Walters, Dorothy. "National Income and Expenditure of the United Kingdom," *Income and Wealth*, Series 5. London: Bowes & Bowes, 1955.

Krogh, D.C. "The National Income and Expenditures of South-West Africa (1920-1956)," *South African Journal of Economics*, 28(1), March 1960, pp. 3-22.

Layton, T. Brent. "New Zealand's Social Accounting Aggregates and Official Trade Statistics, 1859-1939," *Victoria University of Wellington, Working Papers in Economic History*, no. 77/4, 1977 [Working Paper].

Leff, Nathaniel H. "A Technique for Estimating Income Trends from Currency Data and an Application to Nineteenth-Century Brazil," [Translated into Portuguese in Revista Brasileira de Economia, 1972] *Review of Income and Wealth*, 18(4), December 1972, pp. 355-68.

Lineham, B.T. "New Zealand's Gross Domestic Product 1918-38," *New Zealand Economic Papers*, 2, 1968, pp. 15-26.

Mukerjee, Moni. *The National Income of India: Trends and Structure*. Calcutta: Statistical Pub. Society, 1969.

Noda, Tsutomu. "Commodity Prices and Wages, 1880-1965," in Ohkawa and Hayami, eds. *Economic Growth: The Japanese Experience since the Meiji Era*, vol. 1, 1973, pp. 113-32.

Ohkawa, Kazushi and Shinohara, Miyohei., eds. *The Growth Rate of the Japanese Economy since 1878*. Tokyo: Kinokuniya, 1957.

Ohkawa, Kazushi. "National Product and Expenditure, 1885-1969," in Ohkawa and Hayami, eds. *Economic Growth*, vol. 1, 1973, pp. 133-53.

Ohkawa, Kazushi; Shinohara, Miyohei and Umemura, Mataji., eds. *Estimates of Long Term Economic Statistics of Japan since 1868*. Tokyo: Toyo Keizai Shinpo Sha, 1965.

Rosovsky, Henry. "The Statistical Measurement of Japanese Economic

Growth." (Review essay of *The Growth Rate of the Japanese Economy since 1878.* by Kazushi Ohkawa, ed., 1957) *Economic Development and Cultural Change*, 7(1), October 1958, pp. 75-84.

Shinohara, Miyohei. "Personal Consumption Expenditures, 1874-1940," Kazushi Ohkawa and Yujiro Hayami, eds. *Economic Growth: The Japanese Experience since the Meiji Era*, vol. 1. Tokyo: Japan Economic Research Center, 1973, pp. 51-66.

Stadler, J.J. "The Gross Domestic Product of South Africa, 1911-1959," *South African Journal of Economics*, 31(3), September 1963, pp. 185-208.

Yasuba, Yasukichi. "General Comments on Statistical Estimates," in Ohkawa and Hayami, eds. *Economic Growth*, vol. 1, 1973, pp. 165-72.

Other: Capital Formation and Capital Stock

Bagchi, Amiya K. *Private Investment in India, 1900-1939.* Cambridge: Cambridge University Press, 1972.

Butlin, Noel G. *Public Capital Formation in Australia: Estimates 1860-1900.* Canberra: Australian National University, 1954.

Butlin, Noel G. *Private Capital Formation in Australia: Estimates 1860-1900.* Canberra: Australian National University, 1955.

Butlin, Noel G. "Colonial Socialism in Australia 1860-1900," in Aitken, ed. *The State and Economic Growth, 1959.*

Butlin, Noel G. *Australian Domestic Product, Investment and Foreign Borrowing, 1860-1938/39.* Cambridge: Cambridge University Press, 1962.

Butlin, Noel G. "The Growth of Rural Capital, 1860-1890," in Barnard, ed. *A Simple Fleece, 1962,* pp. 322-39.

Butlin, Noel G. *Investment in Australian Economic Development, 1860-1900.* London: Cambridge University Press, 1964.

Emi, Koichi and Rosovsky, Henry. "Seifu Kensetsu toshi no Sokutei, 1868-1940 [The Measurement of Japanese Government Investment in Construction, 1868-1940]," *Keizai Kenkyu*, 9(1), January 1958, pp. 52-60.

Emi, Koichi. "Long Term Movements of Gross Domestic Fixed Capital Formation in Japan, 1869-1940," in Ohkawa and Hayami, eds. *Economic Growth*, vol. 1, 1973, pp. 67-79.

Gould, John D. "A Case of Unbalanced Growth. Review Essay of 'Investment in Australian Economic Development, 1861-1900' by Noel G. Butlin (London: Cambridge University Press, 1964)," *Economic Record*, 42(98), June 1966, pp. 312-20.

Haig, Brian D. "Capital Stock in Manufacturing, 1920 to 1978," *Australian National University Department of Economics/Research School of Social Sciences Series Monograph.* Canberra: Australian National University Press, 1981.

Ishiwata, Shigeru. "Capital Stocks, 1888-1937," in Ohkawa and Hayami, eds. *Economic Growth*, vol. 1, 1973, pp. 101-12.

Kuznets, Simon S. "Quantitative Aspects of the Economic Growth of Nations (Part 6): Long-Term Trends in Capital Formation Proportions," *Economic Development and Cultural Change*, 9(4, Part 2), July 1961, pp. 1-124.

Kuznets, Simon S. "Capital Formation in Modern Economic Growth (and some implications for the past)," *Third International Conference of Economic History, Munich, 1965*, part 1. Paris: Mouton, 1968, pp. 15-53.

Leff, Nathaniel H. *The Brazilian Capital Goods Industry, 1929-1964*. Cambridge: Harvard University Press, 1968.

Morris, Morris D. "Private Industrial Investment on the Indian Subcontinent, 1900-1939: Some Methodological Considerations," (Review essay of *Private Investment in India, 1900-1939*. by A. K. Bagchi, 1972) *Modern Asian Studies*, 8(4), October 1974, pp. 535-55.

Pelaez, Carlos Manuel. "Unbalance in Demand and Supply, and Input-Provision Capital Formation: Brazil, 1920-1951," (Summary of Doctoral Dissertation) *Journal of Economic History*, 25(4), December 1965, pp. 700-703.

Rosovsky, Henry and Emi, K. . "Nihon no Shihon Keisei to Shite no Kensetsu [Construction as a Part of Japanese Capital Formation]," *Nikon Tokei Gakkai Kaiho*, April 1958.

Rosovsky, Henry. "Japanese Capital Formation: The Role of the Public Sector," *Journal of Economic History*, 19(3), September 1959, pp. 350-75.

Rosovsky, Henry. "Nihon no Shihon Keisei to Seifu no Yakuwari [The Role of the State in Japanese Capital Formation]," Tokyo: Japan Economic Planning Agency, June 1960.

Rosovsky, Henry. "Senzen Nihon no Shihon Keisei [Capital Formation in Prewar Japan]," *Shakai Keizai-Shi Gaku*, February 1963.

Sinclair, William A. "Public Capital Formation in Australia: 1919-20 to 1929-30: A Note," *Economic Record*, 31(61), November 1955, pp. 299-310.

Sinclair, William A. "Capital Formation," in Forster, ed. *Australian Economic Development in the Twentieth Century*, 1970.

Other: Sectoral Contributions

Buescu, Mircea. "Medicao das Disparidades Regionais de Renda: Brasil, 1872-1900 [Measurement of Regional Income Disparaties: Brazil, 1872-1900]," *Verbum*, 33(2), December 1977, pp. 199-208.

Keesing, Donald B. "Structural Change Early in Development: Mexico's Changing Industrial and Occupational Structure from 1895 to 1950," *Journal of Economic History*, 29(4), December 1969, pp. 716-38.

Kuznets, Simon S. "Quantitative Aspects of the Economic Growth of Nations (Part 2): Industrial Distribution of National Product and Labor Force," *Economic Development and Cultural Change*, 5(4, Part 2), July 1957, pp. 3-110.

Kuznets, Simon S. "Quantitative Aspects of the Economic Growth of Nations (Part 7): *The Share and Structure of Consumption,*" *Economic Development and Cultural Change*, 10(2, Part 2), January 1962, pp. 1-92.

Singer, H.W. "Quantitative Aspects of the Economic Growth of Nations: A Footnote to Professor Kuznets," *Economic Development and Cultural*

Change, 7(1), October 1958, pp. 73-74.

Zahn, Frank. "Sectorial Labor Migration and Sustained Industrialization in the Japanese Development Experience," *Review of Economics and Statistics*, 53(3), August 1971, pp. 283-87.

Other: Distribution of Income

Fua, Giorgio. "La distribuzione del reddito in Italia, 1862-1970 [Income Distribution in Italy, 1862-1970]," *Studi economici*, (1), 1973.

Haig, Brian D. *Expenditure and Living Standards, Australia 1920-1950* (vol. 1: *Basic Estimates*; vol. 2: *Analysis and Sources*). Canberra: Australian National University, 1980.

Hawke, Gary R. "Acquisitiveness and Equality in New Zealand's Economic Development," *Economic History Review*, Second Series, 32(3), August 1979, pp. 376-90.

Kuznets, Simon S. *Growth, Population, and Income Distribution: Selected Essays*. New York: W.W. Norton, 1979.

McAlpin, Michelle Burge. "The Effects of Expansion of Markets on Rural Income Distribution in Nineteenth Century India," (Symposium on Economic Change in Indian Agriculture. Edited by Morris D. Morris) *Explorations in Economic History*, 12(3), July 1975, pp. 289-301.

Mokyr, Joel and Savin, N. Eugene. "Some Econometric Problems in the Standard of Living Controversy," *Journal of European Economic History*, 7(2-3), Fall/Winter 1978, pp. 517-25.

Morris, Cynthia Taft and Adelman, Irma. *Economic Growth and Social Equity in Developing Countries*. Stanford: Stanford University Press, 1973.

Morris, Cynthia Taft and Adelman, Irma. "An Inquiry into the Course of Poverty in the Ninteenth and Early Twentieth Centuries," in Matthews, ed. *Measurement, History, and Factors of Economic Growth*, 1978.

Phelps Brown, E.H. and Hart, P.E. "The Share of Wages in National Income," *Economic Journal*, 62(246), June 1952, pp. 253-77.

Phelps Brown, E.H. and Hopkins, Sheila V. "Seven Centuries of Building Wages," *Economica*, 22(87), August 1955, pp. 195-206.

Phelps Brown, E.H. and Hopkins, Sheila V. "Seven Centuries of the Prices of Consumables, Compared with Builders' Wage Rates," (Reprinted in Ramsey, ed. *The Price Revolution in the Sixteenth Century*, 1971, pp. 18-41) *Economica*, 23(92), November 1956, pp. 296-314.

Soltow, Lee C. "The Censuses of Wealth of Men in Australia in 1915 and in the United States in 1860 and 1870," *Australian Economic History Review*, 12(2), September 1972, pp. 125-41.

Uselding, Paul J. "Wages and Capital Consumption Levels in England and on the Continent in the 1830's," *Journal of European Economic History*, 4(2), Fall 1975, pp. 501-13.

Yamamura, Kozo. "The Increasing Poverty of the Samurai in Tokugawa

Japan, 1600-1868," *Journal of Economic History*, 31(2), June 1971, pp. 378-406.

Chapter 5

ECONOMIC GROWTH

General

Cameron, Rondo E. "Some Lessons of History for Developing Nations," *American Economic Review, Papers and Proceedings*, 57(2), May 1967, pp. 312-24.

Clark, Colin. *The Conditions of Economic Progress.* (Reprinted in revised Third edition by Macmillan and St.Martin's Press, London and New York, 1957) New York: Macmillan, 1940.

Coats, A.W. *Economic Growth: The Economic and Social Historian's Dilemma.* Nottingham: University of Nottingham Press, 1967.

Deane, Phyllis. "The Long Term Trends in World Economic Growth," *Malayan Economic Review*, 6(2), October 1961, pp. 14-26.

Easterlin, Richard A. "Economic Growth: An Overview," in Sills, ed. *International Encyclopedia of the Social Sciences*, 1968, pp. 395-408.

Easterlin, Richard A. "Some Conceptual Aspects of the Comparative Measurement of Economic Growth," Ph.D. Dissertation, Available on Microfilm, 1953 [Working Paper].

Gould, John D. *Economic Growth in History: Survey and Analysis.* London: Methuen, 1972.

Hughes, Jonathan R.T. "Economic Growth and Change: How and Why," *Journal of Interdisciplinary History*, 2(3), Winter 1972, pp. 263-80.

Kellenbenz, Hermann; Schneider, Jurgen and Gommel, Rainer. *Wirtschaftliches Wachstum im Spiegel der Wirtschaftsgeschichte [Economic Growth in Economic Historical Perspective].* Darmstadt: Wissenschaftliche Buchgesellschaft, 1978.

Kuznets, Simon S., ed. *Problems in the Study of Economic Growth.* New York: National Bureau of Economic Research, 1949.

Kuznets, Simon S. *Economic Change: Selected Essays in Business Cycles, National Income, and Economic Growth.* New York: W.W. Norton, 1953.

Kuznets, Simon S. *Six Lectures on Economic Growth.* Glencoe, Ill.: Free Press, 1960.

Kuznets, Simon S. *Economic Growth of Nations: Total Output and Production Structure.* Cambridge, Mass.: Belknap Press, 1971.

Kuznets, Simon S. *Growth, Population, and Income Distribution: Selected Essays.* New York: W.W. Norton, 1979.

Lewis, W. Arthur. *Growth and Fluctuations, 1870-1913.* London: Allen & Unwin, 1978.

Before the Industrial Revolution

Lewis, W. Arthur. *The Evolution of the International Economic Order.*
Princeton: Princeton University Press, 1978.
North, Douglass C. "Institutional Change and Economic Growth," *Journal of Economic History*, 31(1), March 1971, pp. 118-25.
O'Brien, Patrick K. "Theories of Economic Change for Historians,"
[Working Paper].
Rostow, W.W. *Politics and the Stages of Growth.* Cambridge: Cambridge University Press, 1971.
Rostow, W.W. *Getting from Here to There.* New York: McGraw-Hill, 1978.
Rostow, W.W. and Fordyce, Frederick E. "Growth Rates at Different Levels of Income and Stage of Growth: Reflections on Why the Poor Get Richer and the Rich Slow Down," in Uselding, ed. *Research in Economic History*, vol. 3, 1978, pp. 47-86.
Rostow, W.W. *The World Economy: History & Prospect.* Austin: University of Texas Press, 1978.
Supple, Barry. "Economic History and Economic Growth," *Journal of Economic History*, 20(4), December 1960, pp. 548-56.

Before the Industrial Revolution

Bairoch, Paul. "Estimations du Revenu National dans les societes occidentales durant les periodes pre-industrielles et le XIXe siecle: propositions d'approches indirectes [National Income Estimates for Western Societies in the Pre-Industrial Period and in the Nineteenth Century: Suggestions for Indirect Approaches]," *Revue Economique*, 28(2), March 1977, pp. 177-208.
Bairoch, Paul. "Ecarts internationaux des niveaux de vie avant la revolution industrielle [International Differences in Standards of Living Before the Industrial Revolution]," *Annales*, 34(1), January/February 1979, pp. 145-171.
Freudenberger, Herman and Cummins, J. Gaylord. "Health, Work, and Leisure before the Industrial Revolution," *Explorations in Economic History*, 13(1), January 1976, pp. 1-12.
Jones, Andrew. "The Rise and Fall of the Manorial System: A Critical Comment (on North and Thomas)," *Journal of Economic History*, 32(4), December 1972, pp. 938-44.
Lane, Frederic C. "The Role of Governments in Economic Growth in Early Modern Times," *Journal of Economic History*, 35(1), March 1975, pp. 8-17.
Mendels, Franklin. "Proto-Industrialization: The First Phase of the Industrialization Process," *Journal of Economic History*, 32(1), March 1972, pp. 241-61.
North, Douglass C. and Thomas, Robert P. "An Economic Theory of the Growth of the Western World," *Economic History Review*, Second Series, 23(1), April 1970, pp. 1-17.
North, Douglass C. and Thomas, Robert P. "The Rise and Fall of the Manorial System: A Theoretical Model," *Journal of Economic History*, 31(4), December 1971, pp. 777-803.
North, Douglass C. and Thomas, Robert P. "European Economic Growth: Reply to Professor D. Ringose," *Economic History Review*, Second Series, 26(2), May 1973, pp. 293-94.

North, Douglass C. and Thomas, Robert P. *The Rise of the Western World: A New Economic History.* [Translated into Italian, Spanish, and French] Cambridge: Cambridge University Press, 1975.

North, Douglass C. and Thomas, Robert P. "The Role of Governments in Economic Growth in Early Modern Times: Comment on Lane," *Journal of Economic History*, 35(1), March 1975, pp. 18-19.

Rapp, Richard T. "A Theory of Premodern Economic Growth," (Review essay of 'The Rise of the Western World: A New Economic History' by North and Thomas, 1975) *Reviews in European History*, 2(2), June 1976, pp. 181-8.

Reed, Clyde G. "Transactions Costs and Differential Growth in Seventeenth Century Western Europe," *Journal of Economic History*, 33(1), March 1973, pp. 178-90.

Ringrose, D.R. "European Economic Growth: Comments on the North-Thomas Theory," *Economic History Review*, Second Series, 26(2), May 1973, pp. 285-92.

Roehl, Richard. "Comment on Papers by Reed and Bean Presented to the 32nd Annual Meeting of the Economic History Association," *Journal of Economic History*, 33(1), March 1973, pp. 228-31.

Smith, Vernon L. "The Primitive Hunter Culture, Pleistocene Extinction, and the Rise of Agriculture," *Journal of Political Economy*, 83(4), August 1975, pp. 727-56.

Thomas, Brinley. "The Rhythm of Growth in the Atlantic Economy of the Eighteenth Century," in Uselding, ed. *Research in Economic History*, vol. 3, 1978, pp. 1-46.

Tortella Casares, Gabriel. "El profesor Hicks y la historia economica [Professor Hicks and Economic History]," *Sistema, Revista de Ciencias Sociales*, 1(3), October 1973.

The Industrial Revolution

Bairoch, Paul. "Original Characteristics and Consequences of the Industrial Revolution," *Diogene*, (54), Summer 1966, pp. 47-58.

Chambers, Edward J. and Gordon, Donald F. "Primary Products and Economic Growth: An Empirical Measurement," [Translated into Spanish in *Journal of the Fundacion de Investigationes Economicas Lationoamericanas*] *Journal of Political Economy*, 74(4), August 1966, pp. 315-32.

Chambers, Edward J. and Gordon, Donald F. "Primary Products and Economic Growth: Rejoinder to Dales, McManus, and Watkins," *Journal of Political Economy*, 75(6), December 1967, pp. 881-85.

Dales, John H.; McManus, John C. and Watkins, Melville H. "Primary Products and Economic Growth: A Comment on Chambers and Gordon," *Journal of Political Economy*, 75(6), December 1967, pp. 876-80.

Deane, Phyllis. "The Role of Capital in the Industrial Revolution," *Explorations in Economic History*, 10(4), Summer 1973, pp. 349-64.

Fishlow, Albert. "Empty Economic Stages?" (Review essay of *The Economics of Take-Off into Sustained Growth.*, edited by W.W. Rostow, 1963) *Economic Journal*, 75(297), March 1965, pp. 112-25.

Hoffmann, Walther G. *Stadien und Typen der Industrialisierung: ein Beitrag zur quantitativen Analyse historischer Wirtschaftsprozesse.*

Jena: G. Fischer, 1931.

Hoffmann, Walther G. *The Growth of Industrial Economies.* (translated by W.O. Henderson and W.H. Chaloner) Manchester: Manchester University Press, 1958.

Hoffmann, Walther G. "The Take-Off in Germany," in Rostow, ed. *The Economics of Take-Off into Sustained Growth,* 1963, pp. 95-118.

Holtfrerich, Karl-Ludwig. "Wachstum I: Volkswirtschaftliche Probleme [Growth I: Economic Problems]," *Handworterbuch der Wirtschaftswissenschaften,* 1979.

Hughes, Jonathan R.T. *Industrialization and Economic History: Theses and Conjectures.* New York: McGraw-Hill, 1970.

Hughes, Jonathan R.T. "What Difference Did the Beginning Make?" American Economic Review, Papers and Proceedings, 67(1), February 1977, pp. 15-20.

Kindleberger, Charles P. *Economic Response: Comparative Studies in Trade, Finance, and Growth.* Cambridge: Harvard University Press, 1978.

Kuczynski, Thomas. "Have there been Differences between the Growth Rates in Different Periods of the Development of the Capitalist World Economy since 1850? An Application of Cluster Analysis in Time Series Analysis," *Historisch-Sozialwissenschaftliche Forschungen,* vol. 5. Stuttgart, 1980.

Kuznets, Simon S. "Notes on the Take-off," in Rostow, ed. *The Economics of Take-off into Sustained Growth,* 1963, pp. 22-43.

Kuznets, Simon S. *Economic Growth and Structure.* (Second Edition published by Yale University Press, New Haven, 1970) New York: W.W. Norton, 1965.

Kuznets, Simon S. *Modern Economic Growth: Rate, Structure, and Spread* (Studies in Comparative Economics, no. 7). New Haven: Yale University Press, 1966.

Leff, Nathaniel H. "Entrepreneurship and Economic Development: The Problem Revisited," *Journal of Economic Literature,* 17(1), March 1979, pp. 46-64.

Lewis, W. Arthur. *Growth and Fluctuations, 1870-1913.* London: Allen & Unwin, 1978.

Morris, Cynthia Taft and Adelman, Irma. "Patterns of Industrialization in the Nineteenth and Early Twentieth Centuries: A Cross-Sectional Quantitative Study," in Uselding, ed. *Research in Economic History,* vol. 5, 1980.

Myrdal, Gunnar. "The Theories of 'Stages of Growth'," *Scandinavian Economic History Review,* 15, nos. 1 & 2), 1967, pp. 1-12.

North, Douglass C. "A Note on Professor Rostow's Take-Off into Self-Sustained Growth," *Manchester School of Economic and Social Studies,* 26(1), January 1958, pp. 68-75.

Parker, William N. "Economic History and National Accounts." (Review essay of *Modern Economic Growth,* by Kuznets, 1966) *Review of Income and Wealth,* 13(2), June 1967, pp. 199-204.

Rosenberg, Nathan. "Science, Invention and Economic Growth," *Economic Journal,* 84(333), March 1974, pp. 90-108.

Rosovsky, Henry. "The Take-Off into Sustained Controversy." (Review essay of *The Economics of Take-Off into Sustained Growth,* by Rostow, ed., 1963) *Journal of Economic History,* 25(2), June 1965,

pp. 271-75.

Rostow, W.W. *The Process of Economic Growth.* New York: W.W. Norton, 1952.

Rostow, W.W. "The Stages of Economic Growth," *Economic History Review,* Second Series, 12(1), 1959, pp. 1-16.

Rostow, W.W. *The Stages of Economic Growth: A Non-Communist Manifesto.* Cambridge: Cambridge University Press, 1960.

Rostow, W.W., ed. *The Economics of Take-Off into Sustained Growth: Proceedings of a Conference Held by the International Economic Association.* New York: St. Martin's Press, 1963.

Rostow, W.W. "Leading Sectors and the Take-off," in Rostow, ed. *The Economics of Take-off into Sustained Growth,* 1963, pp. 1-21.

Siengenthaler, Jurg K. "A Scale Analysis of Nineteenth-Century Industrialization," *Explorations in Economic History,* 10(1), Fall 1972, pp. 75-108.

Solow, Robert M. and Temin, Peter. "Introduction: The Inputs for Growth," in Mathias and Postan, eds. *The Cambridge Economic History of Europe,* vol. 7, part 1, 1978, pp. 1-27.

Soltow, James H. "The Entrepreneur in Economic History," *American Economic Review,* 58(2), May 1968, pp. 84-92.

Supple, Barry. "Thinking About Economic Development," in Youngson, ed. *Economic Development in the Long Run,* 1972, pp. 19-35.

Temin, Peter. "A Time-Series Test of Patterns of Industrial Growth," *Economic Development and Cultural Change,* 15(2, Part 1), January 1967, pp. 174-82.

Thomas, Brinley. "Towards an Energy Interpretation of the Industrial Revolution," *Atlantic Economic Journal,* 8(1), March 1980, pp. 1-15.

Post-Industrial Revolution

De Vries, Jan. "Is There an Economics of Decline?" (Summary of 1977 Research Workshop) *Journal of Economic History,* 38(1), March 1978, pp. 256-58.

Hoffmann, Walther G. *The Growth of Industrial Economies.* (translated by W.O. Henderson and W.H. Chaloner) Manchester: Manchester University Press, 1958.

Kindleberger, Charles P. *Economic Response: Comparative Studies in Trade, Finance, and Growth.* Cambridge: Harvard University Press, 1978.

Kuznets, Simon S. *Economic Growth and Structure.* (Second Edition published by Yale University Press, New Haven, 1970) New York: W.W. Norton, 1965.

Lewis, W. Arthur. *Economic Survey, 1919-1939.* (Reprinted by Harper & Row, New York, 1969) London: Allen & Unwin, 1949.

Olson, Mancur L. and Lansberg, Hans. *The No Growth Society.* <Also, Published as the Fall 1973 Issue of *Daedalus,* in Japanese Translation (Tokyo, 1974), and in a Separate British Edition (Woborn Press, 1975)> New York: W.W. Norton, 1974.

Abramovitz, Moses. "Economic Growth in the United States: A Review Article," *American Economic Review*, 52(4), September 1962, pp. 762-82.

Abramovitz, Moses and David, Paul A. "Economic Growth in America: Historical Parables and Realities," *De Economist*, 121(3), 1973, pp. 251-72.

Abramovitz, Moses and David, Paul A. "Reinterpreting Economic Growth: Parables and Realities," *American Economic Review, Papers and Proceedings*, 63(2), May 1973, pp. 428-39.

Bruchey, Stuart. "Douglass C. North on American Economic Growth," *Explorations in Entrepreneurial History*, Second Series, 1(2), Winter 1964, pp. 145-58.

Conrad, Alfred H. "Income Growth and Structural Change," in Harris, ed. *American Economic History*, 1961, pp. 26-64.

David, Paul A. and Abramovitz, Moses. "Economic Growth in America: Historical Parables and Realities," *De Economist*, 121(3), 1973, pp. 251-72.

David, Paul A. and Abramovitz, Moses. "Reinterpreting Economic Growth: Parables and Realities," *American Economic Review, Papers and Proceedings*, 63(2), May 1973, pp. 428-39.

David, Paul A. "Invention and Accumulation in America's Economic Growth: A Nineteenth Century Parable," in Brunner and Meltzer, eds. *International Organization, National Policies and Economic Development*, 1977.

Davis, Lance E. "Capital and Growth," in Davis, Easterlin, and Parker, eds. *American Economic Growth*, 1972, pp. 280-310.

Davis, Lance E. "Capital Immobilities and Economic Growth," Presented at the First International Economic History Conference, Rome, 1965 [Working Paper].

Davis, Lance E. "Directions of Change in American Capitalism," Presented at the First Annual International Seminar on Societies in Transition, Malente, Federal Republic of Germany, July 1978 [Working Paper].

Davis, Lance E. "Monopolies, Speculators, Causal Models, Quantitative Evidence, and American Economic Growth," Presented at the Meetings of the Organization of American Historians, April 1967 [Working Paper].

Gallman, Robert E. "The Pace and Pattern of American Economic Growth," Lance E. Davis, Richard A. Easterlin, and William N. Parker, eds. *American Economic Growth: An Economist's History of the United States*. New York: Harper & Row, 1972, pp. 15-60.

Gallman, Robert E. "Economic Growth," in Porter, ed. *Encyclopedia of American Economic History*, vol. 1, 1980, pp. 133-50.

Kendrick, John W. "Productivity," in Porter, ed. *Encyclopedia of American Economic History*, vol. 1, 1980, pp. 157-66.

Kuznets, Simon S. "Notes on the Pattern of U.S. Economic Growth," in Fogel and Engerman, eds. *The Reinterpretation of American Economic History*, 1971, pp. 17-24.

Lindert, Peter H. *Fertility and Scarcity in America*. Princeton: Princeton University Press, 1978.

North, Douglass C. "The Spatial and Interregional Framework of the

United States Economy: An Historical Perspective," in Carrothers, ed. *Papers and Proceedings of the Regional Science Association, 1956*, vol. 2, 1956, pp. 201-9.

North, Douglass C. "The United States in the International Economy, 1790-1950," in Harris, ed. *American Economic History*, 1961, pp. 181-206.

North, Douglass C. "Douglass C. North on American Economic Growth: Comments on Stuart Bruchey's Paper," *Explorations in Entrepreneurial History*, Second Series, 1(2), Winter 1964, pp. 159-63.

North, Douglass C. *Growth and Welfare in the American Past: A New Economic History*. (Second Edition Printed in 1974) Englewood Cliffs, N.J.: Prentice-Hall, 1966.

North, Douglass C. and Davis, Lance E. *Institutional Change and American Economic Growth*. Cambridge: Cambridge University Press, 1971.

North, Douglass C. "Institutional Change and Economic Growth," *Journal of Economic History*, 31(1), March 1971, pp. 118-25.

Olmstead, Alan L. and Goldberg, Victor P. "Institutional Change and American Economic Growth: A Critique of Davis and North," *Explorations in Economic History*, 12(2), April 1975, pp. 193-210.

America Before the Industrial Revolution

Anderson, Terry L. "Wealth Estimates for the New England Colonies, 1650-1709," *Explorations in Economic History*, 12(2), April 1975, pp. 151-76.

Andreano, Ralph L. "Trends in Economic Welfare, 1790-1860," in Andreano, ed. *New Views on American Economic Development*, 1965, pp. 131-67.

Andreano, Ralph L. "Some Issues in Antebellum U.S. Economic Growth and Welfare," *Cahiers Internationaux d'Histoire Economique et Sociale*, 5, 1975, pp. 357-79.

Bean, Richard N. "Colonial American Economic History," (Summary of 1975 Research Workshop) *Journal of Economic History*, 36(1), March 1976, pp. 32-34.

Bean, Richard N.; Anderson, Terry L. and Thomas, Robert P. "Economic Growth in the 17th Century American Colonies: Application of an Export-Led Growth Model," [Working Paper].

Bruchey, Stuart. "Douglass C. North on American Economic Growth," *Explorations in Entrepreneurial History*, Second Series, vol. 1(2), Winter 1964, pp. 145-58.

David, Paul A. "New Light on a Statistical Dark Age: U.S. Real Product Growth before 1840," *American Economic Review, Papers and Proceedings*, 57(2), May 1967, pp. 294-306.

David, Paul A. "The Growth of Real Product in the United States before 1840: New Evidence, Controlled Conjectures," *Journal of Economic History*, 27(2), June 1967, pp. 151-97.

David, Paul A. "American Economic Growth Before 1840: Comments on Papers by Anderson, Haeger, Kulikoff, and Lindstrom Presented to the 38th Annual Meeting of the Economic History Association,"

Journal of Economic History, 39(1), March 1979, pp. 303-10.

Engerman, Stanley L. "Notes on the Patterns of Economic Growth in the British North American Colonies in the Seventeenth, Eighteenth, and Nineteenth Centuries," *International Economic History Congress, Edinburgh, 1978: Four 'A' Themes*. Edinburgh: Edinburgh University Press, 1978, pp. 187-98 [Working Paper].

Galenson, David W. and Menard, Russell R. "Approaches to the Analysis of Economic Growth in Colonial British America," *Historical Methods*, 13(1), Winter 1980, pp. 3-18.

Gallman, Robert E. *Developing the American Colonies, 1607-1783*. Chicago: Scott, Foresman, 1964.

Gallman, Robert E. "Comment on Papers by Anderson, Haeger, Kulikoff, and Lindstrom Presented to the 38th Annual Meeting of the Economic History Association," *Journal of Economic History*, 39(1), March 1979, pp. 311-12.

Jones, Alice Hanson. "Wealth Estimates for the American Middle Colonies, 1774," *Economic Development and Cultural Change*, 18(4, Part 2), July 1970, pp. 1-172.

Jones, Alice Hanson. "Wealth Estimates for the New England Colonies about 1770," *Journal of Economic History*, 32(1), March 1972, pp. 98-127.

Jones, Alice Hanson. "Components of Private Wealth Per Free Capita for the Thirteen Colonies," in U.S. Bureau of the Census, ed. *Historical Statistics of the United States, Colonial Times to 1970*, vol. 2, 1976, pp. 1175.

Jones, Alice Hanson. *Wealth of a Nation to Be: The American Colonies on the Eve of the Revolution*. New York: Columbia University Press, 1980.

Jones, Alice Hanson. "Wealth Estimates for the Southern Colonies about 1770," *Claremont Economic Papers*, no. 86, December 1973 [Working Paper].

Klingaman, David C. "The Significance of Grain in the Development of the Tobacco Colonies," *Journal of Economic History*, 29(2), June 1969, pp. 268-78.

Kulikoff, Allan. "The Economic Growth of the Eighteenth-Century Chesapeake Colonies," *Journal of Economic History*, 39(1), March 1979, pp. 275-88.

Lindstrom, Diane L. "American Economic Growth before 1840: New Evidence and New Directions," *Journal of Economic History*, 39(1), March 1979, pp. 289-301.

North, Douglass C. *The Economic Growth of the United States, 1790-1860*. Englewood Cliffs, N.J.: Prentice-Hall, 1961.

North, Douglass C. "Douglass C. North on American Economic Growth: Comments on Stuart Bruchey's Paper," *Explorations in Entrepreneurial History*, Second Series, 1(2), Winter 1964, pp. 159-63.

North, Douglass C. and Thomas, Robert P. *A Documentary History of American Economic Growth, 1607-1860*. New York: Harper & Row, 1968.

Parker, William N. and Whartenby, Franklee. "The Growth of Output Before 1840," in Parker, ed. *Trends in the American Economy in the Nineteenth Century* (Studies in Income and Wealth, vol. 24), 1960, pp. 191-212.

Parker, William N. *Commerce, Cotton, and Westward Expansion, 1820-1860.* Chicago: Scott, Foresman, 1964.

Rezneck, Samuel. "The Growth of Output Before 1840: Comment on Parker and Whartenby," in Parker, ed. *Trends in the American Economy in the Nineteenth Century* (Studies in Income and Wealth, vol. 24), 1960, pp. 212-16.

Shepherd, James F. and Walton, Gary M. *The Economic Rise of Early America.* London: Cambridge University Press, 1979.

Shepherd, James F. "The Economy from Revolution to 1815," in Porter, ed. *Encyclopedia of American Economic History,* 1980, pp. 51-65.

Taylor, George Rogers. "American Economic Growth Before 1840: An Exploratory Essay," in Andreano, ed. *New Views on American Economic Development,* 1965, pp. 57-72.

Temin, Peter. *The Jacksonian Economy.* New York: W.W. Norton, 1969.

Walton, Gary M. "The Colonial Economy," in Porter, ed. *Encyclopedia of American Economic History,* vol. 1, 1980, pp. 34-50.

Weiss, Roger W. "Comment on Papers by Jones, Shepherd and Walton, and McCusker Presented to the 31st Annual Meeting of the Economic History Association," *Journal of Economic History,* 32(1), March 1972, pp. 163-64.

The American Industrial Revolution

David, Paul A. "Factories at the Prairie's Edge: A Study of Industrialization in Chicago, 1848-1893," [Working Paper].

Davis, Lance E. "Some Aspects of the Economic Development of Great Britain and the U.S.A., 1820-1914," Presented at the British American Studies Association Meetings, Leeds, 1965 [Working Paper].

Higgs, Robert. *The Transformation of the American Economy, 1865-1914: An Essay in Interpretation.* New York: John Wiley & Sons, 1971.

Hughes, Jonathan R.T. *Industrialization and Economic History: Theses and Conjectures.* New York: McGraw-Hill, 1970.

Kahn, Charles. "The Use of Complicated Models as Explanations: A Re-examination of Williamson's Late Nineteenth Century America," Presented at the Harvard University Workshop in Economic History, no. 7980-1, June 1980 [Working Paper].

Kendrick, John W., assisted by Pech, Maude R. *Productivity Trends in the United States* (National Bureau of Economic Research General Series, no. 71). Princeton: Princeton University Press for the National Bureau of Economic Research, 1961.

North, Douglass C. "Industrialization in the United States (1815-60)," in Rostow, ed. *The Economics of Take-Off into Sustained Growth,* 1963, pp. 44-62.

North, Douglass C. "Industrialization in the United States," in Habakkuk and Postan, eds. *The Cambridge Economic History of Europe,* vol. 6, 1965, pp. 673-705.

Thomas, Brinley. *The Drive to Industrial Maturity: The U.S. Economy 1860-1940.* Westport, Conn.: Greenwood Press, 1975.

Weber, B.A. and Handfield-Jones, Stephen J. "Variations in the Rate of Economic Growth in the U.S.A., 1869-1939," *Oxford Economic Papers,* 6, June 1954, pp. 101-32.

Weiss, Thomas J. "Economies of Scale in Nineteenth-Century Economic Growth," (Summary of 1975 Research Workshop) *Journal of Economic History*, 36(1), March 1976, pp. 39-41.

Williamson, Jeffrey G. "Late Nineteenth Century Retardation: A Neoclassical Analysis," (See the Editor's Note this Journal, 34(2), June 1974, p. 501, for an Errata Statement on this article) *Journal of Economic History*, 33(3), September 1973, pp. 581-607.

The United States After the Industrial Revolution

Abramovitz, Moses. "Resource and Output Trends in the United States Since 1870," *American Economic Review, Papers and Proceedings*, 46(2), May 1956, pp. 5-23.

Davis, Lance E.; Hughes, Jonathan R.T. and McDougall, Duncan. *American Economic History: The Development of a National Economy*. Homewood, Ill.: Richard D. Irwin, 1961.

Denison, Edward F. *The Sources of Economic Growth in the United States and the Alternatives Before Us*. New York: Committee on Economic Development, 1962.

Denison, Edward F. *Accounting for United States Economic Growth, 1929-1969*. Washington, D.C.: The Brookings Institution, 1974.

Kahn, Charles. "The Use of Complicated Models as Explanations: A Re-examination of Williamson's Late Nineteenth Century America," Presented at the Harvard University Workshop in Economic History, no. 7980-1, June 1980 [Working Paper].

Kendrick, John W., assisted by Pech, Maude R. *Productivity Trends in the United States* (National Bureau of Economic Research General Series, no. 71). Princeton: Princeton University Press for the National Bureau of Economic Research, 1961.

Klein, L.R. and Goldberger, A.S. *An Econometric Model of the United States, 1929-52*. Amsterdam: North-Holland, 1955.

Leontief, Wassily. *The Structure of the American Economy, 1919-1939*. New York: Oxford University Press, 1951.

Olmstead, Alan L. "The Cost of Economic Growth," in Porter, ed. *Encyclopedia of American Economic History*, vol. 2, 1980, pp. 863-81.

Poulson, Barry W. "The Dynamic Properties of a Macro Economic Model of U.S. Economic Growth, 1855-1965," Cambridge University Faculty of Economics and Politics Working Paper, December 1975 [Working Paper].

Poulson, Barry W. and Dowling, J. Malcolm. "The Climacteric in U.S. Economic Growth," *Oxford Economic Papers*, New Series, 25(3), November 1973, pp. 420-34.

Smolensky, Eugene. *Adjustments to Depressions and War, 1930-1945*. Chicago: Scott Foresman, 1964.

Uselding, Paul J. and McMullen, Neil J. "The Changing Basis of American Prosperity," *Economia Internazionale*, 29(3-4), August/November 1977, pp. 446-61.

Weber, B.A. and Handfield-Jones, Stephen J. "Variations in the Rate of Economic Growth in the U.S.A., 1869-1939," *Oxford Economic Papers*, 6, June 1954, pp. 101-32.

Williamson, Jeffrey G. "Late Nineteenth Century Retardation: A Neoclassical Analysis," (See the Editor's Note this Journal, 34(2), June 1974, pp. 501, for an Errata Statement on this article) *Journal of Economic History*, 33(3), September 1973, pp. 581-607.

Williamson, Jeffrey G. *Late Nineteenth Century American Development: A General Equilibrium History.* Cambridge: Cambridge University Press, 1974.

Williamson, Jeffrey G. "The Railroads and Midwestern Development, 1870-90: A General Equilibrium History," in Klingaman and Vedder, eds. *Essays in Nineteenth Century Economic History,* 1975, pp. 269-352.

The Rest of the World: The Long View

Bairoch, Paul. *The Economic Development of the Third World since 1900.* London and Berkeley: Methuen and University of California Press, 1975.

Buckley, Kenneth. "Development of Canada's Economy, 1850-1900: Comment on Firestone," in Parker, ed. *Trends in the American Economy in the Nineteenth Century* (Studies in Income and Wealth, vol. 24), 1960, pp. 246-48.

Buescu, Mircea. "Para uma Quantificacao Global da Historia Economica do Brasil [Towards a Global Quantification of Brazilian Economic History]," (Reprinted in *L'Histoire Quantitative du Bresil de 1800 a 1930*, 1973, pp. 109-20) *Verbum*, 29(1), March 1972, pp. 79-99.

Buescu, Mircea. *Evolucao Economica do Brasil* (4th Edition) [*The Economic Evolution of Brazil*]. Rio de Janeiro: APEC, 1979.

Butlin, Noel G. and Tucker, G.S.L. "The Quantitative Study of British Economic Growth: A Review," (Review essay of *British Economic Growth*, by Deane and Cole, 1968) *Economic Record*, 40(91), September 1964, pp. 455-60.

Cole, W.A. "Deane and Cole on Industrialization and Population Change in the Eighteenth Century: A Rejoinder to Neal," *Economic History Review*, Second Series, 24(4), November 1971, pp. 648-52.

Crafts, N.F.R. "English Economic Growth in the Eighteenth Century: A Re-examination of Deane and Cole's Estimates," *Economic History Review*, Second Series, 29(2), May 1976, pp. 226-35.

Deane, Phyllis and Cole, W.A. *British Economic Growth, 1688-1959: Trends and Structure.* Second Edition, 1968 Cambridge: Cambridge University Press, 1962.

Dick, Trevor J.O. "Property Rights, Forest Wealth, and Nineteenth Century Economic Growth in Central Canada," [Working Paper].

Firestone, O.J. *Canada's Economic Development, 1867-1953* (Income and Wealth Series, no. 7). London: Bowes & Bowes for the International Association for Research in Income and Wealth, 1958.

Firestone, O.J. "Development of Canada's Economy, 1850-1900," in Parker, ed. *Trends in the American Economy in the Nineteenth Century* (Studies in Income and Wealth, vol. 24), 1960, pp. 217-46.

Firestone, O.J. "Development of Canada's Economy, 1850-1900: Reply to Buckley and McDougall," in Parker, ed. *Trends in the American Economy in the Nineteenth Century* (Studies in Income and Wealth, vol. 24), 1960, pp. 249-52.

Fishlow, Albert. "Brazilian Development in Long-Term Perrspective," *American Economic Review Papers and Proceedings*, 70(2), May 1980, pp. 102-108.

Freund, W.M. and Shenton, R.W. "'Vent-for-Surplus' Theory and the Economic History of West Africa," *Savanna*, 6(2), December 1977, pp. 191-6.

Heston, Alan W. and Summers, Robert. "Comparative Indian Economic Growth, 1870 to 1970," *American Economic Review Papers and Proceedings*, 70(2), May 1980, pp. 96-101.

Hogendorn, Jan S. "The Vent for Surplus Model and African Cash Agriculture to 1914," *Savanna*, 5(1), June 1976, pp. 15-28.

Hogendorn, Jan S. "Vent-For Surplus Theory: A Reply to Freund and Shenton," *Savanna*, 6(2), December 1977, pp. 196-99.

Kuznets, Simon S.; Moore, Wilbert E. and Spengler, Joseph J., eds. *Economic Growth: Brazil, India, Japan.* Durham, N.C.: Duke University Press, 1955.

Kuznets, Simon S. "Quantitative Aspects of the Economic Growth of Nations (Part 1): Level and Variability of Rates of Growth," *Economic Development and Cultural Change*, 5(1, Part 1), October 1956, pp. 5-94.

Leet, Don R. and Shaw, John A. "French Economic Stagnation, 1700-1960: Old Economic History Revisited," *Journal of Interdisciplinary History*, 8(3), Winter 1978, pp. 531-44.

Leff, Nathaniel H. "Long-Term Brazilian Economic Development," [Translated into Portuguese in El Trimestre Economico, 1970] *Journal of Economic History*, 29(3), September 1969, pp. 473-93.

Leff, Nathaniel H. "Uma Perspectiva a Longo Prazo do Desenvolvimento e do Subdesenvolvimento Brasileiros [A Long Term Perspective on the Development and Underdevelopment of Brazil]," *Revista Brasileira de Economia*, 26(3), July/September 1972, pp. 147-68.

Leff, Nathaniel H. "Economic Retardation in Nineteenth-Century Brazil," *Economic History Review*, Second Series, 25(3), August 1972, pp. 489-507.

Levy-Leboyer, Maurice. "Productivite et croissance economique en France," in Van der Wee, Vinogradov, and Kotovsky, eds. *Fifth International Congress of Economic History*, vol. 7, 1976, pp. 169-91.

Lewis, W. Arthur. *Growth and Fluctuations, 1870-1913.* London: Allen & Unwin, 1978.

McDougall, Duncan. "Development of Canada's Economy, 1850-1900: Comment on Firestone," in Parker, ed. *Trends in the American Economy in the Nineteenth Century* (Studies in Income and Wealth, vol. 24), 1960, pp. 248-49.

Neal, Larry D. "Deane and Cole on Industrialization and Population Change in the Eighteenth Century: Comment," *Economic History Review*, Second Series, 24(4), November 1971, pp. 643-47.

O'Brien, Patrick K. "Economic Growth in Britain and France from the End of the 17th Century to Present Day," in Bedarida, Crouzet, and Johnson, eds. *Dix siecles d'histoire Franco-britannique De Guillaume le conquerant au Marche commun [France and Britain Ten Centuries]*, 1979.

Parker, William N. "Economic Development in Historical Perspective," *Economic Development and Cultural Change*, 10(1), October 1961, pp. 1-7.

Patel, Surendra J. "Rates of Industrial Growth in the Last Century, 1860-1958," *Economic Development and Cultural Change*, 9(3), April 1961, pp. 316-30.

Rosovsky, Henry. "The Economic Position of Japan: Past, Present, and Future," in U.S. Commission on International Trade and Investment Policy, ed. *United States International Economic Policy in an Interdependent World*, 1971.

Rosovsky, Henry. *The Modernization of Japan and Russia*. New York: Free Press, 1975.

Toniolo, Gianni., ed. *Lo sviluppo economico italiano, 1861-1940* [*Italian Economic Development, 1861-1940*]. Bari: Laterza, 1973.

Toniolo, Gianni., ed. *L'economia italiana 1861-1940*. Bari: Laterza, 1978.

Tuma, Elias H. *European Economic History: Tenth Century to the Present; Theory and History of Economic Change*. New York: Harper & Row, 1971.

Yamamura, Kozo. "Recent Research in Japanese Economic History, 1600-1945," in Gallman, ed. *Recent Developments in the Study of Economic and Business History*, 1977, pp. 221-45.

The Rest of the World: Before the Industrial Revolution

Adams, John and West, Robert C. "Money, Prices, and Economic Development in India, 1861-1895," *Journal of Economic History*, 39(1), March 1979, pp. 55-68.

Almquist, Eric L. "Pre-Famine Ireland and the Theory of European Proto-Industrialization: Evidence from the 1841 Census," *Journal of Economic History*, 39(3), September 1979, pp. 699-718.

Butlin, Noel G. and Tucker, G.S.L. "The Quantitative Study of British Economic Growth: A Review," (Review essay of *British Economic Growth*, by Deane and Cole, 1968) *Economic Record*, 40(91), September 1964, pp. 455-60.

Coatsworth, John H. "Obstacles to Economic Growth in Nineteenth Century Mexico," *American Historical Review*, 83(1), February 1978, pp. 80-100.

Cole, W.A. "Deane and Cole on Industrialization and Population Change in the Eighteenth Century: A Rejoinder to Neal," *Economic History Review*, Second Series, 24(4), November 1971, pp. 648-52.

Crafts, N.F.R. "English Economic Growth in the Eighteenth Century: A Re-examination of Deane and Cole's Estimates," *Economic History Review*, Second Series, 29(2), May 1976, pp. 226-35.

Crafts, N.F.R. "The Eighteenth Century: A Survey," in Floud and McCloskey, eds. *The Economic History of Britain since 1700*, vol. 1, 1981, pp. 1-16.

De Vries, Jan. "The Role of the Rural Sector in the Development of the Dutch Economy: 1500-1700," (Summary of Doctoral Dissertation) *Journal of Economic History*, 31(1), March 1971, pp. 266-68.

De Vries, Jan. *The Dutch Rural Economy in the Golden Age, 1500-1700*.

New Haven: Yale University Press, 1974.

Deane, Phyllis. "The Implications of Early National Income Estimates for the Measurement of Long-Term Economic Growth in the United Kingdom," *Economic Development and Cultural Change*, 4(1), October 1955, pp. 3-38.

Deane, Phyllis and Cole, W.A. *British Economic Growth, 1688-1959: Trends and Structure*. Second Edition, 1968 Cambridge: Cambridge University Press, 1962.

Dernberger, Robert F. "The Role of the Foreigner in China's Economic Development, 1840-1949," in Perkins, ed. *China's Modern Economy in Historical Perspective*, 1975, pp. 19-47.

Eckstein, Alexander; Fairbank, John K. and Yang, L.S. "Economic Change in Early Modern China: An Analytic Framework," *Economic Development and Cultural Change*, 9(1, Part 1), October 1960, pp. 1-26.

Eckstein, Alexander; Chao, Kang and Chang, John. "The Economic Development of Manchuria: The Rise of a Frontier Economy," *Journal of Economic History*, 34(1), March 1974, pp. 239-64.

Felix, D. "Profit Inflation and Industrial Growth: The Historic Record and Contemporary Analogies," in Floud, ed. *Essays in Quantitative Economic History*, 1974, pp. 133-51.

Firestone, O.J. "Canada's Subsistence Economy before 1860," *Fourth International Conference of Economic History, Bloomington, 1968.* Paris: Mouton, 1973, pp. 409-18.

Gunderson, Gerald A. "Real Incomes in the Late Middle Ages: A Test of the Common Case for Diminishing Returns," *Social Science History*, 2(1), Fall 1977, pp. 90-118.

Hamilton, Earl J. "Prices, Wages, and the Industrial Revolution," *Economics and Industrial Relations*. Philadelphia: University of Pennsylvania Press, 1941, pp. 99-112.

Hamilton, Earl J. "American Treasure and the Rise of Capitalism (1500-1700)," *Economica*, 9(27), November 1929, pp. 338-57.

Hanley, Susan B. and Yamamura, Kozo. "A Quiet Transformation in Tokugawa Economic History," *Journal of Asian Studies*, 30(2), February 1971, pp. 373-84.

Hanley, Susan B. and Yamamura, Kozo. *Economic and Demographic Change in Preindustrial Japan, 1600-1868.* Princeton: Princeton University Press, 1977.

Harris, John R. "Some Problems in Identifying the Role of Entrepreneurship in Economic Development: The Nigerian Case," *Explorations in Economic History*, 7(3), Spring 1970, pp. 347-70.

Jones, Eric L. "The Constraints on Economic Growth in Southern England, 1650-1850," *Third International Conference of Economic History, Munich, 1965, part 5.* Paris: Mouton, 1974, pp. 423-30.

Kahan, Arcadius. "Continuity in Economic Activity and Policy during the Post-Petrine Period in Russia," *Journal of Economic History*, 25(1), March 1965, pp. 61-85.

Klep, Paul M.M. *Groeidynamiek en Stagnatie in een Agrarisch Grensgebied, De Economische Ontwikkeling in de Noordantwerpse Kempen en de Baronie Van Breda, 1750-1850 [Growth and Stagnation in an Agrarian Borderland, The Economic Development in the Northantwerp Kempen (In Belgium) and the Barony of Breda (The Netherlands), 1750-1850].* Tilburg: Stichting Zuidelijk Historisch

Contact, 1973.

Lampe, John R. "Varieties of Unsuccessful Industrialization: The Balkan States Before 1914," *Journal of Economic History*, 35(1), March 1975, pp. 56-85.

Lewis, W. Arthur. *Aspects of Tropical Trade, 1883-1965.* Stockholm: Almquist, 1969.

Lewis, W. Arthur., ed. *Tropical Development, 1883-1913.* London and Evanston, Ill.: Allen & Unwin and Northwestern University Press, 1970.

Mendels, Franklin F. "Proto-Industrialization: The First Phase of the Industrialization Process," *Journal of Economic History*, 32(1), March 1972, pp. 241-61.

Mendels, Franklin F. "Industrialization and Population Pressure in Eighteenth-Century Flanders," (Summary of Doctoral Dissertation) *Journal of Economic History*, 31(1), March 1971, pp. 269-71.

Miyamoto, Mataji; Sakudo, Yotaro and Yasuba, Yasukichi. "Economic Development in Preindustrial Japan, 1859-1894," *Journal of Economic History*, 25(4), December 1965, pp. 541-64.

Mokyr, Joel. "Industrialization and Poverty in Ireland and the Netherlands," *Journal of Interdisciplinary History*, 10(3), Winter 1980, pp. 429-58.

Morris, Morris D. "Towards a Reinterpretation of Nineteenth-Century Indian Economic History," *Journal of Economic History*, 23(4), December 1963, pp. 606-18.

Neal, Larry D. "Deane and Cole on Industrialization and Population Change in the Eighteenth Century: Comment," *Economic History Review*, Second Series, 24(4), November 1971, pp. 643-47.

North, Douglass C. and Thomas, Robert P. "An Economic Theory of the Growth of the Western World," *Economic History Review*, Second Series, 23(1), April 1970, pp. 1-17.

North, Douglass C. and Thomas, Robert P. "European Economic Growth: Reply to Professor D. Ringose," *Economic History Review*, Second Series, 26(2), May 1973, pp. 293-94.

North, Douglass C. and Thomas, Robert P. "The First Economic Revolution," *Economic History Review*, Second Series, 30(2), May 1977, pp. 229-41.

O'Brien, Patrick K. "Turning Points in the Economic History of Egypt," in Sinor, ed. *Proceedings of the 27th World Congress of Orientalists, 1967.*

O'Brien, Patrick K. "Structural Changes in the Egyptian Economy, 1937-1965," in Cook, ed. *Studies in the Economic History of the Middle East from the Rise of Islam to the Present Day, 1970.*

O'Brien, Patrick K. "Russian Backwardness in European Perspective," [Working Paper].

O'Brien, Patrick K. "The Intersectoral Terms of Trade in European Industrialization, 1660-1820," [Working Paper].

Paquet, Gilles and Wallot, Jean-Pierre. "Canada, 1760-1850: anamorphoses et prospective," *Cahiers de l'Universite de Quebec*, 1-2, September 1969, pp. 255-300.

Paquet, Gilles and Wallot, Jean-Pierre. "Le Bas Canada au debut du XIXe siecle: une hypothese," *Revue d'Histoire de l'Amerique Francaise*, 25(1), June 1971, pp. 39-61.

Pelaez, Carlos M. "World War I and the Economy of Brazil: Some Evidence from Monetary Statistics," *Journal of Interdisciplinary History*, 7(4), Spring 1977, pp. 683-89.

Phelps Brown, E.H. and Hopkins, Sheila V. "Seven Centuries of Building Wages," *Economica*, 22(87), August 1955, pp. 195-206.

Phelps Brown, E.H. and Hopkins, Sheila V. "Seven Centuries of the Prices of Consumables, Compared with Builders' Wage Rates," (Reprinted in Ramsey, ed. *The Price Revolution in the Sixteenth Century*, 1971, pp. 18-41) *Economica*, 23(92), November 1956, pp. 296-314.

Rapp, Richard T. *Industry and Economic Decline in Seventeenth-Century Venice*. Cambridge: Harvard University Press, 1976.

Rawski, Thomas G. "China's Republican Economy: An Introduction," [Working Paper].

Ringrose, D.R. "European Economic Growth: Comments on the North-Thomas Theory," *Economic History Review*, Second Series, 26(2), May 1973, pp. 285-92.

Riskin, Carl. "Surplus and Stagnation in Modern China," in Perkins, ed. *China's Modern Economy in Historical Perspective*, 1975, pp. 49-84.

Roehl, Richard. "Plan and Reality in a Medieval Monastic Economy: The Cistercians," in Adelson, ed. *Studies in Medieval and Renaissance History*, vol. 9, 1972.

Rosovsky, Henry. "L'iniziativa dello stato nell'industriallizzazione giapponese [State Initiative in Japanese Industrialization]," *Mercurio*, June 1960.

Rosovsky, Henry. "Meiji-Ki Nihon no Keizei Hattan to Gendai [Early Japanese Economic Development and Its Modern Implications]," *Nichi-Bei Foramu*, August 1972.

Rudolph, Richard L. "Social Structure and the Beginning of Austrian Economic Growth," *East Central Europe/L'Europe de Centre-Est*, 7(2), 1980, pp. 207-24.

Rudolph, Richard L. "Family Structure and Proto-Industrialization in Russia," *Journal of Economic History*, 40(1), March 1980, pp. 111-18.

Rudolph, Richard L. "Agricultural Structure and Proto-Industrialization in Russia: Economic Development with Serf Labor," in Deyon and Mendels, eds. *Protoindustrialization*, 1982.

Taira, Koji. "Growth, Trends, and Swings in Japanese Agriculture and Industry," (Review essay of *Agriculture and Economic Growth*, by Ohkawa, Johnston, and Kaneda, eds., 1970) *Economic Development and Cultural Change*, 24(2), January 1976, pp. 423-36.

Yamamura, Kozo. "The Development of Za in Medieval Japan," *Business History Review*, 47(4), Winter 1973, pp. 438-65.

Yamamura, Kozo. "Toward a Reexamination of the Economic History of Tokugawa Japan, 1600-1867," *Journal of Economic History*, 33(3), September 1973, pp. 509-46.

The Rest of the World: Modern Economic Growth

Abramovitz, Moses. "Kuznets and Juglar Cycles during the

Industrialization of 1874-1940: Comment on Shinohara," in Ohkawa and Hayami, eds. *Economic Growth: The Japanese Experience since the Meiji Era*, vol. 1, 1973, pp. 253-65.

Anderson, J.L. "Aspects of the Effect on the British Economy of the Wars against France, 1793-1815," *Australian Economic History Review*, 12(1), March 1972, pp. 1-20.

Ankli, Robert E. "The Growth of the Canadian Economy, 1896-1920: Export Led and/or Neoclassical Growth," *Explorations in Economic History*, 17(3), July 1980, pp. 251-74.

Bairoch, Paul. "Niveaux de developpement economique de 1810 a 1910 [Levels of Economic Development: 1810-1910]," *Annales: Economies, Societes, Civilisations*, 20(6), 1965, pp. 1091-117.

Baker, Anita B. "Agriculture and Industrialization in Europe," (Summary of 1978 Research Workshop) *Journal of Economic History*, 39(1), March 1979, pp. 313-15.

Bertram, Gordon W. "Economic Growth in Canadian Industry, 1870-1915: The Staple Model and the Take-Off Hypothesis," *Canadian Journal of Economics and Political Science*, 29, May 1963, pp. 159-84.

Boehm, E.A. "Australia's Economic Depression of the 1930s," *Economic Record*, 49(128), December 1973, pp. 606-23.

Boehm, E.A. "Economic Development and Fluctuation in Australia in the 1920s: A Reply (to Sinclair)," *Economic Record*, 51(135), September 1975, pp. 414-20.

Bos, Roeland W.J.M. "Factorprijzen, technologie en marktstructuur: de groei van de Nederlandse volkshuishouding 1815-1914 [Factor Prices, Technology and Market Structure: The Growth of the Dutch Economy, 1815-1914]," *Afdeling Agrarische Geschiedenis, Bijdragen*, 22, 1979, pp. 109-137.

Bos, Roeland W.J.M. "Kapitaal en industrialisatie in Nederland tijdens de negentiende eeuw [Capital and Industrialization in the Netherlands during the Nineteenth Century]," *Afdeling Agrarische Geschiedenis, Bijdragen*, 22, 1979, pp. 89-105.

Bouvier, Jean. "Capital bancaire, capital industriel, capital financier dans la croissance francaise du 19 eme siecle [Bank Capital, Industrial Capital, and Financial Capital in Nineteenth Century French Growth]," *La Pensee*, 36, December 1974.

Buckley, Kenneth. "Development of Canada's Economy, 1850-1900: Comment on Firestone," in Parker, ed. *Trends in the American Economy in the Nineteenth Century* (Studies in Income and Wealth, vol. 24), 1960, pp. 246-48.

Butlin, Noel G. and Tucker, G.S.L. "The Quantitative Study of British Economic Growth: A Review," (Review essay of *British Economic Growth*, by Deane and Cole, 1968) *Economic Record*, 40(91), September 1964, pp. 455-60.

Cameron, Rondo E.; Crisp, Olga; Patrick, Hugh T. and Tilly, Richard. *Banking in the Early Stages of Industrialization: A Study in Comparative Economic History*. London and New York: Oxford University Press, 1967.

Cameron, Rondo E. "Belgium, 1800-1875," in Cameron et al., *Banking in the Early Stages of Industrialization*, 1967, pp. 129-50.

Chambers, Edward J. and Gordon, Donald F. "Primary Products and Economic Growth: An Empirical Measurement," [Translated into

Spanish in *Journal of the Fundacion de Investigationes Economicas Lationoamericanas*] *Journal of Political Economy*, 74(4), August 1966, pp. 315-32.

Chambers, Edward J. and Gordon, Donald F. "Primary Products and Economic Growth: Rejoinder to Dales, McManus, and Watkins," *Journal of Political Economy*, 75(6), December 1967, pp. 881-85.

Ciocca, Pierluigi. "Formazione dell'Italia industriale e storia econometrica [Industrial Development in Italy and Econometric History]," *Rivista internazionale di scienze sociali*, 40, September/December 1969, pp. 539-53.

Ciocca, Pierluigi. "Capitale e fascismo: una introduzione all'esperienza italiana [Capital and Fascism: An Introduction to the Italian Experience]," in *Conflitti sociali e accumulazione capitalistica da Giolitti alla guerra fascista*, 1975, pp. 11-28.

Ciocca, Pierluigi. "L'Italia nell'economia mondiale, 1922-1940 [Italy in the World Economy, 1922-1940]," *Quaderni storici*, (29/30), May/December 1975, pp. 342-76.

Ciocca, Pierluigi. "L'economia italiana nel contesto internazionale [The Italian Economy in the International Context (under Fascism)]," in Ciocca and Toniolo, eds. *L'economia italiana nel periodo fascista*, 1976, pp. 19-50.

Ciocca, Pierluigi and Toniolo, Gianni., ed. *L'economia italiana nel periodo fascista* [*The Italian Economy during the Fascist Era*]. Bologna: il Mulino, 1976.

Cohen, Jon S. "Finance and Industrialization in Italy, 1894-1914," (Summary of Doctoral Dissertation) *Journal of Economic History*, 16(4), December 1966, pp. 577-78.

Cohen, Jon S. "Financing Industrialization in Italy, 1894-1914: The Partial Transformation of a Late-Comer," *Journal of Economic History*, 27(3), September 1967, pp. 363-82.

Cohen, Jon S. "Banking and Industrialization: The Case of Italy, 1861-1914," in Cameron, ed. *Banking and Industrialization Among the Late-Comers*, 1972.

Cohen, Jon S. "The Rate and Structure of Economic Growth in Italy, 1861-1968," in Tannenbaum and Noerther, eds. *Modern Italy: a topical history since 1861*, 1974.

Cohen, Jon S. *Finance and Industrialization in Italy, 1894-1914*. New York: Arno Press, 1977.

Cole, W.A. "Deane and Cole on Industrialization and Population Change in the Eighteenth Century: A Rejoinder to Neal," *Economic History Review*, Second Series, 24(4), November 1971, pp. 648-52.

Cole, W.A. "Eighteenth-Century Economic Growth Revisited," *Explorations in Economic History*, 10(4), Summer 1973, pp. 327-48.

Crafts, N.F.R. "English Economic Growth in the Eighteenth Century: A Re-examination of Deane and Cole's Estimates," *Economic History Review*, Second Series, 29(2), May 1976, pp. 226-35.

Crafts, N.F.R. "Industrial Revolution in England and France: Some Thoughts on the Question, 'Why Was England First?'," *Economic History Review*, Second Series, 30(3), August 1977, pp. 429-41.

Crafts, N.F.R. "Entrepreneurship and a Probabilistic View of the British Industrial Revolution: A Reply to Rostow," *Economic History Review*, Second Series, 31(4), November 1978, pp. 613-14.

Crafts, N.F.R. "Income Elasticities of Demand and the Release of Labour by Agriculture during the British Industrial Revolution," *Journal of European Economic History*, 9(1), Spring 1980, pp. 153-68.

Crafts, N.F.R. "National Income Estimates and the British Standard of Living Debate: A Reappraisal of 1801-1831," *Explorations in Economic History*, 17(2), April 1980, pp. 176-88.

Dales, John H.; McManus, John C. and Watkins, Melville H. "Primary Products and Economic Growth: A Comment on Chambers and Gordon," *Journal of Political Economy*, 75(6), December 1967, pp. 876-80.

Deane, Phyllis. "The Industrial Revolution and Economic Growth: The Evidence of Early British National Income Estimates," *Economic Development and Cultural Change*, 5(2), January 1957, pp. 159-74.

Deane, Phyllis and Cole, W.A. *British Economic Growth, 1688-1959: Trends and Structure.* (Second Edition, 1968) Cambridge: Cambridge University Press, 1962.

Dowie, Jack A. "Inverse Relations of the Australian and New Zealand Economies, 1871-1900," *Australian Economic Papers*, 2(2), December 1963, pp. 151-79.

Dowie, Jack A. "Inverse Relations of the Australian and New Zealand Economies, 1871-1900: Reply to von Tunzelmann," *Australian Economic Papers*, 5(3), June 1967, pp. 128-29.

Felix, David. "Technological Dualism in Late Industrializers: On Theory, History, and Policy," *Journal of Economic History*, 34(1), March 1974, pp. 194-238.

Fenoaltea, Stefano. "Public Policy and Italian Industrial Development, 1861-1913," (Summary of Doctoral Dissertation) *Journal of Economic History*, 29(1), March 1969, pp. 176-79.

Fenoaltea, Stefano. "Decollo, ciclo, e intervento dello Stato [The Take-off, the Business Cycle, and the Role of the State (in Italy, 1861-1913)]," in Caracciolo, ed. *La Formazione dell'Italia industriale [Italian Industrial Formation]*, 1969, pp. 95-114.

Fenoaltea, Stefano. "Riflessioni sull'esperienza industriale italiana dal Risorgimento alla prima guerra mondiale [Reflections on the Italian Industrial Experience from the Risorgimento to the First World War]," (Reprinted in Toniolo, ed. *L'economia italiana 1861-1940*, 1978 pp. 69-104) in Gianni Toniolo, ed. *Lo sviluppo economico italiano, 1861-1940 [Italian Economic Development, 1861-1940]*. Bari: Laterza, 1973, pp. 121-56.

Fenoaltea, Stefano. *Italian Industrial Production, 1861-1913: A Statistical Reconstruction.* New York: Cambridge University Press, forthcoming.

Fenoaltea, Stefano. *Public Policy and Italian Industrial Development, 1861-1913: A New Economic History.* New York: Cambridge University Press, forthcoming.

Firestone, O.J. *Canada's Economic Development, 1867-1953* (Income and Wealth Series, no. 7). London: Bowes & Bowes for the International Association for Research in Income and Wealth, 1958.

Firestone, O.J. "Development of Canada's Economy, 1850-1900," in Parker, ed. *Trends in the American Economy in the Nineteenth Century* (Studies in Income and Wealth, vol. 24), 1960, pp. 217-46.

Firestone, O.J. "Development of Canada's Economy, 1850-1900: Reply to

Buckley and McDougall," in Parker, ed. *Trends in the American Economy in the Nineteenth Century* (Studies in Income and Wealth, vol. 24), 1960, pp. 249-52.

Fischer, Wolfram. "Government Activity and Industrialization in Germany (1815-70)," in Rostow, ed. *The Economics of Take-off into Sustained Growth,* 1963, pp. 83-94.

Fremdling, Rainer and Tilly, Richard H. "German Banks, German Growth, and Econometric History: A Note on Neuberger and Stokes," *Journal of Economic History,* 36(2), June 1976, pp. 416-24.

Fremdling, Rainer. "Railroads and German Economic Growth: A Leading Sector Analysis with a Comparison to the United States and Great Britain," *Journal of Economic History,* 37(3), September 1977, pp. 583-604.

Fremdling, Rainer. "Die Rolle der Banken im Wachstumsprozess Deutschlands, 1850-1913 [The Role of Banks in the German Growth Process, 1850-1913]," Ph.D. Dissertation, Universitat Munster, West Germany, 1969 [Working Paper].

Fua, Giorgio. *Lo sviluppo economico in Italia* (3 Vols) (2nd ed. rev.: vol. 1 (1981); vol. 2 (1974); vol. 3 (1975)). Milano: Franco Angeli, 1969.

Fua, Giorgio. "Breve sintesi statistica dello sviluppo economico italiano 1861-1940 [Brief Statistical Synthesis of Italian Economic Development, 1861-1940]," in Toniolo, ed. *L'economia italiana 1861-1940,* 1978, pp. 47-67.

Gerschenkron, Alexander. "The Early Phases of Industrialization in Russia: Afterthoughts and Counterthoughts," in Rostow, ed. *The Economics of Take-off into Sustained Growth,* 1963, pp. 151-69.

Goldsmith, Raymond W. "The Economic Growth of Tsarist Russia, 1860-1913," *Economic Development and Cultural Change,* 9(3), April 1961, pp. 441-75.

Good, David F. "Stagnation and 'Take-Off' in Austria, 1873-1913," *Economic History Review,* Second Series, 27(1), February 1974, pp. 72-87.

Good, David F. "The Great Depression and Austrian Economic Growth after 1873: A Reply to Komlos," *Economic History Review,* Second Series, 31(2), May 1978, pp. 290-94.

Good, David F. "Economic Integration and Regional Development in Austria-Hungary, 1867-1913," in Bairoch and Levy-Leboyer, eds. *Disparities in Economic Development since the Industrial Revolution,* 1981, pp. 137-50.

Green, Alan G. "Regional Inequality, Structural Change, and Economic Growth in Canada, 1890-1956," *Economic Development and Cultural Change,* 17(4), July 1969, pp. 567-83.

Green, Alan G. "Regional Inequality, Structural Change, and Economic Growth in Canada, 1890-1956," *Economic Development and Cultural Change,* 17(4), July 1969, pp. 567-83.

Gregory, Paul R. "1913 Russian National Income: Some Insights into Russian Economic Development," *Quarterly Journal of Economics,* 90, August 1976, pp. 445-59.

Gross, Nachum T. "Economic Growth and the Consumption of Coal in Austria and Hungary, 1831-1913," *Journal of Economic History,* 31(4), December 1971, pp. 898-916.

Habakkuk, H.J. and Deane, Phyllis. "The Take-Off in Britain," in Rostow, ed. *The Economics of Take-Off into Sustained Growth,* 1963, pp. 63-82.

Haddad, Claudio L.S. "Crescimento Economico do Brasil, 1900-76 [Economic Growth of Brazil, 1900-76]," in Neuhaus, ed. *A Economia Brasileira [The Brazilian Economy]*, 1979.

Haines, Michael R. "The Role of Agriculture in Economic Development: A Regional Case Study of Prussian Upper Silesia, 1846-1913," *Journal of Economic History.*

Hausman, William J. and Watts, James M. "Structural Change in the 18th-Century British Economy: A Test Using Cubic Splines," Explorations in Economic History, 17), October 1980, pp. 400-410.

Hoffmann, Walther G. "The Take-Off in Germany," in Rostow, ed. *The Economics of Take-Off into Sustained Growth,* 1963, pp. 95-118.

Hoffmann, Walther G.; Gulicher, Herbert and Joksch, H.C., eds. *Studien zur wirtschaftlichen Verfahrensforschung.* Koln: Westdeutscher Verlag, 1964.

Hohorst, Gerd. *Wirtschaftswachstum und Bevolkerungsentwicklung in Preussen 1816 bis 1914 [Economic Growth and Population Expansion in Prussia, 1816 to 1914].* New York: Arno Press, 1977.

Hohorst, Gerd. "Demo-Okonomische Entwicklungsprozesse in Preussen im 19. Jahrhundert: Versuch eines Simulationstheoretischen Ansatzes [Demographic-Economic Development Processes in Prussia in the 19th Century: A Hypothetical Simulation Experiment]," [Working Paper].

Hueckel, Glenn. "War and the British Economy, 1793-1815: A General Equilibrium Analysis," *Explorations in Economic History*, 10(4), Summer 1973, pp. 365-96.

Huertas, Thomas F. "A New Economic History of the Hapsburg Monarchy," *Journal of Economic History*, 35(1), March 1975, pp. 130-33.

Huertas, Thomas F. *Economic Growth and Economic Policy in a Multinational Setting: The Hapsburg Monarchy, 1841-1865.* New York: Arno Press, 1978.

Huertas, Thomas F. "Economic Growth and Economic Policy in a Multinational Setting: The Habsburg Monarchy, 1841-1865," (Summary of Doctoral Dissertation) *Journal of Economic History*, 38(1), March 1978, pp. 281-82.

Hughes, Jonathan R.T. "Measuring British Economic Growth: Review of Deane and Cole," (Reprinted in Hughes, ed. *Purdue Faculty Papers in Economic History, 1956-1966,* 1967, pp. 59-82) *Journal of Economic History*, 24(1), March 1964, pp. 60-82.

Hughes, Jonathan R.T. *Industrialization and Economic History: Theses and Conjectures.* New York: McGraw-Hill, 1970.

Johanson, Hans Chr. *Den okonomiske og sociale udvikling i Danmark, 1864-1901 [Danish Economic and Social Development, 1864-1901].* Copenhagen: Hojres Fond, 1962.

Kelley, Allen C. "Demographic Change and Economic Growth: Australia, 1861-1911," *Explorations in Entrepreneurial History*, Second Series, 5(3), Spring/Summer 1968, pp. 207-77.

Kelley, Allen C. and Williamson, Jeffrey G. "Writing History Backwards: Meiji Japan Revisited," *Journal of Economic History*, 31(4), December 1971, pp. 729-76.

Kelley, Allen C.; Cheetham, Russell J. and Williamson, Jeffrey G.

Dualistic Economic Development: Theory and History. Chicago: University of Chicago Press, 1972.

Kelley, Allen C. and Williamson, Jeffrey G. *Lessons from Japanese Development: An Analytical Economic History*. Chicago: University of Chicago Press, 1974.

Kelley, Allen C. and Williamson, Jeffrey G. "Simple Parables of Japanese Economic Progress: Report on Early Findings," in Ohkawa and Hayami, eds. *Long-Term Analysis of the Japanese Economy*, 1974, pp. 141-85.

Kelley, Allen C. and Williamson, Jeffrey G. "General Equilibrium Analysis of Agricultural Development: The Case of Meiji Japan," in Reynolds, ed. *Agricultural Development and Theory*, 1974.

Kelly, Allen C. and Williamson, Jeffrey G. "Modelling Economic Development and General Equilibrium Histories," *American Economic Review, Papers and Proceedings*, 63(2), May 1973, pp. 450-58.

Kindleberger, Charles P. *Economic Growth in France and Britain, 1851-1950*. Cambridge: Harvard University Press, 1964.

Komlos, John. "Is the Depression in Austria after 1873 a 'Myth'? A Comment on Good," *Economic History Review*, Second Series, 31(2), May 1978, pp. 287-89.

Komlos, John. "German Banks and German Growth: Rejoinder to Neuberger and Stokes," *Journal of Economic History*, 38(2), June 1978, pp. 483-86.

Komlos, John. "The Kreditbanken and German Growth: A Postscript to Neuberger and Stokes," *Journal of Economic History*, 38(2), June 1978, pp. 476-79.

Lee, Pong S. "Unbalanced Growth: The Case of Japan 1878-1918," *Yale Economic Essays*, 6(2), Fall 1966, pp. 479-526.

Levy-Leboyer, Maurice. "La Croissance Economique en France au XIXe Siecle: Resultats Preliminaires [Economic Growth in France in the Nineteenth Century: Preliminary Results]," *Annales*, 23(4), July/August 1968, pp. 788-807.

Levy-Leboyer, Maurice. "La Deceleration de L'Economie Francaise dans la Seconde Moitie Du XIXe Siecle [The French Economic Slowdown in the Second Half of the Nineteenth Century]," *Revue D'Histoire Economique et Sociale*, 49(4), 1971, pp. 485-507.

Lewis, W. Arthur., ed. *Tropical Development, 1883-1913*. London and Evanston, Ill.: Allen & Unwin and Northwestern University Press, 1970.

Lewis, W. Arthur. *Growth and Fluctuations, 1870-1913*. London: Allen & Unwin, 1978.

Marczewski, Jean. "The Take-Off Hypothesis and the French Experience," in Rostow, ed. *The Economics of Take-Off into Sustained Growth*, 1963, pp. 119-38.

Markovitch, Tihomir J. *L'industrie francaise de 1789 a 1964* (4 Vols) [*French Industry, 1789-1964*]. *Cahiers de l'Institute de Science Economique Appliquee*, 1966.

Markovitch, Tihomir J. "La Revolution industrielle: le cas de la France [The Industrial Revolution: The Case of France]," *Revue d'Histoire economique et sociale*, 1(1), 1974, pp. 115-25.

Matis, Herbert. "The Pattern of Austrian Industrial Growth from the Eighteenth to the Early Twentieth Century: Comment on Rudolph,"

Austrian History Yearbook, 11), 1975, pp. 33-36.

Matteuzzi, Massimo. *Aspetti dell'economia italiana dal 1861 al 1967 (da una lezione di Giorgia Fua) [Aspects of the Italian Economy from 1861 to 1967 (from a lesson by Giorgia Fua)].* Bologna: Consorzio provinciale pubblica lettura, 1976.

McCloskey, Donald N. "The Industrial Revolution, 1780-1860: A Survey," in Floud and McCloskey, eds. *The Economic History of Britain since 1700,* vol. 1, 1980, pp. 103-27.

McDougall, Duncan. "Development of Canada's Economy, 1850-1900: Comment on Firestone," in Parker, ed. *Trends in the American Economy in the Nineteenth Century* (Studies in Income and Wealth, vol. 24), 1960, pp. 248-49.

Minami, Ryoshin. "Mechanical Power in the Industrialization of Japan," *Journal of Economic History,* 37(4), December 1977, pp. 935-58.

Mokyr, Joel. "The Industrial Revolution in the Low Countries in the First Half of the Nineteenth Century: A Comparative Case Study," *Journal of Economic History,* 34(2), June 1974, pp. 365-91.

Mokyr, Joel. "Capital, Labor and the Delay of the Industrial Revolution in the Netherlands," *Yearbook of Economic History,* 38, 1975, pp. 280-99.

Mokyr, Joel. *Industrialization in the Low Countries, 1795-1850.* New Haven: Yale University Press, 1976.

Mokyr, Joel and Savin, N. Eugene. "Stagflation in Historical Perspective: The Napoleonic Wars Revisited," in Uselding, ed. *Research in Economic History,* vol. 1, 1976, pp. 198-259.

Mokyr, Joel. "Industrial Growth and Stagnation in the Low Countries," (Summary of Doctoral Dissertation) *Journal of Economic History,* 36(1), March 1976, pp. 276-78.

Mokyr, Joel. "Growing-Up and the Industrial Revolution in Europe," *Explorations in Economic History,* 13(4), October 1976, pp. 371-96.

Morris, Morris D. "Two Classic Cases of Industrialization Reconsidered: A Comment on Kisch and Krause," *Journal of Economic History,* 19(4), December 1959, pp. 565-69.

Morris, Morris D. "Industrialization in South Asia, 1800-1947," in Kumar and Desai, eds. *Cambridge Economic History of India,* vol. 2, 1982, pp. 553-676.

Munoz, Oscar E. "An Essay on the Progress of Industrialization in Chile since 1914," *Yale Economic Essays,* 8(2), Fall 1968, pp. 137-84.

Neal, Larry D. "Deane and Cole on Industrialization and Population Change in the Eighteenth Century: Comment," *Economic History Review,* Second Series, 24(4), November 1971, pp. 643-47.

Neuberger, Hugh M. and Stokes, Houston H. "German Banks and German Growth: Reply to Fremdling and Tilly," *Journal of Economic History,* 36(2), June 1976, pp. 425-27.

Neuberger, Hugh M. and Stokes, Houston H. "German Banks and German Growth: Reply to Komlos," *Journal of Economic History,* 38(2), June 1978, pp. 480-82.

Neuburger, Hugh M. and Stokes, Houston H. "German Banks and German Growth, 1883-1913: an Empirical View," *Journal of Economic History,* 34(3), September 1974, pp. 710-31.

O'Brien, Patrick K. "Agriculture and the Industrial Revolution: An

Essay in Bibliography and Criticism," *Economic History Review*, Second Series, 30(1), February 1977, pp. 166-81.

O'Brien, Patrick K. and Keyder, Caglar. *Economic Growth in Britain and France, 1780-1914: Two Paths to the Twentieth Century*. London: Allen & Unwin, 1978.

O'Brien, Patrick K. and Engerman, Stanley L. "Changes in Income and Its Distribution during the Industrial Revolution," in Floud and McCloskey, eds. *The Economic History of Britain since 1700*, vol. 1, 1980, pp. 164-81.

O'Brien, Patrick K. "Productivity in the Economies of Europe, 1780-1914," [Working Paper].

Ohkawa, Kazushi and Shinohara, Miyohei., ed. *The Growth Rate of the Japanese Economy since 1878*. Tokyo: Kinokuniya, 1957.

Paquet, Gilles and Faucher, Albert. "L'experience economique du Quebec et la Confederation," *Journal of Canadian Studies*, 1, November 1966, pp. 16-30.

Patrick, Hugh T. *Japanese Industrialization and Its Social Consequences*. Berkeley and Los Angeles: University of California Press, 1976.

Patrick, Hugh T. "A Dynamic Model of Japanese Economic Development, 1887-1915: A Review Article," *Journal of Asian Studies*, 35(3), May 1976, pp. 475-82.

Perkins, Dwight H. "The Economic Performance of China and Japan, 1842-1970," H.I.E.R. Paper no. 177 [Working Paper].

Pomfret, Richard W.T. "The Staple Theory and Canadian Economic Development," Concordia University Working Paper no. 77-08, October 1977 [Working Paper].

Roehl, Richard. "L'Industrialisation Francaise: Une Remise en Cause [French Industrialization: A Reconsideration]," *Revue D'Histoire Economique et Sociale*, 54(3), 1976, pp. 406-27.

Roehl, Richard. "French Industrialization: A Reconsideration," *Explorations in Economic History*, 13(3), July 1976, pp. 233-82.

Rosovsky, Henry. "The Statistical Measurement of Japanese Economic Growth," (Review essay of *The Growth Rate of the Japanese Economy since 1878*, by Ohkawa, ed., 1957) *Economic Development and Cultural Change*, 7(1), October 1958, pp. 75-84.

Rosovsky, Henry and Ohkawa, K. *Japanese Economic Growth: Trend Acceleration in the Twentieth Century*. [Japanese Edition Appears in Japanese] Stanford and Tokyo: Stanford University Press and Toyo Keizai Shimpo-Sha, 1973.

Rostow, W.W., ed. *British Economy of the Nineteenth Century: Essays*. Oxford: Clarendon Press, 1948.

Rostow, W.W. "No Random Walk: A Comment on 'Why Was England First?'," *Economic History Review*, Second Series, 31(4), November 1978, pp. 610-12.

Rudolph, Richard L. "Austrian Industrialization: A Case Study in Leisurely Economic Growth," *Sozialismus, Geschichte und Wirtschaft: Festschrift fur Eduard Marz*. Vienna: Europaverlag, 1973.

Rudolph, Richard L. "Quantitative Aspekte der Industrialisierung in Cisleithanien," in Wandruszka and Urbanitsch, eds. *Die Habsburgermonarchie 1848-1918*, vol. 1, 1973.

Rudolph, Richard L. "The Pattern of Austrian Industrial Growth from the Eighteenth to the Early Twentieth Century," *Austrian History Yearbook*, 11, 1975, pp. 3-25.

Rudolph, Richard L. "Economic Revolution in Austria? The Meaning of 1848 in Austrian Economic History," in Komlos, ed. *Essays on the Habsburg Economy.*

Sandberg, Lars G. "The Case of the Impoverished Sophisticate: Human Capital and Swedish Economic Growth before World War I," *Journal of Economic History*, 39(1), March 1979, pp. 225-41.

Saxonhouse, Gary R. "The Supply of Quality Workers and the Demand for Quality in Jobs in Japan's Early Industrialization," *Explorations in Economic History*, 15(1), January 1978, pp. 40-68.

Saxonhouse, Gary R. and Kiyokawa, Yukihiko. "The Supply and Demand for Quality Workers in the Cotton Textile Industries in Japan and India," in Ohkawa and Hayami, eds. *The Comparative Analysis of Japan and the Less Developed Countries.*

Schremmer, Eckart. "Wie Gross war der "Technische Fortschritt" wahrend der Industriellen Revolution in Deutschland, 1850-1913 [How Large was the Technical Progress during the Industrial Revolution in Germany, 1850-1913?]," *Vierteljahrschrift fur Sozial- und Wirtschaftsgeschichte*, 60(4), 1973, pp. 433-58.

Shinohara, Miyohei. "Manufacturing, 1874-1940," in Ohkawa and Hayami, eds. *Economic Growth*, vol. 1, 1973, pp. 26-37.

Sinclair, William A. "Aspects of Economic Growth 1900-1920," in Boxer, ed. *Aspects of the Australian Economy, 1965.*

Sinclair, William A. "Economic Development and Fluctuation in Australia in the 1920s (Comment on Boehm)," *Economic Record*, 51(135), September 1975, pp. 409-13.

Sinclair, William A. *The Process of Economic Development in Australia.* Melbourne: Cheshire, 1976.

Sinclair, William A. *Australian Economic Development: Old Model and New Model.* Nedlands, W.A.: University of Western Australia Press, 1977.

Spree, Reinhard. *Die Wachstumszyklen der Deutschen Wirtschaft von 1840 bis 1880 [Growth Cycles of the German Economy from 1840 to 1880].* Berlin: Duncker & Humblot, 1977.

Spree, Reinhard. "Zur Quantitativ-Historischen Analyse okonomischer Zeitreihen: Trends und Zyklen in der Deutschen Volkswirtschaft von 1820 bis 1913," in Best and Mann, eds. *Quantitative Methoden in der Historisch-Sozialwissenschaftlichen Forschung [On the Quantitative-Historical Analysis of Economic Time Series]*, 1977.

Spree, Reinhard. *Wachstumtrends und Konjunkturzyklen in der Deutschen Wirtschaft von 1820 bis 1913 - Quantitiver Rahmen fur eine Konjunkturgeschichte des 19. Jahrhunderts [Growth Trends and Business Cycles in the German Economy from 1820 to 1913 - A Quantitative Framework for a Business Cycle History of the 19th Century].* Gottingen: Vandenhoeck & Ruprecht, 1978.

Spree, Reinhard. "Veranderungen der Muster zyklischen Wachstums Patternen Wirtschaft von der Fruh- zur Hochindustrialisierung [Changes in the Character of Cyclical Growth in the German Economy from Early to Late Industrialization]," *Geschichte und Gesellschaft*, 5(2), 1979.

Spree, Reinhard. *Wachstumszyklen der Deutschen Wirtschaft im 19. und*

20. *Jahrhundert - Ergebnisse, Methoden, Erklarungsansatze* [*Growth Cycles of the German Economy in the 19th and 20th Centuries - Results, Methods, Explanations*]. Stuttgart: Klett-Cotta, 1980.

Suzigan, Wilson and Villela, Annibal V. *Politica do Governo e Crescimento da Economia Brasileira, 1889-1945* [*Government Policy and the Economic Growth of Brazil, 1889-1945*]. Rio de Janeiro: I.P.E.A., 1973.

Suzigan, Wilson. "Industrializacao e Politica Economica: Uma Interpretacao em Perspectiva Historica [An Interpretation of Brazilian Industrialization and Economic Policy in Historical Perspective]," *Pesquisa e Planejamento Economico*, 5(2), December 1975, pp. 433-74.

Suzigan, Wilson. "Industrialization and Economic Policy in Historical Perspective," *Brazilian Economic Studies*, (2), 1976, pp. 5-33.

Taira, Koji. "Growth, Trends, and Swings in Japanese Agriculture and Industry," (Review essay of *Agriculture and Economic Growth: Japan's Experience.* by Ohkawa, Johnston, and Kaneda, eds., 1970) *Economic Development and Cultural Change*, 24(2), January 1976, pp. 423-36.

Toniolo, Gianni. "Patterns of Industrial Growth and Italy's Industrialization from 1894 to 1913," *Rendiconti*, 1, 1969, pp. 259-83.

Toniolo, Gianni., ed. *Lo sviluppo economico italiano, 1861-1940* [*Italian Economic Development, 1861-1940*]. Bari: Laterza, 1973.

Toniolo, Gianni., ed. *L'economia italiana 1861-1940.* Bari: Laterza, 1978.

Tortella Casares, Gabriel. "Banking and Industry in Spain, 1829-1874," (Summary of Doctoral Dissertation) *Journal of Economic History*, 29(1), March 1969, pp. 163-66.

Tortella Casares, Gabriel. *Los origenes del capitalismo en Espana* [*The Origins of Capitalism in Spain*]. Madrid: Tecnos, 1973.

Tortella Casares, Gabriel. *Banks, Railroads, and Industry in Spain, 1829-1874.* New York: Arno Press, 1977.

Tsuru, Shigeto. "The Take-off in Japan (1868-1900)," in Rostow, ed. *The Economics of Take-off into Sustained Growth,* 1963, pp. 139-50.

Versiani, Flavio Rabelo. "Industrial Investment in an 'Export' Economy: The Brazilian Experience Before 1914," *Journal of Development Economics*, 7(3), September 1980, pp. 307-29.

Von Tunzelmann, G. Nicholas. "Inverse Relations of the Australian and New Zealand Economies, 1871-1900: An Hypothesis Re-Examined," *Australian Economic Papers*, 5(3), June 1967, pp. 124-27.

Von Tunzelmann, G. Nicholas and Savin, N. Eugene. "The Standard of Living Debate and Optimal Economic Growth," [Working Paper].

Williamson, Jeffrey G. and Kelley, Allen C. "Simple Parables of Japanese Economic Progress: Report on Early Findings," in Ohkawa and Hayami, eds. *Nihon Keizai No Chokiteki Bunseki* [*The Long Term Analysis of the Japanese Economy*], 1973.

Williamson, Jeffrey G. and De Bever, Leo J. "Saving, Accumulation and Modern Economic Growth: The Contemporary Relevance of Japanese History," *Journal of Japanese Studies*, 4(1), Winter 1978, pp. 125-67.

Yamamura, Kozo. "Economic Responsiveness in Japanese

Industrialization," in Cain and Uselding, eds. *Business Enterprise and Economic Change,* 1973, pp. 173-97.

Yamamura, Kozo. *A Study of Samurai Income and Entrepreneurship.* Cambridge: Harvard University Press, 1974.

Yamamura, Kozo. "The Agricultural and Commercial Revolution in Japan," in Uselding, ed. *Research in Economic History,* vol. 5, 1980.

The Rest of the World: After the Industrial Revolution

Aldcroft, Derek H. "McCloskey on Victorian Growth: A Comment," *Economic History Review,* Second Series, 27(2), May 1974, pp. 271-74.

Butlin, Noel G. and Tucker, G.S.L. "The Quantitative Study of British Economic Growth: A Review," (Review essay of *British Economic Growth, 1688-1959.* by Deane and Cole, 1968) *Economic Record,* 40(91), September 1964, pp. 455-60.

Butlin, Noel G. "Some Perspectives of Australian Economic Development, 1890-1965," in Forster, ed. *Australian Economic Development in the Twentieth Century,* 1970, pp. 266-327.

Cairncross, Alec K. "The Postwar Years, 1945-77," in Floud and McCloskey, eds. *The Economic History of Britain since 1700,* vol. 2, 1981.

Ciocca, Pierluigi. "Capitale e fascismo: una introduzione all'esperienza italiana [Capital and Fascism: An Introduction to the Italian Experience]," *Conflitti sociali e accumulazione capitalistica da Giolitti alla guerra fascista.* Roma: Alfani, 1975, pp. 11-28.

Ciocca, Pierluigi. "L'Italia nell'economia mondiale, 1922-1940 [Italy in the World Economy, 1922-1940]," *Quaderni storici,* (29/30), May/December 1975, pp. 342-76.

Ciocca, Pierluigi. "L'economia italiana nel contesto internazionale [The Italian Economy in the International Context (under Fascism)]," in Ciocca and Toniolo, eds. *L'economia italiana nel periodo fascista,* 1976, pp. 19-50.

Ciocca, Pierluigi and Toniolo, Gianni., ed. *L'economia italiana nel periodo fascista [The Italian Economy during the Fascist Era].* Bologna: il Mulino, 1976.

Cohen, Jon S. "Rapporti agricoltura-industria e sviluppo agricolo [Agricultural-Industrial Relationships and Agricultural Development]," in Toniolo and Ciocca, eds. *L'economia italiana nel periodo fascista [The Italian Economy during the Fascist Era],* 1976.

Cole, W.A. "Deane and Cole on Industrialization and Population Change in the Eighteenth Century: A Rejoinder to Neal," *Economic History Review,* Second Series, 24(4), November 1971, pp. 648-52.

Coppock, D.J. "The Climacteric of the 1890's: A Critical Note," *Manchester School of Economic and Social Studies,* 24, January 1956, pp. 1-31.

Crafts, N.F.R. "English Economic Growth in the Eighteenth Century: A Re-examination of Deane and Cole's Estimates," *Economic History Review,* Second Series, 29(2), May 1976, pp. 226-35.

Crafts, N.F.R. "Victorian Britain Did Fail," *Economic History Review*, Second Series, 32(4), November 1979, pp. 533-37.

Davis, Lance E. "Some Aspects of the Economic Development of Great Britain and the U.S.A., 1820-1914," Presented at the British American Studies Association Meetings, Leeds, 1965 [Working Paper].

De Brabander, G.L. "De regionaal-industriele specialisatie en haar effect op Ruimtelijke Verschillen in Economische groei in Belgie, van 1846 tot 1970 [Regional-Industrial Specialization and its Effect on Spatial Differences in Economic Growth in Belgium from 1846 to 1970]," (Unpublished Ph.D. Dissertation) University of Antwerp, 1979, [Working Paper].

De Meere, J.M.M. "Inkomensgroei en -ongelijkheid te Amsterdam 1877-1940 [Growth and Inequality in Amsterdam, 1877-1940]," *Tijdschrift voor Sociale Geschiedenis*, 13, March 1979, pp. 3-47.

Deane, Phyllis and Cole, W.A. *British Economic Growth, 1688-1959: Trends and Structure*. (Second Edition, 1968) Cambridge: Cambridge University Press, 1962.

Dowie, Jack A. "Growth in the Inter-war Period: Some More Arithmetic," *Economic History Review*, Second Series, 21(1), April 1968, pp. 93-112.

Dowie, Jack A. "1919-20 is in Need of Attention," *Economic History Review*, Second Series, 28(3), August 1975, pp. 429-50.

Edelstein, Michael. "United Kingdom Savings in the Age of High Imperialism and After," *American Economic Review, Papers and Proceedings*, 67(1), February 1977, pp. 288-94.

Feinstein, Charles H. "Production and Productivity in the United Kingdom, 1920-1962," *L. and C. Economic Bulletin*, (48), December 1963, pp. 12-14.

Filosa, Renato; Rey, Guido M. and Sitzia, Bruno. "Uno schema di analisi quantitativa del'economia italiana durante il fascismo [Outline of a Quantitative Analysis of the Italian Economy under Fascism]," in Ciocca and Toniolo, eds. *L'economia italiana nel periodo fascista [The Italian Economy during the Fascist Era]*, 1976, pp. 51-102.

Floud, Roderick C. "Britain, 1860-1914: A Survey," in Floud and McCloskey, eds. *The Economic History of Britain since 1700*, vol. 2, 1980.

Forster, Colin., ed. *Australian Economic Development in the Twentieth Century*. [Reprinted in a Japanese Translation: *Nijusseiki no Osutoraria Keizai*, 1977] London: Allen & Unwin, 1970.

Friedman, Philip. *The Impact of Trade Destruction Upon National Incomes: A Study of Europe, 1924-1938*. Gainsville: University of Florida Press, 1974.

Fua, Giorgio. "Breve sintesi statistica dello sviluppo economico italiano 1861-1940 [Brief Statistical Synthesis of Italian Economic Development, 1861-1940]," in Toniolo, ed. *L'economia italiana 1861-1940*, 1978, pp. 47-67.

Gordon, Donald F. and Walton, Gary M. "A Theory of Regenerative Growth and the Experience of Post-World War II West Germany," [Working Paper].

Hawke, Gary R. *The Development of the British Economy, 1870-1914*. Auckland: Heinemann, 1970.

Kelley, Allen C. "Demographic Cycles and Economic Growth: The Long Swing Reconsidered," *Journal of Economic History*, 29(4), December 1969, pp. 633-56.

Kennedy, Jr., William P. "Economic Growth and Structural Change in the U.K., 1870-1914," [Working Paper].

Lee, Clive H. *Regional Economic Growth in the United Kingdom since the 1880's.* London: McGraw-Hill, 1971.

Leff, Nathaniel H. "Export Stagnation and Autarkic Development in Brazil, 1947-1962," [Translated into Portugese in *El Trimestre Economico*, 1969] *Quarterly Journal of Economics*, 81(2), May 1967, pp. 286-301.

Leff, Nathaniel H. *The Brazilian Capital Goods Industry, 1929-1964.* Cambridge: Harvard University Press, 1968.

Lewis, W. Arthur. *The Deceleration of British Growth, 1873-1913.* Princeton: Princeton University Development Research Project, 1967.

Lewis, W. Arthur. *Growth and Fluctuations, 1870-1913.* London: Allen & Unwin, 1978.

Matthews, R.C.O. "Some Aspects of Postwar Growth in the British Economy in Relation to Historical Experience," (Reprinted in Floud, ed. *Essays in Quantitative Economic History*, 1974, pp. 228-247) *Transactions of the Manchester Statistical Society*, Session 1964-65, pp. 1-25.

McCloskey, Donald N. "Did Victorian Britain Fail?" Economic History Review, Second Series, 23(3), December 1970, pp. 446-59.

McCloskey, Donald N. and Sandberg, Lars G. "From Damnation to Redemption: Judgements on the Late Victorian Entrepreneur," *Explorations in Economic History*, 9(1), Fall 1971, pp. 89-108.

McCloskey, Donald N. "Victorian Growth: A Rejoinder (to Aldcroft)," *Economic History Review*, Second Series, 27(2), May 1974, pp. 275-77.

McCloskey, Donald N. "No It Did Not: A Reply to Crafts," *Economic History Review*, Second Series, 32(4), November 1979, pp. 538-41.

McCloskey, Donald N. "A Dialogue between William P. Kennedy and McCloskey on Late Victorian Failure or the Lack of It," in McCloskey, *Trade and Enterprise in Victorian Britain*, 1981.

Meyer, John R. "An Input-Output Approach to Evaluating the Influence of Exports on British Industrial Production in the Late 19th Century," *Explorations in Entrepreneurial History*, 8(1), October 1955, pp. 12-34.

Neal, Larry D. "Deane and Cole on Industrialization and Population Change in the Eighteenth Century: Comment," *Economic History Review*, Second Series, 24(4), November 1971, pp. 643-47.

Nicholas, Stephen J. "Measurement of Productivity, Climacterics and Technical Change in the 1870-1939 British Economy," University of New South Wales Working Paper in Economic History, 1976 [Working Paper].

Phelps Brown, E.H. and Handfield-Jones, Stephen J. "The Climacteric of the 1890'S: A Study in the Expanding Economy," *Oxford Economic Papers*, New Series, 4(3), October 1952, pp. 266-307.

Phelps Brown, E.H. and Weber, Brian A. "Accumulation, Productivity and Distribution in the British Economy, 1870-1938," *Economic Journal*, 63(250), June 1953, pp. 263-88.

Rey, Guido M. "Una sintesi dell'economia italiana durante il fascismo [A Synthesis of the Italian Economy under Fascism]," in Toniolo, ed. *L'economia italiana 1861-1940*, 1978, pp. 269-312.

Richardson, H.W. "Retardation in Britain's Industrial Growth, 1870-1913," *Scottish Journal of Political Economy*, 12(2), June 1965, pp. 125-49.

Rostow, W.W., ed. *British Economy of the Nineteenth Century: Essays.* Oxford: Clarendon Press, 1948.

Sandberg, Lars G. "The Entrepreneur and Technological Change," in Floud and McCloskey, eds. *The Economic History of Britain since 1700*, vol. 2, 1980.

Thomas, Brinley. "Migration and the Rhythm of Economic Growth, 1830-1913," *Manchester School of Economic and Social Studies*, 19(3), September 1951, pp. 215-71.

Toniolo, Gianni. *L'economia dell'Italia Fascista [The Economy of Fascist Italy]*. Bari: Laterza, 1980.

Uselding, Paul J. "Britain's Industrial Marathon," *Reviews in European History*, forthcoming.

Von Tunzelmann, G. Nicholas. "Britain, 1900-45: A Survey," in Floud and McCloskey, eds. *The Economic History of Britain since 1700*, vol. 2, 1980.

Chapter 6

TRANSPORTATION

United States: Railways

Barger, Harold. *The Transportation Industries, 1889-1946* (General Series, no. 51). New York: National Bureau of Economic Research, 1951.

Coelho, Philip R.P. "Railroad Social Saving in Nineteenth Century America: Comment on Hunt," American Economic Review, 58(1), March 1968, pp. 184-86.

Cootner, Paul H. "The Role of Railroads in United States Economic Growth," *Journal of Economic History*, 23(4), December 1963, pp. 477-521.

Cootner, Paul H. "The Economic Impact of the Railroad Innovation," in Mazlish, ed. *The Railroad and the Space Program*, 1965, pp. 107-26.

David, Paul A. "Transport Innovation and Economic Growth: Professor Fogel On and Off the Rails," *Economic History Review*, Second Series, 22(3), December 1969, pp. 506-25.

Davis, Lance E. "Professor Fogel and the New Economic History," *Economic History Review*, Second Series, 19(3), December 1966, pp. 657-63.

Dick, Trevor J.O. "Railroad Inventions' Investment: The United States, 1870-1950," (Summary of Doctoral Dissertation) *Journal of Economic History*, 34(1), March 1974, pp. 275-78.

Dick, Trevor J.O. "United States Railroad Inventions' Investment since 1870," *Explorations in Economic History*, 11(3), Spring 1974, pp. 249-70.

Dowie, Jack A. "As If or Not As If: The Economic Historian as Hamlet," *Australian Economic History Review*, 7, March 1967, pp. 69-85.

Driel, M. van. "Zes paragrafen over Robert William Fogel's Railroads [Six Notes on Robert William Fogel's Railroads]," *Economisch- en Sociaal-Historisch Jaarboek*, 39, 1976, pp. 241-308.

Engerman, Stanley L. "Some Economic Issues Relating to Railroad Subsidies and the Evaluation of Land Grants," *Journal of Economic History*, 32(2), June 1972, pp. 443-63.

Fishlow, Albert. *American Railroads and the Transformation of the Antebellum Economy.* Cambridge: Harvard University Press, 1965.

Fishlow, Albert. "Productivity and Technological Change in the Railroad Sector, 1840-1910," in Brady, ed. *Output, Employment, and Productivity in the United States after 1800* (Studies in Income and Wealth, vol. 30), 1966, pp. 583-646.

Fishlow, Albert. "The Dynamics of Railroad Extension into the West," in Fogel and Engerman, eds. *The Reinterpretation of American Economic History*, 1971, pp. 402-16.

Fishlow, Albert. "Internal Transportation," in Davis, Easterlin, and Parker, eds., *American Economic Growth*, 1972, pp. 468-547.

Fleisig, Heywood. "The Union Pacific Railroad and the Railroad Land Grant Controversy," *Explorations in Economic History*, 11(2), Winter 1974, pp. 155-72.

Fleisig, Heywood. "The Central Pacific Railroad and the Railroad Land Grant Controversy," *Journal of Economic History*, 35(3), September 1975, pp. 552-66.

Fogel, Robert W. *The Union Pacific Railroad: A Case of Premature Enterprise.* Baltimore: Johns Hopkins University Press, 1960.

Fogel, Robert W. "A Quantitative Approach to the Study of Railroads in American Economic Growth: A Report of Some Preliminary Findings," (Reprinted in Swierenga, ed. *Quantification in American History*, 1970, pp. 288-316) *Journal of Economic History*, 22(2), June 1962, pp. 163-97.

Fogel, Robert W. *Railroads and American Economic Growth: Essays in Econometric History.* [Translated into Spanish (1972)] Baltimore: Johns Hopkins University Press, 1964.

Fogel, Robert W. "Railroads and the Axiom of Indispensability," in Andreano, ed. *New Views on American Economic Development*, 1965, pp. 225-41.

Fogel, Robert W. "Railroads as an Analogy to the Space Effort: Some Economic Aspects," *Economic Journal*, 76(301), March 1966, pp. 16-43.

Fogel, Robert W. "Railroads and American Economic Growth," in Fogel and Engerman, eds. *The Reinterpretation of American Economic History*, 1971, pp. 187-203.

Fogel, Robert W. "The Union Pacific Railroad: The Questions of Public Policy," in Fogel and Engerman, eds., *The Reinterpretation of American Economic History*, 1971, pp. 417-25.

Fogel, Robert W. "Notes on the Social Saving Controversy," *Journal of Economic History*, 39(1), March 1979, pp. 1-54.

Golden, James R. "Investment Behavior by United States Railroads: 1870-1914," (Summary of Doctoral Dissertation) *Journal of Economic History*, 32(1), March 1972, pp. 412-14.

Gunderson, Gerald A. "The Nature of Social Saving," *Economic History Review*, Second Series, 23(2), August 1970, pp. 207-19.

Hacker, Louis H. "The New Revolution in Economic History," (Review Essay of *Railroads and Economic Growth*, by Fogel, 1964) *Explorations in Entrepreneurial History*, 3(3), Spring 1966, pp. 159-75.

Haddock, David D. "An Empirical Study of the Regulation of the Rail Industry," [Working Paper].

Haddock, David D. "The Advent of Federal Regulation of Railroads," [Working Paper].

Haddock, David D. "The Origins of Regulation: Competing Theories and Critical Tests," [Working Paper].

Hawke, Gary R. "Mr. Hunt's Study of the Fogel Thesis: A Comment," *History*, 53(177), February 1968, pp. 18-23.

Herbst, Lawrence A. "Trade and Transportation in North America,"

(Summary of 1978 Research Workshop) *Journal of Economic History*, 39(1), March 1979, pp. 317-19.

Higgs, Robert. "Railroad Rates and the Populist Uprising," *Agricultural History*, 44(3), July 1970, pp. 291-97.

Hunt, E.H. "Railroad Social Saving in Nineteenth Century America: Comment on Fogel," *American Economic Review*, 57(4), September 1967, pp. 909-10.

Hunt, E.H. "The New Economic History: Professor Fogel's Study of American Railways," *History*, 53(177), February 1968, pp. 3-18.

Kennedy, Charles J. "Railroad Investment Before the Civil War: Comment on Wicker," in Parker, ed. *Trends in the American Economy in the Nineteenth Century* (Studies in Income and Wealth, vol. 24), 1960, pp. 544-45.

Lebergott, Stanley. "United States Transport Advance and Externalities," *Journal of Economic History*, 26(4), December 1966, pp. 437-61.

Lebergott, Stanley. "United States Transport Advance and Externalities: A Reply to Weiss," *Journal of Economic History*, 28(4), December 1968, pp. 635.

MacAvoy, P.W. *The Economic Effects of Regulation*. Cambridge, Mass.: M.I.T. Press, 1965.

Mazlish, Bruce., ed. *The Railroad and the Space Program: An Exploration in Historical Analogy*. Cambridge, Mass.: M.I.T. Press, 1965.

McClelland, Peter D. "Railroads, American Growth, and the New Economic History: A Critique of Fogel and Fishlow," *Journal of Economic History*, 27(1), March 1968, pp. 102-23.

McClelland, Peter D. "Social Rates of Return on American Railroads in the Nineteenth Century," *Economic History Review*, Second Series, 25(3), August 1972, pp. 471-88.

McClelland, Peter D. "Transportation," in Porter, ed. *Encyclopedia of American Economic History*, vol. 1, 1980, pp. 309-34.

Mercer, Lloyd J. "Land Grants to American Railroads: Social Cost or Social Benefits?" *Business History Review*, 43(2), Summer 1969, pp. 134-51.

Mercer, Lloyd J. "Rates of Return for Land-Grant Railroads: The Central Pacific System," *Journal of Economic History*, 30(3), September 1970, pp. 602-26.

Mercer, Lloyd J. "Taxpayers or Investors: Who Paid for the Land-Grant Railroads?" *Business History Review*, 46(3), Autumn 1972, pp. 279-94.

Morgan, W. Douglas. "Investment Behavior by American Railroads, 1897-1914: A Comment on Neal," *Review of Economics and Statistics*, 53(3), August 1971, pp. 294-98.

Neal, Larry D. "Investment Behavior by American Railroads, 1897-1914," *Review of Economics and Statistics*, 51(2), May 1969, pp. 126-35.

Neal, Larry D. "Investment Behavior by American Railroads, 1897-1914: A Reply to Morgan," *Review of Economics and Statistics*, 53(3), August 1971, pp. 299-300.

Nerlove, Marc. "Railroads and American Economic Growth," (Review essay of *Railroads and American Economic Growth*, by Fogel, 1964) *Journal of Economic History*, 26(1), March 1966, pp. 107-15.

O'Brien, Patrick K. *The New Economic History of Railways: A Critique.* London: Croom Helm, 1977.

Royd, J. Hayden and Walten, Gary M. "The Social Savings from Nineteenth-Century Rail Passenger Services," *Explorations in Economic History*, 9(3), Spring 1972, pp. 233-54.

Schaeffer, Donald F. and Weiss, Thomas J. "The Use of Simulation Techniques in Historical Analysis: Railroads Versus Canals," *Journal of Economic History*, 31(4), December 1971, pp. 854-84.

Scheiber, Harry N. "The Role of the Railroads in United States Economic Growth: Discussion of Cootner," *Journal of Economic History*, 23(4), December 1963, pp. 525-28.

Simon, Matthew. "The Role of the Railroads in United States Economic Growth: Discussion of Cootner," *Journal of Economic History*, 23(4), December 1963, pp. 522-24.

Taylor, George Rogers. "Railroad Investment Before the Civil War: Comment on Wicker," in Parker, ed. *Trends in the American Economy in the Nineteenth Century* (Studies in Income and Wealth, vol. 24), 1960, pp. 524-44.

Thomas, Robert P. and Shetler, Douglass D. "Railroad Social Saving: A Comment on Hunt," *American Economic Review*, 58(1), March 1968, pp. 186-89.

Ulmer, Melville J. *Capital in Transportation, Communications, and Public Utilities: Its Formation and Financing.* Princeton: Princeton University Press for the National Bureau of Economic Research, 1960.

Ulmer, Melville J. "Trends and Cycles in Capital Formation by United States Railroads, 1870-1950," National Bureau of Economic Research, Occasional Paper no. 43, 1954 [Working Paper].

Weiss, Thomas J. "United States Transport Advance and Externalities: A Comment on Lebergott," *Journal of Economic History*, 28(4), December 1968, pp. 631-34.

White, Colin M. "The Concept of Social Saving in Theory and Practice," *Economic History Review*, Second Series, 29(1), February 1976, pp. 82-100.

Wicker, Elmus R. "Railroad Investment Before the Civil War," in Parker, ed. *Trends in the American Economy in the Nineteenth Century* (Studies in Income and Wealth, vol. 24), 1960, pp. 503-24.

Williamson, Jeffrey G. and Kmenta, Jan. "Determinants of Investment Behavior: United States Railroads, 1872-1941," *Review of Economics and Statistics*, 48(2), May 1966, pp. 172-81.

Williamson, Jeffrey G. "The Railroads and Midwestern Development, 1870-90: A General Equilibrium History," in Klingaman and Vedder, eds. *Essays in Nineteenth Century Economic History*, 1975, pp. 269-352.

Yamamura, Kozo, Klein, Maury. "The Growth Strategies of Southern Railroads, 1865-1893," *Business History Review*, 41(4), Winter 1967, pp. 358-77.

TRANSPORTATION

United States: Other

Atack, Jeremy; Haites, Erik F.; Mak, James and Walton, Gary M. "The
Profitability of Steamboating on the Western Rivers: 1850,"
Business History Review, 49(3), Autumn 1975, pp. 346-54.
Atack, Jeremy. "Economies of Scale in Western River Steamboating: A
Comment on Haites and Mak," *Journal of Economic History*, 38(2),
June 1978, pp. 457-66.
Barger, Harold. *The Transportation Industries, 1889-1946* (General
Series, no. 51). New York: National Bureau of Economic Research,
1951.
Coelho, Philip R.P. "Railroad Social Saving in Nineteenth Century
America: Comment on Hunt," *American Economic Review*, 58(1), March
1968, pp. 184-86.
Cranmer, H. Jerome. "Canal Investment, 1815-1860," in Parker, ed.
Trends in the American Economy in the Nineteenth Century (Studies
in Income and Wealth, vol. 24), 1960, pp. 547-64.
Evans, Jr., Robert. "'Without Regard to Cost': The Returns on Clipper
Ships," *Journal of Political Economy*, 72(1), February 1964, pp.
32-43.
Fishlow, Albert. "Internal Transportation," in Davis, Easterlin, and
Parker, eds. *American Economic Growth*, 1972, pp. 468-547.
Goodrich, Carter., ed. *Canals and American Economic Development.* New
York: Columbia University Press, 1961.
Goodrich, Carter. "Internal Improvements Reconsidered," *Journal of
Economic History*, 30(2), June 1970, pp. 289-311.
Gunderson, Gerald A. "The Nature of Social Saving," *Economic History
Review*, Second Series, 23(2), August 1970, pp. 207-19.
Hacker, Louis H. "The New Revolution in Economic History," (Review
essay of *Railroads and Economic Growth*, by Fogel, 1964)
Explorations in Entrepreneurial History, 3(3), Spring 1966, pp.
159-75.
Haites, Erik F. and Mak, James. "Ohio and Mississippi River
Transportation, 1810-1860," *Explorations in Economic History*, 8(2),
Winter 1970/71, pp. 153-80.
Haites, Erik F. and Mak, James. "Steamboating on the Mississippi,
1810-1860: A Purely Competitive Industry," *Business History Review*,
45(1), Spring 1971, pp. 52-78.
Haites, Erik F. and Mak, James. "The Decline of Steamboating on the
Antebellum Western Rivers: Some New Evidence and an Alternative
Hypothesis," *Explorations in Economic History*, 11(1), Fall 1973,
pp. 25-36.
Haites, Erik F. and Mak, James. "Economies of Scale in Western River
Steamboating," *Journal of Economic History*, 36(3), September 1976,
pp. 689-703.
Haites, Erik F. and Mak, James. "Economies of Scale in Western River
Steamboating: A Reply to Atack," *Journal of Economic History*,
38(2), June 1978, pp. 467-70.
Hawke, Gary R. "Mr. Hunt's Study of the Fogel Thesis: A Comment,"
History, 53(177), February 1968, pp. 18-23.
Herbst, Anthony F. and Wu, Joseph S.K. "Some Evidence of

Subsidization: the U.S. Trucking Industry, 1900-1920," *Journal of Economic History*, 33(2), June 1973, pp. 417-33.

Herbst, Lawrence A. "Trade and Transportation in North America," (Summary of 1978 Research Workshop) *Journal of Economic History*, 39(1), March 1979, pp. 317-19.

Hunt, E.H. "Railroad Social Saving in Nineteenth Century America: Comment on Fogel," *American Economic Review*, 57(4), September 1967, pp. 909-10.

Hunt, E.H. "The New Economic History: Professor Fogel's Study of American Railways," *History*, 53(177), February 1968, pp. 3-18.

Mak, James and Haites, Erik F. "Steamboating on the Mississippi: A Purely Competitive Industry," *Business History Review*, 45(1), Spring 1971, pp. 52-78.

Mak, James and Walton, Gary M. "Steamboats and the Great Productivity Surge in River Transportation," *Journal of Economic History*, 32(3), September 1972, pp. 619-40.

Mak, James and Walton, Gary M. "On the Persistence of Old Technologies: The Case of Flatboats," *Journal of Economic History*, 33(2), June 1973, pp. 444-51.

Mak, James; Atack, Jeremy; Haites, Erik F. and Walton, Gary M. "The Profitability of Steamboating on Western Rivers: 1850," *Business History Review*, 49(3), Autumn 1975, pp. 346-54.

Mak, James; Haites, Erik F. and Walton, Gary M. *Western River Transportation during the Era of Early Internal Improvements.* Baltimore: Johns Hopkins University Press, 1975.

Mak, James and Haites, Erik F. "Social Savings Due to Western River Steamboats," in Uselding, ed. *Research in Economic History*, vol. 3, 1978, pp. 263-303.

McClelland, Peter D. "Transportation," in Porter, ed. *Encyclopedia of American Economic History*, vol. 1, 1980, pp. 309-34.

McIlwraith, Thomas F. "Freight Capacity and Utilization of the Erie and Great Lakes Canals before 1850," *Journal of Economic History*, 36(4), December 1976, pp. 852-77.

Nerlove, Marc. "Railroads and American Economic Growth," (Review essay of *Railroads and American Economic Growth*, by Fogel, 1964) *Journal of Economic History*, 26(1), March 1966, pp. 107-15.

Niemi, Jr., Albert W. "A Further Look at Interregional Canals and Economic Specialization: 1820-1840," *Explorations in Economic History*, 7(4), Summer 1970, pp. 499-520.

Niemi, Jr., Albert W. "A Closer Look at Canals and Western Manufacturing in the Canal Era: A Reply to Ransom," *Explorations in Economic History*, 9(4), Summer 1972, pp. 423-24.

Niemi, Jr., Albert W. "Interregional Canals and Manufacturing Development in the West before 1840," *International Review of the History of Banking*, 9, 1974, pp. 192-212.

North, Douglass C. and Heston, Alan. "The Estimation of Shipping Earnings in Historical Studies of the Balance of Payments," *Canadian Journal of Economics and Political Science*, 26(2), May 1960, pp. 265-76.

North, Douglass C. "Sources of Productivity Change in Ocean Shipping, 1600-1850," (Reprinted in Fogel and Engerman, eds. *The Reinterpretation of American Economic History*, 1971, pp. 163-174)

Journal of Political Economy, 76(5), September/October 1968, pp. 953-70.

North, Douglass C. "The Role of Transportation in the Economic Development of North America," [Working Paper].

Ransom, Roger L. "Canals and Economic Development: A Discussion of the Issues," *American Economic Review, Papers and Proceedings*, 54(3), May 1964, pp. 365-76.

Ransom, Roger L. "Interregional Canals and Economic Specialization in the Antebellum United States," *Explorations in Entrepreneurial History*, Second Series, 5(1), Fall 1967, pp. 12-35.

Ransom, Roger L. "Social Returns from Public Transport Investment: A Case Study of the Ohio Canal," *Journal of Political Economy*, 78(5), September/October 1970, pp. 1041-60.

Ransom, Roger L. "A Closer Look at Western Manufacturing in the Canal Era: A Comment on Niemi," *Explorations in Economic History*, 8(4), Summer 1971, pp. 501-8.

Ransom, Roger L. "A Closer Look at Canals and Western Manufacturing in the Canal Era: A Rebuttal to Niemi," *Explorations in Economic History*, 9(4), Summer 1972, pp. 425-26.

Ransom, Roger L. "Public Canal Investment and the Opening of the Old Northwest," in Klingaman and Vedder, eds. *Essays in Nineteenth Century Economic History*, 1975, pp. 246-68.

Reed, M.C., ed. *Railways in the Victorian Economy: Studies in Finance and Economic Growth*. Newton Abbot: David & Charles, 1969.

Scheiber, Harry N. *Ohio Canal Era: A Case Study of Government and the Economy, 1820-1861*. Athens: Ohio University Press, 1969.

Segal, Harvey H. "Canal Investment, 1815-1860: Comment on Cranmer," in Parker, ed. *Trends in the American Economy in the Nineteenth Century* (Studies in Income and Wealth, Vol. 24), 1960, pp. 565-70.

Shepherd, James F. and Walton, Gary M. "Estimates of 'Invisible' Earnings in the Balance of Payments of the British North American Colonies, 1768-1772," *Journal of Economic History*, 29(2), June 1969, pp. 230-63.

Shepherd, James F. and Walton, Gary M. *Shipping, Maritime Trade, and the Economic Development of Colonial North America*. London: Cambridge University Press, 1972.

Shepherd, James F. and Walton, Gary M. "The Effects of the American Revolution on American Maritime Trade and Shipping," *The American Revolution and the Sea: Proceedings of the 14th Conference of the International Commission for Maritime History at Greenwich, London, England*. London: National Maritime Museum, 1974, pp. 58-69.

Thomas, Robert P. and Shetler, Douglass D. "Railroad Social Saving: A Comment on Hunt," *American Economic Review*, 58(1), March 1968, pp. 186-89.

Walton, Gary M. "A Quantitative Study of American Colonial Shipping: A Summary," (Summary of Doctoral Dissertation) *Journal of Economic History*, 26(4), December 1966, pp. 595-98.

Walton, Gary M. "Sources of Productivity Change in American Colonial Shipping, 1675-1775," *Economic History Review*, Second Series, 20(1), April 1967, pp. 67-78.

Walton, Gary M. "Colonial Tonnage Measurement: A Comment on McCusker," *Journal of Economic History*, 27(3), September 1967, pp. 392-97.

Walton, Gary M. "A Measure of Productivity Change in American Colonial Shipping," (See this journal 24(4), November 1971, p. 682, for Erratum Statement concerning this article) *Economic History Review*, Second Series, 21(2), August 1968, pp. 268-82.

Walton, Gary M. "New Evidence on Colonial Commerce," *Journal of Economic History*, 28(3), September 1968, pp. 363-89.

Walton, Gary M. "Trade Routes, Ownership Proportions, and American Colonial Shipping Characteristics," *Las Rutas Del Atlantico*. Sevilla: Trabajos del Noveno Coloquio International de Historia Martima, 1969, pp. 471-502.

Walton, Gary M. "Obstacles to Technical Diffusion in Ocean Shipping, 1675-1775," *Explorations in Economic History*, 8(2), Winter 1970/71, pp. 123-40.

Walton, Gary M.; Atack, Jeremy; Haites, Erik F. and Mak, James. "Profitability of Steamboating on Western Rivers: 1850," *Business History Review*, 49(3), Autumn 1975, pp. 346-54.

White, Colin M. "The Concept of Social Saving in Theory and Practice," *Economic History Review*, Second Series, 29(1), February 1976, pp. 82-100.

Williamson, Samuel H. "The Growth of the Great Lakes as a Major Transportation Resource, 1870-1911," in Uselding, ed. *Research in Economic History*, vol. 2, 1977.

Bean, Richard N. "Productivity Changes in 17th Century Ocean Shipping," [Working Paper].

Broder, Albert A. "Quantitative study of the Role of Railways in a Regional Economy: Southern Spain and the Andalous RR Company, 1872-1913," *First Congress on the Industrialization of Spain*. Barcelona, 1970.

Broeze, Frank J.A. "The Cost of Distance: Shipping and the Early Australian Economy, 1788-1850," *Economic History Review*, Second Series, 28(4), November 1975, pp. 580-97.

Coatsworth, John H. *Crecimiento contra desarrollo, el impacto economico de los ferrocarriles en el Porfiriato* (2 Vols) [*Growth Against Development: The Economic Impact of Railroads in Portfirian Mexico*]. [Printed in an English Edition by Northern Illinois University Press, De Kalb, Ill., 1981] Mexico City: Sep Setentas, Nos. 271-272, 1976.

Coatsworth, John H. "Indispensable Railroads in a Backward Economy: The Case of Mexico," *Journal of Economic History*, 39(4), December 1979, pp. 939-60.

Dales, J.H. "Ocean Freight Rates and Economic Development, 1750-1910: Discussion of North," *Journal of Economic History*, 18(4), December 1958, pp. 574-75.

De Vries, Jan. "Barges and Capitalism: Passenger Transportation in the Dutch Economy, 1632-1839," *A.A.G. Bijdragen*(21), 1978, pp. 33-398.

Engerman, Stanley L. "Railways and Economic Growth in England and Wales, 1840-1870: A New Approach to English Railway History,"

(Review essay of *Railways and Economic Growth In England and Wales,* by Hawke) *Business History,* 13(2), July 1971, pp. 124-28.

Fenoaltea, Stefano. "Railroads and Italian Industrial Growth, 1861-1913," (Reprinted as "Le ferrovie e lo sviluppo industriale italiano. 1861-1913" in Gianni Toniolo, ed. *L'economia italiana 1861-1940.* Bari: Laterza, 1978, pp. 105-56) *Explorations in Economic History,* 9(4), Summer 1972, pp. 325-52.

Floud, Roderick C. and Craig, R.S. "The Evolution of Steam Shipping in Britain in the Nineteenth Century," [Working Paper].

Fremdling, Rainer. "Eisenbahnen und Deutsches Wirtschaftswachstum, 1840-1879. Ein Beitrag zur Entwicklungstheorie und zur Theorie der Infrastruktur (Untersuchungen zur Wirtschafts-, Sozial und Technikgeschichte, vol. 2) [Railroads and German Economic Growth, 1840-1879: A Contribution to Development Theory and to the Theory of Infrastructure]," *Gesellschaft fur Westfalische Wirtschaftgeschichte,* 1975.

Fremdling, Rainer. "Railroads and German Economic Growth: A Leading Sector Analysis with a Comparison to the United States and Great Britain," Journal of Economic History, 37(3), September 1977, pp. 583-604.

Fremdling, Rainer. "Freight Rates and State Budget: The Role of the National Prussian Railways, 1880-1913," *Journal of European Economic History,* 9(1), Spring 1980, pp. 21-40.

George, Peter J. "Rates of Return in Railway Investment and Implications for Government Subsidization of the Canadian Pacific Railway: Some Preliminary Results," *Canadian Journal of Economics,* 1(4), November 1968, pp. 740-62.

George, Peter J. "Rates of Return and Government Subsidization of the Canadian Pacific Railway: Some Further Remarks," *Canadian Journal of Economics,* 8(4), November 1975, pp. 591-600.

George, Peter J. *Government Subsidies and Railway Construction: The Building of the Canadian Pacific Railway, 1870-1896.* New York: Arno Press, 1980.

Gjolberg, Ole. "The Substitution of Steam for Sail in Norwegian Shipping, 1866-1914: A Study in the Economics of Diffusion," *Scandinavian Economic History Review,* 28(2), 1980, pp. 135-46.

Gomez-Mendoza, Antonio. "Railways and Spanish Economic Growth, 1875-1914," Ph.D. Dissertation, St. Antony's College, Oxford, 1980 [Working Paper].

Hansen, Bent and Tourk, Khairy. "The Profitability of the Suez Canal as a Private Enterprise, 1859-1956," *Journal of Economic History,* 38(4), December 1978, pp. 938-58.

Harley, C. Knick. "British Shipbuilding and Merchant Shipping: 1850-1890," (Summary of Doctoral Dissertation) *Journal of Economic History,* 30(1), March 1970, pp. 262-66.

Harley, C. Knick. "The Shift from Sailing Ships to Steamships, 1850-1890: A Study in Technological Change and Its Diffusion," in McCloskey, ed. *Essays on a Mature Economy,* 1971, pp. 215-34.

Harley, C. Knick. "On the Persistence of Old Techniques: The Case of North American Wooden Shipbuilding," *Journal of Economic History,* 33(2), June 1973, pp. 372-98.

Harley, C. Knick. "Transportation, the World Wheat Trade and the

Kuznets Cycle, 1850-1913," *Explorations in Economic History*, 17(3), July 1980, pp. 218-50.

Harley, C. Knick. "World Demand and Transportation Cost: Determinants of Prices and Output of Wheat in Exporting and Importing Regions, 1850-1913," University of Western Ontario, Department of Economics Research Report #2901 [Working Paper].

Hawke, Gary R. "Pricing Policy of Railways in England and Wales before 1881," in Reed, ed. *Railways in the Victorian Economy*, 1969, pp. 76-110.

Hawke, Gary R. and Reed, M.C. "Railway Capital in the United Kingdom in the Nineteenth Century," *Economic History Review*, Second Series, 22(2), August 1969, pp. 269-86.

Hawke, Gary R. *Railways and Economic Growth in England and Wales, 1840-1870.* Oxford: Clarendon Press, 1970.

Hawke, Gary R. "Railway Passenger Traffic in 1865," in McCloskey, ed. *Essays on a Mature Economy*, 1971, pp. 367-84.

Hawke, Gary R. and Higgins, J.P.P. "Transport and Social Overhead Capital," in Floud and McCloskey, eds. *The Economic History of Britain since 1700*, vol. 1, 1980, pp. 226-51.

Hawke, Gary R. "A Note on "Some Economic Aspects of Railroad Development in Tsarist Russia" by Jacob Metzer," [Working Paper].

Henning, Graydon R. and Trace, Keith. "Britain and the Motorship: A Case of the Delayed Adoption of New Technology?" *Journal of Economic History*, 35(2), June 1975, pp. 353-85.

Hornby, Ove C. and Nilsson, Carl-Axel. "The Transition from Sail to Steam in the Danish Merchant Fleet, 1865-1910," *Scandinavian Economic History Review*, 28(2), 1980, pp. 109-34.

Huber, Paul B. "Historische Verkehrsanalyse, 1830 bis 1913 [Historical Analysis of Transportation in Germany from 1820 to 1913]," in Nuesser, ed. *Fernverkehrssysteme* (Anlageband III zum Jahresbericht 1976 der Programmleitung Angewandte Systemanalyse), 1977, pp. 289-350.

Huber, Paul B. "Regionale Expansion und Entleerung in Deutschland des Neunzehnten Jahrhunderts: eine Folge der Eisenbahnentwicklung? [Regional Expansion and Evacuation in 19th Century Germany: A Result of Railroad Development?]," in Fremdling and Tilly, eds. *Industrialisierung und Raum*, 1979, pp. 27-53.

Hughes, Jonathan R.T. and Reiter, Stanley. "The First 1,945 British Steamships," (Reprinted in Hughes, ed. *Purdue Faculty Papers in Economic History, 1956-1966*, 1967, pp. 453-483) *Journal of the American Statistical Association*, 53(282), June 1958, pp. 360-81.

Hughes, Jonathan R.T. "Ocean Freight Rates and Economic Development, 1750-1910: Discussion of North," *Journal of Economic History*, 18(4), December 1958, pp. 575-79.

Hurd, II, John. "Railways and the Expansion of Markets in India, 1861-1921," (Symposium on Economic Change in Indian Agriculture. Edited by Morris D. Morris) *Explorations in Economic History*, 12(3), July 1975, pp. 263-88.

Jennings, Jr., Frederic B. "Interdependence, Incentives, and Institutional Bias: An Organizational Perspective on the British Canals," Ph.D. Dissertation, Stanford University, 1982 [Working Paper].

Johansen, Hans Chr. "Den Danske Skibsfart I Sidste Halvdel af Det 18. Arhundrede [Eighteenth Century Danish Shipping]," *Erhvervshistorisk Arbog*, 26, 1975, pp. 62-89.

Johansen, Hans Chr. "Shipping through the Sound, 1784-95," [Working Paper].

Kelly, W. J. "Railroad Development and Market Integration in Tsarist Russia: Evidence on Oil Products and Grain: A Note on Metzer," *Journal of Economic History*, 36(4), December 1976, pp. 908-16.

Knauerhase, Ramon. "The Compound Steam Engine and Productivity in the German Merchant Marine Fleet, 1871-1887," *Journal of Economic History*, 28(3), September 1968, pp. 390-403.

Krantz, Olle. *Studies in the Growth of Swedish Freight Transportation with Special Reference to the Expansion of Road Transportation after 1920*. Lund: University of Lund Press, 1972.

Krantz, Olle. "The Competition between Railways and Domestic Shipping in Sweden, 1870-1914," *Economy and History*, 15, 1972, pp. 19-40.

McAlpin, Michelle Burge. "Railroads, Prices, and Peasant Rationality: India, 1860-1900," *Journal of Economic History*, 34(3), September 1974, pp. 662-84.

McAlpin, Michelle Burge. "Railroads, Cultivation Patterns, and Foodgrain Availability: India, 1860-1900," *Indian Economic and Social History Review*, 12(1), January/March, 1975, pp. 43-60.

Mercer, Lloyd J. "Rates of Return and Government Subsidization of the Canadian Pacific Railway: An Alternate View," *Canadian Journal of Economics*, 6(3), August 1973, pp. 428-37.

Mercer, Lloyd J. "Building Ahead of Demand: Some Evidence for the Land Grant Railroads," *Journal of Economic History*, 34(2), June 1974, pp. 492-500.

Metzer, Jacob. "Some Economic Aspects of Railroad Development in Tsarist Russia," (Summary of Doctoral Dissertation) *Journal of Economic History*, 33(1), March 1973, pp. 314-16.

Metzer, Jacob. "Railroad Development and Market Integration: The Case of Tsarist Russia," (See the Editor's Note this Journal, 35(2), June 1975, pp. 467 for an Erratum statement concerning this article) *Journal of Economic History*, 34(3), September 1974, pp. 529-50.

Metzer, Jacob. "Railroads in Tsarist Russia: Direct Gains and Implications," *Explorations in Economic History*, 13(1), January 1976, pp. 85-112.

Metzer, Jacob. "Railroad Development and Market Integration in Tsarist Russia: A Rejoinder to Kelly," *Journal of Economic History*, 36(4), December 1976, pp. 917-18.

Metzer, Jacob. *Some Economic Aspects of Railroad Development in Tsarist Russia*. New York: Arno Press, 1977.

Minami, Ryoshin. "Railroads and Electric Utilities, 1872-1960," in Ohkawa and Hayami, eds. *Economic Growth*, vol. 1, 1973, pp. 38-50.

Mitchell, B.R. "The Coming of the Railway and United Kingdom Economic Growth," *Journal of Economic History*, 24(3), September 1964, pp. 315-36.

Morris, Morris D. and Dudley, Clyde B. "Selected Railway Statistics for the Indian Subcontinent, 1853-1946/47," *Artha Vijnana*, 17(3), September 1975, pp. 187-298.

Norrie, Kenneth H. "Canadian Pacific Railroad Land Sale: A Model of the Sale and Pricing of the Canadian Pacific Railroad Land Grant," [Working Paper].

North, Douglass C. "Ocean Freight Rates and Economic Development, 1750-1910," *Journal of Economic History*, 18(4), December 1958, pp. 537-55.

North, Douglass C. and Heston, Alan. "The Estimation of Shipping Earnings in Historical Studies of the Balance of Payments," *Canadian Journal of Economics and Political Science*, 26(2), May 1960, pp. 265-76.

North, Douglass C. "Sources of Productivity Change in Ocean Shipping, 1600-1850," (Reprinted in Fogel and Engerman, eds. *The Reinterpretation of American Economic History*, 1971, pp. 163-174) *Journal of Political Economy*, 76(5), September/October 1968, pp. 953-70.

O'Brien, Patrick K. *The New Economic History of Railways: A Critique.* London: Croom Helm, 1977.

Reed, M.C. *Investment in Railways in Britain, 1820-1844: A Study in the Development of the Capital Market.* Oxford: Oxford University Press, 1975.

Tortella Casares, Gabriel. *Banks, Railroads, and Industry in Spain, 1829-1874.* New York: Arno Press, 1977.

Toutain, Jean Claude. "Les transports en France de 1830 a 1965 [The Transportation Sector in the French Economy, 1830-1965]," *Cahiers de L'Institut de Science Economique Appliquee*, 1968.

Vamplew, Wray. "The Railways and the Iron Industry: A Study of Their Relationship in Scotland," in Reed, ed. *Railways in the Victorian Economy*, 1969, pp. 33-75.

Vamplew, Wray. "Sources of Scottish Railway Share Capital before 1860," Scottish Journal of Political Economy, 17(3), November 1970, pp. 425-39.

Vamplew, Wray. "Nihilistic Impressions of British Railway History," in McCloskey, ed. *Essays on a Mature Economy*, 1971, pp. 345-66.

Vamplew, Wray. "Railways and the Transformation of the Scottish Economy," *Economic History Review*, Second Series, 24(1), February 1971, pp. 37-54.

Vamplew, Wray. "The Financing of Scottish Railways before 1860: A Reply to Gourvish and Reed," *Scottish Journal of Political Economy*, 18(2), June 1971, pp. 221-23.

Walton, Gary M. "Productivity Change in Ocean Shipping after 1870: A Comment on Knauerhase," *Journal of Economic History*, 30(2), June 1970, pp. 435-41.

Walton, Gary M. "Obstacles to Technical Diffusion in Ocean Shipping, 1675-1775," *Explorations in Economic History*, 8(2), Winter 1970/71, pp. 123-40.

Weiss, Thomas J. *The Service Sector in the United States, 1839 through 1899.* New York: Arno Press, 1975.

Wogin, Gillian. "The Land Settlement and Freight Rate Policies of the Canadian Pacific Railway: a case study in wealth-maximizing behaviour," Ph.D. Dissertation, Carleton University, Ottawa [Working Paper].

Yasuba, Yasukichi. "Freight Rates and Productivity in Ocean

TRANSPORTATION

Transportation for Japan, 1875-1943," *Explorations in Economic History*, 15(1), January 1978, pp. 11-39.

Chapter 7

COMMODITY PRODUCTION AND INDUSTRIAL ORGANIZATION

United States: General

Ames, Edward. "Trends, Cycles, and Stagnation in U.S. Manufacturing since 1860," (Reprinted in Hughes, ed. *Purdue Faculty Papers in Economic History, 1956-1966*, 1967, pp. 91-102) *Oxford Economic Papers*, 12(3), October 1959, pp. 270-81.

Andreano, Ralph L. "The American Manufacturing Frontier, 1870-1940: A Comment on Severson," *Business History Review*, 35(1), Spring 1961, pp. 105-9.

Atack, Jeremy. "Returns to Scale in Antebellum United States Manufacturing," *Explorations in Economic History*, 14(4), October 1977, pp. 337-59.

Atack, Jeremy. "Estimation of Economies of Scale in Nineteenth-Century United States Manufacturing and the Form of the Production Function," (Summary of Doctoral Dissertation) *Journal of Economic History*, 38(1), March 1978, pp. 268-70.

Atack, Jeremy; Bateman, Fred and Weiss, Thomas J. "The Regional Diffusion and Adoption of the Steam Engine in American Manufacturing," *Journal of Economic History*, 40(2), June 1980, pp. 281-308.

Bateman, Fred; Foust, James D. and Weiss, Thomas J. "Large-Scale Manufacturing in the South and West," *Business History Review*, 45(1), Spring 1971, pp. 18-34.

Bateman, Fred; Foust, James D. and Weiss, Thomas J. "The Participation of Planters in Manufacturing in the Antebellum South," *Agricultural History*, 48(2), April 1974, pp. 277-97.

Bateman, Fred and Weiss, Thomas J. "Market Structure before the Age of Big Business: Concentration and Profit in Early Southern Manufacturing," *Business History Review*, 49(3), Autumn 1975, pp. 312-36.

Bateman, Fred and Weiss, Thomas J. "Comparative Regional Development in Antebellum Manufacturing," *Journal of Economic History*, 35(1), March 1975, pp. 182-208.

Bateman, Fred; Foust, James and Weiss, Thomas J. "Profitability in Southern Manufacturing: Estimates for 1860," *Explorations in Economic History*, 12(3), July 1975, pp. 211-32.

Bateman, Fred and Weiss, Thomas J. "Manufacturing in the Antebellum South," in Uselding, ed. *Research in Economic History*, vol. 1, 1976.

Bateman, Fred and Weiss, Thomas J. "A Sample of Industrial Firms from the Manuscripts of the U.S. Censuses of Manufacturing, 1850-1870," [Working Paper].

Bateman, Fred and Weiss, Thomas J. "Industrialization in the Slave Economy," [Working Paper].

Brady, Dorothy S., ed. *Output, Employment, and Productivity in the United States after 1800* (Studies in Income and Wealth, vol. 30). New York: Columbia University Press for the National Bureau of Economic Research, 1966.

Burns, Arthur F. *Production Trends in the United States since 1870* (General Series, 23). New York: National Bureau of Economic Research, 1934.

Creamer, Daniel; Dobrovolsky, Sergei and Borenstein, Israel. *Capital in Manufacturing and Mining: Its Formation and Financing.* Princeton: Princeton University Press for the National Bureau of Economic Research, 1960.

David, Paul A. "Estimates of Annual Constant Dollar Gross Output and Real Net Output for Chicago Manufacturing Industries," Stanford University Center for Research in Economic Growth, Memoranda Series no. 18, July 1962 [Working Paper].

David, Paul A. "Factories at the Prairie's Edge: A Study of Industrialization in Chicago, 1848-1893," [Working Paper].

David, Paul A. "Locating a Switch-Over in the Structural Relationship Between Variations in the Manufacturing Sector's Terms of Trade with Agriculture and the Volume of Industrial Output in Chicago: A Statistical Procedure," [Working Paper].

Davis, Lance E. *The Growth of Industrial Enterprise.* Chicago: Scott Foresman, 1964.

Fabricant, Solomon. *The Output of Manufacturing Industries, 1899-1937.* (General Series(39) New York: National Bureau of Economic Research, 1940.

Fabricant, Solomon. *Employment in Manufacturing, 1899-1939* (General Series, 41). New York: National Bureau of Economic Research, 1942.

Fenichel, Allen H. "Growth and Diffusion of Power in Manufacturing, 1838-1919," in Brady, ed. *Output, Employment, and Productivity in the United States After 1800* (Studies in Income and Wealth, vol. 30), 1966, pp. 443-78.

Field, Alexander J. "The Relative Stability of German and American Industrial Growth, 1880-1913: A Comparative Analysis," in Schroder and Spree, eds. *Historisch-Sozialwissenschaftliche Forschungen 11,* 1980.

Gallaway, Lowell E. and Vedder, Richard K. "The Profitability of Antebellum Manufacturing: Some New Estimates," *Business History Review*, 54(1), Spring 1980, pp. 92-103.

Gallman, Robert E. "Commodity Output, 1839-1899," in Parker, ed. *Trends in the American Economy in the Nineteenth Century* (Studies in Income and Wealth, vol. 24), 1960, pp. 13-67.

Gallman, Robert E. "Commodity Output, 1839-1899: Reply to Potter," in Parker, ed. *Trends in the American Economy in the Nineteenth Century* (Studies in Income and Wealth, vol. 24), 1960, pp. 69-71.

Green, George D. "Monetary Systems and Regional Economies: Comments on Papers by Rockoff and Bateman/Weiss," *Journal of Economic History*, 35(1), March 1975, pp. 212-15.

Hughes, Jonathan R.T. "Economic Aspects of Industrialization," in Sills, ed. *International Encyclopedia of the Social Sciences*, 1968.

Livesay, Harold C. and Porter, Glenn. "The Financial Role of Merchants in the Development of U.S. Manufacturing, 1815-1860," *Explorations in Economic History*, 9(1), Fall 1971, pp. 63-87.

Niemi, Jr., Albert W. "A Further Look at Interregional Canals and Economic Specialization: 1820-1840," *Explorations in Economic History*, 7(4), Summer 1970, pp. 499-520.

Niemi, Jr., Albert W. "The Development of Industrial Structure in Southern New England: A Note," *Journal of Economic History*, 30(3), September 1970, pp. 657-62.

Niemi, Jr., Albert W. "Structural Shifts in Southern Manufacturing, 1849-1899," *Business History Review*, 45(1), Spring 1971, pp. 79-84.

Niemi, Jr., Albert W. "The Role of Immigration in United States Commodity Production, 1869-1929," *Social Science Quarterly*, 52(1), June 1971, pp. 190-96.

Niemi, Jr., Albert W. "Structural and Labor Productivity Patterns in United States Manufacturing, 1849-1899," *Business History Review*, 46(1), Spring 1972, pp. 67-84.

Niemi, Jr., Albert W. "A Closer Look at Canals and Western Manufacturing in the Canal Era: A Reply to Ransom," *Explorations in Economic History*, 9(4), Summer 1972, pp. 423-24.

Niemi, Jr., Albert W. "Empirical Tests of the Heckscher Ohlin Hypothesis for New England and Southern Manufacturing, 1860-1958," *Review of Regional Studies*, 4(Supplement), 1974, pp. 87-94.

Niemi, Jr., Albert W. *State and Regional Patterns in American Manufacturing, 1860-1900*. Westport, Conn.: Greenwood Press, 1974.

Passell, Peter and Schmundt, Maria. "Pre-Civil War Policy and the Growth of Manufacturing," *Explorations in Economic History*, 9(1), Fall 1971, pp. 35-48.

Potter, Neal. "Commodity Output, 1839-1899: Comment on Gallman," in Parker, ed. *Trends in the American Economy in the Nineteenth Century* (Studies in Income and Wealth, vol. 24), 1960, pp. 67-69.

Poulson, Barry W. "Estimates of the Value of Manufacturing Output in the Early Nineteenth Century," *Journal of Economic History*, 29(3), September 1969, pp. 521-25.

Poulson, Barry W. *Value Added in Manufacturing, Mining, and Agriculture in the American Economy 1809 to 1839*. New York: Arno Press, 1975.

Ransom, Roger L. "A Closer Look at Western Manufacturing in the Canal Era: A Comment on Niemi," *Explorations in Economic History*, 8(4), Summer 1971, pp. 501-8.

Ransom, Roger L. "A Closer Look at Canals and Western Manufacturing in the Canal Era: A Rebuttal to Niemi," *Explorations in Economic History*, 9(4), Summer 1972, pp. 425-26.

Rees, Albert, assisted by Jacobs, Donald P. *Real Wages in Manufacturing, 1890-1914* (General Series, no. 70). Princeton: Princeton University Press for the National Bureau of Economic Research, 1961.

Sands, Saul S. "Changes in Scale of Production in U.S. Manufacturing Industry, 1904-1947," *Review of Economics and Statistics*, 43(4),

November 1961, pp. 365-68.

Severson, Robert F. "The American Manufacturing Frontier, 1870-1940,"
    Business History Review, 34(3), Autumn 1960, pp. 356-72.

Severson, Robert F. "The American Manufacturing Frontier, 1870-1914:
    Reply to Andreano," *Business History Review*, 35(1), Spring 1961,
    pp. 109-13.

Shaw, W.H. *Value of Commodity Output since 1869* (General Series, no.
    48). New York: National Bureau of Economic Research, 1947.

Sokoloff, Kenneth. "Capital Markets and Industrialization in Early
    America," [Working Paper].

Sokoloff, Kenneth. "Industrialization and the Growth of Manufacturing
    in Early America: Evidence from the 1820 Census," [Working Paper].

Temin, Peter. "Manufacturing," in Davis, Parker, and Easterlin, eds.
    American Economic Growth, 1972, pp. 418-67.

Uselding, Paul J. "A Note on the Inter-Regional Trade in Manufactures
    in 1840," *Journal of Economic History*, 36(2), June 1976, pp.
    428-35.

Uselding, Paul J. "Manufacturing," in Porter, ed. *Encyclopedia of
    American Economic History*, vol. 1, 1980, pp. 397-412.

Uselding, Paul J. "Accurate Size Measurement and Precision in the
    'Making' and 'Manufacturing' Systems of the 19th Century," in
    Mayr, ed. *The American System of Manufacturing.*

Vedder, Richard K. and Gallaway, Lowell E. "The Profitability of
    Antebellum Manufacturing: Some New Estimates," *Business History
    Review*, 54(1), Spring 1980, pp. 92-103.

Weiss, Thomas J.; Bateman, Fred and Foust, James D. "Large Scale
    Manufacturing in the South and West, 1850 and 1860," *Business
    History Review*, 45(1), Spring 1971, pp. 18-34.

Weiss, Thomas J.; Bateman, Fred and Foust, James D. "The Participation
    of Planters in Manufacturing in the Antebellum South," *Agricultural
    History*, 48(2), April 1974, pp. 277-97.

Weiss, Thomas J. and Bateman, Fred. "Manufacturing in the Antebellum
    South," in Uselding, ed. *Research in Economic History*, vol. 1,
    1976.

Weiss, Thomas J.; Atack, Jeremy and Bateman, Fred. "Risk, the Rate of
    Return and the Pattern of Investment in 19th Century American
    Industrialization," [Working Paper].

Zevin, Robert B. "The Growth of Manufacturing in Early Nineteenth
    Century New England," (Summary of Doctoral Dissertation) *Journal of
    Economic History*, 25(4), December 1965, pp. 680-82.

Zevin, Robert B. *The Growth of Manufacturing in Early Nineteenth
    Century New England*. New York: Arno Press, 1975.

United States: Extractive

Andreano, Ralph L. and Willliamson, Harold F. "Integration and
    Competition in the Oil Industry: A Review Article," *Journal of
    Political Economy*, 69(4), August 1961, pp. 381-85.

Barger, Harold. *The Mining Industries, 1899-1939* (General Series, no.
    43). New York: National Bureau of Economic Research, 1944.

Barnett, Harold J. "Some Aspects of Development in the Coal Mining

Industry, 1839-1918: Comment on Eliasberg," in Brady, ed. *Output, Employment, and Productivity in the United States after 1800* (Studies in Income and Wealth, vol. 30), 1966, pp. 437-39.

Borenstein, Israel. "Capital and Output Trends in Mining Industries, 1870-1948," National Bureau of Economic Research, Occasional Paper no. 45, 1954 [Working Paper].

Eliasberg, Vera F. "Some Aspects of Development in the Coal Mining Industry, 1839-1918," in Brady, ed. *Output, Employment, and Productivity in the United States After 1800* (Studies in Income and Wealth, vol. 30), 1966, pp. 405-35.

Hallagan, William S. "Share Contracting for California Gold," *Explorations in Economic History*, 15(2), April 1978, pp. 196-210.

Herfindahl, Orris C. "Development of the Major Metal Mining Industries in the United States from 1839 to 1909," in Brady, ed. *Output, Employment, and Productivity in the United States after 1800* (Studies in Income and Wealth, vol. 30), 1966, pp. 293-346.

Libecap, Gary D. *The Evolution of Private Mining Rights: Nevada's Comstock Lode.* New York: Arno Press, 1978.

Libecap, Gary D. "Economic Variables and the Development of the Law: The Case of Western Mineral Rights," *Journal of Economic History*, 38(2), June 1978, pp. 338-62.

Libecap, Gary D. "Government Support of Private Claims to Public Minerals: Western Mineral Rights," *Business History Review*, 53(3), Autumn 1979, pp. 364-85.

McGann, Paul W. "Development of the Major Metal Mining Industries in the United States from 1839 to 1909: Comment on Herfindahl," in Brady, ed. *Output, Employment, and Productivity in the United States After 1800* (Studies in Income and Wealth, vol. 30), 1966, pp. 347-48.

McGann, Paul W. "Some Aspects of Development in the Coal Mining Industry, 1839-1918: Comment on Eliasberg," in Brady, ed. *Output, Employment, and Productivity in the United States After 1800* (Studies in Income and Wealth, vol. 30), 1966, pp. 436-37.

Parker, William N. "The Land, Minerals, Water, and Forests," in Davis, Easterlin, and Parker, eds. *American Economic Growth*, 1972, pp. 93-120.

Umbeck, John. "The California Gold Rush: a Study of Emerging Property Rights," *Explorations in Economic History*, 14(3), July 1977, pp. 197-226.

Williamson, Harold F. and Andreano, Ralph L. *A History of the American Petroleum Industry* (2 Vols.; vol. 1: *1959*; vol. 2: *1963*). Evanston: Northwestern University Press, 1959, 1963.

United States: Iron and Steel

Adams, Jr., Donald R. "Wage Rates in the Iron Industry: A Comment on Zabler," *Explorations in Economic History*, 11(1), Fall 1973, pp. 89-94.

Allen, Robert C. "The Peculiar Productivity History of American Blast Furnaces, 1840-1913," *Journal of Economic History*, 37(3), September 1977, pp. 605-33.

Allen, Robert C. "International Competition in Iron and Steel, 1850-1913," *Journal of Economic History*, 39(4), December 1979, pp. 911-37.

Baack, Bennett D. and Ray, Edward J. "Tariff Policy and Comparative Advantage in the Iron and Steel Industry, 1870-1929," *Explorations in Economic History*, 11(1), Fall 1973, pp. 3-24.

Berck, Peter. "Hard Driving and Efficiency: Iron Production in 1890," *Journal of Economic History*, 38(4), December 1978, pp. 879-900.

Engerman, Stanley L. "The American Tariff, British Exports, and American Iron Production, 1840-1860," in McCloskey, ed. *Essays on a Mature Economy: Britain After 1840*, 1971, pp. 13-38.

Fogel, Robert W. and Engerman, Stanley L. "A Model for the Explanation of Industrial Expansion During the Nineteenth Century: With an Application to the American Iron Industry," (Reprinted in Fogel and Engerman, eds. *The Reinterpretation of American Economic History*, 1971, pp. 148-162) *Journal of Political Economy*, 77(3), May/June 1969, pp. 306-28.

Green, J. "The Effect of the Iron Tariff in the United States," Paper presented to the Cliometrics Conference, Madison, Wisconsin, 1970 [Working Paper].

Hekman, John S. "An Analysis of the Changing Location of Iron and Steel Production in the Twentieth Century," *American Economic Review*, 68(1), March 1978, pp. 123-33.

Joskow, Paul L. and McFelvey, Edward F. "The Fogel-Engerman Iron Model: A Clarifying Note," *Journal of Political Economy*, 81(5), September/October 1973, pp. 1236-40.

McCloskey, Donald N. "International Differences in Productivity? Coal and Steel in America and Britain before World War I," in McCloskey, ed. *Essays on a Mature Economy: Britain after 1840*, 1971, pp. 285-304.

McCloskey, Donald N. *Economic Maturity and Entrepreneurial Decline: British Iron and Steel, 1870-1913*. Cambridge: Harvard University Press, 1973.

Novak, David E. and Perlman, Richard. "The Structure of Wages in the American Iron and Steel Industry, 1860-1890," *Journal of Economic History*, 22(3), September 1962, pp. 334-47.

Paskoff, Paul F. "Labor Productivity and Managerial Efficiency against a Static Technology: The Pennsylvania Iron Industry, 1750-1800," *Journal of Economic History*, 40(1), March 1980, pp. 129-35.

Smolensky, Eugene. "The Composition of Iron and Steel Products, 1869-1909: Discussion of Temin," *Journal of Economic History*, 23(4), December 1963, pp. 472-76.

Sundarajan, V. "The Impact of the Tariff on Some Selected Products of the U.S. Iron and Steel Industry, 1870-1914," *Quarterly Journal of Economics*, 84(4), November 1970, pp. 590-610.

Temin, Peter. "The Composition of Iron and Steel Products, 1869-1909," *Journal of Economic History*, 23(4), December 1963, pp. 447-71.

Temin, Peter. *Iron and Steel in Nineteenth Century America: An Economic Inquiry*. Cambridge: M.I.T. Press, 1964.

Temin, Peter. "A New Look at Hunter's Hypothesis about the Antebellum Iron Industry," (Reprinted in Fogel and Engerman, eds. *The Reinterpretation of American Economic History*, 1971, pp. 116-121)

American Economic Review, Papers and Proceedings, 54(3), May 1964, pp. 344-51.

Walsh, William D. "The Diffusion of Technological Change in the Pennsylvania Pig Iron Industry, 1850-1870: A Summary," (Summary of Doctoral Dissertation) *Journal of Economic History*, 26(4), December 1966, pp. 591-94.

Walsh, William D. "New Technology in the Mid-Nineteenth Century Pennsylvania Pig Iron Industry," *Yale Economic Essays*, 11(1 & 2), Spring/Fall 1971, pp. 3-52.

Zabler, Jeffrey F. "More on the Wage Rates in the Iron Industry: A Reply to Adams," *Explorations in Economic History*, 11(1), Fall 1973, pp. 95-102.

United States: Textiles

Asher, Ephraim. "Industrial Efficiency and Biased Technical Change in American and British Manufacturing: The Case of Textiles in the Nineteenth Century," *Journal of Economic History*, 32(2), June 1972, pp. 431-42.

Carlson, Leonard A. "Manning the Mills of the New South: Labor Force Recruitment in the Post-Bellum Cotton Textile Industry," [Working Paper].

David, Paul A. "Learning by Doing and Tariff Protection: A Reconsideration of the Case of the Antebellum Cotton Textile Industry," *Journal of Economic History*, 30(3), September 1970, pp. 521-601.

David, Paul A. "The Use and Abuse of Prior Information in Econometric History: A Rejoinder to Professor Williamson on the Antebellum Cotton Textile Industry," *Journal of Economic History*, 32(3), September 1972, pp. 706-27.

David, Paul A. "The "Horndal Effect" in Lowell, 1834-1856: A Short-Run Learning Curve for Integrated Cotton Textile Mills," *Explorations in Economic History*, 10(2), Winter 1973, pp. 131-50.

Davis, Lance E. "Sources of Industrial Finance: The American Textile Industry, A Case Study," (Reprinted in Hughes, ed. *Purdue Faculty Papers in Economic History, 1956-1966*, 1967, pp. 625-642) *Explorations in Entrepreneurial History*, 9(4), April 1957, pp. 189-203.

Davis, Lance E. "Stock Ownership in the Early New England Textile Industry," (Reprinted in Hughes, ed. *Purdue Faculty Papers in Economic History, 1956-1966*, 1967, pp. 563-580) *Business History Review*, 32(2), Summer 1958, pp. 204-22.

Davis, Lance E. "The New England Textile Mills and the Capital Markets: A Study of Industrial Borrowing, 1840-1860," (Reprinted in Hughes, ed. *Purdue Faculty Papers in Economic History, 1956-1966*, 1967, pp. 596-624) *Journal of Economic History*, 20(1), March 1960, pp. 1-30.

Davis, Lance E. "Mrs. Vatter on Industrial Borrowing: A Reply," *Journal of Economic History*, 21(2), June 1961, pp. 222-26.

Davis, Lance E. and Stettler, III, H. Louis. "The New England Textile Industry, 1825-60: Reply to McGouldrick," in Brady, ed. *Output,*

Employment, and Productivity in the United States After 1800 (Studies in Income and Wealth, vol. 30), 1966, pp. 240-42.

Denslow, Jr., David and Schulze, David. "Optimal Replacement of Capital Goods in Early New England and British Textile Firms: A Comment (on Williamson)," Journal of Political Economy, 82(3), May/June 1974, pp. 631-37.

Doane, David P. "Regional Cost Differentials and Textile Location: A Statistical Analysis," Explorations in Economic History, 9(1), Fall 1971, pp. 3-34.

Feller, Irwin. "The Draper Loom in New England Textiles, 1894-1914: A Study of Diffusion of an Innovation," Journal of Economic History, 26(3), September 1966, pp. 320-47.

Feller, Irwin. "The Draper Loom in New England Textiles: A Reply to Sandberg," Journal of Economic History, 28(4), December 1968, pp. 628-30.

Galenson, Alice C. The Migration of the Cotton Textile Industry from New England to the South: 1880-1930. Ithaca, N.Y.: Cornell University Press, 1975.

Hekman, John S. "The Product Cycle and New England Textiles in the Nineteenth Century," [Working Paper].

Ishikawa, Tsuneo. "Conceptualization of Learning by Doing: A Note on Paul David's 'Learning by Doing and...the Antebellum United States Textile Industry," Journal of Economic History, 33(4), December 1973, pp. 851-61.

Klingaman, David C.; Vedder, Richard K.; Gallaway, Lowell E. and Uselding Paul. "Discrimination and Exploitation in Antebellum American Cotton Textile Manufacturing," in Uselding, ed. Research in Economic History, vol. 3, 1978, pp. 217-61.

Lazonick, William H. "Industrial Relations and Technical Change: The Case of the Self-Acting Mule," Cambridge Journal of Economics, 3(3), September 1979, pp. 231-62.

McGouldrick, Paul F. "The New England Textile Industry, 1825-60: Comment on Davis and Stettler," in Brady, ed. Output, Employment, and Productivity in the United States After 1800 (Studies in Income and Wealth, vol. 30), 1966, pp. 239-40.

McGouldrick, Paul F. New England Textiles in the Nineteenth Century: Profits and Investment. Cambridge: Harvard University Press, 1968.

Nickless, Pamela J. "Changing Labor Productivity and the Utilization of Native Women Workers in the American Cotton Textile Industry, 1825-1860," (Summary of Doctoral Dissertations) Journal of Economic History, 38(1), March 1978, pp. 287-88.

Nickless, Pamela J. "A New Look at Productivity in the New England Cotton Textile Industry, 1835-1860," Journal of Economic History, 39(4), December 1979, pp. 889-910.

Nickless, Pamela J. "Learning-By-Doing Revisited: The Case of Cotton Textiles," [Working Paper].

Oates, Mary J. "The Role of the Cotton Textile Industry in the Economic Development of the American Southeast: 1900-1940," (Summary of Doctoral Dissertation) Journal of Economic History, 31(1), March 1971, pp. 281-84.

Sandberg, Lars G. "The Draper Loom in New England Textiles: Comment on Feller," Journal of Economic History, 28(4), December 1968, pp.

624-27.

Sandberg, Lars G. "American Rings and English Mules: The Role of Economic Rationality," (Reprinted in Floud, ed. *Essays in Quantitative Economic History*, 1974, pp. 181-195) *Quarterly Journal of Economics*, 83(1), February 1969, pp. 25-43.

Sandberg, Lars G. "A Note on British Cotton Cloth Exports to the United States: 1815-1860 (Comment on Zevin)," *Explorations in Economic History*, 9(4), Summer 1972, pp. 427-28.

Synnott, III, Thomas W. "Investment Policies, Growth, and Profitability in the New England Cotton Textile Industry, 1830-1914," *Yale Economic Essays*, 11, Nos. 1 & 2), Spring/Fall 1971, pp. 97-144.

Vatter, Barbara. "Industrial Borrowing by the New England Textile Mills, 1840-1860: A Comment on Davis," *Journal of Economic History*, 21(2), June 1961, pp. 216-21.

Vedder, Richard K.; Klingman, David C and Gallaway, Lowell E. "Exploitation of Labor in Early American Cotton Textile Manufacturing," in Uselding, ed. *Research in Economic History*, vol. 3, 1978.

Williamson, Jeffrey G. "Optimal Replacement of Capital Goods: The Early New England and British Textile Firm," *Journal of Political Economy*, 79(6), November/December 1971, pp. 1320-34.

Williamson, Jeffrey G. "Embodiment, Disembodiment, Learning by Doing, and Returns to Scale in Nineteenth Century Cotton Textiles: A Comment on David," *Journal of Economic History*, 32(3), September 1972, pp. 691-705.

Williamson, Jeffrey G. "Optimal Replacement of Capital Goods in Early New England and British Textile Firms: Reply to Denslow and Schulze," *Journal of Political Economy*, 82(3), May/June 1974, pp. 638-40.

Wright, Gavin. "Cheap Labor and Southern Textiles before 1880," *Journal of Economic History*, 39(3), September 1979, pp. 655-80.

Wright, Gavin. "Cheap Labor and Southern Progress, 1880-1940," Presented to Meetings of Southern Economics Association, November 1977 [Working Paper].

Wright, Gavin. "Cheap Labor and Southern Textiles before 1880," Presented to the Berkeley-Stanford Economic History Colloquium, June 1978 [Working Paper].

Zevin, Robert B. "The Growth of Cotton Textile Production after 1815," in Fogel and Engerman, eds. *The Reinterpretation of American Economic History*, 1971, pp. 122-47.

United States: Industrial Organization

Aduddell, Robert and Cain, Louis P. "Location and Collusion in the Meatpacking Industry," in Cain and Uselding, eds. *Business Enterprise and Economic Change*, 1973, pp. 85-117.

Bateman, Fred and Weiss, Thomas J. "Market Structure before the Age of Big Business: Concentration and Profit in Early Southern Manufacturing," *Business History Review*, 49(3), Autumn 1975, pp. 312-36.

Bittlingmayer, George. "Merger for Monopoly: The Cast Iron Pipe Industry, 1890-1910, and the Case of Addyston Pipe," Ph.D. Dissertation, University of Chicago, 1981 [Working Paper].

Bunting, David and Barbour, J. "Interlocking Directorates in Large American Corporations, 1896-1964," *Business History Review*, 45), 1971, pp. 317-35.

Bunting, David. "The Truth About 'The Truth About the Trusts'," *Journal of Economic History*, 31), 1971, pp. 664-71.

Bunting, David. *Statistical View of the Trusts: A Manual of Large Industrial and Mining Corporations Active in the United States Around 1900.* Westport, Conn.: Greenwood Press, 1974.

Bunting, David. "Corporate Interlocking: The Money Trust," *Directors & Boards*, 1, Spring 1976, pp. 6-15.

Bunting, David and Mizruchi, M.S. "The Transfer of Control in Large Corporations: 1912-1919 (Summary)," in Uselding, ed. *Business and Economic History*, 2nd Series, vol. 9, 1980, pp. 120-23.

Davis, Lance E. "The Capital Markets and Industrial Concentration: The U.S. and U.K., a Comparative Study," (Reprinted in Hughes, ed. *Purdue Faculty Papers in Economic History, 1956-1966*, 1967, pp. 663-682) *Economic History Review*, Second Series, 19(2), August 1966, pp. 255-72.

Davis, Lance E. "Self-Regulation in Baseball, 1909-1972: Cartel Leadership, Strategy, and Tactics," in Noll, ed. *Economic Policy Aspects of Professional Sports*, 1974.

Davis, Lance E. "Monopolies, Speculators, Causal Models, Quantitative Evidence, and American Economic Growth," Presented at the Meetings of the Organization of American Historians, April 1967 [Working Paper].

Evans, G.H. *Business Incorporations in the United States, 1800-1943* (General Series, no. 49). New York: National Bureau of Economic Research, 1948.

Haddock, David D. "An Empirical Study of the Regulation of the Rail Industry," [Working Paper].

Haddock, David D. "Determinants of Industrial Concentration in the United States Automobile Industry, 1907 to 1979," [Working Paper].

Haddock, David D. "The Advent of Federal Regulation of Railroads," [Working Paper].

Haddock, David D. "The Origins of Regulation: Competing Theories and Critical Tests," [Working Paper].

Hannah, Leslie. "Mergers, Cartels and Concentration: The U.S. and European Experience 1890-1914," in Horn and Kocka, eds. *Recht und Entwicklung der GroBunternehmen im 19. und fruhen 20. Jahrhundert [Law and the Formation of the Big Enterprises in the 19th and Early 20th Centuries]*, 1979, pp. 306-316.

Hannah, Leslie. "Mergers," in Porter, ed. *Encyclopedia of American Economic History*, vol. 2, 1980, pp. 639-51.

Lamoureaux, Naomi R. "Industrial Organization and Market Behavior: The Great Merger Movement in American Industry," (Summary of Doctoral Dissertation) *Journal of Economic History*, 40(1), March 1980, pp. 169-71.

Mariger, Randall. "Predatory Price Cutting: The Standard Oil of New Jersey Case Revisited," *Explorations in Economic History*, 15(4),

October 1978, pp. 341-67.

Nelson, Ralph. *Merger Movements in American Industry* (National Bureau of Economic Research General Series, no. 66). Princeton: Princeton University Press for the National Bureau of Economic Research, 1959.

Porter, Patrick G. and Livesay, Harold C. "Oligopoly in Small Manufacturing Industries," *Explorations in Economic History*, 7(3), Spring 1970, pp. 371-9.

Ulen, Thomas S. "Cartels and Regulation: Late Nineteenth-Century Railroad Collusion and the Creation of the Interstate Commerce Commission," (Summary of Doctoral Dissertation) *Journal of Economic History*, 40(1), March 1980, pp. 179-81.

Ulen, Thomas S. "The Market for Regulation: The ICC from 1887 to 1920," *American Economic Review Papers and Proceedings*, 70(2), May 1980, pp. 306-310 [Working Paper].

Ulen, Thomas S. "Voting Behavior for the Interstate Commerce Act: 1879-1886," [Working Paper].

Ulen, Thomas S. "Was the ICC Necessary as a Cartel Manager?" Presented at the Cliometrics Conference, University of Wisconsin-Madison, May 1977 [Working Paper].

Weiss, Thomas J. and Bateman, Fred. "Market Structure before the Age of Big Business: Concentration and Profit in Early Southern Manufacturing," *Business History Review*, 49(3), Autumn 1975, pp. 312-36.

United States: Other

Aduddell, Robert and Cain, Louis P. "Location and Collusion in the Meatpacking Industry," in Cain and Uselding, eds. *Business Enterprise and Economic Change*, 1973, pp. 85-117.

Dick, Trevor J.O. "Canadian Newsprint: National Design or North American Economy?" [Working Paper].

George, Peter J. and Oksanen, Ernest H. "Saturation in the Automobile Market in the Late Twenties: Some Further Results," *Explorations in Economic History*, 11(1), Fall 1973, pp. 73-86.

Haddock, David D. "Determinants of Industrial Concentration in the United States Automobile Industry, 1907 to 1979," [Working Paper].

McDougall, Duncan. "Machine Tool Ouput, 1861-1910," in Brady, ed. *Output, Employment, and Productivity in the United States After 1800* (Studies in Income and Wealth, vol. 30), 1966, pp. 497-517.

Morgan, W. Douglas and Mercer, Lloyd J. "The American Automobile Industry: Investment Demand, Capacity and Capacity Utilization, 1921-1940," *Journal of Political Economy*, 80(6), November/December 1972, pp. 1214-31.

Robertson, Ross M. "Changing Production of Metalworking Machinery, 1860-1920," in Brady, ed. *Output, Employment, and Productivity in the United States After 1800* (Studies in Income and Wealth, vol. 30), 1966, pp. 479-96.

Rosenberg, Nathan. "Technological Change in the Machine Tool Industry, 1840-1910," (Reprinted in Hughes, ed. *Purdue Faculty Papers in Economic History, 1956-1966*, 1967, pp. 405-430) *Journal of Economic*

History, 23(4), December 1963, pp. 414-43.

Rosenberg, Nathan. "America's Rise to Woodworking Leadership," in Hindle, ed. *America's Wooden Age: Aspects of Its Early Technology*, 1975.

Rosenberg, Nathan. "Machine Tools," in Adams, ed. *Dictionary of American History*, 1976.

Strassmann, W. Paul. "Technological Change in the Machine Tool Industry, 1840-1910: Discussion of Rosenberg," *Journal of Economic History*, 23(4), December 1963, pp. 444-46.

Thomas, Robert P. "Business Failure in the Early Automobile Industry, 1895-1910," in Van Fenstermaker, ed. *Business History Conference*, 1962.

Thomas, Robert P. "The Automobile Industry and Its Tycoon," *Explorations in Entrepreneurial History*, Second Series, 6(2), Winter 1969, pp. 139-57.

Thomas, Robert P. "Style Change and the Automobile Industry during the Roaring Twenties," in Cain and Uselding, eds. *Business Enterprise and Economic Change*, 1973, pp. 118-38.

Thomas, Robert P. *An Analysis of the Pattern of Growth of the Automobile Industry*. New York: Arno Press, 1977.

Vatter, Harold G. "The Closure of Entry in the American Automobile Industry," *Oxford Economic Papers*, New Series, 4(3), October 1952, pp. 213-34.

Vedder, Richard K. "Some Evidence on the Scale of the Antebellum Farm Implement Industry," in Uselding, ed., *Proceedings of the Twenty-Third Annual Meeting of the Business History Conference*, 1976.

Rest of the World: General

Andreano, Ralph L. "The American Manufacturing Frontier, 1870-1940: A Comment on Severson," *Business History Review*, 35(1), Spring 1961, pp. 105-9.

Bos, Roeland W.J.M. "Techniek en industrialisatie: Nederland in de negentiende eeuw [Technology and Industrialization: The Netherlands in the Nineteenth Century]," *Afdeling Agrarische Geschiedenis, Bijdragen*, 22, 1979, pp. 59-88.

Boulle, Pierre H. "Marchandes de Traite et Developpement Industriel dans le France et l'Angleterre du XVIIIe Siecle [Slave Traders and Industrial Development in France and England in the Eighteenth Century]," *Revue Francaise d'Histoire d'Outre-Mer*, 62(226-227), 1975, pp. 309-30.

Ciocca, Pierluigi. "Formazione dell'Italia industriale e storia econometrica [Industrial Development in Italy and Econometric History]," *Rivista internazionale di scienze sociali*, 40, September/December 1969, pp. 539-53.

Covino, Renato; Gallo, Giampaolo and Mantovani, Enrico. "L'industria dall'economia di guerra alla ricostruzione [Industry from the War Economy to Reconstruction]," in Ciocca and Toniolo, eds. *L'economia italiana nel periodo fascista [The Italian Economy during the Fascist Era]*, 1976, pp. 171-270.

Crouzet, Francois. "Essai de Construction d'un Indice Annuel de la Production Industrielle Francaise au XIXe Siecle [A Tentative Annual Index of French Industrial Production in the 19th Century]," (Reprinted in English in Cameron, ed. *Essays in French Economic History*, 1970, pp. 245-78) *Annales: Economies, Societes, Civilisation*, 25(1), January/February 1970, pp. 56-99.

Dales, John H. "Estimates of Canadian Manufacturing Output by Markets, 1870-1915," in Henripin and Asinakopulos, eds. *Canadian Political Science Association Conference on Statistics*, 1964, pp. 61-92.

De Brabander, G.L. "The Distribution of Economic Activities Over Industries and Regions in Belgium, 1846-1910: A Study of the Data [In Dutch with English Summary]," *Bijdragen tot de Geschiedenis*, 61, 1978, pp. 97-184.

De Brabander, G.L. "De regionaal-industriele specialisatie en haar effect op Ruimtelijke Verschillen in Economische groei in Belgie, van 1846 tot 1970 [Regional-Industrial Specialization and its Effect on Spatial Differences in Economic Growth in Belgium from 1846 to 1970]," Unpublished Ph.D. Dissertation, University of Antwerp, 1979 [Working Paper].

Doane, David P. "Regional Cost Differentials and Textile Location: A Statistical Analysis," *Explorations in Economic History*, 9(1), Fall 1971, pp. 3-34.

Fenoaltea, Stefano. "Public Policy and Italian Industrial Development, 1861-1913," (Summary of Doctoral Dissertation) *Journal of Economic History*, 29(1), March 1969, pp. 176-79.

Fenoaltea, Stefano. "Riflessioni sull'esperienza industriale italiana dal Risorgimento alla prima guerra mondiale [Reflections on the Italian Industrial Experience from the Risorgimento to the First World War]," (Reprinted in Toniolo, ed., *L'economia italiana 1861-1940*, 1978, pp. 69-104) in Gianni Toniolo, ed. *Lo sviluppo economico italiano, 1861-1940 [Italian Economic Development, 1861-1940]*. Bari: Laterza, 1973, pp. 121-56.

Fenoaltea, Stefano. *Italian Industrial Production, 1861-1913: A Statistical Reconstruction.* New York: Cambridge University Press.

Fenoaltea, Stefano. *Public Policy and Italian Industrial Development, 1861-1913: A New Economic History.* New York: Cambridge University Press.

Field, Alexander J. "The Relative Stability of German and American Industrial Growth, 1880-1913: A Comparative Analysis," in Schroder and Spree, eds. *Historisch-Sozialwissenschaftliche Forschungen 11*, 1980.

Fischer, Wolfram. "Government Activity and Industrialization in Germany (1815-70)," in Rostow, ed. *The Economics of Take-off into Sustained Growth*, 1963, pp. 83-94.

Foreman-Peck, James S. "The Interdependence of the Manufacturing and Primary Product Sectors, 1881-1913," Presented at the A.P.T.E. Conference, Plymouth, April 1979 [Working Paper].

Forster, Colin. "Australian Manufacturing and the War of 1914-18," *Economic Record*, 29, November 1953, pp. 211-30.

Forster, Colin. *Industrial Development in Australia, 1920-1930.* Canberra: Australian National University Press, 1964.

Forster, Colin. "Economies of Scale and Australian Manufacturing," in

Forster, ed. *Australian Economic Development in the Twentieth Century*, 1970, pp. 123-68.

Fremdling, Rainer and Tilly, Richard H., eds. *Industrialisierung und Raum, Studien zur Regionalen Differenzierung im Deutschland im 19. Jahrhundert* [*Industrialization and Spatial Relationships: Studies on Regional Differentiation in Germany in the 19th Century*] (Historisch-Sozialwissenschaftliche Forschungen, vol. 7). Stuttgart: Klett-Cotta, 1979.

Fremdling, Rainer. "Modernisierung und Wachstum der Schwerindustrie in Deutschland, 1830-1860 [Modernization and Growth of Heavy Industry in Germany, 1830-1860]," *Geschichte und Gesellschaft*, 5(2), 1979.

Haig, Brian D. "Manufacturing Output and Productivity, 1910 to 1948/9," *Australian Economic History Review*, 15(2), September 1975, pp. 136-61.

Haig, Brian D. "Capital Stock in Manufacturing, 1920 to 1978," *Australian National University Department of Economics/Research School of Social Sciences Series Monograph*. Canberra: Australian National University Press, 1981.

Hart, P.E. "A Long-Run Analysis of the Rate of Return on Capital in Manufacturing Industry, United Kingdom, 1920-62," in Hart, ed. *Studies in Profit, Business Saving and Investment in the United Kingdom, 1920-1962* (vol. 2), 1968, pp. 220-83.

Hart, P.E. "A Macroeconometric Analysis of the Appropriation of Profit in Manufacturing," in Hart, ed. *Studies in Profit, Business Saving and Investment in the United Kingdom, 1920-1962* (vol. 2), 1968, pp. 109-43.

Hoffmann, Walther G. *British Industry, 1700-1950*. [translated by W.O. Henderson and W.H.] Chaloner Oxford: Blackwell, 1955.

Kotowitz, Yehuda. "Capital-Labour Substitution in Canadian Manufacturing, 1926-1939 and 1946-1961," *Canadian Journal of Economics*, 1(3), August 1968, pp. 619-32.

Lewis, Kenneth A. and Yamamura, Kozo. "Industrialization and Interregional Interest Rate Structure, The Japanese Case: 1889-1925," *Explorations in Economic History*, 8(4), Summer 1971, pp. 473-99.

Marczewski, Jean. "Le Produit Physique de L'Economie Francaise de 1789 a 1913 (Comparaison Avec la Grande-Bretagne) [The Physical Product of the French Economy, 1789-1913 (Comparison with Great Britain)]," *Cahiers de L'Institut de Science Economique Appliquee, 1965.*

Markovitch, Tihomir J. *L'industrie francaise de 1789 a 1964* (4 Vols) [*French Industry, 1789-1964*]. Cahiers de l'Institute de Science Economique Appliquee, 1966.

Markovitch, Tihomir J. "Les secteurs dominants de L'industrie francaise [The Dominant Sectors in French Industry]," Analyse et Prevision, 1(3), March 1966, pp. 161-75.

Markovitch, Tihomir J. "La Revolution industrielle: le cas de la France [The Industrial Revolution: The Case of France]," *Revue d'Histoire economique et sociale*, 1(1), 1974, pp. 115-25.

Markovitch, Tihomir J. "La croissance industrielle sous l'Ancien Regime [Industrial Growth During the Ancien Regime]," *Annales: Economies, Societes, Civilisations*, 31(3), May/June 1976, pp. 648-55.

Matis, Herbert. "The Pattern of Austrian Industrial Growth from the Eighteenth to the Early Twentieth Century: Comment on Rudolph," *Austrian History Yearbook*, 11), 1975, pp. 33-36.

McDougall, Duncan M. "Canadian Manufactured Commodity Output, 1870-1915," *Canadian Journal of Economics*, 4(1), February 1971, pp. 21-36.

McDougall, Duncan M. "The Domestic Availability of Manufactured Commodity Output: Canada, 1870-1915," *Canadian Journal of Economics*, 6(2), May 1973, pp. 189-206.

Morris, Cynthia Taft and Adelman, Irma. "Patterns of Market Expansion in the Nineteenth Century: A Quantitative Study," in Dalton, ed. *Research in Economic Anthropology*, vol. 1, 1978.

Morris, Morris D. "Industrialization in South Asia, 1800-1947," in Kumar and Desai, eds. *Cambridge Economic History of India*, vol. 2, 1982, pp. 553-676.

Nicholas, Stephen J. and Purcell, W. "Returns to Scale and Imperfect Markets in Australian Manufacturing 1908-1975," University of New South Wales Working Paper in Economic History, 1978 [Working Paper].

Nutter, G. Warren, assisted by Boronstein, Israel, and Kaufman, Adam. *Growth of Industrial Production in the Soviet Union* (General Series, no. 75). Princeton: Princeton University Press for the National Bureau of Economic Research, 1962.

Paradisi, Mariangela. "Il commercio estero e la struttura industriale [Foreign Trade and Industrial Structure]," in Ciocca and Toniolo, eds. *L'economia italiana nel periodo fascista* [*The Italian Economy during the Fascist Era*], 1976, pp. 271-328.

Parks, Richard W. "Price Responsiveness of Factor Utilization in Swedish Manufacturing, 1870-1950," *Review of Economics and Statistics*, 53(2), May 1971, pp. 129-39.

Phelps Brown, E.H. "Levels and Movements of Industrial Productivity and Real Wages Internationally Compared, 1860-1970," *Economic Journal*, 83(329), March 1973, pp. 58-71.

Rapp, Richard T. *Industry and Economic Decline in Seventeenth-Century Venice*. Cambridge: Harvard University Press, 1976.

Rawski, Thomas G. "The Growth of Producer Industries, 1900-1971," in Perkins, ed. *China's Modern Economy in Historical Perspective*, 1975, pp. 203-34.

Rudolph, Richard L. "The Pattern of Austrian Industrial Growth from the Eighteenth to the Early Twentieth Century," *Austrian History Yearbook*, 11, 1975, pp. 3-25.

Schremmer, Eckart. "Standortausweitung der Warenproduktion im Langfristigen Wirtschaftswachstum. Zur Stadt-Land-Arbeitsteilung im Gewerbe des 18. Jahrhunderts [Locational Diffusion of Goods Production in Long-Run Economic Growth: About the Division of Labor in the City and in the Country in the Trade of the 18th Century]," *Vierteljahrschrift fur Sozial- und Wirtschaftsgeschichte*, 59(1), 1972, pp. 1-40.

Severson, Robert F. "The American Manufacturing Frontier, 1870-1940," *Business History Review*, 34(3), Autumn 1960, pp. 356-72.

Severson, Robert F. "The American Manufacturing Frontier, 1870-1914: Reply to Andreano," *Business History Review*, 35(1), Spring 1961,

pp. 109-13.
Toniolo, Gianni and Tattara, Giuseppe. "L'industria manifatturiera: cicli, politiche e mutamenti di struttura (1921-37) [Industrial Manufacturing: Cycles, Policies, and Structural Change (1921-37)]," in Ciocca and Toniolo, ed. *L'economia italiana nel periodo fascista* [*The Italian Economy during the Fascist Era*], 1976.
Von Tunzelmann, G. Nicholas. "Britain's New Industries between the Wars: A New 'Development Block'?" Presented at the Cliometrics Conference, Warwick, 1978 [Working Paper].
Yamamura, Kozo and Duffy, William J. "Monetization and Integration of Markets in Tokugawa Japan: A Spectral Analysis," *Explorations in Economic History*, 8(4), Summer 1971, pp. 395-423.
Yasuba, Yasukichi. "A Revised Index of Industrial Production for Japan, 1905-1935," *Osaka Economic Papers*, 19(34), March 1971, pp. 19-41.

Rest of the World: Extractive

Blainey, Geoffrey. "A Theory of Mineral Discovery: Australia in the Nineteenth Century," *Economic History Review*, Second Series, 23(2), May 1970, pp. 298-313.
Blainey, Geoffrey. "A Theory of Mineral Discovery: A Rejoinder to Morrissey and Burt," *Economic History Review*, Second Series, 26(3), August 1973, pp. 506-9.
Cromar, Peter. "The Coal Industry on Tyneside, 1771-1800: Oligopoly and Spatial Change," *Economic Geography*, 53(1), January 1977, pp. 79-94.
Frankel, S. Herbert. *Investment and the Return to Equity Capital in the South African Gold Mining Industry, 1887-1965: An International Comparison.* Cambridge: Harvard University Press, 1967.
Gross, Nachum T. "Economic Growth and the Consumption of Coal in Austria and Hungary, 1831-1913," *Journal of Economic History*, 31(4), December 1971, pp. 898-916.
Hausman, William J. "Size and Profitability of English Colliers in the Eighteenth Century," *Business History Review*, 51(4), Winter 1977, pp. 460-73.
Hausman, William J. "Public Policy and the Supply of Coal to London, 1700-1770," (Summary of Doctoral Dissertation) *Journal of Economic History*, 37(1), March 1977, pp. 252-54.
Hausman, William J. *Public Policy and the Supply of Coal to London, 1700-1770.* New York: Arno Press, 1980.
Hausman, William J. "A Model of the London Coal Trade in the Eighteenth Century," *Quarterly Journal of Economics*, 94, February 1980, pp. 1-14.
Holtfrerich, Karl-Ludwig. *Quantitative Wirtschaftsgeschichte des Ruhrkohlenbergbaus im 19. Jahrhundert. Eine Fuhrungssektoranalyse* [*Quantitative Economic History of the Ruhr Coal-Mining Industry in the 19th Century: A Leading-Sector Analysis*]. Dortmund: Gesellschaft fur Westfalische Wirtschaftsgeschichte, 1973.
Johnson, Arthur M. "The American Petroleum Industry: Comment on Williamson, Andreano, and Menezes," in Brady, ed. *Output,*

Employment, and Productivity in the United States After 1800 (Studies in Income and Wealth, vol. 30), 1966, pp. 403-4.

Kelly, William J. and Kano, Tsuneo. "Crude Oil Production in the Russian Empire: 1818-1919," *Journal of European Economic History*, 6(2), Fall 1977, pp. 307-38.

McCloskey, Donald N. "International Differences in Productivity? Coal and Steel in America and Britain before World War I," in McCloskey, ed. *Essays on a Mature Economy: Britain after 1840*, 1971, pp. 285-304.

Morrissey, M.J. and Burt, R. "A Theory of Mineral Discovery: A Note on Blainey," *Economic History Review*, Second Series, 26(3), August 1973, pp. 497-505.

Parker, William N. "Nation States and National Development: French and German Ore Mining in the Late Nineteenth Century," in Aitken, ed. *The State and Economic Growth*, 1959, pp. 201-12.

Richards, C.S. "Investment and the Return to Equity Capital in the South African Gold Mining Industry, 1887-1965," *South African Journal of Economics*, 36(4), December 1968, pp. 330-37.

Von Tunzelmann, G. Nicholas. "Technological Diffusion during the Industrial Revolution: The Case of the Cornish Pumping Engine," in Hartwell, ed. *The Industrial Revolution* (Nuffield College Studies in Economic History, vol. 1), 1970, pp. 77-98.

Williamson, Harold F.; Andreano, Ralph L. and Menezes, Carmen. "The American Petroleum Industry," in Brady, ed. *Output, Employment, and Productivity in the United States After 1800* (Studies in Income and Wealth, vol. 30), 1966, pp. 349-403.

Allen, Robert C. "International Competition in Iron and Steel, 1850-1913," *Journal of Economic History*, 39(4), December 1979, pp. 911-37.

Allen, Robert C. "Entrepreneurship and Technical Progress in the Northeast Coast Pig Iron Industry, 1850-1913," in Uselding, ed. *Research in Economic History*, vol. 6, 1981.

Bouvier, Jean; Furet, Francois and Gillet, Marcel., eds. *Le Mouvement du profit en France au XIXe siecle: Materiaux et Etudes [The Movement of Profit in Nineteenth Century France]*. Paris: Mouton, 1965.

Hyde, Charles K. "Technological Change and the Development of the British Iron Industry, 1700-1870," (Summary of Doctoral Dissertation) *Journal of Economic History*, 33(1), March 1973, pp. 312-13.

Hyde, Charles K. "The Adoption of the Hot Blast by the British Iron Industry: A Reinterpretation," *Explorations in Economic History*, 10(3), Spring 1973, pp. 281-94.

Hyde, Charles K. "The Adoption of Coke-Smelting by the British Iron Industry, 1709-1790," *Explorations in Economic History*, 10(4), Summer 1973, pp. 397-418.

Hyde, Charles K. "Technological Change in the British Wrought Iron Industry, 1750-1815: A Reinterpretation," *Economic History Review*, Second Series, 27(2), May 1974, pp. 190-206.

Hyde, Charles K. *Technological Change and the British Iron Industry, 1700-1870.* Princeton: Princeton University Press, 1977.

McCloskey, Donald N. "Productivity Change in British Pig Iron, 1870-1939," *Quarterly Journal of Economics*, 82(2), May 1968, pp. 281-96.

McCloskey, Donald N. "The British Iron and Steel Industry, 1870-1914: A Study of the Climacteric in Productivity," (Summary of Doctoral Dissertation) *Journal of Economic History*, 29(1), March 1969, pp. 173-75.

McCloskey, Donald N. "International Differences in Productivity? Coal and Steel in America and Britain before World War I," in McCloskey, ed. *Essays on a Mature Economy: Britain after 1840*, 1971, pp. 285-304.

McCloskey, Donald N. *Economic Maturity and Entrepreneurial Decline: British Iron and Steel, 1870-1913.* Cambridge: Harvard University Press, 1973.

Niemi, Jr., Albert W. "Some Aspects of the Relative Decline of the British Steel Industry, 1870-1913," *American Economist*, 13(2), Fall 1969, pp. 40-49.

Parker, William N. and Pounds, J.G. *Coal and Steel in Western Europe.* Bloomington: Indiana University Press, 1957.

Parker, William N. "Coal and Steel Output Movements in Western Europe, 1880-1956," *Explorations in Entrepreneurial History*, 9(4), April 1957, pp. 213-30.

Sonnemann, Rolf. *Die Auswirkungen des Schutzzolls auf die Monopolisierung der Deutschen Eisen- und Stahl-Industrie, 1879-1892* [*The Effects of Protective Tariffs on the Monopolization of the German Iron and Steel Industry, 1879-1892*]. Berlin: Akademie Verlag, 1960.

Temin, Peter. "The Relative Decline of the British Steel Industry, 1880-1913," in Rosovsky, ed. *Industrialization in Two Systems*, 1966.

Webb, Steven B. "Tariff Protection for the Iron Industry, Cotton Textiles and Agriculture in Germany, 1879-1914," [Appears in German] *Jahrbucher fur Nationalokonomie und Statistik*, 192(3-4), November 1977, pp. 336-57.

Webb, Steven B. AF:. "Tariffs, Cartels, Technology, and Growth in the German Steel Industry, 1879 to 1914," *Journal of Economic History*, 40(2), June 1980, pp. 309-29.

Rest of the World: Textiles

Asher, Ephraim. "Industrial Efficiency and Biased Technical Change in American and British Manufacturing: The Case of Textiles in the Nineteenth Century," *Journal of Economic History*, 32(2), June 1972, pp. 431-42.

Blaug, M. "The Productivity of Capital in the Lancashire Cotton Industry during the Nineteenth Century," *Economic History Review*,

Second Series, 13(3), 1961, pp. 358-81.

Chao, Kang. "The Growth of a Modern Cotton Textile Industry and the Competition with Handicrafts," in Perkins, ed. *China's Modern Economy in Historical Perspective*, 1975, pp. 167-201.

Cizakca, Murat. "Price History and the Bursa Silk Industry: A Study in Ottoman Industrial Decline, 1550-1650," *Journal of Economic History*, 40(3), September 1980, pp. 533-50.

Coleman, D.C. "An Innovation and its Diffusion: the 'New Draperies'," *Economic History Review*, Second Series, 22(3), December 1969, pp. 417-29.

Coleman, D.C. "G.R. Hawke on -What? (Rejoinder on the New Draperies)," *Economic History Review*, Second Series, 24(2), May 1971, pp. 260-61.

Deane, Phyllis. "The Output of the British Woollen Industry in the Eighteenth Century," *Journal of Economic History*, 17(2), June 1957, pp. 207-23.

Denslow, Jr., David and Schulze, David. "Optimal Replacement of Capital Goods in Early New England and British Textile Firms: A Comment (on Williamson)," *Journal of Political Economy*, 82(3), May/June 1974, pp. 631-37.

Gatrell, V.A.C. "Labour, Power, and the Size of Firms in Lancashire Cotton in the Second Quarter of the Nineteenth Century," *Economic History Review*, Second Series, 30(1), February 1977, pp. 95-139.

Hawke, Gary R. "D.C. Coleman on the Counterfactual History of the New Draperies," *Economic History Review*, Second Series, 24(2), May 1971, pp. 258-59.

Kirchain, Gunter. "Das Wachstum der Deutschen Baumwollindustrie im 19. Jahrhundert [The Growth of the German Cotton Textile Industry in the 19th Century]," Ph.D. Dissertation, Universitat Munster, 1971 [Working Paper].

Kirchhain, Gunter. *Das Wachstum der Deutschen Baumwollindustrie im 19. Jahrhundert [The Growth of the German Cotton Textile Industry in the 19th Century]*. New York: Arno Press, 1977.

Lazonick, William. "Factor Costs and the Diffusion of Ring Spinning in Britain Prior to World War I," *Quarterly Journal of Economics*, 96(1), February 1981, pp. 89-109.

Lee, Clive H. "The British Cotton Industry, 1825-75," in Church, ed. *Victorian Business*, 1980.

Lyons, John S. "The Lancashire Cotton Industry and the Introduction of the Powerloom, 1815-1850," (Summary of Doctoral Dissertation) *Journal of Economic History*, 38(1), March 1978, pp. 283-84.

Lyons, John S. "The Lancashire Cotton Industry and the Introduction of the Powerloom, 1815-1850," Ph.D. Dissertation, University of California-Berkeley, 1977 [Working Paper].

Markovitch, Tihomir J. *L'industrie lainiere francaise au debut du XVIIIe siecle [The French Woolen Industry at the Beginning of the Eighteenth Century]*. *Cahiers de l'Institute de Science Economique Appliquee, 1968*.

Markovitch, Tihomir J. *Les industries lainieres de Colbert a la Revolution [The Woolen Industry From Colbert to the Revolution]*. Geneva: Editions Droz, 1976.

Marvel, Howard P. "Factory Regulation: A Reinterpretation of Early

English Experience," Journal of Law and Economics, 20(2), October 1977, pp. 379-402.

Morris, Morris D. The Emergence of an Industrial Labor Force in India: A Study of the Bombay Cotton Mills, 1854-1947. Berkeley and Los Angeles: University of California Press, 1965.

Ono, Akira and Fujino, Shiro. "Textile Industry, 1890-1945," in Ohkawa and Hayami, eds. Economic Growth, 1973, pp. 154-64.

Sandberg, Lars G. "Movements in the Quality of British Cotton Textile Exports, 1815-1913," Journal of Economic History, 28(1), March 1968, pp. 1-27.

Sandberg, Lars G. "American Rings and English Mules: The Role of Economic Rationality," (Reprinted in Floud, ed. Essays in Quantitative Economic History, 1974, pp. 181-195) Quarterly Journal of Economics, 83(1), February 1969, pp. 25-43.

Sandberg, Lars G. "A Note on British Cotton Cloth Exports to the United States: 1815-1860 (Comment on Zevin)," Explorations in Economic History, 9(4), Summer 1972, pp. 427-28.

Sandberg, Lars G. Lancashire in Decline: A Study in Entrepreneurship, Technology and International Trade. Columbus: Ohio State University Press, 1974.

Saxonhouse, Gary R. "A Tale of Technological Diffusion in the Meiji Period," Journal of Economic History, 36(1), March 1974, pp. 149-65.

Saxonhouse, Gary R. "Country Girls and Communication among Competitors in the Japanese Cotton Spinning Industry," in Patrick, ed. Japanese Industrialization and Its Social Consequences, 1976, pp. 97-125.

Saxonhouse, Gary R. "Productivity Change and Labor Absorption in Japanese Cotton Spinning, 1891-1935," Quarterly Journal of Economics, 91(2), May 1977, pp. 195-219.

Saxonhouse, Gary R. and Ranis, Gustav. "Technology Choice, Adaptation and the Quality Dimension in the Japanese Cotton Textile Industry," in Okhawa and Hayami, eds. The Comparative Analysis of Japan and Less Developed Countries.

Shapiro, Seymour. Capital and the Cotton Industry in the Industrial Revolution. Ithaca: Cornell University Press, 1967.

Vicziany, Antonia Markka. "The Cotton Trade and the Commercial Development of Bombay 1855-1875," (Unpublished Ph.D. Dissertation, University of London, 1975) [Working Paper].

Webb, Steven B. "Tariff Protection for the Iron Industry, Cotton Textiles and Agriculture in Germany, 1879-1914," [Appears in German] Jahrbucher fur Nationalokonomie und Statistik, 192(3-4), November 1977, pp. 336-57.

Williamson, Jeffrey G. "Optimal Replacement of Capital Goods: The Early New England and British Textile Firm," Journal of Political Economy, 79(6), November/December 1971, pp. 1320-34.

Williamson, Jeffrey G. "Optimal Replacement of Capital Goods in Early New England and British Textile Firms: Reply to Denslow and Schulze," Journal of Political Economy, 82(3), May/June 1974, pp. 638-40.

Rest of the World: Industrial Organization

Cromar, Peter. "The Coal Industry on Tyneside, 1771-1800: Oligopoly and Spatial Change," *Economic Geography*, 53(1), January 1977, pp. 79-94.

Davis, Lance E. "The Capital Markets and Industrial Concentration: The U.S. and U.K., a Comparative Study," (Reprinted in Hughes, ed. *Purdue Faculty Papers in Economic History, 1956-1966*, 1967, pp. 663-682) *Economic History Review*, Second Series, 19(2), August 1966, pp. 255-72.

Hannah, Leslie. "Mergers in British Manufacturing Industry, 1880-1918," *Oxford Economic Papers*, New Series, 26(1), March 1974, pp. 1-20.

Hannah, Leslie. *The Rise of the Corporate Economy: The British Experience*. Baltimore: Johns Hopkins University Press, 1976.

Hannah, Leslie and Kay, J.A. *Concentration in Modern Industry: Theory Measurement and the U.K. Experience*. London: Macmillan, 1977.

Hannah, Leslie. "Mergers, Cartels and Concentration: The U.S. and European Experience 1890-1914," in Horn and Kocka, eds. *Recht und Entwicklung der GroBunternehmen im 19. und fruhen 20. Jahrhundert [Law and the Formation of the Big Enterprises in the 19th and Early 20th Centuries]*, 1979, pp. 306-316.

Jones, S.R.H. "Price Associations and Competition in the British Pin Industry, 1814-40," *Economic History Review*, Second Series, 26(2), May 1973, pp. 237-53.

Jones, S.R.H. "The Development of Needle Manufacturing in the West Midlands before 1750," *Economic History Review*, Second Series, 31(3), August 1978, pp. 354-68.

Nicholas, Stephen J. and Purcell, W. "Returns to Scale and Imperfect Markets in Australian Manufacturing 1908-1975," University of New South Wales Working Paper in Economic History, 1978 [Working Paper].

Nicholas, Stephen J. "Technical Change, Returns to Scale and Imperfect Markets in the British Inter-War Economy," University of New South Wales Working Paper in Economic History, 1978 [Working Paper].

Tilly, Richard H. "Das Wachstum Industrieller Grossunternehmen in Deutschland, 1870-1913 [The Growth of Large Industrial Firms in Germany, 1870-1913]," in Kellenbenz, ed. *Wirtschaftliches Wachstum, Energie und Verkehr*, 1981.

Yamamura, Kozo. "The Decline of the Ritsuryo System: Hypotheses on Economic and Institutional Change," *Journal of Japanese Studies*, 1(1), Autumn 1974, pp. 3-38.

Yamamura, Kozo. "General Trading Companies in Japan: Their Origins and Growth," in Patrick, ed. *Industrial Growth and Consequences in Japanese Economic Development*, 1976.

Yamamura, Kozo. "Entrepreneurship, Ownership and Management in Japan," in Mathias and Postan, eds. *The Cambridge Economic History of Europe*, vol. 7, part 2, 1978, pp. 215-64.

Rest of The World: Other

Coatsworth, John H. "Anotaciones Sobre la Produccion de Alimentos Durante el Porfiriato," *Historia Mexicana*, 26(2), October/December 1976, pp. 167-87.

Cooney, E.W. "Long Waves in Building in the British Economy of the Nineteenth Century.," *Economic History Review*, Second Series, 13(2), 1960, pp. 257-69.

David, Paul A. "Building in Ohio between 1837 and 1914: Comment on Gottlieb," in Brady, ed. *Output, Employment and Productivity in the United States After 1800* (Studies in Income and Wealth, vol. 30), 1966, pp. 281-88.

Floud, Roderick C. "Changes in the Productivity of Labour in the British Machine Tool Industry, 1856-1900," in McCloskey, ed. *Essays on a Mature Economy*, 1971, pp. 313-37.

Floud, Roderick C. *The British Machine Tool Industry, 1850-1914.* Cambridge: Cambridge University Press, 1976.

Foreman-Peck, James S. "Tariff Protection and Economies of Scale: The British Motor Industry Before 1939," *Oxford Economic Papers*, New Series, 31(2), July 1979, pp. 237-57.

Foreman-Peck, James S. "Economies of Scale and the Development of the British Motor Industry Before 1939," Ph.D. Dissertation, London School of Economics, University of London, 1978 [Working Paper].

Gottlieb, Manuel. "New Measures of Value of Nonfarm Building for the United States: Annually, 1850-1939," *Review of Economics and Statistics*, 47(4), November 1965, pp. 412-19.

Gottlieb, Manuel. "Building in Ohio Between 1837 and 1914," in Brady, ed. *Output, Employment, and Productivity in the United States After 1800* (Studies in Income and Wealth, vol. 30), 1966, pp. 243-80.

Gottlieb, Manuel. "Building in Ohio Between 1837 and 1914: Reply to David," in Brady, ed. *Output, Employment, and Productivity in the United States After 1800* (Studies in Income and Wealth, vol. 30), 1966, pp. 288-90.

Gross, Nachum T. "Austrian Industrial Statistics 1880/85 and 1911/13," in Giersch and Sauermann, eds. *Quantitative Aspects of Economic History, Zeitschrift fur die gesamte Staatswissenschaft*, 124(1), February 1968, pp. 35-69.

Gross, Nachum T. "An Estimate of Industrial Product in Austria in 1841," *Journal of Economic History*, 28(1), March 1968, pp. 80-101.

Hall, A.R. "Long Waves in Building in the British Economy of the Nineteenth Century: A Comment on Cooney," *Economic History Review*, Second Series, 14(2), 1961, pp. 330-32.

Hart, P.E. "Profits in Non-Manufacturing Industries in the United Kingdom, 1920-1938," *Scottish Journal of Political Economy*, 10(2), June 1963, pp. 167-97.

Hohenberg, Paul M. *Chemicals in Western Europe, 1850-1914: An Economic Study of Technical Change.* Amsterdam and Chicago: North-Holland and Rand-McNally, 1967.

Jackson, R.V. "House Building and the Age Structure of Population in

New South Wales, 1861-1900," *Australian Economic History Review*, 14(2), September 1974, pp. 143-59.

Johnson, H. Thomas. "Relation of Building Volume and Construction Inputs: A Note," *Explorations in Entrepreneurial History*, Second Series, 5(1), Fall 1967, pp. 108-10.

Jones, S.R.H. "Price Associations and Competition in the British Pin Industry, 1814-40," *Economic History Review*, Second Series, 26(2), May 1973, pp. 237-53.

Jones, S.R.H. "The Development of Needle Manufacturing in the West Midlands before 1750," *Economic History Review*, Second Series, 31(3), August 1978, pp. 354-68.

Lindert, Peter H. and Trace, Keith. "Yardsticks for Victorian Entrepreneurs," in McCloskey, ed. *Essays on a Mature Economy*, 1971, pp. 239-74.

Mercer, Lloyd J. and Morgan, W. Douglas. "Alternative Interpretations of Market Saturation: Evaluation for the Automobile Market in the Late Twenties," *Explorations in Economic History*, 9(3), Spring 1972, pp. 269-90.

Mercer, Lloyd J. and Morgan, W. Douglas. "Internal Funds and Automobile Investment: An Evaluation of the Seltzer Hypothesis," *Journal of Economic History*, 32(3), September 1972, pp. 682-90.

Mercer, Lloyd J. and Morgan, W. Douglas. "The American Automobile Industry: Investment Demand, Capacity and Capacity Utilization, 1921-1940," *Journal of Political Economy*, 80(6), November/December 1972, pp. 1214-31.

Pope, David H. "An Index of Melbourne Building Activity, 1896-1939," *Australian Economic Papers*, 11(18), June 1972, pp. 103-11.

Trace, Keith. "The Chemical Industry," in Roderick and Stephens, eds. *Industry, Education and the Economy in Victorian England*, 1980.

Weber, B.A. and Lewis, J. Parry. "New Industrial Building in Great Britain, 1923-1938," *Scottish Journal of Political Economy*, 8(1), February 1961, pp. 57-64.

Williamson, Harold F. and Andreano, Ralph L. "A Reappraisal of the Competitive Structure of the American Petroleum Industry Before 1911," in Andreano, ed. *New Views on American Economic Development*, 1960, pp. 307-16.

Chapter 8

SERVICES AND CONSUMER DEMAND

United States: General

Barger, Harold. *Distribution's Place in the American Economy Since 1869.* New York: National Bureau of Economic Research, 1955.

Easterlin, Richard A. "The Service Industries in the Nineteenth Century: Comment on Gallman and Weiss," in Fuchs, ed. *Production and Productivity in the Service Industries* (Studies in Income and Wealth, vol. 34), 1969, pp. 352-65.

Fabricant, Solomon. "The Service Industries in the Nineteenth Century: Comment on Gallman and Weiss," in Fuchs, ed. *Production and Productivity in the Service Industries* (Studies in Income and Wealth, vol. 34), 1969, pp. 368-71.

Firestone, O.J. "The Service Industries in the Nineteenth Century: Comment on Gallman and Weiss," in Fuchs, ed. *Production and Productivity in the Service Industries* (Studies in Income and Wealth, vol. 34), 1969, pp. 371-72.

Gallman, Robert E. and Weiss, Thomas J. "The Service Industries in the Nineteenth Century," in Fuchs, ed. *Production and Productivity in the Service Industries* (Studies in Income and Wealth, vol. 34), 1969, pp. 287-352.

Gallman, Robert E. and Weiss, Thomas J. "The Service Industries in the Nineteenth Century: Reply to Easterlin, Lebergott, Fabricant, and Firestone," in Fuchs, ed. *Production and Productivity in the Service Industries.* (Studies in Income and Wealth, vol. 34), 1969, pp. 372-81.

Gould, J.M. *Output and Productivity in the Electric and Gas Utilities, 1899-1942* (General Series, 47). New York: National Bureau of Economic Research, 1946.

Lebergott, Stanley. "The Service Industries in the Nineteenth Century: Comment on Gallman and Weiss," in Fuchs, ed. *Production and Productivity in the Service Industries* (Studies in Income and Wealth, vol. 34), 1969, pp. 365-68.

Rotella, Elyce J. "The Expansion of the Clerical Sector in the United States, 1870-1930," [Working Paper].

Sutch, Richard C. and Ransom, Roger L. "Credit Merchandising in the Post-Emancipation South: Structure, Conduct, and Performance," *Explorations in Economic History*, 16(1), January 1979, pp. 64-89.

Ulmer, Melville J. *Capital in Transportation, Communications, and Public Utilities: Its Formation and Financing.* Princeton: Princeton University Press for the National Bureau of Economic

Research, 1960.
Weiss, Thomas J. "The Service Sector in the United States, 1839 to 1899," (Summary of Doctoral Dissertation) *Journal of Economic History*, 27(4), December 1967, pp. 625-28.
Weiss, Thomas J. "Urbanization and the Growth of the Service Workforce," *Explorations in Economic History*, 8(3), Spring 1971, pp. 241-59.

Rest of the World: General

Drummond, Ian M. "Canadian Life Insurance Companies and the Capital Market, 1890-1914," *Canadian Journal of Economics and Political Science*, 28(2), May 1962, pp. 204-24.
Hawke, Gary R. "Economic Decisions and Political Ossification: New Zealand Retail Electricity Tariff," in Peter Munz, ed. *The Feel of Truth: Essays in New Zealand and Pacific History*. Wellington: A.H. & A.W. Reed for Victoria University of Wellington, 1969, pp. 219-33.
Hoffmann, Walther G. "Der tertiare Sektor im Wachstumprozess [The Service Sector in the Growth Process] (with English Summary)," *Jahrbucher fur Nationalokonomie und Statistik*, 183(1), June 1969, pp. 1-29.
Johnston, J. and Murphy, G.W. "The Growth of Life Assurance in the United Kingdom since 1880," *Manchester School of Economic and Social Studies*, 25, May 1957, pp. 107-82.
Minami, Ryoshin. "Railroads and Electric Utilities, 1872-1960," in Ohkawa and Hayami, eds. *Economic Growth*, vol. 1, 1973, pp. 38-50.
Vicziany, Antonia Markka. "The Cotton Trade and the Commercial Development of Bombay 1855-1875," (Unpublished Ph.D. Dissertation, University of London, 1975).

Housing and Building

Adams, Jr., Donald R. "Residential Construction Industry in the Early Nineteenth Century," *Journal of Economic History*, 35(4), December 1975, pp. 794-816.
Blank, David M. "The Volume of Residential Construction, 1889-1950," National Bureau of Economic Research, Technical Paper no. 9, 1954 [Working Paper].
Bloch, Ben; Fels, Rendigs and McMahon, Marshall. "Housing Surplus in the 1920's?" *Explorations in Economic History*, 8(3), Spring 1971, pp. 259-84.
Bloch, Ben; Fels, Rendigs and McMahon, Marshall. "Housing Surplus in the 1920's?" *Explorations in Economic History*, 8(3), Spring 1971, pp. 259-83.
Cairncross, Alec K. and Weber, Brian A. "Fluctuations in Building in Great Britain, 1785-1849," *Economic History Review*, Second Series, 9(2), 1956, pp. 283-97.
Cooney, E.W. "Long Waves in Building in the British Economy of the Nineteenth Century.," *Economic History Review*, Second Series,

13(2), 1960, pp. 257-69.

David, Paul A. "Building in Ohio between 1837 and 1914: Comment on Gottlieb," in Brady, ed. *Output, Employment and Productivity in the United States After 1800* (Studies in Income and Wealth, vol. 30), 1966, pp. 281-88.

Gottlieb, Manuel. "Building in Ohio Between 1837 and 1914," in Brady, ed. *Output, Employment, and Productivity in the United States After 1800* (Studies in Income and Wealth, vol. 30), 1966, pp. 243-80.

Gottlieb, Manuel. "Building in Ohio Between 1837 and 1914: Reply to David," in Brady, ed. *Output, Employment, and Productivity in the United States After 1800* (Studies in Income and Wealth, vol. 30), 1966, pp. 288-90.

Grebler, Leo; Blank, David M. and Winnick, Louis. *Capital Formation in Residential Real Estate: Trends and Prospects.* Princeton: Princeton University Press for the National Bureau of Economic Research, 1956.

Habakkuk, H.J. "Fluctuations in House-Building in Britain and the United States in the Nineteenth Century," *Journal of Economic History*, 22, 1926, pp. 198-230.

Hall, A.R. "Long Waves in Building in the British Economy of the Nineteenth Century: A Comment on Cooney," *Economic History Review*, Second Series, 14(2), 1961, pp. 330-32.

Hoover, Ethel D. "Retail Prices after 1850," in Parker, ed. *Trends in the American Economy in the Nineteenth Century* (Studies in Income and Wealth, vol. 24), 1960, pp. 141-86.

Jackson, R.V. "Owner-occupation of Houses in Sydney, 1871 to 1891," *Australian Economic History Review*, 10(2), September 1970, pp. 138-54.

Kendrick, John W. "Retail Prices after 1850: Comment on Hoover," in Parker, ed. *Trends in the American Economy in the Nineteenth Century* (Studies in Income and Wealth, vol. 24), 1960, pp. 186-90.

Lewis, J. Parry. "Indices of House-Building in the Manchester Conurbation, South Wales and Great Britain, 1851-1913," *Scottish Journal of Political Economy*, 8(2), June 1961, pp. 148-56.

Mercer, Lloyd J. and Morgan, W. Douglas. "Housing Surplus in the 1920s? Another Evaluation," *Explorations in Economic History*, 10(3), Spring 1973, pp. 295-303.

Thomas, Brinley. "Demographic Determinants of British and American Building Cycles, 1870-1913," in McCloskey, ed. *Essays on a Mature Economy*, 1971, pp. 39-74.

Thomas, Brinley. *Migration and Urban Development: A Reappraisal of British and American Long Cycles.* London: Methuen, 1972.

Weber, B.A. "A New Index of House Rents for Great Britain, 1874-1913," *Scottish Journal of Political Economy*, 7(3), November 1960, pp. 232-37.

Consumer Demand

Cole, W.A.   "Factors in Demand, 1700-80," in Floud and McCloskey, eds.
   The Economic History of Britain since 1700, vol. 1, 1981, pp.
   36-65.
Daniere, Andre.   "Feudal Incomes and Demand Elasticity for Bread in
   Late 18th Century France," *Journal of Economic History*, 18(3),
   September 1958, pp. 317-30.
Daniere, Andre.   "Feudal Incomes and Demand Elasticity for Bread in
   Late 18th Century France: A Rejoinder to Landes," *Journal of
   Economic History*, 18(3), September 1958, pp. 339-41.
De Vries, Jan.   "Peasant Demand Patterns and Economic Development:
   Friesland, 1550-1750," in Parker and Jones, eds.   *European Peasants
   and Their Markets*, 1975, pp. 205-66.
Fishlow, Albert.   "Comparative Consumption Patterns, the Extent of the
   Market, and Alternative Development Strategies," in Ayal, ed.
   Micro Aspects of Development, 1973, pp. 41-80.
Goldin, Claudia D.   "Household and Market Production of Families in a
   Late Nineteenth Century American City," *Explorations in Economic
   History*, 16(2), April 1979, pp. 111-31.
Green, George D.   "The Economic Impact of the Stock Market Boom and
   Crash of 1929," in *Consumer Spending and Monetary Policy*, 1972, pp.
   189-220.
Hoover, Ethel D.   "Retail Prices after 1850," in Parker, ed.   *Trends in
   the American Economy in the Nineteenth Century* (Studies in Income
   and Wealth, vol. 24), 1960, pp. 141-86.
Kendrick, John W.   "Retail Prices after 1850: Comment on Hoover," in
   Parker, ed.   *Trends in the American Economy in the Nineteenth
   Century* (Studies in Income and Wealth, vol. 24), 1960, pp. 186-90.
Koenker, Roger.   "Was Bread Giffen? The Demand for Food in England
   Circa 1790," *Review of Economics and Statistics*, 59(2), May 1977,
   pp. 225-29.
Kuznets, Simon S.   "Quantitative Aspects of the Economic Growth of
   Nations (Part 7): The Share and Structure of Consumption," *Economic
   Development and Cultural Change*, 10(2, Part 2), January 1962, pp.
   1-92.
Landes, David S.   "Feudal Incomes and Demand Elasticity for Bread in
   Late 18th Century France: Reply to Mr.   Daniere and Some
   Reflections on the Significance of the Debate," *Journal of Economic
   History*, 18(3), September 1958, pp. 331-38.
Landes, David S.   "Feudal Incomes and Demand Elasticity for Bread in
   Late 18th Century France: A Second Reply to Daniere," *Journal of
   Economic History*, 18(3), September 1958, pp. 342-44.
McAlpin, Michelle Burge.   "Railroads, Cultivation Patterns, and
   Foodgrain Availability: India, 1860-1900," *Indian Economic and
   Social History Review*, 12(1), January/March, 1975, pp. 43-60.
McAlpin, Michelle Burge.   "Dearth, Famine, and Risk: The Changing
   Impact of Crop Failures in Western India, 1870-1920," *Journal of
   Economic History*, 39(1), March 1979, pp. 143-57.

Mokyr, Joel. "Demand vs. Supply in the Industrial Revolution," *Journal of Economic History*, 37(4), December 1977, pp. 981-1008.

Parker, William N. "Comment on Papers by McAlpin, Libecap and Johnson, and Adelman and Morris Presented to the 38th Annual Meeting of the Economic History Association," *Journal of Economic History*, 39(1), March 1979, pp. 177-79.

Phelps Brown, E.H. and Hopkins, Sheila V. "Seven Centuries of the Prices of Consumables, Compared with Builders' Wage Rates," (Reprinted in Ramsey, ed. *The Price Revolution in the Sixteenth Century*, 1971, pp. 18-41) *Economica*, 23(92), November 1956, pp. 296-314.

Roehl, Richard. "Patterns and Structure of Demand, 1000-1500," in Cipolla, ed. *The Fontana Economic History of Europe*, vol. 1, 1970.

Supple, Barry E. "Income and Demand, 1860-1914," in Floud and McCloskey, eds. *The Economic History of Britain since 1700*, vol. 2, 1980.

Toutain, Jean Claude. "La consommation alimentaire de la France de 1789 a 1964 [Food Consumption in France, 1789-1964]," *Cahiers de L'Institut de Science Economique Appliquee*, 1971.

Vatter, Harold G. "Has There Been a Twentieth-Century Consumer Durables Revolution?" *Journal of Economic History*, 27(1), March 1967, pp. 1-16.

Williamson, Jeffrey G. "Consumer Behavior in the Nineteenth Century: Carroll D. Wright's Massachusetts Workers in 1875," *Explorations in Entrepreneurial History*, Second Series, 4(2), Winter 1967, pp. 98-135.

Chapter 9

AGRICULTURE

United States: Inputs and Institutions

Alston, Lee J. "Costs of Contracting and the Decline of Tenancy in the South, 1930-1960," (Summary of Doctoral Dissertation) *Journal of Economic History*, 39(1), March 1979, pp. 324-26.

Alston, Lee J. "A Theory Explaining the Decline in Tenant Contracts Relative to Wage Conracts in the South, 1930-1960," Williams College, Department of Economics Research Paper no. 17, December 1978 [Working Paper].

Anderson, Terry L. and Hill, Peter J. "The Evolution of Property Rights: A Study of the American West," *Journal of Law and Economics*, 18(1), April 1975, pp. 163-80.

Anderson, Terry L. and Hill, Peter J. "The Role of Private Property in the History of American Agriculture, 1776-1976," *American Journal of Agricultural Economics*, 58(5), December 1976, pp. 937-45.

Anderson, Terry L. and Hill, Peter J. "From Free Grass to Fences: Transforming the Commons of the American West," in Hardin and Baden, eds. *Managing the Commons*, 1977, pp. 200-216.

Anderson, Terry L. and Hill, Peter J. "The Role of Private Property in the History of American Agriculture, 1776-1976: Reply to Schmid," *American Journal of Agricultural Economics*, 59(3), August 1977, pp. 590-91.

Anderson, Terry L. and Hill, Peter J. "An American Experiment in Anarcho-Capitalism: The Not So Wild, Wild West," *Journal of Libertarian Studies*, 3(1), 1979, pp. 9-29.

Ankli, Robert E. "Farm-Making Costs in the 1850's," *Agricultural History*, 48(1), January 1974, pp. 51-70.

Ankli, Robert E. "The Coming of the Reaper," in Uselding, ed. *Business and Economic History*, Second Series, vol. 5, 1976, pp. 1-24.

Ankli, Robert E. "Horses Vs. Tractors on the Corn Belt, 1920-1940," *Agricultural History*, 54(1), January 1980, pp. 134-48.

Baack, Ben and Reid, Jr., Joseph D. "Land Tenure Patterns and Property Rights in Agriculture," (Summary of 1975 Research Workshop) *Journal of Economic History*, 36(1), March 1976, pp. 29-32.

Bateman, Fred. "Labor Inputs and Productivity in American Dairy Agriculture, 1850-1910," *Journal of Economic History*, 29(2), June 1969, pp. 206-29.

Bateman, Fred. "Issues in the Measurement of Efficiency of American Dairy Farming, 1850-1910: A Reply to Gunderson," *Journal of*

Economic History, 29(3), September 1969, pp. 506-11.

Bateman, Fred and Foust, James D. "A Sample of Rural Households Selected from the 1860 Manuscript Censuses," *Agricultural History*, 48(1), January 1974, pp. 75-93.

Bateman, Fred. "The 'Marketable Surplus' in Northern Dairy Farming: New Evidence by Size of Farm in 1860," *Agricultural History*, 52(3), July 1978, pp. 345-63.

Battalio, Raymond C. and Kagel, John. "The Structure of Antebellum Southern Agriculture: South Carolina, A Case Study," in Parker, ed. *The Structure of the Cotton Economy of the Antebellum South*, 1970, pp. 25-37.

Bogue, Allan G. *Money at Interest: The Farm Mortgage on the Middle Border.* (Second Edition Published by Russell & Russell, New York, 1968) Ithaca: Cornell University Press, 1955.

Bogue, Allan G. and Bogue, Margaret Beattie. "'Profits' and the Frontier Land Speculator," (Reprinted in Fogel and Engerman, eds. *The Reinterpretation of American Economic History*, 1971, pp. 64-72) *Journal of Economic History*, 17(1), March 1957, pp. 1-24.

Bogue, Allan G. "Financing the Prairie Farmer," in Fogel and Engerman, eds. *The Reinterpretation of American Economic History*, 1971, pp. 301-7.

Bogue, Allan G. "Population Change and Farm Settlement in the Northern United States: Comment on Easterlin," *Journal of Economic History*, 36(1), March 1976, pp. 76-81.

Bowman, John D. "An Economic Analysis of Midwestern Farm Land Values and Farm Land Income, 1860 to 1900," *Yale Economic Essays*, 5(2), Fall 1965, pp. 317-52.

Brown, William W. and Reynolds, Morgan O. "Debt Peonage Re-examined: A Note on Ransom and Sutch," *Journal of Economic History*, 33(4), December 1973, pp. 862-871.

Burford, Roger L. "The Federal Cotton Programs and Farm Labor Force Adjustments," *Southern Economic Journal*, 33(2), October 1966, pp. 223-36.

Carlson, Leonard A. "The Dawes Act and the Decline of Indian Farming," (Summary of Doctoral Dissertation) *Journal of Economic History*, 38(1), March 1978, pp. 274-76.

Cooley, Thomas F. and DeCanio, Stephen J. "Rational Expectations in American Agriculture, 1867-1914," *Review of Economics and Statistics*, 59(1), February 1977, pp. 9-17.

Danhof, Clarence H. "Discussion of Papers by Lang, DeCanio, Ellsworth, and Lindley Presented to the 31st Annual Meeting of the Economic History Association," *Journal of Economic History*, 32(1), March 1972, pp. 421-22.

David, Paul A. "The Mechanization of Reaping in the Antebellum Midwest," in Rosovsky, ed. *Industrialization in Two Systems*, 1966, pp. 3-39.

David, Paul A. "The Landscape and the Machine: Technical Interrelatedness, Land Tenure and the Mechanization of the Corn Harvest in Victorian Britain," in McCloskey, ed. *Essays on a Mature Economy*, 1971, pp. 145-204.

David, Paul A. "Locating a Switch-Over in the Structural Relationship Between Variations in the Manufacturing Sector's Terms of Trade with Agriculture and the Volume of Industrial Output in Chicago: A Statistical Procedure," [Working Paper].

Davis, Ronald L.F. "Southern Merchants and the Origins of Sharecropping: A Case Study," in Soltow, ed. *Essays in Economic and Business History*, 1979.

Dennen, R. Taylor. "Cattle Trailing in the Nineteenth Century: A Note on Galenson," *Journal of Economic History*, 35(2), June 1975, pp. 458-60.

Dennen, R. Taylor. "Cattlemen's Associations and Property Rights in Land in the American West," *Explorations in Economic History*, 13(4), October 1976, pp. 423-36.

DeCanio, Stephen J. "Agricultural Production, Supply and Institutions in the Post-Civil War South," (Summary of Doctoral Dissertation) *Journal of Economic History*, 32(1), March 1972, pp. 396-98.

DeCanio, Stephen J. *Agriculture in the Postbellum South: The Economics of Production and Supply*. Cambridge: M.I.T. Press, 1974.

DeCanio, Stephen J.; Cooley, Thomas F. and Matthews, M. Scott. "ATICS: An Agricultural Time Series-Cross Section Dataset," National Bureau of Economic Research(197, August 1977 [Working Paper].

DeCanio, Stephen J. and Trojanowski, Joseph. "KANATICS: A Kansas Agricultural Time Series-Cross Section Dataset," Inter-University Consortium for Political and Social Research, Ann Arbor, Paper no. 41, November 1977 [Working Paper].

Easterlin, Richard A. "Population Change and Farm Settlement in the Northern United States," *Journal of Economic History*, 36(1), March 1976, pp. 45-75.

Easterlin, Richard A. "Population Change and Farm Settlement in the Northern United States: Reply to Bogue," *Journal of Economic History*, 36(1), March 1976, pp. 81-83.

Feller, Irwin. "Inventive Activity in Agriculture, 1837-1890," *Journal of Economic History*, 22(4), December 1962, pp. 560-77.

Ferleger, Louis. "Productivity Change in the Postbellum Louisiana Sugar Industry," in Anderson and Perryman, eds. *Time Series Analysis*, 1981, pp. 147-61.

Ferleger, Louis. *Farm Mechanization in the Southern Sugar Sector After the Civil War Louisiana History*. forthcoming.

Fitzharris, Joseph C. "Technology in Minnesota Agriculture, 1900-1940: Some Case Studies," University of Minnesota Department of Agricultural and Applied Economics Staff Paper Series [Working Paper].

Fleisig, Heywood. "Mechanizing the Cotton Harvest in the Nineteenth-Century South," (Summary of Doctoral Dissertation) Journal of Economic History, 25(4), December 1965, pp. 704-6.

Fogel, Robert W. and Rutner, Jack L. "The Efficiency Effects of Federal Land Policy, 1850-1900: Some Provisional Findings," in Bogue, Aydelotte, and Fogel, eds. *The Dimensions of Quantitative Research in History*, 1972.

Foust, James D. "The Yeoman Farmer and Westward Expansion of U.S. Cotton Production," (Summary of Doctoral Dissertation) *Journal of Economic History*, 27(4), December 1967, pp. 611-14.

Foust, James D. "The Yeoman Farmer and Westward Expansion of U.S.

Cotton Production," Ph.D. Dissertation, University of North Carolina, 1967 New York: Arno Press, 1976 [Working Paper].

Galenson, David W. "The End of the Chisholm Trail," *Journal of Economic History*, 34(2), June 1974, pp. 350-64.

Galenson, David W. "Cattle Trailing in the Nineteenth Century: A Reply to Dennen," *Journal of Economic History*, 35(2), June 1975, pp. 461-66.

Galenson, David W. "Origins of the Long Drive," *Journal of the West*, 14(3), July 1975, pp. 3-14.

Gallman, Robert E. "Self-Sufficiency in the Cotton Economy of the Antebellum South," (Reprinted in Parker, ed. *The Structure of the Cotton Economy of the Antebellum South*, 1970, pp. 5-23) *Agricultural History*, 44(1), January 1970, pp. 5-23.

Goldin, Claudia D. "Comments on Dissertations by Alston and Shlomovitz Presented to the 38th Annual Meeting of the Economic History Association," *Journal of Economic History*, 39(1), March 1979, pp. 336-38.

Gould, John D. "The Landscape and the Machine: A Comment on David," *Economic History Review*, Second Series, 27(3), August 1974, pp. 455-60.

Gray, Lewis C. *History of Agriculture in the Southern United States to 1860*. (Reprinted by Peter Smith, Gloucester, Mass., 1958) Washington, D.C.: Carnegie Institution of Washington, 1933.

Griliches, Zvi. "Hybrid Corn and the Economics of Innovation," (Reprinted in Fogel and Engerman, eds. *The Reinterpretation of American Economic History*, 1971, pp. 207-213) *Science*, 132, July 29, 1960, pp. 275-80.

Gunderson, Gerald A. "Issues in the Measurement of Efficiency of American Dairy Farming, 1850-1910: A Comment on Bateman," *Journal of Economic History*, 29(3), September 1969, pp. 501-5.

Hallagan, William S. "Labor Contracting in Turn-Of-The-Century California Agriculture," *Journal of Economic History*, 40(4), December 1980, pp. 757-76.

Higgs, Robert. "Race, Tenure, and Resource Allocation in Southern Agriculture, 1910," (See Editor's Notes this Journal, 33(3), September 1973, pp. 668 for Correction of a Printer's Error in This Article) *Journal of Economic History*, 33(1), March 1973, pp. 149-69.

Higgs, Robert. "Patterns of Farm Rental in the Georgia Cotton Belt, 1880-1900," *Journal of Economic History*, 34(2), June 1974, pp. 468-82.

Higgs, Robert. "The Boll Weevil, the Cotton Economy, and Black Migration, 1910-1930," *Agricultural History*, 50(2), April 1976, pp. 335-50.

Higgs, Robert. "Landless by Law: Japanese Immigrants in California Agriculture to 1941," *Journal of Economic History*, 38(1), March 1978, pp. 205-25.

Higgs, Robert. "The Wealth of Japanese Tenant Farmers in California, 1909," *Agricultural History*, 53(2), April 1979, pp. 488-93.

Johnson, Thomas H. "Postwar Optimism and the Rural Financial Crisis of the 1920's," *Explorations in Economic History*, 11(2), Winter 1974, pp. 173-91.

Jones, Donald W. "Land Use and Land Tenure: Theory and Empirical Analysis," [Working Paper].

Jones, Lewis R. "The Mechanization of Reaping and Mowing in American Agriculture, 1833-1870: Comment (on Olmstead)," *Journal of Economic History*, 37(2), June 1977, pp. 451-55.

Klein, Judith V. "Farm-Making Costs in the 1850's: A Comment on Ankli," *Agricultural History*, 48(1), January 1974, pp. 71-4.

Klingaman, David C. "The Significance of Grain in the Development of the Tobacco Colonies," *Journal of Economic History*, 29(2), June 1969, pp. 268-78.

Kunreuther, Howard and Wright, Gavin. "Safety-First, Gambling and the Subsistence Farmer," in Roumasset, Boussard, and Singh, ed. *Risk, Uncertainty and Agricultural Development*, 1979, pp. 213-46.

Leet, Don R. "Human Fertility and Agricultural Opportunities in Ohio Counties: from Frontier to Maturity, 1810-60," in Klingaman and Vedder, eds. *Essays in Nineteenth Century Economic History*, 1975, pp. 138-58.

Leet, Don R. "Agricultural Opportunities in a Frontier Community: Ohio, 1810-1860," Presented at the Annual Cliometrics Conference, University of Wisconsin-Madison, April 1973 [Working Paper].

Lindert, Peter H. "Land Scarcity and American Growth," *Journal of Economic History*, 34(4), December 1974, pp. 851-84.

McClelland, Peter D. "New Perspectives on the Disposal of Western Lands in Nineteenth Century America," *Business History Review*, 43(1), Spring 1969, pp. 77-83.

McGuire, Robert and Higgs, Robert. "Cotton, Corn and Risk in the Nineteenth Century: Another View," *Explorations in Economic History*, 14(2), April 1977, pp. 167-82.

McGuire, Robert A. "A Portfolio Analysis of Crop Diversification and Risk in the Cotton South," *Explorations in Economic History*, 17(4), October 1980, pp. 342-71.

Metzer, Jacob. "Rational Management, Modern Business Practices, and Economies of Scale in the Antebellum Southern Plantations," *Explorations in Economic History*, 12(2), April 1975, pp. 123-50.

Musoke, Moses S. "Technical Change in Cotton Production in the United States, 1925-1960," (Summary of Doctoral Dissertation) *Journal of Economic History*, 37(1), March 1977, pp. 258-60.

Olmstead, Alan L. "The Mechanization of Reaping and Mowing in American Agriculture, 1833-1870," *Journal of Economic History*, 35(2), June 1975, pp. 327-52.

Olmstead, Alan L. "The Civil War as a Catalyst of Technological Change in Agriculture," in Uselding, ed. *Business and Economic History, Second Series*, vol. 5, 1976, pp. 36-50.

Olmstead, Alan L. "The Diffusion of the Reaper: One More Time! (Reply to Jones)," *Journal of Economic History*, 39(2), June 1979, pp. 475-76.

Olmstead, Alan L. and Ankli, Robert E. "The Adoption of the Reaper: The State of the Debate," [Working Paper].

Olmstead, Alan L. "The Civil War, Farm Mechanization, and the Agricultural Machinery Industry," [Working Paper].

Olson, John F. and Fogel, Robert W. "Clock-Time Vs. Real-Time: A Comparison of the Lengths of the Northern and the Southern

Agricultural Work-Years," [Working Paper].

Page, Walter P. "A Study of the Fixed Coefficients Model of Production for Agriculture in a Selected Region of the Great Plains, 1899-1903: Some Tentative Results," *Mississippi Valley Journal of Business and Statistics*, 5(1), Fall 1969, pp. 34-42.

Parker, William N. "Sources of Agricultural Productivity in the Nineteenth Century," *Journal of Farm Economics*, 49(5), December 1967, pp. 1455-68.

Parker, William N. "The Slave Plantation in American Agriculture," in Coats and Robertson, eds. *Essays in American Economic History*, 1969.

Parker, William N., ed. *The Structure of the Cotton Economy of the Antebellum South.* (Originally Published as an Issue of *Agricultural History*, 44(1), January 1970) Washington, D.C.: Agricultural History Society, 1970.

Parker, William N. "Productivity Growth in American Grain Farming: An Analysis of Its 19th Century Sources," in Fogel and Engerman, eds. *The Reinterpretation of American Economic History*, 1971, pp. 175-86.

Parker, William N. "Agriculture," in Davis, Easterlin, and Parker, eds. *American Economic Growth*, 1972, pp. 369-417.

Parker, William N. "The Land, Minerals, Water, and Forests," in Davis, Easterlin, and Parker, eds. *American Economic Growth*, 1972, pp. 93-120.

Parker, William N. and DeCanio, Stephen. "Agricultural Output and Productivity," (Summary of 1976 Research Workshop) *Journal of Economic History*, 37(1), March 1977, pp. 230-31.

Parker, William N. "Labor Productivity in Cotton Farming: The History of a Research," *Agricultural History*, 53(1), January 1979, pp. 228-44.

Passell, Peter. "The Impact of Cotton Land Distribution on the Antebellum Economy," *Journal of Economic History*, 31(4), December 1971, pp. 917-37.

Passell, Peter. *Essays in the Economics of 19th Century Land Policy.* New York: Arno Press, 1975.

Primack, Martin L. "Land Clearing Under Nineteenth-Century Techniques: Some Preliminary Calculations," *Journal of Economic History*, 22(4), December 1962, pp. 484-97.

Primack, Martin L. "Farm Construction as a Use of Farm Labor in the United States, 1850-1910," *Journal of Economic History*, 25(1), March 1965, pp. 114-25.

Primack, Martin L. "Farm Capital Formation as a Use of Farm Labor, 1850-1910," *Journal of Economic History*, 26(3), September 1966, pp. 348-62.

Ransom, Roger L. and Sutch, Richard C. "Debt Peonage in the Cotton South after the Civil War," *Journal of Economic History*, 32(3), September 1972, pp. 641-69.

Ransom, Roger L. and Sutch, Richard C. "The 'Lock-In' Mechanism and Overproduction of Cotton in the Postbellum South," *Agricultural History*, 49(2), April 1975, pp. 405-25.

Ransom, Roger L. and Sutch, Richard C. *One Kind of Freedom: The Economic Consequences of Emancipation.* New York: Cambridge

University Press, 1977.

Ransom, Roger L. and Sutch, Richard C. "Sharecropping: Market Response or Mechanism of Race Control?" in Sansing, ed. *What Was Freedom's Price?*, 1978, pp. 51-69.

Rasmussen, Wayne D. "The Impact of Technological Change on American Agriculture, 1862-1962," *Journal of Economic History*, 22(4), December 1962, pp. 578-91.

Rastatter, Edward H. "Nineteenth Century Public Land Policy: The Case for the Speculator," in Klingaman and Vedder, eds. *Essays in Nineteenth Century Economic History*, 1975, pp. 118-37.

Reid, Jr., Joseph D. "Sharecropping as an Understandable Market Response: The Postbellum South," *Journal of Economic History*, 33(1), March 1973, pp. 106-30.

Reid, Jr., Joseph D. "Sharecropping in History and Theory," *Agricultural History*, 49(2), April 1975, pp. 426-40.

Reid, Jr., Joseph D. "Progress on Agricultural Credit: Comment on Bogue and Parker," *Agricultural History*, 50(1), January 1976, pp. 117-24.

Reid, Jr., Joseph D. "Antebellum Southern Rental Contracts," *Explorations in Economic History*, 13(1), January 1976, pp. 69-84.

Reid, Jr., Joseph D. "Sharecropping and Agricultural Uncertainty," *Economic Development and Cultural Change*, 24(3), April 1976, pp. 549-76.

Reid, Jr., Joseph D. "Tenancy in American History," in Roumasset, Boussard, and Singh, eds. *Risk, Uncertainty and Agricultural Development*, 1979.

Reid, Jr., Joseph D. "The Evaluations and Implications of Southern Tenancy," *Agricultural History*, 53(1), January 1979, pp. 153-69.

Reid, Jr., Joseph D. "White Land, Black Labor, and Agricultural Stagnation: The Causes and Effects of Sharecropping in the Postbellum South," *Explorations in Economic History*, 16(1), January 1979, pp. 31-55.

Rothstein, Morton. "The Cotton Frontier of the Antebellum South: A Methodological Battleground," in Parker, ed. *The Structure of the Cotton Economy of the Antebellum South*, 1970, pp. 149-65.

Schaeffer, Donald F. "Yeoman Farmers and Economic Democracy: A Study of Wealth and Economic Mobility in the Western Tobacco Region, 1850 to 1860," *Explorations in Economic History*, 15(4), October 1978, pp. 421-37.

Schmid, A. Allan. "The Role of Private Property in the History of American Agriculture, 1776-1976: Comment (on Anderson and Hill)," *American Journal of Agricultural Economics*, 59(3), August 1977, pp. 590-91.

Schmitz, Mark D. "Postbellum Developments in the Louisiana Cane Sugar Industry," in Uselding, ed. *Business and Economic History*, Second Series, vol. 5, 1976, pp. 88-101.

Schmitz, Mark D. *Economic Analysis of Antebellum Sugar Plantations in Louisiana.* New York: Arno Press, 1977.

Schmitz, Mark D. "Economies of Scale and Farm Size in the Antebellum Sugar Sector," *Journal of Economic History*, 37(4), December 1977, pp. 959-80.

Schmitz, Mark D. "Farm Interdependence in the Antebellum Sugar

Sector," *Agricultural History*, 52(1), January 1978, pp. 93-103.

Schmitz, Mark D. "The Transformation of the Southern Cane Sugar Sector, 1860-1930," *Agricultural History*, 53(1), January 1979, pp. 270-85.

Shepherd, James F. "The Development of New Wheat Varieties in the Pacific Northwest," *Agricultural History*, 54(1), January 1980, pp. 52-63.

Shlomowitz, Ralph. "New and Old Views on the Rural Economy of the Postbellum American South: A Review Article," [Working Paper].

Sutch, Richard C. and Ransom, Roger L. "The 'Lock-In' Mechanism and Over-Production of Cotton in the Postbellum South," *Agricultural History*, 49(2), April 1975, pp. 405-25.

Sutch, Richard C. and Ransom, Roger L. "Sharecropping: A Market Response or Racial Mechanism?" in Sansing, ed. *What Was Freedom's Price?*, 1978.

Swierenga, Robert P. "Land Speculator 'Profits' Reconsidered: Central Iowa as a Test Case," (Reprinted in Swierenga, ed., *Quantification in American History*, 1970, pp. 317-40) *Journal of Economic History*, 26(1), March 1966, pp. 1-28.

Swierenga, Robert P. *Pioneers and Profits: Land Speculation on the Iowa Frontier.* Ames: Iowa State University Press, 1968.

Swierenga, Robert P. "Land Speculation and Frontier Tax Assessments," *Agricultural History*, 44(3), July 1970, pp. 253-66.

Swierenga, Robert P. "The Equity Effects of Public Land Speculation in Iowa: Large versus Small Speculators," *Journal of Economic History*, 34(4), December 1974, pp. 1008-20.

Swierenga, Robert P. "Land Speculation and Its Impact on American Economic Growth and Welfare: An Historiographical Review," *Western Historical Quarterly*, 8, July 1977, pp. 283-302.

Tostlebe, Alvin S. *Capital in Agriculture: Its Formation and Financing since 1870.* Princeton: Princeton University Press for the National Bureau of Economic Research, 1957.

Tostlebe, Alvin S. "The Growth of Physical Capital in Agriculture, 1870-1950," National Bureau of Economic Research, Occasional Paper no. 44, 1954 [Working Paper].

Winters, Donald L. "Tenant Farming in Iowa, 1860-1900: A Study of the Terms of Rental Leases," *Agricultural History*, 48(1), January 1974, pp. 130-50.

Winters, Donald L. "Tenancy as an Economic Institution: The Growth and Distribution of Agricultural Tenancy in Iowa, 1850-1900," *Journal of Economic History*, 37(2), June 1977, pp. 382-408.

Winters, Donald L. *Farmers Without Farms: Agricultural Tenancy in Nineteenth Century Iowa.* Westport, Conn.: Greenwood Press, 1978.

Wright, Gavin. "Comments on Papers by Reid, Ransom/Sutch, and Higgs on the Postbellum South Presented to the 32nd Annual Meeting of the Economic History Association," *Journal of Economic History*, 33(1), March 1973, pp. 170-76.

Wright, Gavin and Kunreuther, Howard. "Cotton, Corn and Risk in the Nineteenth Century: A Reply to McGuire and Higgs," *Explorations in Economic History*, 14(2), April 1977, pp. 183-95.

Wright, Gavin. *The Political Economy of the Cotton South: Households, Markets, and Wealth in the Nineteenth Century.* New York: W.W.

Norton, 1978.
Wright, Gavin. "Agriculture in the South," in Porter, ed.
Encyclopedia of American Economic History, vol. 1, 1980, pp.
371-85.

United States: Outputs

Aldrich, Terry Mark. "Flexible Exchange Rates, Northern Expansion, and
the Market for Southern Cotton: 1866-1879," *Journal of Economic
History*, 33(2), June 1973, pp. 399-416.
Ankli, Robert E. "Gross Farm Revenue in Pre-Civil War Illinois,"
(Reprinted in *Papers of the Sixteenth Business History Conference*,
1969) *Nebraska Journal of Economics and Business*, 8(3), Summer
1969, pp. 147-78.
Ankli, Robert E. "Problems in Aggregate Agricultural History,"
Agricultural History, 46(1), January 1972, pp. 65-70.
Ankli, Robert E. *Gross Farm Revenue in Pre-Civil War Illinois*. New
York: Arno Press, 1977.
Ankli, Robert E. "Farm Income on the Great Plains and Prairies:
1920-1940," *Agricultural History* , 51(1), January 1977, pp. 92-103.
Atack, Jeremy and Bateman, Fred. "The Profitability of Northern
Agriculture in 1860," in Uselding, ed. *Research in Economic
History*, vol. 4, 1979.
Ball, Duane E. and Walton, Gary M. "Agricultural Productivity Change
in Eighteenth-Century Pennsylvania," *Journal of Economic History*,
36(1), March 1976, pp. 102-17.
Ball, Duane E. "The Adaptiveness and Market Response of Early 19th
Century Chester County, Pennsylvania Farmers," Presented at the
Regional Economic History Conference, Wilmington, Delaware, 1976
[Working Paper].
Barger, Harold. *American Agriculture, 1899-1939 (General Series*, 42).
New York: National Bureau of Economic Research, 1942.
Barton, Glen T. "Productivity Growth in Grain Production in the United
States, 1840-60 and 1900-10: Comment on Parker and Klein," in
Brady, ed. *Output, Employment, and Productivity in the United
States after 1800 (Studies in Income and Wealth*, vol. 30), 1966,
pp. 580-82.
Bateman, Fred. "Improvement in American Dairy Farming, 1850-1910: A
Quantitative Analysis," *Journal of Economic History*, 28(2), June
1968, pp. 255-73.
Bateman, Fred. "Labor Inputs and Productivity in American Dairy
Agriculture, 1850-1910," *Journal of Economic History*, 29(2), June
1969, pp. 206-29.
Bateman, Fred. "Issues in the Measurement of Efficiency of American
Dairy Farming, 1850-1910: A Reply to Gunderson," *Journal of
Economic History*, 29(3), September 1969, pp. 506-11.
Bateman, Fred. "The 'Marketable Surplus' in Northern Dairy Farming:
New Evidence by Size of Farm in 1860," *Agricultural History*, 52(3),
July 1978, pp. 345-63.
Bowman, John D. and Keehn, Richard H. "Agricultural Terms of Trade in
Four Midwestern States, 1870-1900," *Journal of Economic History*,

34(3), September 1974, pp. 592-609.

Callahan, Colleen M. and Hutchinson , William K. "Antebellum Interregional Trade in Agricultural Goods: Preliminary Results," *Journal of Economic History*, 40(1), March 1980, pp. 25-31.

Danhof, Clarence H. "Farm Gross Product and Gross Investment in the Nineteenth Century: Comment on Towne and Rasmussen," in Parker, ed. *Trends in the American Economy in the Nineteenth Century* (*Studies in Income and Wealth*, vol. 24), 1960, pp. 312-15.

Danhof, Clarence H. "Discussion of Papers by Lang, DeCanio, Ellsworth, and Lindley Presented to the 31st Annual Meeting of the Economic History Association," *Journal of Economic History*, 32(1), March 1972, pp. 421-22.

DeCanio, Stephen J. "Agricultural Production, Supply and Institutions in the Post-Civil War South," (Summary of Doctoral Dissertation) *Journal of Economic History*, 32(1), March 1972, pp. 396-98.

DeCanio, Stephen J. "Cotton 'Overproduction' in Late Nineteenth-Century Southern Agriculture," *Journal of Economic History*, 33(3), September 1973, pp. 608-33.

DeCanio, Stephen J. *Agriculture in the Postbellum South: The Economics of Production and Supply.* Cambridge: M.I.T. Press, 1974.

DeCanio, Stephen J. "Economic Losses from Forecasting Error in Agriculture," *Journal of Political Economy*, 88(2), April 1980, pp. 234-58.

DeCanio, Stephen J. and Parker, William N. "Two Hidden Sources of Productivity Growth in American Agriculture, 1860-1930," Presented at the International Economic History Congress, Edinburgh, August 1978 [Working Paper].

Easterlin, Richard A. "Farm Production and Income in Old and New Areas at Mid-Century," in Klingaman and Vedder, eds. *Essays in Nineteenth Century Economic History*, 1975, pp. 77-117.

Fisher, Franklin M. and Temin, Peter. "Regional Specialization and the Supply of Wheat in the United States, 1867-1914," *Review of Economics and Statistics*, 52(2), May 1970, pp. 134-49.

Fisher, Franklin M. and Temin, Peter. "Regional Specialization and the Supply of Wheat in the United States, 1867-1914: A Reply to Higgs," *Review of Economics and Statistics*, 53(1), February 1971, pp. 102-103.

Fitzharris, Joseph C. "Minnesota Agricultural Growth, 1880-1970," University of Minnesota Department of Agricultural and Applied Economics Staff Paper P76-4, June 1976 [Working Paper].

Fitzharris, Joseph C. "The Development of Minnesota Agriculture, 1880-1970: A Study in Productivity Change," University of Minnesota Department of Agricultural and Applied Economics Staff Paper P74-2, October 1974 [Working Paper].

Friedman, Philip. "A Reconstructionist Production Function: Post Civil War South and the Optimal Path to Recovery," Presented at the Meeting of the Western Economic Association, August 1973 [Working Paper].

Galenson, David W. "The Profitability of the Long Drive," *Agricultural History*, 51(4), October 1977, pp. 737-58.

Gallaway, Lowell E.; Vedder, Richard K. and Klingaman, David C. "The Profitability of Antebellum Agriculture in the Cotton Belt: Some

New Evidence," *Atlantic Economic Journal*, 2(2), November 1974, pp. 30-47.

Gallman, Robert E. "A Note on the Patent Office Crop Estimates, 1841-1848," *Journal of Economic History*, 23(2), June 1963, pp. 185-95.

Gallman, Robert E. "Changes in Total U.S. Agricultural Factor Productivity in the Nineteenth Century," *Agricultural History*, 46(1), January 1972, pp. 191-210.

Gallman, Robert E. "The Agricultural Sector and the Pace of Economic Growth: U.S. Experience in the Nineteenth Century," in Klingaman and Vedder, eds. *Essays in Nineteenth Century Economic History*, 1975, pp. 35-76.

Goldin, Claudia D. and Lewis, Frank D. "The Postbellum Recovery of the South and the Cost of the Civil War: Comment on Temin," *Journal of Economic History*, 38(2), June 1978, pp. 487-92.

Gray, Lewis C. *History of Agriculture in the Southern United States to 1860.* (Reprinted by Peter Smith, Gloucester, Mass., 1958) Washington, D.C.: Carnegie Institution of Washington, 1933.

Gunderson, Gerald A. "Issues in the Measurement of Efficiency of American Dairy Farming, 1850-1910: A Comment on Bateman," *Journal of Economic History*, 29(3), September 1969, pp. 501-5.

Hanson, II, John R. "World Demand for Cotton during the Nineteenth Century: Wright's Estimates Re-examined," (See note in this Journal, 40(1), March 1980, for a Corrigenda concerning this article) *Journal of Economic History*, 39(4), December 1979, pp. 1015-21.

Herbst, Lawrence A. "Antebellum Interregional Trade in Agricultural Goods: Discussion of Paper by Callahan and Hutchinson," *Journal of Economic History*, 40(1), March 1980, pp. 43-44.

Higgs, Robert. "Regional Specialization and the Supply of Wheat in the United States, 1867-1914: A Comment on Fisher and Temin," *Review of Economics and Statistics*, 53(1), February 1971, pp. 101-2.

Klingaman, David C.; Vedder, Richard K. and Gallaway, Lowell E. "The Profitability of Antebellum Agriculture in the Cotton Belt: Some New Evidence," *Atlantic Economic Journal*, 2(2), November 1974, pp. 30-47.

Klingaman, David C. *Colonial Virginia's Coastwise and Grain Trade.* New York: Arno Press, 1975.

Lang, Edith M. "The Effect of Net Interregional Migration on Agricultural Income Growth: The United States, 1850-1860," (Summary of Doctoral Dissertation) *Journal of Economic History*, 32(1), March 1972, pp. 393-95.

Lebergott, Stanley. "Comments on Measuring Agricultural Change," *Agricultural History*, 46(1), January 1972, pp. 227-34.

Lebergott, Stanley. "Confederate Cotton Exports," [Working Paper].

Lindstrom, Diane L. "Southern Dependence upon Interregional Grain Supplies: A Review of the Trade Flows, 1840-1860," in Parker, ed. *The Structure of the Cotton Economy of the Antebellum South*, 1970, pp. 101-13.

McGuire, Robert and Higgs, Robert. "Cotton, Corn and Risk in the Nineteenth Century: Another View," *Explorations in Economic History*, 14(2), April 1977, pp. 167-82.

Menard, Russell R. "Agricultural Productivity Change in Eighteenth-Century Pennsylvania: Comment on Ball and Walton," *Journal of Economic History*, 36(1), March 1976, pp. 118-25.

Munyon, Paul G. "Agricultural Income Statistics Since the Civil War," (Summary of 1977 Research Workshop) *Journal of Economic History*, 38(1), March 1978, pp. 265-67.

North, Douglass C. "Agriculture in Regional Economic Growth," (Reprinted in Coben and Hill, eds. *American Economic History*, 1966, pp. 258-267) *Journal of Farm Economics*, 41(5), December 1959, pp. 943-51.

Parker, William N. "The International Market for Agricultural Commodities, 1850-1873: Comment on Rothstein," in Gilchrist and Lewis, eds. *Economic Change in the Civil War Era*, 1965, pp. 73-76.

Parker, William N. and Klein, Judith L.V. "Productivity Growth in Grain Production in the United States, 1840-60 and 1900-10," in Brady, ed. *Output, Employment, and Productivity in the United States after 1800 (Studies in Income and Wealth*, vol. 30), 1966, pp. 523-80.

Parker, William N. "Sources of Agricultural Productivity in the Nineteenth Century," *Journal of Farm Economics*, 49(5), December 1967, pp. 1455-68.

Parker, William N. "Measurement of Productivity in American Agriculture, 1840-1910," *Third International Conference of Economic History, Munich, 1965, part 3.* Paris and The Hague: Mouton, 1969, pp. 37-43.

Parker, William N., ed. *The Structure of the Cotton Economy of the Antebellum South.* (Originally Published as an Issue of *Agricultural History*, 44(1), January 1970) Washington, D.C.: Agricultural History Society, 1970.

Parker, William N. "Problemi e prospettive di storia americana: l'agricoltura negli Stati Uniti del Nord [Problems and Perspectives of American History: Agriculture in the Northern United States]," *Quaderni storici*, (14), August 1970, pp. 393-415.

Parker, William N. "Productivity Growth in American Grain Farming: An Analysis of Its 19th Century Sources," in Fogel and Engerman, eds. *The Reinterpretation of American Economic History*, 1971, pp. 175-86.

Parker, William N. "Agriculture," in Davis, Easterlin, and Parker, eds. *American Economic Growth*, 1972, pp. 369-417.

Ransom, Roger L. and Sutch, Richard C. "The Impact of the Civil War and of Emancipation on Southern Agriculture," *Explorations in Economic History*, 12(1), January 1975, pp. 1-28.

Ransom, Roger L. and Sutch, Richard C. "Economic Dimensions of Reconstruction: An Overview," [Working Paper].

Rothstein, Morton. "The International Market for Agricultural Commodities, 1850-1873," in Gilchrist and Lewis, eds. *Economic Change in the Civil War Era*, 1965, pp. 62-72.

Shepherd, James F. "The Development of Wheat Production in the Pacific Northwest," *Agricultural History*, 49(1), January 1975, pp. 258-71.

Swan, Dale E. "The Structure and Profitability of the Antebellum Rice Industry: 1859," (Summary of Doctoral Dissertation) *Journal of Economic History*, 33(1), March 1973, pp. 321-25.

Temin, Peter. "The Causes of Cotton-Price Fluctuations in the 1830's," *Review of Economics and Statistics*, 46(4), November 1967, pp. 463-70.

Temin, Peter. "The Postbellum Recovery of the South and the Cost of the Civil War," *Journal of Economic History*, 36(4), December 1976, pp. 898-907.

Temin, Peter. "The Postbellum Recovery of the South and the Cost of the Civil War: A Reply to Goldin and Lewis," *Journal of Economic History*, 38(2), June 1978, pp. 493.

Towne, Marvin W. and Rasmussen, Wayne D. "Farm Gross Product and Gross Investment in the Nineteenth Century," in Parker, ed. *Trends in the American Economy in the Nineteenth Century (Studies in Income and Wealth*, vol. 24), 1960, pp. 255-312.

Vedder, Richard K.; Gallaway, Lowell E. and Klingman, David C. "The Profitability of Antebellum Agriculture in the Cotton Belt: Some New Evidence," *Atlantic Economic Journal*, 2(2), November 1974, pp. 30-47.

Whitten, David O. "Tariff and Profit in the Antebellum Louisiana Sugar Industry," (Abstract Appears in the *Journal of Economic Literature*, 9(1), March 1971, pp. 306) *Business History Review*, 44(2), Summer 1970, pp. 226-33.

Wright, Gavin. "Note on the Manuscript Census Samples," William N. Parker, ed. The Structure of the Cotton Economy of the Antebellum South Washington, D.C.: Agricultural History Society, 1970, pp. 95-99.

Wright, Gavin. "An Econometric Study of Cotton Production and Trade, 1830-1860," *Review of Economics and Statistics*, 53(2), May 1971, pp. 111-20.

Wright, Gavin. "Cotton Competition and the Postbellum Recovery of the American South," *Journal of Economic History*, 34(3), September 1974, pp. 610-35.

Wright, Gavin and Kunreuther, Howard. "Cotton, Corn, and Risk in the Nineteenth Century," *Journal of Economic History*, 35(3), September 1975, pp. 526-51.

Wright, Gavin. "Slavery and the Cotton Boom," (Symposium on Time on the Cross. Edited by Gary M. Walton) *Explorations in Economic History*, 12(4), October 1975, pp. 439-52.

Wright, Gavin. *The Political Economy of the Cotton South: Households, Markets, and Wealth in the Nineteenth Century.* New York: W.W. Norton, 1978.

Wright, Gavin. "World Demand for Cotton during the Nineteenth Century: Reply to Hanson," *Journal of Economic History*, 39(4), December 1979, pp. 1023-24.

European Agriculture

Allen, Robert C. "The Efficiency and Distributional Consequences of Eighteenth Century Enclosures," University of British Columbia Department of Economics Discussion Paper no. 79-18, April 1979 [Working Paper].

Baack, Bennett D. and Thomas, Robert P. "The Enclosure Movement and the Supply of Labor During the Industrial Revolution," *Journal of European Economic History*, 3(2), Fall 1974, pp. 401-23.

Baker, A.R.H. "Observations on the Open Fields: The Present Position of Studies in British Field Systems," *Journal of Historical Geography*, 5(3), July 1979, pp. 315-23.

Cohen, Jon S. and Weitzman, Martin L. "A Mathematical Model of Enclosures," in Los and Los, eds. *Mathematical Models in Economics*, 1974.

Cohen, Jon S. and Weitzman, Martin L. "Enclosures and Depopulation: A Marxian Analysis," in Parker and Jones, eds. *European Peasants and Their Markets*, 1975, pp. 161-76.

Cohen, Jon S. and Weitzman, Martin L. "A Marxian Model of Enclosures," *Journal of Development Economics*, 1(4), February 1975, pp. 287-336.

Cohen, Jon S. and Weitzman, Martin L. "A Marxian Model of Enclosures: Reply to Fenoaltea," *Journal of Development Economics*, 3(2), July 1976, pp. 199-200.

Crafts, N.F.R. "Determinants of the Rate of Parliamentary Enclosure," *Explorations in Economic History*, 14(3), July 1977, pp. 227-49.

Crafts, N.F.R. "Enclosure and Labor Supply Revisited," *Explorations in Economic History*, 15(2), April 1978, pp. 172-83.

Dahlman, Carl J. *The Open Field System and Beyond*. New York: Cambridge University Press, 1979.

Dahlman, Carl J. "An Economic Theory of Serfdom," [Working Paper].

Fenoaltea, Stefano. "The Rise and Fall of a Theoretical Model: The Manorial System," *Journal of Economic History*, 35(2), June 1975, pp. 386-409.

Fenoaltea, Stefano. "Authority, Efficiency, and Agricultural Organization in Medieval England and Beyond: A Hypothesis," *Journal of Economic History*, 35(4), December 1975, pp. 693-718.

Fenoaltea, Stefano. "Risk, Transaction Costs, and the Organization of Medieval Agriculture," *Explorations in Economic History*, 13(2), April 1976, pp. 129-51.

Fenoaltea, Stefano. "On a Marxian Model of Enclosures: Comment on Cohen and Weitzman," *Journal of Development Economics*, 3(2), June 1976, pp. 195-98.

Fenoaltea, Stefano. "Fenoaltea on Open Fields: A Reply to McCloskey," *Explorations in Economic History*, 14(4), October 1977, pp. 405-10.

Grantham, George W. "The Persistence of Open-Field Farming in Nineteenth-Century France," *Journal of Economic History*, 40(3), September 1980, pp. 515-31.

Jones, Andrew. "The Rise and Fall of the Manorial System: A Critical Comment (on North and Thomas)," *Journal of Economic History*, 32(4), December 1972, pp. 938-44.

Komlos, John. "The Emancipation of the Hungarian Peasantry and Agricultural Development," in Volgyes, ed. *The East European Peasantry*, 1979, pp. 109-18.

Lazonick, William H. "Karl Marx and Enclosures in England," *Review of Radical Political Economics*, 6(2), Summer 1974, pp. 1-32.

Linneman, Peter D. "An Econometric Examination of the English Parlimentary Enclosure Movement," *Explorations in Economic History*, 15(2), April 1978, pp. 221-28.

Mazur, Michael P. "The Dispersion of Holdings in the Open Fields: An Interpretation in Terms of Property Rights," *Journal of European Economic History*, 6(2), Fall 1977, pp. 461-71.

Mazur, Michael P. "Scattering in Open Fields: Reply to McCloskey," *Journal of European Economic History*, 9(1), Spring 1980, pp. 215-18.

McCloskey, Donald N. "The Enclosure of Open Fields: Preface to a Study of Its Impact on the Efficiency of English Agriculture in the Eighteenth Century," *Journal of Economic History*, 32(1), March 1972, pp. 15-35.

McCloskey, Donald N. "The Economics of Enclosure: A Market Analysis," in Parker and Jones, eds. *European Peasants and Their Markets*, 1975, pp. 123-60.

McCloskey, Donald N. "The Persistence of English Common Fields," in Parker and Jones, eds. *European Peasants and Their Markets*, 1975, pp. 73-119.

McCloskey, Donald N. "English Open Fields as Behavior toward Risk," in Uselding, ed. *Research in Economic History*, vol. 1, 1976.

McCloskey, Donald N. "Fenoaltea on Open Fields: A Comment," *Explorations in Economic History*, 14(4), October 1977, pp. 402-4.

McCloskey, Donald N. "Explaining Open Fields: A Reply to Professor Charles Wilson," *Journal of European Economic History*, 8(1), Spring 1979, pp. 193-202.

McCloskey, Donald N. "Another Way of Observing Open Fields: A Reply to A.R.H. Baker," *Journal of Historical Geography*, 5(4), October 1979, pp. 426-29.

McCloskey, Donald N. "Scattering in Open Fields: A Comment on Mazur," *Journal of European Economic History*, 9(1), Spring 1980, pp. 209-214.

McCloskey, Donald N. "A Working Bibliography on English Open Fields and Enclosure," [Working Paper].

McCloskey, Donald N. "The Mathematics of the Fisheries Case Applied to Open Fields," [Working Paper].

Miller, Edward. "England in the Twelfth and Thirteenth Centuries: An Economic Contrast?" *Economic History Review*, Second Series, 24(1), February 1971, pp. 1-14.

Miller, Edward. "Farming of Manors and Direct Management: Rejoinder (to Reed and Anderson)," *Economic History Review*, Second Series, 26(1), February 1973, pp. 138-40.

Murphy, Earl F. "Comment on Papers by McCloskey, McManus, and Landes and Solmon Presented to the 31st Annual Meeting of the Economic History Association," *Journal of Economic History*, 32(1), March 1972, pp. 95-97.

North, Douglass C. and Thomas, Robert P. "An Economic Theory of the

Growth of the Western World," *Economic History Review*, Second Series, 23(1), April 1970, pp. 1-17.

North, Douglass C. and Thomas, Robert P. "The Rise and Fall of the Manorial System: A Theoretical Model," *Journal of Economic History*, 31(4), December 1971, pp. 777-803.

North, Douglass C. and Thomas, Robert P. "European Economic Growth: Reply to Professor D. Ringose," *Economic History Review*, Second Series, 26(2), May 1973, pp. 293-94.

Philpot, Gordon. "Enclosure and Population Growth in Eighteenth-Century England," *Explorations in Economic History*, 12(1), January 1975, pp. 29-46.

Philpot, Gordon. "Parliamentary Enclosure and Population Change in England, 1750-1830: A Reply to Turner," *Explorations in Economic History*, 13(4), October 1976, pp. 469-71.

Purdum, Jack J. "Profitability and Timing of Parliamentary Land Enclosures," *Explorations in Economic History*, 15(3), July 1978, pp. 313-26.

Reed, Clyde G. and Anderson, Terry L. "An Economic Explanation of English Agricultural Organization in the Twelfth and Thirteenth Centuries: Comment on Miller," *Economic History Review*, Second Series, 26(1), February 1973, pp. 134-37.

Ringrose, D.R. "European Economic Growth: Comments on the North-Thomas Theory," *Economic History Review*, Second Series, 26(2), May 1973, pp. 285-92.

Roehl, Richard. "Plan and Reality in a Medieval Monastic Economy: The Cistercians," (Summary of Doctoral Dissertation) *Journal of Economic History*, 29(1), March 1969, pp. 180-82.

Salsbury, Stephen. "Comment on Papers by McCloskey, McManus, and Landes and Solmon Presented to the 31st Annual Meeting of the Economic History Association," *Journal of Economic History*, 32(1), March 1972, pp. 92-94.

Tomaske, John A. "Enclosures and Population Movement in England, 1700-1830: A Methodological Comment (on White)," *Explorations in Economic History*, 8(2), Winter 1970/71, pp. 223-28.

Turner, Michael. "Parliamentary Enclosure and Population Change in England, 1750-1830: A Comment on Philpot," *Explorations in Economic History*, 13(4), October 1976, pp. 463-68.

White, Lawrence J. "Enclosures and Population Movement in England, 1700-1830," *Explorations in Entrepreneurial History*, Second Series, 6(2), Winter 1969, pp. 175-86.

Wilson, Charles. "Explaining Open Fields: A Letter to Professor McCloskey," *Journal of European Economic History*, 8(1), Spring 1979, pp. 193-202.

Other: Inputs and Institutions

Abramovitz, Moses. "Sources of Agricultural Growth in Japan, 1880-1965: Comment (on Akino and Hayami)," in Ohkawa and Hayami, eds. *Economic Growth*, vol. 1, 1973, pp. 213-19.

Adelman, Irma and Morris, Cynthia Taft. "The Role of Institutional Influences in Patterns of Agricultural Development in the

Nineteenth and Early Twentieth Centuries: A Cross-Section Quantitative Study," *Journal of Economic History*, 39(1), March 1979, pp. 159-76.

Akino, Masakatsu and Hayami, Yujiro. "Sources of Agricultural Growth in Japan, 1880-1965," *Quarterly Journal of Economics*, 88(3), August 1974, pp. 454-79.

Almquist, Eric L. "Mayo and Beyond: Land, Domestic Industry, and Rural Transformation in the Irish West," (Summary of Doctoral Dissertation) *Journal of Economic History*, 39(1), March 1979, pp. 323-24.

Ankli, Robert E. and Litt, R.M. "The Growth of Prairie Agriculture: Economic Considerations," *Canadian Papers in Rural History*, 1, 1978, pp. 35-64.

Borins, S.F. "Econometric Modelling of the Settlement Process in Western Canada and of the Effect of Government Land and Railroad Policy on the Spatial and Temporal Nature of the Process," [Working Paper].

Butlin, Noel G. "Distribution of the Sheep Population: Preliminary Statistical Picture, 1860-1957," A. Barnard, ed. A Simple Fleece Canberra: Australian National University, 1962, pp. 281-307.

Butlin, Noel G. "Pastoral Finance and Capital Requirements, 1860-1960," A. Barnard, ed. A Simple Fleece Canberra: Australian National University, 1962, pp. 383-400.

Chambers, Edward J. and Gordon, Donald F. "Primary Products and Economic Growth: An Empirical Measurement," [Translated into Spanish in *Journal of the Fundacion de Investigationes Economicas Lationoamericanas*] *Journal of Political Economy*, 74(4), August 1966, pp. 315-32.

Chambers, Edward J. and Gordon, Donald F. "Primary Products and Economic Growth: Rejoinder to Dales, McManus, and Watkins," *Journal of Political Economy*, 75(6), December 1967, pp. 881-85.

Cohen, Jon S. "Un esame statistico delle opere di bonifica intraprese durante il regime fascista [A Statistical Examination of Land Reclamation under Fascism]," in Toniolo, ed. *Lo sviluppo economico italiano, 1861-1940 [The Economic Development of Italy, 1861-1940]*, 1973.

Crafts, N.F.R. "Income Elasticities of Demand and the Release of Labour by Agriculture during the British Industrial Revolution," *Journal of European Economic History*, 9(1), Spring 1980, pp. 153-68.

Dales, John H.; McManus, John C. and Watkins, Melville H. "Primary Products and Economic Growth: A Comment on Chambers and Gordon," *Journal of Political Economy*, 75(6), December 1967, pp. 876-80.

Darby, Michael R. "Three and-a-Half Million U.S. Employees Have Been Mislaid: Or, an Explanation of Unemployment, 1934-1941," *Journal of Political Economy*, 84(1), February 1976, pp. 1-16.

David, Paul A. "The Landscape and the Machine: Technical Interrelatedness, Land Tenure and the Mechanization of the Corn Harvest in Victorian Britain," in McCloskey, ed. *Essays on a Mature Economy: Britain after 1840*, 1971, pp. 145-204.

De Vries, Jan. "Conditions of Agricultural Growth: Boserup as Economics and History," *Peasant Studies Newsletter*, 1(2), April

1972, pp. 45-50.

De Vries, Jan. *The Dutch Rural Economy in the Golden Age, 1500-1700.* New Haven: Yale University Press, 1974.

Dickler, Robert A. "Organization and Change in Productivity in Eastern Prussia," in Parker and Jones, eds. *European Peasants and Their Markets,* 1975, pp. 269-92.

Dittrich, Scott R. and Myers, Ramon H. "Resource Allocation in Traditional Agriculture: Republican China, 1937-1940," *Journal of Political Economy,* 79(4), July/August 1971, pp. 887-96.

Eddie, Scott M. "The Changing Pattern of Landownership in Hungary, 1867-1914," *Economic History Review,* Second Series, 20(2), August 1967, pp. 293-310.

Eddie, Scott M. and Puskas, J. "Landownership Structure in Hungary," Hungarian Academy of Sciences Historical Institute Working Paper [Working Paper].

Feeny, David H. "Induced Technical and Institutional Change: A Thai Case Study," in Means, ed. *The Past in Southeast Asia's Present,* 1978, pp. 56-69.

Feeny, David H. "Competing Hypotheses of Underdevelopment: A Thai Case Study," *Journal of Economic History,* 39(1), March 1979, pp. 113-27.

Feeny, David H. "Paddy, Princes, and Productivity: Irrigation and Thai Agricultural Development, 1900-1940," *Explorations in Economic History,* 16(2), April 1979, pp. 132-50.

Feeny, David H. "Technical and Institutional Change in Thai Agriculture, 1880-1940," Ph.D. Dissertation, University of Wisconsin-Madison, 1976 [Working Paper].

Gagan, David P. "The Indivisibility of Land: A Microanalysis of the System of Inheritance in Nineteenth-Century Ontario," *Journal of Economic History,* 36(1), March 1976, pp. 126-41.

Gemery, Henry A. and Hogendorn, Jan S. "Comparative Disadvantage: The Case of Sugar Cultivation in West Africa," *Journal of Interdisciplinary History,* 9(3), Winter 1979, pp. 429-50.

Gould, John D. "The Landscape and the Machine: A Comment on David," *Economic History Review,* Second Series, 27(3), August 1974, pp. 455-60.

Grant, Kenneth G. "The Rate of Settlement of Canadian Provinces, 1870-1911: A Comment on Norrie," *Journal of Economic History,* 38(2), June 1978, pp. 471-73.

Grantham, George W. "Scale and Organization in French Farming, 1840-1880," in Parker and Jones, eds. *European Peasants and Their Markets,* 1975, pp. 293-326.

Grantham, George W. "The Diffusion of the New Husbandry in Northern France, 1815-1840," *Journal of Economic History,* 38(2), June 1978, pp. 311-37.

Hayami, Yujiro and Ruttan, V.W. "Factor Prices and Technical Changes in Agricultural Development: The United States and Japan, 1880-1960," *Journal of Political Economy,* 78(5), September/October 1970, pp. 1115-41.

Hayami, Yujiro. "Elements of Induced Innovation: A Historical Perspective for the Green Revolution," *Explorations in Economic History,* 8(4), Summer 1971, pp. 445-72.

Hayami, Yujiro. "Conditions for the Diffusion of Agricultural

Technology: An Asian Perspective," *Journal of Economic History*, 34(1), March 1974, pp. 131-48.

Hayami, Yujiro; Ruttan, Vernon W.; Binswanger, Hans P.; Wade, W.W. and Weber, A. "Factor Productivity and Growth: A Historical Interpretation," in Binswanger, Ruttan, et al., eds. *Induced Innovation*, 1978.

Higgs, Robert. "Property Rights and Resource Allocation under Alternative Land Tenure Forms: A Comment on Sau," *Oxford Economic Papers*, New Series, 24(3), November 1972, pp. 428-31.

Hogendorn, Jan S. "Economic Initiative and African Cash Farming: Precolonial Origins and Early Colonial Developments," in Duignan and Gann, eds. *Colonialism in Africa, 1870-1960*, vol. 4, 1975.

Hueckel, Glenn. "Relative Prices and Supply Response in English Agriculture during the Napoleonic Wars," *Economic History Review*, Second Series, 29(3), August 1976, pp. 401-14.

Hueckel, Glenn. "Agriculture during Industrialization," in Floud and McCloskey, eds. *The Economic History of Britain since 1700*, vol. 1, 1980, pp. 182-202.

Jones, Eric L. "Agriculture, 1700-80," in Floud and McCloskey, eds. *The Economic History of Britain since 1700*, vol. 1, 1980, pp. 66-86.

Kelley, Allen C. and Williamson, Jeffrey G. "General Equilibrium Analysis of Agricultural Development: The Case of Meiji Japan," in Reynolds, ed. *Agricultural Development and Theory*, 1974.

Kessinger, Tom G. "The Peasant Farm in North India, 1848-1968," (Symposium on Economic Change in Indian Agriculture, edited by Morris D. Morris) *Explorations in Economic History*, 12(3), July 1975, pp. 303-331.

Komlos, John. "The Emancipation of the Hungarian Peasantry and Agricultural Development," in Volgyes, ed. *The East European Peasantry*, 1979, pp. 109-18.

Komlos, John. "Astro-Hungarian Agricultural Development, 1827-1877," *Journal of European Economic History*, 8(1), Spring 1979, pp. 37-60.

Kumar, Dhumar. *Land and Caste in South India: Agricultural Labor in the Madras Presidency during the Nineteenth Century.* Cambridge: Cambridge University Press, 1965.

Levy-Leboyer, Maurice. "Les Inegalites Regionales de Croissance dans L'Agriculture Francaise, 1823-1939 [Regional Inequalities of Growth in French Agriculture, 1823-1939]," in Bairoch and Levy-Leboyer, eds. *Disparities in Economic Development since the Industrial Revolution*, 1980.

Lewis, Frank D. and McInnis, R. Marvin. "The Efficiency of the French-Canadian Farmer in the Nineteenth Century," *Journal of Economic History*, 40(3), September 1980, pp. 497-514.

Lobdell, Richard A. "Patterns of Investment and Sources of Credit in the British West Indian Sugar Industry, 1838-97," *Journal of Caribbean History*, 4, May 1972, pp. 31-53.

Marr, William L. and Percy, Michael. "The Government and the Rate of Canadian Prairie Settlement (Comment on Norrie)," *Canadian Journal of Economics*, 11(4), November 1978, pp. 757-67.

McAlpin, Michelle Burge. "Comments on Dissertations by Almquist and Kussmaul Presented to the 38th Annual Meeting of the Economic

History Association," *Journal of Economic History*, 39(1), March 1979, pp. 338-39.

McAlpin, Michelle Burge. "Railroads, Prices, and Peasant Rationality: India, 1860-1900," *Journal of Economic History*, 34(3), September 1974, pp. 662-84.

McInnis, R. Marvin. "The Indivisibility of Land: A Microanalysis of the System of Inheritance in Nineteenth-Century Ontario (A Comment on Gagan)," *Journal of Economic History*, 36(1), March 1976, pp. 142-46.

McLean, Ian W. "The Adoption of Harvest Machinery in Victoria in the Late Nineteenth Century," *Australian Economic History Review*, 13(1), March 1973, pp. 41-56.

McLean, Ian W. "Growth and Technological Change in Agriculture: Victoria, 1870-1910," Economic Record, 49(128), December 1973, pp. 560-74.

McLean, Ian W. "Growth and Technological Change in Agriculture: A Reply (to Powell)," *Economic Record*, 50(132), December 1974, pp. 620-22.

McLean, Ian W. "Rural Output, Inputs, and Mechanisation in Victoria, 1870-1910," Ph.D. Dissertation, Australian National University, 1971 [Working Paper].

Mendels, Franklin F. "Agriculture and Peasant Industry in Eighteenth-Century Flanders," in Parker and Jones, eds. *European Peasants and Their Markets*, 1975, pp. 179-204.

Mendels, Franklin F. "La Composition du Menage Paysan en France au XIXe Siecle: Une Analyse Economique du Mode de Production Domestique [The Makeup of the French Country Household in the 19th Century: an Economic Analysis along the Line of Domestic Production]," *Annales: Economies, Societes, Civilisations*, 33(4), July/August 1978, pp. 780-802.

Minami, Ryoshin. "Sources of Agricultural Growth in Japan, 1880-1965: Comment on Akino and Hayami," in Ohkawa and Hayami, eds. *Economic Growth*, vol. 1, 1973, pp. 219-31.

Morineau, Michel. "The Agricultural Revolution in Nineteenth-Century France: Comment on Newell," *Journal of Economic History*, 36(2), June 1976, pp. 436-37.

Morris, Morris D. "The Problem of the Peasant Agriculturist in Meiji Japan, 1873-1885," *Far Eastern Quarterly*, 15(3), May 1956, pp. 357-70.

Morris, Morris D. "Economic Change and Agriculture in 19th Century India," *Indian Economic and Social History Review*, 3(2), June 1966, pp. 185-209.

Morris, Morris D. "Introduction to a Symposium on Economic Change in Indian Agriculture," *Explorations in Economic History*, 12(3), July 1975, pp. 253-61.

Newell, William H. "The Agricultural Revolution in Nineteenth-Century France," *Journal of Economic History*, 33(4), December 1973, pp. 697-731.

Newell, William H. "The Agricultural Revolution in Nineteenth-Century France: Reply to Morineau," *Journal of Economic History*, 36(2), June 1976, pp. 438.

Newell, William H. *Population Change and Agricultural Development in*

Nineteenth Century France. New York: Arno Press, 1977.

Nghiep, Le Thanh and Hayami, Yujiro. "Mobilizing Slack Resources for Economic Development: The Summer-Fall Reaping Technology of Sericulture in Japan," *Explorations in Economic History,* 16(2), April 1979, pp. 163-81.

Nicholas, Stephen J. and Dziegielewski, M. "Supply Elasticities, Rationality and Structural Change in Irish Agriculture, 1850-1925: Comment on O'Grada," *Economic History Review,* Second Series, 33(3), August 1980, pp. 411-14.

Nicholas, Stephen J. "The Staple Theory of Economic Development: An Economic Criticism," University of New South Wales Working Paper in Economic History, 1976 [Working Paper].

Nishikawa, Shunsaku. "Productivity, Subsistence, and By-Employment in the Mid-Nineteenth Century Choshu," (Erratum: a correction for this article appears in 15(3), July 1978, p. 338 of this journal) *Explorations in Economic History,* 15(1), January 1978, pp. 69-83.

Norrie, Kenneth H. "Agricultural Implement Tariffs, the National Policy, and Income Distribution in the Wheat Economy," *Canadian Journal of Economics,* 7(3), August 1974, pp. 449-62.

Norrie, Kenneth H. "The Rate of Settlement of the Canadian Prairies, 1870-1911," *Journal of Economic History,* 35(2), June 1975, pp. 410-27.

Norrie, Kenneth H. "Dry Farming and the Economics of Risk Bearing: The Canadian Prairies, 1870-1930," *Agricultural History,* 51(1), January 1977, pp. 134-48.

Norrie, Kenneth H. "The Rate of Settlement of the Canadian Prairies, 1870-1911: A Reply to Grant," *Journal of Economic History,* 38(2), June 1978, pp. 474-75.

Norrie, Kenneth H. "Cultivation Techniques as a Response to Risk in Early Canadian Prairie Agriculture," *Explorations in Economic History,* 17(4), October 1980, pp. 386-99.

Norrie, Kenneth H. "Canadian Pacific Railroad Land Sale: A Model of the Sale and Pricing of the Canadian Pacific Railroad Land Grant," [Working Paper].

North, Douglass C. and Thomas, Robert P. "The First Economic Revolution," *Economic History Review,* Second Series, 30(2), May 1977, pp. 229-41.

O'Brien, Patrick K. and Heath, D., Keyder, C. "Agriculture in Britain and France, 1815-1914," *Journal of European Economic History,* 6(2), Fall 1977, pp. 339-91.

O'Grada, Cormac. "Supply Responsiveness in Irish Agriculture during the Nineteenth Century," *Economic History Review,* Second Series, 28(2), May 1975, pp. 312-17.

O'Grada, Cormac. "The Beginnings of the Irish Creamery System, 1880-1914," *Economic History Review,* Second Series, 30(2), May 1977, pp. 284-305.

O'Grada, Cormac. "The Landlord and Agricultural Transformation, 1870-1900: A Comment on Richard Perren's Hypothesis," *Agricultural History Review,* 27(1), 1979, pp. 40-42.

O'Grada, Cormac. "Agricultural Decline, 1860-1914," in Floud and McCloskey, eds. *The Economic History of Britain since 1700,* vol. 2, 1980.

O'Grada, Cormac. "Supply Elasticities in Irish Agriculture: A Reply to Nicholas and Dziegielewski," *Economic History Review*, Second Series, 33(3), August 1980, pp. 415-16.

Offer, Avner. "Ricardo's Paradox and the Movement of Rent, c. 1870-1910," *Economic History Review*, Second Series, 33(2), May 1980, pp. 236-52.

Olsen, Bernard M. "Measurement of 18th and 19th century agricultural productivity in Sweden," [Working Paper].

Olsson, Carl-Axel. "Estimates of the Aggregate Swedish Farm Supply Function, 1935-1950: Some Preliminary Results," *Economy and History*, 17), 1974, pp. 3-19.

Paquet, Gilles and Wallot, Jean-Pierre. "Crise agricole et tensions socio-techniques dans le Bas Canada au tournant du XIXe siecle," *Revue d'Histoire de l'Amerique Francaise*, 26(2), September 1972, pp. 185-237.

Paquet, Gilles and Wallot, Jean-Pierre. "The Agricultural Crisis in Lower Canada, 1802-1812: mise au point," *Canadian Historical Review*, 56(2), June 1975, pp. 133-61.

Paquet, Gilles and Wallot, Jean-Pierre. "Rentes foncieres, dimes et revenus paysans: le cas canadien," in Ladurie and Goy, eds. *Prestations paysannes, dimes, rente fonciere et mouvement de la production agricole a l'epoque pre-industrielle.*

Parker, William N. and Jones, Eric L., eds. *European Peasants and Their Markets: Essays in European Agrarian History.* Princeton: Princeton University Press, 1975.

Parker, William N. "On a Certain Parallelism in Form between Two Historical Processes of Productivity Growth," *Agricultural History*, 50(1), January 1976, pp. 101-16.

Parker, William N. "Comment on Papers by McAlpin, Libecap and Johnson, and Adelman and Morris Presented to the 38th Annual Meeting of the Economic History Association," *Journal of Economic History*, 39(1), March 1979, pp. 177-79.

Peet, Richard. "Von Thunen Theory and the Dynamics of Agricultural Expansion," *Explorations in Economic History*, 8(2), Winter 1970/71, pp. 181-202.

Perren, Richard. "The Landlord and Agricultural Transformation, 1870-1900," *Agricultural History Review*, 18(1), 1970, pp. 36-51.

Perren, Richard. "The Landlord and Agricultural Transformation, 1870-1900: A Rejoinder (to O'Grada)," *Agricultural History Review*, 27(1), 1979, pp. 43-47.

Pomfret, Richard W.T. "The Mechanization of Reaping in Nineteenth Century Ontario: A Case Study of the Pace and Causes of the Diffusion of Embodied Technical Change," *Journal of Economic History*, 36(2), June 1976, pp. 399-415.

Pomfret, Richard W.T. *The Introduction of the Mechanical Reaper in Canada, 1850-1870.* New York: Arno Press, 1979.

Powell, R.A. "Growth and Technological Change in Agriculture: A Comment (on McLean)," *Economic Record*, 50(132), December 1974, pp. 616-19.

Richards, Alan R. "Accumulation, Distribution and Technical Change in Egyptian Agriculture: 1800-1940," (Summary of Doctoral Dissertation) *Journal of Economic History*, 36(1), March 1976, pp.

279-82.

Richards, Alan R. "Technical and Social Change in Egyptian Agriculture, 1890-1914," *Economic Development and Cultural Change*, 26(4), July 1978, pp. 725-45.

Richards, Alan R. "Land and Labor on Egyptian Cotton Farms: 1882-1940," *Agricultural History*, 52(4), October 1978, pp. 503-18.

Ruttan, Vernon W. "Structural Retardation and the Modernization of French Agriculture: A Skeptical View," *Journal of Economic History*, 38(3), September 1978, pp. 714-28.

Sau, R.K. "Land Tenancy, Rent, and the Optimal Terms of Trade between Industry and Agriculture," *Oxford Economic Papers*, New Series, 23(3), November 1971.

Schremmer, Eckart. "Industrielle Ruckstandigkeit und Strukturstabilisierender Fortschritt. Uber den Einsatz von Produktionsfaktoren in der Deutschen (Land-)Wirtschaft zwischen 1850 und 1913 [Industrial Backwardness and Structure-stabilizing Progress: On the Input of Factors of Production in German Agriculture Between 1850 and 1913]," in Kellenbenz, ed. *Wirtschaftswachstum, Energie und Verkehr vom Mittelalter bis ins 19. Jahrhundert*, 1978, pp. 205-33.

Solow, Barbara Lewis. "The Irish Land Question After 1870," (Summary of Doctoral Dissertation) *Journal of Economic History*, 27(4), December 1967, pp. 618-20.

Solow, Barbara Lewis. *The Land Question and the Irish Economy, 1870-1903*. Cambridge: Harvard University Press, 1971.

Taira, Koji. "*Growth, Trends, and Swings in Japanese Agriculture and Industry*," (Review essay of *Agriculture and Economic Growth*, by Ohkawa, Johnston, and Kaneda, eds., 1970) *Economic Development and Cultural Change*, 24(2), January 1976, pp. 423-36.

Tattara, Giuseppe. "Cerealicultura e politica agraria durante il fascismo [Cereal Production and Agricultural Policy under Fascism]," (Reprinted in Toniolo, ed. *L'economia italiana 1861-1940*, 1978) in Gianni Toniolo, ed. *Lo sviluppo economico italiano 1861-1940 [Italian Economic Development, 1861-1940]*. Bari: Laterza, 1973, pp. 373-405.

Yamamura, Kozo. "A Comparative Analysis of Changes in Preindustrial Landholding Patterns and Systems in Japan and in England," in Craig, ed. *The Japanese Experience*, 1978.

Zamagni, Vera. "Le radici agricole del dualismo italiano [The Agricultural Roots of Italian Dualism]," *Nuova rivista storica*, 59(1-2), January-April 1975, pp. 55-99.

Other: Outputs

Bairoch, Paul. "L'agriculture et le processus d'industrialisation aux XVIIIe et XIXe siecles [Agriculture and the Process of Industrialization in the Eighteenth and Nineteenth Centuries]," *Cahiers de L'Institut de Science Economique Appliquee*, Serie AG(10), May 1972, pp. 1113-32.

Bengtsson, Tommy and Jorberg, Lennart. "Market Integration in Sweden during the 18th and 19th Centuries: Spectral Analysis of Grain

Prices," *Economy and History*, 18(2), 1975, pp. 93-106.

Blyn, George. *Agricultural Trends in India, 1891-1947: Output, Availability, and Productivity.* Philadelphia: University of Pennsylvania Press, 1966.

Cohen, Jon S. "Rapporti agricoltura-industria e sviluppo agricolo [Agricultural-Industrial Relationships and Agricultural Development]," in Toniolo and Ciocca, eds. *L'economia italiana nel periodo fascista [The Italian Economy during the Fascist Era],* 1976.

David, Paul A. "Labour Productivity in English Agriculture, 1850-1914: Some Quantitative Evidence on Regional Differences," *Economic History Review*, Second Series, 23(3), December 1970, pp. 504-14.

Dick, Trevor J.O. "Productivity Change and Grain Farm Practice on the Canadian Prairie, 1900-1930," *Journal of Economic History*, 40(1), March 1980, pp. 105-10.

Dick, Trevor J.O. "Canadian Wheat Production and Trade, 1896-1930," *Explorations in Economic History*, 17(3), July 1980, pp. 275-302.

Dick, Trevor J.O. "Changing Patterns of Grain Farm Practice on the Canadian Prairie, 1885-1930," [Working Paper].

Eddie, Scott M. "Agricultural Production and Output per Worker in Hungary, 1870-1913," *Journal of Economic History*, 28(2), June 1968, pp. 197-222.

Eddie, Scott M. "Die Landwirtschaft als Quelle des Arbeitskraft-Angebots: Mutmassungen aus der Geschichte Ungarns, 1870 BIS 1913," *Vierteljahrschrift fur Sozial-und Wirtschaftsgeschite*, 56(2), September 1969, pp. 215-32.

Eddie, Scott M. "Farmers' Response to Price in Large-Estate Agriculture: Hungary, 1870-1913," *Economic History Review*, Second Series, 24(4), November 1971, pp. 571-88.

Ellman, Michael. "Did Agricultural Surplus Provide for the Increase in Investment in the USSR During the First Five Year Plan?" *Economic Journal*, 85(340), December 1975, pp. 844-63.

Feeny, David H. "Productivity Change and Grain Farm Practice on the Canadian Prairie, 1900-1930: A Discussion of Dick," *Journal of Economic History*, 40(1), March 1980, pp. 119-20.

Fei, John C. "The 'Standard Market' of Traditional China," Dwight H. Perkins, ed. China's Modern Economy in Historical Perspective Stanford: Stanford University Press, 1975, pp. 235-59.

Fremdling, Rainer and Hohorst, Gerd. "Marktintegration der Preussischen Wirtschaft im 19. Jahrhundert: Skizze eines Forschungsansatzes zur Fluktuation der Roggenpreise zwischen 1821 und 1865 [Market Integration of the Prussian Economy in the 19th Century: Preliminary Findings on Fluctuations of Rye Prices Between 1821 and 1865]," in Fremdling and Tilly, eds. *Industrialisierung und Raum: Studien zur Regionalen Differenzierung in Deutschland in 19,* 1979.

Freund, W.M. and Shenton, R.W. "'Vent-for-Surplus' Theory and the Economic History of West Africa," *Savanna*, 6(2), December 1977, pp. 191-6.

Fua, Giorgio. "Declino dell'agricoltura e legge di Engel nell'esperienza italiana, 1897-1967 [Agricultural Decline and Engel's Law in the Italian Experience, 1897-1967]," *Moneta e credito*, (107), September 1974.

Gould, John D. "Agricultural Fluctuations and the English Economy in the Eighteenth Century," *Journal of Economic History*, 22(3), September 1962, pp. 313-33.

Granger, C.W.J. and Elliott, C.M. "A Fresh Look at Wheat Prices and Markets in the Eighteenth Century," *Economic History Review*, Second Series, 20(2), August 1967, pp. 257-65.

Gregory, Paul R. "Grain Marketings and Peasant Consumption, Russia, 1885-1913," *Explorations in Economic History*, 17(2), April 1980, pp. 135-64.

Haines, Michael R. "The Role of Agriculture in Economic Development: A Regional Case Study of Prussian Upper Silesia, 1846-1913," *Journal of Economic History*, forthcoming.

Harley, C. Knick. "Western Settlement and the Price of Wheat, 1872-1913," Journal of Economic History, 38(4), December 1978, pp. 865-78.

Harnetty, Peter. "Cotton Exports and Indian Agriculture, 1861-1870," *Economic History Review*, Second Series, 24(3), August 1971, pp. 414-29.

Hayami, Yujiro and Yamada, Saburo. "Agricultural Productivity at the Beginning of Industrialization," in Ohkawa, Johnston, and Kaneda, eds. *Agriculture and Economic Growth*, 1970, pp. 105-35.

Hayami, Yujiro, in association with Akino, Masakatsu; Shintani, Masahiko and Yamada, Saburo. *A Century of Agricultural Growth in Japan: Its Relevance to Asian Development*. Tokyo and Minneapolis: University of Tokyo Press and University of Minnesota Press, 1975.

Heston, Alan W. "Official Yields Per Acre in India, 1886-1947: Some Questions of Interpretation," *Indian Economic and Social History Review*, 10(4), December 1973, pp. 303-32.

Ho, Samuel Pao-San. "Agricultural Transformation Under Colonialism: The Case of Taiwan," *Journal of Economic History*, 28(3), September 1968, pp. 313-40.

Hogendorn, Jan S. "The Vent for Surplus Model and African Cash Agriculture to 1914," *Savanna*, 5(1), June 1976, pp. 15-28.

Hogendorn, Jan S. "Vent-For Surplus Theory: A Reply to Freund and Shenton," *Savanna*, 6(2), December 1977, pp. 196-99.

Hogendorn, Jan S. and Gemery, Henry A. "Comparative Disadvantage: The Case of Sugar Cultivation in West Africa," *Journal of Interdisciplinary History*, 9(3), Winter 1979, pp. 429-50.

Hueckel, Glenn. "English Farming Profits during the Napoleonic Wars, 1793-1815," *Explorations in Economic History*, 13(3), July 1976, pp. 331-46.

Hueckel, Glenn. "Relative Prices and Supply Response in English Agriculture during the Napoleonic Wars," *Economic History Review*, 29(3), August 1976, pp. 401-14.

Hueckel, Glenn. "Agriculture during Industrialization," in Floud and McCloskey, eds. *The Economic History of Britain since 1700*, vol. 1, 1980, pp. 182-202.

Ippolito, Richard A. "The Effect of the 'Agricultural Depression' on Industrial Demand in England: 1730-1750," *Economica*, 42(167), August 1975, pp. 298-312.

Jones, Eric L. "Agriculture, 1700-80," in Floud and McCloskey, eds.

The Economic History of Britain since 1700, vol. 1, 1980, pp. 66-86.

Jorberg, Lennart and Bengtsson, Tommy. "Market Integration in Sweden during the 18th and 19th Centuries: Spectral Analysis of Grain Prices," *Economy and History*, 18(2), 1975, pp. 93-106.

Kikuchi, Masao and Hayami, Yujiro. "Agricultural Growth against a Land Resource Constraint: A Comparative History of Japan, Taiwan, Korea and the Philippines," *Journal of Economic History*, 38(4), December 1978, pp. 839-64.

Lewis, Frank D. "The Canadian Wheat Boom and Per Capita Income: New Estimates," *Journal of Political Economy*, 83(6), December 1975, pp. 1249-57.

McAlpin, Michelle Burge. "Railroads, Cultivation Patterns, and Foodgrain Availability: India, 1860-1900," *Indian Economic and Social History Review*, 12(1), January/March, 1975, pp. 43-60.

McAlpin, Michelle Burge. "Dearth, Famine, and Risk: The Changing Impact of Crop Failures in Western India, 1870-1920," *Journal of Economic History*, 39(1), March 1979, pp. 143-57.

McAlpin, Michelle Burge. "The Impact of Trade on Agricultural Development: Bombay Presidency, 1855-1920," *Explorations in Economic History*, 17(1), January 1980, pp. 26-47.

McAlpin, Michelle Burge. "Death, Famine and Changes in Risk: A Preliminary Exploration of the Changing Impact of Crop Failures in Bombay Presidency," Presented at the Workshop on 'The Effects of Risk and Uncertainty on Economic and Social Processes in South Asia' of the ACLS-SSRC Joint Committee on South Asia and the University of Pennsylvania, November 1977 [Working Paper].

McCalla, Douglas. "The Wheat Staple and Upper Canadian Development," *Canadian Historical Association: Historical Papers*, 1978, pp. 34-46.

McInnis, R. Marvin and Urquhart, Mac C. "Estimation of Historical Series of Farm Income for Canada," [Working Paper].

Morris, Cynthia Taft. "Productivity Change and Grain Farm Practice on the Canadian Prairie, 1900-1930: A Discussion of Dick," *Journal of Economic History*, 40(1), March 1980, pp. 121-22.

O'Brien, Patrick K. "The Long-Term Growth of Agricultural Production in Egypt, 1821-1962," in Holt, ed. *Political and Social Change in Modern Egypt, 1968.*

O'Brien, Patrick K. *"Agriculture and the Industrial Revolution: An Essay in Bibliography and Criticism,"* Economic History Review, Second Series, 30(1), February 1977, pp. 166-81.

O'Brien, Patrick K. and Heath, D., Keyder, C. "Agriculture in Britain and France, 1815-1914," *Journal of European Economic History*, 6(2), Fall 1977, pp. 339-91.

O'Grada, Cormac. "Agricultural Decline, 1860-1914," in Floud and McCloskey, eds. *The Economic History of Britain since 1700*, vol. 2, 1980.

O'Grada, Cormac. "Productivity Growth in Irish Agriculture, 1845-1926," [Working Paper].

Olson, Mancur L. and Harris, Jr., Curtis C. "Free Trade in 'Corn': A Statistical Study of the Prices and Production of Wheat in Great Britain from 1873 to 1914," (Reprinted in Floud, ed. *Essays in*

Quantitative Economic History, 1974, pp. 196-215) *Quarterly Journal of Economics*, 73(1), February 1959, pp. 145-69.

Olson, Mancur L. *The Economics of the Wartime Shortage: A History of British Food Shortages in the Napoleonic War and World Wars I and II*. Durham: Duke University Press, 1963.

Olson, Mancur L. "The United Kingdom and the World Market in Wheat, 1870-1914," *Explorations in Economic History*, 11(4), Summer 1974, pp. 325-55.

Olsson, Carl-Axel. "Swedish Agriculture during the Interwar Years," *Economy and History*, 11, 1968, pp. 67-107.

Olsson, Carl-Axel. *Om Jordbrukssektorns Ekonomi Med Sarskild Hansyn Till Sverige Under Det Andra Varldskriget*. Lund: University of Lund Press, 1974.

Overton, Mark. "Estimating Crop Yields from Probate Inventories: An Example from East Anglia, 1585-1735," *Journal of Economic History*, 39(2), June 1979, pp. 363-78.

Parker, William N. and Jones, Eric L., eds. *European Peasants and Their Markets: Essays in European Agrarian History*. Princeton: Princeton University Press, 1975.

Parker, William N. "Comment on Papers by McAlpin, Libecap and Johnson, and Adelman and Morris Presented to the 38th Annual Meeting of the Economic History Association," *Journal of Economic History*, 39(1), March 1979, pp. 177-79.

Pelaez, Carlos M. "Analise Economica do Programa Brasileiro de Sustentacao do Cafe, 1906-1945: Teoria, Politica e Medicao [An Economic Analysis of the Brazilian Coffee Support Program, 1906-1945: Theory, Policy and Measurement]," *Revista Brasileira de Economia*, 25(4), October/December 1971, pp. 5-212.

Pelaez, Carlos M. "An Economic Analysis of the Brazilian Coffee Support Program, 1906-1945," in Pelaez, ed. *Essays on Coffee and Economic Development*, 1973, pp. 181-249.

Perkins, Dwight H. *Agricultural Development in China, 1368-1968*. Chicago: Aldine Press, 1969.

Pope, David H. "Viticulture and Phylloxera in North-East Victoria, 1880-1910," *Australian Economic History Review*, 11(1), March 1971, pp. 21-38.

Reed, Clyde G. "The Profits of Cultivation in England during the Later Middle Ages," *Agricultural History*, 50(4), October 1976, pp. 645-48.

Schremmer, Eckart. "Agrareinkommen und Kapitalbildung im 19. Jahrhundert in Sudwestdeutschland [Agricultural Income and Capital Formation in Southwest Germany in the 19th Century]," *Jahrbucher fur Nationalokonomie und Statistik*, 176(3), June 1964, pp. 196-240.

Toutain, Jean Claude. "Le produit de L'Agriculture Francaise de 1700 a 1958 [French Agricultural Product, 1700-1958]," *Cahiers de L'Institut de Science Economique Appliquee*, 1961, pp. 288-96.

Tracy, Michael. "Agriculture in the Great Depression: World Market Developments and European Protectionism," in Van der Wee, ed. *The Great Depression Revisited*, 1972, pp. 91-119.

Umemura, Mataji. "Note on Economic Development in Agriculture in the Tokugawa Period," in Ohkawa and Hayami, eds. *Economic Growth*, vol. 1, 1973, pp. 175-83.

Vamplew, Wray. "The Protection of English Cereal Producers: The Corn Laws Reassessed," *Economic History Review*, Second Series, 33(3), Augustt 1980, pp. 382-95.

Webb, Steven B. "Tariff Protection for the Iron Industry, Cotton Textiles and Agriculture in Germany, 1879-1914," [Appears in German] *Jahrbucher fur Nationalokonomie und Statistik*, 192(3-4), November 1977, pp. 336-57.

Yamada, Saburo and Hayami, Yujiro. "Agriculture, 1880-1965," in Ohkawa and Hayami, eds. *Economic Growth*, vol. 1, 1973, pp. 7-25.

Fishing, Hunting, Logging

Anderson, Terry L. and Hill, Peter J. "The Evolution of Property Rights: A Study of the American West," *Journal of Law and Economics*, 18(1), April 1975, pp. 163-80.

Anderson, Terry L. and Hill, Peter J. "From Free Grass to Fences: Transforming the Commons of the American West," in Hardin and Baden, eds. *Managing the Commons*, 1977, pp. 200-216.

Carlos, Ann. "The Origins and Causes of the Canadian Fur Trade Rivalry, 1808-1810," [Working Paper].

Dick, Trevor J.O. "Property Rights, Forest Wealth, and Nineteenth Century Economic Growth in Central Canada," [Working Paper].

Johnson, Ronald N. and Libecap, Gary D. "Efficient Markets and Great Lakes Timber: A Conservation Issue Reexamined," *Explorations in Economic History*, 17(4), October 1980, pp. 372-85.

Libecap, Gary D. and Johnson, Ronald N. "Property Rights, Nineteenth-Century Federal Timber Policy, and the Conservation Movement," *Journal of Economic History*, 39(1), March 1979, pp. 129-42.

McManus, John C. "An Economic Analysis of Indian Behavior in the North American Fur Trade," *Journal of Economic History*, 32(1), March 1972, pp. 36-53.

Murphy, Earl F. "Comment on Papers by McCloskey, McManus, and Landes and Solmon Presented to the 31st Annual Meeting of the Economic History Association," *Journal of Economic History*, 32(1), March 1972, pp. 95-97.

North, Douglass C. and Thomas, Robert P. "The First Economic Revolution," *Economic History Review*, Second Series, 30(2), May 1977, pp. 229-41.

Parker, William N. "The Land, Minerals, Water, and Forests," in Davis, Easterlin, and Parker, eds. *American Economic Growth*, 1972, pp. 93-120.

Parker, William N. "Comment on Papers by McAlpin, Libecap and Johnson, and Adelman and Morris Presented to the 38th Annual Meeting of the Economic History Association," *Journal of Economic History*, 39(1), March 1979, pp. 177-79.

Paterson, Donald G. and Wilen, J. "Depletion and Diplomacy: The North Pacific Seal Hunt, 1886-1910," in Uselding, ed. *Research in Economic History*, vol. 2, 1977, pp. 81-139.

Paterson, Donald G. "The North Pacific Seal Hunt, 1886-1910: Rights and Regulations," *Explorations in Economic History*, 14(2), April

1977, pp. 97-119.

Salsbury, Stephen. "Comment on Papers by McCloskey, McManus, and Landes and Solmon Presented to the 31st Annual Meeting of the Economic History Association," *Journal of Economic History*, 32(1), March 1972, pp. 92-94.

Smith, Vernon L. "The Primitive Hunter Culture, Pleistocene Extinction, and the Rise of Agriculture," *Journal of Political Economy*, 83(4), August 1975, pp. 727-56.

Sweden Statistika centralbyran. *Historisk statistik for Sverige*, Del. 2: *Vaderlek, lantmateri, jordbruk, skogsbruk, fiske tom ar* [*Historical Statistics of Sweden*, part 2: *Climate, Land Surveying, Agriculture, Forestry, Fisheries*]. Stockholm: National Central Bureau of Statistics, 1955.

Unger, Richard W. "Dutch Herring, Technology, and International Trade in the Seventeenth Century," *Journal of Economic History*, 40(2), June 1980, pp. 253-79.

Chapter 10

INTERNATIONAL FINANCE AND INVESTMENT

Gold Standard

Agherli, Bijan B. "The Balance of Payments and Money Supply under the Gold Standard Regime: United States, 1879-1914," *American Economic Review*, 65(1), March 1975, pp. 40-58.

Barkai, Haim. "The Macro-Economics of Tsarist Russia in the Industrialization Era: Monetary Developments, the Balance of Payments and the Gold Standard," *Journal of Economic History*, 33(2), June 1973, pp. 339-71.

Bloomfield, A. *Monetary Policy under the International Gold Standard.* New York: Federal Reserve Bank of New York, 1959.

Bloomfield, A. *Short-Term Capital Movements Under the Pre-1914 Gold Standard (Princeton Studies in International Finance*, no. 11). Princeton: Princeton University Press, 1963.

Bloomfield, A. *Patterns of Fluctuation in International Investment Before 1914 (Princeton Studies in International Finance*, no. 21). Princeton: Princeton University Press, 1968.

Bordo, Michael D. "John E. Cairnes on the Effects of the Australian Gold Discoveries, 1851-73: An Early Application of the Methodology of Positive Economics," *History of Political Economy*, 7, Fall 1975, pp. 357-59.

Brittain, W.H. Bruce. "Monetary Factors in the French Balance of Payments, 1880-1913," Ph.D. Dissertation, University of Chicago, 1975 [Working Paper].

Dalgaard, Bruce R. "South Africa's Impact on Britain's Return to Gold, 1925 (Abstract)," in Uselding, ed. *Business and Economic History*, Second Series, vol. 7, 1978, pp. 138-41.

Dick, Trevor J.O. "The Canadian Balance of Payments, 1900-1913: Mechanisms of Adjustment," [Working Paper].

Drummond, Ian M. "The Russian Gold Standard, 1897-1914," *Journal of Economic History*, 36(3), September 1976, pp. 663-88.

Flynn, Dennis O. "A New Perspective on the Spanish Price Revolution: The Monetary Approach to the Balance of Payments," *Explorations in Economic History*, 15(4), October 1978, pp. 388-406.

Flynn, Dennis O. "Silver and the Spanish Empire," in Soltow, ed. *Essays in Economic and Business History*, 1979, pp. 197-211.

Flynn, Dennis O. "Spanish-American Silver and World Markets in the Sixteenth Century," *Economic Forum*, 10(2), Winter 1979/80, pp. 46-72.

Flynn, Dennis O. "Sixteenth-Century Inflation from a Production Point of View," in Marcus, ed. *Inflation through the Ages*, 1981.

Ford, A.G. "Notes on the Working of the Gold Standard Before 1914," *Oxford Economic Papers*, New Series, 12(1), February 1960, pp. 52-76.

Ford, A.G. *The Gold Standard, 1880-1914: Britain and Argentina.* [Translated into Spanish (1966)] Oxford: Oxford University Press, 1962.

Ford, A.G. "Bank Rate, the British Balance of Payments and the Burdens of Adjustment, 1870-1914," *Oxford Economic Papers*, New Series, 16(1), March 1964, pp. 24-39.

Ford, A.G. "The Truth About Gold," *Lloyds Bank Review*(71), July 1965, pp. 1-18.

Ford, A.G. "International Financial Policy and the Gold Standard, 1870-1914," in Mathias and Pollard, eds. *The Cambridge Economic History of Europe*, vol. 8.

Goodhart, Charles A.E. *The New York Money Market and the Finance of Trade, 1900-1913.* Cambridge: Harvard University Press, 1969.

Goodhart, Charles A.E. *The Business of Banking, 1891-1914.* London: Weidenfeld & Nicholson, 1972.

Gregory, Paul R. "The Russian Balance of Payments, the Gold Standard, and Monetary Policy: A Historical Example of Foreign Capital Movements," *Journal of Economic History*, 39(2), June 1979, pp. 379-99.

Hanisch, Tore Jorgen. "Okonomiske Virkninger av Paripolitikken. et Essay om Norsk Okonomi i 1920-Arene [Economic Consequences of Restoring the Norwegian Krone to Gold Parity in the 1920s]," *Norsk Historisk Tidsskrift*, (3), 1979.

Hawke, Gary R. "New Zealand and the Return to Gold in 1925," *Australian Economic History Review*, 11(1), March 1971, pp. 48-58.

Hinderliter, Roger H. and Rockoff, Hugh T. "Banking under the Gold Standard: An Analysis of Liquidity Management in the Leading Financial Centers," *Journal of Economic History*, 36(2), June 1976, pp. 379-98.

Jones, Donald W. "Prices, Gold and Interest Rates in Gold Rush California: An Inquiry into Domestic and International Economic Relations of California, 1850-1855," Presented at the Meetings of the North American Economic Studies Association, Atlantic City, New Jersey, September 1976 [Working Paper].

Jones, Donald W. "The Gold Standard in California during the Greenback Period and the Origins of the Specific Contract Act," Presented at the 38th Annual Meeting of the Economic History Association, Toronto, Ontario, September 1978 [Working Paper].

Kindahl, James K. "Economic Factors in Specie Resumption: The United States, 1865-79," (Reprinted in Fogel and Engerman, eds. *The Reinterpretation of American Economic History*, 1971, pp. 468-479) *Journal of Political Economy*, 69(1), February 1961, pp. 30-48.

Klein, Benjamin. "Our New Monetary Standard: The Measurement and Effects of Price Uncertainty, 1800-1973," *Economic Inquiry*, 13(4), December 1975, pp. 461-83.

Lindert, Peter H. *Key Currencies and Gold, 1900-1913.* Princeton: Princeton University Press, 1969.

Martin, David A. "The Impact of Mid-Nineteenth Century Gold Depreciation upon Western Monetary Standards," *Journal of European Economic History*, 6(3), Winter 1977, pp. 641-58.

McCloskey, Donald N. and Zecher, J. Richard. "How the Gold Standard Worked, 1880-1914," in Frenkel and Johnson, eds. *The Monetary Approach to the Balance of Payments*, 1975.

Moggridge, Donald E. *The Return to Gold, 1925: The Formulation of Economic Policy and Its Critics*. Cambridge: Cambridge University Press, 1969.

Moggridge, Donald E. "The Norman Conquest of $4.86: Britain and the Return to Gold, 1925," *Annales D'Etudes Internationales*, 1, 1970, pp. 115-29.

Moggridge, Donald E. "The Bank of England and the Management of the Inter-War Gold Standard," *International Currency Review*, 3(3), August 1971, pp. 17-25.

Moggridge, Donald E. "Bank of England Foreign Exchange Operations 1924-1931," *International Review of the History of Banking*, 5, 1972, pp. 1-23.

Moggridge, Donald E. *British Monetary Policy, 1924-1931: The Norman Conquest of $4.86*. London: Cambridge University Press, 1972.

Moggridge, Donald E. "The Gold Standard and National Economic Policies, 1919-1939," in Mathias and Pollard, eds. *The Cambridge Economic History of Europe*, vol. 8.

Nishimura, Shizuya. "A Study of the International Gold Standard, 1870-1914," [Working Paper].

Rich, Georg. "The Cross of Gold, Money and the Canadian Business Cycle 1867-1913," [Working Paper].

Shearer, Ronald A. and Clark, Carolyn. "Statistics of Canada's International Gold Flows, 1920-1934," Presented at the Eighth Conference on Quantitative Methods in Canadian Economic History, Hamilton, Ontario, October 1976 [Working Paper].

Shearer, Ronald A. and Clark, Carolyn. "The Suspension of the Gold Standard, 1928-1931," University of British Columbia, Department of Economics Discussion Paper no. 79-36, 1979 [Working Paper].

Williamson, Jeffrey G. *American Growth and the Balance of Payments, 1820-1913: A Study of the Long Swing*. Chapel Hill: University of North Carolina Press, 1964.

Wimmer, Larry T. "The Gold Crisis of 1869: Stabilizing or Destabilizing Speculation under Floating Exchange Rates?" *Explorations in Economic History*, 12(2), April 1975, pp. 105-22.

Wimmer, Larry T. "The Gold Crisis of 1869," Ph.D. Dissertation, University of Chicago, 1968.

International Investment

Ball, R.J. "Mr. Rosenberg on Capital Imports and Growth: A Further Comment," *Economic Journal*, 71(284), December 1961, pp. 853-55.

Bentick, Brian L. "Foreign Borrowing and Relative Prices: Victoria, 1872-1893," *Yale Economic Essays*, 10(2), Fall 1970, pp. 3-44.

Bonomo, Vittorio. "International Capital Movements and Economic Activity: The United States Experience, 1870-1968," *Explorations in*

Economic History, 8(3), Spring 1971, pp. 321-42.
Bouvier, Jean. "A propos des approches micro et macro economiques des exportations de capitaux avant 1914 [Regarding Micro- and Macro-Economic Approaches to Capital Exports Before 1914]," in Levy-Leboyer, ed. *La position internationale de la France*, 1977.
Broder, Albert A. "Les Investissements etrangers en Espagne au XIXe siecle: Methodologie et quantification [Foreign Investment in Spain in the 19th Century: Methods and Findings]," *Revue d'Histoire Economique et Sociale*, 54(1), 1976, pp. 29-63.
Broder, Albert A. "Les Investissements Francais en Espagne [French Investments in Spain]," in Levy-Leboyer, ed. *La Position Internationale de la France*, 1977.
Cairncross, Alec K. *Home and Foreign Investment, 1870-1913: Studies in Capital Accumulation.* Cambridge: Cambridge University Press, 1953.
Cairncross, Alec K. "Investment in Canada, 1900-13," in Hall, ed. *The Export of Capital from Britain, 1870-1914*, 1968, pp. 153-86.
Carstensen, Fred V. "Numbers and Reality: A Critique of Foreign Investment Estimates in Tsarist Russia," in Levy-Leboyer, ed. *La Position Internationale de la France*, 1977, pp. 275-83.
Delivanis, D.J. "Mr. Rosenberg on Capital Imports and Growth: Comment," *Economic Journal*, 71(284), December 1961, pp. 852-53.
Dernberger, Robert F. "The Role of the Foreigner in China's Economic Development, 1840-1949," in Perkins, ed. *China's Modern Economy in Historical Perspective*, 1975, pp. 19-47.
Drummond, Ian M. "Government Securities on Colonial New Issue Markets: Australia and Canada, 1895-1914," *Yale Economic Essays*, 1(1), Spring 1961, pp. 137-75.
Edelstein, Michael. "Rigidity and Bias in the British Capital Market, 1870-1913," in McCloskey, ed. *Essays on a Mature Economy*, 1971, pp. 83-112.
Edelstein, Michael. "The Determinants of U.K. Investment Abroad, 1870-1913: The U.S. Case," *Journal of Economic History*, 34(4), December 1974, pp. 980-1007.
Edelstein, Michael. "Realized Rates of Return on U.K. Home and Overseas Portfolio Investment in the Age of High Imperialism," *Explorations in Economic History*, 13(3), July 1976, pp. 283-330.
Edelstein, Michael. "Foreign Investment and Empire, 1860-1914," in Floud and McCloskey, eds. *The Economic History of Britain Since 1700*, vol. 2, 1980.
Esbitt, Milton. *International Capital Flows and Domestic Economic Fluctuation: The United States During the 1830's.* New York: Arno Press, 1978.
Ford, A.G. "The Transfer of British Foreign Lending, 1870-1913," *Economic History Review*, Second Series, 11(2), 1958, pp. 302-8.
Ford, A.G. "Capital Exports and Growth for Argentina, 1880-1914," *Economic Journal*, 68(271), September 1958, pp. 589-93.
Ford, A.G. "Capital Exports and Growth for Argentina: A Rejoinder (to Knapp)," *Economic Journal*, 70(279), September 1960, pp. 630-33.
Ford, A.G. "Notes on the Transfer of Overseas Lending and Grants," *Oxford Economic Papers*, New Series, 14(1), February 1962, pp. 94-102.
Ford, A.G. "Overseas Lending and Internal Fluctuations: 1870-1914,"

(Reprinted in Hall, ed. *The Export of Capital from Britain,*
1870-1914, 1968, pp. 84-102) *Yorkshire Bulletin of Economic and*
Social Research, 17(1), May 1965, pp. 19-31.

Ford, A.G. "British Overseas Investment in Argentina and Long Swings,
1880-1914," (Reprinted in Floud, ed. *Essays in Quantitative*
Economic History, 1974, pp. 216-227) *Journal of Economic History*,
31(3), September 1971, pp. 650-63.

Ford, A.G. "British Investment and ARgentine Economic Development,
1880-1914," in Rock, ed. *Argentina in the Twentieth Century*, 1975,
pp. 12-40.

Gregory, Paul R. "The Russian Balance of Payments, the Gold Standard,
and Monetary Policy: A Historical Example of Foreign Capital
Movements," *Journal of Economic History*, 39(2), June 1979, pp.
379-99.

Hall, A.R. *The London Capital Market and Australia, 1870-1914.*
Canberra: Australian National University Press, 1963.

Hall, A.R. "Capital Imports and the Composition of Investment in a
Borrowing Country," in Hall, ed. *The Export of Capital from*
Britain, 1870-1914, 1968.

Hall, A.R., ed. *The Export of Capital from Britain, 1870-1914.*
London: Methuen, 1968.

Holtfrerich, Karl-Ludwig. "Amerikanischer Kapitalexport und
Wiederaufbau der Deutschen Wirtschaft 1919-23 im Vergleich zu
1924-29 [American Capital Export and the Reconstruction of the
German Economy, 1919-23 in Comparison with 1924-29]," (Reprinted in
Sturmer, ed. *Die Weimarer Republik*, 1980) *Vierteljahrschrift fur*
Sozial- und Wirtschaftsgeschichte, 64(4), 1977, pp. 497-529.

Imlah, Albert H. "British Balance of Payments and Export of Capital,
1816-1913," *Economic History Review*, Second Series, 5(2), 1952, pp.
208-39.

Imlah, A.H. *Economic Elements in the Pax Britannica.* Cambridge:
Harvard University Press, 1958.

Kennedy, Jr., William P. "Foreign Investment, Trade, and Growth in the
United Kingdom, 1870-1913," *Explorations in Economic History*,
11(4), Summer 1974, pp. 415-44.

Knapp, J. "Capital Exports and Growth for Argentina: A Comment (on
Ford)," *Economic Journal*, 69(275), September 1959, pp. 593-97.

Mauro, F. "Towards an 'Intercontinental Model: European Overseas
Expansion between 1500 and 1800," *Economic History Review*, Second
Series, 14(1), 1961, pp. 1-17.

North, Douglass C. "International Capital Flows and the Development of
the American West," *Journal of Economic History*, 16(4), December
1956, pp. 493-505.

North, Douglass C. "International Capital Movements in Historical
Perspective," in Mikesell, ed. *U.S. Private and Government*
Investment Abroad, 1962.

Paterson, Donald G. *British Direct Investment in Canada, 1890-1914:*
Estimates and Determinants. Toronto and Buffalo: University of
Toronto Press, 1976.

Rapp, Richard T. and Ames, Edward. "Capital Transfers and Foreign
Indebtedness: The Long-Term Experience," [Working Paper].

Richardson, H.W. "British Emigration and Overseas Investment,

1870-1914," *Economic History Review*, Second Series, 25(1), February 1972, pp. 99-113.

Rosenberg, W. "Capital Imports and Growth - The Case of New Zealand: Foreign Investment in New Zealand, 1840-58," *Economic Journal*, 71(281), March 1961, pp. 93-114.

Rosenberg, W. "Mr. Rosenberg on Capital Imports and Growth: A Rejoinder to Delivanis," *Economic Journal*, 71(284), December 1961, pp. 855-56.

Rosenberg, W. "Mr. Rosenberg on Capital Imports and Growth: A Rejoinder to Ball," *Economic Journal*, 71(284), December 1961, pp. 855-56.

Simon, Matthew. "The Pattern of New British Portfolio Foreign Investment, 1865-1914," in Hall, ed. *The Export of Capital from Britain, 1870-1914*, 1968, pp. 15-44.

Stone, Irving. "British Long-Term Investment in Latin America, 1865-1913," *Business History Review*, 42(3), Autumn 1968, pp. 311-39.

Stone, Irving. "La distribuzione geografica degli investimenti inglesi nell'America Latina (1825-1913) [The Geographic Distribution of British Investment in Latin America, 1825-1913]," *Storia contemporanea*, 2(3), 1971, pp. 495-518.

Stone, Irving. "British Investment in Argentina: A Note on Ford," *Journal of Economic History*, 32(2), June 1972, pp. 546-47.

Stone, Irving. "British Direct and Portfolio Investment in Latin America before 1914," *Journal of Economic History*, 37(3), September 1977, pp. 690-722.

Stone, Irving. "Global Export of Capital from Great Britain, 1865-1914," [Working Paper].

Stone, Irving. "The (Annual) Export of Capital from Great Britain to Latin America, 1865-1914," Presented at the Seventh International Congress on Economic History at Edinburgh, Scotland, August, 1978 [Working Paper].

Thomas, Brinley. "International Factor Movements and Unequal Rates of Growth," *Manchester School of Economic and Social Studies*, 29(1), January 1961, pp. 1-21.

Thomas, Brinley. "Intra-Commonwealth Flows of Capital and Skills," in Hamilton, Robinson, and Goodwin, eds. *a Decade of the Commonwealth, 1955-1964*, 1966, pp. 407-27.

Thomas, Brinley. "The Historical Record of International Capital Movements to 1913," in Adler, ed. *Capital Movements and Economic Development*, 1967, pp. 3-32.

Thomas, Brinley. "Migration and International Investment," in Hall, ed. *The Export of Capital from Britain, 1870-1914*, pp. 45-54.

Other Topics

Aldrich, Terry Mark. "Flexible Exchange Rates, Northern Expansion, and the Market for Southern Cotton: 1866-1879," *Journal of Economic History*, 33(2), June 1973, pp. 399-416.

Aliber, Robert Z. "Speculation in the Foreign Exchanges: The European Experience, 1919-1926," *Yale Economic Essays*, 2, Spring 1962, pp.

170-245.

Aliber, Robert Z. "Speculation in the Flexible Exchange Revisited," *Kyklos*, 23(2), 1970, pp. 303-14.

Aliber, Robert Z. "Speculation in the Flexible Exchange Re-Revisited: Reply to Pippenger," *Kyklos*, 26(3), 1973, pp. 619-20.

Aliber, Robert Z. "Floating Exchange Rates: The Twenties and the Seventies," in Chipman and Kindleberger, eds. *Flexible Exchange Rates and the Balance of Payments*, 1980, pp. 81-97.

Ames, Edward. "The Sterling Crisis of 1337-1339," (Reprinted in Floud, ed. *Essays in Quantitative Economic History*, 1974, pp. 36-58) *Journal of Economic History*, 25(4), December 1965, pp. 496-522.

Baxter, Stephen B. "Domestic and International Integration of the London Money Market, 1731-1789: Comment on Eagly and Smith," *Journal of Economic History*, 36(1), March 1976, pp. 213-16.

Bentick, Brian L. "Foreign Borrowing and Relative Prices: Victoria, 1872-1893," *Yale Economic Essays*, 10(2), Fall 1970, pp. 3-44.

Bonomo, Vittorio. "International Capital Movements and Economic Activity: The United States Experience, 1870-1968," *Explorations in Economic History*, 8(3), Spring 1971, pp. 321-42.

Bordo, Michael D. and Schwartz, Anna J. "Money and Prices in the Nineteenth Century: Was Thomas Tooke Right?" UCLA Discussion Paper, 1980 [Working Paper].

Chen, Chau-nan. "Flexible Bimetallic Exchange Rates in China, 1650-1850: A Historical Example of Optimum Currency Areas," *Journal of Money, Credit and Banking*, 7(3), August 1975, pp. 359-76.

Cohen, Jon S. "The 1927 Revaluation of the Lira: A Study in Political Economy," (Reprinted as "La rivalutazione della lira del 1927: uno studio sulla politica economica fascista," in Toniolo, ed. *L'economia italiana 1861-1940*, 1978, pp. 313-36) *Economic History Review*, Second Series, 25(4), November 1972, pp. 642-54.

Davis, Lance E. and Hughes, Jonathan R.T. "A Dollar-Sterling Exchange, 1803-1895," (Reprinted in Hughes, ed. *Purdue Faculty Papers in Economic History*, 1956-1966, 1967, pp. 235-268) *Economic History Review*, Second Series, 13(1), August 1960, pp. 52-78.

Eagly, Robert V. and Smith, V. Kerry. "Domestic and International Integration of the London Money Market, 1731-1789," *Journal of Economic History*, 36(1), March 1976, pp. 198-212.

Edelstein, Michael. "Factor and Commodity Flows in the International Economy of 1870-1914: Discussion of Papers by Eagly/Smith and Green/Urquhart," *Journal of Economic History*, 36(1), March 1976, pp. 253-58.

Edelstein, Michael. "Money: A Discussion of Papers by Keehn, Howson, and Bordo/Schwartz Presented to the 39th Annual Meeting of the Economic History Association," *Journal of Economic History*, 40(1), March 1980, pp. 68-69.

Eichengreen, Barry J. "Did Speculation Destabilize the French Franc During the 1920s?" [Working Paper].

Esbitt, Milton . "A Note on the Sources of American Specie Imports During the 1830's," [Working Paper].

Esbitt, Milton. "Using Monthly Money-Market Rates to Test the Davis-Hughes and Perkins Analyses of the Dollar-Sterling Exchange Rates," [Working Paper].

Falkus, Malcolm E. "United States Economic Policy and the 'Dollar Gap' of the 1920's," *Economic History Review*, Second Series, 24(4), November 1971, pp. 599-623.

Ford, A.G. "Flexible Exchange Rates and Argentina, 1885-1900," *Oxford Economic Papers*, New Series, 10(3), October 1958, pp. 316-38.

Frenkel, Jacob A. "The Forward Exchange Rate, Expectations and the Demand for Money: The German Hyperinflation," *American Economic Review*, 67, September 1977, pp. 653-70.

Frenkel, Jacob A. "Purchasing Power Parity: Doctrinal Perspective and Evidence from the 1920's," *Journal of International Economics*, 8, May 1978, pp. 169-91.

Frenkel, Jacob A. "Exchange Rates, Prices, and Money: Lessons from the 1920's," *American Economic Review Papers and Proceedings*, 70(2), May 1980, pp. 235-42.

Friedman, Milton. "Prices of Money and Goods Across Frontiers: The Pound and the Dollar Over a Century," *The World Economy*, 2, February 1980, pp. 497-511.

Glynn, Sean and Lougheed, Alan L. "A Comment on United States Economic Policy and the "Dollar Gap" of the 1920's," *Economic History Review*, Second Series, 26(4), November 1973, pp. 692-94.

Goodhart, Charles A.E. *The Business of Banking, 1891-1914.* London: Weidenfeld & Nicholson, 1972.

Gould, John D. "Currency and the Exchange Rate in Sixteenth-Century England," *Journal of European Economic History*, 2(1), Spring 1973, pp. 149-59.

Hanson, II, John R. "Exchange-Rate Movements and Economic Development in the Late Nineteenth Century: A Critique," *Journal of Political Economy*, 83(4), August 1975, pp. 859-62.

Hartland, Penelope. "Canadian Balance of Payments since 1868," in Parker, ed. *Trends in the American Economy in the Nineteenth Century* (*Studies in Income and Wealth*, vol. 24), 1960, pp. 717-53.

Howson, Susan. "The Managed Floating Pound, 1932-39," *Banker*, 126(601), March 1976, pp. 249-55.

Howson, Susan. "The Management of Sterling, 1932-1939," *Journal of Economic History*, 40(1), March 1980, pp. 53-60.

Klein, Benjamin. "Our New Monetary Standard: The Measurement and Effects of Price Uncertainty, 1800-1973," *Economic Inquiry*, 13(4), December 1975, pp. 461-83.

Lampard, Eric E. "The United States Balance of Payments, 1861-1900: Comment on Simon," in Parker, ed. *Trends in the American Economy in the Nineteenth Century* (*Studies in Income and Wealth*, vol. 24), 1960, pp. 711-15.

Moggridge, Donald E. "British Controls on Long Term Capital Movements, 1924-1931," in McCloskey, ed. *Essays on a Mature Economy*, 1971, pp. 113-38.

North, Douglass C. "Canadian Balance of Payments Since 1868: Comment on Hartland," in Parker, ed. *Trends in the American Economy in the Nineteenth Century* (*Studies in Income and Wealth*, vol. 24), 1960, pp. 754-55.

North, Douglass C. "The United States Balance of Payments, 1790-1860," in Parker, ed. *Trends in the American Economy in the Nineteenth Century* (*Studies in Income and Wealth*, vol. 24), 1960, pp. 573-627.

North, Douglass C. and Heston, Alan. "The Estimation of Shipping Earnings in Historical Studies of the Balance of Payments," *Canadian Journal of Economics and Political Science*, 26(2), May 1960, pp. 265-76.

Nugent, Jeffrey B. "Exchange-Rate Movements and Economic Development in the Late Nineteenth Century," *Journal of Political Economy*, 81(5), September/October 1973, pp. 1110-35.

O'Leary, Paul M. "The Scene of the Crime of 1873 Revisited: A Note," *Journal of Political Economy*, 68(4), August 1960, pp. 388-92.

Patrick, Hugh T. "External Equilibrium and Internal Convertibility: Financial Policy in Meiji Japan," *Journal of Economic History*, 25(2), June 1965, pp. 187-213.

Pelaez, Carlos M. "As Consequencias Economicas da Ortodoxia Monetaria, Cambial e Fiscal no Brasil entre 1889 e 1945 [The Economic Consequences of Monetary, Exchange and Fiscal Orthodoxy in Brasil, 1889-1945]," *Revista Brasileira de Economia*, 25(3), July/September 1971, pp. 5-82.

Perkins, Edwin J. "The Emergence of a Futures Market for Foreign Exchange in the United States," *Explorations in Economic History*, 11(3), Spring 1974, pp. 193-212.

Perkins, Edwin J. "Foreign Interest Rates in American Financial Markets: A Revised Series of Dollar-Sterling Exchange Rates, 1835-1900," *Journal of Economic History*, 38(2), June 1978, pp. 392-417.

Pippenger, John E. "Speculation in the Flexible Exchange Re-Revisited: Comment (on Aliber)," *Kyklos*, 26(3), 1973, pp. 613-18.

Redmond, John. "An Indicator of the Effective Exchange Rate of the Pound in the Nineteen-Thirties," *Economic History Review*, Second Series, 33(1), February 1980, pp. 83-91.

Reed, Clyde G. "Price Movements, Balance of Payments, Bullion Flows, and Unemployment in the Fourteenth and Fifteenth Centuries," *Journal of European Economic History*, 8(2), Fall 1979, pp. 479-86.

Sheppard, David K. *The Growth and Role of U.K. Financial Institutions, 1880-1962.* London: Methuen, 1971.

Silber, Jacques and Rozenberg, Yakov. "The Monetary Approach to the Balance of Payments of Palestine," [In Hebrew] *Quarterly Banking Review*, 18(69), November 1978, pp. 32-51.

Silber, Jacques and Rozenberg, Yakov. "Adaptation Process of the Balance of Payments of Palestine: 1922-1935," Topics in Economics: Proceedings of the Israeli Economic Association, April 1979, pp. 201-18.

Silber, Jacques and Rozenberg, Yakov. "The Balance of Payments of Palestine under the British Mandate: A Monetary Approach," [Working Paper].

Simon, Matthew. "The United States Balance of Payments, 1861-1900," in Parker, ed. *Trends in the American Economy in the Nineteenth Century* (Studies in Income and Wealth, vol. 24), 1960, pp. 629-711.

Suzigan, Wilson. "A Politica Cambial Brasileira, 1889-1946 [Analysis of Brazilian Exchange Rate Policy, 1889-1946]," *Revista Brasileira de Economia*, 25(3), July/September 1971, pp. 93-111.

Sylla, Richard E. "Money: A Discussion of Papers by Keehn, Howson, and Bordo/Schwartz Presented to the 39th Annual Meeting of the Economic

History Association," *Journal of Economic History*, 40(1), March 1980, pp. 70-72.

Tanner, J. Ernest and Bonomo, Vittorio. "Gold, Capital Flows and Long Swings in American Business Activity," *Journal of Political Economy*, 76(1), January/February 1968, pp. 44-52.

Thomas, Lloyd B. "Behavior of Flexible Exchange Rates: Additional Tests from the Post-World War I Episode," *Southern Economic Journal*, 40(2), October 1973, pp. 167-82.

Triffin, Robert. *The Evolution of the International Monetary System: Historical Reappraisal and Future Perspectives* (Princeton Studies in International Finance, no. 12). Princeton, N.J.: Princeton University, Department of Economics, 1964.

Whitaker, John K. and Hudgins, Jr., Maxwell W. "The Floating Pound Sterling of the Nineteen-thirties: An Econometric Study," *Southern Economic Journal*, 44(1), July 1977, pp. 1478-85.

Williamson, Jeffrey G. "The Long Swing: Comparisons and Interactions between British and American Balance of Payments, 1820-1913," (Reprinted in Hall, ed. *The Export of Capital from Britain, 1870-1914*, 1968, pp. 55-83) *Journal of Economic History*, 22(1), March 1962, pp. 21-46.

Williamson, Jeffrey G. "Real Growth, Monetary Disturbances and the Transfer Process: The United States, 1879-1900," *Southern Economic Journal*, 29(3), January 1963, pp. 167-80.

Williamson, Jeffrey G. "Dollar Scarcity and Surplus in Historical Perspective," *American Economic Review*, 53(2), May 1963, pp. 519-29.

Williamson, Jeffrey G. *American Growth and the Balance of Payments, 1820-1913: A Study of the Long Swing*. Chapel Hill: University of North Carolina Press, 1964.

Yeager, Leland B. "Fluctuating Exchange Rates in the Nineteenth Century: The Experiences of Austria and Russia," in Mundell and Swoboda, eds. *Monetary Problems and the International Economy*, 1969, pp. 61-89.

Yeager, LeLand B. *International Monetary Relations: Theory, History and Policy* (Second Edition). New York: Harper & Row, 1976.

Chapter 11

FINANCIAL MARKETS

United States: General

Curran, Christopher and Johnston, Jack. "The Antebellum Money Market and the Economic Impact of the Bank War: A Comment on Sushka," *Journal of Economic History*, 39(2), June 1979, pp. 461-66.

Davis, Lance E. "Sources of Industrial Finance: The American Textile Industry, A Case Study," (Reprinted in Hughes, ed. *Purdue Faculty Papers in Economic History, 1956-1966*, 1967, pp. 625-642) *Explorations in Entrepreneurial History*, 9(4), April 1957, pp. 189-203.

Davis, Lance E. "Stock Ownership in the Early New England Textile Industry," (Reprinted in Hughes, ed. *Purdue Faculty Papers in Economic History, 1956-1966*, 1967, pp. 563-580) *Business History Review*, 32(2), Summer 1958, pp. 204-22.

Davis, Lance E. "The New England Textile Mills and the Capital Markets: A Study of Industrial Borrowing, 1840-1860," (Reprinted in Hughes, ed. *Purdue Faculty Papers in Economic History, 1956-1966*, 1967, pp. 596-624) *Journal of Economic History*, 20(1), March 1960, pp. 1-30.

Davis, Lance E. "Mrs. Vatter on Industrial Borrowing: A Reply," *Journal of Economic History*, 21(2), June 1961, pp. 222-26.

Davis, Lance E. "Capital Immobilities and Finance Capitalism: A Study of Economic Evolution in the United States, 1820-1920," (Reprinted in Hughes, ed. *Purdue Faculty Papers in Economic History, 1956-1966*, 1967, pp. 581-595) *Explorations in Entrepreneurial History*, Second Series, 1(1), Fall 1963, pp. 88-105.

Davis, Lance E. "The Investment Market, 1870-1914: The Evolution of a National Market," (Reprinted in Hughes, ed. *Purdue Faculty Papers in Economic History, 1956-1966*, 1967, pp. 119-160) *Journal of Economic History*, 25(3), September 1965, pp. 355-99.

Davis, Lance E. "The Capital Markets and Industrial Concentration: The U.S. and U.K., a Comparative Study," (Reprinted in Hughes, ed. *Purdue Faculty Papers in Economic History, 1956-1966*, 1967, pp. 663-682) *Economic History Review*, Second Series, 19(2), August 1966, pp. 255-72.

Davis, Lance E. "Capital Immobilities, Institutional Adaptation, and Financial Development: The United States and England, An International Comparison," in Giersch, Herbert, and Sauermann, eds. *Quantitative Aspects of Economic History*, 1968, pp. 14-34.

Davis, Lance E. "Savings Sources and Utilization," in Davis,

Easterlin, and Parker, eds. *American Economic Growth*, 1972, pp. 311-39.

Davis, Lance E. "The Evolution of the American Capital Market, 1860-1940: A Case Study in Institutional Change," in Silber, ed. *Financial Innovation*, 1975.

Edwards, Richard C. "Stages in Corporate Stability and the Risks of Corporate Failure," *Journal of Economic History*, 35(2), June 1975, pp. 428-57.

Fleisig, Heywood. *Long Term Capital Flows and the Great Depression: The Role of the United States, 1927-1933.* New York: Arno Press, 1975.

Goldsmith, Raymond W. *Financial Intermediaries in the American Economy Since 1900.* Princeton: Princeton University Press, 1958.

Goldsmith, Raymond W. "The Share of Financial Intermediaries in National Wealth and National Assets, 1900-1949," National Bureau of Economic Research, Occasional Paper no. 42, 1954 [Working Paper].

Green, George D. "Financial Intermediaries," in Porter, ed. *Encyclopedia of American Economic History*, vol. 2, 1980, pp. 707-26.

Gurley, John G. and Shaw, E.S. "The Growth of Debt and Money in the United States, 1800-1950: A Suggested Interpretation," *Review of Economics and Statistics*, 39(3), August 1957, pp. 250-62.

Gurley, John G. and Shaw, E.S. "Money," in Harris, ed. *American Economic History*, 1961, pp. 101-29.

James, John A. *Money and Capital Markets in Postbellum America.* Princeton: Princeton University Press, 1978.

Johnson, Thomas H. "Postwar Optimism and the Rural Financial Crisis of the 1920's," *Explorations in Economic History*, 11(2), Winter 1974, pp. 173-91.

Livesay, Harold C. and Porter, Glenn. "The Financial Role of Merchants in the Development of U.S. Manufacturing, 1815-1860," *Explorations in Economic History*, 9(1), Fall 1971, pp. 63-87.

McGouldrick, Paul F. *New England Textiles in the Nineteenth Century: Profits and Investment.* Cambridge: Harvard University Press, 1968.

Smiley, Gene. "The 1898-1902 Expansion of the Securities Market," *Journal of Economics*, 4), 1978, pp. 193-96.

Sushka, Marie E. "An Economic Model of the Money Market in the United States, 1823-1859," (Summary of Doctoral Dissertation) *Journal of Economic History*, 35(1), March 1975, pp. 280-85.

Sushka, Marie E. "The Antebellum Money Market and the Economic Impact of the Bank War," *Journal of Economic History*, 36(4), December 1976, pp. 809-35.

Sushka, Marie E. "The Antebellum Money Market and the Economic Impact of the Bank War: A Reply to Curran and Johnston," *Journal of Economic History*, 39(2), June 1979, pp. 467-74.

Sutch, Richard C. and Ransom, Roger L. "Credit Merchandising in the Post-Emancipation South: Structure, Conduct, and Performance," *Explorations in Economic History*, 16(1), January 1979, pp. 64-89.

Sylla, Richard E. *The American Capital Market, 1846-1914.* New York: Arno Press, 1975.

Sylla, Richard E. "Financial Intermediaries in Economic History: Quantitative Research on the Seminal Hypotheses of Lance Davis and

Alexander Gerschenkron," in Gallman, ed. *Recent Developments in the Study of Business and Economic History*, 1977.
Vatter, Barbara. "Industrial Borrowing by the New England Textile Mills, 1840-1860: A Comment on Davis," *Journal of Economic History*, 21(2), June 1961, pp. 216-21.

United States: Banking

Adams, Jr., Donald R. "The Bank of Stephen Girard, 1812-1831," *Journal of Economic History*, 32(4), December 1972, pp. 841-68.
Adams, Jr., Donald R. "The Role of Banks in the Economic Development of the Old Northwest," in Klingaman and Vedder, eds. *Essays in Nineteenth Century Economic History*, 1975, pp. 208-45.
Adams, Jr., Donald R. *Finance and Enterprise in Early America: A Study of Stephen Girard's Bank, 1812-1831.* Philadelphia: University of Pennsylvania Press, 1978.
Adams, Jr., Donald R. "Portfolio Management and Profitability in Early Nineteenth Century Banking," *Business History Review*, 52(1), Spring 1978, pp. 61-79.
Adams, Jr., Donald R. "The Beginning of Investment Banking in the United States," *Pennsylvania History*, 45(2), April 1978, pp. 99-116.
Cameron, Rondo E.; Crisp, Olga; Patrick, Hugh T. and Tilly, Richard. *Banking in the Early Stages of Industrialization: A Study in Comparative Economic History.* London and New York: Oxford University Press, 1967.
Cameron, Rondo E. *Banking and Economic Development: Some Lessons of History.* New York and London: Oxford University Press, 1972.
Curran, Christopher and Johnston, Jack. "The Antebellum Money Market and the Economic Impact of the Bank War: A Comment on Sushka," *Journal of Economic History*, 39(2), June 1979, pp. 461-66.
Davis, Lance E. and Payne, Peter L. "From Benevolence to Business: The Story of Two Savings Banks," (Reprinted in Hughes, ed. *Purdue Faculty Papers in Economic History, 1956-1966*, 1967, pp. 643-662) *Business History Review*, 32(4), Winter 1958, pp. 386-406.
Davis, Lance E. "Banks and Their Economic Effects," in Davis, Easterlin, and Parker, eds. *American Economic Growth*, 1972, pp. 340-67.
Davis, Lance E. "Forgotten Men of Money, Private Bankers in Early U.S. History: Comment on Sylla," *Journal of Economic History*, 36(1), March 1976, pp. 189-93.
Edelstein, Michael. "Money: A Discussion of Papers by Keehn, Howson, and Bordo/Schwartz Presented to the 39th Annual Meeting of the Economic History Association," *Journal of Economic History*, 40(1), March 1980, pp. 68-69.
Eichengreen, Barry J. "Regional Differentials in the Use of Credit Instruments Prior to the Establishment of the Federal Reserve System," [Working Paper].
Engerman, Stanley L. "A Note on the Economic Consequences of the Second Bank of the United States," *Journal of Political Economy*, 78(4, Part 1), July/August 1970, pp. 725-28.

Esbitt, Milton. "An Antebellum Attempt at National Bank Regulation: Deposit Banks," in Soltow, ed. *Essays in Economic and Business History*, 1979, pp. 174-96.

Esbitt, Milton. "The New York City Banking Suspension of 1837," in Soltow, ed. *Essays in Economic and Business History*, 1979, pp. 163-73.

Esbitt, Milton. "Bank Failures and Economic Welfare: The Impact of Bank Failures on Local Communities During the Great Depression," [Working Paper].

Esbitt, Milton. "Federal Government Regulation of Banking in the Antebellum Period: Depository and Non-depository Banks in the 1830's," [Working Paper].

Esbitt, Milton. "Politics and Bank Reopenings After the Banking Holiday of 1933," [Working Paper].

Esbitt, Milton. "The Causes of Bank Failures in 1930: Illinois Banks," [Working Paper].

Fishlow, Albert. "Trustee Savings Banks, 1817-1861," *Journal of Economic History*, 21(1), March 1961, pp. 26-40.

Fraas, Arthur. "The Second Bank of the United States: An Instrument for an Interregional Monetary Union," *Journal of Economic History*, 34(2), June 1974, pp. 447-67.

Friedman, Philip. "Financial Intermediation and the Neutrality of Money: The Impact of Institutional Change Upon a Banker's Response, Post Civil War to the Great Depression," [Working Paper].

Goldsmith, Raymond W. *Financial Intermediaries in the American Economy Since 1900.* Princeton: Princeton University Press, 1958.

Goldsmith, Raymond W. "The Share of Financial Intermediaries in National Wealth and National Assets, 1900-1949," National Bureau of Economic Research, Occasional Paper no. 42, 1954 [Working Paper].

Goodhart, Charles A.E. "Profit on National Bank Notes, 1900-1913," *Journal of Political Economy*, 73(5), October 1965, pp. 516-22.

Goodhart, Charles A.E. *The New York Money Market and the Finance of Trade, 1900-1913.* Cambridge: Harvard University Press, 1969.

Green, George D. "Banking and Finance in Antebellum Louisiana: Their Influence on the Course of Economic Development," (Summary of Doctoral Dissertation) *Journal of Economic History*, 26(4), December 1966, pp. 579-81.

Green, George D. "The Louisiana Bank Act of 1842: Policy Making during Financial Crisis," *Explorations in Economic History*, 7(4), Summer 1970, pp. 399-412.

Green, George D. *Finance and Economic Development in the Old South: Louisiana Banking, 1804-1861.* Stanford: Stanford University Press, 1972.

Green, George D. "Louisiana, 1804-61," in Cameron, ed. *Banking and Economic Development*, 1972, pp. 199-231.

Green, George D. "Monetary Systems and Regional Economies: Comments on Papers by Rockoff and Bateman/Weiss," *Journal of Economic History*, 35(1), March 1975, pp. 212-15.

Hinderliter, Roger H. and Rockoff, Hugh T. "The Management of Reserves by Banks in Antebellum Eastern Financial Centers," *Explorations in Economic History*, 11(1), Fall 1973, pp. 37-54.

Hinderliter, Roger H. and Rockoff, Hugh T. "Banking under the Gold

Standard: An Analysis of Liquidity Management in the Leading Financial Centers," *Journal of Economic History*, 36(2), June 1976, pp. 379-98.

Horwich, George. "Effective Reserves, Credit, and Causality in the Banking System of the Thirties," in Hughes, ed. *Purdue Faculty Papers in Economic History, 1956-1966*, 1967, pp. 269-89.

James, John A. "The Evolution of the National Money Market, 1888-1911," (Summary of Doctoral Dissertation) *Journal of Economic History*, 36(1), March 1976, pp. 271-75.

James, John A. "The Conundrum of the Low Issue of National Bank Notes," *Journal of Political Economy*, 84(2), April 1976, pp. 359-67.

James, John A. "A Note on Interest Paid on New York Bankers' Balances in the Postbellum Period," *Business History Review*, 50(2), Summer 1976, pp. 198-202.

James, John A. "Banking Market Structure, Risk and the Pattern of Local Interest Rates in the United States, 1893-1911," *Review of Economics and Statistics*, 58(4), November 1976, pp. 453-62.

James, John A. "The Development of the National Money Market, 1893-1911," *Journal of Economic History*, 36(4), December 1976, pp. 878-97.

James, John A. "Cost Functions of Postbellum National Banks," *Explorations in Economic History*, 15(2), April 1978, pp. 184-95.

Jones, Homer. "Banking Reforms in the 1930s," in Walton, ed. *Regulatory Change in an Atmosphere of Crisis*, 1979, pp. 79-92.

Keehn, Richard H. "Market Structure and Bank Performance: Wisconsin, 1870-1900," *Transactions of the Wisconsin Academy of Sciences, Arts and Letters*, 56, 1973, pp. 149-56.

Keehn, Richard H. "Federal Bank Policy, Bank Market Structure, and Bank Performance: Wisconsin, 1863-1914," *Business History Review*, 48(1), Spring 1974, pp. 1-27.

Keehn, Richard H. and Smiley, Gene. "A Note on John A. James' Analysis of Interest Paid on Bankers' Balances in the Postbellum Period," *Business History Review*, 51(3), Autumn 1977, pp. 367-69.

Keehn, Richard H. and Smiley, Gene. "Mortgage Lending by National Banks, 1870-1914," *Business History Review*, 51(4), Winter 1977, pp. 474-91.

Keehn, Richard H. "Market Power and Bank Lending: Some Evidence from Wisconsin, 1870-1900," *Journal of Economic History*, 40(1), March 1980, pp. 45-52.

McGuire, William J. and Vedder, Richard K. "Bank Failures, 1929-1933: An Empirical Analysis," Ohio University Economic History Research Paper no. F-37 [Working Paper].

Olmstead, Alan L. "New York City Mutual Savings Banks in the Antebellum Years," (Summary of Doctoral Dissertation) *Journal of Economic History*, 31(1), March 1971, pp. 272-75.

Olmstead, Alan L. "Investment Constraints and New York City Mutual Savings Bank Financing of Antebellum Development," *Journal of Economic History*, 32(4), December 1972, pp. 811-40.

Olmstead, Alan L. "New York City Mutual Savings Bank Portfolio Management and Trustee Objectives," *Journal of Economic History*, 34(4), December 1974, pp. 815-34.

Olmstead, Alan L. "Mutual Savings Bank Depositors in New York," *Business History Review*, 49(3), Autumn 1975, pp. 287-311.

Olmstead, Alan L. *New York City Mutual Savings Banks, 1819-1861.* Chapel Hill: University of North Carolina Press, 1976.

Ransom, Roger L. and Sutch, Richard C. "Credit Merchandising in the Post-Emancipation South: Structure, Conduct, and Performance," *Explorations in Economic History*, 16(1), January 1979, pp. 64-89.

Redlich, Fritz. "American Banking and Growth in the Nineteenth Century: Epistemological Reflections (Comment on Sylla)," *Explorations in Economic History*, 10(3), Spring 1973, pp. 305-14.

Rockoff, Hugh T. "American Free Banking before the Civil War: A Re-Examination," (Summary of Doctoral Dissertation) *Journal of Economic History*, 32(1), March 1972, pp. 417-20.

Rockoff, Hugh T. "The Free Banking Era: A Re-Examinaton," *Journal of Money, Credit and Banking*, 6(2), May 1974, pp. 141-67.

Rockoff, Hugh T. *The Free Banking Era: A Re-Examination.* New York: Arno Press, 1975.

Rockoff, Hugh T. "Varieties of Banking and Regional Economic Development in the United States, 1840-1860," *Journal of Economic History*, 35(1), March 1975, pp. 160-81.

Rockoff, Hugh T. "Regional Interest Rates and Bank Failures, 1870-1914," *Explorations in Economic History*, 14(1), January 1977, pp. 90-95.

Rockoff, Hugh T. "Banking in the South," in Twyman and Roller, eds. *Encyclopedia of Southern History*, 1979.

Schwartz, Anna J. "The Beginning of Competitive Banking in Philadelphia, 1782-1809," *Journal of Political Economy*, 55(5), October 1947, pp. 417-31.

Schwartz, Anna J. "The Banking Reforms of the 1930s: Discussion (of Jones)," in Walton, ed. *Regulatory Change in an Atmosphere of Crisis*, 1979, pp. 93-99.

Smiley, Gene. "Regional Cost Differences among Country National Banks, 1888-1913," Marquette University Department of Economics Working Paper, August 1978 [Working Paper].

Sushka, Marie E. "The Antebellum Money Market and the Economic Impact of the Bank War," *Journal of Economic History*, 36(4), December 1976, pp. 809-35.

Sushka, Marie E. "The Antebellum Money Market and the Economic Impact of the Bank War: A Reply to Curran and Johnston," *Journal of Economic History*, 39(2), June 1979, pp. 467-74.

Sylla, Richard E. "The United States, 1863-1913," in Cameron, ed. *Banking and Economic Development*, 1972, pp. 232-62.

Sylla, Richard E. "American Banking and Growth in the Nineteenth Century: A Partial View of the Terrain," *Explorations in Economic History*, 9(2), Winter 1971/72, pp. 197-227.

Sylla, Richard E. "Economic History 'von unten nach oben' and 'von oben nach unten': A Reply to Fritz Redlich," *Explorations in Economic History*, 10(3), Spring 1973, pp. 315-18.

Sylla, Richard E. *The American Capital Market, 1846-1914.* New York: Arno Press, 1975.

Sylla, Richard E. "Forgotten Men of Money: Private Bankers in Early U.S. History," *Journal of Economic History*, 36(1), March 1976, pp.

173-88.

Sylla, Richard E. "Small-Business Banking in the United States, 1780-1920," in Bruchey, ed. *Small Business in American Life*, 1980, pp. 240-62.

Sylla, Richard E. "Money: A Discussion of Papers by Keehn, Howson, and Bordo/Schwartz Presented to the 39th Annual Meeting of the Economic History Association," *Journal of Economic History*, 40(1), March 1980, pp. 70-72.

Sylla, Richard E. "The Concept of the Corporation in Early British and American Banking," [Working Paper].

Temin, Peter. "The Economic Consequences of the Bank War," *Journal of Political Economy*, 76(2), March/April 1968, pp. 257-74.

Updike, Helen Hill. *The National Banks and American Economic Development, 1870-1900*. New York: Arno Press, 1977.

Warburton, Clark. "Variations in Economic Growth and Banking Developments in the United States from 1835 to 1885," *Journal of Economic History*, 18(3), September 1958, pp. 283-97.

White, Eugene N. "State Deposit Insurance before the FDIC," [Working Paper].

United States: Interest Rates

James, John A. "A Note on Interest Paid on New York Bankers' Balances in the Postbellum Period," *Business History Review*, 50(2), Summer 1976, pp. 198-202.

James, John A. "Banking Market Structure, Risk and the Pattern of Local Interest Rates in the United States, 1893-1911," *Review of Economics and Statistics*, 58(4), November 1976, pp. 453-62.

James, John A. "The Development of the National Money Market, 1893-1911," *Journal of Economic History*, 36(4), December 1976, pp. 878-97.

Keehn, Richard H. and Smiley, Gene. "A Note on John A. James' Analysis of Interest Paid on Bankers' Balances in the Postbellum Period," *Business History Review*, 51(3), Autumn 1977, pp. 367-69.

Keehn, Richard H. and Smiley, Gene. "Short Term Interest Rates in New York City and San Francisco, 1872-1898," [Working Paper].

National Bureau of Economic Research. *Corporate Bond Statistics, 1900-1938*. New York: National Bureau of Economic Research, 1941.

Neuberger, Hugh M. and Stokes, Houston H. "The Effect of Monetary Changes on the Interest Rates during the National Banking Period, 1875-1907: A Box-Jenkins Approach," Presented at the Seminar on Economic History, Columbia University, May 1976 [Working Paper].

Olmstead, Alan L. "Davis Vs. Bigelow Revisited: Antebellum American Interest Rates," *Journal of Economic History*, 34(2), June 1974, pp. 483-91.

Rockoff, Hugh T. "Regional Interest Rates and Bank Failures, 1870-1914," *Explorations in Economic History*, 14(1), January 1977, pp. 90-95.

Roll, Richard. "Interest Rates and Price Expectations During the Civil War," *Journal of Economic History*, 32(2), June 1972, pp. 476-98.

Smiley, Gene and Britton, Charles R. "Interregional Resource

Allocation: Mid-South Resource Flows during the 1880-1913 Period," *Annals of the Midsouth Academy of Economists*, 3, 1975, pp. 175-96.

Smiley, Gene. "Interest Rate Movement in the United States, 1888-1913," *Journal of Economic History*, 35(3), September 1975, pp. 591-620.

Smiley, Gene and Keehn, Richard H. "A Note on Interest Paid on New York Bankers' Balances in the Postbellum Period: A Note on James," *Business History Review*, 51(3), Autumn 1977, pp. 367-69.

Smiley, Gene and Keehn, Richard H. "Mortgage Lending by National Banks," *Business History Review*, 51(4), Winter 1977, pp. 474-91.

Smiley, Gene. "Revised Estimates of Short Term Interest Rates of National Banks for States and Reserve Cities, 1888-1913," Marquette University Department of Economics Working Paper, October 1976 [Working Paper].

Smiley, Gene. "Risk, Market Structure, and Transactions Costs in the Development of the National Short Term Capital Market, 1888-1913," Marquette University Department of Economics Working Paper, August 1978 [Working Paper].

Smiley, Gene and Keehn, Richard H. "Short Term Interest Rates in New York City and San Francisco, 1872-1898," Marquette University Department of Economics Working Paper, July 1978 [Working Paper].

Stigler, George J. *Capital and Rates of Return in Manufacturing Industries* (*General Series*, no. 78) Princeton: Princeton University Press for the National Bureau of Economic Research, 1963.

Sylla, Richard E. "Finance and Capital in the United States, 1850-1900," (Summary of Doctoral Dissertation) *Journal of Economic History*, 27(4), December 1967, pp. 621-24.

Sylla, Richard E. "Federal Policy, Banking Market Structure, and Capital Mobilization in the United States, 1863-1913," *Journal of Economic History*, 29(4), December 1969, pp. 657-86.

Sylla, Richard E. *The American Capital Market, 1846-1914*. New York: Arno Press, 1975.

Sylla, Richard E. "Financial Intermediaries in Economic History: Quantitative Research on the Seminal Hypotheses of Lance Davis and Alexander Gerschenkron," in Gallman, ed. *Recent Developments in the Study of Business and Economic History*, 1977.

Yamamura, Kozo. "Evolution of a Unified Capital Market in Japan, 1889-1925: A Statistical Analysis," [in Japanese] *Shakai Keizai Shigaku* (Tokyo University), 35(2), Spring 1970.

Rest of the World: General

Adie, Douglas K. "English Bank Deposits before 1844," (Reprinted in Floud, ed. *Essays in Quantitative Economic History*, 1974), p. 166-180 *Economic History Review*, Second Series, 23(2), August 1970, pp. 285-97.

Barsby, Steven. "Economic Backwardness and the Characteristics of Development," *Journal of Economic History*, 29(3), September 1969, pp. 449-50.

Baxter, Stephen B. "Domestic and International Integration of the London Money Market, 1731-1789: Comment on Eagly and Smith,"

Journal of Economic History, 36(1), March 1976, pp. 213-16.

Bouvier, Jean. "Sur les dimensions mesurables du fait financier, XIXe et XXe siecles [On the Measureable Achievements of Financiers, Nineteenth and Twentieth Centuries]," *Revue d'Histoire Economique et Sociale*, 46(2), 1968, pp. 161-84.

Bouvier, Jean. *Un siecle de banque francaise [A Century of French Banking]*. Paris: Hachette, 1973.

Bouvier, Jean. "Capital bancaire, capital industriel, capital financier dans la croissance francaise du 19 eme siecle [Bank Capital, Industrial Capital, and Financial Capital in Nineteenth Century French Growth]," *La Pensee*, 36), December 1974.

Bouvier, Jean. "Le Credit Lyonnais de 1863 a 1882: Les Annees de Formation d'Une Banque de Depots [The "Credit Lyonnais", 1863-1882: The Formative Years of a Bank-of-Deposit]," Ph.D. Dissertation, SEVPEN, 1961 [Working Paper].

Butlin, S.J.; Hall, A.R. and White, R.C. *Australian Banking and Monetary Statistics, 1817-1945.* (Reserve Bank Occasional Paper no. 4A) Sydney: Reserve Bank of Australia, 1971.

Burstein, M.L. "Homer on the History of Interest Rates," *Explorations in Entrepreneurial History*, Second Series, 2(1), Fall 1964, pp. 56-67.

Cairncross, Alec K. *Home and Foreign Investment, 1870-1913: Studies in Capital Accumulation.* Cambridge: Cambridge University Press, 1953.

Cairncross, Alec K. "The English Capital Market Before 1914: Comment on Hall," *Economica*, 25(98), May 1958, pp. 142-46.

Cameron, Rondo E. "Theoretical Bases of a Comparative Study of the Role of Financial Institutions in the Early Stages of Industrialization," *Second International Conference of Economic History, Aix-en-Provence, 1962*, vol. 2. Paris and The Hague: Mouton, 1965, pp. 567-86.

Cameron, Rondo E.; Crisp, Olga; Patrick, Hugh T. and Tilly, Richard. *Banking in the Early Stages of Industrialization.* London and New York: Oxford University Press, 1967.

Cameron, Rondo E. "Belgium, 1800-1875," in Cameron et al., *Banking in the Early Stages of Industrialization*, 1967, pp. 129-50.

Cameron, Rondo E. "Editor's Conclusion," in Cameron et al., *Banking in the Early Stages of Industrialization*, 1967, pp. 290-321.

Cameron, Rondo E. "England, 1750-1844," in Cameron et al., *Banking in the Early Stages of Industrialization*, 1967, pp. 15-59.

Cameron, Rondo E. "France, 1800-1870," in Cameron et al., *Banking in the Early Stages of Industrialization*, 1967, pp. 100-128.

Cameron, Rondo E. "Scotland, 1750-1845," in Cameron et al., *Banking in the Early Stages of Industrialization*, 1967, pp. 60-99.

Cameron, Rondo E. "Banking and Credit as Factors in Economic Growth," in Van der Wee, Vinogradov, and Kotovsky, eds. *Fifth International Congress of Economic History*, vol. 4, 1976, pp. 45-57.

Ciocca, Pierluigi. "Note sulla politica monetaria italiana 1900-1913 [Notes on Italian Monetary Policy, 1900-1913]," (Reprinted in Toniolo, ed. *l'economia italiana 1861-1940*, 1978, pp. 179-222) in Gianni Toniolo, ed. *Lo sviluppo economico italiano 1861-1940 [Italian Economic Development, 1861-1940]*. Bari: Laterza, 1973, pp. 241-82.

Ciocca, Pierluigi. "Introduzione all'edizione italiana [Introduction to the Italian Edition]," in Cameron et al., *Le banche e lo sviluppo del sistema industriale*, 1975, pp. 9-35.

Ciocca, Pierluigi and Biscaini Cotula, Anna Maria. "Le strutture finanziarie: aspetti quantitativi di lungo periodo (1870-1970) [Financial Structures: Long Run Quantitative Features (1870-1970)]," in Vicarelli, ed. *Capitale industriale e capitale finanziario: il caso italiano [Industrial Capital and Financial Capital: The Case of Italy]*, 1979, pp. 61-136.

Cohen, Jon S. "Finance and Industrialization in Italy, 1894-1914," (Summary of Doctoral Dissertation) *Journal of Economic History*, 16(4), December 1966, pp. 577-78.

Cohen, Jon S. "Financing Industrialization in Italy, 1894-1914: The Partial Transformation of a Late-Comer," *Journal of Economic History*, 27(3), September 1967, pp. 363-82.

Cohen, Jon S. "Banking and Industrialization: The Case of Italy, 1861-1914," Rondo E. Cameron, ed. Banking and Industrialization Among the Late-Comers Oxford: Oxford University Press, 1972.

Cohen, Jon S. *Finance and Industrialization in Italy, 1894-1914*. New York: Arno Press, 1977.

Collins, Michael. "English Bank Deposits before 1844: A Comment on Adie," *Economic History Review*, Second Series, 32(1), February 1979, pp. 114-17.

Crisp, Olga. "Russia, 1860-1914," in Cameron et al., *Banking in the Early Stages of Industrialization*, 1967, pp. 183-238.

David, Paul A. "Behavior of British Investment, 1860-1869," Center for Research in Economic Growth: Research Memo. 17 (Stanford University), 1961 [Working Paper].

Davis, Lance E. "The Capital Markets and Industrial Concentration: The U.S. and U.K., a Comparative Study," (Reprinted in Hughes, ed. *Purdue Faculty Papers in Economic History, 1956-1966*, 1967, pp. 663-682) *Economic History Review*, Second Series, 19(2), August 1966, pp. 255-72.

Davis, Lance E. "Capital Immobilities, Institutional Adaptation, and Financial Development: The United States and England, An International Comparison," in Giersch, Herbert, and Sauermann, eds. *Quantitative Aspects of Economic History*, 1968, pp. 14-34.

Drummond, Ian M. "Financial Institutions in Historical Perspective," *Canadian Banker*, 74(1), Spring 1966, pp. 150-58.

Eagly, Robert V. "Monetary Policy and Politics in Mid-Eighteenth Century Sweden," *Journal of Economic History*, 29(4), December 1969, pp. 739-57.

Eagly, Robert V. "Monetary Policy and Politics in Mid-Eighteenth-Century Sweden: A Reply to Sandberg," *Journal of Economic History*, 30(3), September 1970, pp. 655-56.

Eagly, Robert V. and Smith, V. Kerry. "Domestic and International Integration of the London Money Market, 1731-1789," *Journal of Economic History*, 36(1), March 1976, pp. 198-212.

Edelstein, Michael. "Rigidity and Bias in the British Capital Market, 1870-1913," in McCloskey, ed. *Essays on a Mature Economy*, 1971, pp. 83-112.

Edelstein, Michael. "Factor and Commodity Flows in the International

Economy of 1870-1914: Discussion of Papers by Eagly/Smith and Green/Urquhart," *Journal of Economic History*, 36(1), March 1976, pp. 253-58.

Edelstein, Michael. "Realized Rates of Return on U.K. Home and Overseas Portfolio Investment in the Age of High Imperialism," *Explorations in Economic History*, 13(3), July 1976, pp. 283-330.

Fetter, Frank W. "Some Pitfalls in the Use of Bank of England Credit Statistics: 1794-1832," *Review of Economics and Statistics*, 49(4), November 1967, pp. 619-23.

Fremdling, Rainer and Tilly, Richard H. "German Banks, German Growth, and Econometric History: A Note on Neuberger and Stokes," *Journal of Economic History*, 36(2), June 1976, pp. 416-24.

Fremdling, Rainer. "Die Rolle der Banken im Wachstumsprozess Deutschlands, 1850-1913 [The Role of Banks in the German Growth Process, 1850-1913]," Ph.D. Dissertation, Universitat Munster, West Germany, 1969 [Working Paper].

Goldsmith, Raymond W. "The Quantitative International Comparison of Financial Structure and Development," *Journal of Economic History*, 35(1), March 1975, pp. 216-37.

Good, David F. "Backwardness and the Role of Banking in Nineteenth-Century European Industrialization: A Note on Gerschenkron," *Journal of Economic History*, 33(4), December 1973, pp. 845-50.

Good, David F. "National Bias in the Austrian Capital Market before World War I," *Explorations in Economic History*, 14(2), April 1977, pp. 141-66.

Good, David F. "Financial Integration in Late Nineteenth-Century Austria," *Journal of Economic History*, 37(4), December 1977, pp. 890-910.

Good, David F. "Discrimination in the Austrian Capital Market? A Reply to Komlos," *Explorations in Economic History*, 17(4), October 1980, pp. 428-33.

Goodhart, Charles A.E. *The Business of Banking, 1891-1914*. London: Weidenfeld & Nicholson, 1972.

Hall, A.R. "A Note on the English Capital Market as a Source of Funds for Home Investment before 1914," *Economica*, 24(93), February 1957, pp. 59-66.

Hall, A.R. "The English Capital Market before 1914: A Reply to Cairncross," *Economica*, 25(100), November 1958, pp. 339-43.

Hall, A.R.; Butlin, S.J. and White, R.C. *Australian Banking and Monetary Statistics, 1817-1945*. Sydney: Reserve Bank of Australia, 1971.

Harley, C. Knick. "Goschen's Conversion of the National Debt and the Yield on Consols," *Economic History Review*, Second Series, 29(1), February 1976, pp. 101-6.

Harley, C. Knick. "The Interest Rate and Prices in Britain, 1873-1913: A Study of the Gibson Paradox," *Explorations in Economic History*, 14(1), January 1977, pp. 69-89.

Hawke, Gary R. *Between Governments and Banks: A History of the Reserve Bank of New Zealand*. Wellington: Government Printer, 1973.

Jonung, Lars. "The Legal Framework and the Economics of Private Bank Notes in Sweden, 1831-1902," in Skogh, ed. *Law and Economics*,

1978, pp. 185-201.

Kennedy, Jr., William P. "Institutional Response to Economic Growth: Capital Markets in Britain to 1914," in Hannah, ed. *Management Strategy and Business Development*, 1976, pp. 151-83.

Kirchhain, Gunter. "Geldmenge, Zinssatze und Wachstum in Deutschland, 1870-1913 [Money Supply, Interest Rates and Economic Growth in Germany, 1870-1913]," Diploma Thesis, Universitat Munster, 1968 [Working Paper].

Komlos, John. "German Banks and German Growth: Rejoinder to Neuberger and Stokes," *Journal of Economic History*, f8(2), June 1978, pp. 483-86.

Komlos, John. "The Kreditbanken and German Growth: A Postscript to Neuberger and Stokes," *Journal of Economic History*, 38(2), June 1978, pp. 476-79.

Komlos, John. "Discrimination in the Austrian Capital Market? Comment on Good," *Explorations in Economic History*, 17(4), October 1980, pp. 421-27.

Lewis, Kenneth A. and Yamamura, Kozo. "Industrialization and Interregional Interest Rate Structure, The Japanese Case: 1889-1925," *Explorations in Economic History*, 8(4), Summer 1971, pp. 473-99.

Mirowski, Philip. "The Rise (and Retreat) of a Market: English Joint Stocks in the Eighteenth Century," *Journal of Economic History*, 41(3), September 1981.

Neuberger, Hugh M. and Stokes, Houston H. "German Banking and Japanese Banking: A Comparative Analysis," *Journal of Economic History*, 35(1), March 1975, pp. 238-52.

Neuberger, Hugh M. and Stokes, Houston H. "German Banks and German Growth: Reply to Fremdling and Tilly," *Journal of Economic History*, 36(2), June 1976, pp. 425-27.

Neuberger, Hugh M. *German Banks and German Economic Growth from Unification to World War I.* New York: Arno Press, 1977.

Neuberger, Hugh M. and Stokes, Houston H. "German Banks and German Growth: Reply to Komlos," *Journal of Economic History*, 38(2), June 1978, pp. 480-82.

Neuburger, Hugh M. and Stokes, Houston H. "German Banks and German Growth, 1883-1913: an Empirical View," *Journal of Economic History*, 34(3), September 1974, pp. 710-31.

Neuhaus, Paulo. "A Doutrina do Credito Legitimo e o Primeiro Banco Central Brasileiro [The Real Bills Doctrine and the First Brazilian Central Bank]," *Revista Brasileira de Mercado de Capitais*, 1(1), 1974.

Nishimura, Shizuya. *The Decline of Inland Bills of Exchange in the London Money Market, 1855-1913.* Cambridge: Cambridge University Press, 1971.

Nishimura, Shizuya; Wood, G.E. and Mills, T. "The Estimates of Bank Deposits in the U.K., 1870-1913," [Working Paper].

Nye, William W. "The Old Lady Shows Her Metals: The British Money Market in the 1860's," [Working Paper].

Olmstead, Alan L. and Judd, John. "Saved from Sociology: The Frugal Scot and His Banking System," [Working Paper].

Patrick, Hugh T. "Japan, 1868-1914," in Cameron, Crisp, Patrick, and

Tilly, eds. *Banking in the Early Stages of Industrialization*, 1967, pp. 239-89.

Reed, M.C. *Investment in Railways in Britain, 1820-1844: A Study in the Development of the Capital Market.* Oxford: Oxford University Press, 1975.

Rudolph, Richard L. "Austria, 1800-1914," in Cameron, ed. *Banking and Economic Development*, 1972.

Rudolph, Richard L. *Banking and Industrialization in Austria-Hungary.* Cambridge: Cambridge University Press, 1976.

Sandberg, Lars G. "Monetary Policy and Politics in Mid-Eighteenth Century Sweden: A Comment on Eagly," *Journal of Economic History*, 30(3), September 1970, pp. 653-54.

Sandberg, Lars G. "Banking and Economic Growth in Sweden before World War I," *Journal of Economic History*, 38(3), September 1978, pp. 650-80.

Sayers, Richard S. *Central Banking after Bagehot.* Oxford: Oxford University Press, 1957.

Sayers, Richard S. *The Bank of England, 1891-1944* (3 vols). Cambridge: Cambridge University Press, 1976.

Sheppard, David K. *The Growth and Role of U.K. Financial Institutions, 1880-1962.* London: Methuen, 1971.

Tilly, Richard H. "Germany, 1815-1870," in Cameron, ed. *Banking in the Early Stages of Industrialization*, 1967, pp. 151-82.

Tilly, Richard H. "Zur Entwicklung des Kapitalmarktes und Industrialisierung im 19. Jahrhundert unter Besonderer Berucksichtigung Deutschlands [The Development of the Capital Market and Industrialization in the 19th Century: the Case of Germany]," (Reprinted in Kellenbenz, Schneider, and Gommel, eds. *Wirtschaftliches Wachstum im Spiegel der Wirtschaftsgeschichte*, 1978) *Vierteljahrschrift fur Sozial- und Wirtschaftsgeschichte*, 60(2), 1973, pp. 145-65.

Tortella Casares, Gabriel. "Banking and Industry in Spain, 1829-1874," (Summary of Doctoral Dissertation) *Journal of Economic History*, 29(1), March 1969, pp. 163-66.

Tortella Casares, Gabriel. "La evolution del sistema financiero espanol de 1856 a 1868 [The Evolution of the Spanish Financial System from 1856 to 1868]," in Giron, ed. *Ensayos sobre la economia espanola a mediados del siglo XIX*, 1970, pp. 17-146.

Tortella Casares, Gabriel. *La Banca espanola en la Restauracion* (vol. 1: *Politica y Finanzas*; vol. 2: *Datos para una historia economica*) [*The Spanish Banking System during the Restoration Period*]. Madrid: Banco de Espana, 1974.

Tortella Casares, Gabriel. *Banks, Railroads, and Industry in Spain, 1829-1874.* New York: Arno Press, 1977.

Tremblay, Rodrique. "L'Equilibre de la Balance des Paiements et L'Integration des Marches de Capitaux le Cas du Canada, 1923-1930 [The Equilibrium of the Balance of Payments and the Integration of Capital Markets: the Case of Canada, 1923-1930]," *Canadian Journal of Economics*, 1(4), November 1968, pp. 805-15.

Yamamura, Kozo. "The Role of the Samurai in the Development of Modern Banking in Japan," *Journal of Economic History*, 27(2), June 1967, pp. 198-220.

Yamamura, Kozo. "Japan, 1868-1912: A Revised View," in Cameron, ed. *Banking and Economic Development*, 1972.
Yamamura, Kozo. "The Role of Banking in Japan's Industrialization," in Cameron, ed. *Banking and Economic Development*, 1972.

Chapter 12

PRICE INDICES, INFLATION, AND THE MONEY SUPPLY

United States: Price Indices

Bean, Richard N. "The Importance of Regional Cost of Living Differentials in Estimating Gini-Coefficients for U.S. Income Inequality," [Working Paper].

Brady, Dorothy S. "Price Deflators for Final Product Estimates," in Brady, ed. *Output, Employment, and Productivity in the United States after 1800* (Studies in Income and Wealth, vol. 30), 1966, pp. 91-115.

Coelho, Philip R.P. and Shepherd , James F. "Differences in Regional Prices: The United States, 1851-1880," *Journal of Economic History*, 34(3), September 1974, pp. 551-91.

David, Paul A. and Solar, Peter. "A Bicentenary Contribution to the History of the Cost of Living in America," in Uselding, ed. *Research in Economic History*, vol. 2, 1977, pp. 1-80.

Hoover, Ethel D. "Retail Prices after 1850," in Parker, ed. *Trends in the American Economy in the Nineteenth Century* (Studies in Income and Wealth, vol. 24), 1960, pp. 141-86.

Kendrick, John W. "Retail Prices after 1850: Comment on Hoover," in Parker, ed. *Trends in the American Economy in the Nineteenth Century* (Studies in Income and Wealth, vol. 24), 1960, pp. 186-90.

Rees, Albert, assisted by Jacobs, Donald P. *Real Wages in Manufacturing, 1890-1914* (General Series, no. 70). Princeton: Princeton University Press for the National Bureau of Economic Research, 1961.

Rothenberg, Winifred B. "A Price Index for Rural Massachusetts, 1750-1855," (See note in this Journal, 40(1), March 1980, for a Corregenda concerning this article) *Journal of Economic History*, 39(4), December 1979, pp. 975-1001.

Williamson, Jeffrey G. "American Prices and Urban Inequality Since 1820," *Journal of Economic History*, 36(2), June 1976, pp. 303-33.

Rest of the World: Price Indices

Bean, Richard N. "Surrogate Price Indices for Several Countries in the Nineteenth Century," [Working Paper].

Desai, Ashok V. *Real Wages in Germany, 1871-1913*. Oxford: Oxford University Press, 1968.

Inflation

Good, David F. "The Cost-Of-Living in Austria, 1874-1913," *Journal of European Economic History*, 5(2), Fall 1976, pp. 391-400.

Hamilton, Earl J. "Use and Misuse of Price History," *Journal of Economic History*, 4, Supplement), 1944, pp. 47-60.

Hamilton, Earl J. "Price History," in Sills, ed., *International Encyclopedia of the Social Sciences*, vol. 12, 1968, pp. 471-77.

Jonung, Lars and Wadensjo, Eskil. "Wages and Prices in Sweden, 1912-1922: A Retrospective Test," *Scandinavian Journal of Economics*, 81(1), 1979, pp. 60-71.

Jorberg, Lennart. *A History of Prices in Sweden, 1732-1914* (vol. 1: *Sources, Methods, Tables*; vol. 2: *Description, Analysis*). Lund: University of Lund Press, 1972.

Noda, Tsutomu. "Commodity Prices and Wages, 1880-1965," in Ohkawa and Hayami, eds. *Economic Growth*, vol. 1, 1973, pp. 113-32.

Thornton, Judith G. "The Index Number Problem in the Measurement of Soviet National Income: A Review Article," (Review essay of *The Real National Income of Soviet Russia Since 1928*, by Bergson, 1961) *Journal of Economic History*, 22(3), September 1962, pp. 379-89.

Inflation

Buescu, Mircea. "A Inflacao Brasileira de 1850 a 1870: Monetarismo e Estruturalismo [The Brazilian Inflation from 1850 to 1870: Monetarism and Structuralism]," (Reprinted in *L'Histoire Quantitative du Bresil de 1800 a 1930*, 1973) *Revista Brasileira de Economia*, 26(4), October/December 1972, pp. 125-47.

Buescu, Mircea. *300 Anos de Inflacao [300 Years of Inflation]*. Rio de Janeiro: APEC, 1973.

Bustelo, Francisco and Tortella Casares, Gabriel. "Monetary Inflation in Spain, 1800-1970," *Journal of European Economic History*, 5(1), Spring 1976, pp. 141-50.

Cagan, Philip. "The Monetary Dynamics of the Hyper-Inflation," in Friedman, ed. *Studies in the Quantity Theory of Money*, 1956.

Chevallier, Dominique. "Western Development and Eastern Crisis in the Mid-Nineteenth Century: Syria Confronted with the European Economy," in Polk and Chambers, ed. *Beginnings of Modernization in the Middle East*, 1968, pp. 205-22.

Ciocca, Pierluigi. "L'ipotesi del "ritardo" dei salari rispetto ai prezzi in periodi di inflazione: alcune considerazioni generali (Part 2) [The Hypothesis that Wages Lag Prices in Periods of Inflation: Some General Comments]," *Bancaria*, (5), May 1969, pp. 572-83.

Davis, Tom E. "Eight Decades of Inflation in Chile, 1879-1959: A Political Interpretation," *Journal of Political Economy*, 71(4), August 1963, pp. 389-97.

Deane, Phyllis. "History of Inflation," in Heathfield, ed. *Perspectives on Inflation*, 1979.

Doughty, Robert A. "Industrial Prices and Inflation in Southern England, 1401-1640," *Explorations in Economic History*, 12(2), April 1975, pp. 177-92.

Frenkel, Jacob A. "The Forward Exchange Rate, Expectations and the Demand for Money: The German Hyperinflation," *American Economic Review*, 67, September 1977, pp. 653-70.

Friedman, Philip. "An Analysis of the International Transmission of Hyper-inflation: Central Europe, 1922-1925," [Working Paper].

Friedman, Philip. "Inflation, Deflation, and Forward Markets: The Effects of Trade and Exchange Markets on the German Hyper-inflation," [Working Paper].

Gayer, Arthur D.; Rostow, W.W. and Schwartz, Anna J. *The Growth and Fluctuation of the British Economy, 1790-1850.* (Revised Second Edition, New York: Barnes & Noble, 1975) Oxford: Clarendon Press, 1953.

Gerber, Haim and Gross, Nachum T. "Inflation or Deflation in Nineteenth-Century Syria and Palestine: A Note on Chevallier," *Journal of Economic History*, 40(2), June 1980, pp. 351-57.

Gordon, Robert J. "A Consistent Characterization of a Near-Century of Price Behavior," *American Economic Review Papers and Proceedings*, 70(2), May 1980, pp. 243-49.

Gould, John D. "The 'Price Revolution': Comments on a Comment," *Australian Economic History Review*, 9(2), September 1969, pp. 179-81.

Haddad, Claudio L.S. and Contador, Claudio R. "Produto Real, Moeda e Precos: A Experiencia Brasileira no Periodo 1861-1970 [Real Product, Money and Prices: The Brazilian Experience in the Period 1861-1970]," *Revista Brasileira de Estatistica*, 36(143), July/September 1975, pp. 407-40.

Hamilton, Earl J. *American Treasure and the Price Revolution in Spain, 1501-1650.* Cambridge: Harvard University Press, 1934.

Hamilton, Earl J. *Money, Prices, and Wages in Valencia, Aragon, and Navarre, 1351-1500.* Cambridge: Harvard University Press, 1936.

Hamilton, Earl J. "Prices, Wages, and the Industrial Revolution," in *Economics and Industrial Relations*, 1941, pp. 99-112.

Hamilton, Earl J. *War and Prices in Spain, 1651-1800.* Cambridge: Harvard University Press, 1947.

Hamilton, Earl J. "Prices as a Factor in Business Growth: Prices and Progress," *Journal of Economic History*, 12(4), Fall 1952, pp. 325-49.

Hamilton, Earl J. "The History of Prices before 1750," *XIe Congres International des Sciences Historiques, Stockholm, 1960.* Stockholm: Almqvist & Wiksell, 1962, pp. 144-64.

Hamilton, Earl J. "American Treasure and the Rise of Capitalism (1500-1700)," *Economica*, 9(27), November 1929, pp. 338-57.

Hamilton, Earl J. "Price History," in Sills, ed., *International Encyclopedia of the Social Sciences*, vol. 12, 1968, pp. 471-77.

Hines, A.G. "Trade Unions and Wage Inflation in the United Kingdom, 1893-1961," *Review of Economic Studies*, 31, 1964, pp. 221-52.

Hines, A.G. "Unemployment and the Rate of Change of Money Wage Rates in the United Kingdom, 1862-1963: A Reappraisal," *Review of Economics and Statistics*, 50(1), February 1968, pp. 60-67.

Hoffmann, Walther G. "Die "Phillips-Kurve" in Deutschland (with English Summary)," *Kyklos*, 22(2), 1969, pp. 219-31.

Holtfrerich, Karl-Ludwig. "Internationale Verteilungsfolgen der

Deutschen Inflation 1918-1923 [International Distributional Consequences of the German Inflation, 1918-1923]," *Kyklos*, 30(2), August 1977, pp. 271-92.

Holtfrerich, Karl-Ludwig. "Reichsbankpolitik 1918-1923 zwischen Zahlungsbilanz- und Quantitats theorie," *Zeitschrift fur Wirtsschafts- und Sozialwissenschaften*, 1977, pp. 193-214.

Holtfrerich, Karl-Ludwig. "Die Diskontpolitik der Reichsbank wahrend der Inflation 1918 bis 1923. Ein Beurteilungsraster [The Discount Policy of the Reichsbank during the Inflation, 1918 to 1923: A Framework for Judgement]," in Henning, ed. *Entwicklung und Aufgaben von Versicherung und Banken in der Industrialisierung* (*Schriften des Vereins fur Sozialpolitik*, n.s., 105), 1980, pp. 283-95.

Holtfrerich, Karl-Ludwig. "Domestic and Foreign Expectations and the Demand for Money During the German Inflation 1920-1923," [Working Paper].

Jonung, Lars and Wadensjo, Eskil. "A Model of the Determination of Wages and Prices in Sweden, 1922-1971," Economy and History, 21(2), 1978, pp. 104-13.

Kessel, Reuben A. and Alchian, Armen A. "Real Wages in the North During the Civil War: Mitchell's Data Reinterpreted," (Reprinted in Fogel and Engerman, eds. *The Reinterpretation of American Economic History*, 1971, pp. 459-467) *Journal of Law and Economics*, 2, October 1959, pp. 95-113.

Klein, John J. "German Money and Prices, 1932-44," in Friedman, ed., *Studies in the Quantity Theory of Money*, 1956, pp. 121-59.

Lerner, Eugene M. "Inflation in the Confederacy, 1861-65," in Friedman, ed. *Studies in the Quantity Theory of Money*, 1956, pp. 163-75.

Lipsey, Richard G. "The Relation between Unemployment and the Rate of Change of Money Wage Rates in the United Kingdom, 1862-1957: A Further Analysis," *Economica*, 27(105), February 1960, pp. 1-31.

Mokyr, Joel and Savin, N. Eugene. "Stagflation in Historical Perspective: The Napoleonic Wars Revisited," in Uselding, ed. *Research in Economic History*, vol. 1, 1976, pp. 198-259.

Phelps Brown, E.H. and Hopkins, Sheila V. "Seven Centuries of the Prices of Consumables, Compared with Builders' Wage Rates," (Reprinted in Ramsey, ed. *The Price Revolution in the Sixteenth Century*, 1971, pp. 18-41) *Economica*, 23(92), November 1956, pp. 296-314.

Phillips, A.W. "The Relation between Unemployment and the Rate of Change of Money Wage Rates in the United Kingdom, 1861-1957," *Economica*, 25(100), November 1958, pp. 283-99.

Pickersgill, Joyce E. "Hyperinflation and Monetary Reform in the Soviet Union, 1921-1926," *Journal of Political Economy*, 76(5), September/October 1968, pp. 1037-48.

Rockoff, Hugh T. "History of Price Controls in the United States," [Working Paper].

Schwartz, Anna J. "Secular Price Change in Historical Perspective," *Journal of Money, Credit and Banking*, 5(1, Part 2), February 1973, pp. 243-69.

Spencer, Austin H. "An Examination of the Relative Downward Industrial

185

Price Flexibility, 1870-1921," (Summary of Doctoral Dissertation) *Journal of Economic History*, 34(1), March 1974, pp. 300-303.

Spencer, Austin H. "Relative Downward Industrial Price Flexibility, 1870-1921," *Explorations in Economic History*, 14(1), January 1977, pp. 1-19.

Spencer, Austin H. *Relative Downward Price Flexibility, 1870-1921*. New York: Arno Press, 1978.

Sylla, Richard E. "The Public Sector and the Price Level in America, 1720-1977," [Working Paper].

United States: Money Supply

Agherli, Bijan B. "The Balance of Payments and Money Supply under the Gold Standard Regime: United States, 1879-1914," *American Economic Review*, 65(1), March 1975, pp. 40-58.

Bordo, Michael D. and Schwartz, Anna J. "Issues in Monetary Economics and their Impact on Research," in Gallman, ed. *Recent Developments in the Study of Economic and Business History*, 1977.

Bordo, Michael D. "The Income Effects of the Sources of New Money: A Comparison of the United States and the United Kingdom, 1870-1913," *Explorations in Economic History*, 14(1), January 1977, pp. 20-43.

Bordo, Michael D. and Schwartz, Anna J. "Money and Prices in the Nineteenth Century: An Old Debate Rejoined," *Journal of Economic History*, 40(1), March 1980, pp. 61-67.

Brunner, Karl. "Institutions, Policy, and Monetary Analysis," (Review essay of *A Monetary History of the United States*, by Friedman and Schwartz, 1963) *Journal of Political Economy*, 73(2), April 1965.

Cagan, Philip. *Determinants and Effects of Changes in the Stock of Money, 1875-1960*. New York: Columbia University Press for the National Bureau of Economic Research, 1965.

Edelstein, Michael. "Money: A Discussion of Papers by Keehn, Howson, and Bordo/Schwartz Presented to the 39th Annual Meeting of the Economic History Association," *Journal of Economic History*, 40(1), March 1980, pp. 68-69.

Esbitt, Milton. "A Re-examination of the Relationship Between Specie Flows and the Money Supply in the 1830's," Presented at the University of Chicago Workshop in Economic History, Paper #7273-1, October 1972 [Working Paper].

Falkus, Malcolm E. "United States Economic Policy and the 'Dollar Gap' of the 1920's," *Economic History Review*, Second Series, 24(4), November 1971, pp. 599-623.

Finkelstein, Stanley S. "The Currency Act of 1764: A Quantitative Reappraisal," *American Economist*, 12(2), Fall 1968, pp. 38-47.

Friedman, Milton and Schwartz, Anna J. *A Monetary History of the United States, 1867-1960*. Princeton: Princeton University Press for the National Bureau of Economic Research, 1963.

Friedman, Milton and Schwartz, Anna J. "Money and Business Cycles," *Review of Economics and Statistics*, 45(1, Part 2 Supplement), February 1963, pp. 32-78.

Friedman, Milton and Schwartz, Anna J. *Monetary Statistics of the United States: Estimates, Sources, Methods*. New York: Columbia

University Press for the National Bureau of Economic Research, 1970.

Friedman, Milton. "Monetary Trends in the United States and United Kingdom," *American Economist*, 16(1), Spring 1972, pp. 4-18.

Gandolfi, Arthur E. "Stability of the Demand for Money during the Great Contraction, 1929-1933," *Journal of Political Economy*, 82(5), September 1974, pp. 969-84.

Glynn, Sean and Lougheed, Alan L. "A Comment on United States Economic Policy and the "Dollar Gap" of the 1920's," *Economic History Review*, Second Series, 26(4), November 1973, pp. 692-94.

Gurley, John G. and Shaw, E.S. "The Growth of Debt and Money in the United States, 1800-1950: A Suggested Interpretation," *Review of Economics and Statistics*, 39(3), August 1957, pp. 250-62.

Gurley, John G. and Shaw, E.S. "Money," in Harris, ed. *American Economic History*, 1961, pp. 101-29.

Hanson, II, John R. "Money in the Colonial American Economy: An Extension," *Economic Inquiry*, 17(2), April 1979, pp. 281-86.

Hanson, II, John R. "Small Notes in the American Colonies," *Explorations in Economic History*, 17(4), October 1980, pp. 411-20.

James, John A. *Money and Capital Markets in Postbellum America.* Princeton: Princeton University Press, 1978.

Johnson, Harry G. "A Quantity Theorist's Monetary History of the United States," (Review essay of *A Monetary History of the United States, 1867-1960*, by Friedman and Schwartz, 1963) *Economic Journal*, 75(298), June 1965, pp. 388-96.

Khan, Mohsin S. "The Stability of the Demand-For-Money Function in the United States, 1901-1965," *Journal of Political Economy*, 82(6), November/December 1974, pp. 1205-20.

Lester, Richard. "Currency Issues to Overcome Depressions in Pennsylvania," in Andreano, ed. *New Views on American Economic Development*, 1965, pp. 73-118.

Macesich, George. "Sources of Monetary Disturbances in the United States, 1834-1845," *Journal of Economic History*, 20(3), September 1960, pp. 407-34.

Martin, David A. "Bimetallism in the United States before 1850," *Journal of Political Economy*, 76(3), May/June 1968, pp. 428-42.

Martin, David A. "Did the 'Crime of 1873' Really Occur in 1853?" *Papers and Proceedings of the New York State Economics Association*, vol. 1. December 1968, pp. 43-76.

Martin, David A. "1853: The End of Bimetallism in the United States," *Journal of Economic History*, 33(4), December 1973, pp. 825-44.

Martin, David A. "Metallism, Small Notes, and Jackson's War with the B.U.S.," *Explorations in Economic History*, 11(3), Spring 1974, pp. 227-48.

Martin, David A. "United States Gold Production Prior to the California Gold Rush," *Explorations in Economic History*, 13(4), October 1976, pp. 437-50.

Martin, David A. "The Changing Role of Foreign Money in the United States, 1782-1857," *Journal of Economic History*, 37(4), December 1977, pp. 1009-27.

Neuberger, Hugh M. and Stokes, Houston H. "The Effect of Monetary Changes on the Interest Rates during the National Banking Period,

1875-1907: A Box-Jenkins Approach," Presented at the Seminar on Economic History, Columbia University, May 1976 [Working Paper].

Schwartz, Anna J. "Monetary Trends in the United States and the United Kingdom, 1878-1970: Selected Findings," *Journal of Economic History*, 35(1), March 1975, pp. 138-59.

Schwartz, Anna J. and Bordo, Michael D. "Issues in Monetary Economics and Their Impact on Research in Economic History," in Gallman, ed. *Recent Developments in the Study of Economic and Business History*, 1977, pp. 81-129.

Stevens, Edward J. "Composition of the Money Stock Prior to the Civil War," *Journal of Money, Credit and Banking*, 3(1), February 1971, pp. 84-101.

Sylla, Richard E. "Money: A Discussion of Papers by Keehn, Howson, and Bordo/Schwartz Presented to the 39th Annual Meeting of the Economic History Association," *Journal of Economic History*, 40(1), March 1980, pp. 70-72.

Temin, Peter. "Money, Money Everywhere: A Retrospective," (Review essay of *The Monetary History of the United States, 1867-1960*, by Friedman and Schwartz, 1963) *Reviews in American History*, 5(2), June 1977, pp. 151-59.

Timberlake, Richard H. "Denominational Factors in Nineteenth-Century Currency Experience," *Journal of Economic History*, 34(4), December 1974, pp. 835-50.

Timberlake, Jr., Richard H. "The Specie Circular and the Distribution of the Surplus," *Journal of Political Economy*, 68(2), April 1960, pp. 109-17.

Timberlake, Jr., Richard H. "The Independent Treasury and Monetary Policy before the Civil War," *Southern Economic Journal*, 27(2), October 1960, pp. 92-103.

Timberlake, Jr., Richard H. "Mr. Shaw and His Critics: Monetary Policy in the Golden Era Reviewed," *Quarterly Journal of Economics*, 77(1), February 1963, pp. 40-54.

Timberlake, Jr., Richard H. "Ideological Factors in Specie Resumption and Treasury Policy," *Journal of Economic History*, 24(1), March 1964, pp. 29-52.

Timberlake, Jr., Richard H. "The Resumption Act and the Money Supply," *Journal of Monetary Economics*, 1(3), July 1975, pp. 343-54.

Timberlake, Jr., Richard H. "Repeal of Silver Monetization in the Late Nineteenth Century," *Journal of Money, Credit, and Banking*, 10(1), February 1978, pp. 27-45.

Tobin, James. "The Monetary Interpretation of History: A Review Article," *American Economic Review*, 55(3), June 1965, pp. 464-85.

Weiss, Roger W. "The Issue of Paper Money in the American Colonies, 1720-1774," *Journal of Economic History*, 30(4), December 1970, pp. 770-84.

Weiss, Roger W. "The Colonial Monetary Standard of Massachusetts," *Economic History Review*, Second Series, 27(4), November 1974, pp. 577-92.

Willett, Thomas D. "International Specie Flows and American Monetary Stability, 1834-1860," *Journal of Economic History*, 28(1), March 1968, pp. 28-50.

Rest of the World: Money Supply

Adie, Douglas K. "English Bank Deposits before 1844," (Reprinted in Floud, ed. *Essays in Quantitative Economic History*, 1974, pp. 166-180) *Economic History Review*, Second Series, 23(2), August 1970, pp. 285-97.

Adie, Douglas K. "The English Money Stock, 1834-1844," *Explorations in Economic History*, 9(2), Winter 1971/72, pp. 111-43.

Barber, Clarence L. "The Quantity Theory and the Income Expenditure Theory in an Open Economy, 1926-1958: A Comment (on Macesich)," *Canadian Journal of Economics and Political Science*, 32(3), August 1966, pp. 375-7.

Barrett, C.R. and Walters, A.A. "The Stability of Keynesian and Monetary Multipliers in the United Kingdom," *Review of Economics and Statistics*, 38, November 1966, pp. 395-405.

Bordo, Michael D. "The Income Effects of Monetary Change: A Historical Approach," *Economic Inquiry*, 13, December 1974, pp. 505-25.

Bordo, Michael D. and Schwartz, Anna J. "Issues in Monetary Economics and their Impact on Research," in Gallman, ed. *Recent Developments in the Study of Economic and Business History*, 1977.

Bordo, Michael D. "The Income Effects of the Sources of New Money: A Comparison of the United States and the United Kingdom, 1870-1913," *Explorations in Economic History*, 14(1), January 1977, pp. 20-43.

Bordo, Michael D. and Schwartz, Anna J. "Money and Prices in the Nineteenth Century: An Old Debate Rejoined," *Journal of Economic History*, 40(1), March 1980, pp. 61-67.

Bordo, Michael D. and Jonung, Lars. "The Long Run Behavior of the Income Velocity of Money: A Cross Country Comparison of Five Advanced Countries, 1870-1975," [Working Paper].

Buescu, Mircea. "A Inflacao Brasileira de 1850 a 1870: Monetarismo e Estruturalismo [The Brazilian Inflation from 1850 to 1870: Monetarism and Structuralism]," (Reprinted in *L'Histoire Quantitative du Bresil de 1800 a 1930*, 1973) *Revista Brasileira de Economia*, 26(4), October/December 1972, pp. 125-47.

Butlin, S.J., Hall, A.R. and White, R.C., eds. *Australian Banking and Monetary Statistics, 1817-1945* (Reserve Bank Occasional Paper no. 4A). Sydney: Reserve Bank of Australia, 1971.

Cagan, Philip. "The Monetary Dynamics of the Hyper-Inflation," in Friedman, ed. *Studies in the Quantity Theory of Money*, 1956.

Ciocca, Pierluigi. "Note sulla politica monetaria italiana 1900-1913 [Notes on Italian Monetary Policy, 1900-1913]," (Reprinted in Toniolo, ed. *l'economia italiana 1861-1940*, 1978, pp. 179-222) in Gianni Toniolo, ed. *Lo sviluppo economico italiano 1861-1940 [Italian Economic Development, 1861-1940]*. Bari: Laterza, 1973, pp. 241-82.

Collins, Michael. "Monetary Policy and the Supply of Trade Credit, 1830-44," *Economica*, 45, November 1978, pp. 379-89.

Collins, Michael. "English Bank Deposits before 1844: A Comment on Adie," *Economic History Review*, Second Series, 32(1), February 1979, pp. 114-17.

Coppietiers, E. *English Bank Note Circulation 1694-1954*. The Hague:

Louvain Institute of Economics and Social Research, 1955.

Courchene, Thomas J. "An Analysis of the Canadian Money Supply, 1925-1934," *Journal of Political Economy*, 77(3), May/June 1969, pp. 363-91.

Eagly, Robert V. "Monetary Policy and Politics in Mid-Eighteenth Century Sweden," *Journal of Economic History*, 29(4), December 1969, pp. 739-57.

Eagly, Robert V. "Monetary Policy and Politics in Mid-Eighteenth-Century Sweden: A Reply to Sandberg," *Journal of Economic History*, 30(3), September 1970, pp. 655-56.

Edelstein, Michael. "Money: A Discussion of Papers by Keehn, Howson, and Bordo/Schwartz Presented to the 39th Annual Meeting of the Economic History Association," *Journal of Economic History*, 40(1), March 1980, pp. 68-69.

Friedman, Milton. "Monetary Data and National Income Estimates," *Economic Development and Cultural Change*, 9(3), April 1961, pp. 267-86.

Friedman, Milton. "Monetary Trends in the United States and United Kingdom," *American Economist*, 16(1), Spring 1972, pp. 4-18.

Goodhart, Charles A.E. "The Determination of the Volume of Bank Deposits 1891-1914," Ph.D. Dissertation, University of Cambridge, 1963 [Working Paper].

Gould, John D. *The Great Debasement: Currency and the Economy in Mid-Tudor Emgland.* Oxford: Clarendon Press, 1970.

Gregory, Paul and Sailors, Joel W. "Russian Monetary Policy and Industrialization, 1861-1913," *Journal of Economic History*, 36(4), December 1976, pp. 836-51.

Haddad, Claudio L.S. and Contador, Claudio R. "Produto Real, Moeda e Precos: A Experiencia Brasileira no Periodo 1861-1970 [Real Product, Money and Prices: The Brazilian Experience in the Period 1861-1970]," *Revista Brasileira de Estatistica*, 36(143), July/September 1975, pp. 407-40.

Hall, A.R., Butlin, S.J. and White, R.C. *Australian Banking and Monetary Statistics, 1817-1945.* Sydney: Reserve Bank of Australia, 1971.

Hamilton, Earl J. *American Treasure and the Price Revolution in Spain, 1501-1650.* Cambridge: Harvard University Press, 1934.

Hamilton, Earl J. *Money, Prices, and Wages in Valencia, Aragon, and Navarre, 1351-1500.* Cambridge: Harvard University Press, 1936.

Hamilton, Earl J. *War and Prices in Spain, 1651-1800.* Cambridge: Harvard University Press, 1947.

Hamilton, Earl J. "The History of Prices before 1750," *XIe Congres International des Sciences Historiques, Stockholm, 1960.* Stockholm: Almqvist & Wiksell, 1962, pp. 144-64.

Hamilton, Earl J. "Imports of American Gold and Silver into Spain, 1503-1660," *Quarterly Journal of Economics*, 43, May 1929, pp. 436-72.

Hamilton, Earl J. "American Treasure and Andalusian Prices, 1503-1660: A Study in the Spanish Price Revolution," in Ramsey, ed. *The Price Revolution in the Sixteenth Century*, 1971, pp. 147-81.

Hawke, Gary R. "Income Estimation from Monetary Data: Further Explorations," *Review of Income and Wealth*, 21(3), September 1975,

pp. 301-308.

Heckscher, Eli. "Natural and Money Economy as Illustrated from Swedish History in the Sixteenth Century," *Journal of Economic and Business History*, 3(1), November 1930, pp. 1-29.

Higonnet, Renc P. "Bank Deposits in the United Kingdom, 1870-1914," *Quarterly Journal of Economics*, 71(3), August 1957, pp. 329-67.

Howson, Susan. "The Origins of Dear Money, 1919-20," *Economic History Review*, Second Series, 27(1), February 1974, pp. 88-107.

Howson, Susan. *Domestic Monetary Management in Britain, 1919-38.* Cambridge: Cambridge University Press, 1975.

Johnson, Harry G. *Clearing Bank Holdings of Public Debt, 1930-50* (Reprint Series no. 54). Cambridge: Cambridge University Press, 1952.

Jonson, P.D. "Money and Economic Activity in the Open Economy: The United Kingdom, 1880-1970," *Journal of Political Economy*, 84(5), October 1976, pp. 979-1012.

Jonson, Peter D. "Monetary and Economic Activity in the Open Economy: The United Kingdom, 1880-1970," *Journal of Political Economy*, 84, October 1976, pp. 979-1012.

Jonson, Peter D. "Inflation and Growth in the United Kingdom: A Longer Run Perspective," *Journal of Monetary Economics*, 3, January 1977, pp. 1-23.

Jonung, Lars. "Money and Prices in Sweden, 1732-1972," *Scandinavian Journal of Economics*, 78(1), 1976, pp. 40-58.

Jonung, Lars. "Sources of growth in the Swedish money stock, 1871-1971," *Scandinavian Journal of Economics*, 78(4), 1976, pp. 611-27.

Kavanagh, N.J. and Walters, A.A. "The Demand for Money in the U.K., 1877-1961: Some Preliminary Findings," *Oxford Bulletin of Economics and Statistics*, 28, May 1966, pp. 98-116.

Klein, John J. "German Money and Prices, 1932-44," in Friedman, ed. *Studies in the Quantity Theory of Money*, 1956, pp. 121-59.

Larna, K. *The Money Supply, Money Flows, and Domestic Product in Finland, 1910-1956.* Helsinki: Finnish Economic Association, 1959.

Leff, Nathaniel H. "A Technique for Estimating Income Trends from Currency Data and an Application to Nineteenth-Century Brazil," [Translated into Portuguese in *Revista Brasileira de Economia*, 1972] *Review of Income and Wealth*, 18(4), December 1972, pp. 355-68.

Lerner, Eugene M. "Inflation in the Confederacy, 1861-65," in Friedman, ed. *Studies in the Quantity Theory of Money*, 1956, pp. 163-75.

Lindert, Peter H. "A Century of International Monetary Evolution," in Van der Wee, Vinogradov, and Kotovsky, eds. *Fifth International Congress of Economic History*, Vol. 4, 1976, pp. 167-77.

Lothian, James R. and Huffman, Wallace. "Money in the United Kingdom, 1833-80," *Journal of Money, Credit and Banking*, 12, May 1980, pp. 155-74.

Macesich, George. "The Quantity Theory and the Income Expenditure Theory in an Open Economy: Canada, 1926-1958," *Canadian Journal of Economics and Political Science*, 30(3), August 1964, pp. 368-90.

Macesich, George. "Empirical Testing and the Income Expenditure Theory

(Reply to Barber)," *Canadian Journal of Economics and Political Science*, 32(3), August 1966, pp. 377-79.

Martin, David A. "The Impact of Mid-Nineteenth Century Gold Depreciation upon Western Monetary Standards," *Journal of European Economic History*, 6(3), Winter 1977, pp. 641-58.

Maxwell, Thomas. "The Long Run Demand for Money in South Africa, 1918-1960: Some Preliminary Findings," *South African Journal of Economics*, 39(1), March 1971, pp. 18-30.

Neuhaus, Paulo. *Historia Monetaria do Brasil, 1900-1945* [*The Monetary History of Brazil, 1900-1945*]. Rio de Janeiro: IBMEC, 1975.

Nwani Okonkwo A. "The Quantity Theory in the Early Monetary System of West Africa with Particular Emphasis on Nigeria, 1850-1895," *Journal of Political Economy*, 83(1), February 1975, pp. 185-94.

Nye, William W. "The Old Lady Shows Her Metals: The British Money Market in the 1860's," [Working Paper].

Ohkura, Takehiko and Shimbo, Hiroshi. "The Tokugawa Monetary Policy in the Eighteenth and Nineteenth Centuries," *Explorations in Economic History*, 15(1), January 1978, pp. 101-24.

Olson, Mancur L. "Reports of 'Shortages of Money' in Medieval Europe," [Working Paper].

Patterson, C.C. "Silver Stocks and Losses in Ancient and Medieval Times," *Economic History Review*, Second Series, 25(2), May 1972, pp. 205-35.

Pelaez, Carlos M. "As Consequencias Economicas da Ortodoxia Monetaria, Cambial e Fiscal no Brasil entre 1889 e 1945 [The Economic Consequences of Monetary, Exchange and Fiscal Orthodoxy in Brasil, 1889-1945]," *Revista Brasileira de Economia*, 25(3), July/September 1971, pp. 5-82.

Pelaez, Carlos M. and Suzigan, Wilson. "Bases para a Interpretacao Monetaria da Historia Economica Brasileira [Basis for a Monetary Interpretation of Brazilian Economic History]," *Revista Brasileira de Economia*, 26(4), October/December 1972, pp. 57-94.

Pelaez, Carlos M. and Suzigan, Wilson. *Historia Monetaria do Brasil: Analise da Politica, Comportamento e Instituicoes Monetarias* [*Monetary History of Brasil: Analysis of Policy Behavior and Monetary Institutions*] (IPEA Serie Monografica no. 23). Rio de Janeiro: Instituto de Planejamento Economico e Social, 1976.

Pelaez, Carlos M. "A Comparison of Long-Term Monetary Behaviour and Institutions in Brazil, Europe, and the United States," *Journal of European Economic History*, 5(2), Fall 1976, pp. 439-50.

Pelaez, Carlos M. "World War I and the Economy of Brazil: Some Evidence from Monetary Statistics," *Journal of Interdisciplinary History*, 7(4), Spring 1977, pp. 683-89.

Pelaez, Carlos M. and Suzigan, Wilson. "Comportamento e Instituicoes Monetarias no Brasil, 1852-1972 [Monetary Institutions and their Behavior in Brazil, 1852-1872]," in Neuhaus, ed. *A Economia Brasileira* [*The Brazilian Economy*], 1979, pp. 161-90.

Pickersgill, Joyce E. "Hyperinflation and Monetary Reform in the Soviet Union, 1921-1926," *Journal of Political Economy*, 76(5), September/October 1968, pp. 1037-48.

Rich, Georg. "The Cross of Gold, Money and the Canadian Business Cycle 1867-1913," [Working Paper].

Rockoff, Hugh T. "Money Supply," in Porter, ed. *Encyclopedia of American Economic History*, vol. 1, 1980, pp. 424-38.

Sandberg, Lars G. "Monetary Policy and Politics in Mid-Eighteenth Century Sweden: A Comment on Eagly," *Journal of Economic History*, 30(3), September 1970, pp. 653-54.

Schwartz, Anna J. "Monetary Trends in the United States and the United Kingdom, 1878-1970: Selected Findings," *Journal of Economic History*, 35(1), March 1975, pp. 138-59.

Schwartz, Anna J. and Bordo, Michael D. "Issues in Monetary Economics and Their Impact on Research in Economic History," in Gallman, ed. *Recent Developments in the Study of Economic and Business History*, 1977, pp. 81-129.

Smith, David. "A Monetary Model of the British Economy 1880-1975," *National Westminster Bank Quarterly Review*, February 1977, pp. 18-32.

Sylla, Richard E. "Money: A Discussion of Papers by Keehn, Howson, and Bordo/Schwartz Presented to the 39th Annual Meeting of the Economic History Association," *Journal of Economic History*, 40(1), March 1980, pp. 70-72.

Tilly, Richard H. "Zeitreihen zum Geldumlauf in Deutschland, 1870-1913 [Time Series on the Money Circulation in Germany, 1870-1913]," *Jahrbucher fur Nationalokonomie und Statistik*, 187(4), May 1973, pp. 330-63.

Triffin, Robert. *The Evolution of the International Monetary System: Historical Reappraisal and Future Perspectives* (Princeton Studies in International Finance, no. 12). Princeton, N.J.: Princeton University, Department of Economics, 1964.

Walters, A.A. "Money Multipliers in the United Kingdom, 1880-1962," *Oxford Economic Papers*, 18(3), November 1966, pp. 270-83.

Yamamura, Kozo and Crawcour, E.S. "The Tokugawa Monetary System: 1787-1868," *Economic Development and Cultural Change*, 18(4, Part 1), July 1970, pp. 489-518.

Chapter 13

FOREIGN TRADE

General

Adams, N.A. "Notes on 'Trade as a Handmaiden of Growth'," *Economic Journal*, 83(329), March 1973, pp. 210-12.

Baxter, Stephen B. "Domestic and International Integration of the London Money Market, 1731-1789: Comment on Eagly and Smith," *Journal of Economic History*, 36(1), March 1976, pp. 213-16.

Cairncross, Alec K. "World Trade in Manufactures since 1900," *Economia Internationale*, 8(4), November 1955, pp. 715-41.

Caves, Richard E. "Export-Led Growth and the New Economic History," in Bhagwati, ed. *Trade, Balance of Payments and Growth*, 1971, pp. 403-42.

Caves, Richard E.; North, Douglass C. and Price, Jacob M. "Introduction: Exports and Economic Growth," *Explorations in Economic History*, 17(1), January 1980, pp. 1-5.

Chambers, Edward J. and Gordon, Donald F. "Primary Products and Economic Growth: An Empirical Measurement," [Translated into Spanish in *Journal of the Fundacion de Investigationes Economicas Lationoamericanas*] *Journal of Political Economy*, 74(4), August 1966, pp. 315-32.

Chambers, Edward J. and Gordon, Donald F. "Primary Products and Economic Growth: Rejoinder to Dales, McManus, and Watkins," *Journal of Political Economy*, 75(6), December 1967, pp. 881-85.

Cooper, Richard N. "Growth and Trade: Some Hypotheses About Long-Term Trends," *Journal of Economic History*, 24(4), December 1964, pp. 609-28.

Crafts, N.F.R. "Trade as a Handmaiden of Growth: An Alternative View," *Economic Journal*, 83(331), September 1973, pp. 875-84.

Dales, John H.; McManus, John C. and Watkins, Melville H. "Primary Products and Economic Growth: A Comment on Chambers and Gordon," *Journal of Political Economy*, 75(6), December 1967, pp. 876-80.

Drummond, Ian M. "Empire Trade and Russian Trade: Economic Diplomacy in the Nineteen-Thirties," *Canadian Journal of Economics*, 5(1), February 1972, pp. 35-47.

Eagly, Robert V. and Smith, V. Kerry. "Domestic and International Integration of the London Money Market, 1731-1789," *Journal of Economic History*, 36(1), March 1976, pp. 198-212.

Edelstein, Michael. "Factor and Commodity Flows in the International Economy of 1870-1914: Discussion of Papers by Eagly/Smith and Green/Urquhart," *Journal of Economic History*, 36(1), March 1976,

pp. 253-58.
Green, Alan G. and Urquhart, M.C. "Factor and Commodity Flows in the International Economy of 1870-1914: A Multi-Country View," *Journal of Economic History*, 26(1), March 1976, pp. 217-52.
Hanson, II, John R. "More on Trade as a Handmaiden of Growth," *Economic Journal*, 87(347), September 1977, pp. 554-57.
Hanson, II, John R. "Export Instability in Historical Perspective," *Explorations in Economic History*, 14(4), October 1977, pp. 293-310.
Harley, C. Knick. "World Demand and Transportation Cost: Determinants of Prices and Output of Wheat in Exporting and Importing Regions, 1850-1913," University of Western Ontario, Department of Economics Research Report #2901 [Working Paper].
Hughes, Jonathan R.T. "Foreign Trade and Balanced Growth: The Historical Framework," (Reprinted in Hughes, ed. *Purdue Faculty Papers in Economic History, 1956-1966*, 1967, pp. 83-90) *American Economic Review, Papers and Proceedings*, 49(2), May 1959, pp. 330-37.
Kravis, Irving B. "Trade as a Handmaiden of Growth: Similarities between the Nineteenth and Twentieth Centuries," *Economic Journal*, 80(320), December 1970, pp. 850-72.
Kravis, Irving B. "Trade as a Handmaiden of Growth: A Reply to Crafts," *Economic Journal*, 83(329), March 1973, pp. 885-89.
Kravis, Irving B. "Trade as a Handmaiden of Growth: Reply to Adams," *Economic Journal*, 83(329), March 1973, pp. 212-17.
Kuznets, Simon S. "Quantitative Aspects of the Economic Growth of Nations (Part 10): Level and Structure of Foreign Trade: Long Term Trends," *Economic Development and Cultural Change*, 15(2, Part 2), January 1967, pp. 1-140.
Lewis, W. Arthur. "International Competition in Manufactures," *American Economic Review Papers and Proceedings*, 47(2), May 1957, pp. 578-87.
Lewis, W. Arthur. *The Evolution of the International Economic Order*. Princeton: Princeton University Press, 1978.
Lewis, W. Arthur. "The Slowing Down of the Engine of Growth," *American Economic Review*, 70(3), September 1980, pp. 555-64.
Maizels, Alfred. *Industrial Growth and World Trade*. (Second Edition, with corrections, published 1969) Cambridge: Cambridge University Press, 1965.
Williamson, Jeffrey G. "Growth and Trade: Some Hypotheses About Long-Term Trade: Discussion of Cooper," *Journal of Economic History*, 24(4), December 1964, pp. 629-33.

United States: General

Adams, Jr., Donald R. "Franco-American Trade, 1790-1815," Presented at the Conference on Franco-American Commerce, Eleutherian Mills-Hagley Foundation, Greenville, Wilmington, Delaware, 1977 [Working Paper].
Barger, Harold. "Income Originating in Trade, 1869-1929," in Parker, ed. *Trends in the American Economy in the Nineteenth Century* (Studies in Income and Wealth, vol. 24), 1960, pp. 327-33.

Bean, Richard N.; Anderson, Terry L. and Thomas, Robert P. "Economic Growth in the 17th Century American Colonies: Application of an Export-Led Growth Model," [Working Paper].

Berry, Thomas S. "Income Originating in Trade, 1869-1929: Comment on Barger," in Parker, ed. *Trends in the American Economy in the Nineteenth Century* (Studies in Income and Wealth, vol. 24), 1960, pp. 333-36.

Bruchey, Stuart. "Douglass C. North on American Economic Growth," *Explorations in Entrepreneurial History*, Second Series, vol. 1(2), Winter 1964, pp. 145-58.

Gilbert, Geoffrey N. "Baltimore's Flour Trade to the Carribean, 1750-1815," (Summary of Doctoral Dissertation) *Journal of Economic History*, 37(1), March 1977, pp. 249-51.

Gilbert, Geoffrey N. "The Role of Breadstuffs in American Trade, 1770-1790," *Explorations in Economic History*, 14(4), October 1977, pp. 378-87.

Goldin, Claudia D. and Lewis, Frank D. "The Role of Exports in American Economic Growth during the Napoleonic Wars, 1793 to 1807," *Explorations in Economic History*, 17(1), January 1980, pp. 6-25.

Goldin, Claudia D. and Lewis, Frank D. "Growth and Exports, 1793 to 1807, and a Re-Examination of Growth before 1840," [Working Paper].

Hutchinson, William K. "Regional Exports to Foreign Countries, U.S. 1870-1910: A Structural Analysis," [Working Paper].

Klingaman, David C. "The Coastwise Trade of Virginia in the Late Colonial Period," *Virginia Magazine of History and Biography*, 77(1), January 1969, pp. 26-45.

Klingaman, David C. "Food Surpluses and Deficits in the American Colonies, 1768-1772," *Journal of Economic History*, 31(3), September 1971, pp. 553-69.

Klingaman, David C. "The Coastwise Trade of Colonial Massachusetts," *Essex Institute Historical Collections*, 108(3), July 1972, pp. 217-34.

Klingaman, David C. *Colonial Virginia's Coastwise and Grain Trade.* New York: Arno Press, 1975.

Kravis, Irving B. "The Role of Exports in Nineteenth-Century United States Growth," *Economic Development and Cultural Change*, 20(3), April 1972, pp. 387-405.

Lampard, Eric E. "The United States Balance of Payments, 1861-1900: Comment on Simon," in Parker, ed. *Trends in the American Economy in the Nineteenth Century* (Studies in Income and Wealth, vol. 24), 1960, pp. 711-15.

Lindstrom, Diane L. "Southern Dependence upon Interregional Grain Supplies: A Review of the Trade Flows, 1840-1860," in Parker, ed. *The Structure of the Cotton Economy of the Antebellum South*, 1970, pp. 101-13.

Lipsey, R.E. *Price and Quantity Trends in the Foreign Trade Sector of the United States.* Princeton: Princeton University Press, 1963.

Lipsey, Robert E. "Foreign Trade," in Davis, Easterlin, and Parker, eds. *American Economic Growth*, 1972, pp. 548-81.

Macesich, George. "International Trade and United States Economic Development Revisited: Reply to Williamson," (Reprinted in Coben

and Hill, eds. *American Economic History*, 1966, pp. 256-258)
Journal of Economic History, 21(3), September 1961, pp. 384-85.

Marburg, Theodore F. "Income Originating in Trade, 1799-1869," in
Parker, ed. *Trends in the American Economy in the Nineteenth
Century* (Studies in Income and Wealth, vol. 24), 1960, pp. 317-26.

Mintz, Ilse. *Cyclical Flucuations in the Exports of the United States
since 1879*. New York: Columbia University Press for the National
Bureau of Economic Research, 1967.

Nicholas, Stephen J. "The American Export Invasion of Britain: The
Case of the Engineering Industry, 1870-1914," *Technology and
Culture*, 21(4), October 1980, pp. 570-88.

Niemi, Jr., Albert W. "Empirical Tests of the Heckscher Ohlin
Hypothesis for New England and Southern Manufacturing, 1860-1958,"
Review of Regional Studies, 4(Supplement), 1974, pp. 87-94.

North, Douglass C. "The United States in the International Economy,
1790-1950," in Harris, ed. *American Economic History*, 1961, pp.
181-206.

North, Douglass C. "Douglass C. North on American Economic Growth:
Comments on Stuart Bruchey's Paper," *Explorations in
Entrepreneurial History*, Second Series, 1(2), Winter 1964, pp.
159-63.

Nugent, Jeffrey B. "Exchange-Rate Movements and Economic Development
in the Late Nineteenth Century," *Journal of Political Economy*,
81(5), September/October 1973, pp. 1110-35.

Olson, Mancur L. "The Economic Growth of the Chesapeake and the
European Market, 1697-1775: Discussion of Price," *Journal of
Economic History*, 24(4), December 1964, pp. 512-16.

Parker, William N. "The International Market for Agricultural
Commodities, 1850-1873: Comment on Rothstein," in Gilchrist and
Lewis, eds. *Economic Change in the Civil War Era*, 1965, pp. 73-76.

Price, Jacob M. "A Note on the Value of Colonial Exports of Shipping,"
Journal of Economic History, 36(3), September 1976, pp. 704-24.

Rothstein, Morton. "The International Market for Agricultural
Commodities, 1850-1873," in Gilchrist and Lewis, eds. *Economic
Change in the Civil War Era*, 1965, pp. 62-72.

Rothstein, Morton. "Foreign Trade," in Porter, ed. *Encylopedia of
American Economic History*, vol. 1, 1980, pp. 247-63.

Shepherd, James F. "A Balance of Payments for the Thirteen Colonies,
1768-1772: A Summary," (Summary of Doctoral Dissertation) *Journal
of Economic History*, 25(4), December 1965, pp. 691-95.

Shepherd, James F. and Walton, Gary M. "Estimates of 'Invisible'
Earnings in the Balance of Payments of the British North American
Colonies, 1768-1772," *Journal of Economic History*, 29(2), June
1969, pp. 230-63.

Shepherd, James F. "Commodity Exports from the British North American
Colonies to Overseas Areas, 1768-1772: Magnitudes and Patterns of
Trade," *Explorations in Economic History*, 8(1), Fall 1970, pp.
5-76.

Shepherd, James F. and Walton, Gary M. *Shipping, Maritime Trade, and
the Economic Development of Colonial North America*. London:
Cambridge University Press, 1972.

Shepherd, James F. and Walton, Gary M. "Trade, Distribution and

Economic Growth in Colonial America," *Journal of Economic History*, 32(1), March 1972, pp. 128-45.

Shepherd, James F. and Williamson, Samuel H. "The Coastal Trade of the British North American Colonies, 1768-1772," *Journal of Economic History*, 32(4), December 1972, pp. 783-810.

Shepherd, James F. and Walton, Gary M. "The Effects of the American Revolution on American Maritime Trade and Shipping," *The American Revolution and the Sea: Proceedings of the 14th Conference of the International Commission for Maritime History at Greenwich, London, England.* London: National Maritime Museum, 1974, pp. 58-69.

Shepherd, James F. and Walton, Gary M. "Economic Change after the Revolution: Pre- and Post-War Comparisons of Maritime Shipping and Trade," *Explorations in Economic History*, 13(4), October 1976, pp. 397-422.

Simon, Matthew. "The United States Balance of Payments, 1861-1900," in Parker, ed. *Trends in the American Economy in the Nineteenth Century* (Studies in Income and Wealth, vol. 24), 1960, pp. 629-711.

Simon, Matthew and Novack, David. "Some Dimensions of the American Commercial Invasion of Europe, 1871-1914: An Introductory Essay," *Journal of Economic History*, 24(4), December 1964, pp. 591-605.

Vanek, Jaroslav. "The Natural Resource Content of Foreign Trade, 1870-1955, and the Relative Abundance of Natural Resources in the United States," *Review of Economics and Statistics*, 41(1), February 1959, pp. 146-53.

Vatter, Harold G. "An Estimate of Import Substitution for Manufactured Products in the U.S. Economy, 1859 and 1899," *Economic Development and Cultural Change*, 18(1, Part 1), October 1969, pp. 40-43.

Weiss, Roger W. "Comment on Papers by Jones, Shepherd and Walton, and McCusker Presented to the 31st Annual Meeting of the Economic History Association," *Journal of Economic History*, 32(1), March 1972, pp. 163-64.

Williamson, Jeffrey G. "International Trade and United States Economic Development, 1827-1843: Comment on Macesich," (Reprinted in Cohen and Hill, eds. *American Economic History*, 1966, pp. 245-256) *Journal of Economic History*, 21(3), September 1961, pp. 372-83.

Williamson, Jeffrey G. *American Growth and the Balance of Payments, 1820-1913: A Study of the Long Swing.* Chapel Hill: University of North Carolina Press, 1964.

Williamson, Jeffrey G. "Greasing the Wheels of Sputtering Export Engines: Midwestern Grains and American Growth," *Explorations in Economic History*, 17(3), July 1980, pp. 189-217.

United States: Tariffs

Baack, Bennett D. and Ray, Edward J. "Tariff Policy and Comparative Advantage in the Iron and Steel Industry, 1870-1929," *Explorations in Economic History*, 11(1), Fall 1973, pp. 3-24.

Baack, Bennett D. and Ray, Edward J. "Tariff Policy and Income Distribution: The Case of the U.S., 1830-1860," *Explorations in Economic History*, 11(2), Winter 1974, pp. 103-22.

David, Paul A. "Learning by Doing and Tariff Protection: A

Reconsideration of the Case of the Antebellum Cotton Textile Industry," *Journal of Economic History*, 30(3), September 1970, pp. 521-601.

David, Paul A. "The Use and Abuse of Prior Information in Econometric History: A Rejoinder to Professor Williamson on the Antebellum Cotton Textile Industry," *Journal of Economic History*, 32(3), September 1972, pp. 706-27.

Edwards, Richard C. "Economic Sophistication in Nineteenth-Century Congressional Tariff Debates," *Journal of Economic History*, 30(4), December 1970, pp. 802-38.

Engerman, Stanley L. "The American Tariff, British Exports, and American Iron Production, 1840-1860," in McCloskey, ed. *Essays on a Mature Economy*, 1971, pp. 13-38.

Fogel, Robert W. and Engerman, Stanley L. "A Model for the Explanation of Industrial Expansion During the Nineteenth Century: With an Application to the American Iron Industry," (Reprinted in Fogel and Engerman, eds. *The Reinterpretation of American Economic History*, 1971, pp. 148-162) *Journal of Political Economy*, 77(3), May/June 1969, pp. 306-28.

Green, J. "The Effect of the Iron Tariff in the United States," Paper presented to the Cliometrics Conference, Madison, Wisconsin, 1970 [Working Paper].

Hawke, Gary R. "The United States Tariff and Industrial Protection in the Late Nineteenth Century," *Economic History Review*, Second Series, 28(1), February 1975, pp. 84-99.

Ishikawa, Tsuneo. "Conceptualization of Learning by Doing: A Note on Paul David's 'Learning by Doing and...the Antebellum United States Textile Industry," *Journal of Economic History*, 33(4), December 1973, pp. 851-61.

James, John A. "The Welfare Effects of the Antebellum Tariff: A General Equilibrium Analysis," *Explorations in Economic History*, 15(3), July 1978, pp. 231-56.

Joskow, Paul L. and McFelvey, Edward F. "The Fogel-Engerman Iron Model: A Clarifying Note," *Journal of Political Economy*, 81(5), September/October 1973, pp. 1236-40.

Passell, Peter and Schmundt, Maria. "Pre-Civil War Policy and the Growth of Manufacturing," *Explorations in Economic History*, 9(1), Fall 1971, pp. 35-48.

Pincus, Jonathan J. "A Positive Theory of Tariff Formation Applied to Nineteenth Century United States," (Summary of Doctoral Dissertation) *Journal of Economic History*, 34(1), March 1974, pp. 273-74.

Pincus, Jonathan J. "Pressure Groups and the Pattern of Tariffs," *Journal of Political Economy*, 83(4), August 1975, pp. 757-78.

Pincus, Jonathan J. *Pressure Groups and Politics in Antebellum Tariffs*. New York: Columbia University Press, 1977.

Pincus, Jonathan J. "Tariffs," in Porter, ed. *Encyclopedia of American Economic History*, vol. 1, pp. 439-50.

Pope, Clayne L. "The Impact of the Antebellum Tariff on Income Distribution," (Summary of Doctoral Dissertation) *Journal of Economic History*, 31(1), March 1971, pp. 276-78.

Pope, Clayne L. "The Impact of the Antebellum Tariff on Income

Distribution," *Explorations in Economic History*, 9(4), Summer 1972, pp. 375-422.

Pope, Clayne L. *The Impact of the Antebellum Tariff on Income Distribution*. New York: Arno Press, 1975.

Sundarajan, V. "The Impact of the Tariff on Some Selected Products of the U.S. Iron and Steel Industry, 1870-1914," *Quarterly Journal of Economics*, 84(4), November 1970, pp. 590-610.

Williamson, Jeffrey G. "Embodiment, Disembodiment, Learning by Doing, and Returns to Scale in Nineteenth Century Cotton Textiles: A Comment on David," *Journal of Economic History*, 32(3), September 1972, pp. 691-705.

Williamson, Jeffrey G. "What Should the Civil War Tariffs Have Done Anyway?" Presented at the Social System Research Institute Workshop, Madison, Wisconsin, October 1973 [Working Paper].

Rest of the World: General

Adams, John. "A Statistical Test of the Impact of the Suez Canal on the Growth of India's Trade," *Indian Economic and Social History Review*, 8(3), September 1971, pp. 229-40.

Aitken, Hugh G.J. "The Role of Staple Industries in Canada's Economic Development: Discussion of Buckley," *Journal of Economic History*, 18(4), December 1958, pp. 451-52.

Ankli, Robert E. "The Growth of the Canadian Economy, 1896-1920: Export Led and/or Neoclassical Growth," *Explorations in Economic History*, 17(3), July 1980, pp. 251-74.

Bairoch, Paul. "Commerce exterieur et developpement economique. Les enseignements de l'experience libre-echangiste de la France au XIXe siecle [Foreign Trade and Economic Development: The Lessons from the French Interlude of Free Trade in the Nineteenth Century]," *Revue Economique*, 21(1), January 1970, pp. 1-33.

Bairoch, Paul. "Free Trade and European Economic Development in the 19th Century," *European Economic Review*, 3(3), November 1972, pp. 211-45.

Bairoch, Paul. "Le role du commerce exterieur dans la Genese de la revolution industrielle anglaise [The Role of Foreign Trade in the Origins of the Industrial Revolution in England]," *Annales: Economies, Societes, Civilisations*, 28(2), March/April 1973, pp. 541-71.

Bairoch, Paul. "European Foreign Trade in the 19th Century: The Development of the Value and Volume of Exports (Preliminary Results)," *Journal of European Economic History*, 2(1), Spring 1973, pp. 5-36.

Bairoch, Paul. "Geographical Structure and Trade Balance of European Foreign Trade from 1800 to 1870," *Journal of European Economic History*, 3(3), Winter 1974, pp. 557-608.

Bairoch, Paul. *Commerce exterieur et developpement economique de l'Europe au XIXe siecle [Foreign Trade and Economic Development: Europe in the Nineteenth Century]*. Paris and The Hague: Mouton, 1976.

Bairoch, Paul. "La place de la France sur les marches internationaux au XIXe siecle: presentation de quelques faits [The Position of France in International Markets in the Nineteenth Century: Presentation of Some Facts]," in Levy-Leboyer, ed. *La position internationale de la France*, 1977, pp. 37-52.

Baldwin, R.E. *Economic Development and Export Growth: A Study of Northern Rhodesia, 1920-1960.* Berkeley: University of California Press, 1966.

Bertram, Gordon W. "Economic Growth in Canadian Industry, 1870-1915: The Staple Model and the Take-Off Hypothesis," *Canadian Journal of Economics and Political Science*, 29, May 1963, pp. 159-84.

Brockstedt, Jurgen. *Die Schiffahrts- und Handelsbeziehungen Schleswig-Holsteins nach Lateinamerika, 1815-1848 [The Shipping and Trade Relationships of Schleswig-Holstein with Latin America, 1815-1848].* Koln: Bohlau, 1975.

Buckley, Kenneth. "The Role of Staple Industries in Canada's Economic Development," *Journal of Economic History*, 18(4), December 1958, pp. 439-50.

Capie, Forrest and Tucker, K.A. "British and New Zealand Trading Relationships, 1841-1852," *Economic History Review*, Second Series, 25(2), May 1972, pp. 293-302.

Chambers, Edward J. and Gordon, Donald F. "Primary Products and Economic Growth: An Empirical Measurement," [Translated into Spanish in *Journal of the Fundacion de Investigationes Economicas Lationoamericanas*] *Journal of Political Economy*, 74(4), August 1966, pp. 315-32.

Chambers, Edward J. and Gordon, Donald F. "Primary Products and Economic Growth: Rejoinder to Dales, McManus, and Watkins," *Journal of Political Economy*, 75(6), December 1967, pp. 881-85.

Chaudhuri, K.N. "India's International Economy in the Nineteenth Century: An Historical Survey," *Modern Asian Studies*, 2(1), January 1968, pp. 31-50.

Chaudhuri, K.N. "The Economic and Monetary Problem of European Trade with Asia during the Seventeenth and Eighteenth Centuries," *Journal of European Economic History*, 4(2), Fall 1975, pp. 323-58.

Cypher, J.M. "The Economic Significance of the Slave Trade in England, 1700-1760," (Abstract of Paper Presented to the 44th Annual Conference of the Western Economic Association) *Western Economic Journal*, 7(3), September 1969, pp. 255.

Dales, John H.; McManus, John C. and Watkins, Melville H. "Primary Products and Economic Growth: A Comment on Chambers and Gordon," *Journal of Political Economy*, 75(6), December 1967, pp. 876-80.

Dick, Trevor J.O. "The Specification Problem in Theories of Resource Determined Economic Growth," [Working Paper].

Dowie, Jack A. "Inverse Relations of the Australian and New Zealand Economies, 1871-1900," *Australian Economic Papers*, 2(2), December 1963, pp. 151-79.

Dowie, Jack A. "Inverse Relations of the Australian and New Zealand Economies, 1871-1900: Reply to von Tunzelmann," *Australian Economic Papers*, 5(3), June 1967, pp. 128-29.

Drummond, Ian. "Britain and the World Economy, 1900-45," in Floud and McCloskey, eds. *The Economic History of Britain since 1700*, vol. 2, 1980.

Dumke, Rolf H. "Intra-German Trade in 1837 and Regional Economic Development," *Vierteljahrschrift fur Sozial- und Wirtschaftsgeschichte*, 64(4), 1977, pp. 468-96.

Dumke, Rolf H. "Anglo-Deutscher Handel und Fruhindustrialisierung in Deutschland, 1822-1865 [Anglo-German Trade and Early Industrialization in Germany, 1822-1865]," *Geschichte und Gesellschaft*, 5(2), 1979.

Eddie, Scott M. "The Terms of Trade as a Tax on Agriculture: Hungary's Trade With Austria, 1883-1913," *Journal of Economic History*, 32(1), March 1972, pp. 298-315.

Eddie, Scott M. "The Terms and Patterns of Hungarian Foreign Trade, 1882-1913," *Journal of Economic History*, 37(2), June 1977, pp. 329-58.

Eddie, Scott M. "Die Auswirkung der Preisanderungen auf Ungarns Aussenhandel Wahrend der Schutzzollara [The Consequences of Price Fluctuations on Hungary's Foreign Trade during the Protectionist Period]," [Working Paper].

Eddie, Scott M. "Industrialization and Exports of Manufactures from Hungary During the Protectionist Period (1882-1913)," [Working Paper].

Firestone, O.J. "Canada's External Trade and Net Foreign Balance, 1851-1900," in Parker, ed. *Trends in the American Economy in the Nineteenth Century* (Studies in Income and Wealth, vol. 24), 1960, pp. 757-71.

Ford, A.G. "Notes on the Role of Exports in British Economic Fluctuations, 1870-1914," *Economic History Review*, Second Series, 16(2), December 1963, pp. 328-37.

Ford, A.G. "A Note on British Export Performance, 1899-1913," *Economic History Review*, Second Series, 22(1), April 1969, pp. 120-21.

Freund, W.M. and Shenton, R.W. "'Vent-for-Surplus' Theory and the Economic History of West Africa," *Savanna*, 6(2), December 1977, pp. 191-6.

Friedman, Philip. *The Impact of Trade Destruction Upon National Incomes: A Study of Europe, 1924-1938*. Gainsville: University of Florida Press, 1974.

Friedman, Philip. "The Welfare Costs of Bilateralism: German-Hungarian Trade, 1933-1938," *Explorations in Economic History*, 13(1), January 1976, pp. 113-25.

Friedman, Philip. "An Econometric Model of National Income, Commercial Policy and the Level of International Trade: The Open Economies of Europe, 1924-1938," *Journal of Economic History*, 38(1), March 1978, pp. 148-80.

Hansen, Bert and Lucas, Edward F. "Egyptian Foreign Trade, 1885-1961: A New Set of Trade Indices," *Journal of European Economic History*, 7(2-3), Fall/Winter 1978, pp. 429-60.

Hanson, II, John R. "The Nineteenth Century Exports of the Less Developed Countries," (Summary of Doctoral Dissertation) *Journal of Economic History*, 33(1), March 1973, pp. 305-8.

Hanson, II, John R. "The Leff Conjecture: Some Contrary Evidence," *Journal of Political Economy*, 84(2), April 1976, pp. 401-5.

Hanson, II, John R. "Diversification and Concentration of LDC Exports: Victorian Trends," *Explorations in Economic History*, 14(1), January

1977, pp. 44-68.
Hanson, II, John R. "Export Instability in Historical Perspective: Further Results," *Journal of Economic History*, 40(1), March 1980, pp. 17-23.
Harley, C. Knick and McCloskey, Donald N. "Foreign Trade, Competition and the Expanding International Economy," in Floud and McCloskey, eds. *The Economic History of Britain since 1700*, vol. 2, 1980.
Hawke, Gary R. "Long-Term Trends in New Zealand Imports," *Australian Economic History Review*, 18(1), March 1978, pp. 1-28.
Hogendorn, Jan S. and Brown, Wilson B. "Agricultural Export Growth and Myint's Model: Nigeria and Peru, 1900-1920," *Agricultural History*, 46(2), April 1972, pp. 313-24.
Hogendorn, Jan S. "The Vent for Surplus Model and African Cash Agriculture to 1914," *Savanna*, 5(1), June 1976, pp. 15-28.
Hogendorn, Jan S. "Vent-For Surplus Theory: A Reply to Freund and Shenton," *Savanna*, 6(2), December 1977, pp. 196-99.
Hogendorn, Jan S. *Nigerian Groundnut Exports: Origins and Early Development*. London and Zaria: Oxford University Press and Ahmadu Bello University Press, 1978.
Huber, J. Richard. "The Effect on Prices of Japanese Entry into World Commerce after 1858," *Journal of Political Economy*, 79(3), May/June 1971, pp. 614-28.
Huertas, Thomas F. "A New Economic History of the Hapsburg Monarchy," *Journal of Economic History*, 35(1), March 1975, pp. 130-33.
Hymer, Stephen H. "Economic Forms in Pre-Colonial Ghana," *Journal of Economic History*, 30(1), March 1970, pp. 33-50.
Imlah, A.H. *Economic Elements in the Pax Britannica*. Cambridge: Harvard University Press, 1958.
Johansen, Hans Chr. "Ostersohandelen og den Svensk-Russiske Krig 1788-90 [Baltic Trade and the Swedish-Russian War, 1788-90]," *Erhvervshistorisk Arbog*, 27, 1976/77, pp. 35-54.
Kindleberger, Charles P., assisted by Van der Tak, Herman G., and Vanek, Jaroslav. *The Terms of Trade: A European Case Study*. Cambridge, Mass. and New York: Technology Press of M.I.T. and Wiley, 1956.
Latham, A.J.H. *The International Economy and the Undeveloped World, 1886-1914*. London: Croom Helm, 1978.
Latham, A.J.H. "Merchandise Trade Imbalances and Uneven Economic Development in India and China," *Journal of European Economic History*, 7(1), Spring 1978, pp. 33-60.
Layton, T. Brent. "New Zealand's Social Accounting Aggregates and Official Trade Statistics, 1859-1939," Victoria University of Wellington, Working Papers in Economic History, no. 77/4, 1977 [Working Paper].
Leff, Nathaniel H. "Export Stagnation and Autarkic Development in Brazil, 1947-1962," [Translated into Portugese in El Trimestre Economico, 1969] *Quarterly Journal of Economics*, 81(2), May 1967, pp. 286-301.
Leff, Nathaniel H. "Tropical Trade and Development in the Nineteenth Century: The Brazilian Experience," *Journal of Political Economy*, 81(3), May/June 1973, pp. 678-96.
Levy-Leboyer, Maurice. "L'Heritage de Simiand: prix, profit et termes

d'echange au XXXe siecle," *Revue Historique*, (493), January/March 1970, pp. 77-120.

Lewis, Frank D. "The Canadian Wheat Boom and Per Capita Income: New Estimates," *Journal of Political Economy*, 83(6), December 1975, pp. 1249-57.

Lewis, W. Arthur. *Aspects of Tropical Trade, 1883-1965*. Stockholm: Almquist, 1969.

Mauro, F. "Towards an "Intercontinental Model": European Overseas Expansion between 1500 and 1800.," *Economic History Review*, Second Series, 14(1), 1961, pp. 1-17.

McAlpin, Michelle Burge. "The Impact of Trade on Agricultural Development: Bombay Presidency, 1855-1920," *Explorations in Economic History*, 17(1), January 1980, pp. 26-47.

McCloskey, Donald N. "Britain's Loss from Foreign Industrialization: A Provisional Estimate," *Explorations in Economic History*, 8(2), Winter 1970/71, pp. 141-52.

McCloskey, Donald N. "Markets Abroad and British Economic Growth, 1820-1913," [Working Paper].

McLean, Ian W. "The Australian Balance of Payments on Current Account, 1901 to 1964-65," *Australian Economic Papers*, 7(10), June 1968, pp. 77-90.

McLean, Ian W. "Anglo-American Engineering Competition, 1870-1914: Some Third-Market Evidence," *Economic History Review*, Second Series, 29(3), August 1976, pp. 452-64.

McRandle, James H. and Quirk, James P. "An Interpretation of the German Risk Fleet Concept, 1899-1914," in Hughes, ed. *Purdue Faculty Papers in Economic History, 1956-1966*, 1967, pp. 484-537.

Meyer, John R. "An Input-Output Approach to Evaluating the Influence of Exports on British Industrial Production in the Late 19th Century," *Explorations in Entrepreneurial History*, 8(1), October 1955, pp. 12-34.

Moggridge, Donald E. "Comments on Papers by Friedman and Vandagna Presented to the 37th Annual Meeting of the Economic History Association," *Journal of Economic History*, 38(1), March 1978, pp. 202-4.

Morgan, Theodore. "The Decline of Rural Industry Under Export Expansion: A Comparison among Burma, Philippines, and Thailand, 1870-1938 and Economic Forms in Pre-Colonial Ghana: Comments (on Resnick and Hymer)," *Journal of Economic History*, 30(2), June 1970, pp. 442-45.

Morris, Cynthia Taft and Adelman, Irma. "Patterns of Market Expansion in the Nineteenth Century: A Quantitative Study," in Dalton, ed. *Research in Economic Anthropology*, vol. 1, 1978.

Neal, Larry D. "The Economics and Finance of Bilateral Clearing Agreements: Germany, 1934-8," *Economic History Review*, Second Series, 32(3), August 1979, pp. 391-404.

Neill, R.F. "The Nature and Measurement of Canada's Reliance on Primary Product Exports," Carleton University Economic Working Paper no. 79-15, July 1979 [Working Paper].

Nicholas, Stephen J. "The American Export Invasion of Britain: The Case of the Engineering Industry, 1870-1914," *Technology and Culture*, 21(4), October 1980, pp. 570-88.

Paquet, Gilles and Wallot, Jean-Pierre. "Apercu sur le commerce international et les prix domestique dans le Bas Canada, 1793-1812," *Revue d'Histoire de l'Amerique Francaise*, 21(3), December 1967, pp. 447-73.

Paquet, Gilles and Wallot, Jean-Pierre. "International Circumstances of Lower Canada, 1786-1810: Prolegomena," *Canadian Historical Review*, 53(4), December 1972, pp. 371-401.

Paradisi, Mariangela. "Il commercio estero e la struttura industriale [Foreign Trade and Industrial Structure]," in Ciocca and Toniolo, eds. *L'economia italiana nel periodo fascista [The Italian Economy during the Fascist Era]*, 1976, pp. 271-328.

Pomfret, Richard W.T. "The Staple Theory and Canadian Economic Development," Concordia University Working Paper no. 77-08, October 1977 [Working Paper].

Rapp, Richard T. "The Unmaking of the Mediterranean Trade Hegemony: International Trade Rivalry and the Commercial Revolution," *Journal of Economic History*, 35(3), September 1975, pp. 499-525.

Rapp, William V. "A Theory of Changing Trade Patterns under Economic Growth: Tested for Japan," *Yale Economic Essays*, 7(2), Fall 1967, pp. 69-138.

Resnick, Stephen A. "The Decline of Rural Industry under Export Expansion: A Comparison among Burma, Philippines, and Thailand, 1870-1938," *Journal of Economic History*, 30(1), March 1970, pp. 51-73.

Schlote, Werner. *British Overseas Trade from 1700 to the 1930s*. [translated by W.O. Henderson and W.H. Chaloner] Oxford: Basil Blackwell, 1952.

Shepherd, James F. "Newfoundland and the Staple Theory: Export-Led Growth or Decline?" Presented at the Ninth Conference on the Application of Economic Theory and Quantitative Methods to Canadian Economic History, University of Western Ontario, London, Ontario, March 1978 [Working Paper].

Simon, Matthew and Novack, David. "Some Dimensions of the American Commercial Invasion of Europe, 1871-1914: An Introductory Essay," *Journal of Economic History*, 24(4), December 1964, pp. 591-605.

Sweden Statistika centralbyran. *Historisk Statistik for Sverige*, Del. 3: *Utrikeshandel, 1732-1970 [Historical Statistics of Sweden*, part 3: *Foreign Trade, 1732-1970]*. Stockholm: National Central Bureau of Statistics, 1972.

Thomas, Brinley. "The Rhythm of Growth in the Atlantic Economy," in Hegeland, ed. *Money, Growth and Methodology*, 1961, pp. 39-48.

Thomas, Brinley. *The Changing Pattern of Anglo-Danish Trade, 1913-1963*. Aarhus, Denmark: Erhvervshistorisk Arbog, 1966.

Thomas, Robert P. and McCloskey, Donald N. "Overseas Trade and Empire, 1700-1860," in Floud and McCloskey, eds. *The Economic History of Britain since 1700*, vol. 1, 1980, pp. 87-102.

Thomas, Robert P.; Anderson, Terry L. and Bean, Richard N. "Economic Growth in the Seventeenth Century American Colonies: Applications of an Export-Led Growth Model," [Working Paper].

Tortella Casares, Gabriel. "Las balanzas del comercio exterior espanol: un experimento historico-estadistico [The Spanish Foreign Trade Balances: a Statistical-Historical Experiment]," in Segura

and Delgado, eds. *Realidad Social y Analisis Economico*, 1978.
Toutain, Jean Claude. "Les structures du commerce exterieur de la France, 1789-1970 [The Structure of French Foreign Commerce, 1789-1970]," in Levy-Leboyer, ed. *La Position Internationale de la France*, 1977.
Tremblay, Rodrique. "L'Equilibre de la Balance des Paiements et L'Integration des Marches de Capitaux le Cas du Canada, 1923-1930 [The Equilibrium of the Balance of Payments and the Integration of Capital Markets: the Case of Canada, 1923-1930]," *Canadian Journal of Economics*, 1(4), November 1968, pp. 805-15.
Unger, Richard W. "Dutch Herring, Technology, and International Trade in the Seventeenth Century," *Journal of Economic History*, 40(2), June 1980, pp. 253-79.
Versiani, Flavio Rabelo. "Industrial Investment in an 'Export' Economy: The Brazilian Experience Before 1914," *Journal of Development Economics*, 7(3), September 1980, pp. 307-29.
Von Tunzelmann, G. Nicholas. "Inverse Relations of the Australian and New Zealand Economies, 1871-1900: An Hypothesis Re-Examined," *Australian Economic Papers*, 5(3), June 1967, pp. 124-27.
Weisskoff, Richard and Wolff, Edward. "Development and Trade Dependence: The Case of Puerto Rico, 1848-1963," *Review of Economics and Statistics*, 57(4), November 1975, pp. 470-77.

Rest of the World: Tariffs

Ankli, Robert E. "Canadian-American Reciprocity: A Comment on Officer and Smith," *Journal of Economic History*, 30(2), June 1970, pp. 427-31.
Ankli, Robert E. "The Reciprocity Treaty of 1854," *Canadian Journal of Economics and Political Science*, 4(1), February 1971, pp. 1-20.
Bairoch, Paul. "Free Trade and European Economic Development in the 19th Century," *European Economic Review*, 3(3), November 1972, pp. 211-45.
Bairoch, Paul. "Protectionnisme et expansion economique en Europe de 1892 a 1914 [Protectionism and Economic Expansion in Europe, 1892-1914]," *Relations Internationales*, (15), Autumn 1978, pp. 227-233.
Capie, Forrest. "The British Tariff and Industrial Protection in the 1930's," *Economic History Review*, Second Series, 31(3), August 1978, pp. 399-409.
Coats, A.W. "Political Economy and the Tariff Reform Campaign of 1903," *Journal of Law and Economics*, 11, April 1968, pp. 181-229.
Dales, John H. *The Protective Tariff in Canada's Development: Eight Essays on Trade and Tariffs when Factors Move with Special Reference to Canadian Protectionism, 1870-1955.* Toronto: University of Toronto Press, 1966.
Diaz Alejandro, Carlos F. "The Argentine Tariff, 1906-1940," *Oxford Economic Papers*, 19(1), March 1967, pp. 75-98.
Dick, Trevor J.O. "Approaches to Tariff Formation: The Case of Late Nineteenth Century Canadian Tariffs," [Working Paper].
Dumke, Rolf H. "The Political Economy of German Economic Unification:

Tariffs, Trade and Politics of the Zollverein Era," (Summary of Doctoral Dissertation) *Journal of Economic History*, 37(1), March 1977, pp. 56-58.

Dumke, Rolf H. "The Political Economy of German Economic Unification: Tariffs, Trade and Politics of the Zollverein Era," (Summary of Doctoral Dissertation) *Journal of Economic History*, 38(1), March 1978, pp. 277-78.

Dumke, Rolf H. "The Political Economy of Economic Integration: the Case of the German Zollverein of 1834," Queen's University, Institute for Economic Research Discussion Paper no. 153, Ontario, 1974 [Working Paper].

Dumke, Rolf H. "The Political Economy of German Economic Unification: Tariffs, Trade and Politics of the Zollverein Era," Ph.D. Dissertation, University of Wisconsin-Madison, 1976 [Working Paper].

Eddie, Scott M. "Cui Bono? Magyarorszag es a Dualista Monarchia vedovampolitikaja [Cui Bono? Hungary and the Protectionist Policy of the Dual Monarchy]," *Tortenelmi Szemle*, 19(1-2), 1976, pp. 156-66.

Eddie, Scott M. "Austria in the Dual Monarchy: Her Trade Within and Without the Customs Union," *East Central Europe*, 7(part 2), 1980, pp. 225-47.

Eddie, Scott M. "Economic Policy and Economic Development in Austria-Hungary, 1867-1913," in Mathias and Pollard, eds. *The Cambridge Economic History of Europe*, vol. 8.

Eichengreen, Barry J. "Economic Analysis And the Development of British Commercial Policy, 1929-1932," [Working Paper].

Eichengreen, Barry J. "The Macroeconomic Effects of the British General Tariff of 1932," [Working Paper].

Eichengreen, Barry J. "The Origins of Protection, 1923-1931," [Working Paper].

Foreman-Peck, James S. "Tariff Protection and Economies of Scale: The British Motor Industry Before 1939," *Oxford Economic Papers*, New Series, 31(2), July 1979, pp. 237-57.

Forster, Colin. "Federation and the Tariff," *Australian Economic History Review*, 17(2), September 1977, pp. 95-116.

Friedman, Philip. *The Impact of Trade Destruction Upon National Incomes: A Study of Europe, 1924-1938*. Gainsville: University of Florida Press, 1974.

Huertas, Thomas F. "Economic Growth and Economic Policy in a Multinational Setting: The Habsburg Monarchy, 1841-1865," (Summary of Doctoral Dissertation) *Journal of Economic History*, 38(1), March 1978, pp. 281-82.

Imlah, A.H. *Economic Elements in the Pax Britannica*. Cambridge: Harvard University Press, 1958.

Kindleberger, Charles P. "The Rise of Free Trade in Western Europe, 1820-1875," *Journal of Economic History*, 35(1), March 1975, pp. 20-55.

Komlos, John. "The Habsburg Monarchy as a Customs Union: Economic Development in Austria-Hungary in the Nineteenth Century," Ph.D. Dissertation, University of Chicago, 1978 [Working Paper].

McCloskey, Donald N. "Magnanimous Albion: Free Trade and British

National Income, 1841-1881," *Explorations in Economic History*, 17(3), July 1980, pp. 303-20.

Norrie, Kenneth H. "Agricultural Implement Tariffs, the National Policy, and Income Distribution in the Wheat Economy," *Canadian Journal of Economics*, 7(3), August 1974, pp. 449-62.

Officer, Lawrence H. and Smith, Lawrence B. "The Canadian-American Reciprocity Treaty of 1855 to 1866," *Journal of Economic History*, 28(4), December 1968, pp. 598-623.

Officer, Lawrence H. and Smith, Lawrence B. "Canadian-American Reciprocity: A Reply to Ankli," *Journal of Economic History*, 30(2), June 1970, pp. 432-34.

Olson, Mancur L. and Harris, Jr., Curtis C. "Free Trade in 'Corn': A Statistical Study of the Prices and Production of Wheat in Great Britain from 1873 to 1914," (Reprinted in Floud, ed. *Essays in Quantitative Economic History*, 1974, pp. 196-215) *Quarterly Journal of Economics*, 73(1), February 1959, pp. 145-69.

Sinclair, William A. "The Tariff and Manufacturing Employment in Victoria, 1860-1900: A Note," *Economic Record*, 31(60), May 1955, pp. 100-104.

Sinclair, William A. "The Tariff and Economic Growth in Pre-Federation Victoria," *Economic Record*, 47(117), March 1971, pp. 77-92.

Sonnemann, Rolf. *Die Auswirkungen des Schutzzolls auf die Monopolisierung der Deutschen Eisen- und Stahl-Industrie, 1879-1892* [*The Effects of Protective Tariffs on the Monopolization of the German Iron and Steel Industry, 1879-1892*]. Berlin: Akademie Verlag, 1960.

Toniolo, Gianni. "Effective Protection and Industrial Growth: The Case of Italian Engineering, 1898-1913," *Journal of European Economic History*, 6(3), Winter 1977, pp. 659-73.

Vamplew, Wray. "The Protection of English Cereal Producers: The Corn Laws Reassessed," *Economic History Review*, Second Series, 33(3), Augustt 1980, pp. 382-95.

Webb, Steven B. "Tariff Protection for the Iron Industry, Cotton Textiles and Agriculture in Germany, 1879-1914," [Appears in German] *Jahrbucher fur Nationalokonomie und Statistik*, 192(3-4), November 1977, pp. 336-57.

Webb, Steven B. "Tariffs, Cartels, Technology, and Growth in the German Steel Industry, 1879 to 1914," *Journal of Economic History*, 40(2), June 1980, pp. 309-29.

Webb, Steven B. "The Economic Effects of Protective Tarrifs in Imperial Germany, 1879-1914," Ph.D. Dissertation, University of Chicago, 1978 [Working Paper].

Chapter 14

TECHNOLOGY

United States: General

Ames, Edward and Rosenberg, Nathan. "The Enfield Arsenal in Theory and History," *Economic Journal*, 78(312), December 1968, pp. 827-42.

Atack, Jeremy; Bateman, Fred and Weiss, Thomas J. "The Regional Diffusion and Adoption of the Steam Engine in American Manufacturing," *Journal of Economic History*, 40(2), June 1980, pp. 281-308.

Ball, R.J. "Mr. Rosenberg on Capital Imports and Growth: A Further Comment," *Economic Journal*, 71(284), December 1961, pp. 853-55.

David, Paul A. "The "Horndal Effect" in Lowell, 1834-1856: A Short-Run Learning Curve for Integrated Cotton Textile Mills," *Explorations in Economic History*, 10(2), Winter 1973, pp. 131-50.

David, Paul A. *Technical Choice, Innovation and Economic Growth: Essays on American and British Experience in the Nineteenth Century.* Cambridge and New York: Cambridge University Press, 1975.

David, Paul A. "Invention and Accumulation in America's Economic Growth: A Nineteenth Century Parable," in Brunner and Meltzer, eds. *International Organization, National Policies and Economic Development*, 1977.

Delivanis, D.J. "Mr. Rosenberg on Capital Imports and Growth: Comment," *Economic Journal*, 71(284), December 1961, pp. 852-53.

Dick, Trevor J.O. *An Economic Theory of Technological Change: The Case of Patents and United States Railroads.* New York: Arno Press, 1978.

Engelbourg, Saul. "Energy and Industrialization: The Case of Southern New England," in Soltow, ed. *Essays in Economic and Business History*, 1979, pp. 268-82.

Feller, Irwin. "The Urban Location of United States Invention, 1860-1910," *Explorations in Economic History*, 8(3), Spring 1971, pp. 285-304.

Fisher, Franklin M. and Temin, Peter. "Returns to Scale in Research and Development: What does the Schumpeterian Hypothesis Imply?" *Journal of Political Economy*, 81(1), January/February 1973, pp. 56-70.

Flueckiger, Gerald. "Observation and Measurement of Technical Change," *Explorations in Economic History*, 9(2), Winter 1971/72, pp. 145-77.

Hayami, Yujiro and Ruttan, V.W. "Factor Prices and Technical Changes in Agricultural Development: The United States and Japan, 1880-1960," *Journal of Political Economy*, 78(5), September/October

1970, pp. 1115-41.

Higgs, Robert. "American Inventiveness, 1870-1920," *Journal of Political Economy*, 79(3), May/June 1971, pp. 661-67.

Hughes, Jonathan R.T. "Eight Tycoons: The Entrepreneur and American History," (Reprinted in Andreano, ed. *New Views on American Economic Development*, 1965, pp. 261-276) *Explorations in Entrepreneurial History*, Second Series, 1(3), Spring/Summer 1964, pp. 213-31.

Hughes, Jonathan R.T. "Entrepreneurship and the American Economy: A Sketch," in Uselding, ed. *Research in Economic History*, vol. 3, 1978, pp. 361-68.

Hughes, Jonathan R.T. "Entrepreneurship," in Porter, ed. *Encyclopedia of American Economic History*, vol. 1, 1980, pp. 214-28.

Kelley, Allen C. "Scale Economies, Inventive Activity, and the Economics of American Population Growth," *Explorations in Economic History*, 10(1), Fall 1972, pp. 35-52.

Klingaman, David C.; Vedder, Richard K. and Gallaway, Lowell E. "The Ames-Rosenberg Hypothesis Revisited: A Note on Uselding," *Explorations in Economic History*, 11(3), Spring 1974, pp. 311-14.

Lazonick, William H. "Industrial Relations and Technical Change: The Case of the Self-Acting Mule," *Cambridge Journal of Economics*, 3(3), September 1979, pp. 231-62.

North, Douglass C. "Innovation and the Diffusion of Technology (a Theoretical Framework)," *Fourth International Conference of Economic History, Bloomington, 1968*. Paris and The Hague: Mouton, 1973, pp. 221-31.

Poulson, Barry W. "Quantitative Aspects of Technological Innovation in American Industry before the Civil War," *Rocky Mountain Social Science Journal*, 4(1), April 1967, pp. 1-11.

Rosenberg, Nathan and Ames, Edward. "The Enfield Arsenal in Theory and History," *Economic Journal*, 78(312), December 1968, pp. 827-42.

Rosenberg, Nathan. *The American System of Manufactures: The Report of the Committee on the Machinery of the United States 1855, and the Special Reports of George Wallis and Joseph Whitworth 1854*. Edinburgh: University of Edinburgh Press, 1969.

Rosenberg, Nathan. "The Direction of Technological Change: Inducement Mechanisms and Focusing Devices," *Economic Development and Cultural Change*, 18(1, Part 1), October 1969, pp. 1-24.

Rosenberg, Nathan. "Economic Development and the Transfer of Technology: Some Historical Perspectives," *Technology and Culture*, 11(4), October 1970, pp. 550-75.

Rosenberg, Nathan. "Technological Change," in Davis, Easterlin, and Parker, eds. *American Economic Growth*, 1972, pp. 233-79.

Rosenberg, Nathan. *Technology and American Economic Growth*. New York: Harper & Row, 1972.

Rosenberg, Nathan. "Factors Affecting the Diffusion of Technology," *Explorations in Economic History*, 10(1), Fall 1972, pp. 3-34.

Rosenberg, Nathan. "Innovative Responses to Materials Shortages," *American Economic Review, Papers and Proceedings*, 63(2), May 1973, pp. 111-18.

Rosenberg, Nathan. "Science, Invention and Economic Growth," *Economic Journal*, 84(333), March 1974, pp. 90-108.

Rosenberg, Nathan. *Perspectives on Technology*. New York: Cambridge University Press, 1976.

Rosenberg, Nathan. "American Technology: Imported or Indigenous?" *American Economic Review, Papers and Proceedings*, 67(1), February 1977, pp. 21-26.

Rosenberg, Nathan. "The Role of Science and Technology in the National Development of the U.S.," in Beranek and Ranis, eds. *Science, Technology and Economic Development*, 1978.

Rosenberg, W. "Capital Imports and Growth - The Case of New Zealand: Foreign Investment in New Zealand, 1840-58," *Economic Journal*, 71(281), March 1961, pp. 93-114.

Rosenberg, W. "Mr. Rosenberg on Capital Imports and Growth: A Rejoinder to Delivanis," *Economic Journal*, 71(284), December 1961, pp. 855-56.

Rosenberg, W. "Mr. Rosenberg on Capital Imports and Growth: A Rejoinder to Ball," *Economic Journal*, 71(284), December 1961, pp. 855-56.

Schmookler, Jacob. "Economic Sources of Inventive Activity," *Journal of Economic History*, 22(1), March 1962, pp. 1-20.

Schmookler, Jacob. *Invention and Economic Growth*. Cambridge: Harvard University Press, 1966.

Smith, V. Kerry. "The Ames-Rosenberg Hypothesis and the Role of Natural Resources in the Production Technology," *Explorations in Economic History*, 15(3), July 1978, pp. 257-68.

Temin, Peter. "Steam and Waterpower in the Early Nineteenth Century," (Reprinted in Fogel and Engerman, eds. *The Reinterpretation of American Economic History*, 1971, pp. 228-237) *Journal of Economic History*, 26(2), June 1966, pp. 187-205.

Thompson, Alexander M. *Technology, Labor, and Industrial Structure in the U.S. Coal Industry*. New York: Garland Press, 1979.

Thompson, Alexander M. "Technological Change and the Control of Work," [Working Paper].

Thompson, Alexander M. "Workers' Control and the Fracturing of Miners' Skills in Appalachian Coal Mining," [Working Paper].

Uselding, Paul J. "Studies in the Technological Development of the American Economy during the First Half of the Nineteenth Century," (Summary of Doctoral Dissertation) *Journal of Economic History*, 31(1), March 1971, pp. 264-65.

Uselding, Paul J. "Technical Progress at the Springfield Armory, 1820-1850," *Explorations in Economic History*, 9(3), Spring 1972, pp. 291-316.

Uselding, Paul J. "Factor Substitution and Labor Productivity Growth in American Manufacturing, 1839-1899," *Journal of Economic History*, 32(3), September 1972, pp. 670-81.

Uselding, Paul J. and Juba, Bruce. "Biased Technical Progress in American Manufacturing, 1839-1899," *Explorations in Economic History*, 11(1), Fall 1973, pp. 55-72.

Uselding, Paul J. "The Ames-Rosenberg Hypothesis Revisited: A Rejoinder to Klingaman, Vedder, and Gallaway," *Explorations in Economic History*, 11(3), Spring 1974, pp. 315-16.

Uselding, Paul J. *Studies in the Technological Development of the American Economy during the First Half of the Nineteenth Century*.

New York: Arno Press, 1975.

Uselding, Paul J. "Studies of Technology in Economic History," in Gallman, ed. *Recent Developments in the Study of Business and Economic History*, 1977, pp. 159-220.

Weiher, Kenneth. "Slavery and Southern Urbanization: A Reformulation of the Argument," in Soltow, ed. *Essays in Economic and Business History*, 1979, pp. 259-67.

Williamson, Jeffrey G. "Technology, Growth, History," *Journal of Political Economy*, 84(4, Part 1), August 1976, pp. 809-20.

Habbakuk Controversy

Cain, Louis P. and Paterson Donald G. "Factor Biases and Technical Change in Manufacturing: The American System, 1850-1919," [Working Paper].

David, Paul A. and Klundert, TH. van de. "Biased Efficiency Growth and Capital-Labor Substitution in the U.S., 1899-1960," *American Economic Review*, 55(3), June 1965, pp. 357-94.

Drummond, Ian M. "Labor Scarcity and the Problem of American Industrial Efficiency in the 1850'S: A Comment on Temin," *Journal of Economic History*, 27(3), September 1967, pp. 383-90.

Field, Alexander J. "Habakkuk on American and British Technology: A Reexamination from a Capital-Theoretic Perspective," [Working Paper].

Fogel, Robert W. "The Specification Problem in Economic History," (A Correction for this article appears in this Journal, 28(1), March 1968, pp. 126) *Journal of Economic History*, 27(3), September 1967, pp. 283-308.

Habakkuk, H.J. *American and British Technology in the 19th Century: The Search for Labour-Saving Inventions.* Cambridge: Cambridge University Press, 1962.

Harley, C. Knick. "Skilled Labour and the Choice of Technique in Edwardian Industry," *Explorations in Economic History*, 11(4), Summer 1974, pp. 391-414.

James, John A. "Some Evidence on Relative Labor Scarcity in Nineteenth-Century American Manufacturing," [Working Paper].

Klingaman, David C.; Vedder, Richard K. and Gallaway, Lowell E. "The Ames-Rosenberg Hypothesis Revisited: A Note on Uselding," *Explorations in Economic History*, 11(3), Spring 1974, pp. 311-14.

Swan, Peter L. "Optimum Replacement of Capital Goods with Labor-Saving Technical Progress: A Comparison of the Early New England and British Textile Firm," *Journal of Political Economy*, 84(6), December 1976, pp. 1293-304.

Temin, Peter. "Labor Scarcity and the Problem of American Industrial Efficiency in the 1850's," *Journal of Economic History*, 26(3), September 1966, pp. 277-98.

Temin, Peter. "Labor Scarcity and the Problem of American Industrial Efficiency in the 1850's: A Reply to Drummond," *Journal of Economic History*, 28(1), March 1968, pp. 124-25.

Temin, Peter. "Labor Scarcity in America," *Journal of Interdisciplinary History*, 1(2), Winter 1971, pp. 251-64.

Uselding, Paul J. and Juba, Bruce. "Biased Technical Progress in American Manufacturing, 1839-1899," *Explorations in Economic History*, 11(1), Fall 1973, pp. 55-72.
Uselding, Paul J. "The Ames-Rosenberg Hypothesis Revisited: A Rejoinder to Klingaman, Vedder, and Gallaway," *Explorations in Economic History*, 11(3), Spring 1974, pp. 315-16.

Rest of the World: General

Bos, Roeland W.J.M. "Techniek en industrialisatie: Nederland in de negentiende eeuw [Technology and Industrialization: The Netherlands in the Nineteenth Century]," *Afdeling Agrarische Geschiedenis, Bijdragen*, 22, 1979, pp. 59-88.
Cameron, Rondo E. "The International Diffusion of Technology and Economic Development in the Modern Economic Epoch," in Glamann, Hornby, and Larsen, eds. *Sixth International Congress on Economic History*, 1974, pp. 83-92.
David, Paul A. "The Landscape and the Machine: Technical Interrelatedness, Land Tenure and the Mechanization of the Corn Harvest in Victorian Britain," in McCloskey, ed. *Essays on a Mature Economy*, 1971, pp. 145-204.
Field, Alexander J. "Habakkuk on American and British Technology: A Reexamination from a Capital-Theoretic Perspective," [Working Paper].
Freudenberger, Herman and Wolff, Klaus. "Transfer of Technology," (Summary of 1976 Research Workshop) *Journal of Economic History*, 37(1), March 1977, pp. 231-34.
Gould, John D. "The Landscape and the Machine: A Comment on David," *Economic History Review*, Second Series, 27(3), August 1974, pp. 455-60.
Harley, C. Knick. "The Shift from Sailing Ships to Steamships, 1850-1890: A Study in Technological Change and Its Diffusion," in McCloskey, ed. *Essays on a Mature Economy*, 1971, pp. 215-34.
Hayami, Yujiro, Ruttan, V.W. "Factor Prices and Technical Changes in Agricultural Development: The United States and Japan, 1880-1960," *Journal of Political Economy*, 78(5), September/October 1970, pp. 1115-41.
Hayami, Yujiro; Ruttan, Vernon W.; Binswanger, Hans P.; Wade, W.W. and Weber A. "Factor Productivity and Growth: A Historical Interpretation," in Binswanger, Ruttan, et al., eds. *Induced Innovation*, 1978.
Hohenberg, Paul M. *Chemicals in Western Europe, 1850-1914: An Economic Study of Technical Change*. Amsterdam and Chicago: North-Holland and Rand-McNally, 1967.
Hyde, Charles K. *Technological Change and the British Iron Industry, 1700-1870*. Princeton: Princeton University Press, 1977.
Klep, Paul M.M. "Technologische Modernisering in de Noordelijke en Zuidelijke Nederlanden Gedurende de Eerste Helft Van de Negentiende Eeuw [Technological Modernization in the Northern and Southern Netherlands during the First Half of the Nineteenth Century]," [Working Paper].

Kuczynski, Thomas. "Uberproduktion und Innovation [Overproduction and Innovation]," *Jahrbuch fur Wirtschaftsgeschichte*, (4), 1979, pp. 139-45.

Leff, Nathaniel H. "Entrepreneurship and Economic Development: The Problem Revisited," *Journal of Economic Literature*, 17(1), March 1979, pp. 46-64.

Lundgreen, Peter. "Wissenschaft und Wirtschaft. Methodische Ansatze und Empirische Ergebnisse (unter besonderer Berucksichtigung Deutschlands im 19. Jahrhundert) [Science and the Economy: Methods and Empirical Results]," *Technikgeschichte*, 44, 1977, pp. 302-14.

Nicholas, Stephen J. "Technical Change, Returns to Scale and Imperfect Markets in the British Inter-War Economy," University of New South Wales Working Paper in Economic History, 1978 [Working Paper].

Nicholas, Stephen J. "The Theory and Measurement of Technological Change in the British Inter-War Economy, 1920-1938," University of New South Wales Working Paper in Economic History, 1977 [Working Paper].

Parker, William N. "Entrepreneurship, Industrial Organization, and Economic Growth: A German Example," *Journal of Economic History*, 14(4), December 1954, pp. 380-400.

Parker, William N.; Strassman, W. Paul; Wilkening, E.A. and Merrill, Robert S. *The Diffusion of Technical Knowledge as an Instrument of Economic Development* (Symposia Studies Series no. 13) *National Institute of Social and Behavioral Science*, 1962.

Parker, William N. "Technology, Resources and Economic Change in the West," in Youngson, ed. *Economic Development in the Long Run*, 1972, pp. 62-78.

Rice, Richard. "Success Illgotten? The Role of Meiji Militarism in Japan's Technological Progress: Comment (on Yamamura)," Journal of Economic History, 37(1), March 1977, pp. 136-38.

Saxonhouse, Gary R. "A Tale of Technological Diffusion in the Meiji Period," *Journal of Economic History*, 36(1), March 1974, pp. 149-65.

Sayers, Richard S. "The Springs of Technical Progress, 1919-39," *Economic Journal*, 60(238), June 1950, pp. 275-91.

Schremmer, Eckart. "Wie Gross war der 'Technische Fortschritt' wahrend der Industriellen Revolution in Deutschland, 1850-1913 [How Large was the Technical Progress during the Industrial Revolution in Germany, 1850-1913?]," *Vierteljahrschrift fur Sozial- und Wirtschaftsgeschichte*, 60(4), 1973, pp. 433-58.

Spree, Reinhard. "Probleme der Messung des Technischen Fortschritts im Wachstum der Deutschen Volkswirtschaft seit 1850 mit Hilfe Makrookonomischer Produktionsfunktionen [Problems of Measuring Technical Progress in the Growth of the German Economy since 1850 with the Help of Macroeconomic Production Functions]," (Ph.D. Dissertation, Freie Universitat Berlin, 1969) [Working Paper].

Swan, Peter L. "Optimum Replacement of Capital Goods with Labor-Saving Technical Progress: A Comparison of the Early New England and British Textile Firm," Journal of Political Economy, 84(6), December 1976, pp. 1293-304.

Von Tunzelmann, G. Nicholas. "Technological Diffusion during the Industrial Revolution: The Case of the Cornish Pumping Engine," in

Hartwell, ed. *The Industrial Revolution* (Nuffield College Studies in Economic History, vol. 1), 1970, pp. 77-98.

Von Tunzelmann, G. Nicholas. *Steam Power and British Industrialization to 1860.* New York and London: Oxford University Press, 1978.

Von Tunzelmann, G. Nicholas. "Technical Progress during the Industrial Revolution," in Floud and McCloskey, eds. *The Economic History of Britain since 1700*, vol. 1, 1980, pp. 143-63.

Yamamura, Kozo. "A Reexamination of Entrepreneurship in Meiji Japan (1868-1912)," *Economic History Review*, Second Series, 21(1), April 1968, pp. 144-58.

Yamamura, Kozo. "The Role of the Merchant Class as Entrepreneurs and Capitalists in Meiji Japan," *Sozial und Wirtschaftsgeschichte*, June 1969.

Yamamura, Kozo and Rosovsky, Henry. "Entrepreneurial Studies in Japan: An Introduction," *Business History Review*, 44(1), Spring 1970, pp. 1-12.

Yamamura, Kozo. *A Study of Samurai Income and Entrepreneurship.* Cambridge: Harvard University Press, 1974.

Yamamura, Kozo. "Success Illgotten?: The Role of Meiji Militarism in Japan's Technological Change," *Journal of Economic History*, 37(1), March 1977, pp. 113-38.

Yoshihara, Kunio. "Productivity Change in the Manufacturing Sector, 1906-1965," in Ohkawa and Hayami, eds. *Economic Growth*, vol. 1, 1973, pp. 269-85.

Aldcroft, Derek H. "McCloskey on Victorian Growth: A Comment," *Economic History Review*, Second Series, 27(2), May 1974, pp. 271-74.

Allen, Robert C. "International Competition in Iron and Steel, 1850-1913," *Journal of Economic History*, 39(4), December 1979, pp. 911-37.

Allen, Robert C. "Entrepreneurship and Technical Progress in the Northeast Coast Pig Iron Industry, 1850-1913," in Uselding, ed. *Research in Economic History*, vol. 6, 1981.

Crafts, N.F.R. "Victorian Britain Did Fail," *Economic History Review*, Second Series, 32(4), November 1979, pp. 533-37.

Floud, Roderick C. "Britain, 1860-1914: A Survey," in Floud and McCloskey, eds. *The Economic History of Britain since 1700*, vol. 2, 1980.

Harley, C. Knick. "The Shift from Sailing Ships to Steamships, 1850-1890: A Study in Technological Change and Its Diffusion," in McCloskey, ed. *Essays on a Mature Economy*, 1971, pp. 215-34.

Henning, Graydon R. and Trace, Keith. "Britain and the Motorship: A Case of the Delayed Adoption of New Technology?" *Journal of Economic History*, 35(2), June 1975, pp. 353-85.

Kennedy, Jr., William P. "Foreign Investment, Trade, and Growth in the United Kingdom, 1870-1913," *Explorations in Economic History*, 11(4), Summer 1974, pp. 415-44.

Kennedy, Jr., William P. "Economic Growth and Structural Change in the U.K., 1870-1914," [Working Paper].

Lewis, W. Arthur. *The Deceleration of British Growth, 1873-1913.* Princeton: Princeton University Development Research Project, 1967.

Lindert, Peter H. and Trace, Keith. "Yardsticks for Victorian Entrepreneurs," in McCloskey, ed. *Essays on a Mature Economy,* 1971, pp. 239-74.

McCloskey, Donald N. "The British Iron and Steel Industry, 1870-1914: A Study of the Climacteric in Productivity," (Summary of Doctoral Dissertation) *Journal of Economic History,* 29(1), March 1969, pp. 173-75.

McCloskey, Donald N. "Did Victorian Britain Fail?" *Economic History Review,* Second Series, 23(3), December 1970, pp. 446-59.

McCloskey, Donald N. "International Differences in Productivity? Coal and Steel in America and Britain before World War I," in McCloskey, ed. *Essays on a Mature Economy,* 1971, pp. 285-304.

McCloskey, Donald N. and Sandberg, Lars G. "From Damnation to Redemption: Judgements on the Late Victorian Entrepreneur," *Explorations in Economic History,* 9(1), Fall 1971, pp. 89-108.

McCloskey, Donald N. *Economic Maturity and Entrepreneurial Decline: British Iron and Steel, 1870-1913.* Cambridge: Harvard University Press, 1973.

McCloskey, Donald N. "Victorian Growth: A Rejoinder (to Aldcroft)," *Economic History Review,* Second Series, 27(2), May 1974, pp. 275-77.

McCloskey, Donald N. "No It Did Not: A Reply to Crafts," *Economic History Review,* Second Series, 32(4), November 1979, pp. 538-41.

McCloskey, Donald N. "A Dialogue between William P. Kennedy and McCloskey on Late Victorian Failure or the Lack of It," in McCloskey, *Trade and Enterprise in Victorian Britain,* 1981.

Nicholas, Stephen J. "Measurement of Productivity, Climacterics and Technical Change in the 1870-1939 British Economy," University of New South Wales Working Paper in Economic History, 1976 [Working Paper].

Paterson, Donald G. "The Failure of British Business in Canada, 1890-1914," in Krooss, ed. *Proceedings of the Business History Conference, 1974,* Second Series, Vol. 3, 1975, pp. 14-31.

Richardson, H.W. "Retardation in Britain's Industrial Growth, 1870-1913," *Scottish Journal of Political Economy,* 12(2), June 1965, pp. 125-49.

Sandberg, Lars G. *Lancashire in Decline: A Study in Entrepreneurship, Technology and International Trade.* Columbus: Ohio State University Press, 1974.

Sandberg, Lars G. "The Entrepreneur and Technological Change," in Floud and McCloskey, eds. *The Economic History of Britain since 1700,* vol. 2, 1980.

Chapter 15

LABOR SUPPLY

United States: General

Adams, Jr., Donald R. "Wages Rates in Philadelphia, 1790-1830," (Summary of Doctoral Dissertation) *Journal of Economic History*, 27(4), December 1967, pp. 608-10.

Adams, Jr., Donald R. "Wages Rates in the Early National Period: Philadelphia, 1785-1830," *Journal of Economic History*, 28(3), September 1968, pp. 404-26.

Adams, Jr., Donald R. "Some Evidence on English and American Wage Rates, 1790-1830," *Journal of Economic History*, 30(3), September 1970, pp. 499-520.

Adams, Jr., Donald R. "Wage Rates in the Iron Industry: A Comment on Zabler," *Explorations in Economic History*, 11(1), Fall 1973, pp. 89-94.

Adams, Jr., Donald R. *Wage Rates in Philadelphia, 1790-1830.* New York: Arno Press, 1975.

Adams, Jr., Donald R. "Prices and Wages," in Porter, ed. *Encyclopedia of American Economic History*, vol. 1, 1980, pp. 229-46.

Allison, Chris and McGuire, William J. "Wage Discrimination and Economies of Scale in the American Manufacturing Sector, 1820-1920," Ohio University Economic History Research Paper no. G-6 [Working Paper].

Ashenfelter, Orley and Pencavel, John H. "American Trade Union Growth: 1900-1960," *Quarterly Journal of Economics*, 83(3), August 1964, pp. 434-48.

Bean, Richard N. "The Rate of Return on the Ownership of Indentured Servant Contracts in Colonial America," [Working Paper].

Brito, D.L. and Williamson, Jeffrey G. "Skilled Labor and Nineteenth-Century Anglo-American Managerial Behavior," *Explorations in Economic History*, 10(3), Spring 1973, pp. 235-52.

Burford, Roger L. "The Federal Cotton Programs and Farm Labor Force Adjustments," *Southern Economic Journal*, 33(2), October 1966, pp. 223-36.

Campbell, Mildred. "The Social Origins of Some Early Americans: Response to Galenson," *William and Mary Quarterly*, 3rd ser., 35(3), July 1978, pp. 525-40.

Campbell, Mildred. "The Social Origins of Some Early Americans: Reply to Galenson," *William and Mary Quarterly*, 3rd ser., 36(2), April 1979, pp. 277-86.

Cebula, Richard J. and Vedder, Richard K. "An Empirical Analysis of

Income Expectations and Interstate Migration," *Review of Regional Studies*, 5(1), Spring 1975, pp. 19-28.

Coelho, Philip R.P. and Ghali, Moheb A. "The End of the North-South Wage Differential," *American Economic Review*, 61(5), December 1971, pp. 932-37.

Coelho, Philip R.P. and Ghali, Moheb A. "The End of the North-South Wage Differential: Reply (to Ladenson)," *American Economic Review*, 63(4), September 1973, pp. 757-62.

Coelho, Philip R.P. and Shepherd, James F. "Regional Differences in Real Wages: The United States, 1851-1880," *Explorations in Economic History*, 13(2), April 1976, pp. 203-30.

Coen, Robert M. "Labor Force and Unemployment in the 1920's and 1930's: A Re-examination based on Postwar Experience," *Review of Economics and Statistics*, 55(1), February 1973, pp. 46-55.

Coen, Robert M. "Labor Force and Unemployment in the 1920's and 1930's: A Reply to Lebergott," *Review of Economics and Statistics*, 55(4), November 1973, pp. 527-28.

Darby, Michael R. "Three and-a-Half Million U.S. Employees Have Been Mislaid: Or, an Explanation of Unemployment, 1934-1941," *Journal of Political Economy*, 84(1), February 1976, pp. 1-16.

David, Paul A. "Estimates of the U.S. Labor Force, Industrial and Regional Distribution, 1800-1840," [Working Paper].

Earle, Carville V. "Entering the Modern Age: A Geographical Interpretation of Labor Economics, Industrialization, and the 'Working Class' in the Antebellum United States," Presented at the Annual Cliometrics Conference, University of Chicago, Chicago, June 1979 [Working Paper].

Ermisch, John and Weiss, Thomas J. "The Impact of the Rural Market on the Growth of the Urban Workforce: U.S., 1870-1900," *Explorations in Economic History*, 11(2), Winter 1974, pp. 137-54.

Estey, Marten S. "Trends in Concentration of Union Membership, 1897-1962," *Quarterly Journal of Economics*, 80(3), August 1966, pp. 343-60.

Fabricant, Solomon. *Employment in Manufacturing, 1899-1939* (General Series, no. 41). New York: National Bureau of Economic Research, 1942.

Galenson, David W. "Immigration and the Colonial Labor System: An Analysis of the Length of Indenture," *Explorations in Economic History*, 14(4), October 1977, pp. 360-77.

Galenson, David W. "British Servants and the Colonial Indenture System in the Eighteenth Century," *Journal of Southern History*, 44(1), February 1978, pp. 41-66.

Galenson, David W. "'Middling People' or 'Common Sort'?: The Social Origins of Some Early Americans Reexamined," *William and Mary Quarterly*, Third Series, 35(3), July 1978, pp. 499-524.

Galenson, David W. "The Social Origins of Some Early Americans: Rejoinder," *William and Mary Quarterly*, Third Series, 36(2), April 1979, pp. 264-77.

Galenson, David W. "Literacy and the Social Origins of Some Early Americans," *Historical Journal*, 22(1), May 1979, pp. 75-96.

Galenson, David W. "Demographic Aspects of White Servitude in Colonial British America," *Annales de Demographic Historique*, 1980, pp.

239-52.

Galenson, David W. *White Servitude in Colonial America: An Economic Analysis.* Cambridge and New York: Cambridge University Press, 1981.

Gemery, Henry A. "Emigration from the British Isles to the New World, 1630-1700: Inferences from Colonial Populations," in Uselding, ed. *Research in Economic History*, vol. 5, 1980, pp. 179-232.

Hallagan, William S. "Labor Contracting in Turn-Of-The-Century California Agriculture," *Journal of Economic History*, 40(4), December 1980, pp. 757-76.

Hannon, Joan Underhill. "The Immigrant Worker in the Promised Land: Human Capital and Ethnic Discrimination in the Michigan Labor Market, 1888-1890," Ph.D. Dissertation, University of Wisconsin-Madison, 1978 [Working Paper].

Hartwell, R.M. "Slave Labour and Factory Labour," Presented at the MSSB-University of Rochester Conference, Time on the Cross: A First Appraisal, October 1974 [Working Paper].

Heavner, Robert O. "Indentured Servitude: The Philadelphia Market, 1771-1773," *Journal of Economic History*, 38(3), September 1978, pp. 701-13.

Hill, Peter J. "The Economic Impact of Immigration into the United States," (Summary of Doctoral Dissertation) *Journal of Economic History*, 31(1), March 1971, pp. 260-63.

Hill, Peter J. *The Economic Impact of Immigration into the United States.* New York: Arno Press, 1975.

Hill, Peter J. "Relative Skill and Income Levels of Native and Foreign Born Workers in the United States," *Explorations in Economic History*, 12(1), January 1975, pp. 47-60.

Jones, Ethel B. "State Legislation and Hours of Work in Manufacturing," *Southern Economic Journal*, 41(4), April 1975, pp. 602-12.

Keat, Paul G. "Long-Run Changes in Occupational Wage Structure, 1900-1956," *Journal of Political Economy*, 68(6), December 1960, pp. 584-600.

Kendrick, John W. "Productivity," in Porter, ed. *Encyclopedia of American Economic History*, vol. 1, 1980, pp. 157-66.

Kessel, Reuben A. and Alchian, Armen A. "Real Wages in the North During the Civil War: Mitchell's Data Reinterpreted," (Reprinted in Fogel and Engerman, eds. *The Reinterpretation of American Economic History*, 1971, pp. 459-467) *Journal of Law and Economics*, 2, October 1959, pp. 95-113.

Kuznets, Simon S. "Quantitative Aspects of the Economic Growth of Nations (Part 2): Industrial Distribution of National Product and Labor Force," *Economic Development and Cultural Change*, 5(4, Part 2), July 1957, pp. 3-110.

Kuznets, Simon S. "Quantitative Aspects of the Economic Growth of Nations (Part 3): Industrial Distribution of Income and Labor Force by States, United States, 1919-1921 to 1955," *Economic Development and Cultural Change*, 6(4, Part 2), July 1958, pp. 1-128.

Kuznets, Simon S. "The Contribution of Immigration to the Growth of the Labor Force," in Fogel and Engerman, eds. *The Reinterpretation of American Economic History*, 1971, pp. 396-401.

Ladenson, Mark L. "The End of the North-South Wage Differential: Comment on Coelho and Ghali," *American Economic Review*, 63(4), September 1973, pp. 754-56.

Lazonick, William H. and Cannings, Kathleen. "The Development of the Nursing Labor Force in the United States: A Basic Analysis," *International Journal of Health Services*, 5(2), 1975, pp. 185-216.

Lebergott, Stanley. "Earnings of Nonfarm Employees in the U.S., 1890-1946," *Journal of the American Statistical Association*, 43(241), March 1948, pp. 74-93.

Lebergott, Stanley. "Annual Estimates of Unemployment in the United States, 1900-1954," in Universities-National Bureau Committee for Economic Research, ed. *The Measurement and Behavior of Unemployment*, 1957.

Lebergott, Stanley. "Long Term Factors in Labor Mobility and Unemployment," *Monthly Labor Review*, 82(8), August 1959, pp. 876-81.

Lebergott, Stanley. "Wage Trends, 1800-1900," in Parker, ed. *Trends in the American Economy in the Nineteenth Century* (Studies in Income and Wealth, vol. 24), 1960, pp. 449-98.

Lebergott, Stanley. "The Pattern of Employment since 1800," in Harris, ed. *American Economic History*, 1961, pp. 281-310.

Lebergott, Stanley. *Manpower in Economic Growth: The American Record since 1800*. New York: McGraw-Hill, 1964.

Lebergott, Stanley. "Labor Force Mobility and Unemployment, 1800-1960," in Andreano, ed. *New Views on American Economic Development*, 1965, pp. 362-76.

Lebergott, Stanley. "Long Term Factors in Labor Mobility and Unemployment," in Andreano, ed. *New Views on American Economic Development*, 1965.

Lebergott, Stanley. "Labor Force and Employment, 1800-1960," in Brady, ed. *Output, Employment and Productivity in the United States after 1800* (Studies in Income and Wealth, vol. 30), 1966, pp. 117-204.

Lebergott, Stanley. "Changes in Unemployment 1800-1960," in Fogel and Engerman, eds. *The Reinterpretation of American Economic History*, 1971, pp. 73-83.

Lebergott, Stanley. "The American Labor Force," in Davis, Easterlin, and Parker, eds. *American Economic Growth*, 1972, pp. 184-232.

Lebergott, Stanley. "A New Technique for Time Series: A Comment on Coen," *Review of Economics and Statistics*, 55(4), February 1973, pp. 525-27.

Lebergott, Stanley. "Industrialization, Regional Change, and the Sectoral Distribution of the U.S. Labor Force, 1850-1880: A Reply (to Vatter)," *Economic Development and Cultural Change*, 23(4), July 1975, pp. 749-50.

Lewis, Frank D. "Explaining the Shift of Labor from Agriculture to Industry in the United States: 1869 to 1899," *Journal of Economic History*, 39(3), September 1979, pp. 681-98.

Lindstrom, Diane. "Another Look at Industry and Agricultural Wage Differentials, 1800-1830," in Cain, ed. *Proceedings of the Business History Conference*, Vol. 1, 1973, pp. 111-14.

Long, Clarence D. *Wages and Earnings in the United States, 1860-1890* (General Series, no. 67). Princeton: Princeton University Press for the National Bureau of Economic Research, 1960.

Mancke, R.B. "American Trade Union Growth, 1900-1960: A Comment on Ashenfelter and Pencavel," *Quarterly Journal of Economics*, 85(1), February 1971, pp. 187-93.

Meeker, Edward F. "The Improving Health of the United States, 1850-1915," *Explorations in Economic History*, 9(4), Summer 1972, pp. 353-74.

Meeker, Edward F. "The Social Rate of Return on Investment in Public Health, 1880-1910," *Journal of Economic History*, 34(2), June 1974, pp. 392-421.

Niemi, Jr., Albert W. "Structural and Labor Productivity Patterns in United States Manufacturing, 1849-1899," *Business History Review*, 46(1), Spring 1972, pp. 67-84.

Novak, David E. and Perlman, Richard. "The Structure of Wages in the American Iron and Steel Industry, 1860-1890," *Journal of Economic History*, 22(3), September 1962, pp. 334-47.

Orsagh, Thomas J. and Mooney, Peter J. "A Model for the Dispersion of the Migrant Labor Force and Some Results for the United States, 1880-1920," *Review of Economics and Statistics*, 52(3), August 1970, pp. 306-12.

Rees, Albert. "Wage Trends, 1800-1900: Comment on Lebergott," in Parker, ed. *Trends in the American Economy in the NIneteenth Century* (Studies in Income and Wealth, vol. 24), 1960, pp. 498-99.

Rosenberg, Nathan. "Anglo-American Wage Differences in the 1820's," *Journal of Economic History*, 27(2), June 1967, pp. 221-29.

Sanderson, Allen R. "Child-Labor Legislation and the Labor Force Participation of Children," (Summary of Doctoral Dissertation) *Journal of Economic History*, 34(1), March 1974, pp. 297-99.

Scott, Robert H. "A 'Liquidity' Factor Contributing to Those Downward Sloping Yield Curves, 1900-1916," *Review of Economics and Statistics*, 45(3), August 1963, pp. 328-29.

Scully, Gerald W. "The North-South Manufacturing Wage Differential, 1869-1919," *Journal of Regional Science*, 11(2), August 1971, pp. 235-52.

Thompson, Alexander M. *Technology, Labor, and Industrial Structure in the U.S. Coal Industry*. New York: Garland Press, 1979.

Thompson, Alexander M. "Workers' Control and the Fracturing of Miners' Skills in Appalachian Coal Mining," [Working Paper].

Uselding, Paul J. "Conjectural Estmates of Gross Human Capital Inflows to the American Economy: 1790-1860," *Explorations in Economic History*, 9(1), Fall 1971, pp. 49-61.

Uselding, Paul J. "Occupational Mortality in the United States: 1890-1910," in Uselding, ed. *Research in Economic History*, vol. 1, 1976, pp. 334-71.

Vatter, Harold G. "Industrialization, Regional Change, and the Sectoral Distribution of the U.S. Labor Force, 1850-1880," *Economic Development and Cultural Change*, 23(3), April 1975, pp. 739-47.

Vatter, Harold G. "Industrialization, Regional Change, and the Sectoral Distribution of the U.S. Labor Force, 1850-1880: Comment on Lebergott," *Economic Development and Cultural Change*, 23(4), July 1975, pp. 739-47.

Vatter, Harold G. "U.S. Economic Development and the Sectoral Distribution of the Labor Force, 1850-1880," in Van der Wee, Vinogradov, and Kotovsky, eds. *Fifth International Congress of Economic History*, vol. 3, 1976, pp. 28-49.

Vedder, Richard K.; Klingman, David C. and Gallaway, Lowell E. "Exploitation of Labor in Early American Cotton Textile Manufacturing," in Uselding, ed. *Research in Economic History*, vol. 3, 1978.

Weiss, Thomas J. "The Industrial Distribution of the Urban and Rural Workforces: Estimates for the United States, 1870-1910," *Journal of Economic History*, 32(4), December 1972, pp. 919-37.

Wilkinson, Maurice. "European Migration to the United States: An Econometric Analysis of Aggregate Labor Supply and Demand," *Review of Economics and Statistics*, 52(3), August 1970, pp. 272-79.

Wright, Gavin. "Cheap Labor and Southern Textiles before 1880," *Journal of Economic History*, 39(3), September 1979, pp. 655-80.

Zabler, Jeffrey F. "Another Look at Industry and Agricultural Wage Differentials, 1800-1830," in Cain, ed. *Proceedings of the Business History Conference*, Vol. 1, 1973, pp. 98-110.

United States: Discrimination

Brown, William W. and Reynolds, Morgan O. "Debt Peonage Re-examined: A Note on Ransom and Sutch," *Journal of Economic History*, 33(4), December 1973, pp. 862-871.

Carlson, Leonard A. "Indians, Asians, and Blacks: Racial Minorities in North American Economic History," (Summary of 1978 Research Workshops) *Journal of Economic History*, 39(1), March 1979, pp. 315-17.

DeCanio, Stephen J. "Accumulation and Discrimination in the Postbellum South," *Explorations in Economic History*, 16(2), April 1979, pp. 182-206.

Goldin, Claudia D. "'N' Kinds of Freedom: An Introduction to the Issues," *Explorations in Economic History*, 16(1), January 1979, pp. 8-30.

Hannon, Joan Underhill. "The Economics of the Melting Pot: Discussion of Papers by Higgs, Kirk/Kirk, and Kahan Presented to the 37th Annual Meeting of the Economic History Association," *Journal of Economic History*, 38(1), March 1978, pp. 252-55.

Hannon, Joan Underhill. "The Immigrant Worker in the Promised Land: Human Capital and Ethnic Discrimination in the Michigan Labor Market, 1888-1891," (Summary of Doctoral Dissertation) *Journal of Economic History*, 38(1), March 1978, pp. 279-80.

Hannon, Joan Underhill. "The Immigrant Worker in the Promised Land: Human Capital and Ethnic Discrimination in the Michigan Labor Market, 1888-1890," Ph.D. Dissertation, University of Wisconsin-Madison, 1978 [Working Paper].

Higgs, Robert. "Williamson and Swanson on City Growth: A Critique," *Explorations in Economic History*, 8(2), Winter 1970/71, pp. 203-11.

Higgs, Robert. "Race, Skills, and Earnings: American Immigrants in 1909," *Journal of Economic History*, 31(2), June 1971, pp. 420-28.

Higgs, Robert. "Cities and Yankee Ingenuity, 1870-1920," in Jackson and Schultz, eds. *Cities in American History*, 1972, pp. 16-22.

Higgs, Robert. "Did Southern Farmers Discriminate?" *Agricultural History*, 46(2), April 1972, pp. 325-28.

Higgs, Robert. "Race, Tenure, and Resource Allocation in Southern Agriculture, 1910," (See Editor's Notes this Journal, 33(3), September 1973, pp. 668 for Correction of a Printer's Error in This Article) *Journal of Economic History*, 33(1), March 1973, pp. 149-69.

Higgs, Robert. "Urbanization and Inventiveness in the United States, 1870-1920," in Schnore, ed. *The New Urban History*, 1975, pp. 247-59.

Higgs, Robert. "Did Southern Farmers Discriminate?: Interpretive Problems and Further Evidence," *Agricultural History*, 49(2), April 1975, pp. 445-47.

Higgs, Robert. "Participation of Blacks and Immigrants in the American Merchant Class, 1890-1910: Some Demographic Relations," *Explorations in Economic History*, 13(2), April 1976, pp. 153-64.

Higgs, Robert. *Competition and Coercion: Blacks in the American Economy, 1865-1914*. New York: Cambridge University Press, 1977.

Higgs, Robert. "Firm-Specific Evidence on Racial Wage Differentials and Workforce Segregation," *American Economic Review*, 67(2), March 1977, pp. 236-45.

Higgs, Robert. "Race and Economy in the South, 1890-1950," in Haws, ed. *The Age of Segregation*, 1978.

Higgs, Robert. "Landless by Law: Japanese Immigrants in California Agriculture to 1941," *Journal of Economic History*, 38(1), March 1978, pp. 205-25.

Higgs, Robert. "Racial Wage Differentials in Agriculture: Evidence from North Carolina in 1887," *Agricultural History*, 52(2), April 1978, pp. 308-11.

Higgs, Robert, Booth, David. "Mortality Differentials Within Large American Cities in 1890," *Human Ecology*, 7(4), December 1979, pp. 353-370.

Higgs, Robert. "Urbanization and Invention in the Process of Economic Growth: Simultaneous Equations Estimates for the United States, 1880-1920," in Simon and Davanzo, eds. *Research in Population Economics*, vol. 2, 1980.

Klingaman, David C.; Vedder, Richard K.; Gallaway, Lowell E. and Uselding, Paul. "Discrimination and Exploitation in Antebellum American Cotton Textile Manufacturing," in Uselding, ed. *Research in Economic History*, vol. 3, 1978, pp. 217-61.

Lampard, Eric E. "The Evolving System of Cities in the United States: Urbanization and Economic Development," in Perloff and Wingo, eds. *Issues in Urban Economics*, 1968, pp. 81-139.

Mandle, Jay R. "The Reestablishment of the Plantation Economy in the South, 1865-1970," *Review of Black Political Economy*, 3(2), Winter 1973, pp. 68-88.

McGouldrick, Paul F. and Tannen, Michael B. "Did American Manufacturers Discriminate against Immigrants before 1914?" *Journal of Economic History*, 37(3), September 1977, pp. 723-46.

Meeker, Edward F. "Freedom, Economic Opportunity, and Fertility: Black

Americans, 1860-1910," *Economic Inquiry*, 15(3), July 1977, pp. 397-412.

Meeker, Edward F. and Kau, James. "Racial Discrimination and Occupational Attainment at the Turn of the Century," *Explorations in Economic History*, 14(3), July 1977, pp. 250-76.

Ransom, Roger L. and Sutch, Richard C. "Debt Peonage in the Cotton South after the Civil War," *Journal of Economic History*, 32(3), September 1972, pp. 641-69.

Ransom, Roger L. and Sutch, Richard C. *One Kind of Freedom: The Economic Consequences of Emancipation.* New York: Cambridge University Press, 1977.

Ransom, Roger L. and Sutch, Richard C. "Sharecropping: Market Response or Mechanism of Race Control?" in Sansing, ed. *What Was Freedom's Price?*, 1978, pp. 51-69.

Reid, Jr., Joseph D. "Sharecropping as an Understandable Market Response: The Postbellum South," *Journal of Economic History*, 33(1), March 1973, pp. 106-30.

Reid, Jr., Joseph D. "Sharecropping in History and Theory," *Agricultural History*, 49(2), April 1975, pp. 426-40.

Reid, Jr., Joseph D. "Sharecropping and Agricultural Uncertainty," *Economic Development and Cultural Change*, 24(3), April 1976, pp. 549-76.

Reid, Jr., Joseph D. "Tenancy in American History," in Roumasset, Boussard, and Singh, eds. *Risk, Uncertainty and Agricultural Development*, 1979.

Reid, Jr., Joseph D. "The Evaluations and Implications of Southern Tenancy," *Agricultural History*, 53(1), January 1979, pp. 153-69.

Reid, Jr., Joseph D. "White Land, Black Labor, and Agricultural Stagnation: The Causes and Effects of Sharecropping in the Postbellum South," *Explorations in Economic History*, 16(1), January 1979, pp. 31-55.

Shergold, Peter R. "Relative Skill and Income Levels of Native and Foreign Born Workers: A Reexamination," *Explorations in Economic History*, 13(4), October 1976, pp. 451-62.

Shlomowitz, Ralph. "New and Old Views on the Rural Economy of the Postbellum American South: A Review Article," [Working Paper].

Soltow, Lee C. "A Century of Personal Wealth Accumulation," in Vatter and Palm, eds. *The Economics of Black America*, 1972.

Soltow, Lee C. and May, Dean L. "Accumulation and Discrimination in the Postbellum South," *Explorations in Economic History*, 16(2), April 1979, pp. 151-62.

Temin, Peter. "Freedom and Coercion: Notes on the Analysis of Debt Peonage in 'One Kind of Freedom'," *Explorations in Economic History*, 16(1), January 1979, pp. 56-63.

Wright, Gavin. "Comments on Papers by Reid, Ransom/Sutch, and Higgs on the Postbellum South Presented to the 32nd Annual Meeting of the Economic History Association," *Journal of Economic History*, 33(1), March 1973, pp. 170-76.

United States: Slavery

Aitken, Hugh G.J., ed. *Did Slavery Pay? Readings in the Economics of Black Slavery in the United States.* Boston: Houghton Mifflin, 1971.

Aufhauser, R. Keith. "Slavery and Technological Change," *Journal of Economic History*, 34(1), March 1974, pp. 36-50.

Bateman, Fred and Weiss, Thomas J. "Industrialization in the Slave Economy," [Working Paper].

Bean, Richard N. "The British Transatlantic Slave Trade, 1650-1775," (Summary of Doctoral Dissertation) *Journal of Economic History*, 32(1), March 1972, pp. 409-11.

Bean, Richard N. *The British Transatlantic Slave Trade, 1650-1775.* New York: Arno Press, 1975.

Bean, Richard N. and Thomas, Robert P. "The Adoption of Slave Labor in British America," in Gemery and Hogendorn, eds. *The Uncommon Market*, 1979, pp. 377-98.

Brown, William W. and Reynolds, Morgan O. "Debt Peonage Re-examined: A Note on Ransom and Sutch," *Journal of Economic History*, 33(4), December 1973, pp. 862-871.

Brownlee, W. Elliot. "The Economics of Urban Slavery," (Review essay of *Urban Slavery in the American South, 1820-1860: A Quantitative History,* by Claudia Dale Goldin, 1976) *Reviews in American History*, 5(2), June 1977, pp. 230-35.

Butlin, Noel G. *Antebellum Slavery: A Critique of a Debate.* Canberra: Australian National University, 1971.

Canarella, Giorgio and Tomaske, John A. "The Optimal Utilization of Slaves," *Journal of Economic History*, 35(3), September 1975, pp. 621-29.

Carmagnani, Marcello. "Una visione deformata della schiavitu americana: a proposito dello studio di Fogel e Engerman sull'economia della schiavitu [A Distorted View of American Slavery: the Fogel and Engerman Study on the Slavery Economy]," *Quaderni storici*, (31), April 1976, pp. 445-61.

Carstensen, Fred V. "Trouble on the Auction Block: Interregional Slave Sales and the Reliability of a Linear Equation," *Journal of Interdisciplinary History*, 7(2), Autumn 1977, pp. 315-18.

Conrad, Alfred H. and Meyer, John R. "The Economics of Slavery in the Antebellum South," Reprinted in Fogel and Engerman, eds. *The Reinterpretation of American Economic History*, 1971, pp. 342-361) *Journal of Political Economy*, 66(2), April 1958, pp. 95-130.

Conrad, Alfred H. and Meyer, John R. "The Economics of Slavery in the Antebellum South: A Reply to Dowd," *Journal of Political Economy*, 66(5), October 1958, pp. 442-3.

Conrad, Alfred H. and Meyer, John R. "The Economics of Slavery in the Antebellum South: Reply to Moes," *Journal of Political Economy*, 68(2), April 1960, pp. 187-89.

Conrad, Alfred H. and Meyer, John R. *The Economics of Slavery and Other Essays on the Quantitative Study of Economic History.* Chicago: Aldine Press, 1964.

Conrad, Alfred H. and Meyer, John R. "Slavery as an Obstacle to

Economic Growth in the United States: A Panel Discussion of Conrad and Meyer," (Reprinted in Aitken, ed. *Did Slavery Pay?*, 1971, pp. 270-287) *Journal of Economic History*, 27(4), December 1967, pp. 518-31.

David, Paul A. and Temin, Peter. "Slavery: The Progressive Institution?" (Review essay of *Time on the Cross* (2 Vols). by Fogel and Engerman, 1974) (Reprinted in David, et. al., *Reckoning with Slavery*, 1976, pp. 165-230) *Journal of Economic History*, 34(3), September 1974, pp. 739-83.

David, Paul A. and Temin, Peter. "Capitalist Masters, Bourgeois Slaves," (Review essay of *Time on the Cross* (2 Vols). by Fogel and Engerman, 1974) (Reprinted in David, et. al., *Reckoning with Slavery*, , 1976, pp. 33-54) *Journal of Interdisciplinary History*, 5(3), Winter 1975, pp. 445-57.

David, Paul A.; Gutman, Herbert; Sutch, Richard C.; Temin, Peter and Wright, Gavin. *Reckoning with Slavery: A Critical Study in the Quantitative History of American Negro Slavery.* New York: Oxford University Press, 1976.

David, Paul A.; Gutman, Herbert G.; Sutch, Richard C.; Temin, Peter and Wright, Gavin. "Time on the Cross and the Burden of Quantitative History," in David, et. al., *Reckoning with Slavery*, 1976, pp. 339-57.

David, Paul A. and Temin, Peter. "Explaining the Relative Efficiency of Slave Agriculture in the Antebellum South: Comment on Fogel and Engerman," *American Economic Review*, 69(1), March 1979, pp. 213-18.

David, Paul A. "Child-Care in the Slave Quarters: A Critical Note on Some Uses of Demography in 'Time on the Cross'," [Working Paper].

Davis, Lance E. "One Potato Two Potato Sweet Potato Pie: Clio Looks at Slavery and the South," Presented at the MSSB-University of Rochester Conference, Time on the Cross: A First Appraisal, October 1974 [Working Paper].

Desai, Meghnad. "The Consolation of Slavery," (Review essay of *Time on the Cross* (2 Vols), by Fogel and Engerman, 1974) *Economic History Review*, Second Series, 29(3), August 1976, pp. 491-503.

DeCanio, Stephen J. "A New Economic History of Slavery," (Review essay of *Time on the Cross* (2 Vols), by Fogel and Engerman, 1974) *Reviews in American History*, 2(4), December 1974, pp. 474-87.

DeCanio, Stephen J. "New Directions and Old Questions in the Economic History of the Postbellum South, Time on the Cross: A First Appraisal," Presented at the MSSB-University of Rochester Conference, Time on the Cross: A First Appraisal, October 1974 [Working Paper].

Dowd, Douglas F. "The Economics of Slavery in the Antebellum South: A Comment on Conrad and Meyer," *Journal of Political Economy*, 66(5), October 1958, pp. 440-2.

Dowd, Douglas F. "Slavery as an Obstacle to Economic Growth in the United States: A Panel Discussion of Conrad and Meyer," (Reprinted in Aitken, ed. *Did Slavery Pay?*, 1971, pp. 287-295) *Journal of Economic History*, 27(4), December 1967, pp. 531-38.

Earle, Carville V. "A Staple Interpretation of Slavery and Free Labor," *Geographical Review*, 68(1), January 1978, pp. 51-65.

Engelbourg, Saul. "Energy and Industrialization: The Case of Southern

New England," in Soltow, ed. *Essays in Economic and Business History*, 1979, pp. 268-82.

Engerman, Stanley L. "The Effects of Slavery upon the Southern Economy: A Review of the Recent Debate," (Reprinted in Aitken, ed. *Did Slavery Pay?*, 1971, pp. 295-327) *Explorations in Entrepreneurial History*, Second Series, 4(2), Winter 1967, pp. 71-97.

Engerman, Stanley L. "Slavery as an Obstacle to Economic Growth in the United States: A Panel Discussion of Conrad and Meyer," *Journal of Economic History*, 27(4), December 1967, pp. 541-44.

Engerman, Stanley L. "The Antebellum South: What Probably Was and What Should Have Been," (Reprinted in Parker, ed. *The Structure of the Cotton Economy of the Antebellum South*, 1970) *Agricultural History*, 44(1), January 1970, pp. 127-42.

Engerman, Stanley L. "Some Economic Factors in Southern Backwardness in the Nineteenth Century," in Kain and Meyer, eds. *Essays in Regional Economics*, 1971, pp. 279-306.

Engerman, Stanley L. "Some Considerations Relating to Property Rights in Man," *Journal of Economic History*, 33(1), March 1973, pp. 43-65.

Engerman, Stanley L. and Genovese, Eugene D., eds. *Race and Slavery in the Western Hemisphere: Quantitative Studies.* Princeton: Princeton University Press, 1975.

Engerman, Stanley L. "A Reconsideration of Southern Economic Growth, 1770-1860," *Agricultural History*, 49(2), April 1975, pp. 343-61.

Engerman, Stanley L. "The Southern Slave Economy," in Owens, ed. *Perspectives and Irony in American Slavery*, 1976.

Engerman, Stanley L. "The Height of Slaves in the United States," *Local Population Studies*, (16), Spring 1976, pp. 45-50.

Engerman, Stanley L. "Some Economic and Demographic Comparisons of Slavery in the United States and the British West Indies," *Economic History Review*, Second Series, 29(2), May 1976, pp. 258-75.

Engerman, Stanley L. "Introduction to Special Issue on Colonial Slavery in the Chesapeake Region," *Southern Studies*, 16(4), Winter 1977, pp. 347-54.

Engerman, Stanley L. "Black Fertility and Family Structure in the United States, 1880-1940," *Journal of Family History*, 2(2), Summer 1977, pp. 117-38.

Engerman, Stanley L. "Relooking at the Slave Community," in Gilmore, ed. *Revisiting John Blassingame's Slave Community*, 1978.

Engerman, Stanley L. "Marxist Economic Studies of the Slave South," *Marxist Perspectives*, 1(1), Spring 1978, pp. 148-64.

Engerman, Stanley L. "Studying the Black Family," (Review essay of *The Black Family In Slavery and Freedom*, by Gutman, 1976) *Journal of Family History*, 3(1), Spring 1978, pp. 78-101.

Engerman, Stanley L. "The Realities of Slavery: A Review of Recent Evidence," *International Journal of Comparative Sociology*, 20(1-2), March/June 1979, pp. 46-66.

Evans, Jr., Robert. "Some Economic Aspects of the Domestic Slave Trade, 1830-1860," *Southern Economic Journal*, 27(4), April 1961, pp. 329-37.

Evans, Jr., Robert. "The Economics of American Negro Slavery, 1830-1860," *Aspects of Labor Economics* (Special Conference Series,

no. 14). Princeton: Princeton University Press for the National
Bureau of Economic Research, 1962, pp. 221-27.

Fenoaltea, Stefano. "Negative Incentives, Authority, and Slavery: A
Comparative Perspective," [Working Paper].

Fenoaltea, Stefano. "The Slavery Debate: A Note from the Sidelines,"
[Working Paper].

Fischbaum, Marvin and Rubin, Julius. "Slavery and the Economic
Development of the American South: Comment on Engerman," (Reprinted
in Aitken, ed. *Did Slavery Pay?*, 1971, pp. 327-341) *Explorations
in Entrepreneurial History*, Second Series, 6(1), Fall 1968, pp.
116-27.

Fleisig, Heywood. "Slavery and Technological Change: Comment on
Aufhauser," *Journal of Economic History*, 34(1), March 1974, pp.
79-83.

Fleisig, Heywood. "Slavery, the Supply of Agricultural Labor, and the
Industrialization of the South," *Journal of Economic History*,
36(3), September 1976, pp. 572-97.

Fogel, Robert W. and Engerman, Stanley L. "The Economics of Slavery,"
in Fogel and Engerman, eds. *The Reinterpretation of American
Economic History*, 1971, pp. 311-41.

Fogel, Robert W. and Engerman, Stanley L. "The Relative Efficiency of
Slavery: A Comparison of Northern and Southern Agriculture in
1860," *Explorations in Economic History*, 8(3), Spring 1971, pp.
353-67.

Fogel, Robert W. and Engerman, Stanley L. *Time on the Cross* (vol. 1:
The Economics of American Negro Slavery; vol. 2: *Evidence and
Methods: A Supplement*). [Translated into Spanish (1977), Italian
(1977), Japanese (1978)] Boston: Little, Brown, 1974.

Fogel, Robert W. and Engerman, Stanley L. "Philanthropy at Bargain
Prices: Notes on the Economics of Gradual Emancipation," *Journal of
Legal Studies*, 3(2), June 1974, pp. 377-401.

Fogel, Robert W. "Three Phases of Cliometric Research on Slavery and
Its Aftermath," *American Economic Review, Papers and Proceedings*,
65(2), May 1975, pp. 37-46.

Fogel, Robert W. and Engerman, Stanley L. "A Comparison of the
Relative Efficiency of Slave and Free Agriculture in the United
States during 1860," in Van der Wee, Vinogradov, and Kotovsky, eds.
Fifth International Congress of Economic History, vol. 7, 1976, pp.
141-46.

Fogel, Robert W. and Engerman, Stanley L. "Explaining the Relative
Efficiency of Slave Agriculture in the Antebellum South," *American
Economic Review*, 67(3), June 1977, pp. 275-96.

Fogel, Robert W. "Cliometrics and Culture: Some Recent Developments in
the Historiography of Slavery," *Journal of Social History*, 11(1),
Fall 1977, pp. 34-51.

Fogel, Robert W. and Engerman, Stanley L. "Explaining the Relative
Efficiency of Slave Agriculture in the Antebellum South: Reply (to
David and Temin, Wright, and Schaefer and Schmitz)," *American
Economic Review*, 70(4), September 1980, pp. 672-90.

Foust, James D. and Swan, Dale E. "Productivity and Profitability of
Antebellum Slave Labor: A Micro-Approach," in Parker, ed. *The
Structure of the Cotton Economy of the Antebellum South*, 1970, pp.

39-62.

Fox-Genovese, Elizabeth. "Poor Richard at Work in the Cotton Fields: A Critique of the Psychological and Ideological Presuppositions of 'Time on the Cross'," *Review of Radical Political Economics*, 7(4), Fall 1975, pp. 67-83.

Friedman, Gerald. "Slave Heights: Trinidad and the United States," [Working Paper].

Friedman, Gerald. "Slave Occupations in Trinidad and Eight Southern States," [Working Paper].

Friedman, Gerald and Medoff, James. "Slavery and the Termination of Implicit Contracts," [Working Paper].

Gallman, Robert E. "Slavery, the Supply of Agricultural Labor, and the Industrialization of the South: Comment on Fleisig," *Journal of Economic History*, 37(2), June 1977, pp. 473-74.

Gallman, Robert E. and Anderson, Ralph V. "Slaves as Fixed Capital: Slave Labor and Southern Economic Development," *Journal of American History*, 64(1), June 1977, pp. 24-46.

Gallman, Robert E. "Slavery and Southern Economic Growth," *Southern Economic Journal*, 45(4), April 1979, pp. 1007-22.

Gemery, Henry A. and Hogendorn, Jan S. "Editor's Introduction," in Gemery and Hogendorn, eds. *The Uncommon Market*, 1979, pp. 1-19.

Ginzberg, Eli. "Slavery as an Obstacle to Economic Growth in the United States: A Panel Discussion of Conrad and Meyer," *Journal of Economic History*, 27(4), December 1967, pp. 538-40.

Goldin, Claudia D. "The Economics of Emancipation," *Journal of Economic History*, 33(1), March 1973, pp. 66-85.

Goldin, Claudia D. "A Model to Explain the Relative Decline of Urban Slavery: Empirical Results," in Engerman and Genovese, eds. *Race and Slavery in the Western Hemisphere*, 1975, pp. 427-50.

Goldin, Claudia D. "Cities and Slavery: The Issue of Compatibility," in Schnore, ed. *The New Urban History*, 1975.

Goldin, Claudia D. *Urban Slavery in the American South, 1820-1860: A Quantitative History*. Chicago: University of Chicago Press, 1976.

Goldin, Claudia D. "'N' Kinds of Freedom: An Introduction to the Issues," *Explorations in Economic History*, 16(1), January 1979, pp. 8-30.

Goldin, Claudia D. "Comments on Dissertations by Alston and Shlomovitz Presented to the 38th Annual Meeting of the Economic History Association," *Journal of Economic History*, 39(1), March 1979, pp. 336-38.

Gray, Ralph and Wood, Betty. "The Transition from Indentured to Involuntary Servitude in Colonial Georgia," *Explorations in Economic History*, 13(4), October 1976, pp. 353-70.

Gunderson, Gerald A. "Slavery," in Porter, ed. *Encyclopedia of American Economic History*, vol. 2, 1980, pp. 552-61.

Gutman, Herbert G. and Sutch, Richard C. "Sambo Makes Good, or Were Slaves Imbued with the Protestant Work Ethic?" in David, Gutman, Sutch, Temin, and Wright, eds. *Reckoning with Slavery*, 1976, pp. 55-93.

Gutman, Herbert G. and Sutch, Richard C. "The Slave Family: Protected Agent of Capitalist Masters or Victim of the Slave Trade?" in David, Gutman, Sutch, Temin, and Wright, eds. *Reckoning with*

Slavery, 1976, pp. 94-133.
Gutman, Herbert G. and Sutch, Richard C. "Victorians All? The Sexual Mores and Conduct of Slaves and Their Masters," in David, Gutman, Sutch, Temin, and Wright, eds. *Reckoning with Slavery*, 1976, pp. 134-64.
Hartwell, R.M. "Slave Labour and Factory Labour," Presented at the MSSB-University of Rochester Conference, Time on the Cross: A First Appraisal, October 1974 [Working Paper].
Hellie, Richard. "Time on the Cross from a Comparative Perspective of Early Modern Russian Slavery," Presented at the MSSB-University of Rochester Conference, Time on the Cross: A First Appraisal, October 1974 [Working Paper].
Hogendorn, Jan S. and Gemery, Henry A. "Technological Change, Slavery, and the Slave Trade," in Dewey and Hopkins, eds. *The Imperial Impact*, 1978.
Hopkins, Mark M. and Cardell, Nicholas S. "The Effect of Milk Intolerance on the Consumption of Milk by Slaves in 1860," *Journal of Interdisciplinary History*, 8(3), Winter 1978, pp. 507-14.
Hopkins, Mark M. "Emancipation: The Dominant Cause of Southern Stagnation," Presented at the 18th Annual Cliometrics Conference, University of Chicago, May 1978 [Working Paper].
Hunt, E.H. "The 'New' Economics of Slavery," (Review essay of *Time on the Cross* (2 Vols), by Fogel and Engerman, 1974) *Review of Social Economy*, 33(2), October 1975, pp. 166-73.
Kelso, Charles. "Slavery as an Obstacle of Economic Growth in the United States: A Panel Discussion of Conrad and Meyer," *Journal of Economic History*, 27(4), December 1967, pp. 544-47.
Klein, Herbert S. "Reflections on the Viability of Slavery and the Causes of Abolition in 19th Century Cuba," Presented at the MSSB-University of Rochester Conference, Time on the Cross: A First Appraisal, October 1974 [Working Paper].
Kotlikoff, Laurence J. and Pinera, Sebastian E. "The Old South's Stake in the Inter-Regional Movement of Slaves, 1850-1860," *Journal of Economic History*, 37(2), June 1977, pp. 434-50.
Kotlikoff, Laurence J. "Towards a Quantitative Description of the New Orleans Slave Market," Presented at the Annual Cliometrics Conference, University of Wisconsin-Madison, 1976 [Working Paper].
Leiman, M. "A Note on Slave Profitability and Economic Growth: An Examination of the Conrad-Meyer Thesis," *Social and Economic Studies*, 16(2), June 1967, pp. 211-15.
LeVeen, E. Phillip. "A Quantitative Analysis of the Impact of British Suppression Policies on the Volume of the Nineteenth Century Atlantic Slave Trade," in Engerman and Genovese, eds. *Race and Slavery in the Western Hemisphere*, 1975, pp. 51-81.
Luraghi, Raimondo. "Wage Labor in the "Rice Belt" of Northern Italy and Slave Labor in the American South: A First Approach," Presented at the MSSB-University of Rochester Conference, Time on the Cross: A First Appraisal, October 1974 [Working Paper].
Mandle, Jay R. "The Reestablishment of the Plantation Economy in the South, 1865-1970," *Review of Black Political Economy*, 3(2), Winter 1973, pp. 68-88.
Mandle, Jay R. "Strength and Growth in the Plantation Economy: An

Appraisal of Time on the Cross," Presented at the MSSB-University of Rochester Conference, Time on the Cross: A First Appraisal, October 1974 [Working Paper].

Margo, Robert A. "Civilian Occupation of Ex-Slaves in the Union Army, 1862-1865," in Fogel and Engerman, eds. *Without Consent or Contract.*

Marr, William L. "The Economics of Lincoln's Proposal for Compensated Emancipation: Comment on Weintraub," *American Journal of Economics and Sociology*, 35(1), January 1976, pp. 105-7.

Meeker, Edward F. "Mortality Trends of Southern Blacks, 1850-1910: Some Preliminary Findings," *Explorations in Economic History*, 13(1), January 1976, pp. 13-42.

Metzer, Jacob. "Rational Management, Modern Business Practices, and Economies of Scale in the Antebellum Southern Plantations," *Explorations in Economic History*, 12(2), April 1975, pp. 123-50.

Metzer, Jacob. "Institutional Change and Economic Analysis: Some Issues Related to American Slavery," *Louisiana Studies*, 15(4), Winter 1976, pp. 321-43.

Meyer, John R. "Slavery as an Obstacle to Economic Growth in the United States: A Panel Discussion of Conrad and Meyer," *Journal of Economic History*, 27(4), December 1967, pp. 549-51.

Meyer, John R. "Comment on Papers by Engerman, Goldin, and Kahan presented to the 32nd Annual Meeting of the Economic History Association," *Journal of Economic History*, 33(1), March 1973, pp. 100-105.

Miller, William L. "Slavery and the Population of the South," *Southern Economic Journal*, 28), July 1961, pp. 46-54.

Miller, William L. "A Note on the Importance of the Interstate Slave Trade of the Antebellum South," *Journal of Political Economy*, 73(2), April 1965, pp. 181-87.

Moes, John E. "The Economics of Slavery in the Antebellum South: Another Comment on Conrad and Meyer," *Journal of Political Economy*, 68(2), April 1960, pp. 183-87.

Neal, Larry D. and Simon, Julian. "A Calculation of the Black Reparations Bill," *Review of Black Political Economy*, 4(2), Winter 1974, pp. 75-86.

Niemi, Jr., Albert W. "Inequality in the Distribution of Slave Wealth: The Cotton South and Other Southern Agricultural Regions," *Journal of Economic History*, 37(3), September 1977, pp. 747-54.

Olson, John F. and Fogel, Robert W. "Clock-Time Vs. Real-Time: A Comparison of the Lengths of the Northern and the Southern Agricultural Work-Years," [Working Paper].

Olson, John F. "The Occupational Structure and Characteristics of Skilled Slave Labor in the Late Antebellum Plantation Economy," Ph.D. Dissertation, University of Rochester [Working Paper].

Parker, William N. "The Slave Plantation in American Agriculture," in Coats and Robertson, eds. *Essays in American Economic History*, 1969.

Parker, William N., ed. *The Structure of the Cotton Economy of the Antebellum South.* (Originally Published as an Issue of *Agricultural History*, 44(1), January 1970) Washington, D.C.: Agricultural History Society, 1970.

Parker, William N. "Slavery and Southern Economic Development: An Hypothesis and Some Evidence," (Reprinted in Parker, ed. *The Structure of the Cotton Economy of the Antebellum South*, 1970) *Agricultural History*, 44(1), January 1970, pp. 115-25.

Ransom, Roger L. and Sutch, Richard C. "Debt Peonage in the Cotton South after the Civil War," *Journal of Economic History*, 32(3), September 1972, pp. 641-69.

Ransom, Roger L. and Sutch, Richard C. "The Ex-Slave in the Postbellum South: A Study of the Economic Impact of Racism in a Market Environment," *Journal of Economic History*, 33(1), March 1973, pp. 131-47.

Ransom, Roger L. and Sutch, Richard C. *One Kind of Freedom: The Economic Consequences of Emancipation*. New York: Cambridge University Press, 1977.

Rothstein, Morton. "Measurement Calculus and Direction: Prometheus in the Antebellum Southland," Presented at the MSSB-University of Rochester Conference, Time on the Cross: A First Appraisal, October 1974 [Working Paper].

Ryan, Terrance C.I. "The Economics of Trading in Slaves," (Summary of Doctoral Dissertation) *African Economic History*, 1, Spring 1976, pp. 40-1.

Ryan, Terrance C.I. "The Economics of Trading in Slaves," Ph.D. Dissertation, Massachusetts Institute of Technology, 1975 [Working Paper].

Sanderson, Warren C. "Herbert G. Gutman's The Black Family in Slavery and Freedom, 1750-1925: A Cliometric Reconsideration," *Social Science History*, 3(3-4), October 1979, pp. 66-85.

Saraydar, Edward. "A Note on the Profitability of Antebellum Slavery," (Reprinted in Aitken, ed. *Did Slavery Pay?*, 1971, pp. 209-220) *Southern Economic Journal*, 30(4), April 1964, pp. 325-32.

Saraydar, Edward. "The Profitability of Antebellum Slavery: A Reply to Sutch," (Reprinted in Aitken, ed. *Did Slavery Pay?*, 1971, pp. 242-250) *Southern Economic Journal*, 31(4), April 1965, pp. 377-83.

Schaeffer, Donald F. and Schmitz, Mark D. "The Relative Efficiency of Slave Agriculture: A Comment on Fogel and Engerman," *American Economic Review*, 69(1), March 1979, pp. 208-12.

Scheiber, Harry N. "Slavery as an Obstacle to Economic Growth in the United States: A Panel Discussion of Conrad and Meyer," *Journal of Economic History*, 27(4), December 1967, pp. 547-49.

Scheiber, Harry N. "Black Is Computable: An Essay on 'Time on the Cross' and Its Critics," *American Scholar*, 44(4), Autumn 1975, pp. 656-73.

Schmitz, Mark D. and Schaeffer, Donald F. "Slavery, Freedom, and the Elasticity of Substitution," *Explorations in Economic History*, 15(3), July 1978, pp. 327-37.

Seagrave, Charles E. "The Southern Negro Agricultural Worker: 1850-1870," (Summary of Doctoral Dissertation) *Journal of Economic History*, 31(1), March 1971, pp. 279-80.

Shlomovitz, Ralph. "The Transition from Slave to Freedman Labor Arrangements in Southern Agriculture, 1865-1870," (Summary of Doctoral Dissertation) *Journal of Economic History*, 39(1), March 1979, pp. 333-36.

Stampp, Kenneth M. "Introduction: A Humanistic Perspective," in David, Gutman, Sutch, Temin, and Wright, eds. *Reckoning with Slavery*, 1976, pp. 1-30.

Steckel, Richard H. *The Economics of U.S. Slave and Southern White Fertility.* New York: Arno Press, 1977.

Steckel, Richard H. and Trussell, James. "The Age of Slaves at Menarche and Their First Birth," *Journal of Interdisciplinary History*, 8(3), Winter 1978, pp. 477-505.

Steckel, Richard H. "The Economics of U.S. Slave and Southern White Fertility," (Summary of Doctoral Dissertation) *Journal of Economic History*, 38(1), March 1978, pp. 289-91.

Sutch, Richard C. "The Profitability of Antebellum Slavery: Revisited (Comment on Saraydar)," (Reprinted in Aitken, ed. *Did Slavery Pay?*, 1971, pp. 221-241 *Southern Economic Journal*, 31(4), April 1965, pp. 365-77.

Sutch, Richard C. "Slavery as an Obstacle to Economic Growth in the United States: A Panel Discussion of Conrad and Meyer," *Journal of Economic History*, 27(4), December 1967, pp. 540-41.

Sutch, Richard C. "Comments on Papers by Smith and Vinovskis Presented to the 31st Annual Meeting of the Economic History Association," *Journal of Economic History*, 32(1), March 1972, pp. 216-18.

Sutch, Richard C. "The Breeding of Slaves for Sale and the Westward Expansion of Slavery, 1850-1860," in Engerman and Genovese, eds. *Race and Slavery in the Western Hemisphere*, 1975, pp. 173-210.

Sutch, Richard C. "The Treatment Received by American Slaves: A Critical Review of Evidence Presented in Time on the Cross," (Symposium on Time on the Cross. Edited by Gary M. Walton) *Explorations in Economic History*, 12(4), October 1975, pp. 335-438.

Sutch, Richard C.; David, Paul A.; Gutman, Herbert G.; Temin, Peter and Wright, Gavin. "'Time on the Cross' and the Burden of Quantitative History," in David, Gutman, Sutch, Temin, and Wright, eds. *Reckoning with Slavery*, 1976, pp. 339-82.

Sutch, Richard C. "The Care and Feeding of Slaves," in David, Gutman, Sutch, Temin, and Wright, ed. *Reckoning with Slavery*, 1976, pp. 231-301.

Vedder, Richard K. and Stockdale, David E. "The Profitability of Slavery Revisited: A Different Approach," *Agricultural History*, 49(2), April 1975, pp. 392-404.

Vedder, Richard K. "The Slave Exploitation (Expropriation) Rate," (Symposium on Time on the Cross. Edited by Gary M. Walton) *Explorations in Economic History*, 12(4), October 1975, pp. 453-58.

Vinovskis, Maris A. "The Demography of the Slave Population in Antebellum America: A Critique of 'Time on the Cross'," *Journal of Interdisciplinary History*, 5(3), Winter 1975, pp. 459-67.

Weiher, Kenneth. "Slavery and Southern Urbanization: A Reformulation of the Argument," in Soltow, ed. *Essays in Economic and Business History*, 1979, pp. 259-67.

Weintraub, Andrew. "Economics of Lincoln's Proposal for Compensated Emancipation," *American Journal of Economics and Sociology*, 35(2), April 1973, pp. 171-8.

Whitten, David O. "A Black Entrepreneur in Antebellum Louisiana," *Business History Review*, 45(2), Summer 1971, pp. 201-19.

Whitten, David O. "Sugar Slavery: A Profitability Model of Slave Investments in the Antebellum Louisiana Sugar Industry," *Louisiana Studies*, 12(2), Summer 1973, pp. 423-42.

Whitten, David O. "Medical Care of Slaves: Louisiana Sugar Region and South Carolina Rice District," *Southern Studies: An Interdisciplinary Journal of the South*, 16(2), Summer 1977, pp. 153-80.

Woodman, Harold D. "The Profitability of Slavery: A Historical Perennial," (Reprinted in Aitken, ed. *Did Slavery Pay?*, 1971, pp. 1-25) *Journal of Southern History*, 29, August 1963, pp. 303-25.

Woodman, Harold D. "The Old South and the New History," Presented at the MSSB-University of Rochester Conference, Time on the Cross: A First Appraisal, October 1974 [Working Paper].

Woodman, Harold D. "A Model to Explain the Relative Decline of Urban Slavery: Comment on Goldin," in Engerman and Genovese, eds. *Race and Slavery in the Western Hemisphere*, 1975, pp. 451-54.

Woodman, Harold D. "The Slave and Free Person of Color in an Urban Environment: General Comment," in Engerman and Genovese, eds. *Race and Slavery in the Western Hemisphere*, 1975, pp. 451-54.

Wright, Gavin and Passell, Peter. "The Effects of Pre-Civil War Territorial Expansion on the Price of Slaves," *Journal of Political Economy*, 80(6), November/December 1972, pp. 1188-202.

Wright, Gavin. "Comments on Papers by Reid, Ransom/Sutch, and Higgs on the Postbellum South Presented to the 32nd Annual Meeting of the Economic History Association," *Journal of Economic History*, 33(1), March 1973, pp. 170-76.

Wright, Gavin. "New and Old Views on the Economics of Slavery: A Review Article," *Journal of Economic History*, 33(2), June 1973, pp. 452-66.

Wright, Gavin. "Slavery and the Cotton Boom," (Symposium on *Time on the Cross*. Edited by Gary M. Walton) *Explorations in Economic History*, 12(4), October 1975, pp. 439-52.

Wright, Gavin. "Prosperity, Progress, and American Slavery," in David, Gutman, Sutch, Temin, and Wright, eds. *Reckoning with Slavery*, 1976, pp. 302-38.

Wright, Gavin. *The Political Economy of the Cotton South: Households, Markets, and Wealth in the Nineteenth Century*. New York: W.W. Norton, 1978.

Wright, Gavin. "Freedom and the Southern Economy," *Explorations in Economic History*, 16(1), January 1979, pp. 90-108.

Wright, Gavin. "The Efficiency of Slavery: Another Interpretation," *American Economic Review*, 69(1), March 1979, pp. 219-26.

Yasuba, Yasukichi. "The Profitability and Viability of Plantation Slavery in the United States," (Reprinted in Fogel and Engerman, eds. *The Reinterpretation of American Economic History*, 1971, pp. 362-368) *Economic Studies Quarterly*, 12(1), September 1961, pp. 60-67.

Zepp, Thomas M. "On Returns to Scale and Input Substitutability in Slave Agriculture," *Explorations in Economic History*, 13(2), April 1976, pp. 165-78.

United States: Education

Aldrich, Terry Mark. "Rates of Return Earned on Formal Technical Education in the Antebellum American Economy," (Summary of Doctoral Dissertation) *Journal of Economic History*, 30(1), March 1970, pp. 251-55.

Aldrich, Terry Mark. "Earnings of American Civil Engineers, 1820-1859," *Journal of Economic History*, 31(2), June 1971, pp. 407-19.

Aldrich, Terry Mark. *Rates of Return on Investment in Technical Education in the Antebellum American Economy.* New York: Arno Press, 1975.

Bowman, Mary Jean and Anderson, C. Arnold. "Human Capital and Economic Modernization in Historical Perspective," *Fourth International Conference of Economic History, Bloomington, 1968.* Paris: Mouton, 1973, pp. 247-72.

Easterlin, Richard A. "A Note on the Evidence of History," in Anderson and Bowman, eds. *Education and Economic Growth*, 1965, pp. 422-29.

Engerman, Stanley L. "Human Capital, Education, and Economic Growth," in Fogel and Engerman, eds. *The Reinterpretation of American Economic History*, 1971, pp. 241-56.

Field, Alexander J. "Educational Reform and Manufacturing Development in Mid-Nineteenth Century Massachusetts," (Summary of Doctoral Dissertation) *Journal of Economic History*, 36(1), March 1976, pp. 263-66.

Field, Alexander J. "Educational Expansion in Mid-Nineteenth Century Massachusetts: Human Capital Formation or Structural Reinforcement?" *Harvard Educational Review*, 46(4), November 1976, pp. 521-52.

Field, Alexander J. "Education and Social Programs," (Summary of 1977 Research Workshop) *Journal of Economic History*, 38(1), March 1978, pp. 258-61.

Field, Alexander J. "Economic and Demographic Determinants of Educational Commitment: Massachusetts, 1855," *Journal of Economic History*, 39(2), June 1979, pp. 439-59.

Field, Alexander J. "Industrialization and Skill Intensity: The Case of Massachusetts," *Journal of Human Resources*, 15(2), Spring 1980, pp. 149-75.

Fishlow, Albert. "The American Common School Revival, Fact or Fancy?" in Rosovsky, ed. *Industrialization in Two Systems*, 1966.

Fishlow, Albert. The Growth of American Educational Investment in the Nineteenth Century," *Third International Conference of Economic History, Munich, 1965*, part 1. Paris: Mouton, 1968, pp. 761-2.

Floud, Roderick C. "The Adolescence of American Engineering Competition, 1860-1900," *Economic History Review*, Second Series, 27(1), February 1974, pp. 57-71.

Gallman, Robert E. "Human Capital in the First 80 Years of the Republic: How Much Did America Owe the Rest of the World?" *American Economic Review, Papers and Proceedings*, 67(1), February 1977, pp. 27-31.

Kendrick, John W., assisted by Lethem, Yvonne, and Rowley, Jennifer. *The Formation and Stocks of Total Capital* (National Bureau of

Economic Research General Series, no. 100) New York: Columbia University Press for the National Bureau of Economic Research, 1976.

Landes, William M. and Solmon, Lewis C. "Compulsory Schooling Legislation: An Economic Analysis of Law and Social Change in the Nineteenth Century," *Journal of Economic History*, 32(1), March 1972, pp. 54-91.

Margo, Robert A. "School Finance and the Economics of Segregated Schools in the U.S. South, 1890-1920," [Working Paper].

Murphy, Earl F. "Comment on Papers by McCloskey, McManus, and Landes and Solmon Presented to the 31st Annual Meeting of the Economic History Association," *Journal of Economic History*, 32(1), March 1972, pp. 95-97.

Salsbury, Stephen. "Comment on Papers by McCloskey, McManus, and Landes and Solmon Presented to the 31st Annual Meeting of the Economic History Association," *Journal of Economic History*, 32(1), March 1972, pp. 92-94.

Solmon, Lewis C. "Capital Formation by Expenditures on Formal Education, 1880 and 1890," (Summary of Doctoral Dissertation) *Journal of Economic History*, 29(1), March 1969, pp. 167-72.

West, E.G. "Tom Paine's Voucher Scheme for Education," *Southern Economic Journal*, 33(3), January 1967, pp. 378-82.

United States: Women

Aldrich, Terry Mark and Albelda, Randy. "Determinants of Working Women's Wages during the Progressive Era," *Explorations in Economic History*, 17(4), October 1980, pp. 323-41.

Fraundorf, Martha Norby. "Relative Earnings of Native- and Foreign-born Women," *Explorations in Economic History*, 15(2), April 1978, pp. 211-20.

Goldin, Claudia D. "Female Labor Force Participation: The Origin of Black and White Differences, 1870 and 1880," *Journal of Economic History*, 37(1), March 1977, pp. 87-108.

Goldin, Claudia D. "The Work and Wages of Single Women, 1870 to 1920," *Journal of Economic History*, 40(1), March 1980, pp. 81-88.

Goldin, Claudia D. "Family Strategies and the Family Economy in the Late Nineteenth Century: The Role of Secondary Workers," in Hershberg, ed. *Philadelphia*, 1981, pp. 240-76.

McGouldrick, Paul F. and Tannen, Michael. "The Increasing Pay Gap for Women in the Textile and Clothing Industries, 1910 to 1970," *Journal of Economic History*, 40(4), December 1980, pp. 799-814.

Nickless, Pamela J. "Changing Labor Productivity and the Utilization of Native Women Workers in the American Cotton Textile Industry, 1825-1860," (Summary of Doctoral Dissertations) *Journal of Economic History*, 38(1), March 1978, pp. 287-88.

Nickless, Pamela J. "The Work and Wages of Single Women, 1870 to 1920: A Discussion of Goldin," *Journal of Economic History*, 40(1), March 1980, pp. 96-97.

Rotella, Elyce J. "Women's Labor Force Participation and the Growth of Clerical Employment in the United States, 1870-1930," (Summary of

Doctoral Dissertation) *Journal of Economic History*, 39(1), March 1979, pp. 331-33.

Rotella, Elyce J. "Women's Labor Force Participation and the Decline of the Family Economy in the United States," *Explorations in Economic History*, 17(2), April 1980, pp. 95-117.

Rotella, Elyce J. "The Expansion of the Clerical Sector in the United States, 1870-1930," [Working Paper].

Rotella, Elyce J. "Women's Labor Force Participation and the Growth of Clerical Employment in the United States, 1870-1930," Ph.D. Dissertation, University of Pennsylvania, 1977 [Working Paper].

Rotella, Elyce J. "Women's Participation in the U.S. Labor Force, 1870-1930: The Decline of the Family Economy and the Rise of the Clerical Sector," Presented at the Annual Meetings of the Social Science History Association, 1977 [Working Paper].

Strober, Myra H. and Best, Laura. "Female-Male Salary Differential in Public Schools: Some Lessons from San Francisco, 1879," *Economic Inquiry*, 17(2), April 1979, pp. 218-36.

Tannen, Michael B. and McGouldrick, Paul. "Further Results on Male and Female Pay Differentials, 1910 to 1970," [Working Paper].

Vinovskis, Maris A.; Mason, Karen and Hareven, Tamara K. "Determinants of Women's Labor Force Participation in Late Nineteenth-Century America," Family Transitions and the Life Course in Historical Perspective New York: Academic Press, 1978.

Woodman, Harold D. "Female Labor Force Participation: The Origin of Black and White Differences, 1870 and 1880: Comment on Paper by Goldin," *Journal of Economic History*, 37(1), March 1977, pp. 109-12.

Yeager, Mary. "Comment on Dissertations by Rotella and Easton Presented to the 38th Annual Meeting of the Economic History Association," *Journal of Economic History*, 39(1), March 1979, pp. 339-40.

Rest of the World: General

Adams, Jr., Donald R. "Some Evidence on English and American Wage Rates, 1790-1830," *Journal of Economic History*, 30(3), September 1970, pp. 499-520.

Almquist, Eric L. "Labor Specialization and the Irish Economy in 1841: An Aggregate Occupational Analysis," [Working Paper].

Baines, Dudley E. "The Labour Supply and the Labour Market, 1860-1914," in Floud and McCloskey, eds. *The Economic History of Britain since 1700*, vol. 2, 1980.

Bairoch, Paul. "Structure de la population active mondiale de 1700 a 1970 [Structure of the Labor Force Internationally, 1700-1970]," *Annales: Economies, Societes, Civilisations*, 26(5), September/October 1971, pp. 960-76.

Benjamin, Daniel K. and Kochin, Levis A. "Searching for an Explanation of Unemployment in Interwar Britain," *Journal of Political Economy*, 87(3), June 1979, pp. 441-78.

Benjamin, Daniel K. and Kochin, Levis A. "What Went Right with Juvenile Unemployment Policy between the Wars: A Comment (on

Garside)," *Economic History Review*, Second Series, 32(4), November 1979, pp. 523-28.

Bertram, Gordon W. and Percy, Michael B. "Real Wage Trends in Canada, 1900-1926: Some Provisional Estimates," *Canadian Journal of Economics*, 12(2), May 1979, pp. 299-312.

Blaug, Mark. "The Myth of the Old Poor Law and the Making of the New," *Journal of Economic History*, 23(1), March 1963, pp. 151-84.

Branson, William H. "Social Legislation and the Birth Rate in Nineteenth Century Britain," *Western Economic Journal*, 6(2), March 1968, pp. 134-44.

Branson, William H. "Social Legislation and the Demand for Children: Reply to West," *Western Economic Journal*, 6(5), December 1968, pp. 424.

Butlin, Noel G. and Dowie, J.A. "Estimates of Australian Workforce and Employment, 1861-1961," (Erratum: see this Review, 10(1), March 1970, for corrections of this article) *Australian Economic History Review*, 9(2), September 1969, pp. 138-55.

De Vries, Jan. "An Inquiry into the Behaviour of Wages in the Dutch Republic and Southern Netherlands, 1580-1800," *Acta Historiae Neerlandica [Studies in the History of the Netherlands]*, 10), 1978, pp. 79-97.

Duggan, Edward P. "The Impact of Industrialization on an Urban Labor Market: Birmingham, England, 1770-1860," (Summary of Doctoral Dissertation) *Journal of Economic History*, 34(1), March 1974, pp. 279-82.

Dutta, Amita. "An Econometric Study of Indo-Ceylon Labor Migration, 1920-1938: A Critique," *Economic Development and Cultural Change*, 21(1), October 1972, pp. 142-56.

Easton, Stephen T. "The Outdoor Relief System in England and Wales," in Grubel and Walker, eds. *Unemployment Insurance*, 1978, pp. 320-28.

Easton, Stephen T. "Aggregate Aspects of Unemployment, Unemployment Insurance and the Poor Laws in Great Britain, 1855-1940," (Summary of Doctoral Dissertation) *Journal of Economic History*, 39(1), March 1979, pp. 326-29.

Engerman, Stanley L. and Hartwell, Ronald M. "Models of Immiseration: The Theoretical Basis of Pessimism," in Taylor, ed. *The Standard of Living in Britain in the Industrial Revolution*, 1975.

Engerman, Stanley L. "Some Economic and Demographic Comparisons of Slavery in the United States and the British West Indies," *Economic History Review*, Second Series, 29(2), May 1976, pp. 258-75.

Evans, Jr., Robert. "Evolution of the Japanese System of Employer-Employee Relations, 1868-1945," *Business History Review*, 44(1), Spring 1970, pp. 110-25.

Flinn, M.W. "Trends in Real Wages, 1750-1850," *Economic History Review*, Second Series, 27(3), August 1974, pp. 395-413.

Flinn, M.W. "Real Wage Trends in Britain, 1750-1850: A Reply (to Gourvish)," *Economic History Review*, Second Series, 29(1), February 1976, pp. 143-45.

Forster, Colin. "Australian Unemployment, 1900-1940," *Economic Record*, 41(95), September 1965, pp. 426-50.

Forster, Colin. "Indexation and the Commonwealth Basic Wage, 1907-22,"

Australian Economic History Review, 20(2), September 1980, pp. 99-118.

Freudenberger, Herman and Cummins, J. Gaylord. "Health, Work, and Leisure before the Industrial Revolution," *Explorations in Economic History*, 13(1), January 1976, pp. 1-12.

Friedman, Gerald. "Slave Heights: Trinidad and the United States," [Working Paper].

Garside, W.R. "Juvenile Unemployment and Public Policy between the Wars," *Economic History Review*, Second Series, 30(2), May 1977, pp. 322-39.

Garside, W.R. "Juvenile Unemployment between the Wars: A Rejoinder (to Benjamin and Kochin)," *Economic History Review*, Second Series, 32(4), November 1979, pp. 529-32.

Gourvish, T.R. "Flinn and Real Wage Trends in Britain, 1750-1850: A Comment," *Economic History Review*, Second Series, 29(1), February 1976, pp. 136-42.

Green, Alan G. "Is Foreign Labour Complementary or Competitive (In Terms of Skill) with Native-Born Labour? The Canadian Case, 1911-1941," *International Migration*, 12(1-2), 1974, pp. 49-60.

Greenwood, Michael J. and Thomas, Lloyd B. "Geographic Labor Mobility in Nineteenth Century England and Wales," *Annals of Regional Science*, 7(2), December 1973, pp. 90-105.

Haines, Michael R. *Fertility and Occupation: Population Patterns in Industrialization*. New York: Academic Press, 1979.

Harley, C. Knick. "Skilled Labour and the Choice of Technique in Edwardian Industry," *Explorations in Economic History*, 11(4), Summer 1974, pp. 391-414.

Hilton, George W. "The British Truck System in the Nineteenth Century," *Journal of Political Economy*, 65(3), June 1957, pp. 237-56.

Hines, A.G. "Trade Unions and Wage Inflation in the United Kingdom, 1893-1961," *Review of Economic Studies*, 31, 1964, pp. 221-52.

Jonung, Lars and Wadensjo, Eskil. "Wages and Prices in Sweden, 1912-1922: A Retrospective Test," *Scandinavian Journal of Economics*, 81(1), 1979, pp. 60-71.

Jorberg, Lennart and Bengtsson, Tommy. "Regional Wages in Sweden during the 19th Century," in Bairoch and Levy-Leboyer, eds. *Disparities in Economic Development since the Industrial Revolution*, 1980.

Keating, M. and Haig, Brian D. "A Comment on the Butlin-Dowie Australian Work Force and Employment Estimates," *Australian Economic History Review*, 11(1), March 1971, pp. 59-62.

Kelley, Allen C. and Weisbrod, Burton A. "Disease and Economic Development: The Impact of Parasitic Disease in St. Lucia," *Journal of Social Economics*, Fall 1973.

Klep, Paul M.M. *Bevolking en Arbeid in Transformatie, Brabant 1700-1900. Een Analyse Van Ongelijktijdige Ontwikkelingen in een Maatschappij Opweg Naar Moderne Economische Groei* [*Population and Labour in Transformation, Brabant 1700-1900. An Analysis of Uneven Development in a Society on Its Way to Modern Economic Growth*]. Nijmegen: Socialistiese Vitgeverij, 1981.

Klep, Paul M.M. and Daems, Herman. "The Effect of Population, Exports and Rents on the Employment Structure of Agrarian Economy," Presented at the Workshop on Quantitative Economic History, Leuven, 1974 [Working Paper].

Kochin, Louis A. "Unemployment and Dole: Evidence from Interwar Britain," in Brabel and Walker, eds. *Unemployment Insurance*, 1978.

Korpelainen, Lauri. "Trends and Cyclical Movements in Industrial Employment in Finland, 1885-1952," Scandinavian Economic History Review, 5(1), 1957, pp. 26-48.

Krishnamurty, J. "Some Aspects of the Distribution of the Working Force in the Indian States, 1911-1961," in Van der Wee, Vinogradov, and Kotovsky, eds. *Fifth International Congress of Economic History*, vol. 3, 1976, pp. 62-74.

Kumar, Dhumar. *Land and Caste in South India: Agricultural Labor in the Madras Presidency during the Nineteenth Century*. Cambridge: Cambridge University Press, 1965.

Lazonick, William H. "Industrial Relations and Technical Change: The Case of the Self-Acting Mule," *Cambridge Journal of Economics*, 3(3), September 1979, pp. 231-62.

Lee, Clive H. *British Regional Employment Statistics, 1841-1971*. Cambridge: Cambridge University Press, 1980.

Lindert, Peter H. "English Occupations, 1670-1811," *Journal of Economic History*, 40(4), December 1980, pp. 685-712.

Luraghi, Raimondo. "Wage Labor in the 'Rice Belt' of Northern Italy and Slave Labor in the American South: A First Approach," Presented at the MSSB-University of Rochester Conference, Time on the Cross: A First Appraisal, October 1974 [Working Paper].

Marvel, Howard P. "Factory Regulation: A Reinterpretation of Early English Experience," *Journal of Law and Economics*, 20(2), October 1977, pp. 379-402.

McCloskey, Donald N. "New Perspectives on the Old Poor Law," *Explorations in Economic History*, 10(4), Summer 1973, pp. 419-36.

McInnis, R. Marvin. "Long-Run Changes in the Industrial Structure of the Canadian Work Force," *Canadian Journal of Economics*, 4(3), August 1971, pp. 353-61.

Morris, Morris D. "The Recruitment of an Industrial Labor Force in Asia, with British and American Comparisons," *Comparative Studies in Society and History*, 2(3), April 1960, pp. 305-28.

Morris, Morris D. *The Emergence of an Industrial Labor Force in India: A Study of the Bombay Cotton Mills, 1854-1947*. Berkeley and Los Angeles: University of California Press, 1965.

Nardinelli, Clark. "Child Labor and the Factory Acts," *Journal of Economic History*, 40(4), December 1980, pp. 739-55.

Nardinelli, Clark. "An Economic History of the Factory Acts," Unpublished Ph.D. Dissertation, University of Chicago, 1979 [Working Paper].

Neal, Larry D. "The Cost of Impressment during the Seven Years War," *Mariner's Mirror*, 64(1), February 1978, pp. 45-56.

Nishikawa, Shunsaku. "Productivity, Subsistence, and By-Employment in the Mid-Nineteenth Century Choshu," (Erratum: a correction for this article appears in 15(3), July 1978, p. 338 of this journal) *Explorations in Economic History*, 15(1), January 1978, pp. 69-83.

O'Grada, Cormac. "Demographic Adjustment and Seasonal Migration in

Nineteenth-Century Ireland," in Cullen and Furet, eds. *Ireland and France in the 17th-20th Centuries*, 1981, pp. 181-93.

Ohlsson, Rolf. *Invandrarna pa Arbetsmarknadan [Immigrants on the Labour Market]*. [Contains an English Summary] Lund: University of Lund Press, 1975.

Phelps Brown, E.H. and Hopkins, Sheila V. "The Course of Wage-Rates in Five Countries, 1860-1939," *Oxford Economic Papers*, New Series, 2(2), June 1950, pp. 226-96.

Phelps Brown, E.H. and Hart, P.E. "The Share of Wages in National Income," *Economic Journal*, 62(246), June 1952, pp. 253-77.

Phelps Brown, E.H. and Hopkins, Sheila V. "Seven Centuries of Building Wages," *Economica*, 22(87), August 1955, pp. 195-206.

Phelps Brown, E.H. and Hopkins, Sheila V. "Seven Centuries of the Prices of Consumables, Compared with Builders' Wage Rates," (Reprinted in Ramsey, ed. *The Price Revolution in the Sixteenth Century*, 1971, pp. 18-41) *Economica*, 23(92), November 1956, pp. 296-314.

Phelps Brown, E.H. "The Long Term Movement in Real Wages," in Dunlop, ed. *The Theory of Wage Determination*, 1957.

Phelps Brown, E.H. and Hopkins, Sheila V. "Wage-Rates and Prices: Evidence for Population Pressure in the Sixteenth Century," *Economica*, 24(96), November 1957, pp. 289-306.

Phelps Brown, E.H. and Hopkins, Sheila V. "Builders' Wage-Rates, Prices and Population: Some Further Evidence," *Economica*, 26(101), February 1959, pp. 18-38.

Phelps Brown, E.H. and Hopkins, Sheila V. "Seven Centuries of Wages and Prices: Some Earlier Estimates," *Economica*, 28(109), February 1961, pp. 30-36.

Phelps Brown, E.H. "Levels and Movements of Industrial Productivity and Real Wages Internationally Compared, 1860-1970," *Economic Journal*, 83(329), March 1973, pp. 58-71.

Phelps-Brown, E.H. *A Century of Pay*. London: Macmillan, 1968.

Pope, David H. "The Contribution of United Kingdom Migrants to Australia's Population, Employment and Economic Growth: Federation to the Depression," *Australian Economic Papers*, 16(29), December 1977, pp. 194-210.

Pope, David H. "Some Aspects of the Australian Labour Market and the Standard of Living, 1900-30," [Working Paper].

Reed, Clyde G. and Devoretz, Donald. "Evidence from the Skilled-Unskilled Canadian Wage Index: 1930-1972," [Working Paper].

Richards, G.M. "Wages and the Wage Share: Australian Manufacturing in the 1920s," *Australian Economic History Review*, 20(2), September 1980, pp. 119-35.

Saito, Osamu. "The Labor Market in Tokugawa Japan: Wage Differentials and the Real Wage Level, 1727-1830," *Explorations in Economic History*, 15(1), January 1978, pp. 84-100.

Sapsford, D. "A Time Series Analysis of U.K. Industrial Disputes," *Industrial Relations*, 14(2), May 1975, pp. 242-49.

Saxonhouse, Gary R. "The Supply of Quality Workers and the Demand for Quality in Jobs in Japan's Early Industrialization," *Explorations in Economic History*, 15(1), January 1978, pp. 40-68.

Saxonhouse, Gary R. and Kiyokawa, Yukihiko. "The Supply and Demand fo Quality Workers in the Cotton Textile Industries in Japan and India," in Ohkawa and Hayami, eds. *The Comparative Analysis of Japan and the Less Developed Countries.*

Saxonhouse, Gary R. "The Colonial Labor Force and Korean Economic Development," in Sato, ed. *The Japan Economy in the Interwar Years.*

Sinclair, William A. "Was Labour Scarce in the 1830'S?" *Australian Economic History Review*, 11(2), September 1971, pp. 115-32.

Thomas, Brinley. "The Migration of Labour into Glamorganshire Coalfield, 1861-1911," in Minchinton, ed. *Industrial South Wales, 1750-1914*, 1969, pp. 37-56.

Tipton, Jr., Frank B. "Farm Labor and Power Politics: Germany, 1850-1914," *Journal of Economic History*, 34(4), December 1974, pp. 951-79.

Tranter, N.L. "The Labour Supply, 1780-1860," in Floud and McCloskey, eds. *The Economic History of Britain since 1700*, vol. 1, 1980, pp. 203-25.

Tucker, G.S.L. "The Old Poor Law Revisited," *Explorations in Economic History*, 12(3), July 1975, pp. 233-52.

Tussing, Arlon. "The Labor Force in Meiji Economic Growth: A Quantitative Study of Yamanashi Prefecture," (Reprinted in Ohkawa, Johnston, and Kaneda, eds. *Agriculture and Economic Growth*, 1970, pp. 198-221) *Journal of Economic History*, 26(1), March 1966, pp. 59-92.

Umemura, Mataji. "Gainful Workers, 1870-1940," in Ohkawa and Hayami, eds. *Economic Growth*, vol. 1, 1973, pp. 95-100.

Vedder, Richard K. and Cooper, David C. "Nineteenth Century English and Welsh Geographic Labor Mobility: Some Further Evidence," *Annals of Regional Science*, 8(2), June 1974, pp. 131-39.

Von Tunzelmann, G. Nicholas. "Trends in Real Wages, 1750-1850, Revisited," *Economic History Review*, Second Series, 32(1), February 1979, pp. 33-49.

West, E.G. "Social Legislation and the Demand for Children: A Comment on Branson," *Western Economic Journal*, 6(5), December 1968, pp. 419-24.

Williams, L.J. and Boyns, T. "Occupation in Wales, 1851-1971," *Bulletin of Economic Research*, 29(2), November 1977, pp. 71-83.

Woroby, Tamara. "An Examination of Wage Inequality Changes in Canada, 1901-1921," Ph.D. Dissertation, Queen's University, Kingston, Ontario [Working Paper].

Yasuba, Yasukichi. "THE Evolution of Dualistic Wage Structure," in Patrick, ed. *Japanese Industrialization and its Social Consequences*, 1976.

Yeager, Mary. "Comment on Dissertations by Rotella and Easton Presented to the 38th Annual Meeting of the Economic History Association," *Journal of Economic History*, 39(1), March 1979, pp. 339-40.

Zamagni, Vera. "La dinamica dei salari nel settore industriale [Wage Movements in the Industrial Sector]," in Ciocca and Toniolo, eds. *L'economia italiana nel periodo fascista [The Italian Economy during the Fascist Era]*, 1976, pp. 329-78.

Rest of the World: Slavery and Serfdom

Bean, Richard N. "The British Transatlantic Slave Trade, 1650-1775," (Summary of Doctoral Dissertation) *Journal of Economic History*, 32(1), March 1972, pp. 409-11.

Bean, Richard N. *The British Transatlantic Slave Trade, 1650-1775.* New York: Arno Press, 1975.

Bean, Richard N. and Thomas, Robert P. "The Adoption of Slave Labor in British America," in Gemery and Hogendorn, eds. *The Uncommon Market*, 1979, pp. 377-98.

Buescu, Mircea. "Notas Sobre o Custo da Mao-De-Obra Escrava [Remarks on the Slave Manpower Cost]," *Verbum*, 31(3), September 1975, pp. 33-44.

Dahlman, Carl J. "An Economic Theory of Serfdom," [Working Paper].

De Mello, Pedro C. "Aspectos Economicos da Organizacao do Trabalho da Economia Cafeeira do Rio de Janeiro, 1850-88 [Economic Aspects of the Organization of Labor in the Coffee Economy of Rio de Janeiro, 1850-88]," *Revista Brasileira de Economia*, 32(1), January/March 1978, pp. 19-67.

De Mello, Pedro C. and Slenes, Robert W. "Analise Economica da Escravidao no Brasil [Economic Analysis of Slavery in Brazil]," in Paulo Neuhaus, ed. *A Economia Brasileira: Uma Visao Historica [The Brazilian Economy: An Historical View]*, 1979, pp. 89-122.

Domar, Evsey D. "The Causes of Slavery Or Serfdom: A Hypothesis," *Journal of Economic History*, 30(1), March 1970, pp. 18-32.

Domar, Evsey D. "The Profitability of Russian Serfdom Prior to its Abolition," [Working Paper].

Engerman, Stanley L. and Genovese, Eugene D., eds. *Race and Slavery in the Western Hemisphere: Quantitative Studies.* Princeton: Princeton University Press, 1975.

Engerman, Stanley L. "Some Economic and Demographic Comparisons of Slavery in the United States and the British West Indies," *Economic History Review*, Second Series, 29(2), May 1976, pp. 258-75.

Evans, Jr., Robert. "Some Notes on Coerced Labor," *Journal of Economic History*, 30(4), December 1970, pp. 861-66.

Feeny, David H. "The Decline in Slavery and Rise in Property Rights in Land in Mainland Southeast Asia, 1850-1940," [Working Paper].

Friedman, Gerald. "Slave Heights: Trinidad and the United States," [Working Paper].

Friedman, Gerald. "Slave Occupations in Trinidad and Eight Southern States," [Working Paper].

Friedman, Gerald. "The Demography of Trinidad Slavery," [Working Paper].

Friedman, Gerald. "The Registration of Slaves in Trinidad, 1813: More Numbers for the Slavery Game," [Working Paper].

Galenson, David W. "The Slave Trade to the English West Indies, 1673-1724: Evidence from Royal African Company Records," *Economic History Review*, Second Series, 32(2), May 1979, pp. 241-49.

Gemery, Henry A. and Hogendorn, Jan S. "The Atlantic Slave Trade: A Tentative Economic Model," *Journal of African History*, 15(2), 1974,

pp. 223-46.

Gemery, Henry A. and Hogendorn, Jan S. "Elasticity of Slave Labor Supply and the Development of Slave Economies in the British Carribean: The 17th Century Experience," in Rubin and Tuden, ed. *Comparative Perspectives on Slavery in New World Plantation Societies* (Annals of the New York Academy of Sciences, vol. 292), 1977, pp. 72-83.

Gemery, Henry A. and Hogendorn, Jan S. "Technological Change, Slavery, and the Slave Trade," in Dewey and Hopkins, eds. *The Imperial Impact*, 1978, pp. 243-58.

Gemery, Henry A. and Hogendorn, Jan S. "The Economic Costs of West African Participation in the Atlantic Slave Trade: A Preliminary Sampling for the Eighteenth Century," in Gemery and Hogendorn, eds. *The Uncommon Market*, 1979, pp. 143-61.

Gemery, Henry A. and Hogendorn, Jan S., eds. *The Uncommon Market: Essays in the Economic History of the Atlantic Slave Trade.* New York: Academic Press, 1979.

Hartwell, R.M. "Slave Labour and Factory Labour," Presented at the MSSB-University of Rochester Conference, Time on the Cross: A First Appraisal, October 1974 [Working Paper].

Hellie, Richard. "Time on the Cross from a Comparative Perspective of Early Modern Russian Slavery," Presented at the MSSB-University of Rochester Conference, Time on the Cross: A First Appraisal, October 1974 [Working Paper].

Hogendorn, Jan S. and Gemery, Henry A. "The Atlantic Slave Trade: A Tentative Economic Model," *Journal of African History*, 15(2), 1974, pp. 223-46.

Hogendorn, Jan S. and Gemery, Henry A. "Slave Labor Supply Elasticity and the Development of Slave Economies in the British Caribbean: The 17th Century Experience," in Rubin and Tuden, eds. *Comparative Perspectives on Slavery in New World Plantation Societies* (Annals of the New York Academy of Sciences, vol. 292), 1977.

Hogendorn, Jan S. "The Economics of Slave Use on Two 'Plantations' in the Zaria Emirate of the Sokoto Caliphate," *International Journal of African Historical Studies*, 10(3), 1977, pp. 369-83.

Hogendorn, Jan S. and Gemery, Henry A. "Technological Change, Slavery, and the Slave Trade," in Dewey and Hopkins, eds. *The Imperial Impact*, 1978.

Hogendorn, Jan S. "Slave Acquisition and Delivery in Precolonial Hausaland," in Schwartz and Dumett, eds. *West African Culture Dynamics*, 1980, pp. 477-93.

Kahan, Arcadius. "Notes on Serfdom in Western and Eastern Europe," *Journal of Economic History*, 33(1), March 1973, pp. 86-99.

Klein, Herbert S. "Reflections on the Viability of Slavery and the Causes of Abolition in 19th Century Cuba," Presented at the MSSB-University of Rochester Conference, Time on the Cross: A First Appraisal, October 1974 [Working Paper].

Klein, Herbert S. "The Cuban Slave Trade in a Period of Transition, 1790-1843," *Revue Francaise D'Histoire D'Outre-Mer*, 62(226-227), 1975, pp. 67-89.

Komlos, John. "The Emancipation of the Hungarian Peasantry and Agricultural Development," in Volgyes, ed. *The East European*

Peasantry, 1979, pp. 109-18.

LeVeen, E. Phillip. "British Slave Trade Suppression Policies, 1821-1865: Impact and Implications," (Summary of Doctoral Dissertation) *Journal of Economic History*, 32(1), March 1972, pp. 415-16.

LeVeen, E. Phillip. "The African Slave Supply Response," *African Studies Review*, 18, 1975, pp. 9-28.

Leff, Nathaniel H. "Long-Term Viability of Slavery in a Backward Closed Economy," *Journal of Interdisciplinary History*, 5(1), Summer 1974, pp. 103-8.

LeVeen, E. Phillip. "A Quantitative Analysis of the Impact of British Suppression Policies on the Volume of the Nineteenth Century Atlantic Slave Trade," in Engerman and Genovese, eds. *Race and Slavery in the Western Hemisphere*, 1975, pp. 51-81.

Postma, Johannes. "The Dutch Slave Trade: A Quantitative Assessment," *Revue Francaise D'Histoire D'Outre-Mer*, 62(226-227), 1975, pp. 232-44.

Rudolph, Richard L. "Agricultural Structure and Proto-Industrialization in Russia: Economic Development with Serf Labor," in Deyon and Mendels, eds. *Protoindustrialization*, 1982.

Ryan, Terrance C.I. "The Economics of Trading in Slaves," (Summary of Doctoral Dissertation) *African Economic History*, 1, Spring 1976, pp. 40-1.

Ryan, Terrance C.I. "The Economics of Trading in Slaves," Ph.D. Dissertation, Massachusetts Institute of Technology, 1975 [Working Paper].

Thomas, Robert P. and Bean, Richard N. "The Fishers of Men: The Profits of the Slave Trade," *Journal of Economic History*, 34(4), December 1974, pp. 885-914.

Rest of the World: Education

Bowman, Mary Jean and Anderson, C. Arnold. "Human Capital and Economic Modernization in Historical Perspective," *Fourth International Conference of Economic History, Bloomington, 1968.* Paris: Mouton, 1973, pp. 247-72.

Field, Alexander J. "Occupational Structure, Dissent, and Educational Commitment: Lancashire, 1841," in Uselding, ed. *Research in Economic History*, vol. 4, 1979.

Floud, Roderick C. "The Adolescence of American Engineering Competition, 1860-1900," *Economic History Review*, Second Series, 27(1), February 1974, pp. 57-71.

Floud, Roderick C. "Technical Education and Economic Performance: Engineering in the Late 19th Century," [Working Paper].

Hurt, J.S. "Professor West on Early Nineteenth-Century Education," *Economic History Review*, Second Series, 24(4), November 1971, pp. 624-32.

Lundgreen, Peter. "Technicians and the Labour Market in Prussia, 1810-1850," *Annales Cisalpines d'Histoire Sociale*, 1(2), 1971, pp. 9-29.

Lundgreen, Peter. *Bildung und Wirtschaftswachstum im*

Industrialisierungsprozess des 19. Jahrhunderts. Methodische Ansatze, Empirische Studien und Internationale Vergleiche (Historische und Padagogische Studien, vol. 5) [*Education and Economic Growth in the Industrialization Process of the 19th Century: Methodology, Empirical Studies and International Comparisons*]. Berlin: Colloqium-Verlag, 1973.

Lundgreen, Peter and Thirlwall, A.P. "Educational Expansion and Economic Growth in Nineteenth Century Germany: A Quantitative Study," in Stone, ed. *Schooling and Society*, 1976, pp. 20-66.

Lundgreen, Peter. "Quantifizierung in der Sozialgeschichte der Bildung [Quantification in the Social History of Education]," *Vierteljahrschrift fur Sozial- und Wirtschaftsgeschichte*, 63(4), 1976, pp. 433-53.

Mitch, David F. "Education as Consumption and Investment in Britain during the Nineteenth Century," [Working Paper].

Schultz, Theodore W. "Capital Formation by Education," (Reprinted in Fogel and Engerman, eds. *The Reinterpretation of American Economic History*, 1971, pp. 257-264) *Journal of Political Economy*, 68(6), December 1960, pp. 571-83.

Solmon, Lewis C. "Estimates of the Costs of Schooling in 1880 and 1890," *Explorations in Economic History*, 7(4, Supplement), Summer 1970, pp. 531-81.

Solmon, Lewis C. "Opportunity Costs and Models of Schooling in the Nineteenth Century," *Southern Economic Journal*, 37(1), July 1970, pp. 66-83.

Solmon, Lewis C. and Tierney, Michael. "Education," in Porter, ed. *Encyclopedia of American Economic History*, vol. 3, 1980, pp. 1012-27.

Soltow, Lee C. and Stevens, Edward. "Economic Aspects of School Participation in Mid-Nineteenth Century United States," *Journal of Interdisciplinary History*, 8(2), Autumn 1977, pp. 221-43.

West, E.G. "Resource Allocation and Growth in Early Nineteenth-Century British Education," *Economic History Review*, Second Series, 23(1), April 1970, pp. 68-95.

West, E.G. "The Interpretation of Early Nineteenth-Century Education Statistics: Reply to Hurt," *Economic History Review*, Second Series, 24(4), November 1971, pp. 633-42.

West, E.G. *Education and the Industrial Revolution*. London: Batsford's, 1975.

West, E.G. "Educational Slowdown and Public Intervention in Nineteenth Century Britain: A Study in the Economics of Bureaucracy," *Explorations in Economic History*, 12(1), January 1975, pp. 61-88.

West, E.G. "The Political Economy of American Public School Legislation," *Journal of Law and Economics*, 19(1), April 1976, pp. 101-28.

West, E.G. "Literacy and the Industrial Revolution," *Economic History Review*, Second Series, 31(3), August 1978, pp. 369-83.

Zamagni, Vera. "Istruzione e sviluppo economico. Il caso italiano 1861-1913 [Education and Economic Development: The Case of Italy, 1861-1913]," (Reprinted in Toniolo, ed. *L'economia italiana 1861-1940*, 1978, pp. 157-78) in Gianni Toniolo, ed. *Lo sviluppo economico italiano 1861-1940 [Italian Economic Development,*

1861-1940].   Laterza: Bari, 1973, pp. 187-240.

Chapter 16

United States: The South

Aldrich, Terry Mark. "Flexible Exchange Rates, Northern Expansion, and the Market for Southern Cotton: 1866-1879," *Journal of Economic History*, 33(2), June 1973, pp. 399-416.

Anderson, Terry L. and Thomas, Robert P. "The Growth of Population and Labor Force in the 17th-Century Chesapeake," *Explorations in Economic History*, 15(3), July 1978, pp. 290-312.

Bruchey, Stuart. "Econometrics and Southern History: Comment on Conrad," *Explorations in Entrepreneurial History*, Second Series, 6(1), Fall 1968, pp. 59-65.

Callahan, Colleen M. and Hutchinson, William K. "Antebellum Interregional Trade in Agricultural Goods: Preliminary Results," *Journal of Economic History*, 40(1), March 1980, pp. 25-31.

Chandler, Jr., Alfred D. "Econometrics and Southern History: Comment on Conrad," *Explorations in Entrepreneurial History*, Second Series, 6(1), Fall 1968, pp. 66-74.

Chandler, Jr., Alfred D. "Comment on Econometrics and Southern History," in Andreano, ed. *The New Economic History*, 1970, pp. 143-50.

Coelho, Philip R.P. and Ghali, Moheb A. "The End of the North-South Wage Differential," *American Economic Review*, 61(5), December 1971, pp. 932-37.

Coelho, Philip R.P. and Ghali, Moheb A. "The End of the North-South Wage Differential: Reply (to Ladenson)," *American Economic Review*, 63(4), September 1973, pp. 757-62.

Conrad, Alfred H. "Econometrics and Southern History," *Explorations in Entrepreneurial History*, Second Series, 6(1), Fall 1968, pp. 34-53.

DeCanio, Stephen J. "Productivity and Income Distribution in the Postbellum South," *Journal of Economic History*, 34(2), June 1974, pp. 422-46.

Earle, Carville V. and Hoffman, Ronald. "Staple Crops and Urban Development in the Eighteenth Century South," *Perspectives in American History*, 10), 1976, pp. 7-78.

Engerman, Stanley L. "The Effects of Slavery upon the Southern Economy: A Review of the Recent Debate," (Reprinted in Aitken, ed. *Did Slavery Pay?*, 1971, pp. 295-327) *Explorations in Entrepreneurial History*, Second Series, 4(2), Winter 1967, pp. 71-97.

Engerman, Stanley L. "The Antebellum South: What Probably Was and What

Should Have Been," (Reprinted in Parker, ed. *The Structure of the Cotton Economy of the Antebellum South*, 1970) *Agricultural History*, 44(1), January 1970, pp. 127-42.

Engerman, Stanley L. "Some Economic Factors in Southern Backwardness in the Nineteenth Century," in Kain and Meyer, eds. *Essays in Regional Economics*, 1971, pp. 279-306.

Engerman, Stanley L. "A Reconsideration of Southern Economic Growth, 1770-1860," *Agricultural History*, 49(2), April 1975, pp. 343-61.

Fischbaum, Marvin and Rubin, Julius. "Slavery and the Economic Development of the American South: Comment on Engerman," (Reprinted in Aitken, ed. *Did Slavery Pay?*, 1971, pp. 327-341) *Explorations in Entrepreneurial History*, Second Series, 6(1), Fall 1968, pp. 116-27.

FitzRandolph, Peter W. "The Rural Furnishing Merchant in the Postbellum United States: A Study in Spatial Economics," Ph.D. Dissertation, Tufts University, 1979 [Working Paper].

Fleisig, Heywood. "Slavery, the Supply of Agricultural Labor, and the Industrialization of the South," *Journal of Economic History*, 36(3), September 1976, pp. 572-97.

Fogel, Robert W. "Econometrics and Southern History: Comment on Conrad," *Explorations in Entrepreneurial History*, Second Series, 6(1), Fall 1968, pp. 54-58.

Gallman, Robert E. "Self-Sufficiency in the Cotton Economy of the Antebellum South," (Reprinted in Parker, ed. *The Structure of the Cotton Economy of the Antebellum South*, 1970, pp. 5-23) *Agricultural History*, 44(1), January 1970, pp. 5-23.

Gallman, Robert E. "Southern Antebellum Income Reconsidered: A Note on Gunderson," *Explorations in Economic History*, 12(1), January 1975, pp. 89-99.

Gallman, Robert E. "Slavery, the Supply of Agricultural Labor, and the Industrialization of the South: Comment on Fleisig," *Journal of Economic History*, 37(2), June 1977, pp. 473-74.

Gallman, Robert E. and Anderson, Ralph V. "Slaves as Fixed Capital: Slave Labor and Southern Economic Development," *Journal of American History*, 64(1), June 1977, pp. 24-46.

Gallman, Robert E. "Slavery and Southern Economic Growth," *Southern Economic Journal*, 45(4), April 1979, pp. 1007-22.

Gunderson, Gerald A. "Southern Antebellum Income Reconsidered," *Explorations in Economic History*, 10(2), Winter 1973, pp. 151-76.

Gunderson, Gerald A. "Southern Income Reconsidered: A Reply to Gallman," *Explorations in Economic History*, 12(1), January 1975, pp. 101-2.

Herbst, Lawrence A. "Interregional Commodity Trade from the North to the South and American Economic Development in the Antebellum Period," (Summary of Doctoral Dissertation) *Journal of Economic History*, 35(1), March 1975, pp. 264-70.

Herbst, Lawrence A. *Interregional Commodity Trade from the North to the South and American Economic Development in the Antebellum Period*. New York: Arno Press, 1978.

Herbst, Lawrence A. "Patterns of American Interregional Commodity Trade North to South, 1824-1839," *American Economist*, 12(2), Fall 1978, pp. 61-66.

Herbst, Lawrence A. "Antebellum Interregional Trade in Agricultural Goods: Discussion of Paper by Callahan and Hutchinson," *Journal of Economic History*, 40(1), March 1980, pp. 43-44.

Huertas, Thomas F. "Damnifying Growth in the Antebellum South," *Journal of Economic History*, 39(1), March 1979, pp. 87-100.

Hutchinson, William K. and Williamson, Samual H. "The Self-Sufficiency of the Antebellum South: Estimates of the Food Supply," *Journal of Economic History*, 31(3), September 1971, pp. 591-612.

Jones, Alice Hanson. "Wealth Estimates for the Southern Colonies about 1770," Claremont Economic Papers, no. 86, December 1973 [Working Paper].

Ladenson, Mark L. "The End of the North-South Wage Differential: Comment on Coelho and Ghali," *American Economic Review*, 63(4), September 1973, pp. 754-56.

Mandle, Jay R. "The Plantation States as a Sub-Region of the Postbellum South: A Note," *Journal of Economic History*, 34(3), September 1974, pp. 732-38.

Mellman, Robert. "A Reinterpretation of the Economic History of the Post-Reconstruction South, 1877-1919," Ph.D. Dissertation, Massachusetts Institute of Technology, 1975 [Working Paper].

Oates, Mary J. "The Role of the Cotton Textile Industry in the Economic Development of the American Southeast: 1900-1940," (Summary of Doctoral Dissertation) *Journal of Economic History*, 31(1), March 1971, pp. 281-84.

Olson, Mancur L. "The Causes and Quality of Southern Growth," in Liner and Lynch, eds. *The Economics of Southern Growth*, 1977, pp. 107-30.

Persky, Joseph. "The Dominance of the Rural-Industrial South, 1900-1930," *Journal of Regional Science*, 13(3), December 1973, pp. 409-19.

Ransom, Roger L. and Sutch, Richard C. "Growth and Welfare in the American South of the Nineteenth Century," *Explorations in Economic History*, 16(2), April 1979, pp. 207-36.

Rothstein, Morton. "Measurement Calculus and Direction: Prometheus in the Antebellum Southland," Presented at the MSSB-University of Rochester Conference, Time on the Cross: A First Appraisal, October 1974 [Working Paper].

Schaeffer, Donald F. "Productivity in the Antebellum South: The Western Tobacco Region," in Uselding, ed. *Research in Economic History*, vol. 3, 1978.

Shepherd, James F. and Walton, Gary M., eds. *Market Institutions and Economic Progress in the New South, 1865-1900*. New York: Academic Press, 1980.

Vedder, Richard K.; Gallaway, Lowell E. and Klingman, David C. "The Profitability of Antebellum Agriculture in the Cotton Belt: Some New Evidence," *Atlantic Economic Journal*, 2(2), November 1974, pp. 30-47.

Walton, Gary M. "Regenerative Failings of the New South: An Introduction," in Shepherd and Walton, eds. *Market Institutions and Economic Progress in the New South, 1865-1900*, 1980.

Weiss, Thomas J.; Bateman, Fred and Foust, James D. "Large Scale Manufacturing in the South and West, 1850 and 1860," *Business*

History Review, 45(1), Spring 1971, pp. 18-34.

Weiss, Thomas J.; Bateman, Fred and Foust, James D. "The Participation of Planters in Manufacturing in the Antebellum South," *Agricultural History*, 48(2), April 1974, pp. 277-97.

Weiss, Thomas J. and Bateman, Fred. "Manufacturing in the Antebellum South," in Uselding, ed. *Research in Economic History*, vol. 1, 1976.

Woodman, Harold D. "New Perspectives on Southern Economic Development: A Comment on Engerman and Rubin," *Agricultural History*, 49(2), April 1975, pp. 374-80.

Wright, Gavin. "'Economic Democracy' and the Concentration of Agricultural Wealth in the Cotton South, 1850-1860," (Reprinted in Parker, ed. *The Structure of the Cotton Economy in the Antebellum South*, 1970) *Agricultural History*, 44(1), January 1970, pp. 63-94.

Wright, Gavin. "Comments on Papers by Reid, Ransom/Sutch, and Higgs on the Postbellum South Presented to the 32nd Annual Meeting of the Economic History Association," *Journal of Economic History*, 33(1), March 1973, pp. 170-76.

Wright, Gavin. *The Political Economy of the Cotton South: Households, Markets, and Wealth in the Nineteenth Century.* New York: W.W. Norton, 1978.

Wright, Gavin. "Freedom and the Southern Economy," *Explorations in Economic History*, 16(1), January 1979, pp. 90-108.

Wright, Gavin. "Cheap Labor and Southern Textiles before 1880," *Journal of Economic History*, 39(3), September 1979, pp. 655-80.

Wright, Gavin. "Agriculture in the South," in Porter, ed. *Encyclopedia of American Economic History*, vol. 1, 1980, pp. 371-85.

United States: Other Regions

Adams, Jr., Donald R. "The Role of Banks in the Economic Development of the Old Northwest," in Klingaman and Vedder, eds. *Essays in Nineteenth Century Economic History*, 1975, pp. 208-45.

Anderson, Terry L. "The Economic Growth of Seventeenth-Century New England: A Measurement of Regional Income," (Summary of Doctoral Dissertation) *Journal of Economic History*, 33(1), March 1973, pp. 299-301.

Anderson, Terry L. and Hill, Peter J. "The Evolution of Property Rights: A Study of the American West," *Journal of Law and Economics*, 18(1), April 1975, pp. 163-80.

Anderson, Terry L. "Wealth Estimates for the New England Colonies, 1650-1709," *Explorations in Economic History*, 12(2), April 1975, pp. 151-76.

Anderson, Terry L. and Hill, Peter J. "From Free Grass to Fences: Transforming the Commons of the American West," in Hardin and Baden, eds. *Managing the Commons*, 1977, pp. 200-216.

Anderson, Terry L. and Hill, Peter J. "The Role of Private Property in the History of American Agriculture, 1776-1976: Reply to Schmid," *American Journal of Agricultural Economics*, 59(3), August 1977, pp. 590-91.

Anderson, Terry L. and Hill, Peter J. "An American Experiment in Anarcho-Capitalism: The Not So Wild, Wild West," *Journal of Libertarian Studies*, 3(1), 1979, pp. 9-29.

Anderson, Terry L. "Economic Growth in Colonial New England: 'Statistical Renaissance'," *Journal of Economic History*, 39(1), March 1979, pp. 243-57.

Ankli, Robert E. "Gross Farm Revenue in Pre-Civil War Illinois," (Reprinted in *Papers of the Sixteenth Business History Conference*, 1969) *Nebraska Journal of Economics and Business*, 8(3), Summer 1969, pp. 147-78.

Ankli, Robert E. "Agricultural Growth in Antebellum Illinois," *Journal of the Illinois State Historical Society*, 63(4), Winter 1970, pp. 387-98.

Ankli, Robert E. *Gross Farm Revenue in Pre-Civil War Illinois*. New York: Arno Press, 1977.

Ball, Duane E. "The Process of Settlement in Eighteenth-Century Chester County, Pennsylvania: A Social and Economic History," (Summary of Doctoral Dissertation) *Journal of Economic History*, 35(1), March 1975, pp. 253-55.

Ball, Duane E. "Dynamics of Population and Wealth in Eighteenth-Century Chester County, Pennsylvania," *Journal of Interdisciplinary History*, 6(4), Spring 1976, pp. 621-44.

Bateman, Fred and Weiss, Thomas J. "Comparative Regional Development in Antebellum Manufacturing," *Journal of Economic History*, 35(1), March 1975, pp. 182-208.

Bean, Richard N. "The Importance of Regional Cost of Living Differentials in Estimating Gini-Coefficients for U.S. Income Inequality," [Working Paper].

Bjorle, G.C. "Regional Adjustment to Economic Growth: The United States, 1880-1950," *Oxford Economic Papers*, 20(1), March 1968, pp. 81-97.

Bowman, John D. "An Economic Analysis of Midwestern Farm Land Values and Farm Land Income, 1860 to 1900," *Yale Economic Essays*, 5(2), Fall 1965, pp. 317-52.

Bowman, John D. and Keehn, Richard H. "Agricultural Terms of Trade in Four Midwestern States, 1870-1900," *Journal of Economic History*, 34(3), September 1974, pp. 592-609.

Bowman, John D. and Danhof, Clarence H. "An Industrial Income Distribution for New York State, 1865," [Working Paper].

Bowman, John D. "Gross Agricultural Output, Value Added and Factor Shares in the Twelve Midwestern States, 1870 to 1900," [Working Paper].

Brownlee, W. Elliot. "Income Taxation and Capital Formation in Wisconsin, 1911-1929," *Explorations in Economic History*, 8(1), Fall 1970, pp. 77-102.

Coelho, Philip R.P. and Shepherd, James F. "The Impact of Regional Differences in Prices and Wages on Economic Growth: The United States in 1890," *Journal of Economic History*, 39(1), March 1979, pp. 69-85.

Coelho, Philip R.P. and Shepherd, James F. "Differences in Regional Prices: The United States, 1851-1880," *Journal of Economic History*, 34(3), September 1974, pp. 551-91.

Coelho, Philip R.P. and Shepherd, James F. "Regional Differences in Real Wages: The United States, 1851-1880," *Explorations in Economic History*, 13(2), April 1976, pp. 203-30.

Coelho, Philip R.P. and Shepherd, James F. "The Impact of Regional Differences in Prices and Wages on Economic Growth: The United States in 1890," *Journal of Economic History*, 39(1), March 1979, pp. 69-85.

Cohn, Raymond L. "Location Theory, Regional Growth Theory and Manufacturing in the Antebellum South and Midwest," *Review of Regional Studies*, 8(1), Spring 1978, pp. 20-27.

Cohn, Raymond L. "Local Manufacturing in the Antebellum South and Midwest," *Business History Review*, 54(1), Spring 1980, pp. 80-91.

Cohn, Raymond L. "Antebellum Regional Incomes: Another Look," [Working Paper].

Daniels, Bruce C. "Long Range Trends of Wealth Distribution in 18th Century New England," *Explorations in Economic History*, 11(2), Winter 1974, pp. 123-36.

David, Paul A. "American Economic Growth Before 1840: Comments on Papers by Anderson, Haeger, Kulikoff, and Lindstrom Presented to the 38th Annual Meeting of the Economic History Association," *Journal of Economic History*, 39(1), March 1979, pp. 303-10.

David, Paul A. "Factories at the Prairie's Edge: A Study of Industrialization in Chicago, 1848-1893," [Working Paper].

Davis, Lance E. and Legler, John B. "The Regional Impact of the Federal Budget, 1815-1900: A Preliminary Survey (Summary)," *Third International Conference of Economic History, Munich, 1965*, part 1. Paris and The Hague: Mouton, 1968, pp. 753-59.

Davis, Lance E. and Legler, J. "The Regional Impact of the Federal Budget, 1815-1900," Presented at the Third International Economic History Conference, Munich, 1965 [Working Paper].

Easterlin, Richard A. "Interregional Differences in Per Capita Income, Population, and Total Income, 1840-1950," in Parker, ed. *Trends in the American Economy in the Nineteenth Century* (Studies in Income and Wealth, vol. 24), 1960, pp. 73-140.

Easterlin, Richard A. "Regional Income Trends, 1840-1950," in Harris, ed. *American Economic History*, 1961, pp. 525-47.

Easterlin, Richard A. "Suggestions for the Study of the Economic Growth of the Delaware Valley Area," in Porter, ed. *Regional Economic History*, 1976, pp. 17-24.

Engelbourg, Saul. "Energy and Industrialization: The Case of Southern New England," in Soltow, ed. *Essays in Economic and Business History*, 1979, pp. 268-82.

Field, Alexander J. "Sectoral Shift in Antebellum Massachusetts: A Reconsideration," *Explorations in Economic History*, 15(2), April 1978, pp. 146-71.

Fishlow, Albert. "Antebellum Interregional Trade Reconsidered," (Reprinted in Andreano, ed. *New Views on American Economic Development*, 1965, pp. 187-200) *American Economic Review, Papers and Proceedings*, 54(3), May 1964, pp. 352-64.

Fishlow, Albert. "Postscript on Antebellum Interregional Trade," in Andreano, ed. *New Views on American Economic Development*, 1965, pp. 209-12.

Fogel, Robert W. "American Interregional Trade in the 19th Century," in Andreano, ed. *New Views on American Economic Development*, 1965, pp. 213-24.

Gallman, Robert E. "Comment on Papers by Anderson, Haeger, Kulikoff, and Lindstrom Presented to the 38th Annual Meeting of the Economic History Association," *Journal of Economic History*, 39(1), March 1979, pp. 311-12.

Grant, Kenneth G. "The Rate of Settlement of Canadian Provinces, 1870-1911: A Comment on Norrie," *Journal of Economic History*, 38(2), June 1978, pp. 471-73.

Green, Alan G. "Regional Aspects of Canada's Economic Growth, 1890-1929," *Canadian Journal of Economics and Political Science*, 33(2), May 1967, pp. 232-245.

Green, George D. "Louisiana, 1804-61," in Cameron, ed. *Banking and Economic Development*, 1972, pp. 199-231.

Green, George D. "Monetary Systems and Regional Economies: Comments on Papers by Rockoff and Bateman/Weiss," *Journal of Economic History*, 35(1), March 1975, pp. 212-15.

Higgs, Robert and Stettler III, H. Louis. "Colonial New England Demography: A Sampling Approach," *William and Mary Quarterly*, Third Series, 27(2), April 1970, pp. 282-94.

Higgs, Robert. "The Wealth of Japanese Tenant Farmers in California, 1909," *Agricultural History*, 53(2), April 1979, pp. 488-93.

Jones, Alice Hanson. "La Fortune Privee en Pennsylvanie, New Jersey, Delaware (1774) [The Private Wealth in Pennsylvania, New Jersey, and Delaware (1774)]," *Annales: Economies, Societes, Civilisations*, 24(2), March/April 1969, pp. 235-49.

Jones, Alice Hanson. "Wealth Estimates for the American Middle Colonies, 1774," *Economic Development and Cultural Change*, 18(4, Part 2), July 1970, pp. 1-172.

Jones, Alice Hanson. "Wealth Estimates for the New England Colonies about 1770," *Journal of Economic History*, 32(1), March 1972, pp. 98-127.

Jones, Donald W. "Prices, Gold and Interest Rates in Gold Rush California: An Inquiry into Domestic and International Economic Relations of California, 1850-1855," Presented at the Meetings of the North American Economic Studies Association, Atlantic City, New Jersey, September 1976 [Working Paper].

Kearl, J.R.; Pope, Clayne L. and Wimmer, Larry T. "Household Wealth in a Settlement Economy: Utah, 1850-1870," *Journal of Economic History*, 40(3), September 1980, pp. 477-96.

Klingaman, David C. "Individual Wealth in Ohio in 1860," in Klingaman and Vedder, eds. *Essays in Nineteenth Century Economic History*, 1975, pp. 177-90.

Laurent, Jerome K. "Sources of Capital and Expenditures for Internal Improvements in a Developing Region: The Case of Wisconsin Lake Ports, 1836-1910," *Exploration in Economic History*, 13(2), April 1976, pp. 179-201.

Lebergott, Stanley. "Migration in the United States, 1800-1960: Some New Estimates," *Journal of Economic History*, 30(4), December 1970, pp. 839-47.

Lebergott, Stanley. "Industrialization, Regional Change, and the

Sectoral Distribution of the U.S. Labor Force, 1850-1880: A Reply (to Vatter)," *Economic Development and Cultural Change*, 23(4), July 1975, pp. 749-50.

Lindstrom, Diane. "Domestic Trade and Regional Specialization," in Porter, ed. *Encyclopedia of American Economic History*, vol. 1, 1980, pp. 264-80.

Mak, James, Matsuba, S. "A Concise Economic History of the Hawaiian Islands," [Working Paper].

Munyon, Paul G. "A Critical Review of Estimates of Net Income from Agriculture for 1880 and 1900: New Hampshire, a Case Study," *Journal of Economic History*, 37(3), September 1977, pp. 634-54.

Niemi, Jr., Albert W. "The Development of Industrial Structure in Southern New England: A Note," *Journal of Economic History*, 30(3), September 1970, pp. 657-62.

Niemi, Jr., Albert W. "Structural Shifts in Southern Manufacturing, 1849-1899," *Business History Review*, 45(1), Spring 1971, pp. 79-84.

Niemi, Jr., Albert W. "Empirical Tests of the Heckscher Ohlin Hypothesis for New England and Southern Manufacturing, 1860-1958," *Review of Regional Studies*, 4, Supplement), 1974, pp. 87-94.

Niemi, Jr., Albert W. *State and Regional Patterns in American Manufacturing, 1860-1900*. Westport, Conn.: Greenwood Press, 1974.

Norrie, Kenneth H. "The Rate of Settlement of the Canadian Prairies, 1870-1911," *Journal of Economic History*, 35(2), June 1975, pp. 410-27.

Norrie, Kenneth H. "The Rate of Settlement of the Canadian Prairies, 1870-1911: A Reply to Grant," *Journal of Economic History*, 38(2), June 1978, pp. 474-75.

North, Douglass C. "Location Theory and Regional Economic Growth," *Journal of Political Economy*, 63(3), June 1955, pp. 243-58.

North, Douglass C. "The Spatial and Interregional Framework of the United States Economy: An Historical Perspective," in Carrothers, ed. *Papers and Proceedings of the Regional Science Association, 1956*, vol. 2, 1956, pp. 201-9.

North, Douglass C. "International Capital Flows and the Development of the American West," *Journal of Economic History*, 16(4), December 1956, pp. 493-505.

North, Douglass C. "Agriculture in Regional Economic Growth," (Reprinted in Coben and Hill, eds. *American Economic History*, 1966, pp. 258-267) *Journal of Farm Economics*, 41(5), December 1959, pp. 943-51.

Olson, Mancur L. "The Economic Growth of the Chesapeake and the European Market, 1697-1775: Discussion of Price," *Journal of Economic History*, 24(4), December 1964, pp. 512-16.

Peet, Richard. "Von Thunen Theory and the Dynamics of Agricultural Expansion," *Explorations in Economic History*, 8(2), Winter 1970/71, pp. 181-202.

Peklar, Conrad. "Wealth in Colonial Connecticut, 1650-1760," Ohio University Economic History Research Paper no. G-10 [Working Paper].

Perloff, Harvey S.; Muth, Richard F. and Lampard, Eric E. *Regions, Resources, and Economic Growth*. Baltimore: Johns Hopkins University Press, 1960.

Price, Jacob M. "A Note on the Value of Colonial Exports of Shipping," *Journal of Economic History*, 36(3), September 1976, pp. 704-24.

Roberts, Charles A. "Interregional Per Capita Income Differentials and Convergence: 1880-1950," *Journal of Economic History*, 39(1), March 1979, pp. 101-12.

Rockoff, Hugh T. "Varieties of Banking and Regional Economic Development in the United States, 1840-1860," *Journal of Economic History*, 35(1), March 1975, pp. 160-81.

Rothenberg, Winifred B. "A Price Index for Rural Massachusetts, 1750-1855," (See note in this Journal, 40(1), March 1980, for a Corregenda concerning this article) *Journal of Economic History*, 39(4), December 1979, pp. 975-1001.

Schmid, A. Allan. "The Role of Private Property in the History of American Agriculture, 1776-1976: Comment (on Anderson and Hill)," *American Journal of Agricultural Economics*, 59(3), August 1977, pp. 590-91.

Shaw, John A. "Railroads, Irrigation, and Economic Growth: The San Joaquin Valley of California," *Explorations in Economic History*, 10(2), Winter 1973, pp. 211-28.

Soltow, Lee C. *Patterns of Wealthholding in Wisconsin since 1850*. Madison: University of Wisconsin Press, 1971.

Soltow, Lee C. "The Economic Heritage of an Iowa County," *Annals of Iowa*, Third Series, 43(1), Summer 1975, pp. 24-38.

Thomas, Robert P. and Anderson, Terry L. "White Population, Labor Force and Extensive Growth of the New England Economy in the Seventeenth Century," *Journal of Economic History*, 33(3), September 1973, pp. 634-67.

Vatter, Harold G. "Industrialization, Regional Change, and the Sectoral Distribution of the U.S. Labor Force, 1850-1880," *Economic Development and Cultural Change*, 23(3), April 1975, pp. 739-47.

Vatter, Harold G. "Industrialization, Regional Change, and the Sectoral Distribution of the U.S. Labor Force, 1850-1880: Comment on Lebergott," *Economic Development and Cultural Change*, 23(4), July 1975, pp. 739-47.

Vedder, Richard K. and Gallaway, Lowell E. "Migration and the Old Northwest," in Klingaman and Vedder, eds. *Essays in Nineteenth Century Economic History*, 1975, pp. 159-76.

Weiher, Kenneth. "Slavery and Southern Urbanization: A Reformulation of the Argument," in Soltow, ed. *Essays in Economic and Business History*, 1979, pp. 259-67.

Weiss, Roger W. "Comment on Papers by Jones, Shepherd and Walton, and McCusker Presented to the 31st Annual Meeting of the Economic History Association," *Journal of Economic History*, 32(1), March 1972, pp. 163-64.

Weiss, Thomas J.; Bateman, Fred and Foust, James D. "Large Scale Manufacturing in the South and West, 1850 and 1860," *Business History Review*, 45(1), Spring 1971, pp. 18-34.

Williamson, Jeffrey G. "Regional Inequality and the Process of National Development: A Description of Patterns," (Reprinted in Needleman, ed. *Regional Analysis*, 1968, pp. 99-158) *Economic Development and Cultural Change*, 13(4, Part 2), July 1965, pp.

1-84.
Williamson, Jeffrey G. "Unbalanced Growth, Inequality and Regional Development: Some Lessons from American History," in Arnold, ed. *Alternatives to Confrontation*, 1980, pp. 3-62.
Williamson, Jeffrey G. "Inequality and Regional Development: The View from America," in Bairoch and Levy-Leboyer, eds. *Disparities in Economic Development Since the Industrial Revolution*, 1981, pp. 373-91.
Wimmer, Larry T.; Hill, Marvin S. and Rooker, C. Keith. *The Kirtland Economy Revisited.* Provo, Utah: Brigham Young University Press, 1978.

Adams, Jr., Donald R. "Wage Rates in the Iron Industry: A Comment on Zabler," *Explorations in Economic History*, 11(1), Fall 1973, pp. 89-94.
Bean, Richard N. "An Explanation of Chicago Urban Density Based on Relative Prices at Time of First Development - Or the Putty-Clay Theory of Capital Refuted," [Working Paper].
Booms, Bernard H. "Impact of Urban Market Structure on the Level of Inventive Activity in Cities in the Early Nineteen-Hundreds," *Land Economics*, 49, August 1973, pp. 318-25.
Cain, Louis P. The Sanitary District of Chicago: A Case Study in Water Use and Conservation," (Summary of Doctoral Dissertation) *Journal of Economic History*, 30(1), March 1970, pp. 256-61.
Cain, Louis P. "An Economic History of Urban Location and Sanitation," in Uselding, ed. *Research in Economic History*, vol. 2, 1977, pp. 337-89.
Crowther, Simeon J. "Urban Growth in the Mid-Atlantic States, 1785-1850," *Journal of Economic History*, 36(3), September 1976, pp. 624-44.
Goldin, Claudia D. "A Model to Explain the Relative Decline of Urban Slavery: Empirical Results," in Engerman and Genovese, eds. *Race and Slavery in the Western Hemisphere*, 1975, pp. 427-50.
Goldin, Claudia D. "Cities and Slavery: The Issue of Compatibility," in Schnore, ed. *The New Urban History*, 1975.
Goldin, Claudia D. *Urban Slavery in the American South, 1820-1860: A Quantitative History.* Chicago: University of Chicago Press, 1976.
Goldin, Claudia D. "Household and Market Production of Families in a Late Nineteenth Century American City," *Explorations in Economic History*, 16(2), April 1979, pp. 111-31.
Haines, Michael R. "Fertility and Marriage in a Nineteenth-Century Industrial City: Philadelphia, 1850-1880," *Journal of Economic History*, 40(1), March 1980, pp. 151-58.
Haines, Michael R. "Poverty, Economic Stress, and the Family in a Late Nineteenth-Century American City: Whites in Philadelphia, 1880," in Hershberg, ed. *Philadelphia*, 1981, pp. 240-76.
Haines, Michael R. "Why Were Nineteenth Century U.S. Urban Black Fertility Rates So Low? (Evidence from Philadelphia, 1850-1880)," Presented at the University of Chicago, Workshop in Economic

History, no. 8081-4, October 1980 [Working Paper].

Higgs, Robert. "The Growth of Cities in a Midwestern Region, 1870-1900," *Journal of Regional Science*, 9(3), December 1969, pp. 369-75.

Jones, Donald W. "Migration and Urban Unemployment in Dualistic Economic Development," University of Chicago, Department of Geography Research Series #165, 1975 [Working Paper].

Lebergott, Stanley. "Industrialization, Regional Change, and the Sectoral Distribution of the U.S. Labor Force, 1850-1880: A Reply (to Vatter)," *Economic Development and Cultural Change*, 23(4), July 1975, pp. 749-50.

Leet, Don R. "Interrelations of Population Density, Urbanization, Literacy, and Fertility," *Explorations in Economic History*, 14(4), October 1977, pp. 388-401.

Lindstrom, Diane and Sharpless, John. "Urban Growth and Economic Structure in Antebellum America," in Uselding, ed. *Research in Economic History*, vol. 3, 1978, pp. 161-216.

Lindstrom, Diane L. "Demand, Markets, and Eastern Economic Development: Philadelphia, 1815-1840," (Summary of Doctoral Dissertation) *Journal of Economic History*, 35(1), March 1975, pp. 271-73.

Olmstead, Alan L. and Smolensky, Eugene. *The Urbanization of the United States.* Morristown, N.J.: General Learning, 1973.

Riefler, Roger F. "Nineteenth-Century Urbanization Patterns in the United States," *Journal of Economic History*, 39(4), December 1979, pp. 961-74.

Roehl, Richard and Sutch, Richard. "Urban Migration during the Process of Industrialization: The United States and England in the Nineteenth Century," Presented at the International Econometric Society Meetings, September 1970 [Working Paper].

Schmitz, Mark D. and Laurie, Bruce. "Manufacture and Productivity: The Making of an Industrial Base," in Hershberg, ed. *Toward an Interdisciplinary History of the City*, 1978.

Smolensky, Eugene. "Industrial Location and Urban Growth," in Davis, Easterlin, and Parker, eds. *American Economic Growth*, 1972, pp. 582-610.

Smolensky, Eugene. "The Management of Urban Agglomeration," in Davis, Easterlin, and Parker, eds. *American Economic Growth*, 1972, pp. 611-35.

Swanson, Joseph A. and Williamson, Jeffrey G. "A Model of Urban Capital Formation and the Growth of Cities in History," *Explorations in Economic History*, 8(2), Winter 1970/71, pp. 213-22.

Thomas, Brinley. *Migration and Urban Development: A Reappraisal of British and American Long Cycles.* London: Methuen, 1972.

Vatter, Harold G. "Industrialization, Regional Change, and the Sectoral Distribution of the U.S. Labor Force, 1850-1880," *Economic Development and Cultural Change*, 23(3), April 1975, pp. 739-47.

Vatter, Harold G. "Industrialization, Regional Change, and the Sectoral Distribution of the U.S. Labor Force, 1850-1880: Comment on Lebergott," *Economic Development and Cultural Change*, 23(4), July 1975, pp. 739-47.

Weiss, Thomas J. "Urbanization and the Growth of the Service Workforce," *Explorations in Economic History*, 8(3), Spring 1971, pp. 241-59.

Williamson, Jeffrey G. "Antebellum Urbanization in the American Northeast," (Reprinted in Fogel and Engerman, eds. *The Reinterpretation of American Economic History*, 1971, pp. 426-436) *Journal of Economic History*, 25(4), December 1965, pp. 592-608.

Williamson, Jeffrey G. and Swanson, Joseph A. "The Growth of Cities in the American Northeast, 1820-1870," *Explorations in Entrepreneurial History*, Second Series, 4(1, Supplement), Fall 1966, pp. 1-101.

Williamson, Jeffrey G.; Smith, Kenneth R. and Swanson, Joseph A. "The Size Distribution of Cities and Optimal City Size," *Journal of Urban Economics*, 1(4), October 1974, pp. 395-409.

Williamson, Jeffrey G. and Swanson, Joseph A. "Firm Location and Optimal City Size in American History," in Schnore, ed. *The New Urban History*, 1975, pp. 260-73.

Woodman, Harold D. "A Model to Explain the Relative Decline of Urban Slavery: Comment on Goldin," in Engerman and Genovese, eds. *Race and Slavery in the Western Hemisphere*, 1975, pp. 451-54.

Yeates, Maurice H. "Some Factors Affecting the Spatial Distribution of Chicago Land Values, 1910-1960," *Economic Geography*, 41(1), January 1965, pp. 57-70.

Rest of the World: Regions and Cities

Anderson, Isabel. "The Temporal Characteristics of the Growth of Manufacturing in Urbanized Areas of Canada," [Working Paper].

Borchardt, Knut. "Regional Differentiation in the Development of Germany throughout the 19th Century with Special Regard to the East/West Differential," *Third International Conference of Economic History, Munich, 1965*, part 5. Paris: Mouton, 1974, pp. 441-43.

Brockstedt, Jurgen. "Die Wirtschaftsentwicklung Kiels in vor- und fruhindustrieller Zeit (1800-1864) [The Economic Development of Kiel in the Pre- and Early-Industrial Period (1800-1864)]," in Schneider, ed. *Wirtschaftskrafte und Wirtschaftswege*, vol. 3 [*Economic Forces and Economic Paths*, part 3], 1978, pp. 251-64.

Brockstedt, Jurgen. *Regionale Mobilitat in Schleswig-Holstein 1600-1900. Theorie, Fallstudien, Quellenkunde, Bibliographie* [*Regional Mobility in Schleswig-Holstein 1600-1900: Theory, Case Studies, Sources, Bibliography*]. Neumunster: Wachholtz, 1980.

Brockstedt, Jurgen. "Wirtschaftsentwicklung, Sozialstruktur und Mobilitat in Schleswig-Holstein (1800-1864) [Economic Development, Social Structure, and Mobility in Schleswig-Holstein, 1800-1864]," in Schroder, ed. *Sozialwissenschaftliche Ansatze in der modernen Stadtgeschichte*, 1979, pp. 179-97.

Broder, Albert A. "Quantitative study of the Role of Railways in a Regional Economy: Southern Spain and the Andalous RR Company, 1872-1913," *First Congress on the Industrialization of Spain*. Barcelona, 1970.

Buescu, Mircea. "Medicao das Disparidades Regionais de Renda: Brasil, 1872-1900 [Measurement of Regional Income Disparaties: Brazil,

1872-1900]," *Verbum*, 33(2), December 1977, pp. 199-208.

Buescu, Mircea. "Disparites Regionales au Bresil dans la Seconde Moitie du XIX Siecle [Regional Disparaties in Brazil during the Second Half of the 19th Century]," *Proceedings of the International Congress on Economic History, 7th, Edinburgh, 1978.* London: Macmillan.

Costanzia, Dario. "Popolazione, attivita edilizia e mercato immobiliare a Torino tra il 1850 ed il 1880 [Population, Building Activity, and the Real Estate Market in Turin, 1850-1880]," *Storia urbana*, (6), September/December 1978, pp. 3-53.

De Brabander, G.L. "The Distribution of Economic Activities Over Industries and Regions in Belgium, 1846-1910: A Study of the Data [In Dutch with English Summary]," *Bijdragen tot de Geschiedenis*, 61, 1978, pp. 97-184.

De Brabander, G.L. "De regionaal-industriele specialisatie en haar effect op Ruimtelijke Verschillen in Economische groei in Belgie, van 1846 tot 1970 [Regional-Industrial Specialization and its Effect on Spatial Differences in Economic Growth in Belgium from 1846 to 1970] [Working Paper]," Unpublished Ph.D. Dissertation, University of Antwerp, 1979.

De Meere, J.M.M. "Inkomensgroei en -ongelijkheid te Amsterdam 1877-1940 [Growth and Inequality in Amsterdam, 1877-1940]," Tijdschrift voor Sociale Geschiedenis, 13, March 1979, pp. 3-47.

Falkus, Malcolm E. and Jones, Eric L. "Urban Improvement and the English Economy in the Seventeenth and Eighteenth Centuries," in Uselding, ed. *Research in Economic History*, vol. 4, 1979.

Fremdling, Rainer and Tilly, Richard H., eds. *Industrialisierung und Raum, Studien zur Regionalen Differenzierung im Deutschland im 19. Jahrhundert [Industrialization and Spatial Relationships: Studies on Regional Differentiation in Germany in the 19th Century]* (Historisch-Sozialwissenschaftliche Forschungen, vol. 7). Stuttgart: Klett-Cotta, 1979.

Fremdling, Rainer; Pierenkemper, Toni and Tilly, Richard H. "Regionale Differenzierung in Deutschland als Schwerpunkt Wirtschaftshistorischer Forschung [Regional Differentiation in Germany as the Central Focus of Research in Economic History]," in Fremdling and Tilly, eds. *Industiralisierung und Raum* (Historisch-Sozialwissenschaftliche Forschungen, vol. 7), 1979.

Gommel, Rainer. *Wachstum und Konjunktur der Nurnberger Wirtschaft (1815-1914) [Growth and Business Cycles of the Nurembergian Economy, 1815-1914]*. Stuttgart: Klett-Cotta, 1978.

Gommel, Rainer. "The Development of a Growth Pole in the Nineteenth Century illustrated by the Example of Nuremberg," in Bairoch and Levy-Leboyer, eds. *Disparities in Economic Development since the Industrial Revolution*, 1980.

Good, David F. "Economic Integration and Regional Development in Austria-Hungary, 1867-1913," in Bairoch and Levy-Leboyer, eds. *Disparities in Economic Development since the Industrial Revolution*, 1981, pp. 137-50.

Haines, Michael R. "Economic-Demographic Interrelations in Developing Agricultural Regions: A Case Study of Prussian Upper Silesia, 1840-1914," (Summary of Doctoral Dissertation) *Journal of Economic*

History, 33(1), March 1973, pp. 302-4.

Huber, Paul B. "Regionale Expansion und Entleerung in Deutschland des
Neunzehnten Jahrhunderts: eine Folge der Eisenbahnentwicklung?
[Regional Expansion and Evacuation in 19th Century Germany: A
Result of Railroad Development?]," in Fremdling and Tilly, eds.
Industrialisierung und Raum, 1979, pp. 27-53.

Lee, Clive H. *Regional Economic Growth in the United Kingdom since the
1880's*. London: McGraw-Hill, 1971.

Lee, Clive H. "Regional Structural Change in the Long Run: Great
Britain, 1841-1971," in Pollard, ed. *Region und
Industrialisierung*, 1980.

Leff, Nathaniel H. "Economic Development and Regional Inequality:
Origins of the Brazilian Case," [Translated into Portuguese in
Revista Brasileira de Economia, 1972] *Quarterly Journal of
Economics*, 86(2), May 1972, pp. 243-62.

Levy-Leboyer, Maurice. "Les Inegalites Regionales de Croissance dans
L'Agriculture Francaise, 1823-1939 [Regional Inequalities of Growth
in French Agriculture, 1823-1939]," in Bairoch and Levy-Leboyer,
eds. *Disparities in Economic Development since the Industrial
Revolution*, 1980.

Lewis, J. Parry. "Indices of House-Building in the Manchester
Conurbation, South Wales and Great Britain, 1851-1913," *Scottish
Journal of Political Economy*, 8(2), June 1961, pp. 148-56.

Loschky, David J. "Urbanization and England's Eighteenth Century Crude
Death and Birth Rates," *Journal of European Economic History*, 1(3),
Winter 1972, pp. 697-712.

McClelland, Peter D. "The New Brunswick Economy in the Nineteenth
Century," (Summary of Doctoral Dissertation) *Journal of Economic
History*, 25(4), December 1965, pp. 686-90.

McInnis, R. Marvin. "Regional Income Differentials in Canada,
1911-1961," (Summary of Doctoral Dissertation) *Journal of Economic
History*, 26(4), December 1966, pp. 586-88.

McInnis, R. Marvin. "The Trend of Regional Income Differentials in
Canada," *Canadian Journal of Economics*, 1(2), May 1968, pp. 440-70.

Paterson, Donald G.; Blain, L. and Rae, J.D. "The Regional Impact of
Economic Fluctuations during the Inter-War Period: The Case of
British Columbia," *Canadian Journal of Economics*, 7(3), August
1974, pp. 381-401.

Sanchez-Albornoz, Nicolas. "Congruence Among Spanish Economic Regions
in the Nineteenth Century," *Journal of European Economic History*,
3(3), Winter 1974, pp. 725-45.

Schremmer, Eckart. "Agrareinkommen und Kapitalbildung im 19.
Jahrhundert in Sudwestdeutschland [Agricultural Income and Capital
Formation in Southwest Germany in the 19th Century]," *Jahrbucher
fur Nationalokonomie und Statistik*, 176(3), June 1964, pp. 196-240.

Shepherd, James F. "Newfoundland and the Staple Theory: Export-Led
Growth or Decline?" Presented at the Ninth Conference on the
Application of Economic Theory and Quantitative Methods to Canadian
Economic History, University of Western Ontario, London, Ontario,
March 1978 [Working Paper].

Sinclair, William A. "Economic Growth and Well-Being: Melbourne,
1870-1914," *Economic Record*, 51(134), June 1975, pp. 153-73.

Snooks, G.D. "Regional Estimates of Gross Domestic Product and Capital Formation: Western Australia, 1923/24-1938/39," *Economic Record*, 48(124), December 1972, pp. 536-53.

Snooks, G.D. "Depression and Recovery in Western Australia 1928-29 to 1938-39: A Deviation from the Norm," *Economic Record*, 49(127), September 1973, pp. 420-39.

Snooks, G.D. *Depression and Recovery in Western Australia, 1928/29 to 1938/39: A Study in Cyclical and Structural Change.* Nedlands, W.A.: University of Western Australia Press, 1974.

Snooks, G.D. "Development in Adversity, (Western Australia) 1913 to 1946," in Appleyard, Bolton, de Garis, and Stannage, eds. *New History of Western Australia*, 1979.

Snooks, G.D. "The Arithmetic of Regional Growth: Western Australia, 1912/13 to 1957/58," *Australian Economic History Review*, 19(1), March 1979, pp. 63-84.

Spechler, Martin C. "The Regional Concentration of Industry in Imperial Russia, 1854-1917," *Journal of European Economic History*, 9(2), Fall 1980, pp. 401-430.

Thomas, Brinley., eds. *The Welsh Economy: Studies in Expansion.* Cardiff: University of Wales Press, 1962.

Thomas, Brinley. *Migration and Urban Development: A Reappraisal of British and American Long Cycles.* London: Methuen, 1972.

Toninelli, Pier Angelo. "Innovazioni tecniche, mutamenti strutturali e accumulazione capitalistica nelle campagne cremonesi (1861-1914) [Technical Innovation, Structural Change, and Capitalistic Accumulation in the Cremonan Countryside, 1861-1914]," *Rivista di storia dell'agricoltura*, (2), August 1973.

Toniolo, Gianni. "Cento anni di economia portuale a Venezia [One Hundred Years of Harbour Economy in Venice]," *CoSES Informazioni*, 3, 1972, pp. 33-73.

Vaillancourt, Francois and Ferron, Jean-Olivier. "Qui Perd Sa Langue, Perd Sa Foi [He Who Loses His Language Loses Faith]," *Revue D'Histoire de L'Amerique Francaise*, 33(2), September 1979, pp. 263-65.

Von Tunzelmann, G. Nicholas. "Steam Power and Smoke Pollution in English Cities to 1870," [Working Paper].

Zamagni, Vera. *Industrializzazione e squilibri regionali in Italia. Bilancio dell'eta giolittiana [Industrialization and Regional Imbalance in Italy: An Evaluation of the Giolitti Years].* Bologna: il Mulino, 1978.

Chapter 17

GOVERNMENT AND POLITICS

United States: General and Taxation

Anderson, Terry L. and Hill, Peter J. "The Role of Private Property in the History of American Agriculture, 1776-1976," *American Journal of Agricultural Economics*, 58(5), December 1976, pp. 937-45.

Anderson, Terry L. and Hill, Peter J. "The Role of Private Property in the History of American Agriculture, 1776-1976: Reply to Schmid," *American Journal of Agricultural Economics*, 59(3), August 1977, pp. 590-91.

Benston, George J. "On Understanding the Birth and Evolution of the Securities and Exchange Commission: Where Are We in the Theory of Regulation? Discussion of MacKay and Reid," in Walton, ed. *Regulatory Change in an Atmosphere of Crisis*, 1979, pp. 123-27.

Brown, E. Cary. "Fiscal Policy in the Thirties: A Reappraisal," (Reprinted in Fogel and Engerman, eds. *The Reinterpretation of American Economic History*, 1971, pp. 480-487) *American Economic Review*, 46, December 1956, pp. 857-79.

Cagan, Phillip. "Some Macroeconomic Impacts of the National Industrial Recovery Act, 1933-35: Comment on Weinstein," in Brunner, ed. *The Great Depression Revisited* (Rochester Studies in Economics and Policy Issues, vol. 2), 1981, pp. 282-285.

Copeland, Morris A. *Trends in Government Financing.* Princeton: Princeton University Press for the National Bureau of Economic Research, 1961.

Curran, Christopher and Swanson, Joseph S. "The Fiscal Behavior of Municipal Governments: 1905-1930," *Journal of Urban Economics*, 3(4), October 1976, pp. 344-56.

Davis, Lance E. and Legler, John. "The Government in the American Economy, 1815-1902: A Quantitative Study," *Journal of Economic History*, 26(4), December 1966, pp. 514-52.

Davis, Lance E. and Legler, John B. "The Regional Impact of the Federal Budget, 1815-1900: A Preliminary Survey (Summary)," *Third International Conference of Economic History, Munich, 1965*, part 1. Paris and The Hague: Mouton, 1968, pp. 753-59.

Davis, Lance E. "It's a Long, Long Road to Tipperary, or Reflections on Organized Violence, Protection Rates, and Related Topics: The New Political History," *Journal of Economic History*, 40(1), March 1980, pp. 1-16.

Davis, Lance E. and Legler, J. "The Regional Impact of the Federal Budget, 1815-1900," Presented at the Third International Economic

History Conference, Munich, 1965 [Working Paper].

DeCanio, Stephen J. "The Economics of Political Change: Comments on Papers by Reid, Metzer, and Berkowitz/McQuaid Presented to the 37th Annual Meeting of the Economic History Association," *Journal of Economic History*, 38(1), March 1978, pp. 143-47.

Emi, Koichi. "Government Expenditure," in Ohkawa and Hayami, eds. *Economic Growth*, vol. 1, 1973, pp. 80-94.

Fabricant, Solomon. *The Trend of Government Activity in the United States since 1900* (General Series, no. 56). New York: National Bureau of Economic Research, 1952.

Firestone, John M. *Federal Receipts and Expenditures during Business Cycles, 1879-1958*. Princeton: Princeton University Press for the National Bureau of Economic Research, 1960.

Fogel, Robert W. "The Union Pacific Railroad: The Questions of Public Policy," in Fogel and Engerman, eds. *The Reinterpretation of American Economic History*, 1971, pp. 417-25.

Fogel, Robert W. and Rutner, Jack L. "The Efficiency Effects of Federal Land Policy, 1850-1900: Some Provisional Findings," in Bogue, Aydelotte, and Fogel, eds. *The Dimensions of Quantitative Research in History*, 1972.

Haddock, David D. "An Empirical Study of the Regulation of the Rail Industry," [Working Paper].

Haddock, David D. "The Advent of Federal Regulation of Railroads," [Working Paper].

Haddock, David D. "The Origins of Regulation: Competing Theories and Critical Tests," [Working Paper].

Hill, Peter J. and Anderson, Terry L. *The Birth of a Transfer Society*. Stanford: Hoover Institute Press, 1980.

Holt, Charles F. *The Role of State Government in the Nineteenth-Century American Economy, 1820-1902: A Quantitative Study*. New York: Arno Press, 1977.

Hughes, Jonathan R.T. "The Colonial Origins of Modern Social Control," in Krooss, ed. *Proceedings of the Business History Conference, 1974*, Second Series, Vol. 3, 1975, pp. 67-95.

Hughes, Jonathan R.T. *Social Control in the Colonial Economy*. Charlottesville: University Press of Virginia, 1976.

Hughes, Jonathan R.T. "Transference and Development of Constraints Upon Economic Activity," in Uselding, ed. *Research in Economic History*, vol. 1, 1976.

Hughes, Jonathan R.T. *The Governmental Habit: Economic Control from Colonial Times to the Present*. New York: Basic Books, 1977.

Hughes, Jonathan R.T. "Roots of Regulation: The New Deal," in Walton, ed. *Regulatory Change in an Atmosphere of Crisis*, 1979, pp. 31-55.

James, John A. and Sylla, Richard E. "The Changing Nature of American Public Debt, 1690-1835," in *La Dette Publique aux XVIIIe et XIXe Siecles*, 1980.

Legler, John B. "Regional Distribution of Federal Receipts and Expenditures in the Nineteenth Century," *Regional Science Association, Papers and Proceedings*, 19, 1967, pp. 141-60.

MacAvoy, P.W. *The Economic Effects of Regulation*. Cambridge, Mass.: M.I.T. Press, 1965.

MacKay, Robert J. and Reid, Jr., Joseph D. "On Understanding the Birth and Evolution of the Securities and Exchange Commission: Where Are We in the Theory of Regulation?" in Walton, ed. *Regulatory Change in an Atmosphere of Crisis*, 1979, pp. 101-21.

North, Douglass C. "Government and the American Economy," in Davis, Easterlin, and Parker, eds. *American Economic Growth*, 1972, pp. 636-64.

Olson, Mancur L. *The Economics of the Wartime Shortage: A History of British Food Shortages in the Napoleonic War and World Wars I and II.* Durham: Duke University Press, 1963.

Ratner, Sidney. "Taxation," in Porter, ed. *Encyclopedia of American Economic History*, vol. 1, 1980, pp. 451-67.

Reid, Jr., Joseph D. "Government Regulatory Institutions: Origin and Evolution," (Summary of 1978 Research Workshop) *Journal of Economic History*, 39(1), March 1979, pp. 321-22.

Schmid, A. Allan. "The Role of Private Property in the History of American Agriculture, 1776-1976: Comment (on Anderson and Hill)," *American Journal of Agricultural Economics*, 59(3), August 1977, pp. 590-91.

Schweitzer, Mary McKinney. "Economic Regulation and the Colonial Economy: The Maryland Tobacco Inspection Act of 1747," *Journal of Economic History*, 40(3), September 1980, pp. 551-69.

Sylla, Richard E. "The Public Sector and the Price Level in America, 1720-1977," [Working Paper].

Temin, Peter. "Roots of Regulation: The New Deal (Discussion of Hughes)," in Walton, ed. *Regulatory Change in an Atmosphere of Crisis*, 1979, pp. 57-62.

Temin, Peter. "The Origin of Compulsory Drug Prescriptions," *Journal of Law and Economics*, 22(1), April 1979, pp. 91-106.

Trace, Keith. "The New Deal: Some Trends in Re-interpretation," *Proceedings of the Australian and New Zealand Society for the Advancement of American Studies*, 1965, pp. 60-71.

Trescott, Paul B. "The United States Government and National Income, 1790-1860," in Parker, ed. *Trends in the American Economy in the Nineteenth Century* (Studies in Income and Wealth, vol. 24), 1960, pp. 337-61.

Walton, Gary M., ed. *Regulatory Change in an Atmosphere of Crisis: Current Implications of the Roosevelt Years.* New York: Academic Press, 1979.

Weinstein, Michael M. "Some Macroeconomic Impacts of the National Industrial Recovery Act, 1933-1935," in Brunner, ed. *The Great Depression Revisited* (Rochester Studies in Economics and Policy Issues, vol. 2), 1981, pp. 262-81.

Williamson, Jeffrey G. "Watersheds and Turning Points: Conjectures on the Long-Term Impact of Civil War Financing," Journal of Economic History, 34(3), September 1974, pp. 636-61.

Wright, Gavin. "The Political Economy of New Deal Spending: An Econometric Analysis," *Review of Economics and Statistics*, 56(1), February 1974, pp. 30-38.

Other Countries

Abramovitz, Moses and Eliasberg, Vera F. *The Growth of Public Employment in Great Britain* (General Series, no. 60). Princeton: Princeton University Press for the National Bureau of Economic Research, 1957.

Ames, Edward and Rapp, Richard T. "The Birth and Death of Taxes: A Hypothesis," *Journal of Economic History*, 37(1), March 1977, pp. 161-78.

Anderson, J.L. "A Measure of the Effect of British Public Finance, 1793-1815," *Economic History Review*, Second Series, 27(4), November 1974, pp. 610-19.

Benjamin, Daniel K. and Kochin, Levis A. "What Went Right with Juvenile Unemployment Policy between the Wars: A Comment (on Garside)," *Economic History Review*, Second Series, 32(4), November 1979, pp. 523-28.

Butlin, Noel G. "Colonial Socialism in Australia 1860-1900," in Aitken, ed. *The State and Economic Growth*, 1959.

Carlson, Leonard A. "The Dawes Act and the Decline of Indian Farming," (Summary of Doctoral Dissertation) *Journal of Economic History*, 38(1), March 1978, pp. 274-76.

Cohen, Jon S. "Fascism and Agriculture in Italy: Policies and Consequences," *Economic History Review*, Second Series, 32(1), February 1979, pp. 70-87.

Dick, Trevor J.O. "Approaches to Tariff Formation: The Case of Late Nineteenth Century Canadian Tariffs," [Working Paper].

Dick, Trevor J.O. "Economy, Ideology, and the Growth of Government Spending in Canada Since 1867," [Working Paper].

Eddie, Scott M. "Economic Policy and Economic Development in Austria-Hungary, 1867-1913," in Mathias and Pollard, eds. *The Cambridge Economic History of Europe*, vol. 8.

Emi, Koichi and Rosovsky, Henry. "Seifu Kensetsu toshi no Sokutei, 1868-1940 [The Measurement of Japanese Government Investment in Constructon, 1868-1940]," *Keizai Kenkyu*, 9(1), January 1958, pp. 52-60.

Fenoaltea, Stefano. "Public Policy and Italian Industrial Development, 1861-1913," (Summary of Doctoral Dissertation) *Journal of Economic History*, 29(1), March 1969, pp. 176-79.

Fenoaltea, Stefano. *Public Policy and Italian Industrial Development, 1861-1913: A New Economic History*. New York: Cambridge University Press.

Fischer, Wolfram. "Government Activity and Industrialization in Germany (1815-70)," in Rostow, ed. *The Economics of Take-off into Sustained Growth*, 1963, pp. 83-94.

Forster, Colin. "Federation and the Tariff," *Australian Economic History Review*, 17(2), September 1977, pp. 95-116.

Fremdling, Rainer. "Freight Rates and State Budget: The Role of the National Prussian Railways, 1880-1913," *Journal of European Economic History*, 9(1), Spring 1980, pp. 21-40.

Fritsch, Winston. "Aspectos da Politica Economica no Brasil, 1906-1914 [Aspects of Economic Politics in Brazil, 1906-1914]," in Neuhaus, ed. *A Economia Brasileira* [*Brazilian Economy*], 1979.

Garside, W.R. "Juvenile Unemployment and Public Policy between the Wars," *Economic History Review*, Second Series, 30(2), May 1977, pp. 322-39.

Garside, W.R. "Juvenile Unemployment between the Wars: A Rejoinder (to Benjamin and Kochin)," *Economic History Review*, Second Series, 32(4), November 1979, pp. 529-32.

Goldin, Claudia D. "War," in Porter, ed. *Encyclopedia of American Economic History*, vol. 3, 1980, pp. 935-57.

Gross, Nachum T. and Metzer, Jacob. "Public Finance in the Jewish Economy 1918-1939," [In Hebrew] *Israel Economic Papers*, 1976, pp. 36-49.

Gross, Nachum T. and Metzer, Jacob. "Public Finance in the Jewish Economy in Interwar Palestine," in Uselding, ed. *Research in Economic History*, vol. 3, 1978, pp. 87-159.

Gunderson, Gerald A. "Economic Change and the Demise of the Roman Empire," *Explorations in Economic History*, 13(1), January 1976, pp. 43-68.

Hamilton, Earl J. "The Role of War in Modern Inflation," *Journal of Economic History*, 37(1), March 1977, pp. 13-36.

Hartwell, R.M. and North, Douglass C. "Law, Property Rights, Legal Institutions, and the Performance of Economies," in Flinn, ed. *Proceedings of the Seventh International Economic History Congress*, 1978.

Hausman, William J. "Public Policy and the Supply of Coal to London, 1700-1770," (Summary of Doctoral Dissertation) *Journal of Economic History*, 37(1), March 1977, pp. 252-54.

Holt, Charles F. *The Role of State Government in the Nineteenth-Century American Economy, 1820-1902: A Quantitative Study.* New York: Arno Press, 1977.

Huertas, Thomas F. *Economic Growth and Economic Policy in a Multinational Setting: The Hapsburg Monarchy, 1841-1865.* New York: Arno Press, 1978.

Johansen, Hans Chr. *Dansk Okonomisk Politik I Arene efter 1784 [Danish Economic Policy after 1784].* [Contains English Summary] Aarhus: Universitetsforlaget, 1968.

Kochin, Levis A. and Benjamin, Daniel K. "The British National Debt," [Working Paper].

Lane, Frederic C. "The Role of Governments in Economic Growth in Early Modern Times," *Journal of Economic History*, 35(1), March 1975, pp. 8-17.

Liu, Ts'ui-Jung and Fei, John C.H. "An Analysis of the Land Tax Burden in China, 1650-1865," *Journal of Economic History*, 37(2), June 1977, pp. 359-81.

Marr, William L. "The Expanding Role of Government and Wars: A Further Elaboration," *Public Finance*, 29(3-4), 1974, pp. 416-21.

Marr, William L. and Percy, Michael. "The Government and the Rate of Canadian Prairie Settlement (Comment on Norrie)," *Canadian Journal of Economics*, 11(4), November 1978, pp. 757-67.

Marvel, Howard P. "Factory Regulation: A Reinterpretation of Early English Experience," *Journal of Law and Economics*, 20(2), October 1977, pp. 379-402.

Mathias, Peter and O'Brien, Patrick. "Taxation in Britain and France, 1715-1810: A Comparison of the Social and Economic Incidence of Taxes Collected for the Central Governments," *Journal of European Economic History*, 5(3), Winter 1976, pp. 601-50.

McCloskey, Donald N. "A Mismeasurement of the Incidence of Taxation in Britain and France, 1715-1810: Comment on O'Brien and Mathias," *Journal of European Economic History*, 7(1), Spring 1978, pp. 209-10.

Metzer, Jacob. *National Capital for a National Home: The Formation of the Zionist Public Sector in the Early Mandate Period.* Jerusalem: Ben Zvi Press, 1979.

Millar, James. "The Birth and Death of Taxes: Comment (on Ames and Rapp)," *Journal of Economic History*, 37(1), March 1977, pp. 179-81.

Mokyr, Joel. "Government Finance, Taxation, and Economic Policy in Old Regime Europe," (Summary of the 1975 Research Workshop) *Journal of Economic History*, 36(1), March 1976, pp. 28-29.

Nardinelli, Clark. "Child Labor and the Factory Acts," *Journal of Economic History*, 40(4), December 1980, pp. 739-55.

Nardinelli, Clark. "An Economic History of the Factory Acts," Unpublished Ph.D. Dissertation, University of Chicago, 1979 [Working Paper].

Neal, Larry D. "Interpreting Power and Profit in Economic History: A Case Study of the Seven Years War," *Journal of Economic History*, 27(1), March 1977, pp. 20-35.

Norrie, Kenneth H. "The National Policy and Prairie Economic Discrimination in Canada, 1870-1930," *Canadian Papers in Rural History*, 1, 1978, pp. 13-32.

Norrie, Kenneth H. "Canadian Pacific Railroad Land Sale: A Model of the Sale and Pricing of the Canadian Pacific Railroad Land Grant," [Working Paper].

North, Douglass C. "The State of Economic History," *American Economic Review, Papers and Proceedings*, 55(2), May 1965, pp. 86-91.

North, Douglass C. and Thomas, Robert P. "An Economic Theory of the Growth of the Western World," *Economic History Review*, Second Series, 23(1), April 1970, pp. 1-17.

North, Douglass C. and Davis, Lance E. *Institutional Change and American Economic Growth.* Cambridge: Cambridge University Press, 1971.

North, Douglass C. "Institutional Change and Economic Growth," *Journal of Economic History*, 31(1), March 1971, pp. 118-25.

North, Douglass C. and Thomas, Robert P. "European Economic Growth: Reply to Professor D. Ringose," *Economic History Review*, Second Series, 26(2), May 1973, pp. 293-94.

North, Douglass C. and Thomas, Robert P. *The Rise of the Western World: A New Economic History.* [Translated into Italian, Spanish, and French] Cambridge: Cambridge University Press, 1975.

North, Douglass C. and Thomas, Robert P. "The Role of Governments in Economic Growth in Early Modern Times: Comment on Lane," *Journal of Economic History*, 35(1), March 1975, pp. 18-19.

O'Brien, Patrick K. and Mathias, Peter. "The Incidence of Taxes and the Burden of Proof: Reply to McCloskey," *Journal of European Economic History*, 7(1), Spring 1978, pp. 211-13.

O'Brien, Patrick K. "British Public Finances in the Wars against France, 1793-1815," Ph.D. Dissertation, Oxford University, 1966 [Working Paper].

Olmstead, Alan L. and Goldberg, Victor P. "Institutional Change and American Economic Growth: A Critique of Davis and North," *Explorations in Economic History*, 12(2), April 1975, pp. 193-210.

Olson, Mancur L. "Some Historic Variations in Property Institutions," [Working Paper].

Patrick, Hugh T. "The Government Sector in Japan's Development and Growth: Comment," in Ohkawa and Hayami, eds. *Economic Growth*, vol. 2, 1973, pp. 389-96.

Pettengill, John S. "The Impact of Military Technology on European Income Distribution," *Journal of Interdisciplinary History*, 10(2), Autumn 1979, pp. 201-25.

Pincus, Jonathan J.; Barnard, A. and Butlin, Noel G. "Public and Private Sector Employment in Australia, 1901-1974," *Australian Economic Review*, 10(37), 1st Quarter 1977, pp. 43-52.

Pincus, Jonathan J.; Barnard, A. and Butlin, Noel G. "Big Government in Australia, 1901-1978," [Working Paper].

Reid, Jr., Joseph D. "The Economic Costs of War: Comment on Papers by Neal and Hamilton," *Journal of Economic History*, 37(1), March 1977, pp. 52-55.

Ringrose, D.R. "European Economic Growth: Comments on the North-Thomas Theory," *Economic History Review*, Second Series, 26(2), May 1973, pp. 285-92.

Rockoff, Hugh T. "History of Price Controls in the United States," [Working Paper].

Rosovsky, Henry. "L'iniziativa dello stato nell'industriallizzazione giapponese [State Initiative in Japanese Industrialization]," *Mercurio*, June 1960.

Rosovsky, Henry. *Nihon no Shihon Keisei to Seifu no Yakuwari [The Role of the State in Japanese Capital Formation]*," Tokyo: Japan Economic Planning Agency, June 1960.

Schremmer, Eckart. "Zusammenhange Zwischen Katastersteuersystem, Wirtschaftswachstum und Wirtschaftsstruktur im 19. Jahrhundert; das Beispiel Wurttemberg; 1821-1877/1903 [Relationships between the Kataster Tax System, Economic Growth and Economic Structure in the 19th Century: The Case of Wurttemberg, 1821-1877/1903]," in Bog, Franz, Kaufhold, Kellenbenz, and Zorn, eds. *Wirtschaftliche und soziale Strukturen im sakularen Wandel*, 1974, pp. 679-706.

Toninelli, Pier Angelo; Wagner, J.R. and Glazier, I.A. "Fiscal Policy, Public Sector and Economic Growth: The Case of Italy (1879-1913)," *Seventh International Economic History Congress, Edinburgh, 1978*. Edinburgh: Edinburgh University Press, 1978.

Toninelli, Pier Angelo; Pavese, Claudio and Violante, Sante. *Fiscalita e finanza pubblica in Italia (1861-1913) [Taxation and Public Budgets in Italy, 1861-1913]*. Milano: Unicopli Universitaria, 1979.

Toniolo, Gianni. "Alcune considerazioni sull'uso della teoria nella storia economica [Some Comments on the Use of Theory in Economic History]," Annali della Fondazione Luigi Einaudi, 8, 1974, pp. 143-50.

Toniolo, Gianni. "Politica economica fascista e industrializzazione del Mezzogiorno: alcune considerazioni [Fascist Economic Policy and the Industrialization of the South: Some Comments]," *Ricerche economiche*, 31, 1977, pp. 177-89.

Veverka, J. "The Growth of Government Expenditure in the United Kingdom since 1790," *Scottish Journal of Political Economy*, 10(1), February 1963, pp. 111-27.

Walton, Gary M. "Monetary Crisis and Government Reliance in Modern Times," in Walton, ed. *Regulatory Change in an Atmosphere of Crisis*, 1979, pp. 1-11.

Weinstein, Paul A. "Occupational Convergence and the Role of the Military in Economic Development," *Explorations in Economic History*, 7(3), Spring 1970, pp. 325-46.

Wolpin, Kenneth I. "An Economic Analysis of Crime and Punishment in England and Wales, 1894-1967," *Journal of Political Economy*, 84(6), December 1976.

Other: Imperialism

Bairoch, Paul. "Le bilan economique du colonialisme: mythes et realites [The Economic Impact of Colonialism: Myths and Realities]," in Blusse, Wesseling, and Winius, eds. *History and Under-Development*, 1980, pp. 29-41.

Boulding, Kenneth E. and Mukerjee, Tapan. see Boulding and Munroe.

Boulding, Kenneth E. and Munroe, Tapan. "Unprofitable Empire: Britain in India, 1800-1967: A Critique of the Hobson-Lenin Thesis on Imperialism," *Peace Research Society Papers*, 16, 1970.

Boulding, Kenneth E. and Munroe, Tapan., eds. *Economic Imperialism*. Ann Arbor: University of Michigan Press, 1972.

Coelho, Philip R.P. "The Profitability of Colonialism: The British West Indies, 1768-1772," (Summary of Paper Presented at the Meetings of the Western Economic Association) *Western Economic Journal*, 9(3), September 1971, pp. 327.

Coelho, Philip R.P. "The Profitability of Imperialism: The British Experience in the West Indies, 1768-1772," *Explorations in Economic History*, 10(3), Spring 1973, pp. 253-79.

Davis, Lance E. and Huttenback, Robert A. "Public Expenditure and Private Profit: Budgetary Decision in the British Empire, 1860-1912," *American Economic Review, Papers and Proceedings*, 67(1), February 1977, pp. 282-87.

Davis, Lance E. and Huttenback, Robert A. "Aspects of Late-Nineteenth Century Imperialism," Presented at the Annual Meetings of the Organization of American Historians, New Orleans, April 1979 [Working Paper].

Davis, Lance E. and Huttenback, Robert A. "British Imperialism and Military Expenditure," Presented at the Anglo-American Conference of Historians, London, July 1978 [Working Paper].

Davis, Lance E. and Huttenback, Robert A. "Social Choice and Public Welfare: British and Colonial Expenditure in the Late Nineteenth Century," Presented at the 14th International Congress of Historical Societies, San Francisco, August 1975 [Working Paper].

Drummond, Ian M. *British Economic Policy and the Empire, 1919-1939.* London: Allen & Unwin, 1972.

Drummond, Ian M. *Imperial Economic Policy 1917-1939: Studies in Expansion and Protection.* London and Toronto: Allen & Unwin and University of Toronto Press, 1974.

Edelstein, Michael. "Foreign Investment and Empire, 1860-1914," in Floud and McCloskey, eds. *The Economic History of Britain Since 1700,* vol. 2, 1980.

Lebergott, Stanley. "The Returns to U.S. Imperialism, 1890-1929," *Journal of Economic History,* 40(2), June 1980, pp. 229-52.

McAlpin, Michelle Burge. "Speculations on the Social and Economic Consequences of British Famine Policy in Bombay Presidency, 1870-1920," Presented at the Meetings of the Association for Asian Studies, Toronto, Canada, March 1976 [Working Paper].

Mukerjee, Tapan. see Munroe, Tapan.

Munroe, Tapan. "The Theory of Economic Drain: Britain in India in the Nineteenth Century (Abstract)," *Western Economic Journal,* 7(3), September 1969, pp. 255.

Munroe, Tapan and Fennel, Lee. "The Myth of the Dependency Paradigm: A Study in Grants Economics," International Studies Association, Working Paper no. 48, 1975 [Working Paper].

Munroe, Tapan. "A Critique of Theories of Imperialism," in Pfaff, ed. *Frontiers of Social Thought,* 1976.

Pelaez, Carlos Manuel. "The Theory and Reality of Imperialism in the Coffee Economy of Nineteenth-Century Brazil," *Economic History Review,* Second Series, 29(2), May 1976, pp. 276-90.

Resnick, Stephen A. and Birnberg, Thomas. *Colonial Development: An Econometric Study.* New Haven: Yale University Press, 1975.

Thomas, Robert P. "The Sugar Colonies of the Old Empire: Profit or Loss for Great Britain?" *Economic History Review,* Second Series, 21(1), April 1968, pp. 30-45.

Zevin, Robert B. "An Interpretation of American Imperialism," *Journal of Economic History,* 32(1), March 1972, pp. 316-60.

The American Revolution

Broeze, Frank J.A. "The New Economic History, the Navigation Acts, and the Continental Tobacco Market, 1770-90: Comment on Walton," *Economic History Review,* Second Series, 26(4), November 1973, pp. 668-78.

DeCanio, Stephen J. "The Economics of Political Change: Comments on Papers by Reid, Metzer, and Berkowitz/McQuaid Presented to the 37th Aual Meeting of the Economic History Association," *Journal of Economic History,* 38(1), March 1978, pp. 143-47.

Harder, K. Peter. "The American Economy in 1776: Some Perspectives," in Soltow, ed. *Essays in Economic and Business History,* 1979, pp. 251-58.

Loschky, David J. "Studies of the Navigation Acts: New Economic Non-History?" *Economic History Review,* Second Series, 26(4), November 1973, pp. 689-91.

McClelland, Peter D. "The Cost to America of British Imperial Policy,"

American Economic Review, Papers and Proceedings, 59(2), May 1969, pp. 370-81.

McClelland, Peter D.   "On Navigating the Navigation Acts with Peter McClelland: Reply to Reid," *American Economic Review,* 60(5), December 1970, pp. 956-58.

McClelland, Peter D.   "The New Economic History and the Burdens of the Navigation Acts: A Comment on Walton," *Economic History Review,* Second Series, 26(4), November 1973, pp. 679-86.

Ransom, Roger L.   "British Policy and Colonial Growth: Some Implications of the Burden of the Navigation Acts," *Journal of Economic History,* 28(3), September 1968, pp. 427-35.

Reid, Jr., Joseph D.   "On Navigating the Navigation Acts with Peter D. McClelland: Comment," *American Economic Review,* 60(5), December 1970, pp. 949-55.

Reid, Jr., Joseph D.   "Understanding Political Events in the New Economic History," *Journal of Economic History,* 37(2), June 1977, pp. 302-28.

Reid, Jr., Joseph D.   "Economic Burden: Spark to the American Revolution?" *Journal of Economic History,* 38(1), March 1978, pp. 81-100.

Thomas, Robert P.   "A Quantitative Approach to the Study of the Effects of British Imperial Policy upon Colonial Welfare: Some Preliminary Findings," *Journal of Economic History,* 25(4), December 1965, pp. 615-38.

Thomas, Robert P.   "British Imperial Policy and the Economic Interpretation of the American Revolution: Reply to Ransom," *Journal of Economic History,* 28(3), September 1968, pp. 436-40.

Walton, Gary M.   "The New Economic History and the Burdens of the Navigation Acts," *Economic History Review,* Second Series, 24(4), November 1971, pp. 533-42.

Walton, Gary M.   "The Burdens of the Navigation Acts: A Reply to Broeze and McClelland," *Economic History Review,* Second Series, 26(4), November 1973, pp. 687-88.

The American Civil War

Andreano, Ralph L.   *The Economic Impact of the American Civil War.* Cambridge, Mass.: Schenkman, 1967.

DeCanio, Stephen J. and Mokyr, Joel.   "Inflation and the Wage Lag during the American Civil War," *Explorations in Economic History,* 14(4), October 1977, pp. 311-36.

Engerman, Stanley L.   "The Economic Impact of the Civil War," *Explorations in Entrepreneurial History,* Second Series, 3, Spring/Summer 1966, pp. 179-99.

Friedman, Philip.   "A Reconstructionist Production Function: Post Civil War South and the Optimal Path to Recovery," Presented at the Meeting of the Western Economic Association, August 1973 [Working Paper].

Goldin, Claudia D. and Lewis, Frank D.   "The Economic Cost of the American Civil War: Estimates and Implications," *Journal of Economic History,* 35(2), June 1975, pp. 299-326.

Other: American Political Economy

Goldin, Claudia D. and Lewis, Frank D. "The Postbellum Recovery of the South and the Cost of the Civil War: Comment on Temin," *Journal of Economic History*, 38(2), June 1978, pp. 487-92.

Gunderson, Gerald A. "The Origin of the American Civil War," *Journal of Economic History*, 34(4), December 1974, pp. 915-50.

Kessel, Reuben A. and Alchian, Armen A. "Real Wages in the North During the Civil War: Mitchell's Data Reinterpreted," (Reprinted in Fogel and Engerman, ed. *The Reinterpretation of American Economic History*, 1971, pp. 459-467) *Journal of Law and Economics*, 2, October 1959, pp. 95-113.

Lerner, Eugene M. "Inflation in the Confederacy, 1861-65," in Friedman, ed. *Studies in the Quantity Theory of Money*, 1956, pp. 163-75.

Murphy, G.S. "On the Costs and Benefits of the American Civil War (Abstract)," *Western Economic Journal*, 3(3), September 1970, pp. 277.

Olmstead, Alan L. "The Civil War as a Catalyst of Technological Change in Agriculture," in Uselding, ed. *Business and Economic History, Second Series*, vol. 5, University of Illinois, 1976, pp. 36-50.

Ransom, Roger L. and Sutch, Richard C. "The Impact of the Civil War and of Emancipation on Southern Agriculture," *Explorations in Economic History*, 12(1), January 1975, pp. 1-28.

Ransom, Roger L. and Sutch, Richard C. "Economic Dimensions of Reconstruction: An Overview," [Working Paper].

Temin, Peter. "The Postbellum Recovery of the South and the Cost of the Civil War," *Journal of Economic History*, 36(4), December 1976, pp. 898-907.

Temin, Peter. "The Postbellum Recovery of the South and the Cost of the Civil War: A Reply to Goldin and Lewis," *Journal of Economic History*, 38(2), June 1978, pp. 493.

Williamson, Jeffrey G. "Watersheds and Turning Points: Conjectures on the Long-Term Impact of Civil War Financing," *Journal of Economic History*, 34(3), September 1974, pp. 636-61.

Williamson, Jeffrey G. "What Should the Civil War Tariffs Have Done Anyway?" Presented at the Social System Research Institute Workshop, Madison, Wisconsin, October 1973 [Working Paper].

Other: American Political Economy

Adams, Jr., Donald R. "American Neutrality and Prosperity, 1793-1808: A Reconsideration," *Journal of Economic History*, 40(4), December 1980, pp. 713-37.

Engerman, Stanley L. "A Note on the Economic Consequences of the Second Bank of the United States," *Journal of Political Economy*, 78(4, Part 1), July/August 1970, pp. 725-28.

Higgs, Robert. "Railroad Rates and the Populist Uprising," *Agricultural History*, 44(3), July 1970, pp. 291-97.

Klepper, Robert. "The Economic Bases for Agrarian Protest Movements in the United States, 1870-1900," (Summary of Doctoral Dissertation) *Journal of Economic History*, 34(1), March 1974, pp. 283-85.

O'Leary, Paul M. "The Scene of the Crime of 1873 Revisited: A Note,"

Journal of Political Economy, 68(4), August 1960, pp. 388-92.

Schmitz, Mark D. "Agricultural Uncertainty and Discontent in the Populist era," [Working Paper].

Temin, Peter. "The Economic Consequences of the Bank War," *Journal of Political Economy*, 76(2), March/April 1968, pp. 257-74.

Walton, Gary M., ed. *Regulatory Change in an Atmosphere of Crisis: Current Implications of the Roosevelt Years*. New York: Academic Press, 1979.

Whitten, David O. "An Economic Inquiry into the Whisky Rebellion of 1794," *Agricultural History*, 49(3), Summer 1975, pp. 491-504.

Zevin, Robert B. "The Economics of Normalcy," [Working Paper].

Other: Non-American Political Economy

Anderson, J.L. "Aspects of the Effect on the British Economy of the Wars against France, 1793-1815," *Australian Economic History Review*, 12(1), March 1972, pp. 1-20.

Bean, Richard N. "War and the Birth of the Nation State," *Journal of Economic History*, 33(1), March 1973, pp. 203-21.

Coats, A.W. "The Interpretation of Mercantilist Economics: Some Historiographical Problems," *History of Political Economy*, 5(2), Fall 1973.

Gordon, Donald F. and Walton, Gary M. "A Theory of Regenerative Growth and the Experience of Post-World War II West Germany," [Working Paper].

Haddock, David D. "The Black Death, the Voyages of Columbus, and Other Timely Acts of God," [Working Paper].

Hueckel, Glenn. "The Napoleonic Wars and Their Impact on Factor Returns and Output Growth in England, 1793-1815," (Summary of Doctoral Dissertation) *Journal of Economic History*, 33(1), March 1973, pp. 309-11.

Hueckel, Glenn. "War and the British Economy, 1793-1815: A General Equilibrium Analysis," *Explorations in Economic History*, 10(4), Summer 1973, pp. 365-96.

Hueckel, Glenn. "English Farming Profits during the Napoleonic Wars, 1793-1815," *Explorations in Economic History*, 13(3), July 1976, pp. 331-46.

Hueckel, Glenn. "Relative Prices and Supply Response in English Agriculture during the Napoleonic Wars," *Economic History Review*, 29(3), August 1976, pp. 401-14.

Katz, Barbara G. "Purges and Production: Soviet Economic Growth, 1928-1940," *Journal of Economic History*, 35(3), September 1975, pp. 567-90.

McRandle, James H. and Quirk, James P. "An Interpretation of the German Risk Fleet Concept, 1899-1914," in Hughes, ed. *Purdue Faculty Papers in Economic History, 1956-1966*, 1967, pp. 484-537.

Mokyr, Joel and Savin, N. Eugene. "Stagflation in Historical Perspective: The Napoleonic Wars Revisited," in Uselding, ed. *Research in Economic History*, vol. 1, 1976, pp. 198-259.

Neal, Larry D. "Interpreting Power and Profit in Economic History: A Case Study of the Seven Years War," *Journal of Economic History*,

27(1), March 1977, pp. 20-35.

Neal, Larry D. "The Cost of Impressment during the Seven Years War," *Mariner's Mirror*, 64(1), February 1978, pp. 45-56.

Olson, Mancur L. *The Economics of the Wartime Shortage: A History of British Food Shortages in the Napoleonic War and World Wars I and II.* Durham: Duke University Press, 1963.

Reid, Jr., Joseph D. "The Economic Costs of War: Comment on Papers by Neal and Hamilton," *Journal of Economic History*, 37(1), March 1977, pp. 52-55.

Roehl, Richard. "Comment on Papers by Reed and Bean Presented the 32nd Annual Meeting of the Economic History Association," *Journal of Economic History*, 33(1), March 1973, pp. 228-31.

Webb, Steven B. "Motives for Emancipation: A Statistical Analysis of the British Parliament of 1834," [Working Paper].

Alphabetical Listings

Abramovitz, Moses. "Resource and Output Trends in the United States Since 1870," *American Economic Review, Papers and Proceedings,* 46(2), May 1956, pp. 5-23.

Abramovitz, Moses. "The Nature and Significance of Kuznets Cycles," *Economic Development and Cultural Change,* 9, April 1961, pp. 225-48.

Abramovitz, Moses. "Economic Growth in the United States: A Review Article," *American Economic Review,* 52(4), September 1962, pp. 762-82.

Abramovitz, Moses. *Evidence of Long Swings in Aggregate Construction since the Civil War* (Occasional Papers 90). New York: Columbia University Press for the National Bureau of Economic Research, 1964.

Abramovitz, Moses. "Long Swings in American Economic Growth," in Andreano (ed), *New Views,* 1965, pp. 377-434.

Abramovitz, Moses. "The Passing of the Kuznets Cycle," *Economica,* 35(140), November 1968, pp. 349-67.

Abramovitz, Moses. "Kuznets and Juglar Cycles during the Industrialization of 1874-1940: Comment on Shinohara," in Ohkawa and Hayami (eds), *Economic Growth,* 1973, pp. 253-65.

Abramovitz, Moses. "Sources of Agricultural Growth in Japan, 1880-1965: Comment (on Akino and Hayami)," in Ohkawa and Hayami (eds), *Economic Growth,* 1973, pp. 213-9.

Abramovitz, Moses. "Likenesses and Contrasts between the Investment Booms of the Postwar Period and Earlier Periods in Relation to Long Swings in Economic Growth," in Richards (ed), *Population, Factor Movements and Economic Development,* 1976.

Abramovitz, Moses. "The Monetary Side of Long Swings in U.S. Economic Growth," Stanford University, Center for Research in Economic Growth Working Paper no. 146, April 1973.

Abramovitz, Moses and David, Paul A. "Reinterpreting Economic Growth: Parables and Realities," *American Economic Review, Papers and Proceedings,* 63(2), May 1973, pp. 428-39.

Abramovitz, Moses and David, Paul A. "Economic Growth in America: Historical Parables and Realities," *De Economist,* 121(3), 1973, pp. 251-72.

Abramovitz, Moses and Eliasberg, Vera F. *The Growth of Public Employment in Great Britain* (General Series 60). Princeton: Princeton University Press for the National Bureau of Economic Research, 1957.

Adams, A.A. and Prest, A.R. *Consumers' Expenditure in the United Kingdom, 1900-1919.* Cambridge: Cambridge University Press, 1954.

Adams, John. "A Statistical Test of the Impact of the Suez Canal on the Growth of India's Trade," *Indian Economic and Social History Review,* 8(3), September 1971, pp. 229-40.

Adams, John and West, Robert C. "Money, Prices, and Economic Development in India, 1861-1895," *Journal of Economic History,* 39(1), March 1979, pp. 55-68.

Adams, N.A. "Notes on 'Trade as a Handmaiden of Growth'," *Economic Journal,* 83(329), March 1973, pp. 210-2.

Adams, Donald R., Jr. "Wages Rates in Philadelphia, 1790-1830,"

(Summary of Doctoral Dissertation) *Journal of Economic History,* 27(4), December 1967, pp. 608-10.

Adams, Donald R., Jr. "Wages Rates in the Early National Period: Philadelphia, 1785-1830," *Journal of Economic History,* 28(3), September 1968, pp. 404-26.

Adams, Donald R., Jr. "Some Evidence on English and American Wage Rates, 1790-1830," *Journal of Economic History,* 30(3), September 1970, pp. 499-520.

Adams, Donald R., Jr. "The Bank of Stephen Girard, 1812-1831," *Journal of Economic History,* 32(4), December 1972, pp. 841-68.

Adams, Donald R., Jr. "Wage Rates in the Iron Industry: A Comment on Zabler," *Explorations in Economic History,* 11(1), Fall 1973, pp. 89-94.

Adams, Donald R., Jr. "The Role of Banks in the Economic Development of the Old Northwest," in Klingaman and Vedder (eds), *Essays in Nineteenth Century Economic History,* 1975, pp. 208-45.

Adams, Donald R., Jr. *Wage Rates in Philadelphia, 1790-1830.* New York: Arno Press, 1975.

Adams, Donald R., Jr. "Residential Construction Industry in the Early Nineteenth Century," *Journal of Economic History,* 35(4), December 1975, pp. 794-816.

Adams, Donald R., Jr. *Finance and Enterprise in Early America: A Study of Stephen Girard's Bank, 1812-1831.* Philadelphia: University of Pennsylvania Press, 1978.

Adams, Donald R., Jr. "Portfolio Management and Profitability in Early Nineteenth Century Banking," *Business History Review,* 52(1), Spring 1978, pp. 61-79.

Adams, Donald R., Jr. "The Beginning of Investment Banking in the United States," *Pennsylvania History,* 45(2), April 1978, pp. 99-116.

Adams, Donald R., Jr. "Prices and Wages," in Porter (ed), *Encyclopedia of American Economic History,* 1980, pp. 229-46.

Adams, Donald R., Jr. "Earnings and Savings in the Early 19th Century," *Explorations in Economic History,* 17(2), April 1980, pp. 118-34.

Adams, Donald R., Jr. "American Neutrality and Prosperity, 1793-1808: A Reconsideration," *Journal of Economic History,* 40(4), December 1980, pp. 713-37.

Adams, Donald R., Jr. "Franco-American Trade, 1790-1815," presented at the Conference on Franco-American Commerce, Eleutherian Mills-Hagley Foundation, Greenville, Wilmington, Delaware, 1977.

Adelman, Irma and Morris, Cynthia Taft. *Economic Growth and Social Equity in Developing Countries.* Stanford: Stanford University Press, 1973.

Adelman, Irma and Morris, Cynthia Taft. "An Inquiry into the Course of Poverty in the Ninteenth and Early Twentieth Centuries," in Matthews (ed), *Measurement, History, and Factors of Economic Growth,* 1978.

Adelman, Irma and Morris, Cynthia Taft. "Patterns of Market Expansion in the Nineteenth Century: A Quantitative Study," in Dalton (ed), *Research in Economic Anthropology,* 1978.

Adelman, Irma and Morris, Cynthia Taft. "The Role of Institutional Influences in Patterns of Agricultural Development in the Nineteenth and Early Twentieth Centuries: A Cross-Section

Quantitative Study," *Journal of Economic History,* 39(1), March 1979, pp. 159-76.

Adelman, Irma and Morris, Cynthia Taft. "Patterns of Industrialization in the Nineteenth and Early Twentieth Centuries: A Cross-Sectional Quantitative Study," in Uselding (ed), *Research in Economic History,* 1980.

Adie, Douglas K. "English Bank Deposits before 1844," reprinted in Floud (ed), *Essays in Quantitative Economic History,* 1974, pp. 166-80. *Economic History Review,* Second Series, 23(2), August 1970, pp. 285-97

Adie, Douglas K. "The English Money Stock, 1834-1844," *Explorations in Economic History,* 9(2), Winter 1971/72, pp. 111-43.

Aduddell, Robert and Cain, Louis P. "Location and Collusion in the Meatpacking Industry," in Cain and Uselding (eds), *Business Enterprise and Economic Change,* 1973, pp. 85-117

Aduddell, Robert and Cain, Louis P. "The Consent Decree in the Meat-Packing Industry." [Working Paper]

Agherli, Bijan B. "The Balance of Payments and Money Supply under the Gold Standard Regime: United States, 1879-1914," *American Economic Review,* 65(1), March 1975, pp. 40-58.

Aitken, Hugh G.J. "The Role of Staple Industries in Canada's Economic Development: Discussion of Buckley," *Journal of Economic History,* 18(4), December 1958, pp. 451-2.

Aitken, Hugh G.J., ed. *Did Slavery Pay? Readings in the Economics of Black Slavery in the United States.* Boston: Houghton Mifflin, 1971.

Akerman, Sune; Johansen, Hans Chr. and Gaunt, David, eds. *Chance and Change: Social and Economic Studies in Historical Demography in the Baltic Area.* Odense: Odense University Press, 1978.

Akino, Masakatsu and Hayami, Yujiro. "Sources of Agricultural Growth in Japan, 1880-1965," *Quarterly Journal of Economics,* 88(3), August 1974, pp. 454-79.

Albelda, Randy and Aldcroft, Terry Mark. "Determinants of Working Women's Wages during the Progressive Era," *Explorations in Economic History,* 17(4), October 1980, pp. 323-41.

Alchian, Armen A. and Kessel, Reuben A. "Real Wages in the North During the Civil War: Mitchell's Data Reinterpreted," reprinted in Fogel and Engerman (eds), *The Reinterpretation of American Economic History,* 1971, pp. 459-67. *Journal of Law and Economics,* 2, October 1959, pp. 95-113.

Aldcroft, Derek H. "McCloskey on Victorian Growth: A Comment," *Economic History Review,* Second Series, 27(2), May 1974, pp. 271-4.

Aldrich, Terry Mark. "Rates of Return Earned on Formal Technical Education in the Antebellum American Economy," (Summary of Doctoral Dissertation) *Journal of Economic History,* 30(1), March 1970, pp. 251-5.

Aldrich, Terry Mark. "Earnings of American Civil Engineers, 1820-1859," *Journal of Economic History,* 31(2), June 1971, pp. 407-19.

Aldrich, Terry Mark. "Flexible Exchange Rates, Northern Expansion, and the Market for Southern Cotton: 1866-1879," *Journal of Economic History,* 33(2), June 1973, pp. 399-416.

Aldrich, Terry Mark. *Rates of Return on Investment in Technical*

Education in the Antebellum American Economy. New York: Arno Press, 1975.

Aldrich, Terry Mark and Albelda, Randy. "Determinants of Working Women's Wages during the Progressive Era," *Explorations in Economic History*, 17(4), October 1980, pp. 323-41.

Alford, B.W.E. "New Industries for Old? British Industry between the Wars," in Floud and McCloskey (eds), *The Economic History of Britain since 1700*, 1981.

Aliber, Robert Z. "Speculation in the Foreign Exchanges: The European Experience, 1919-1926," *Yale Economic Essays*, 2, Spring 1962, pp. 170-245.

Aliber, Robert Z. "Speculation in the Flexible Exchange Revisited," *Kyklos*, 23(2), 1970, pp. 303-14.

Aliber, Robert Z. "Speculation in the Flexible Exchange Re-Revisited: Reply to Pippenger," *Kyklos*, 26(3), 1973, pp. 619-20.

Aliber, Robert Z. "Floating Exchange Rates: The Twenties and the Seventies," in Chipman and Kindleberger (eds), *Flexible Exchange Rates and the Balance of Payments*, 1980, pp. 81-97.

Allen, Robert C. "The Peculiar Productivity History of American Blast Furnaces, 1840-1913," *Journal of Economic History*, 37(3), September 1977, pp. 605-33.

Allen, Robert C. "International Competition in Iron and Steel, 1850-1913," *Journal of Economic History*, 39(4), December 1979, pp. 911-37.

Allen, Robert C. "The Efficiency and Distributional Consequences of Eighteenth Century Enclosures," University of British Columbia Department of Economics Discussion Paper no. 79-18, April 1979.

Allen, Robert C. "Entrepreneurship and Technical Progress in the Northeast Coast Pig Iron Industry, 1850-1913," in Uselding (ed), *Research in Economic History*, 1981.

Allison, Chris and McGuire, William J. "Wage Discrimination and Economies of Scale in the American Manufacturing Sector, 1820-1920," Ohio University Economic History Research Paper no. G-6.

Almquist, Eric L. "Mayo and Beyond: Land, Domestic Industry, and Rural Transformation in the Irish West," (Summary of Doctoral Dissertation) *Journal of Economic History*, 39(1), March 1979, pp. 323-4.

Almquist, Eric L. "Pre-Famine Ireland and the Theory of European Proto-Industrialization: Evidence from the 1841 Census," *Journal of Economic History*, 39(3), September 1979, pp. 699-718.

Almquist, Eric L. "Labor Specialization and the Irish Economy in 1841: An Aggregate Occupational Analysis."

Alston, Lee J. "Costs of Contracting and the Decline of Tenancy in the South, 1930-1960," (Summary of Doctoral Dissertation) *Journal of Economic History*, 39(1), March 1979, pp. 324-6.

Alston, Lee J. "A Theory Explaining the Decline in Tenant Contracts Relative to Wage Conracts in the South, 1930-1960," Williams College, Department of Economics Research Paper no. 17, December 1978.

Ames, Edward. "Trends, Cycles, and Stagnation in U.S. Manufacturing since 1860," reprinted in Hughes (ed), *Purdue Faculty Papers in Economic History*, 1967, pp. 91-102. *Oxford Economic Papers*, 12(3), October 1959, pp. 270-81.

Ames, Edward. "The Sterling Crisis of 1337-1339," reprinted in Floud (ed), *Essays in Quantitative Economic History*, 1974, pp. 36-58. *Journal of Economic History*, 25(4), December, 1965, pp. 496-522.

Ames, Edward and Rapp, Richard T. "The Birth and Death of Taxes: A Hypothesis," *Journal of Economic History*, 37(1), March 1977, pp. 161-78.

Ames, Edward and Rapp, Richard T. "Capital Transfers and Foreign Indebtedness: The Long-Term Experience." [Working Paper]

Ames, Edward and Rosenberg, Nathan. "The Enfield Arsenal in Theory and History," *Economic Journal*, 78(312), December 1968, pp. 827-42.

Anderson, C. Arnold and Bowman, Mary Jean. "Human Capital and Economi Modernization in Historical Perspective," *Fourth International Conference of Economic History, Bloomington, 1968*. Paris: Mouton, 1973, pp. 247-72.

Anderson, Isabel. "The Temporal Characteristics of the Growth of Manufacturing in Urbanized Areas of Canada." [Working Paper]

Anderson, J.L. "Aspects of the Effect on the British Economy of the Wars against France, 1793-1815," *Australian Economic History Review*, 12(1), March 1972, pp. 1-20.

Anderson, J.L. "A Measure of the Effect of British Public Finance, 1793-1815," *Economic History Review*, Second Series, 27(4), November 1974, pp. 610-9.

Anderson, Ralph V. and Gallman, Robert E. "Slaves as Fixed Capital: Slave Labor and Southern Economic Development," *Journal of American History*, 64(1), June 1977, pp. 24-46.

Anderson, Terry L. "The Economic Growth of Seventeenth-Century New England: A Measurement of Regional Income," (Summary of Doctoral Dissertation) *Journal of Economic History*, 33(1), March 1973, pp. 299-301.

Anderson, Terry L. "Wealth Estimates for the New England Colonies, 1650-1709," *Explorations in Economic History*, 12(2), April 1975, pp. 151-76.

Anderson, Terry L. "Economic Growth in Colonial New England: 'Statistical Renaissance'," *Journal of Economic History*, 39(1), March 1979, pp. 243-57.

Anderson, Terry L.; Bean, Richard N. and Thomas, Robert P. "Economic Growth in the 17th Century American Colonies: Application of an Export-Led Growth Model." [Working Paper]

Anderson, Terry L. and Hill, Peter J. "The Evolution of Property Rights: A Study of the American West," *Journal of Law and Economics*, 18(1), April 1975, pp. 163-80.

Anderson, Terry L. and Hill, Peter J. "The Role of Private Property in the History of American Agriculture, 1776-1976: Reply (to Schmid)," *American Journal of Agricultural Economics*, 59(3), August 1977, pp. 590-1.

Anderson, Terry L. and Hill, Peter J. "An American Experiment in Anarcho-Capitalism: The Not So Wild, Wild West," *Journal of Libertarian Studies*, 3(1), 1979, pp. 9-29.

Anderson, Terry L. and Hill, Peter J. "The Role of Private Property in the History of American Agriculture, 1776-1976," *American Journal of Agricultural Economics*, 58(5), December 1976, pp. 937-45.

Anderson, Terry L. and Hill, Peter J. "From Free Grass to Fences: Transforming the Commons of the American West," in Hardin and Baden (eds), *Managing the Commons*, 1977, pp. 200-16.

Anderson, Terry L. and Hill, Peter J. *The Birth of a Transfer Society.* Stanford: Hoover Institute Press, 1980.

Anderson, Terry L. and Reed, Clyde G. "An Economic Explanation of English Agricultural Organization in the Twelfth and Thirteenth Centuries: Comment (on Miller)," *Economic History Review,* Second Series, 26(1), February 1973, pp. 134-7.

Anderson, Terry L. and Thomas, Robert P. "White Population, Labor Force and Extensive Growth of the New England Economy in the Seventeenth Century," *Journal of Economic History,* 33(3), September 1973, pp. 634-67.

Anderson, Terry L. and Thomas, Robert P. "The Growth of Population and Labor Force in the 17th-Century Chesapeake," *Explorations in Economic History,* 15(3), July 1978, pp. 290-312.

Andreano, Ralph L. "The American Manufacturing Frontier, 1870-1940: A Comment on Severson," *Business History Review,* 35(1), Spring 1961, pp. 105-9.

Andreano, Ralph L. and Williamson, Harold F. "Integration and Competition in the Oil Industry: A Review Article," *Journal of Political Economy,* 69(4), August 1961, pp. 381-5.

Andreano, Ralph L. "Recent Research in Quantitative Economic History: Some Conceptual Implications," *Proceedings, Indiana Academy of Science,* 1963

Andreano, Ralph L. "Editor's Introduction: The New Economic History/What is New?/An Appraisal," in Andreano (ed), *New Views,* 1965, pp. 3-8.

Andreano, Ralph L. "Four Recent Studies in American Economic History: Some Conceptual Implications," in Andreano (ed), *New Views,* 1965, pp. 13-6.

Andreano, Ralph L., ed. *New Views on American Economic Development: A Selective Anthology of Recent Work.* Cambridge, Mass.: Schenkman, 1965.

Andreano, Ralph L. "Trends in Economic Welfare, 1790-1860," in Andreano (ed), *New Views,* 1965, pp. 131-67.

Andreano, Ralph L. "Reflections on the History of Poverty in America," *Earlham Review,* 1(2), Fall 1966, pp. 51-60.

Andreano, Ralph L., ed. *The Economic Impact of the American Civil War.* Cambridge, Mass.: Schenkman, 1967.

Andreano, Ralph L. *The New Economic History: Recent Papers on Methodology.* New York: John Wiley & Sons, 1970.

Andreano, Ralph L. "Some Issues in Antebellum U.S. Economic Growth and Welfare," *Cahiers Internationaux d'Histoire Economique et Sociale,* 5, 1975, pp. 357-79.

Andreano, Ralph L. and Williamson, Harold F. *A History of the American Petroleum Industry* (Appears in Two volumes: vol. 1, 1959; vol. 2, 1963). Evanston: Northwestern University Press, 1959, 1963.

Andreano, Ralph L.; Williamson, Harold F. and Menezes, Carmen. "The American Petroleum Industry," in Brady (ed), *Output, Employment, and Productivity in the United States After 1800,* 1966, pp. 349-403.

Ankli, Robert E. "Gross Farm Revenue in Pre-Civil War Illinois," reprinted in *Papers of the Sixteenth Business History Conference* (Lincoln, Neb.: College of Business Administration, University of Nebraska for the Business History Conference, 1969). *Nebraska Journal of Economics and Business,* 8(3), Summer 1969, pp. 147-78.

Ankli, Robert E. "Agricultural Growth in Antebellum Illinois," *Journal of the Illinois State Historical Society,* 63(4), Winter 1970, pp. 387-98.

Ankli, Robert E. "Canadian-American Reciprocity: A Comment on Officer and Smith," *Journal of Economic History,* 30(2), June 1970, pp. 427-31.

Ankli, Robert E. "The Reciprocity Treaty of 1854," *Canadian Journal of Economics and Political Science,* 4(1), February 1971, pp. 1-20.

Ankli, Robert E. "Problems in Aggregate Agricultural History," *Agricultural History,* 46(1), January 1972, pp. 65-70.

Ankli, Robert E. "Farm-Making Costs in the 1850's," *Agricultural History,* 48(1), January 1974, pp. 51-70.

Ankli, Robert E. "The Coming of the Reaper," in Uselding (ed), *Business and Economic History,* 1976, pp. 1-24.

Ankli, Robert E. *Gross Farm Revenue in Pre-Civil War Illinois.* New York: Arno Press, 1977.

Ankli, Robert E. "Farm Income on the Great Plains and Prairies: 1920-1940," *Agricultural History,* 51(1), January 1977, pp. 92-103.

Ankli, Robert E. and Litt, R.M. "The Growth of Prairie Agriculture: Economic Considerations," *Canadian Papers in Rural History,* 1, 1978, pp. 35-64.

Ankli, Robert E. "Horses vs. Tractors on the Corn Belt, 1920-1940," *Agricultural History,* 54(1), January 1980, pp. 134-48.

Ankli, Robert E. "The Growth of the Canadian Economy, 1896-1920: Export Led and/or Neoclassical Growth," *Explorations in Economic History,* 17(3), July 1980, pp. 251-74.

Ankli, Robert E. and Olmstead, Alan L. "The Adoption of the Reaper: The State of the Debate." [Working Paper]

Ashenfelter, Orley; Pencavel, John H. "American Trade Union Growth: 1900-1960," *Quarterly Journal of Economics,* 83(3), August 1964, pp. 434-48.

Asher, Ephraim. "Industrial Efficiency and Biased Technical Change in American and British Manufacturing: The Case of Textiles in the Nineteenth Century," *Journal of Economic History,* 32(2), June 1972, pp. 431-42.

Ashton, T.S. and Sayers, Richard S. *Papers in English Monetary History.* Oxford: Oxford University Press, 1953.

Atack, Jeremy. "Returns to Scale in Antebellum United States Manufacturing," *Explorations in Economic History,* 14(4), October 1977, pp. 337-59.

Atack, Jeremy. "Estimation of Economies of Scale in Nineteenth-Century United States Manufacturing and the Form of the Production Function," (Summary of Doctoral Dissertation) *Journal of Economic History,* 38(1), March 1978, pp. 268-70.

Atack, Jeremy. "Economies of Scale in Western River Steamboating: A Comment on Haites and Mak," *Journal of Economic History,* 38(2), June 1978, pp. 457-66.

Atack, Jeremy and Bateman, Fred. "The Profitability of Northern Agriculture in 1860," in Uselding (ed), *Research in Economic History,* 1979.

Atack, Jeremy; Bateman, Fred and Weiss, Thomas J. "The Regional Diffusion and Adoption of the Steam Engine in American Manufacturing," *Journal of Economic History,* 40(2), June 1980, pp. 281-308.

Atack, Jeremy; Haites, Erik F.; Mak, James and Walton, Gary M. "The Profitability of Steamboating on the Western Rivers: 1850," *Business History Review*, 49(3), Autumn 1975, pp. 346-54.

Atack, Jeremy; Weiss, Thomas J. and Bateman, Fred. "Risk, the Rate of Return and the Pattern of Investment in 19th Century American Industrialization." [Working Paper]

Atack, Jeremy; Weiss, Thomas J. and Bateman, Fred. "The Manuscript Census as a Nineteenth Century Data Source." [Working Paper]

Aufhauser, R. Keith. "Slavery and Technological Change," *Journal of Economic History*, 34(1), March 1974, pp. 36-50.

Aukrust, Odd and Bjerke, Juul. "Real Capital in Norway, 1900-56," in Goldsmith and Saunders (eds), *The Measurement of National Wealth*, 1959, pp. 80-118.

Baack, Bennett D. and Ray, Edward J. "Tariff Policy and Comparative Advantage in the Iron and Steel Industry, 1870-1929," *Explorations in Economic History*, 11(1), Fall 1973, pp. 3-24.

Baack, Bennett D. and Ray, Edward J. "Tariff Policy and Income Distribution: The Case of the U.S., 1830-1860," *Explorations in Economic History*, 11(2), Winter 1974, pp. 103-22.

Baack, Ben and Reid, Joseph D., Jr. "Land Tenure Patterns and Property Rights in Agriculture," (Summary of 1975 Research Workshop) *Journal of Economic History*, 36(1), March 1976, pp. 29-32.

Baack, Bennett D. and Thomas, Robert P. "The Enclosure Movement and the Supply of Labor During the Industrial Revolution," *Journal of European Economic History*, 3(2), Fall 1974, pp. 401-23.

Bagchi, Amiya K. *Private Investment in India, 1900-1939.* Cambridge: Cambridge University Press, 1972.

Baines, Dudley E. "Birthplace Statistics and the Analysis of Internal Migration," in Lawton (ed), *The Census and Social Structure*, 1978, pp. 146-64.

Baines, Dudley E. "The Labour Supply and the Labour Market, 1860-1914," in Floud and McCloskey (eds), *The Economic History of Britain since 1700*, 1981.

Bairoch, Paul. "Niveaux de developpement economique de 1810 a 1910 [Levels of Economic Development: 1810-1910]," *Annales: Economies, Societes, Civilisations*, 20(6), 1965, pp. 1091-117.

Bairoch, Paul. "Original Characteristics and Consequences of the Industrial Revolution," *Diogene*, 54, Summer 1966, pp. 47-58.

Bairoch, Paul. "Commerce exterieur et developpement economique. Les enseignements de l'experience libre-echangiste de la France au XIXe siecle," [Foreign Trade and Economic Development: The Lessons from the French Interlude of Free Trade in the Nineteenth Century] *Revue Economique*, 21(1), January 1970, pp. 1-33.

Bairoch, Paul. "Structure de la population active mondiale de 1700 a 1970," [Structure of the Labor Force Internationally, 1700-1970] *Annales: Economies, Societes, Civilisations*, 26(5), September/October 1971, pp. 960-76.

Bairoch, Paul. "L'agriculture et le processus d'industrialisation aux XVIIIe et XIXe siecles," [Agriculture and the Process of Industrialization in the Eighteenth and Nineteenth Centuries]

Cahiers de L'Institut de Science Economique Appliquee, Serie AG(10), May 1972, pp. 1113-32.

Bairoch, Paul. "Free Trade and European Economic Development in the 19th Century," *European Economic Review,* 3(3), November 1972, pp. 211-45.

Bairoch, Paul. "Le role du commerce exterieur dans la Genese de la revolution industrielle anglaise," [The Role of Foreign Trade in the Origins of the Industrial Revolution in England] *Annales: Economies, Societes, Civilisations,* 28(2), March/April 1973, pp. 541-71.

Bairoch, Paul. "European Foreign Trade in the 19th Century: The Development of the Value and volume of Exports (Preliminary Results)," *Journal of European Economic History,* 2(1), Spring 1973, pp. 5-36.

Bairoch, Paul. "Geographical Structure and Trade Balance of European Foreign Trade from 1800 to 1870," *Journal of European Economic History,* 3(3), Winter 1974, pp. 557-608.

Bairoch, Paul. *The Economic Development of the Third World since 1900.* London and Berkeley: Methuen and University of California Press, 1975.

Bairoch, Paul. *Commerce exterieur et developpement economique de l'Europe au XIXe siecle* [Foreign Trade and Economic Development: Europe in the Nineteenth Century]. Paris and The Hague: Mouton, 1976.

Bairoch, Paul. "Europe's Gross National Product, 1800-1975," *Journal of European Economic History,* 5(2), Fall 1976, pp. 273-313.

Bairoch, Paul. "La place de la France sur les marches internationaux au XIXe siecle: presentation de quelques faits," [The Position of France in International Markets in the Nineteenth Century: Presentation of Some Facts] in Levy-Leboyer (ed), *La position internationale de la France,* 1977, pp. 37-52.

Bairoch, Paul. "Estimations du Revenu National dans les societes occidentales durant les periodes pre-industrielles et le XIXe siecle: propositions d'approches indirectes," [National Income Estimates for Western Societies in the Pre-Industrial Period and in the Nineteenth Century: Suggestions for Indirect Approaches] *Revue Economique,* 28(2), March 1977, pp. 177-208.

Bairoch, Paul. "Die Landwirtschaft, der fur die Einleitung der Entwicklung bestimmende Faktor," [Agriculture, the Factor that is Crucial for the Beginning of Development] in Kellenbenz, Schneider, and Gommel (eds), *Wirtschaftliches Wachstum im Spiegel der Wirtschaftsgeschichte,* 1978.

Bairoch, Paul. "Protectionnisme et expansion economique en Europe de 1892 a 1914," [Protectionism and Economic Expansion in Europe, 1892-1914] *Relations Internationales,* 15, Autumn 1978, pp. 227-233.

Bairoch, Paul. "Ecarts internationaux des niveaux de vie avant la revolution industrielle," [International Differences in Standards of Living Before the Industrial Revolution] *Annales: Economies, Societes, Civilisations,* 34(1), January/February 1979, pp. 145-71.

Bairoch, Paul. "Le bilan economique du colonialisme: mythes et realites," [The Economic Impact of Colonialism: Myths and Realities] in Blusse, Wesseling, and Winius (eds), *History and Under-Development,* 1980, pp. 29-41.

Baker, A.R.H. "Observations on the Open Fields: The Present Position of Studies in British Field Systems," *Journal of Historical Geography,* 5(3), July 1979, pp. 315-23.

Baker, Anita B. "Agriculture and Industrialization in Europe," (Summary of 1978 Research Workshop) *Journal of Economic History,* 39(1), March 1979, pp. 313-5.

Balderston, T. "The German Business Cycle in the 1920's: A Comment on Falkus and Temin," *Economic History Review,* Second Series, 30(1), February 1977, pp. 159-61.

Baldwin, R.E. *Economic Development and Export Growth: A Study of Northern Rhodesia, 1920-1960.* Berkeley: University of California Press, 1966.

Ball, Duane E. "The Process of Settlement in Eighteenth-Century Chester County, Pennsylvania: A Social and Economic History," (Summary of Doctoral Dissertation) *Journal of Economic History,* 35(1), March 1975, pp. 253-5.

Ball, Duane E. "Dynamics of Population and Wealth in Eighteenth-Century Chester County, Pennsylvania," *Journal of Interdisciplinary History,* 6(4), Spring 1976, pp. 621-44.

Ball, Duane E. "The Adaptiveness and Market Response of Early 19th Century Chester County, Pennsylvania Farmers," presented at the Regional Economic History Conference, Wilmington, Delaware, 1976.

Ball, Duane E. "The Process of Settlement in 18th Century Chester County, Pennsylvania: A Social and Economic History." [Working Paper]

Ball, Duane E. and Walton, Gary M. "Agricultural Productivity Change in Eighteenth-Century Pennsylvania," *Journal of Economic History,* 36(1), March 1976, pp. 102-17.

Ball, R.J. "Mr. Rosenberg on Capital Imports and Growth: A Further Comment," *Economic Journal,* 71(284), December 1961, pp. 853-5.

Ballestoros, Marto A. and Davis, Thomas E. "The Growth of Output and Employment in Basic Sectors of the Chilean Economy, 1908-1957," *Economic Development and Cultural Change,* 11(2), January 1963, pp. 152-76.

Bank of Japan, Statistics Department, ed. *Hundred Year Statistics of the Japanese Economy.* Tokyo: Bank of Japan, 1966.

Barber, Clarence L. "The Quantity Theory and the Income Expenditure Theory in an Open Economy, 1926-1958: A Comment (on Macesich)," *Canadian Journal of Economics and Political Science,* 32(3), August 1966, pp. 375-7.

Barber, Clarence L. "On the Origins of the Great Depression," *Southern Economic Journal,* 44(3), January 1978, pp. 432-56.

Barbour, J. and Bunting, David. "Interlocking Directorates in Large American Corporations, 1896-1964," *Business History Review,* 45, 1971, pp. 317-35.

Barger, Harold. *American Agriculture, 1899-1939* (General Series 42). New York: National Bureau of Economic Research, 1942.

Barger, Harold. *The Mining Industries, 1899-1939* (General Series 43). New York: National Bureau of Economic Research, 1944.

Barger, Harold. *The Transportation Industries, 1889-1946* (General Series 51). New York: National Bureau of Economic Research, 1951.

Barger, Harold. *Distribution's Place in the American Economy Since 1869.* New York: National Bureau of Economic Research, 1955.

Barger, Harold. "Income Originating in Trade, 1869-1929," in Parker (ed), *Trends in the American Economy in the Nineteenth Century,*

1960, pp. 327-33.

Barkai, Haim. "The Macro-Economics of Tsarist Russia in the Industrialization Era: Monetary Developments, the Balance of Payments and the Gold Standard," *Journal of Economic History,* 33(2), June 1973, pp. 339-71.

Barnard, A.; Pincus, Jonathan J. and Butlin, Noel G. "Public and Private Sector Employment in Australia, 1901-1974," *Australian Economic Review,* 10(37), 1st Quarter 1977, pp. 43-52.

Barnard, A.; Pincus, Jonathan J. and Butlin, Noel G. "Big Government in Australia, 1901-1978." [Working Paper]

Barnett, Harold J. "Some Aspects of Development in the Coal Mining Industry, 1839-1918: Comment on Eliasberg," in Brady (ed), *Output, Employment, and Productivity in the United States after 1800,* 1966, 437-39.

Barrett, C.R. and Walters, A.A. "The Stability of Keynesian and Monetary Multipliers in the United Kingdom," *Review of Economics and Statistics,* 38, November 1966, pp. 395-405.

Barsby, Steven. "Economic Backwardness and the Characteristics of Development," *Journal of Economic History,* 29(3), September 1969, pp. 449-50.

Barton, Glen T. "Productivity Growth in Grain Production in the United States, 1840-60 and 1900-10: Comment on Parker and Klein," in Brady (ed), *Output, Employment, and Productivity in the United States after 1800,* 1966, pp. 580-2.

Basmann, R.L. "The Role of the Economic Historian in Predictive Testing of Proffered 'Economic Laws'," reprinted in Hughes (ed), *Purdue Faculty Papers in Economic History,* 1967, pp. 11- 34. *Explorations in Enterpreneurial History,* Second Series, 2(3), Spring/Summer 1965, pp. 159-86.

Bateman, Fred. "Improvement in American Dairy Farming, 1850-1910: A Quantitative Analysis," *Journal of Economic History,* 28(2), June 1968, pp. 255-73.

Bateman, Fred. "Labor Inputs and Productivity in American Dairy Agriculture, 1850-1910," *Journal of Economic History,* 29(2), June 1969, pp. 206-29.

Bateman, Fred. "Issues in the Measurement of Efficiency of American Dairy Farming, 1850-1910: A Reply to Gunderson," *Journal of Economic History,* 29(3), September 1969, pp. 506-11.

Bateman, Fred. "Comments on Dissertations Presented to the 36th Annual Meeting of the Economic History Association," *Journal of Economic History,* 37(1), March 1977, pp. 276-80.

Bateman, Fred. "The 'Marketable Surplus' in Northern Dairy Farming: New Evidence by Size of Farm in 1860," *Agricultural History,* 52(3), July 1978, pp. 345-63.

Bateman, Fred and Atack, Jeremy. "The Profitability of Northern Agriculture in 1860," in Uselding (ed), *Research in Economic History,* 1979.

Bateman, Fred; Atack, Jeremy and Weiss, Thomas J. "The Regional Diffusion and Adoption of the Steam Engine in American Manufacturing," *Journal of Economic History,* 40(2), June 1980, pp. 281-308.

Bateman, Fred; Atack, Jeremy and Weiss, Thomas J. "Risk, the Rate of Return and the Pattern of Investment in 19th Century American Industrialization." [Working Paper]

286

Bateman, Fred; Atack, Jeremy and Weiss, Thomas J. "The Manuscript Census as a Nineteenth Century Data Source." [Working Paper]

Bateman, Fred; Foust, James D. and Weiss, Thomas J. "Large-Scale Manufacturing in the South and West, 1850-1860," *Business History Review*, 45(1), Spring 1971, pp. 18-34.

Bateman, Fred and Foust, James D. "A Sample of Rural Households Selected from the 1860 Manuscript Censuses," *Agricultural History*, 48(1), January 1974, pp. 75-93.

Bateman, Fred; Foust, James D. and Weiss, Thomas J. "The Participation of Planters in Manufacturing in the Antebellum South," *Agricultural History*, 48(2), April 1974, pp. 277-97.

Bateman, Fred; Foust, James and Weiss, Thomas J. "Profitability in Southern Manufacturing: Estimates for 1860," *Explorations in Economic History*, 12(3), July 1975, pp. 211-32.

Bateman, Fred and Weiss, Thomas J. "Market Structure before the Age of Big Business: Concentration and Profit in Early Southern Manufacturing," *Business History Review*, 49(3), Autumn 1975, pp. 312-36.

Bateman, Fred and Weiss, Thomas J. "Comparative Regional Development in Antebellum Manufacturing," *Journal of Economic History*, 35(1), March 1975, pp. 182-208.

Bateman, Fred and Weiss, Thomas J. "Manufacturing in the Antebellum South," in Uselding (ed), *Research in Economic History*, 1976.

Bateman, Freda and Weiss, Thomas J. "A Sample of Industrial Firms from the Manuscripts of the U.S. Censuses of Manufacturing, 1850-1870." [Working Paper]

Bateman, Fred and Weiss, Thomas J. "Industrialization in the Slave Economy." [Working Paper]

Battalio, Raymond C. and Kagel, John. "The Structure of Antebellum Southern Agriculture: South Carolina, A Case Study," in Parker (ed), *The Structure of the Cotton Economy of the Antebellum South*, 1970, pp. 25-37.

Baxter, Stephen B. "Domestic and International Integration of the London Money Market, 1731-1789: Comment on Eagly and Smith," *Journal of Economic History*, 36(1), March 1976, pp. 213-6.

Bean, Richard N. "The British Transatlantic Slave Trade, 1650-1775," (Summary of Doctoral Dissertation) *Journal of Economic History*, 32(1), March 1972, pp. 409-11.

Bean, Richard N. "War and the Birth of the Nation State," *Journal of Economic History*, 33(1), March 1973, pp. 203-21.

Bean, Richard N. *The British Transatlantic Slave Trade, 1650-1775*. New York: Arno Press, 1975.

Bean, Richard N. "Colonial American Economic History," (Summary of 1975 Research Workshop) *Journal of Economic History*, 36(1), March 1976, pp. 32-4.

Bean, Richard N. "An Explanation of Chicago Urban Density Based on Relative Prices at Time of First Development - Or the Putty-Clay Theory of Capital Refuted." [Working Paper]

Bean, Richard N. "New Estimates of European Migration to British America in the Colonial Period." [Working Paper]

Bean, Richard N. "Productivity Changes in 17th Century Ocean Shipping." [Working Paper]

Bean, Richard N. "Surrogate Price Indices for Several Countries in the Nineteenth Century." [Working Paper]

Bean, Richard N. "The Importance of Regional Cost of Living Differentials in Estimating Gini-Coefficients for U.S. Income Inequality." [Working Paper]

Bean, Richard N. "The Rate of Return on the Ownership of Indentured Servant Contracts in Colonial America." [Working Paper]

Bean, Richard N.; Anderson, Terry L. and Thomas, Robert P. "Economic Growth in the 17th Century American Colonies: Application of an Export-Led Growth Model." [Working Paper]

Bean, Richard N. and Thomas, Robert P. "The Fishers of Men: The Profits of the Slave Trade," *Journal of Economic History*, 34(4), December 1974, pp. 885-914.

Bean, Richard N. and Thomas, Robert P. "The Adoption of Slave Labor in British America," in Gemery and Hogendorn (eds), *The Uncommon Market*, 1979, pp. 377-98.

Benda, Gyula. "New Economic History," *Torteneti Statisztikai Kozlemenyek*, 1977, pp. 261-76.

Bengtsson, Tommy and Jorberg, Lennart. "Market Integration in Sweden during the 18th and 19th Centuries: Spectral Analysis of Grain Prices," *Economy and History*, 18(2), 1975, pp. 93-106.

Bengtsson, Tommy and Jorberg, Lennart. "Regional Wages in Sweden during the 19th Century," in Bairoch and Levy-Leboyer (eds), *Disparities in Economic Development since the Industrial Revolution*, 1980.

Bengtsson, Tommy and Ohlsson, Rolf. "Population and Economic Fluctuations in Sweden, 1749-1914: Spectral Analysis on National Data." [Working Paper]

Benjamin, Daniel K. and Kochin, Levis A. "Searching for an Explanation of Unemployment in Interwar Britain," *Journal of Political Economy*, 87(3), June 1979, pp. 441-78.

Benjamin, Daniel K. and Kochin, Levis A. "What Went Right with Juvenile Unemployment Policy between the Wars: A Comment (on Garside)," *Economic History Review*, Second Series, 32(4), November 1979, pp. 523-8.

Benjamin, Daniel K. and Kochin, Levis A. "The British National Debt." [Working Paper]

Benston, George J. "On Understanding the Birth and Evolution of the Securities and Exchange Commission: Where Are We in the Theory of Regulation? Discussion of MacKay and Reid," in Walton (ed), *Regulatory Change in an Atmosphere of Crisis*, 1979, pp. 123-7.

Bentick, Brian L. "Foreign Borrowing and Relative Prices: Victoria, 1872-1893," *Yale Economic Essays*, 10(2), Fall 1970, pp. 3-44.

Berck, Peter. "Hard Driving and Efficiency: Iron Production in 1890," *Journal of Economic History*, 38(4), December 1978, pp. 879-900.

Bergmann, J. and Spree, Reinhard. "Die konjunkturelle Entwicklung der Deutschen Wirtschaft 1840 bis 1864," [The Cyclical (Business) Process in the German Economy, 1840 to 1864] in Wehler (ed), *Sozialgeschichte Heute*, 1974.

Berry, Thomas S. "Income Originating in Trade, 1869-1929: Comment on Barger," in Parker (ed), *Trends in the American Economy in the Nineteenth Century*, 1960, pp. 333-6.

Bertram, Gordon W. "Economic Growth in Canadian Industry, 1870-1915: The Staple Model and the Take-Off Hypothesis," *Canadian Journal of Economics and Political Science*, 29, May 1963, pp. 159-84.

Bertram, Gordon W. and Percy, Michael B. "Real Wage Trends in Canada,

1900-1926: Some Provisional Estimates," *Canadian Journal of Economics*, 12(2), May 1979, pp. 299-312.

Best, H. and Mann, R. *Quantitative Methoden in der Historisch-Sozialwissenschaftlichen Forschung* [Quantitative Methods in Historical and Sociological Research]. Stuttgart: Klett-Cotta, 1977.

Best, Laura and Strober, Myra H. "Female-Male Salary Differential in Public Schools: Some Lessons from San Francisco, 1879," *Economic Inquiry*, 17(2), April 1979, pp. 218-36.

Binswanger, Hans P.; Ruttan, Vernon W. and Hayami, Yujiro; Wade, W.W. and Weber, A. "Factor Productivity and Growth: A Historical Interpretation," in Binswanger et al (ed), *Induced Innovation: Technology, Institutions, and Development*, 1978.

Birnberg, Thomas and Resnick, Stephen A. *Colonial Development: An Econometric Study*. New Haven: Yale University Press, 1975.

Biscaini Cotula, Anna Maria and Ciocca, Pierluigi. "Le strutture finanziarie: aspetti quantitativi di lungo periodo (1870-1970)," [Financial Structures: Long Run Quantitative Features (1870-1970)] in Vicarelli (ed), *Capitale industriale e capitale finanziario*, 1979, pp. 61-136.

Bittlingmayer, George. "Merger for Monopoly: The Cast Iron Pipe Industry, 1890-1910, and the Case of Addyston Pipe," Ph.D. Dissertation, University of Chicago, 1981.

Bjerke, Kjeld and Ussing, Niels. *Studier over Danmarks Nationalprodukt 1870-1950*. Kobenhavn: Universitits Okonomiske Institut, 1958.

Bjerke, Juul and Aukrust, Odd. "Real Capital in Norway, 1900-56," in Goldsmith and Saunders (eds), *The Measurement of National Wealth*, 1959, pp. 80-118.

Bjorle, G.C. "Regional Adjustment to Economic Growth: The United States, 1880-1950," *Oxford Economic Papers*, 20(1), March 1968, pp. 81-97.

Blain, Larry. "Regional Cyclical Behavior and Sensitivity in Canada, 1919-1973," (Summary of Doctoral Dissertation) *Journal of Economic History*, 38(1), March 1978, pp. 271-3.

Blain, Larry; Paterson, Donald G. and Rae, J.D. "The Regional Impact of Economic Fluctuations during the Inter-War Period: The Case of British Columbia," *Canadian Journal of Economics*, 7(3), August 1974, pp. 381-401.

Blainey, Geoffrey. "A Theory of Mineral Discovery: Australia in the Nineteenth Century," *Economic History Review*, Second Series, 23(2), May 1970, pp. 298-313.

Blainey, Geoffrey. "A Theory of Mineral Discovery: A Rejoinder to Morrissey and Burt," *Economic History Review*, Second Series, 26(3), August 1973, pp. 506-9.

Blank, David M. "The volume of Residential Construction, 1889-1950," National Bureau of Economic Research, Technical Paper no. 9, 1954.

Blank, David M.; Grebler, Leo and Winnick, Louis. *Capital Formation in Residential Real Estate: Trends and Prospects*. Princeton: Princeton University Press for the National Bureau of Economic Research, 1956.

Blaug, Mark. "The Productivity of Capital in the Lancashire Cotton Industry during the Nineteenth Century," *Economic History Review*, Second Series, 13(3), 1961, pp. 358-81.

Blaug, Mark. "The Myth of the Old Poor Law and the Making of the New,"

Journal of Economic History, 23(1), March 1963, pp. 151-84.

Bolch, Ben W.; Fels, Rendigs and McMahon, Marshall. "Housing Surplus in the 1920's?," *Explorations in Economic History,* 8(3), Spring 1971, pp. 259-84.

Blok, L. and De Meere, J.M.M. "Welstand, Ongelijkheid in Welstand en Censuskiesrecht in Nederland Omstreeks Het Midden van de 19de Eeuw," [Prosperity, Wealth Inequality, and Franchise in the Netherlands in the Middle of Nineteenth Century] *Economisch-en Sociaal-Historisch Jaarboek,* 41, 1978, pp. 175-293.

Bloomfield, A. *Monetary Policy under the International Gold Standard.* New York: Federal Reserve Bank of New York, 1959.

Bloomfield, A. *Short-Term Capital Movements Under the Pre-1914 Gold Standard.* Princeton Studies in International Finance no. 11. Princeton: Princeton University Press, 1963.

Bloomfield, A. *Patterns of Fluctuation in International Investment Before 1914.* Princeton Studies in International Finance no. 21. Princeton: Princeton University Press, 1968.

Blyn, George. *Agricultural Trends in India, 1891-1947: Output, Availability, and Productivity.* Philadelphia: University of Pennsylvania Press, 1966.

Boehm, E.A. *Prosperity and Depression in Australia, 1887-1897.* Oxford: Oxford University Press, 1971.

Boehm, E.A. "Australia's Economic Depression of the 1930s," *Economic Record,* 49(128), December 1973, pp. 606-23.

Boehm, E.A. "Economic Development and Fluctuation in Australia in the 1920s: A Reply (to Sinclair)," *Economic Record,* 51(135), September 1975, pp. 414-20.

Bogue, Allan G. *Money at Interest: The Farm Mortgage on the Middle Border* (Second Edition Published by Russell & Russell, New York, 1968). Ithaca: Cornell University Press, 1955.

Bogue, Allan G. "Financing the Prairie Farmer," in Fogel and Engerman (eds), *The Reinterpretation of American Economic History,* 1971, pp. 301-7.

Bogue, Allan G. "Population Change and Farm Settlement in the Northern United States: Comment on Easterlin," *Journal of Economic History,* 36(1), March 1976, pp. 76-81.

Bogue, Allan G. and Bogue, Margaret Beattie. "'Profits' and the Frontier Land Speculator," reprinted in Fogel and Engerman (eds), *The Reinterpretation of American Economic History,* 1971, pp. 64-72. *Journal of Economic History,* 17(1), March 1957, pp. 1-24.

Bolch, Ben W. and Pilgrim, John D. "A Reappraisal of Some Factors Associated with Fluctuations in the United States in the Interwar Period," *Southern Economic Journal,* 39(3), January 1973, pp. 327-44.

Bolino, August C. "Population and Fertility in the Nineteenth Century: A Discussion of Papers by Vedder/Gallaway, Haines, and Mokyr Presented to the 39th Annual Meeting of the Economic History Association," *Journal of Economic History,* 40(1), March 1980, pp. 167-8.

Bonomo, Vittorio. "International Capital Movements and Economic Activity: The United States Experience, 1870-1968," *Explorations in Economic History,* 8(3), Spring 1971, pp. 321-42.

Bonomo, Vittorio and Tanner, J. Ernest. "Gold, Capital Flows and Long Swings in American Business Activity," *Journal of Political*

Economy, 76(1), January/February 1968, pp. 44-52.

Booms, Bernard H. "Impact of Urban Market Structure on the Level of Inventive Activity in Cities in the Early Nineteen-Hundreds," *Land Economics,* 49, August 1973, pp. 318-25.

Booth, David and Higgs, Robert. "Mortality Differentials Within Large American Cities in 1890," *Human Ecology,* 7(4), December 1979, pp. 353-70.

Borchardt, Knut. "Regional Differentiation in the Development of Germany throughout the 19th Century with Special Regard to the East/West Differential," *Third International Conference of Economic History, Munich, 1965, part 5.* Paris: Mouton, 1974, pp. 441-3.

Bordo, Michael D. "The Income Effects of Monetary Change: A Historical Approach," *Economic Inquiry,* 13, December 1974, pp. 505-25.

Bordo, Michael D. "John E. Cairnes on the Effects of the Australian Gold Discoveries, 1851-73: An Early Application of the Methodology of Positive Economics," *History of Political Economy,* 7, Fall 1975, pp. 357-9.

Bordo, Michael D. "The Income Effects of the Sources of New Money: A Comparison of the United States and the United Kingdom, 1870-1913," *Explorations in Economic History,* 14(1), January 1977, pp. 20-43.

Bordo, Michael D. and Jonung, Lars. "The Long Run Behavior of the Income Velocity of Money: A Cross Country Comparison of Five Advanced Countries, 1870-1975." [Working Paper]

Bordo, Michael D. and Schwartz, Anna J. "Issues in Monetary Economics and their Impact on Research," in Gallman (ed), *Recent Developments in the Study of Economic and Business History,* 1977.

Bordo, Michael D. and Schwartz, Anna J. "Money and Prices in the Nineteenth Century: An Old Debate Rejoined," *Journal of Economic History,* 40(1), March 1980, pp. 61-7.

Bordo, Michael D. and Schwartz, Anna J. "Money and Prices in the Nineteenth Century: Was Thomas Tooke Right?," UCLA Discussion Paper, 1980.

Borenstein, Israel. "Capital and Output Trends in Mining Industries, 1870-1948," National Bureau of Economic Research, Occasional Paper no. 45, 1954.

Borenstein, Israel; Creamer, Daniel and Dobrovolsky, Sergei. *Capital in Manufacturing and Mining: Its Formation and Financing.* Princeton: Princeton University Press for the National Bureau of Economic Research, 1960.

Borins, S.F. "Econometric Modelling of the Settlement Process in Western Canada and of the Effect of Government Land and Railroad Policy on the Spatial and Temporal Nature of the Process." [Working Paper]

Bos, Roeland W.J.M. "Factorprijzen, technologie en marktstructuur: de groei van de Nederlandse volkshuishouding 1815-1914," [Factor Prices, Technology and Market Structure: The Growth of the Dutch Economy, 1815-1914] *Afdeling Agrarische Geschiedenis,* Bijdragen 22, 1979, pp. 109-37.

Bos, Roeland W.J.M. "Kapitaal en industrialisatie in Nederland tijdens de negentiende eeuw," [Capital and Industrialization in the Netherlands during the Nineteenth Century] *Afdeling Agrarische Geschiedenis,* Bijdragen 22, 1979, pp. 89-105.

Bos, Roeland W.J.M. "Techniek en industrialisatie: Nederland in de negentiende eeuw," [Technology and Industrialization: The

291

Netherlands in the Nineteenth Century] *Afdeling Agrarische Geschiedenis,* Bijdragen 22, 1979, pp. 59-88.

Boschan, Charlotte and Bry, Gerhard. *Wages in Germany, 1871-1945* (National Bureau of Economic Research General Series 68). Princeton: Princeton University Press for the National Bureau of Economic Research, 1960.

Boschan, Charlotte and Bry, Gerhard. "Secular Trends and Recent Changes in Real Wages and Wage Differentials in Three Western Industrial Countries: The United States, Great Britain, and Germany," *Second International Conference on Economic History, Aix-en-Provence, 1962,* vol. 2. Paris: Mouton, 1965, pp. 175-208.

Boskins, Michael; Roehl, Richard; Lyons, John and Sutch, Richard C. "Urban Migration in the Process of Industrialization: Britain and the United States in the Nineteenth Century," University of California-Berkeley, Center for Research in Management Science, Working Papers in Economic Theory and Econometrics no. 162, August 1970.

Boulding, Kenneth E. and Munroe, Tapan. "Unprofitable Empire: Britain in India, 1800-1967: A Critique of the Hobson-Lenin Thesis on Imperialism," *Peace Research Society Papers,* 16, 1970.

Boulding, Kenneth E. and Munroe, Tapan, eds. *Economic Imperialism.* Ann Arbor: University of Michigan Press, 1972.

Boulle, Pierre H. "Marchandes de Traite et Developpement Industriel dans le France et l'Angleterre du XVIIIe Siecle," [Slave Traders and Industrial Development in France and England in the Eighteenth Century] *Revue Francaise d'Histoire d'Outre-Mer,* 62(226-227), 1975, pp. 309-30.

Bouvier, Jean. "Sur les dimensions mesurables du fait financier, XIXe et XXe siecles," [On the Measureable Achievements of Financiers, Nineteenth and Twentieth Centuries], *Revue d'Histoire Economique et Sociale,* 46(2), 1968, pp. 161-84.

Bouvier, Jean. *Un siecle de banque francaise* [A Century of French Banking]. Paris: Hachette, 1973.

Bouvier, Jean. "Capital bancaire, capital industriel, capital financier dans la croissance francaise du 19 eme siecle," [Bank Capital, Industrial Capital, and Financial Capital in Nineteenth Century French Growth] *La Pensee,* 36, December 1974.

Bouvier, Jean. "A propos des approches micro et macro economiques des exportations de capitaux avant 1914," [Regarding Micro- and Macro-Economic Approaches to Capital Exports Before 1914] in Levy-Leboyer (ed), *La position internationale de la France,* 1977.

Bouvier, Jean. "Le Credit Lyonnais de 1863 a 1882: Les Annees de Formation d'Une Banque de Depots," [The "Credit Lyonnais", 1863-1882: The Formative Years of a Bank-of-Deposit] Ph.D. Dissertation, Sevpen, 1961.

Bouvier, Jean; Furet, Francois and Gillet, Marcel, eds. *Le Mouvement du profit en France au XIXe siecle: Materiaux et Etudes* [The Movement of Profit in Nineteenth Century France]. Paris: Mouton, 1965.

Bowman, John D. "An Economic Analysis of Midwestern Farm Land Values and Farm Land Income, 1860 to 1900," *Yale Economic Essays,* 5(2), Fall 1965, pp. 317-52.

Bowman, John D. "Gross Agricultural Output, Value Added and Factor Shares in the Twelve Midwestern States, 1870 to 1900." [Working

Paper]

Bowman, Mary Jean and Anderson, C. Arnold. "Human Capital and Economic Modernization in Historical Perspective," *Fourth International Conference of Economic History, Bloomington, 1968.* Paris: Mouton, 1973, pp. 247-72.

Bowman, John D. and Danhof, Clarence H. "An Industrial Income Distribution for New York State, 1865." [Working Paper]

Bowman, John D. and Keehn, Richard H. "Agricultural Terms of Trade in Four Midwestern States, 1870-1900," *Journal of Economic History,* 34(3), September 1974, pp. 592-609.

Boyns, T. and Williams, L.J. "Occupation in Wales, 1851-1971," *Bulletin of Economic Research,* 29(2), November 1977, pp. 71-83.

Brady, Dorothy S. "Family Saving, 1888 to 1950," in Goldsmith et al (eds), *A Study of Saving in the United States,* 1957, pp. 139-276.

Brady, Dorothy S, ed. *Output, Employment, and Productivity in the United States after 1800* (Studies in Income and Wealth, vol. 30). New York: Columbia University Press for the National Bureau of Economic Research, 1966.

Brady, Dorothy S. "Price Deflators for Final Product Estimates," in Brady (ed), *Output, Employment, and Productivity in the United States after 1800,* 1966, pp. 91-115.

Brady, Dorothy S. "Consumption and the Style of Life," in Davis, Easterlin, and Parker (eds), *American Economic Growth,* 1972, pp. 61-91.

Brady, Dorothy S.; Goldsmith, Raymond W. and Menderhausen, Horst. *A Study of Saving in the United States, vol. 3: Special Studies.* Princeton: Princeton University Press, 1957.

Brainerd, Carol P.; Lee, Everett S.; Miller, Ann Ratner and Easterlin, Richard A. *Population, Redistribution and Economic Growth: United States, 1870-1950, vol. 1: Methodological Considerations and Reference Tables* (Series edited by Simon S. Kuznets and Dorothy Swaine Thomas). Philadelphia: American Philosophical Society, 1957.

Brainerd, Carol P. and Miller, Ann Ratner. "Labor Force Estimates," in Lee et al (ed), *Population, Redistribution and Economic Growth,* 1957, pp. 363-633.

Branson, William H. "Social Legislation and the Birth Rate in Nineteenth Century Britain," *Western Economic Journal,* 6(2), March 1968, pp. 134-44.

Branson, William H. "Social Legislation and the Demand for Children: Reply to West," *Western Economic Journal,* 6(5), December 1968, pp. 424-7.

Brito, D.L. and Williamson, Jeffrey G. "Skilled Labor and Nineteenth-Century Anglo-American Managerial Behavior," *Explorations in Economic History,* 10(3), Spring 1973, pp. 235-52.

Brittain, W.H. Bruce. "Monetary Factors in the French Balance of Payments, 1880-1913," Ph.D. Dissertation, University of Chicago, 1975.

Britton, Charles R. and Smiley, Gene. "Interregional Resource Allocation: Mid-South Resource Flows during the 1880-1913 Period," *Annals of the Midsouth Academy of Economists,* 3, 1975, pp. 175-96.

Brockstedt, Jurgen. *Die Schiffahrts-und Handelsbeziehungen Schleswig-Holsteins nach Lateinamerika, 1815-1848* [The Shipping and Trade Relationships of Schleswig-Holstein with Latin America,

293

1815-1848]. Koln: Bohlau, 1975.

Brockstedt, Jurgen. *Statistik der Schiffahrtsbeziehungen Schleswig-Holsteins nach Lateinamerika 1815-1848* [Statistics of the Shipping Relationships of Schleswig-Holstein with Latin America, 1815-1848]. Kiel, 1976.

Brockstedt, Jurgen. "Wirtschafts- und Sozialstatistik," [Economic and Social Statistics] in Bracher (ed), *Die Krise Europas*, 1976, pp. 420-35.

Brockstedt, Jurgen. "Wirtschafts- und Sozialstatistik," [Economic and Social Statistics] in Schieder (ed), *Staatensystem als Vormacht der Welt*, 1977, pp. 430-7.

Brockstedt, Jurgen. "Die Wirtschaftsentwicklung Kiels in vor- und fruhindustrieller Zeit (1800-1864)," [The Economic Development of Kiel in the Pre-and Early-Industrial Period (1800-1864)] in Schneider (ed), *Wirtschaftskrafte und Wirtschaftswege, 1978, pp. 251-64.*

Brockstedt, Jurgen. "Wirtschafts- und Sozialstatistik," [Economic and Social Statistics] in Weis (ed), Der Durchbruch des Burgertums, 1978, pp. 435-53.

Brockstedt, Jurgen. *Regionale Mobilitat in Schleswig-Holstein 1600-1900. Theorie, Fallstudien, Quellenkunde, Bibliographie* [Regional Mobility in Schleswig-Holstein 1600-1900: Theory, Case Studies, Sources, Bibliography]. Neumunster: Wacholtz, 1980.

Brockstedt, Jurgen. "Wirtschaftssentwicklung, Sozialstruktur und Mobilitat in Schleswig-Holstein (1800-1864)," [Economic Development, Social Structure, and Mobility in Schleswig-Holstein, 1800-1864] in Schroder (ed), *Sozialwissenschaftliche Ansatze in der modernen Stadtgeschichte*, 1979, pp. 179-97.

Broder, Albert A. "Quantitative Study of the Role of Railways in a Regional Economy: Southern Spain and the Andalous RR Company, 1872-1913," in First Congress on the Industrialization of Spain Barcelona, 1970.

Broder, Albert A. "Les Investissements etrangers en Espagne au XIXe siecle: Methodologie et quantification," [Foreign Investment in Spain in the 19th Century: Methods and Findings] *Revue d'Histoire Economique et Sociale*, 54(1), 1976, pp. 29-63.

Broder, Albert A. "Les Investissements Francais en Espagne," [French Investments in Spain] in Levy-Leboyer (ed), *La Position Internationale de la France*, 1977.

Broeze, Frank J.A. "The Cost of Distance: Shipping and the Early Australian Economy, 1788-1850," *Economic History Review*, Second Series, 28(4), November 1975, pp. 580-97.

Broeze, Frank J.A. "The New Economic History, the Navigation Acts, and the Continental Tobacco Market, 1770-90: Comment on Walton," *Economic History Review*, Second Series, 26(4), November 1973, pp. 668-78.

Brown, E. Cary. "Fiscal Policy in the Thirties: A Reappraisal," reprinted in Fogel and Engerman (eds), *The Reinterpretation of American Economic History*, 1971, pp. 480-7. *American Economic Review*, 46, December 1956, pp. 857-79.

Brown, William W. and Reynolds, Morgan O. "Debt Peonage Re-examined: A Note (on Ransom and Sutch)," *Journal of Economic History*, 33(4), December 1973, pp. 862-71.

Brown, Wilson B. and Hogendorn, Jan S. "Agricultural Export Growth and

Myint's Model: Nigeria and Peru, 1900-1920," *Agricultural History,* 46(2), April 1972, pp. 313-24.

Brownlee, W. Elliot. "Income Taxation and Capital Formation in Wisconsin, 1911-1929," *Explorations in Economic History,* 8(1), Fall 1970, pp. 77-102.

Brownlee, W. Elliot. "The Economics of Urban Slavery. Review Essay of 'Urban Slavery in the American South, 1820-1860: A Quantitative History' by Claudia Dale Goldin (Chicago: University of Chicago Press, 1976)," *Reviews in American History,* 5(2), June 1977, pp. 230-5.

Brownlee, W. Elliot. *Dynamics of Ascent: A History of the American Economy.* New York: Alfred A. Knopf, 1979.

Bruchey, Stuart. "Douglass C. North on American Economic Growth," *Explorations in Entrepreneurial History,* Second Series, 1(2), Winter 1964, pp. 145-58.

Bruchey, Stuart. "Econometrics and Southern History: Comment on Conrad," *Explorations in Entrepreneurial History,* Second Series, 6(1), Fall 1968, pp. 59-65.

Brunner, Karl. "Institutions, Policy, and Monetary Analysis. Review Essay of 'A Monetary History of the United States, 1867-1960' by Milton Friedman and Anna J. Schwartz (Princeton: Princeton University Press for the NBER, 1963)," *Journal of Political Economy,* 73(2), April 1965,.

Brunner, Karl, ed. *The Great Depression Revisited* (Rochester Studies in Economics and Policy Issues, vol. 2). Boston: Martinus Nijhoff, 1981.

Bry, Gerhard and Boschan, Charlotte. *Wages in Germany, 1871-1945* (National Bureau of Economic Research General Series 68). Princeton: Princeton University Press for the National Bureau of Economic Research, 1960.

Bry, Gerhard and Boschan, Charlotte. "Secular Trends and Recent Changes in Real Wages and Wage Differentials in Three Western Industrial Countries: The United States, Great Britain, and Germany," *Second International Conference on Economic History, Aix-en-Provence, 1962,* vol. 2. Paris: Mouton, 1965, pp. 175-208.

Buckley, Kenneth. *Capital Formation in Canada, 1896-1930.* Reprinted by Mclelland & Stewart, Toronto, 1974. Toronto: University of Toronto Press, 1955.

Buckley, Kenneth. "The Role of Staple Industries in Canada's Economic Development," *Journal of Economic History,* 18(4), December 1958, pp. 439-50.

Buckley, Kenneth. "Development of Canada's Economy, 1850-1900: Comment on Firestone," in Parker (ed), *Trends in the American Economy in the Nineteenth Century,* 1960, pp. 246-8.

Buckley, K.A.H.; Urquhart, M.C., eds. *Historical Statistics of Canada.* Toronto: Macmillan, 1965.

Budd, Edward C. "Factor Shares, 1850-1910," in Parker (ed),' *Trends in the American Economy in the Nineteenth Century,* 1960, pp. 365-98.

Budd, Edward C. "Factor Shares, 1850-1910: Reply to Denison," in Parker (ed), *Trends in the American Economy in the Nineteenth Century,* 1960, pp. 403-6.

Buescu, Mircea. "Para uma Quantificacao Global da Historia Economica do Brasil," [Towards a Global Quantification of Brazilian Economic History] reprinted in *L'Histoire Quantitative du Bresil,* 1973, pp.

109-20. *Verbum*, 29(1), March 1972, pp. 79-99.

Buescu, Mircea. "A Inflacao Brasileira de 1850 a 1870: Monetarismo e Estruturalismo," [The Brazilian Inflation from 1850 to 1870: Monetarism and Structuralism] reprinted in *L'Histoire Quantitative du Bresil*, 1973. *Revista Brasileira de Economia*, 26(4), October/December 1972, pp. 125-47.

Buescu, Mircea. *300 Anos de Inflacao* [300 Years of Inflation]. Rio de Janeiro: APEC, 1973.

Buescu, Mircea. "Notas Sobre o Custo da Mao-De-Obra Escrava," [Remarks on the Slave Manpower Cost] *Verbum*, 31(3), September 1975, pp. 33-44.

Buescu, Mircea. "Medicao das Disparidades Regionais de Renda: Brasil, 1872-1900," [Measurement of Regional Income Disparaties: Brazil, 1872-1900] *Verbum*, 33(2), December 1977, pp. 199-208.

Buescu, Mircea. "Bresil, 1907: Un Exercice Macro-Economique," [Brazil, 1907: A Macroeconomic Essay] in Schneider (ed), *Festschrift fur Hermann Kellenbenz*, 1978, pp. 461-70.

Buescu, Mircea. *Evolucao Economica do Brasil* (4th Edition) [The Economic Evolution of Brazil]. Rio de Janeiro: APEC, 1979.

Buescu, Mircea. "Disparites Regionales au Bresil dans la Seconde Moitie du XIX Siecle," [Regional Disparaties in Brazil during the Second Half of the 19th Century] *Proceedings of the International Congress on Economic History, 7th, Edinburgh, 1978.* London: Macmillan.

Bulferetti, Luigi and Itzcovitch, Oscar. *Orientamenti della storiografia quantitativa* [Trends in Quantitative Historiography]. Roma: Citta nuova editrice.

Bunting, David. "The Truth About 'The Truth About the Trusts'," *Journal of Economic History*, 31, 1971, pp. 664-71.

Bunting, David. *Statistical View of the Trusts: A Manual of Large Industrial and Mining Corporations Active in the United States Around 1900.* Westport, Conn.: Greenwood Press, 1974.

Bunting, David. "Corporate Interlocking: The Money Trust," *Directors & Boards*, 1, Spring 1976, pp. 6-15.

Bunting, David; Barbour, J. "Interlocking Directorates in Large American Corporations, 1896-1964," *Business History Review*, 45, 1971, pp. 317-35.

Bunting, David and Mizruchi, M.S. "The Transfer of Control in Large Corporations: 1912-1919 (Summary)," in Uselding (ed), *Business and Economic History*, 1980, pp. 120-3.

Burford, Roger L. "The Federal Cotton Programs and Farm Labor Force Adjustments," *Southern Economic Journal*, 33(2), October 1966, pp. 223-36.

Burns, Arthur F. *Production Trends in the United States since 1870* (General Series 23). New York: National Bureau of Economic Research, 1934.

Burstein, M.L. "Homer on the History of Interest Rates," *Explorations in Entrepreneurial History*, Second Series, 2(1), Fall 1964, pp. 56-67.

Burt, R. and Morrissey, M.J. "A Theory of Mineral Discovery: A Note on Blainey," *Economic History Review*, Second Series, 26(3), August 1973, pp. 497-505.

Bustelo, Francisco and Tortella Casares, Gabriel. "Monetary Inflation in Spain, 1800-1970," *Journal of European Economic History*, 5(1),

Spring 1976, pp. 141-50.

Butlin, Noel G. *Public Capital Formation in Australia: Estimates 1860-1900.* Canberra: Australian National University, 1954.

Butlin, Noel G. *Private Capital Formation in Australia: Estimates 1860-1900.* Canberra: Australian National University, 1955.

Butlin, Noel G. "Colonial Socialism in Australia 1860-1900," in Aitken (ed), *The State and Economic Growth,* 1959.

Butlin, Noel G. *Australian Domestic Product, Investment and Foreign Borrowing, 1860-1938/39.* Cambridge: Cambridge University Press, 1962.

Butlin, Noel G. "Distribution of the Sheep Population: Preliminary Statistical Picture, 1860-1957," in Barnard (ed), *A Simple Fleece,* 1962, pp. 281-307.

Butlin, Noel G. "Pastoral Finance and Capital Requirements, 1860-1960," in Barnard (ed), *A Simple Fleece,* 1962, pp. 383-400.

Butlin, Noel G. "The Growth of Rural Capital, 1860-1890," in Barnard (ed), *A Simple Fleece,* 1962, pp. 322-39.

Butlin, Noel G. *Investment in Australian Economic Development, 1860-1900.* London: Cambridge University Press, 1964.

Butlin, Noel G. "Long-Run Trends in Australia Per Capita Consumption," in Hancock (ed), *The National Income and Social Welfare,* 1965.

Butlin, Noel G. "Kaser on England and Wales Gross Product," *Bulletin of the Oxford University Institute of Economics and Statistics,* 30(1), February 1968, pp. 67-8.

Butlin, Noel G. "A New Plea for the Separation of Ireland," *Journal of Economic History,* 28(2), June 1968, pp. 274-91.

Butlin, Noel G. "Some Perspectives of Australian Economic Development, 1890-1965," in Forster (ed), *Australian Economic Development,* 1970, pp. 43-52.

Butlin, Noel G. *Antebellum Slavery: A Critique of a Debate.* Canberra: Australian National University, 1971.

Butlin, Noel G. and Dowie, Jack A. "Estimates of Australian Workforce and Employment, 1861-1961," (Erratum: see this Review, 10(1) March 1970, for corrections of this article) *Australian Economic History Review,* 9(2), September 1969, pp. 138-55.

Butlin, S.J.; Hall, A.R. and White, R.C., eds. *Australian Banking and Monetary Statistics, 1817-1945* (Reserve Bank Occasional Paper no. 4A). Sydney: Reserve Bank of Australia, 1971.

Butlin, Noel G.; Pincus, Jonathan J. and Barnard, A. "Public and Private Sector Employment in Australia, 1901-1974," *Australian Economic Review,* 10(37), 1st Quarter 1977, pp. 43-52.

Butlin, Noel G.; Pincus, Jonathan J. and Barnard, A. "Big Government in Australia, 1901-1978." [Working Paper]

Butlin, Noel G. and Tucker, G.S.L. "The Quantitative Study of British Economic Growth: A Review. Review Essay of 'British Economic Growth, 1688-1959' by Phyllis Deane and W.A. Cole (Cambridge: Cambridge University Press, 1968)," *Economic Record,* 40(91), September 1964, pp. 455-60.

Cagan, Philip. "The Monetary Dynamics of the Hyper-Inflation," in Friedman (ed), *Studies in the Quantity Theory of Money,* 1956.

Cagan, Philip. *Determinants and Effects of Changes in the Stock of Money, 1875-1960.* New York: Columbia University Press for the National Bureau of Economic Research, 1965.

Cagan, Phillip. "Some Macroeconomic Impacts of the National Industrial Recovery Act, 1933-35: Comment on Weinstein," in Brunner (ed), *The Great Depression Revisited*, 1981, pp. 282-5.

Cain, Louis P. "The Sanitary District of Chicago: A Case Study in Water Use and Conservation," (Summary of Doctoral Dissertation) *Journal of Economic History*, 30(1), March 1970, pp. 256-61.

Cain, Louis P. "An Economic History of Urban Location and Sanitation," in Uselding (ed), *Research in Economic History*, 1977, pp. 337-89.

Cain, Louis P. and Aduddell, Robert. "Location and Collusion in the Meatpacking Industry," in Cain and Uselding (eds), *Business Enterprise and Economic Change*, 1973, pp. 85-117.

Cain, Louis P. and Aduddell, Robert. "The Consent Decree in the Meat-Packing Industry." [Working Paper]

Cain, Louis P. and Paterson, Donald G. "Factor Biases and Technical Change in Manufacturing: The American System, 1850-1919." [Working Paper]

Cairncross, Alec K. *Home and Foreign Investment, 1870-1913: Studies in Capital Accumulation.* Cambridge: Cambridge University Press, 1953.

Cairncross, Alec K. "World Trade in Manufactures since 1900," *Economia Internationale*, 8(4), November 1955, pp. 715-41.

Cairncross, Alec K. "The English Capital Market Before 1914: Comment on Hall," *Economica*, 25(98), May 1958, pp. 142-6.

Cairncross, Alec K. "Investment in Canada, 1900-13," in Hall (ed), *The Export of Capital from Britain*, 1968, pp. 153-86.

Cairncross, Alec K. "The Postwar Years, 1945-77," in Floud and McCloskey (eds), *The Economic History of Britain since 1700*, 1981.

Cairncross, Alec K. and Weber, Brian A. "Fluctuations in Building in Great Britain, 1785-1849," *Economic History Review*, Second Series, 9(2), 1956, pp. 283-97.

Callahan, Colleen M. and Hutchinson, William K. "Antebellum Interregional Trade in Agricultural Goods: Preliminary Results," *Journal of Economic History*, 40(1), March 1980, pp. 25-31.

Cameron, Rondo E. "Theoretical Bases of a Comparative Study of the Role of Financial Institutions in the Early Stages of Industrialization," *Second International Conference of Economic History, Aix-en-Provence, 1962*, vol. 2. Paris and The Hague: Mouton, 1965, pp. 567-86.

Cameron, Rondo E. "Has Economic History a Role in an Economist's Education?," *American Economic Review*, Papers and Proceedings, 55(2), May 1965, pp. 112-5.

Cameron, Rondo E. "Belgium, 1800-1875," in Cameron et al (eds), *Banking in the Early Stages of Industrialization*, 1967, pp. 129-50.

Cameron, Rondo E. "Editor's Conclusion," in Cameron et al (eds), *Banking in the Early Stages of Industrialization*, 1967, pp. 290-321.

Cameron, Rondo E. "England, 1750-1844," in Cameron et al (eds), *Banking in the Early Stages of Industrialization*, 1967, pp. 15-59.

Cameron, Rondo E. "France, 1800-1870," in Cameron et al (eds), *Banking in the Early Stages of Industrialization*, 1967, pp. 100-28.

Cameron, Rondo E. "Scotland, 1750-1845," in Cameron et al (eds), *Banking in the Early Stages of Industrialization*, 1967, pp. 60-99.

Cameron, Rondo E. "Some Lessons of History for Developing Nations," *American Economic Review, Papers and Proceedings,* 57(2), May 1967, pp. 312-24.

Cameron, Rondo E., ed. *Banking and Economic Development: Some Lessons of History.* New York and London: Oxford University Press, 1972.

Cameron, Rondo E. "The International Diffusion of Technology and Economic Development in the Modern Economic Epoch," in Glamann, Hornby, and Larsen (eds), *Sixth International Congress on Economic History, Copenhagen,* 1974, pp. 83-92.

Cameron, Rondo E. "Banking and Credit as Factors in Economic Growth," Van der Wee, Vinogradov, and Kotovsky (eds), *Fifth International Congress of Economic History, Leningrad,* 1976, pp. 45-57.

Cameron, Rondo E. "Economic History, Pure and Applied," *Journal of Economic History,* 36(1), March 1976, pp. 3-27.

Cameron, Rondo E.; Crisp, Olga; Patrick, Hugh T. and Tilly, Richard. *Banking in the Early Stages of Industrialization: A Study in Comparative Economic History.* London and New York: Oxford University Press, 1967.

Campbell, Mildred. "The Social Origins of Some Early Americans: Response to Galenson," *William and Mary Quarterly,* Third Series, 35(3), July 1978, pp. 525-40.

Campbell, Mildred. "The Social Origins of Some Early Americans: Reply to Galenson," *William and Mary Quarterly,* Third Series, 36(2), April 1979, pp. 277-86.

Canarella, Giorgio and Tomaske, John A. "The Optimal Utilization of Slaves," *Journal of Economic History,* 35(3), September 1975, pp. 621-9.

Cannings, Kathleen and Lazonick, William H. "The Development of the Nursing Labor Force in the United States: A Basic Analysis," *International Journal of Health Services,* 5(2), 1975, pp. 185-216.

Capie, Forrest. "The British Tariff and Industrial Protection in the 1930's," *Economic History Review,* Second Series, 31(3), August 1978, pp. 399-409.

Capie, Forrest and Tucker, K.A. "British and New Zealand Trading Relationships, 1841-1852," *Economic History Review,* Second Series, 25(2), May 1972, pp. 293-302.

Cardell, Nicholas S. and Hopkins, Mark M. "The Effect of Milk Intolerance on the Consumption of Milk by Slaves in 1860," *Journal of Interdisciplinary History,* 8(3), Winter 1978, pp. 507-14.

Cargill, Thomas F. "The Long Cycle in Wages and Prices for the United States, 1860-1965: A Spectral Approach (Abstract)," *Western Economic Journal,* 6(4), September 1968, pp. 316.

Carlisle, William T. "Theories of the Great Depression: 1929-1933," in Soltow (ed), *Essays in Economic and Business History,* 1979, pp. 221-32.

Carlos, Ann. "The Origins and Causes of the Canadian Fur Trade Rivalry, 1808-1810." [Working Paper]

Carlson, Leonard A. "The Dawes Act and the Decline of Indian Farming," (Summary of Doctoral Dissertation) *Journal of Economic History,* 38(1), March 1978, pp. 274-6.

Carlson, Leonard A. "Indians, Asians, and Blacks: Racial Minorities in North American Economic History," (Summary of 1978 Research Workshops) *Journal of Economic History,* 39(1), March 1979, pp. 315-7.

Carlson, Leonard A. "Manning the Mills of the New South: Labor Force Recruitment in the Post-Bellum Cotton Textile Industry." [Working Paper]

Carmagnani, Marcello. "Una visione deformata della schiavitu americana: a proposito dello studio di Fogel e Engerman sull'economia della schiavitu," [A Distorted View of American Slavery: the Fogel and Engerman Study on the Slavery Economy], *Quaderni storici,* 31, April 1976, pp. 445-61.

Carstensen, Fred V. "Numbers and Reality: A Critique of Foreign Investment Estimates in Tsarist Russia," in Levy-Leboyer (ed), *La Position Internationale de la France,* 1977, pp. 275- 83.

Carstensen, Fred V. "Trouble on the Auction Block: Interregional Slave Sales and the Reliability of a Linear Equation," *Journal of Interdisciplinary History,* 7(2), Autumn 1977, pp. 315-8.

Caves, Richard E. "Export-Led Growth and the New Economic History," in Bhagwati (ed), *Trade, Balance of Payments and Growth,* 1971, pp. 403-42.

Caves, Richard E.; North, Douglass C. and Price, Jacob M. "Introduction: Exports and Economic Growth," *Explorations in Economic History,* 17(1), January 1980, pp. 1-5.

Cebula, Richard J. and Vedder, Richard K. "An Empirical Analysis of Income Expectations and Interstate Migration," *Review of Regional Studies,* 5(1), Spring 1975, pp. 19-28.

Chambers, Edward J. and Gordon, Donald F. "Primary Products and Economic Growth: An Empirical Measurement," [Translated into Spanish in Journal of the Fundacion de Investigationes Economicas Lationoamericanas] *Journal of Political Economy,* 74(4), August 1966, pp. 315-32.

Chambers, Edward J. and Gordon, Donald F. "Primary Products and Economic Growth: Rejoinder to Dales, McManus, and Watkins," *Journal of Political Economy,* 75(6), December 1967, pp. 881-5.

Chandler, Alfred D., Jr. "Econometrics and Southern History: Comment on Conrad," *Explorations in Entrepreneurial History,* Second Series, 6(1), Fall 1968, pp. 66-74.

Chandler, Alfred D., Jr. "Comment on Econometrics and Southern History," in Andreano (ed), *The New Economic History,* 1970, pp. 143-50.

Chao, Kang; Eckstein, Alexander and Chang, John. "The Economic Development of Manchuria: The Rise of a Frontier Economy," *Journal of Economic History,* 34(1), March 1974, pp. 239-64.

Chao, Kang. "The Growth of a Modern Cotton Textile Industry and the Competition with Handicrafts," in Perkins (ed), *China's Modern Economy in Historical Perspective,* 1975, pp. 167-201.

Chapman, A.L. and Knight, R. *Wages and Salaries in the United Kingdom 1920-1938.* Cambridge: Cambridge University Press, 1953.

Chaudhuri, K.N. "India's International Economy in the Nineteenth Century: An Historical Survey," *Modern Asian Studies,* 2(1), January 1968, pp. 31-50.

Chaudhuri, K.N. "The Economic and Monetary Problem of European Trade with Asia during the Seventeenth and Eighteenth Centuries," *Journal of European Economic History,* 4(2), Fall 1975, pp. 323-58.

Cheetham, Russell J.; Kelley, Allen C. and Williamson, Jeffrey G. *Dualistic Economic Development: Theory and History.* Chicago: University of Chicago Press, 1972.

Chen, Chau-nan. "Flexible Bimetallic Exchange Rates in China, 1650-1850: A Historical Example of Optimum Currency Areas," *Journal of Money, Credit and Banking*, 7(3), August 1975, pp. 359-76.

Chevallier, Dominique. "Western Development and Eastern Crisis in the Mid-Nineteenth Century: Syria Confronted with the European Economy," in Polk and Chambers (ed), *Beginnings of Modernization in the Middle East*, 1968, pp. 205-22.

Choudri, Ehsan and Kochin, Levis A. "The International Transmission of Business Cycles: Evidence from Spain and the Gold Standard Countries in the Great Depression." [Working Paper]

Ciocca, Pierluigi. "L'ipotesi del 'ritardo' dei salari rispetto ai prezzi in periodi di inflazione: alcune considerazioni generali (Part 2)," [The Hypothesis that Wages Lag Prices in Periods of Inflation: Some General Comments] *Bancaria*, 5, May 1969, pp. 572-83.

Ciocca, Pierluigi. "Formazione dell'Italia industriale e storia econometrica," [Industrial Development in Italy and Econometric History] *Rivista internazionale di scienze sociali*, 40, September/December 1969, pp. 539-53.

Ciocca, Pierluigi. "Note sulla politica monetaria italiana 1900-1913," [Notes on Italian Monetary Policy, 1900-1913] in Toniolo, (ed), *Lo sviluppo economico italiano*, 1973, pp. 241-82. Reprinted in Toniolo (ed), *L'economia italiana, 1978, pp. 179-222.*

Ciocca, Pierluigi. "Capitale e fascismo: una introduzione all'esperienza italiana," [Capital and Fascism: An Introduction to the Italian Experience] in *Conflitti sociali e accumulazione capitalistica da Giolitti alla guerra fascista.* Roma: Alfani, 1975, pp. 11-28.

Ciocca, Pierluigi. "Introduzione all'edizione italiana," [Introduction to the Italian Edition] in Cameron et al (eds), *Le banche e lo sviluppo del sistema industriale*, 1975, pp. 9-35.

Ciocca, Pierluigi. "L'Italia nell'economia mondiale, 1922-1940," [Italy in the World Economy, 1922-1940] *Quaderni storici*, 29/30, May/December 1975, pp. 342-76.

Ciocca, Pierluigi. "L'economia italiana nel contesto internazionale," [The Italian Economy in the International Context (under Fascism)] in Ciocca and Toniolo (eds), *L'economia italiana nel periodo fascista*, 1976, pp. 19-50.

Ciocca, Pierluigi and Biscaini Cotula, Anna Maria. "Le strutture finanziarie: aspetti quantitativi di lungo periodo (1870-1970)," [Financial Structures: Long Run Quantitative Features (1870-1970)] in Vicarelli (ed), *Capitale industriale e capitale finanziario*, 1979, pp. 61-136.

Ciocca, Pierluigi and Toniolo, Gianni, eds. *L'economia italiana nel periodo fascista* [The Italian Economy during the Fascist Era]. Bologna: il Mulino, 1976.

Cizakca, Murat. "Price History and the Bursa Silk Industry: A Study in Ottoman Industrial Decline, 1550-1650," *Journal of Economic History*, 40(3), September 1980, pp. 533-50.

Clark, Carolyn and Shearer, Ronald A. "Statistics of Canada's International Gold Flows, 1920-1934," presented at the Eighth Conference on Quantitative Methods in Canadian Economic History, Hamilton, Ontario, October 1976.

Clark, Carolyn and Shearer, Ronald A. "The Suspension of the Gold

Standard, 1928-1931," University of British Columbia, Department of Economics Discussion Paper no. 79-36, 1979.

Clark, Colin. *The Conditions of Economic Progress*. Reprinted in revised Third edition by Macmillan and St.Martin's Press, London and New York, 1957. New York: Macmillan, 1940.

Climo, T.A. and Howells, P.G. "Cause and Counterfactuals," *Economic History Review*, Second Series, 27(3), August 1974, pp. 461-8.

Clough, Shepard B. and Rapp, Richard T. *European Economic History: The Economic Development of Western Civilization*. New York: McGraw-Hill, 1975.

Coats, A.W. *Economic Growth: The Economic and Social Historian's Dilemma*. Nottingham: University of Nottingham Press, 1967.

Coats, A.W. "Political Economy and the Tariff Reform Campaign of 1903," *Journal of Law and Economics*, 11, April 1968, pp. 181-229.

Coats, A.W. "The Interpretation of Mercantilist Economics: Some Historiographical Problems," *History of Political Economy*, 5(2), Fall 1973.

Coats, A.W. "The Historical Context of the 'New' Economic History," *Journal of European Economic History*, 9(1), Spring 1980, pp. 185-207.

Coatsworth, John H. *Crecimiento contra desarrollo, el impacto economico de los ferrocarriles en el Porfiriato* (2 vols) [Growth Against Development: The Economic Impact of Railroads in Portfirian Mexico] [Printed in an English Edition by Northern Illinois University Press, De Kalb, Ill., 1981]. Mexico City: Sep Setentas, 1976.

Coatsworth, John H. "Anotaciones Sobre la Produccion de Alimentos Durante el Porfiriato," *Historia Mexicana*, 26(2), October/December 1976, pp. 167-87.

Coatsworth, John H. "Obstacles to Economic Growth in Nineteenth Century Mexico," *American Historical Review*, 83(1), February 1978, pp. 80-100.

Coatsworth, John H. "Indispensable Railroads in a Backward Economy: The Case of Mexico," *Journal of Economic History*, 39(4), December 1979, pp. 939-60.

Cochran, Thomas C. "Economic History, Old and New," *American Historical Review*, 74(5), June 1969, pp. 1561-72.

Coelho, Philip R.P. "Railroad Social Saving in Nineteenth Century America: Comment on Hunt," *American Economic Review*, 58(1), March 1968, pp. 184-6.

Coelho, Philip R.P. "The Profitability of Colonialism: The British West Indies, 1768-1772," (Summary of Paper Presented at the Meetings of the Western Economic Association) *Western Economic Journal*, 9(3), September 1971, pp. 327.

Coelho, Philip R.P. "The Profitability of Imperialism: The British Experience in the West Indies, 1768-1772," *Explorations in Economic History*, 10(3), Spring 1973, pp. 253-79.

Coelho, Philip R.P. and Ghali, Moheb A. "The End of the North-South Wage Differential," *American Economic Review*, 61(5), December 1971, pp. 932-7.

Coelho, Philip R.P. and Ghali, Moheb A. "The End of the North-South Wage Differential: Reply (to Ladenson)," *American Economic Review*, 63(4), September 1973, pp. 757-62.

Coelho, Philip R.P. and Shepherd, James F. "Differences in Regional

Prices: The United States, 1851-1880," *Journal of Economic History*, 34(3), September 1974, pp. 551-91.

Coelho, Philip R.P. and Shepherd, James F. "Regional Differences in Real Wages: The United States, 1851-1880," *Explorations in Economic History*, 13(2), April 1976, pp. 203-30.

Coelho, Philip R.P. and Shepherd, James F. "The Impact of Regional Differences in Prices and Wages on Economic Growth: The United States in 1890," *Journal of Economic History*, 39(1), March 1979, pp. 69-85.

Coen, Robert M. "Labor Force and Unemployment in the 1920's and 1930's: A Re-examination based on Postwar Experience," *Review of Economics and Statistics*, 55(1), February 1973, pp. 46-55.

Coen, Robert M. "Labor Force and Unemployment in the 1920's and 1930's: A Reply to Lebergott," *Review of Economics and Statistics*, 55(4), November 1973, pp. 527-8.

Cohen, Jon S. "Finance and Industrialization in Italy, 1894-1914," (Summary of Doctoral Dissertation) *Journal of Economic History*, 16(4), December 1966, pp. 577-8.

Cohen, Jon S. "Financing Industrialization in Italy, 1894-1914: The Partial Transformation of a Late-Comer," *Journal of Economic History*, 27(3), September 1967, pp. 363-82.

Cohen, Jon S. "Banking and Industrialization: The Case of Italy, 1861-1914," in Cameron (ed), *Banking and Industrialization*, 1972.

Cohen, Jon S. "The 1927 Revaluation of the Lira: A Study in Political Economy," reprinted as "La rivalutazione della lira del 1927: uno studio sulla politica economica fascista" in Toniolo (ed), *L'economia italiana*, 1978, pp. 313-36. *Economic History Review*, Second Series, 25(4), November 1972, pp. 642-54.

Cohen, Jon S. "Un esame statistico delle opere di bonifica intraprese durante il regime fascista," [A Statistical Examination of Land Reclamation under Fascism] in Toniolo (ed), *Lo sviluppo economico italiano*, 1973, pp. 351-72.

Cohen, Jon S. "The Rate and Structure of Economic Growth in Italy, 1861-1968," in Tannenbaum and Noerther (eds), *Modern Italy*, 1974.

Cohen, Jon S. "Rapporti agricoltura-industria e sviluppo agricolo," [Agricultural-Industrial Relationships and Agricultural Development] in Toniolo and Ciocca (eds), *L'economia italiana nel periodo fascista*, 1976.

Cohen, Jon S. *Finance and Industrialization in Italy, 1894-1914*. New York: Arno Press, 1977.

Cohen, Jon S. "The Achievements of Economic History: The Marxist School," *Journal of Economic History*, 38(1), March 1978, pp. 29-57.

Cohen, Jon S. "Fascism and Agriculture in Italy: Policies and Consequences," *Economic History Review*, Second Series, 32(1), February 1979, pp. 70-87.

Cohen, Jon S. and Weitzman, Martin L. "A Mathematical Model of Enclosures," in Los and Los (eds), *Mathematical Models in Economics*, 1974.

Cohen, Jon S. and Weitzman, Martin L. "Enclosures and Depopulation: A Marxian Analysis," in Parker and Jones (eds), *European Peasants and Their Markets*, 1975, pp. 161-76.

Cohen, Jon S. and Weitzman, Martin L. "A Marxian Model of Enclosures," *Journal of Development Economics*, 1(4), February 1975, pp. 287-336.

Cohen, Jon S. and Weitzman, Martin L. "A Marxian Model of Enclosures:

303

Reply to Fenoaltea," *Journal of Development Economics,* 3(2), July 1976, pp. 199-200.

Cohn, Raymond L. "Location Theory, Regional Growth Theory and Manufacturing in the Antebellum South and Midwest," *Review of Regional Studies,* 8(1), Spring 1978, pp. 20-7.

Cohn, Raymond L. "Local Manufacturing in the Antebellum South and Midwest," *Business History Review,* 54(1), Spring 1980, pp. 80-91.

Cohn, Raymond L. "Antebellum Regional Incomes: Another Look." [Working Paper]

Cole, W.A. "Economic History as a Social Science," in Harte (ed), *The Study of Economic History,* 1971.

Cole, W.A. "Deane and Cole on Industrialization and Population Change in the Eighteenth Century: A Rejoinder to Neal," *Economic History Review,* Second Series, 24(4), November 1971, pp. 648-52.

Cole, W.A. "Eighteenth-Century Economic Growth Revisited," *Explorations in Economic History,* 10(4), Summer 1973, pp. 327-48.

Cole, W.A. "Changes in British Industrial Structure, 1850-1960," in Van der Wee, Vinogradov, and Kotovsky (eds), *Fifth International Congress of Economic History,* 1976, pp. 112-29.

Cole, W.A. "Factors in Demand, 1700-80," in Floud and McCloskey (eds), *The Economic History of Britain since 1700,* 1981, pp. 36-65.

Cole, W.A. and Deane, Phyllis. *British Economic Growth, 1688-1959: Trends and Structure* (Second Edition, 1968). Cambridge: Cambridge University Press, 1962.

Cole, W.A. and Deane, Phyllis. "The Growth of National Incomes," in Habukkuk and Postan (eds), *The Cambridge Economic History of Europe,* 1965, pp. 1-55.

Coleman, D.C. "G.R. Hawke on-What? (Rejoinder on the New Draperies)," *Economic History Review,* Second Series, 24(2), May 1971, pp. 260-1.

Coleman, D.C. "The Model Game. Review Essay of 'Causal Explanation and Model Building in History, Economics, and the New Economic History' by Peter D. McClelland (Ithaca: Cornell University Press, 1975)," *Economic History Review,* Second Series, 30(2), May 1977, pp. 346-51.

Collins, Michael. "Monetary Policy and the Supply of Trade Credit, 1830-44," *Economica,* 45, November 1978, pp. 379-89.

Collins, Michael. "English Bank Deposits before 1844: A Comment on Adie," *Economic History Review,* Second Series, 32(1), February 1979, pp. 114-7.

Conrad, Alfred H. "Income Growth and Structural Change," in Harris (ed), *American Economic History,* 1961, pp. 26-64.

Conrad, Alfred H. "Econometrics and Southern History," *Explorations in Entrepreneurial History,* Second Series, 6(1), Fall 1968, pp. 34-53.

Conrad, Alfred H. and Meyer, John R. "Economic Theory, Statistical Inference, and Economic History," *Journal of Economic History,* 17(4), December 1957, pp. 524-44.

Conrad, Alfred H. and Meyer, John R. "The Economics of Slavery in the Antebellum South," reprinted in Fogel and Engerman (eds), *The Reinterpretation of American Economic History,* 1971, pp. 342-61. *Journal of Political Economy,* 66(2), April 1958, pp. 95-130.

Conrad, Alfred H. and Meyer, John R. "The Economics of Slavery in the Antebellum South: A Reply to Dowd," *Journal of Political Economy,* 66(5), October 1958, pp. 442-3.

Conrad, Alfred H. and Meyer, John R. "The Economics of Slavery in the

Antebellum South: Reply to Moes," *Journal of Political Economy,*
68(2), April 1960, pp. 187-9.

Conrad, Alfred H. and Meyer, John R. *The Economics of Slavery and
Other Essays on the Quantitative Study of Economic History.*
Chicago: Aldine Press, 1964.

Conrad, Alfred H. and Meyer, John R. "Slavery as an Obstacle to
Economic Growth in the United States: A Panel Discussion of Conrad
and Meyer," reprinted in Aitken (ed), *Did Slavery Pay?,* 1971, pp.
270-87. *Journal of Economic History,* December 1967, pp. 518-31.

Contador, Claudio R. and Haddad, Claudio L.S. "Produto Real, Moeda e
Precos: A Experiencia Brasileira no Periodo 1861-1970," [Real
Product, Money and Prices: The Brazilian Experience in the Period
1861-1970] *Revista Brasileira de Estatistica,* 36(143),
July/September 1975, pp. 407-40.

Cooley, Thomas F. and DeCanio, Stephen J. "Rational Expectations in
American Agriculture, 1867-1914," *Review of Economics and
Statistics,* 59(1), February 1977, pp. 9-17.

Cooley, Thomas F.; DeCanio, Stephen J. and Matthews, M. Scott. "Atics:
An Agricultural Time Series-Cross Section Dataset," National Bureau
of Economic Research, 197, August 1977.

Cooney, E.W. "Long Waves in Building in the British Economy of the
Nineteenth Century.," *Economic History Review,* Second Series,
13(2), 1960, pp. 257-69.

Cooper, David C. and Vedder, Richard K. "Nineteenth Century English
and Welsh Geographic Labor Mobility: Some Further Evidence," *Annals
of Regional Science,* 8(2), June 1974, pp. 131-9.

Cooper, Richard N. "Growth and Trade: Some Hypotheses About Long-Term
Trends," *Journal of Economic History,* 24(4), December 1964, pp.
609-28.

Cootner, Paul H. "The Role of Railroads in United States Economic
Growth," *Journal of Economic History,* 23(4), December 1963, pp.
477-521.

Cootner, Paul H. "The Economic Impact of the Railroad Innovation," in
Mazlish (ed), *The Railroad and the Space Program,* 1965, pp. 107-26.

Copeland, Morris A. *Trends in Government Financing.* Princeton:
Princeton University Press for the National Bureau of Economic
Research, 1961.

Coppietiers, E. *English Bank Note Circulation 1694-1954.* The Hague:
Louvain Institute of Economics and Social Research, 1955.

Coppock, D.J. "The Climacteric of the 1890's: A Critical Note,"
Manchester School of Economic and Social Studies, 24, January 1956,
pp. 1-31.

Costanzia, Dario. "Popolazione, attivita edilizia e mercato
immobiliare a Torino tra il 1850 ed il 1880," [Population, Building
Activity, and the Real Estate Market in Turin, 1850-1880] *Storia
Urbana,* 6, September/December 1978, pp. 3-53.

Courchene, Thomas J. "An Analysis of the Canadian Money Supply,
1925-1934," *Journal of Political Economy,* 77(3), May/June 1969, pp.
363-91.

Covino, Renato; Gallo, Giampaolo and Mantovani, Enrico. "L'industria
dall'economia di guerra alla ricostruzione," [Industry from the War
Economy to Reconstruction] in Ciocca and Toniolo (eds), *L'economia
italiana nel periodo fascista,* 1976, pp. 171-270.

Crafts, N.F.R. "Trade as a Handmaiden of Growth: An Alternative View,"

Economic Journal, 83(331), September 1973, pp. 875-84.

Crafts, N.F.R. "Some Aspects of Interactions between Population Growth and Economic Circumstances in the Eighteenth Century," in Minchinton (ed), *Exeter Papers in Economic History,* 1976, pp. 49-64.

Crafts, N.F.R. "English Economic Growth in the Eighteenth Century: A Re-examination of Deane and Cole's Estimates," *Economic History Review,* Second Series, 29(2), May 1976, pp. 226-35.

Crafts, N.F.R. "Determinants of the Rate of Parliamentary Enclosure," *Explorations in Economic History,* 14(3), July 1977, pp. 227-49.

Crafts, N.F.R. "Industrial Revolution in England and France: Some Thoughts on the Question, 'Why Was England First?'," *Economic History Review,* Second Series, 30(3), August 1977, pp. 429-41.

Crafts, N.F.R. "Enclosure and Labor Supply Revisited," *Explorations in Economic History,* 15(2), April 1978, pp. 172-83.

Crafts, N.F.R. "Entrepreneurship and a Probabilistic View of the British Industrial Revolution: A Reply to Rostow," *Economic History Review,* Second Series, 31(4), November 1978, pp. 613-4.

Crafts, N.F.R. "Victorian Britain Did Fail," *Economic History Review,* Second Series, 32(4), November 1979, pp. 533-7.

Crafts, N.F.R. "Income Elasticities of Demand and the Release of Labour by Agriculture during the British Industrial Revolution," *Journal of European Economic History,* 9(1), Spring 1980, pp. 153-68.

Crafts, N.F.R. "National Income Estimates and the British Standard of Living Debate: A Reappraisal of 1801-1831," *Explorations in Economic History,* 17(2), April 1980, pp. 176-88.

Crafts, N.F.R. "The Eighteenth Century: A Survey," in Floud and McCloskey (eds), *The Economic History of Britain since 1700,* 1981, pp. 1-16.

Crafts, N.F.R. and Ireland, N.J. "Family Limitation and the English Demographic Revolution: A Simulation Approach," *Journal of Economic History,* 36(3), September 1976, pp. 598-623.

Craig, R.S. and Floud, Roderick C. "The Evolution of Steam Shipping in Britain in the Nineteenth Century." [Working Paper]

Cranmer, H. Jerome. "Canal Investment, 1815-1860," in Parker (ed), *Trends in the American Economy in the Nineteenth Century,* 1960, pp. 547-64.

Crawcour, E.S. and Yamamura, Kozo. "The Tokugawa Monetary System: 1787-1868," *Economic Development and Cultural Change,* 18(4), (Part 1), July 1970, pp. 489-518.

Creamer, Daniel. "Capital and Output Trends in Manufacturing Industries, 1880-1948," National Bureau of Economic Research, Occasional Paper no. 41, 1954.

Creamer, Daniel; Dobrovolsky, Sergei and Borenstein, Israel. *Capital in Manufacturing and Mining: Its Formation and Financing.* Princeton: Princeton University Press for the National Bureau of Economic Research, 1960.

Crisp, Olga. "Russia, 1860-1914," in Cameron et al (eds), *Banking in the Early Stages of Industrialization,* 1967, pp. 183-238.

Crisp, Olga; Cameron, Rondo E.; Patrick, Hugh T. and Tilly, Richard. *Banking in the Early Stages of Industrialization: A Study in Comparative Economic History.* London and New York: Oxford University Press, 1967.

Cromar, Peter. "The Coal Industry on Tyneside, 1771-1800: Oligopoly and Spatial Change," *Economic Geography*, 53(1), January 1977, pp. 79-94.

Crouzet, Francois. "Essai de Construction d'un Indice Annuel de la Production Industrielle Francaise au XIXe Siecle," [A Tentative Annual Index of French Industrial Production in the 19th Century] reprinted (in English) in Cameron (ed), *Essays in French Economic History*, 1970, pp. 245-78. *Annales: Economies, Societes, Civilisation*, 1, January/February 1970, pp. 56-99.

Crowther, Simeon J. "Urban Growth in the Mid-Atlantic States, 1785-1850," *Journal of Economic History*, 36(3), September 1976, pp. 624-44.

Cummins, J. Gaylord and Freudenberger, Herman. "Health, Work, and Leisure before the Industrial Revolution," *Explorations in Economic History*, 13(1), January 1976, pp. 1-12.

Curran, Christopher and Johnston, Jack. "The Antebellum Money Market and the Economic Impact of the Bank War: A Comment on Sushka," *Journal of Economic History*, 39(2), June 1979, pp. 461-6.

Curran, Christopher and Swanson, Joseph A. "The Fiscal Behavior of Municipal Governments: 1905-1930," *Journal of Urban Economics*, 3(4), October 1976, pp. 344-56.

Cypher, J.M. "The Economic Significance of the Slave Trade in England, 1700-1760," (Abstract of Paper Presented to the 44th Annual Conference of the Western Economic Association) *Western Economic Journal*, 7(3), September 1969, pp. 255.

Daems, Herman and Klep, Paul M.M. "The Effect of Population, Exports and Rents on the Employment Structure of Agrarian Economy," presented at the Workshop on Quantitative Economic History, Leuven, 1974.

Dahlman, Carl J. *The Open Field System and Beyond*. New York: Cambridge University Press, 1979.

Dahlman, Carl J. "An Economic Theory of Serfdom." [Working Paper]

Dales, John H. "Ocean Freight Rates and Economic Development, 1750-1910: Discussion of North," *Journal of Economic History*, 18(4), December 1958, pp. 574-5.

Dales, John H. "Estimates of Canadian Manufacturing Output by Markets, 1870-1915," in Henripin and Asinakopulos (eds), *Canadian Political Science Association Conference on Statistics*, 1964, pp. 61-92.

Dales, John H. *The Protective Tariff in Canada's Development: Eight Essays on Trade and Tariffs when Factors Move with Special Reference to Canadian Protectionism, 1870-1955*. Toronto: University of Toronto Press, 1966.

Dales, John H.; McManus, John C. and Watkins, Melville H. "Primary Products and Economic Growth: A Comment on Chambers and Gordon," *Journal of Political Economy*, 75(6), December 1967, pp. 876-80.

Dalgaard, Bruce R. "South Africa's Impact on Britain's Return to Gold, 1925," (Abstract) in Uselding (ed), *Business and Economic History*, 1978, pp. 138-41.

Danhof, Clarence H. "Farm Gross Product and Gross Investment in the Nineteenth Century: Comment on Towne and Rasmussen," in Parker (ed), *Trends in the American Economy in the Nineteenth Century*, 1960, pp. 312-5.

Danhof, Clarence H. "Discussion of Papers by Lang, DeCanio, Ellsworth, and Lindley Presented to the 31st Annual Meeting of the Economic History Association," *Journal of Economic History*, 32(1), March 1972, pp. 421-2.

Danhof, Clarence H. and Bowman, John D. "An Industrial Income Distribution for New York State, 1865." [Working Paper]

Daniels, Bruce C. "Long Range Trends of Wealth Distribution in 18th Century New England," *Explorations in Economic History*, 11(2), Winter 1974, pp. 123-36.

Daniere, Andre. "Feudal Incomes and Demand Elasticity for Bread in Late 18th Century France," *Journal of Economic History*, 18(3), September 1958, pp. 317-30.

Daniere, Andre. "Feudal Incomes and Demand Elasticity for Bread in Late 18th Century France: A Rejoinder to Landes," *Journal of Economic History*, 18(3), September 1958, pp. 339-41.

Darby, Michael R. "Three and-a-Half Million U.S. Employees Have Been Mislaid: Or, an Explanation of Unemployment, 1934-1941," *Journal of Political Economy*, 84(1), February 1976, pp. 1-16.

David, Paul A. "Economic History Through the Looking-Glass," Summary of Paper Presented at the Meeting of the Econometric Society, Boston, December 1963. *Econometrica*, 32(4), October 1964, pp. 694-6.

David, Paul A. "Building in Ohio between 1837 and 1914: Comment on Gottlieb," in Brady (ed), *Output, Employment and Productivity in the United States After 1800*, 1966, pp. 281-8.

David, Paul A. "The Mechanization of Reaping in the Antebellum Midwest," in Rosovsky (ed), *Industrialization in Two Systems*, 1966, pp. 3-39.

David, Paul A. "New Light on a Statistical Dark Age: U.S. Real Product Growth before 1840," *American Economic Review*, Papers and Proceedings, 57(2), May 1967, pp. 294-306.

David, Paul A. "The Growth of Real Product in the United States before 1840: New Evidence, Controlled Conjectures," *Journal of Economic History*, 27(2), June 1967, pp. 151-97.

David, Paul A. "Transport Innovation and Economic Growth: Professor Fogel On and Off the Rails," *Economic History Review*, Second Series, 22(3), December 1969, pp. 506-25.

David, Paul A. "Learning by Doing and Tariff Protection: A Reconsideration of the Case of the Antebellum Cotton Textile Industry," *Journal of Economic History*, 30(3), September 1970, pp. 521-601.

David, Paul A. "Labour Productivity in English Agriculture, 1850-1914: Some Quantitative Evidence on Regional Differences," *Economic History Review*, Second Series, 23(3), December 1970, pp. 504-14.

David, Paul A. "The Future of Econometric History: Comments on Wright," in Intrilligator (ed), *Frontiers of Quantitative Economics*, 1971, pp. 459-67.

David, Paul A. "The Landscape and the Machine: Technical Interrelatedness, Land Tenure and the Mechanization of the Corn Harvest in Victorian Britain," in McCloskey (ed), *Essays on a Mature Economy*, 1971, pp. 145-204.

David, Paul A. "The Use and Abuse of Prior Information in Econometric

History: A Rejoinder to Professor Williamson on the Antebellum Cotton Textile Industry," *Journal of Economic History*, 32(3), September 1972, pp. 706-27.

David, Paul A. "The 'Horndal Effect' in Lowell, 1834-1856: A Short-Run Learning Curve for Integrated Cotton Textile Mills," *Explorations in Economic History*, 10(2), Winter 1973, pp. 131-50.

David, Paul A. "Fortune, Risk and the Microeconomics of Migration," in David and Reder (eds), *Households and Nations in Economic Growth*, 1974.

David, Paul A. *Technical Choice, Innovation and Economic Growth: Essays on American and British Experience in the Nineteenth Century.* Cambridge and New York: Cambridge University Press, 1975.

David, Paul A. "Invention and Accumulation in America's Economic Growth: A Nineteenth Century Parable," in Brunner and Meltzer (eds), *International Organization, National Policies and Economic Development*, 1977.

David, Paul A. "American Economic Growth Before 1840: Comments on Papers by Anderson, Haeger, Kulikoff, and Lindstrom Presented to the 38th Annual Meeting of the Economic History Association," *Journal of Economic History*, 39(1), March 1979, pp. 303-10.

David, Paul A. "Behavior of British Investment, 1860-1869," Center for Research in Economic Growth: Research Memo. 17 (Stanford University), 1961.

David, Paul A. "Child-Care in the Slave Quarters: A Critical Note on Some Uses of Demography in 'Time on the Cross'." [Working Paper]

David, Paul A. "Estimates of the U.S. Labor Force, Industrial and Regional Distribution, 1800-1840." [Working Paper]

David, Paul A. "Estimates of Annual Constant Dollar Gross Output and Real Net Output for Chicago Manufacturing Industries," Stanford University Center for Research in Economic Growth, Memoranda Series no. 18, July 1962.

David, Paul A. "Factories at the Prairie's Edge: A Study of Industrialization in Chicago, 1848-1893." [Working Paper]

David, Paul A. "Locating a Switch-Over in the Structural Relationship Between Variations in the Manufacturing Sector's Terms of Trade with Agriculture and the volume of Industrial Output in Chicago: A Statistical Procedure." [Working Paper]

David, Paul A. and Abramovitz, Moses. "Economic Growth in America: Historical Parables and Realities," *De Economist*, 121(3), 1973, pp. 251-72.

David, Paul A. and Abramovitz, Moses. "Reinterpreting Economic Growth: Parables and Realities," *American Economic Review*, Papers and Proceedings, 63(2), May 1973, pp. 428-39.

David, Paul A.; Gutman, Herbert; Sutch, Richard C.; Temin, Peter and Wright, Gavin. *Reckoning with Slavery: A Critical Study in the Quantitative History of American Negro Slavery.* New York: Oxford University Press, 1976.

David, Paul A.; Gutman, Herbert G.; Sutch, Richard C.; Temin, Peter and Wright, Gavin. "Time on the Cross and the Burden of Quantitative History," in David, et al (eds), *Reckoning with Slavery*, 1976, pp. 339-57.

David, Paul A. and Reder, Melvyn W., eds. *Nations and Households in Economic Growth: Essays in Honor of Moses Abramovitz.* New York: Academic Press, 1974.

309

David, Paul A. and Sanderson, Warren C. "The Effectiveness of Nineteenth Century Contraceptive Practices: An Application of Microdemographic Modelling Approaches," in International Economic History Association (ed), *Proceedings of the Seventh International Economic History Congress,* 1978, pp. 60-70.

David, Paul A. and Sanderson, Warren C. "Contraceptive Technology and Family Limiting Behavior: Towards a Quantitative History of the Diffusion of Contraceptive Practices in America, 1850-1920." [Working Paper]

David, Paul A. and Sanderson, Warren C. "How Did They Do It?: Strategies of Marital Fertility Control among the Urban Middle Class in Victorian America," Stanford Project on the History of Fertility Control Working Paper no. 6, November 1979.

David, Paul A. and Solar, Peter. "A Bicentenary Contribution to the History of the Cost of Living in America," in Uselding (ed), *Research in Economic History,* 1977, pp. 1-80.

David, Paul A. and Temin, Peter. "Slavery: The Progressive Institution? Review Essay of 'Time on the Cross (2 vols)'," by Robert W. Fogel and Stanley L. Engerman, (Boston: Little, Brown, 1974), reprinted in David, et al (eds), *Reckoning with Slavery,* 1976, pp. 165-230. *Journal of Economic History,* 34(3), September 1974, pp. 739-83.

David, Paul A. and Temin, Peter. "Capitalist Masters, Bourgeois Slaves. Review Essay of 'Time on the Cross (2 vols)' by Robert W. Fogel and Stanley L. Engerman (Boston: Little, Brown, 1974)," reprinted in David, et al (eds), *Reckoning with Slavery,* 1976, pp. 33-54. *Journal of Interdisciplinary History,* 5(3), Winter 1975, pp. 445-57.

David, Paul A. and Temin, Peter. "Explaining the Relative Efficiency of Slave Agriculture in the Antebellum South: A Comment (on Fogel and Engerman)," *American Economic Review,* 69(1), March 1979, pp. 213-8.

David, Paul A. and van de Klundert, Th. "Biased Efficiency Growth and Capital-Labor Substitution in the U.S., 1899-1960," *American Economic Review,* 55(3), June 1965, pp. 357-94.

Davis, Lance E. "Sources of Industrial Finance: The American Textile Industry, A Case Study," reprinted in Hughes (ed), *Purdue Faculty Papers in Economic History,* 1967, pp. 625-42. *Explorations in Enterpreneurial History,* 9(4), April 1957, pp. 189-203.

Davis, Lance E. "Stock Ownership in the Early New England Textile Industry," reprinted in Hughes (ed), *Purdue Faculty Papers in Economic History,* 1967, pp. 563-80. *Business History Review,* 32(2), Summer 1958, pp. 204-22.

Davis, Lance E. "The New England Textile Mills and the Capital Markets: A Study of Industrial Borrowing, 1840-1860," reprinted in Hughes (ed), *Purdue Faculty Papers in Economic History,* 1967, pp. 596-624. *Journal of Economic History,* 20(1), March 1960, pp. 1-30.

Davis, Lance E. "Mrs. Vatter on Industrial Borrowing: A Reply," *Journal of Economic History,* 21(2), June 1961, pp. 222-6.

Davis, Lance E. "Capital Immobilities and Finance Capitalism: A Study of Economic Evolution in the United States, 1820-1920," reprinted in Hughes (ed), *Purdue Faculty Papers in Economic History,* 1967, pp. 581-95. *Explorations in Enterpreneurial History,* Second Series, 1(1), Fall 1963, pp. 88-105.

Davis, Lance E. *The Growth of Industrial Enterprise.* Chicago: Scott Foresman, 1964.

Davis, Lance E. "Capital Formation in the United States During the Early Period of Industrialization: Comment on North," *Second International Conference of Economic History, Aix-en-Provence, 1962,* vol. 2. Paris and The Hague: Mouton, 1965, pp. 657-71.

Davis, Lance E. "The Investment Market, 1870-1914: The Evolution of a National Market," reprinted in Hughes (ed), *Purdue Faculty Papers in Economic History,* 1967, pp. 119-60. *Journal of Economic History,* 25(3), September 1965, pp. 355-99.

Davis, Lance E. "The Capital Markets and Industrial Concentration: The U.S. and U.K., a Comparative Study," reprinted in Hughes (ed), *Purdue Faculty Papers in Economic History,* 1967, pp. 663-82. *Economic History Review,* Second Series, 19(2), August 1966, pp. 255-72.

Davis, Lance E. "Professor Fogel and the New Economic History," *Economic History Review,* Second Series, 19(3), December 1966, pp. 657-63.

Davis, Lance E. "Capital Immobilities, Institutional Adaptation, and Financial Development: The United States and England, An International Comparison," in Giersch, Herbert, and Sauermann (eds), *Quantitative Aspects of Economic History,* 1968, pp. 14-34.

Davis, Lance E. "'And It Will Never Be Literature' - The New Economic History: A Critique," reprinted in Swierenga (ed), *Quantification in American History,* 1970, pp. 274-87. *Explorations in Enterpreneurial History,* Second Series, 6(1), Fall 1968, pp. 75-92.

Davis, Lance E. "Five Neophytes in Search of a Mentor: Discussion of Dissertations Presented at the 28th Annual Meeting of the Economic History Association," *Journal of Economic History,* 29(1), March 1969, pp. 183-8.

Davis, Lance E. "Capital Mobility and American Growth," in Robert W. Fogel and Engerman (eds), *The Reinterpretation of American Economic History,* 1971, pp. 285-300.

Davis, Lance E. "Specification, Identification, and Analysis in Economic History," in Taylor and Ellsworth (eds), *Approaches to American Economic History,* 1971, pp. 106-20.

Davis, Lance E. "Banks and Their Economic Effects," in Davis, Easterlin, and Parker (eds), *American Economic Growth,* 1972, pp. 340-67.

Davis, Lance E. "Capital and Growth," in Davis, Easterlin, and Parker (eds), *American Economic Growth,* 1972, pp. 280-310.

Davis, Lance E. "Savings Sources and Utilization," in Davis, Easterlin, and Parker (eds), *American Economic Growth,* 1972, pp. 311-39.

Davis, Lance E. "Self-Regulation in Baseball, 1909-1972: Cartel Leadership, Strategy, and Tactics," in Noll (ed), *Economic Policy Aspects of Professional Sports,* 1974.

Davis, Lance E. "The Evolution of the American Capital Market, 1860-1940: A Case Study in Institutional Change," in Silber (ed), *Financial Innovation,* 1975.

Davis, Lance E. "Forgotten Men of Money, Private Bankers in Early U.S. History: Comment on Sylla," *Journal of Economic History,* 36(1), March 1976, pp. 189-93.

Davis, Lance E. "Savings and Investment," in Porter (ed), *Encyclopedia of American Economic History,* 1980, pp. 183-201.

Davis, Lance E. "It's a Long, Long Road to Tipperary, or Reflections on Organized Violence, Protection Rates, and Related Topics: The New Political History," *Journal of Economic History,* 40(1), March 1980, pp. 1-16.

Davis, Lance E. "Capital Immobilities and Economic Growth," presented at the First International Economic History Conference, Rome, 1965.

Davis, Lance E. "Monopolies, Speculators, Causal Models, Quantitative Evidence, and American Economic Growth," presented at the Meetings of the Organization of American Historians, April 1967.

Davis, Lance E. "One Potato Two Potato Sweet Potato Pie: Clio Looks at Slavery and the South," presented at the MSSB-University of Rochester Conference Time on the Cross: A First Appraisal, October 1974.

Davis, Lance E. "Directions of Change in American Capitalism," presented at the First Annual International Seminar on Societies in Transition, Malente, Federal Republic of Germany, July 1978.

Davis, Lance E. "Some Aspects of the Economic Development of Great Britain and the U.S.A., 1820-1914," presented at the British American Studies Association Meetings, Leeds, 1965.

Davis, Lance E. "The New Economic History Re-examined," presented at the Meetings of the Pacific Historical Association, Palo Alto, California, August 1967.

Davis, Lance E.; Easterlin, Richard A. and Parker, William N., eds. *American Economic Growth: An Economist's History of the United States.* New York: Harper & Row, 1972.

Davis, Lance E. and Gallman, Robert E. "The Share of Savings and Investment in Gross National Product during the Nineteenth Century in the United States of America," Fourth International Conference of Economic History, Bloomington, 1968. Paris and The Hague: Mouton, 1973, pp. 437-66.

Davis, Lance E. and Gallman, Robert E. "Capital Formation in the United States during the 19th Century," in Mathias and Postan (eds), *The Cambridge Economic History of Europe,* 1978.

Davis, Lance E. and Hughes, Jonathan R.T. "A Dollar-Sterling Exchange, 1803-1895," reprinted in Hughes (ed), *Purdue Faculty Papers in Economic History,* 1967, pp. 235-68. *Economic History Review,* Second Series, 13(1), August 1960, pp. 52-78.

Davis, Lance E.; Hughes, Jonathan R.T. and Reiter, Stanley. "Aspects of Quantitative Research in Economic History," reprinted in Hughes (ed), *Purdue Faculty Papers in Economic History,* 1967, pp. 3-10. *Journal of Economic History,* 20(4), December 1960, pp. 539-47.

Davis, Lance E.; Hughes, Jonathan R.T. and McDougall, Duncan. *American Economic History: The Development of a National Economy.* Homewood, Ill.: Richard D. Irwin, 1961.

Davis, Lance E. and Huttenback, Robert A. "Public Expenditure and Private Profit: Budgetary Decision in the British Empire, 1860-1912," *American Economic Review,* Papers and Proceedings, 67(1), February 1977, pp. 282-7.

Davis, Lance E. and Huttenback, Robert A. "Aspects of Late-Nineteenth Century Imperialism," presented at the Annual Meetings of the Organization of American Historians, New Orleans, April 1979.

Davis, Lance E. and Huttenback, Robert A. "British Imperialism and

Military Expenditure," presented at the Anglo-American Conference of Historians, London, July 1978.

Davis, Lance E. and Huttenback, Robert A. "Social Choice and Public Welfare: British and Colonial Expenditure in the Late Nineteenth Century," presented at the 14th International Congress of Historical Societies, San Francisco, August 1975.

Davis, Lance E. and Legler, John. "The Government in the American Economy, 1815-1902: A Quantitative Study," *Journal of Economic History*, 26(4), December 1966, pp. 514-52.

Davis, Lance E. and Legler, John B. "The Regional Impact of the Federal Budget, 1815-1900: A Preliminary Survey (Summary)," *Third International Conference of Economic History, Munich, 1965*, part 1. Paris and The Hague: Mouton, 1968, pp. 753-9.

Davis, Lance E. and Legler, J. "The Regional Impact of the Federal Budget, 1815-1900," presented at the Third International Economic History Conference, Munich, 1965.

Davis, Lance E. and North, Douglass C. *Institutional Change and American Economic Growth.* Cambridge: Cambridge University Press, 1971.

Davis, Lance E. and Payne, Peter L. "From Benevolence to Business: The Story of Two Savings Banks," reprinted in Hughes (ed), *Purdue Faculty Papers in Economic History, 1967*, pp. 643-62. *Business History Review*, 32(4) Winter 1958, pp. 386-406.

Davis, Lance E. and Stettler, H. Louis, III. "The New England Textile Industry, 1825-60: Reply to McGouldrick," in Brady (ed), *Output, Employment, and Productivity in the United States After 1800*, 1966, pp. 240-2.

Davis, Ronald L.F. "Southern Merchants and the Origins of Sharecropping: A Case Study," in Soltow (ed), *Essays in Economic and Business History*, 1979.

Davis, Thomas E. "Eight Decades of Inflation in Chile, 1879-1959: A Political Interpretation," *Journal of Political Economy*, 71(4), August 1963, pp. 389-97.

Davis, Thomas E. and Ballestoros, Marto A. "The Growth of Output and Employment in Basic Sectors of the Chilean Economy, 1908-1957," *Economic Development and Cultural Change*, 11(2), January 1963, pp. 152-76.

De Bever, Leo J. and Williamson, Jeffrey G. "Saving, Accumulation and Modern Economic Growth: The Contemporary Relevance of Japanese History," *Journal of Japanese Studies*, 4(1), Winter 1978, pp. 125-67.

De Brabander, G.L. "The Distribution of Economic Activities Over Industries and Regions in Belgium, 1846-1910: A Study of the Data," [In Dutch with English Summary], *Bijdragen tot de Geschiedenis*, 61, 1978, pp. 97-184.

De Brabander, G.L. "De regionaal-industriele specialisatie en haar effect op Ruimtelijke Verschillen in Economische groei in Belgie, van 1846 tot 1970," [Regional-Industrial Specialization and its Effect on Spatial Differences in Economic Growth in Belgium from 1846 to 1970] Unpublished Ph.D. Dissertation, University of Antwerp, 1979.

De Brabander, G.L. "The 19th Century Belgian General Censuses as Sources for the Quantification of Regional Industrial Patterns of Specialization," presented at the Workshop on Quantitative Economic

History, Centrum voor Economische Studien, Paper #7502, 1975.
De Meere, J.M.M. "Inkomensgroei en -ongelijkheid te Amsterdam 1877-1940," [Growth and Inequality in Amsterdam, 1877-1940], *Tijdschrift voor Sociale Geschiedenis*, 13, March 1979, pp. 3-47.
De Meere, J.M.M. and Blok, L. "Welstand, Ongelijkheid in Welstand en Censuskiesrecht in Nederland Omstreeks Het Midden van de 19de Eeuw," [Prosperity, Wealth Inequality, and Franchise in the Netherlands in the Middle of the Nineteenth Century] *Economisch-en Sociaal-Historisch Jaarbook*, 41, 1978, pp. 175-293.
De Mello, Pedro C. "Aspectos Economicos da Organizacao do Trabalho da Economia Cafeeira do Rio de Janeiro, 1850-88," [Economic Aspects of the Organization of Labor in the Coffee Economy of Rio de Janeiro, 1850-88] *Revista Brasileira de Economia*, 32(1), January/March 1978, pp. 19-67.
De Mello, Pedro C. and Slenes, Robert W. "Analise Economica da Escravidao no Brasil," [Economic Analysis of Slavery in Brazil] in Neuhaus (ed), *A Economia Brasileira*, 1979, pp. 89-122.
De Vries, Jan. "The Role of the Rural Sector in the Development of the Dutch Economy: 1500-1700," (Summary of Doctoral Dissertation) *Journal of Economic History*, 31(1), March 1971, pp. 266-8.
De Vries, Jan. "Conditions of Agricultural Growth: Boserup as Economics and History," *Peasant Studies Newsletter*, 1(2), April 1972, pp. 45-50.
De Vries, Jan. *The Dutch Rural Economy in the Golden Age, 1500-1700*. New Haven: Yale University Press, 1974.
De Vries, Jan. "Peasant Demand Patterns and Economic Development: Friesland, 1550-1750," in Parker and Jones (eds), *European Peasants and Their Markets*, 1975, pp. 205-66.
De Vries, Jan. "Comments on Dissertations Presented to the 35th Annual Meeting of the Economic History Association," *Journal of Economic History*, 36(1), March 1976, pp. 297-300.
De Vries, Jan. "An Inquiry into the Behaviour of Wages in the Dutch Republic and Southern Netherlands, 1580-1800," *Acta Historiae Neerlandica*, 10, 1978, pp. 79-97.
De Vries, Jan. "Barges and Capitalism: Passenger Transportation in the Dutch Economy, 1632-1839," *A.A.G. Bijdragen*, 21, 1978, pp. 333-98.
De Vries, Jan. "Is There an Economics of Decline?," (Summary of 1977 Research Workshop) *Journal of Economic History*, 38(1), March 1978, pp. 256-8.
Deane, Phyllis. *The Measurement of Colonial National Incomes: An Experiment*. National Institute of Economic and Social Research Occasional Paper Series 12. Cambridge: Cambridge University Press, 1948.
Deane, Phyllis. *Colonial Social Accounting*. National Institute of Economic and Social Research, Economic and Social Studies Series 11. Cambridge: Cambridge University Press, 1953.
Deane, Phyllis. "The Implications of Early National Income Estimates for the Measurement of Long-Term Economic Growth in the United Kingdom," *Economic Development and Cultural Change*, 4(1), October 1955, pp. 3-38.
Deane, Phyllis. "Contemporary Estimates of National Income in the First Half of the Nineteenth Century," *Economic History Review*, Second Series, 8(3), 1956, pp. 339-54.
Deane, Phyllis. "The Industrial Revolution and Economic Growth: The

Evidence of Early British National Income Estimates," *Economic Development and Cultural Change*, 5(2), January 1957, pp. 159-74.

Deane, Phyllis. "The Output of the British Woollen Industry in the Eighteenth Century," *Journal of Economic History*, 17(2), June 1957, pp. 207-23.

Deane, Phyllis. "Capital Formation in Britain Before the Railway Age," *Economic Development and Cultural Change*, 9(3), April 1961, pp. 352-68.

Deane, Phyllis. "The Long Term Trends in World Economic Growth," *Malayan Economic Review*, 6(2), October 1961, pp. 14-26.

Deane, Phyllis. "Long-Term Trends in Capital Formation and Financing. Review Essay of 'Capital in the American Economy: Its Formation and Financing since 1870' by Simon S. Kuznets (Princeton: Princeton University Press for the NBER, 1962)," *Economic Journal*, 72(288), December 1962, pp. 926-30.

Deane, Phyllis. "New Estimates of Gross National Product for the United Kingdom, 1830-1914," *Review of Income and Wealth*, 14(2), June 1968, pp. 95-112.

Deane, Phyllis. "The Role of Capital in the Industrial Revolution," *Explorations in Economic History*, 10(4), Summer 1973, pp. 349-64.

Deane, Phyllis. "The Relevance of New Trends in Economic History to the Information Needs of Research Workers," in Perlman (ed), *The Organization and Retrieval of Economic Knowledge*, 1977.

Deane, Phyllis. "History of Inflation," in Heathfield (ed), *Perspectives on Inflation*, 1979.

Deane, Phyllis and Cole, W.A. *British Economic Growth, 1688-1959: Trends and Structure* (Second Edition, 1968). Cambridge: Cambridge University Press, 1962.

Deane, Phyllis and Cole, W.A. "The Growth of National Incomes," in Habukkuk and Postan (eds), *The Cambridge Economic History of Europe*, 1965, pp. 1-55.

Deane, Phyllis and Habakkuk, H.J. "The Take-Off in Britain," in Rostow (ed), *The Economics of Take-Off into Sustained Growth*, 1963, pp. 63-82.

Delivanis, D.J. "Mr. Rosenberg on Capital Imports and Growth: Comment," *Economic Journal*, 71(284), December 1961, pp. 852-3.

Denison, Edward F. "Factor Shares, 1850-1910: Comment on Budd," in Parker (ed), *Trends in the American Economy in the Nineteenth Century*, 1960, pp. 399-403.

Denison, Edward F. *The Sources of Economic Growth in the United States and the Alternatives Before Us*. New York: Committee on Economic Development, 1962.

Denison, Edward F. *Accounting for United States Economic Growth, 1929-1969*. Washington, D.C.: The Brookings Institution, 1974.

Dennen, R. Taylor. "Cattle Trailing in the Nineteenth Century: A Note on Galenson," *Journal of Economic History*, 35(2), June 1975, pp. 458-60.

Dennen, R. Taylor. "Cattlemen's Associations and Property Rights in Land in the American West," *Explorations in Economic History*, 13(4), October 1976, pp. 423-36.

Denslow, David, Jr., and Schulze, David. "Optimal Replacement of Capital Goods in Early New England and British Textile Firms: A Comment (on Williamson)," *Journal of Political Economy*, 82(3), May/June 1974, pp. 631-7.

315

Deprey, Paul; Hum, Derek and Spencer, Barbara. "Spectral Analysis and the Study of Seasonal Fluctuations in Historical Demography," *Journal of European Economic History,* 5(1), Spring 1976, pp. 171-90.

Dernberger, Robert F. "The Role of the Foreigner in China's Economic Development, 1840-1949," in Perkins (ed), *China's Modern Economy in Historical Perspective,* 1975, pp. 19-47.

Desai, Ashok V. *Real Wages in Germany, 1871-1913.* Oxford: Oxford University Press, 1968.

Desai, Meghnad. "Some Issues in Econometric History," *Economic History Review,* Second Series, 21(1), April 1968, pp. 1-16.

Desai, Meghnad. "The Consolation of Slavery. Review Essay of 'Time on the Cross (2 vols)' by Robert W. Fogel and Stanley L. Engerman (Boston: Little, Brown, 1974)," *Economic History Review,* Second Series, 29(3), August 1976, pp. 491-503.

Desai, Meghnad. "Malthusian Crisis in Medieval England? A Critique of the Postan-Titow Hypothesis," presented at the Social Science Research Council Cliometrics Conference, University of Warwick, January 1978.

Devoretz, Donald and Reed, Clyde G. "Evidence from the Skilled-Unskilled Canadian Wage Index: 1930-1972." [Working Paper]

DeCanio, Stephen J. "Agricultural Production, Supply and Institutions in the Post-Civil War South," (Summary of Doctoral Dissertation) *Journal of Economic History,* 32(1), March 1972, pp. 396-8.

DeCanio, Stephen J. "Cotton 'Overproduction' in Late Nineteenth-Century Southern Agriculture," *Journal of Economic History,* 33(3), September 1973, pp. 608-33.

DeCanio, Stephen J. *Agriculture in the Postbellum South: The Economics of Production and Supply.* Cambridge: M.I.T. Press, 1974.

DeCanio, Stephen J. "Productivity and Income Distribution in the Postbellum South," *Journal of Economic History,* 34(2), June 1974, pp. 422-46.

DeCanio, Stephen J. "A New Economic History of Slavery. Review Essay of 'Time on the Cross (2 vols)' by Robert W. Fogel and Stanley L. Engerman (Boston: Little, Brown, 1974)," *Reviews in American History,* 2(4), December 1974, pp. 474-87.

DeCanio, Stephen J. "The Economics of Political Change: Comments on Papers by Reid, Metzer, and Berkowitz/McQuaid Presented to the 37th Annual Meeting of the Economic History Association," *Journal of Economic History,* 38(1), March 1978, pp. 143-7.

DeCanio, Stephen J. "Accumulation and Discrimination in the Postbellum South," *Explorations in Economic History,* 16(2), April 1979, pp. 182-206.

DeCanio, Stephen J. "Economic Losses from Forecasting Error in Agriculture," *Journal of Political Economy,* 88(2), April 1980, pp. 234-58.

DeCanio, Stephen J. "Business Confidence and the Causes of the Great Depression." [Working Paper]

DeCanio, Stephen J. "New Directions and Old Questions in the Economic History of the Postbellum South, Time on the Cross: A First Appraisal," presented at the MSSB-University of Rochester Conference Time on the Cross: A First Appraisal, October 1974.

DeCanio, Stephen J. "The Inadequacy of Economic Explanations of Major Historical Events." [Working Paper]

DeCanio, Stephen J. and Cooley, Thomas F. "Rational Expectations in American Agriculture, 1867-1914," *Review of Economics and Statistics*, 59(1), February 1977, pp. 9-17.

DeCanio, Stephen J.; Cooley, Thomas F. and Matthews, M. Scott. "Atics: An Agricultural Time Series-Cross Section Dataset," National Bureau of Economic Research, no. 197, August 1977.

DeCanio, Stephen J. and Mokyr, Joel. "Inflation and the Wage Lag during the American Civil War," *Explorations in Economic History*, 14(4), October 1977, pp. 311-36.

DeCanio, Stephen and Parker, William N. "Agricultural Output and Productivity," (Summary of 1976 Research Workshop) *Journal of Economic History*, 37(1), March 1977, pp. 230-1.

DeCanio, Stephen J. and Parker, William N. "Two Hidden Sources of Productivity Growth in American Agriculture, 1860-1930," presented at the International Economic History Congress, Edinburgh, August 1978.

DeCanio, Stephen J. and Trojanowski, Joseph. "Kanatics: A Kansas Agricultural Time Series-Cross Section Dataset," Inter-University Consortium for Political and Social Research, Ann Arbor, Paper no. 41, November 1977.

Diamond, Arthur M., Jr. "Age and the Acceptance of Cliometrics: A Note," *Journal of Economic History*, 40(4), December 1980, pp. 838-41.

Diaz Alejandro, Carlos F. "The Argentine Tariff, 1906-1940," *Oxford Economic Papers*, 19(1), March 1967, pp. 75-98.

Dick, Trevor J.O. "Railroad Inventions' Investment: The United States, 1870-1950," (Summary of Doctoral Dissertation), *Journal of Economic History*, 34(1), March 1974, pp. 275-8.

Dick, Trevor J.O. "United States Railroad Inventions' Investment since 1870," *Explorations in Economic History*, 11(3), Spring 1974, pp. 249-70.

Dick, Trevor J.O. "Frontiers in Canadian Economic History," (Summary of 1975 Research Workshop), *Journal of Economic History*, 36(1), March 1976, pp. 34-9.

Dick, Trevor J.O. *An Economic Theory of Technological Change: The Case of Patents and United States Railroads.* New York: Arno Press, 1978.

Dick, Trevor J.O. *Economic History of Canada: A Guide to Information Sources.* Detroit: Gale Research, 1978.

Dick, Trevor J.O. "Productivity Change and Grain Farm Practice on the Canadian Prairie, 1900-1930," *Journal of Economic History*, 40(1), March 1980, pp. 105-10.

Dick, Trevor J.O. "Canadian Wheat Production and Trade, 1896-1930," *Explorations in Economic History*, 17(3), July 1980, pp. 275-302.

Dick, Trevor J.O. "Approaches to Tariff Formation: The Case of Late Nineteenth Century Canadian Tariffs." [Working Paper]

Dick, Trevor J.O. "Canadian Newsprint: National Design or North American Economy?." [Working Paper]

Dick, Trevor J.O. "Changing Patterns of Grain Farm Practice on the Canadian Prairie, 1885-1930." [Working Paper]

Dick, Trevor J.O. "Economy, Ideology, and the Growth of Government Spending in Canada Since 1867." [Working Paper]

Dick, Trevor J.O. "Growth and Canadian Welfare: A History of the Canadian Economy." [Working Paper]

Dick, Trevor J.O. "Output, Prices, and Real Wages: The Canadian Experience, 1870-1914." [Working Paper]

Dick, Trevor J.O. "Property Rights, Forest Wealth, and Nineteenth Century Economic Growth in Central Canada." [Working Paper]

Dick, Trevor J.O. "The Canadian Balance of Payments, 1900-1913: Mechanisms of Adjustment." [Working Paper]

Dick, Trevor J.O. "The Specification Problem in Theories of Resource Determined Economic Growth." [Working Paper]

Dickler, Robert A. "Organization and Change in Productivity in Eastern Prussia," in Parker and Jones (eds), *European Peasants and Their Markets*, 1975, pp. 269-92.

Dittrich, Scott R. and Myers, Ramon H. "Resource Allocation in Traditional Agriculture: Republican China, 1937-1940," *Journal of Political Economy*, 79(4), July/August 1971, pp. 887-96.

Doane, David P. "Regional Cost Differentials and Textile Location: A Statistical Analysis," *Explorations in Economic History*, 9(1), Fall 1971, pp. 3-34.

Dobrovolsky, Sergei; Creamer, Daniel and Borenstein, Israel. *Capital in Manufacturing and Mining: Its Formation and Financing*. Princeton: Princeton University Press for the National Bureau of Economic Research, 1960.

Dodd, Donald B. and Dodd, Wynelle S. *Historical Statistics of the United States, 1790-1970* (2 vols) (vol. 1: The South, 1790-1970; vol. 2: The Midwest, 1790-1970). University: University of Alabama Press, 1973.

Dodd, Wynelle S. and Dodd, Donald B. *Historical Statistics of the United States, 1790-1970* (2 vols) (vol. 1: The South, 1790-1970; vol. 2: The Midwest, 1790-1970). University: University of Alabama Press, 1973.

Domar, Evsey D. "The Causes of Slavery Or Serfdom: A Hypothesis," *Journal of Economic History*, 30(1), March 1970, pp. 18-32.

Domar, Evsey D. "The Profitability of Russian Serfdom Prior to its Abolition." [Working Paper]

Doughty, Robert A. "Industrial Prices and Inflation in Southern England, 1401-1640," *Explorations in Economic History*, 12(2), April 1975, pp. 177-92.

Dowd, Douglas F. "The Economics of Slavery in the Antebellum South: A Comment on Conrad and Meyer," *Journal of Political Economy*, 66(5), October 1958, pp. 440-2.

Dowd, Douglas F. "Slavery as an Obstacle to Economic Growth in the United States: A Panel Discussion of Conrad and Meyer," reprinted in Aitken (ed), *Did Slavery Pay?*, 1971, pp. 287-95. *Journal of Economic History*, 27(4), December, 1967, pp. 531-8.

Dowie, Jack A. "Inverse Relations of the Australian and New Zealand Economies, 1871-1900," *Australian Economic Papers*, 2(2), December 1963, pp. 151-79.

Dowie, Jack A. "As If or Not As If: The Economic Historian as Hamlet," *Australian Economic History Review*, 7, March 1967, pp. 69-85.

Dowie, Jack A. "Inverse Relations of the Australian and New Zealand Economies, 1871-1900: Reply to von Tunzelmann," *Australian Economic Papers*, 5(3), June 1967, pp. 128-9.

Dowie, Jack A. "Growth in the Inter-war Period: Some More Arithmetic," *Economic History Review*, Second Series, 21(1), April 1968, pp. 93-112.

318

Dowie, Jack A. and Butlin, Noel G. "Estimates of Australian Workforce and Employment, 1861-1961," (Erratum: see this Review, 10(1), March 1970), for corrections of this article) *Australian Economic History Review*, 9(2), September 1969, pp. 138-55.

Dowie, Jack A. "1919-20 is in Need of Attention," *Economic History Review*, Second Series, 28(3), August 1975, pp. 429-50.

Dowling, J. Malcolm and Poulson, Barry W. "Background Conditions and the Spectral Analytic Test of the Long Swings Hypothesis," *Explorations in Economic History*, 8(3), Spring 1971, pp. 343-52.

Eagly, Robert V. "Monetary Policy and Politics in Mid-Eighteenth Century Sweden," *Journal of Economic History*, 29(4), December 1969, pp. 739-57.

Eagly, Robert V. "Monetary Policy and Politics in Mid-Eighteenth-Century Sweden: A Reply to Sandberg," *Journal of Economic History*, 30(3), September 1970, pp. 655-6.

Eagly, Robert V. and Smith, V. Kerry. "Domestic and International Integration of the London Money Market, 1731-1789," *Journal of Economic History*, 36(1), March 1976, pp. 198-212.

Earle, Carville V. "A Staple Interpretation of Slavery and Free Labor," *Geographical Review*, 68(1), January 1978, pp. 51-65.

Earle, Carville V. "Entering the Modern Age: A Geographical Interpretation of Labor Economics, Industrialization, and the 'Working Class' in the Antebellum United States," presented at the Annual Cliometrics Conference, University of Chicago, Chicago, June 1979.

Earle, Carville V. and Hoffman, Ronald. "Staple Crops and Urban Development in the Eighteenth Century South," *Perspectives in American History*, 10, 1976, pp. 7-78.

Easley, David and O'Hara, Maureen. "The Postal Savings System in the Depression," *Journal of Economic History*, 39(3), September 1979, pp. 741-53.

Easterlin, Richard A. "Estimates of Manufacturing Activity," in Lee et al (eds), *Population, Redistribution and Economic Growth*, 1957, pp. 635-701.

Easterlin, Richard A. "State Income Estimates," in Lee et al (eds), *Population, Redistribution and Economic Growth*, 1957, pp. 703-59.

Easterlin, Richard A. "Redistribution of Manufacturing," in Kuznets, Miller, and Easterlin (eds), *Population, Redistribution and Economic Growth*, 1960, pp. 103-39.

Easterlin, Richard A. "Regional Growth of Income: Long Term Tendencies, 1880-1950," in Kuznets, Miller, and Easterlin (eds), *Population, Redistribution and Economic Growth*, 1960, pp. 141-203.

Easterlin, Richard A. "Interregional Differences in Per Capita Income, Population, and Total Income, 1840-1950," in Parker (ed), *Trends in the American Economy in the Nineteenth Century*, 1960, pp. 73-140.

Easterlin, Richard A. "Regional Income Trends, 1840-1950," in Harris (ed), *American Economic History*, 1961, pp. 525-47.

Easterlin, Richard A. "Influences in European Emigration Before World War I," reprinted in Fogel and Engerman (eds), *The Reinterpretation of American Economic History*, 1971, pp. 384-95. *Economic*

Development Cultural Change, 9(3), April 1961, pp. 331-51.

Easterlin, Richard A. "A Note on the Evidence of History," in Anderson and Bowman (eds), *Education and Economic Growth*, 1965, pp. 422-9.

Easterlin, Richard A. "Is There Need for Historical Research in Underdevelopment?," *American Economic Review*, Papers and Proceedings, 55(2), May 1965, pp. 104-8.

Easterlin, Richard A. "Gross National Product in the United States, 1834-1909: Comment on Gallman," in Brady (ed), *Output, Employment, and Productivity in the United States After 1800*, 1966, pp. 76-90.

Easterlin, Richard A. "Economic Growth: An Overview," in Sills (ed), *International Encyclopedia of the Social Sciences*, 1968, pp. 395-408.

Easterlin, Richard A. *Population, Labor Force, and Long Swings in Economic Growth: The American Experience* (General Series 86). New York: Columbia University Press for the National Bureau of Economic Research, 1968.

Easterlin, Richard A. "The Service Industries in the Nineteenth Century: Comment on Gallman and Weiss," in Fuchs (ed), *Production and Productivity in the Service Industries*, 1969, pp. 352-65.

Easterlin, Richard A. "The American Population," in Davis, Easterlin, and Parker (eds), *American Economic Growth*, 1972, pp. 121-83.

Easterlin, Richard A. "Farm Production and Income in Old and New Areas at Mid-Century," in Klingaman and Vedder (eds), *Essays in Nineteenth Century Economic History*, 1975, pp. 77-117.

Easterlin, Richard A. "Suggestions for the Study of the Economic Growth of the Delaware Valley Area," in Porter (ed), *Regional Economic History*, 1976, pp. 17-24.

Easterlin, Richard A. "Population Change and Farm Settlement in the Northern United States," *Journal of Economic History*, 36(1), March 1976, pp. 45-75.

Easterlin, Richard A. "Population Change and Farm Settlement in the Northern United States: Reply to Bogue," *Journal of Economic History*, 36(1), March 1976, pp. 81-3.

Easterlin, Richard A. "Factors in the Decline of Farm Family Fertility in the United States: Some Preliminary Results," *Journal of American History*, 63(3), December 1976, pp. 600-14.

Easterlin, Richard A. "Population Issues in American Economic History: A Survey and Critique," in Gallman (ed), *Recent Developments in the Study of Business and Economic History*, 1977, pp. 131-58.

Easterlin, Richard A. "Population," in Porter (ed), *Encyclopedia of American Economic History*, 1980, pp. 167-82.

Easterlin, Richard A. "Some Conceptual Aspects of the Comparative Measurement of Economic Growth," Ph.D. Dissertation (Available on Microfilm), 1953.

Easterlin, Richard A.; Davis, Lance E. and Parker, William N., eds. *American Economic Growth*, 1972

Easterlin, Richard A.; Miller, Ann Ratner; Brainerd, Carol P. and Lee, Everett S. *Population, Redistribution and Economic Growth: United States, 1870-1950, vol. 1: Methodological Considerations and Reference Tables* (Series edited by Simon S. Kuznets and Dorothy Swaine Thomas). Philadelphia: American Philosophical Society, 1957.

Easterlin, Richard A.; Miller, Ann Ratner and Kuznets, Simon S. *Population, Redistribution and Economic Growth: United States,*

1870-1950, vol. 2: Analyses of Economic Change (Series edited by Simon S. Kuznets and Dorothy Swaine Thomas). Philadelphia: American Philosophical Society, 1960.

Easton, Stephen T. "The Outdoor Relief System in England and Wales," in Grubel and Walker (eds), *Unemployment Insurance*, 1978, pp. 320-8.

Easton, Stephen T. "Continuing Themes in Economic History: A Report on the Meetings of the Economic History Association," *Journal of European Economic History*, 8(3), Winter 1979, pp. 761-72.

Easton, Stephen T. "Aggregate Aspects of Unemployment, Unemployment Insurance and the Poor Laws in Great Britain, 1855-1940," (Summary of Doctoral Dissertation) *Journal of Economic History*, 39(1), March 1979, pp. 326-9.

Eckstein, Alexander; Chao, Kang and Chang, John. "The Economic Development of Manchuria: The Rise of a Frontier Economy," *Journal of Economic History*, 34(1), March 1974, pp. 239-64.

Eckstein, Alexander; Fairbank, John K. and Yang, L.S. "Economic Change in Early Modern China: An Analytic Framework," *Economic Development and Cultural Change*, 9(1), Part 1, October 1960, pp. 1-26.

Eddie, Scott M. "The Changing Pattern of Landownership in Hungary, 1867-1914," *Economic History Review*, Second Series, 20(2), August 1967, pp. 293-310.

Eddie, Scott M. "Agricultural Production and Output per Worker in Hungary, 1870-1913," *Journal of Economic History*, 28(2), June 1968, pp. 197-222.

Eddie, Scott M. "Die Landwirtschaft als Quelle des Arbeitskraft-Angebots: Mutmassungen aus der Geschichte Ungarns, 1870 bis 1913," *Vierteljahrschrift fur Sozial-und Wirtschaftsgeschichte*, 56(2), September 1969, pp. 215-32.

Eddie, Scott M. "Farmers' Response to Price in Large-Estate Agriculture: Hungary, 1870-1913," *Economic History Review*, Second Series, 24(4), November 1971, pp. 571-88.

Eddie, Scott M. "The Terms of Trade as a Tax on Agriculture: Hungary's Trade With Austria, 1883-1913," *Journal of Economic History*, 32(1), March 1972, pp. 298-315.

Eddie, Scott M. "Cui Bono? Magyarorszag es a Dualista Monarchia vedovampolitikaja," [Cui Bono? Hungary and the Protectionist Policy of the Dual Monarchy] *Tortenelmi Szemle*, 19(1-2), 1976, pp. 156-66.

Eddie, Scott M. "The Terms and Patterns of Hungarian Foreign Trade, 1882-1913," *Journal of Economic History*, 37(2), June 1977, pp. 329-58.

Eddie, Scott M. "Austria in the Dual Monarchy: Her Trade Within and Without the Customs Union," *East Central Europe*, 7, part 2 1980, pp. 225-47.

Eddie, Scott M. "Die Auswirkung der Preisanderungen auf Ungarns Aussenhandel Wahrend der Schutzzollara," [The Consequences of Price Fluctuations on Hungary's Foreign Trade during the Protectionist Period]. [Working Paper]

Eddie, Scott M. "Industrialization and Exports of Manufactures from Hungary During the Protectionist Period (1882-1913)." [Working Paper]

Eddie, Scott M. "Economic Policy and Economic Development in Austria-Hungary, 1867-1913," in Mathias and Pollard (eds), *The*

Cambridge Economic History of Europe.

Eddie, Scott M. and Puskas, J. "Landownership Structure in Hungary," Hungarian Academy of Sciences Historical Institute Working Paper.

Edelstein, Michael. "Rigidity and Bias in the British Capital Market, 1870-1913," in McCloskey (ed), *Essays on a Mature Economy*, 1971, pp. 83-112.

Edelstein, Michael. "The Determinants of U.K. Investment Abroad, 1870-1913: The U.S. Case," *Journal of Economic History*, 34(4), December 1974, pp. 980-1007.

Edelstein, Michael. "Factor and Commodity Flows in the International Economy of 1870-1914: Discussion of Papers by Eagly/Smith and Green/Urquhart," *Journal of Economic History*, 36(1), March 1976, pp. 253-8.

Edelstein, Michael. "Realized Rates of Return on U.K. Home and Overseas Portfolio Investment in the Age of High Imperialism," *Explorations in Economic History*, 13(3), July 1976, pp. 283-330.

Edelstein, Michael. "United Kingdom Savings in the Age of High Imperialism and After," *American Economic Review*, Papers and Proceedings, 67(1), February 1977, pp. 288-94.

Edelstein, Michael. "Foreign Investment and Empire, 1860-1914," in Floud and McCloskey (eds), *The Economic History of Britain Since 1700*, 1981.

Edelstein, Michael. "Money: A Discussion of Papers by Keehn, Howson, and Bordo/Schwartz Presented to the 39th Annual Meeting of the Economic History Association," *Journal of Economic History*, 40(1), March 1980, pp. 68-9.

Edelstein, Michael and O'Grada, Cormac. "Property Rights and History: A Report of the Meetings of the Economic History Association," *Journal of European Economic History*, 2(2), Fall 1973, pp. 439-46.

Edelstein, Michael and Rapp, Richard T. "Comparative Economic History: Promises and Problems. A Report of the Meetings of the Economic History Association," *Journal of European Economic History*, 4(1), Spring 1975, pp. 209-14.

Edwards, Richard C. "Economic Sophistication in Nineteenth-Century Congressional Tariff Debates," *Journal of Economic History*, 30(4), December 1970, pp. 802-38.

Edwards, Richard C. "Stages in Corporate Stability and the Risks of Corporate Failure," *Journal of Economic History*, 35(2), June 1975, pp. 428-57.

Eichengreen, Barry J. "Did Speculation Destabilize the French Franc During the 1920s?." [Working Paper]

Eichengreen, Barry J. "Economic Analysis And the Development of British Commercial Policy, 1929-1932." [Working Paper]

Eichengreen, Barry J. "Regional Differentials in the Use of Credit Instruments Prior to the Establishment of the Federal Reserve System." [Working Paper]

Eichengreen, Barry J. "The Macroeconomic Effects of the British General Tariff of 1932." [Working Paper]

Eichengreen, Barry J. "The Origins of Protection, 1923-1931." [Working Paper]

Eldridge, Hope T. "Demographic Analyses," in Eldridge and Thomas (eds), *Population, Redistribution and Economic Growth*, 1964, pp. 3-18.

Eldridge, Hope T. and Thomas, Dorothy Swaine. *Population*

*Redistribution and Economic Growth, United States, 1870-1950, vol.
3: Demographic Analyses and Interrelations* (Series edited by Simon
S. Kuznets and Dorothy Swaine Thomas). Philadelphia: American
Philosophical Society, 1964.

Eliasberg, Vera F. "Some Aspects of Development in the Coal Mining
Industry, 1839-1918," in Brady (ed), *Output, Employment, and
Productivity in the United States After 1800,* 1966, pp. 405-35.

Eliasberg, Vera F. and Abramovitz, Moses. *The Growth of Public
Employment in Great Britain* (General Series 60). Princeton:
Princeton University Press for the National Bureau of Economic
Research, 1957.

Elliott, C.M. and Granger, C.W.J. "A Fresh Look at Wheat Prices and
Markets in the Eighteenth Century," *Economic History Review,* Second
Series, 20(2), August 1967, pp. 257-65.

Ellman, Michael. "Did Agricultural Surplus Provide for the Increase in
Investment in the USSR During the First Five Year Plan?," *Economic
Journal,* 85(340), December 1975, pp. 844-63.

Ellsworth, Robert A. "Migration of Native Americans: New Data of the
Pre-1850 Period," *Inter-Mountain Economic Review,* 5(1), Spring
1974, pp. 13-57.

Emi, Koichi. "Government Expenditure," in Ohkawa and Hayami (eds),
Economic Growth, 1973, pp. 80-94.

Emi, Koichi. "Long Term Movements of Gross Domestic Fixed Capital
Formation in Japan, 1869-1940," in Ohkawa and Hayami (eds),
Economic Growth, 1973, pp. 67-79.

Emi, Koichi and Rosovsky, Henry. "Seifu Kensetsu toshi no Sokutei,
1868-1940," [The Measurement of Japanese Government Investment in
Constructon, 1868-1940] *Keizai Kenkyu,* 9(1), January 1958, pp.
52-60.

Emi, Koichi and Rosovsky, Henry. "Nihon no Shihon Keisei to Shite no
Kensetsu," [Construction as a Part of Japanese Capital Formation]
Nikon Tokei Gakkai Kaiho, April 1958.

Engelbourg, Saul. "Energy and Industrialization: The Case of Southern
New England," in Soltow (ed), *Essays in Economic and Business
History,* 1979, pp. 268-82.

Engerman, Stanley L. "The Economic Impact of the Civil War,"
Explorations in Entrepreneurial History, Second Series, 3,
Spring/Summer 1966, pp. 179-99.

Engerman, Stanley L. "The Effects of Slavery upon the Southern
Economy: A Review of the Recent Debate," reprinted in Aitken (ed),
Did Slavery Pay?, 1971, pp. 295-327. *Explorations in
Enterpreneurial History,* Second Series, 4(2), Winter 1967, pp. 71-
97.

Engerman, Stanley L. "Discussion: Papers in Economic History,"
American Economic Review, Papers and Proceedings, 57(2), May 1967,
pp. 307-10.

Engerman, Stanley L. "Slavery as an Obstacle to Economic Growth in the
United States: A Panel Discussion of Conrad and Meyer," *Journal of
Economic History,* 27(4), December 1967, pp. 541-4.

Engerman, Stanley L. "The Antebellum South: What Probably Was and What
Should Have Been," reprinted in Parker (ed), *The Structure of the
Cotton Economy of the Antebellum South,* 1970. *Agricultural
History,* 44(1), January 1970, pp. 127-42.

Engerman, Stanley L. "A Note on the Economic Consequences of the

Second Bank of the United States," *Journal of Political Economy*, 78(4), Part 1, July/August 1970, pp. 725-8.

Engerman, Stanley L. "Human Capital, Education, and Economic Growth," in Fogel and Engerman (eds), *The Reinterpretation of American Economic History*, 1971, pp. 241-56.

Engerman, Stanley L. "Some Economic Factors in Southern Backwardness in the Nineteenth Century," in Kain and Meyer (eds), *Essays in Regional Economics*, 1971, pp. 279-306.

Engerman, Stanley L. "The American Tariff, British Exports, and American Iron Production, 1840-1860," in McCloskey (ed), *Essays on a Mature Economy*, 1971, pp. 13-38.

Engerman, Stanley L. "Comments on Dissertations Presented at the 30th Annual Meeting of the Economic History Association," *Journal of Economic History*, 31(1), March 1971, pp. 285-88.

Engerman, Stanley L. "Railways and Economic Growth in England and Wales, 1840-1870: A New Approach to English Railway History. Review Essay of 'Railways and Economic Growth In England and Wales, 1840-1870' by Gary R. Hawke (Oxford: Clarendon Press)," *Business History*, 13(2), July 1971, pp. 124-8.

Engerman, Stanley L. "Some Economic Issues Relating to Railroad Subsidies and the Evaluation of Land Grants," *Journal of Economic History*, 32(2), June 1972, pp. 443-63.

Engerman, Stanley L. "Some Considerations Relating to Property Rights in Man," *Journal of Economic History*, 33(1), March 1973, pp. 43-65.

Engerman, Stanley L. "A Reconsideration of Southern Economic Growth, 1770-1860," *Agricultural History*, 49(2), April 1975, pp. 343-61.

Engerman, Stanley L. "The Southern Slave Economy," in Owens (ed), *Perspectives and Irony in American Slavery*, 1976.

Engerman, Stanley L. "The Height of Slaves in the United States," *Local Population Studies*, 16 Spring 1976, pp. 45-50.

Engerman, Stanley L. "Some Economic and Demographic Comparisons of Slavery in the United States and the British West Indies," *Economic History Review*, Second Series, 29(2), May 1976, pp. 258-75.

Engerman, Stanley L. "Introduction to Special Issue on Colonial Slavery in the Chesapeake Region," *Southern Studies*, 16(4), Winter 1977, pp. 347-54.

Engerman, Stanley L. "Black Fertility and Family Structure in the United States, 1880-1940," *Journal of Family History*, 2(2), Summer 1977, pp. 117-38.

Engerman, Stanley L. "Recent Developments in American Economic History," *Social Science History*, 2(1), Fall 1977, pp. 72-89.

Engerman, Stanley L. "Relooking at the Slave Community," in Gilmore (ed), *Revisiting John Blassingame's Slave Community*.

Engerman, Stanley L. "Marxist Economic Studies of the Slave South," *Marxist Perspectives*, 1(1), Spring 1978, pp. 148-64.

Engerman, Stanley L. "Studying the Black Family. Review Essay of 'The Black Family In Slavery and Freedom, 1750-1925' by Herbert G. Gutman (New York: Pantheon, 1976)," *Journal of Family History*, 3(1), Spring 1978, pp. 78-101.

Engerman, Stanley L. "The Realities of Slavery: A Review of Recent Evidence," *International Journal of Comparative Sociology*, 20(1-2), March/June 1979, pp. 46-66.

Engerman, Stanley L. "Counterfactuals and the New Economic History," *Inquiry*, 23(2), June 1980, pp. 157-72.

Engerman, Stanley L. "Notes on the Patterns of Economic Growth in the British North American Colonies in the Seventeenth, Eighteenth, and Nineteenth Centuries," International Economic History Congress, Edinburgh, 1978: Four 'A' Themes. Edinburgh Edinburgh University Press 1978, pp. 187-98.

Engerman, Stanley L. and Fogel, Robert W. "A Model for the Explanation of Industrial Expansion During the Nineteenth Century: With an Application to the American Iron Industry," reprinted in Fogel and Engerman (eds), *The Reinterpretation of American Economic History*, 1971, pp. 148-62. *Journal of Political Economy*, 77(3), May/June 1969, pp. 306-28.

Engerman, Stanley L. and Fogel, Robert W. "The Economics of Slavery," in Fogel and Engerman (eds), *The Reinterpretation of American Economic History*, 1971, pp. 311-41.

Engerman, Stanley L. and Fogel, Robert W, eds. *The Reinterpretation of American Economic History*. New York: Harper & Row, 1971.

Engerman, Stanley L. and Fogel, Robert W. "The Relative Efficiency of Slavery: A Comparison of Northern and Southern Agriculture in 1860," *Explorations in Economic History*, 8(3), Spring 1971, pp. 353-67.

Engerman, Stanley L. and Fogel, Robert W. *Time on the Cross* (vol. 1: The Economics of American Negro Slavery; vol. 2: Evidence and Methods: A Supplement) [Translated into Spanish (1977), Italian (1977), Japanese (1978)]. Boston: Little, Brown, 1974.

Engerman, Stanley L. and Fogel, Robert W. "Philanthropy at Bargain Prices: Notes on the Economics of Gradual Emancipation," *Journal of Legal Studies*, 3(2), June 1974, pp. 377-401.

Engerman, Stanley L. and Fogel, Robert W. "A Comparison of the Relative Efficiency of Slave and Free Agriculture in the United States during 1860," in Van der Wee, Vinogradov, and Kotovsky (eds), *Fifth International Congress of Economic History*, 1976, pp. 141-6.

Engerman, Stanley L. and Fogel, Robert W. "Explaining the Relative Efficiency of Slave Agriculture in the Antebellum South," *American Economic Review*, 67(3), June 1977, pp. 275-96.

Engerman, Stanley L.; Fogel, Robert W.; Floud, Roderick C.; Wimmer, Larry T.; Trussell, James and Pope, Clayne L. "The Economics of Mortality in North America, 1650-1910: A Description of a Research Project," *Historical Methods*, 11(2), June 1978, pp. 75-108.

Engerman, Stanley L. and Fogel, Robert W. "Explaining the Relative Efficiency of Slave Agriculture in the Antebellum South: Reply (to David and Temin, Wright, and Schaefer and Schmitz)," *American Economic Review*, 70(4), September 1980, pp. 672-90.

Engerman, Stanley L. and Genovese, Eugene D. *Race and Slavery in the Western Hemisphere: Quantitative Studies*. Princeton: Princeton University Press, 1975.

Engerman, Stanley L. and Hartwell, Ronald M. "Models of Immiseration: The Theoretical Basis of Pessimism," in Taylor (ed), *The Standard of Living in Britain in the Industrial Revolution*, 1975.

Engerman, Stanley L. and O'Brien, Patrick K. "Changes in Income and Its Distribution during the Industrial Revolution," in Floud and McCloskey (eds), *The Economic History of Britain since 1700*, 1981, pp. 164-81.

Enke, S. "Economic Consequences of Rapid Population Growth," *Economic*

Journal, 81(324), December 1971, pp. 800-11.

Enke, S. "Economic Consequences of Rapid Population Growth: A Reply to Mr. Hanson," *Economic Journal,* 83(329), March 1973, pp. 219-21.

Ermisch, John and Weiss, Thomas J. "The Impact of the Rural Market on the Growth of the Urban Workforce: U.S., 1870-1900," *Explorations in Economic History,* 11(2), Winter 1974, pp. 137-54.

Esbitt, Milton. *International Capital Flows and Domestic Economic Fluctuation: The United States During the 1830's.* New York: Arno Press, 1978.

Esbitt, Milton. "An Antebellum Attempt at National Bank Regulation: Deposit Banks," in Soltow (ed), *Essays in Economic and Business History,* 1979, pp. 174-96.

Esbitt, Milton. "The New York City Banking Suspension of 1837," in Soltow (ed), *Essays in Economic and Business History,* 1979, pp. 163-73.

Esbitt, Milton. "A Note on the Sources of American Specie Imports During the 1830's." [Working Paper]

Esbitt, Milton. "A Re-examination of the Relationship Between Specie Flows and the Money Supply in the 1830's," presented at the University of Chicago Workshop in Economic History, Paper #7273-1, October 1972.

Esbitt, Milton. "Bank Failures and Economic Welfare: The Impact of Bank Failures on Local Communities During the Great Depression." [Working Paper]

Esbitt, Milton. "Federal Government Regulation of Banking in the Antebellum Period: Depository and Non-depository Banks in the 1830's." [Working Paper]

Esbitt, Milton. "Politics and Bank Reopenings After the Banking Holiday of 1933." [Working Paper]

Esbitt, Milton. "The Causes of Bank Failures in 1930: Illinois Banks." [Working Paper]

Esbitt, Milton. "Using Monthly Money-Market Rates to Test the Davis-Hughes and Perkins Analyses of the Dollar-Sterling Exchange Rates." [Working Paper]

Estey, Marten S. "Trends in Concentration of Union Membership, 1897-1962," *Quarterly Journal of Economics,* 80(3), August 1966, pp. 343-60.

Evans, G.H. *Business Incorporations in the United States, 1800-1943* (General Series 49). New York: National Bureau of Economic Research, 1948.

Evans, Robert, Jr. "Some Economic Aspects of the Domestic Slave Trade, 1830-1860," *Southern Economic Journal,* 27(4), April 1961, pp. 329-37.

Evans, Robert, Jr. "The Economics of American Negro Slavery, 1830-1860," in *Aspects of Labor Economics* (Special Conference Series (14)). Princeton: Princeton University Press for the National Bureau of Economic Research, 1962, pp. 221-7.

Evans, Robert, Jr. "'Without Regard to Cost': The Returns on Clipper Ships," *Journal of Political Economy,* 72(1), February 1964, pp. 32-43.

Evans, Robert, Jr. "Evolution of the Japanese System of Employer-Employee Relations, 1868-1945," *Business History Review,* 44(1), Spring 1970, pp. 110-25.

Evans, Robert, Jr. "Some Notes on Coerced Labor," *Journal of Economic*

History, 30(4), December 1970, pp. 861-6.

Fabricant, Solomon. *The Output of Manufacturing Industries, 1899-1937* (General Series 39). New York: National Bureau of Economic Research, 1940.

Fabricant, Solomon. *Employment in Manufacturing, 1899-1939* (General Series 41). New York: National Bureau of Economic Research, 1942.

Fabricant, Solomon. *The Trend of Government Activity in the United States since 1900* (General Series 56). New York: National Bureau of Economic Research, 1952.

Fabricant, Solomon. "The Service Industries in the Nineteenth Century: Comment on Gallman and Weiss," in Fuchs (ed), *Production and Productivity in the Service Industries*, 1969, pp. 368-71.

Falkus, Malcolm E. "Russia's National Income, 1913: A Reevaluation," *Economica*, 35(137), February 1968, pp. 52-73.

Falkus, Malcolm E. "United States Economic Policy and the 'Dollar Gap' of the 1920's," *Economic History Review*, Second Series, 24(4), November 1971, pp. 599-623.

Falkus, Malcolm E. "The German Business Cycle in the 1920's," *Economic History Review*, Second Series, 28(3), August 1975, pp. 451-65.

Falkus, Malcolm E. "The German Business Cycle in the 1920's: A Reply to Temin," *Economic History Review*, Second Series, 30(1), February 1977, pp. 165.

Falkus, Malcolm E. and Jones, Eric L. "Urban Improvement and the English Economy in the Seventeenth and Eighteenth Centuries," in Uselding (ed), *Research in Economic History*, 1979.

Farren, Michael A. "Regression Analysis of Factors Influencing Net Migration in the United States," Ohio University Economic History Research Paper no. G-1.

Faucci, Riccardo. "'Vecchia' e 'nuova' storia economica: quarant'anni di discussioni," ['Old' and 'New' Economic History: Forty Years of Discussion] in Toniolo (ed), *Lo sviluppo economico italiano*, 1973, pp. 71-118.

Faucher, Albert and Paquet, Gilles. "L'experience economique du Quebec et la Confederation," *Journal of Canadian Studies*, 1, November 1966, pp. 16-30.

Feeny, David H. "Induced Technical and Institutional Change: A Thai Case Study," in Means (ed), *The Past in Southeast Asia's Present*, 1978, pp. 56-69.

Feeny, David H. "Competing Hypotheses of Underdevelopment: A Thai Case Study," *Journal of Economic History*, 39(1), March 1979, pp. 113-27.

Feeny, David H. "Paddy, Princes, and Productivity: Irrigation and Thai Agricultural Development, 1900-1940," *Explorations in Economic History*, 16(2), April 1979, pp. 132-50.

Feeny, David H. "Productivity Change and Grain Farm Practice on the Canadian Prairie, 1900-1930: A Discussion of Dick," *Journal of Economic History*, 40(1), March 1980, pp. 119-20.

Feeny, David H. "Technical and Institutional Change in Thai Agriculture, 1880-1940," Ph.D. Dissertation, University of Wisconsin-Madison, 1976.

Feeny, David H. "The Decline in Slavery and Rise in Property Rights in

Land in Mainland Southeast Asia, 1850-1940." [Working Paper]

Fei, John C. "The 'Standard Market' of Traditional China," in Perkins (ed), *China's Modern Economy in Historical Perspective*, 1975, pp. 235-59.

Fei, John C. and Liu, Ts'ui-Jung. "An Analysis of the Land Tax Burden in China, 1650-1865," *Journal of Economic History*, 37(2), June 1977, pp. 359-81.

Feinstein, Charles H. "Income and Investment in the United Kingdom, 1856-1914," *Economic Journal*, 71(282), June 1961, pp. 367-85.

Feinstein, Charles H. "Income and Investment in the United Kingdom, 1856-1914: A Reply (to Maywald)," *Economic Journal*, 71(284), December 1961, pp. 857-9.

Feinstein, Charles H. "Production and Productivity in the United Kingdom, 1920-1962," *L. and C. Economic Bulletin*, 48, December 1963, pp. 12-4.

Feinstein, Charles H. "Production and Productivity in the United Kingdom, 1920-1962," reprinted in Aldcroft and Fearon (eds), *Economic Growth in Twentieth Century Britain*, 1969. *Times Review of Industry and Technology*, December 1963.

Feinstein, Charles H. *Domestic Capital Formation in the United Kingdom, 1920-1938*. Cambridge: Cambridge University Press, 1965.

Feinstein, Charles H. *Key Statistics of the British Economy, 1900-1962* (Second Edition). London: London and Cambridge Economic Service, 1965.

Feinstein, Charles H. "Evolution of the Distribution of the National Income in the U.K. Since 1860," in Marchal and Ducros (eds), *The Distribution of National Income*, 1968.

Feinstein, Charles H. "The Compilation of Gross Domestic Fixed Capital Formation Statistics, 1856-1913," in Higgins and Pollard (eds), *Aspects of Capital Investment in Great Britain*, 1971.

Feinstein, Charles H. *National Income, Expenditure and Output of the United Kingdom, 1855-1965*. Cambridge: Cambridge University Press, 1972.

Feinstein, Charles H. "Capital Formation in Great Britain," in Mathias and Postan (eds), *The Cambridge Economic History of Europe*, 1978, pp. 28-96.

Feinstein, Charles H. "Capital Accumulation and the Industrial Revolution," in Floud and McCloskey (eds), *The Economic History of Britain since 1700*, 1981, pp. 128-42.

Felix, David. "Profit Inflation and Industrial Growth: The Historic Record and Contemporary Analogies," in Floud (ed), *Essays in Quantitative Economic History*, 1974, pp. 133-51.

Felix, David. "Technological Dualism in Late Industrializers: On Theory, History, and Policy," *Journal of Economic History*, 34(1), March 1974, pp. 194-238.

Feller, Irwin. "Inventive Activity in Agriculture, 1837-1890," *Journal of Economic History*, 22(4), December 1962, pp. 560-77.

Feller, Irwin. "The Draper Loom in New England Textiles, 1894-1914: A Study of Diffusion of an Innovation," *Journal of Economic History*, 26(3), September 1966, pp. 320-47.

Feller, Irwin. "The Draper Loom in New England Textiles: A Reply to Sandberg," *Journal of Economic History*, 28(4), December 1968, pp. 628-30.

Feller, Irwin. "The Urban Location of United States Invention,

328

1860-1910," *Explorations in Economic History,* 8(3), Spring 1971, pp. 285-304.

Fels, Rendigs. *American Business Cycles, 1865-1897.* Chapel Hill: University of North Carolina Press, 1959.

Fels, Rendigs; Bolch, Ben W. and McMahon, Marshall. "Housing Surplus in the 1920's?," *Explorations in Economic History,* 8(3), Spring 1971, pp. 259-84.

Fenichel, Allen H. "Growth and Diffusion of Power in Manufacturing, 1838-1919," in Brady (ed), *Output, Employment, and Productivity in the United States After 1800,* 1966, pp. 443-78.

Fennel, Lee and Munroe, Tapan. "The Myth of the Dependency Paradigm: A Study in Grants Economics," International Studies Association, Working Paper no. 48, 1975.

Fenoaltea, Stefano. "Public Policy and Italian Industrial Development, 1861-1913," (Summary of Doctoral Dissertation) *Journal of Economic History,* 29(1), March 1969, pp. 176-9.

Fenoaltea, Stefano. "Decollo, ciclo, e intervento dello Stato," [The Take-off, the Business Cycle, and the Role of the State] in Caracciolo (ed), *La Formazione dell'Italia industriale,* 1969, pp. 95-114.

Fenoaltea, Stefano. "Railroads and Italian Industrial Growth, 1861-1913," reprinted as "Le ferrovie e lo sviluppo industriale italiano, 1861-1913" in Toniolo (ed), *L'economia italiana,* 1978, pp. 105-56. *Explorations in Economic History,* 9(4), Summer 1972, pp. 325-52.

Fenoaltea, Stefano. "Riflessioni sull'esperienza industriale italiana dal Risorgimento alla prima guerra mondiale," [Reflections on the Italian Industrial Experience from the Risorgimento to the First World War] in Toniolo (ed), *Lo sviluppo economico italiano,* 1973, pp. 121-56. Reprinted in Toniolo (ed), *L'economia italiana,* 1978, pp. 69-104.

Fenoaltea, Stefano. "The Discipline and They: Notes on Counterfactual Methodology and the 'New' Economic History," *Journal of European Economic History,* 2(3), Winter 1973, pp. 729-46.

Fenoaltea, Stefano. "The Rise and Fall of a Theoretical Model: The Manorial System," *Journal of Economic History,* 35(2), June 1975, pp. 386-409.

Fenoaltea, Stefano. "Authority, Efficiency, and Agricultural Organization in Medieval England and Beyond: A Hypothesis," *Journal of Economic History,* 35(4), December 1975, pp. 693-718.

Fenoaltea, Stefano. "Risk, Transaction Costs, and the Organization of Medieval Agriculture," *Explorations in Economic History,* 13(2), April 1976, pp. 129-51.

Fenoaltea, Stefano. "On a Marxian Model of Enclosures: Comment on Cohen and Weitzman," *Journal of Development Economics,* 3(2), June 1976, pp. 195-8.

Fenoaltea, Stefano. "Fenoaltea on Open Fields: A Reply to McCloskey," *Explorations in Economic History,* 14(4), October 1977, pp. 405-10.

Fenoaltea, Stefano. "Negative Incentives, Authority, and Slavery: A Comparative Perspective." [Working Paper]

Fenoaltea, Stefano. "The Slavery Debate: A Note from the Sidelines." [Working Paper]

Fenoaltea, Stefano. *Italian Industrial Production, 1861-1913: A Statistical Reconstruction.* Cambridge and New York: Cambridge

University Press.

Fenoaltea, Stefano. *The Industrialization of Italy, 1861-1913.* New York: Cambridge University Press.

Ferleger, Louis. "Productivity Change in the Postbellum Louisiana Sugar Industry," in Anderson and Perryman (eds), *Time Series Analysis,* 1981, pp. 147-61.

Ferleger, Louis. "Farm Mechanization in the Southern Sugar Sector After the Civil War," Louisiana History.

Ferron, Jean-Olivier and Vaillancourt, Francois. "Qui Perd Sa Langue, Perd Sa Foi," [He Who Loses His Language Loses Faith] *Revue D'Histoire de L'Amerique Francaise,* 33(2), September 1979, pp. 263-5.

Fetter, Frank W. "Some Pitfalls in the Use of Bank of England Credit Statistics: 1794-1832," *Review of Economics and Statistics,* 49(4), November 1967, pp. 619-23.

Field, Alexander J. "Educational Reform and Manufacturing Development in Mid-Nineteenth Century Massachusetts," (Summary of Doctoral Dissertation) *Journal of Economic History,* 36(1), March 1976, pp. 263-6.

Field, Alexander J. "Educational Expansion in Mid-Nineteenth Century Massachusetts: Human Capital Formation or Structural Reinforcement?," *Harvard Educational Review,* 46(4), November 1976, pp. 521-52.

Field, Alexander J. "Education and Social Programs," (Summary of 1977 Research Workshop) *Journal of Economic History,* 38(1), March 1978, pp. 258-61.

Field, Alexander J. "Sectoral Shift in Antebellum Massachusetts: A Reconsideration," *Explorations in Economic History,* 15(2), April 1978, pp. 146-71.

Field, Alexander J. "Occupational Structure, Dissent, and Educational Commitment: Lancashire, 1841," in Uselding (ed), *Research in Economic History,* 1979.

Field, Alexander J. "Economic and Demographic Determinants of Educational Commitment: Massachusetts, 1855," *Journal of Economic History,* 39(2), June 1979, pp. 439-59.

Field, Alexander J. "The Relative Stability of German and American Industrial Growth, 1880-1913: A Comparative Analysis," in Schroder and Spree (eds), *Historisch-Sozialwissenschaftliche Forschungen,* 1980.

Field, Alexander J. "Industrialization and Skill Intensity: The Case of Massachusetts," *Journal of Human Resources,* 15(2), Spring 1980, pp. 149-75.

Field, Alexander J. "Habakkuk on American and British Technology: A Reexamination from a Capital-Theoretic Perspective." [Working Paper]

Field, Alexander J. "Notes on the Use of Explanatory Models in European Economic History." [Working Paper]

Filosa, Renato; Rey, Guido M. and Sitzia, Bruno. "Uno schema di analisi quantitativa del'economia italiana durante il fascismo," [Outline of a Quantitative Analysis of the Italian Economy under Fascism] in Ciocca and Toniolo (eds), *L'economia italiana nel periodo fascista,* 1976, pp. 51-102.

Finkelstein, Stanley S. "The Currency Act of 1764: A Quantitative Reappraisal," *American Economist,* 12(2), Fall 1968, pp. 38-47.

Firestone, John M. *Federal Receipts and Expenditures during Business Cycles, 1879-1958.* Princeton: Princeton University Press for the National Bureau of Economic Research, 1960.

Firestone, O.J. *Canada's Economic Development, 1867-1953* (Income and Wealth Series (7)). London: Bowes & Bowes for the International Association for Research in Income and Wealth, 1958.

Firestone, O.J. "Canada's External Trade and Net Foreign Balance, 1851-1900," in Parker (ed), *Trends in the American Economy in the Nineteenth Century,* 1960, pp. 757-71.

Firestone, O.J. "Development of Canada's Economy, 1850-1900," in Parker (ed), *Trends in the American Economy in the Nineteenth Century,* 1960, pp. 217-46.

Firestone, O.J. "Development of Canada's Economy, 1850-1900: Reply to Buckley and McDougall," in Parker (ed), *Trends in the American Economy in the Nineteenth Century,* 1960, pp. 249-52.

Firestone, O.J. "The Service Industries in the Nineteenth Century: Comment on Gallman and Weiss," in Fuchs (ed), *Production and Productivity in the Service Industries,* 1969, pp. 371-2.

Firestone, O.J. "Canada's Subsistence Economy before 1860," *Fourth International Conference of Economic History, Bloomington, 1968.* Paris: Mouton, 1973, pp. 409-18.

Fischbaum, Marvin and Rubin, Julius. "Slavery and the Economic Development of the American South: Comment on Engerman," reprinted in Aitken (ed), *Did Slavery Pay?,* 1971, pp. 327-41. *Explorations in Enterpreneurial History,* Second Series, 6(1), Fall 1968, pp. 116-27.

Fischer, Wolfram. "Government Activity and Industrialization in Germany (1815-70)," in Rostow (ed), *The Economics of Take-off into Sustained Growth,* 1963, pp. 83-94.

Fischer, Wolfram. "Some Recent Developments in the Study of Economic and Business History in Western Germany," in Gallman (ed), *Recent Developments in the Study of Economic and Business History,* 1977, pp. 247-85.

Fisher, Franklin M. and Temin, Peter. "Regional Specialization and the Supply of Wheat in the United States, 1867-1914," *Review of Economics and Statistics,* 52(2), May 1970, pp. 134-49.

Fisher, Franklin M. and Temin, Peter. "Regional Specialization and the Supply of Wheat in the United States, 1867-1914: A Reply to Higgs," *Review of Economics and Statistics,* 53(1), February 1971, pp. 102-3.

Fisher, Franklin M. and Temin, Peter. "Returns to Scale in Research and Development: What does the Schumpeterian Hypothesis Imply?," *Journal of Political Economy,* 81(1), January/February 1973, pp. 56-70.

Fishlow, Albert. "Trustee Savings Banks, 1817-1861," *Journal of Economic History,* 21(1), March 1961, pp. 26-40.

Fishlow, Albert. "Trends in the American Economy in the Nineteenth Century: A Review Article. Review of William N. Parker (ed), *Studies in Income and Wealth,* vol. 24 (Princeton: Princeton University Press, 1960)," *Journal of Economic History,* 22(1), March 1962, pp. 71-80.

Fishlow, Albert. "Antebellum Interregional Trade Reconsidered," reprinted in Andreano (ed), *New Views,* 1965, pp. 187-200. *American Economic Review,* Papers and Proceedings, 54(3), May 1964, pp.

331

352-64.

Fishlow, Albert. *American Railroads and the Transformation of the Antebellum Economy.* Cambridge: Harvard University Press, 1965.

Fishlow, Albert. "Postscript on Antebellum Interregional Trade," in Andreano (ed), *New Views on American Economic Development,* 1965, pp. 209-12.

Fishlow, Albert. "Empty Economic Stages? Review Essay of 'The Economics of Take-Off into Sustained Growth' Edited by W.W. Rostow (London: Macmillan, 1963)," *Economic Journal,* 75(297), March 1965, pp. 112-25.

Fishlow, Albert. "Productivity and Technological Change in the Railroad Sector, 1840-1910," in Brady (ed), *Output, Employment, and Productivity in the United States after 1800,* 1966, pp. 583-646.

Fishlow, Albert. "The American Common School Revival, Fact or Fancy?," in Rosovsky (ed), *Industrialization in Two Systems,* 1966.

Fishlow, Albert. "Levels of Nineteenth Century American Investment in Education," reprinted in Fogel and Engerman (eds), *The Reinterpretation of American Economic History,* 1971, pp. 265-73. *Journal of Economic History,* 26(4), December 1966, pp. 418-36.

Fishlow, Albert. "The Growth of American Educational Investment in the Nineteenth Century," *Third International Conference of Economic History, Munich, 1965, part 1.* Paris: Mouton, 1968, pp. 761-2.

Fishlow, Albert. "The Dynamics of Railroad Extension into the West," in Fogel and Engerman (eds), *The Reinterpretation of American Economic History,* 1971, pp. 402-16.

Fishlow, Albert. "Internal Transportation," in Davis, Easterlin, and Parker (eds), *American Economic Growth,* 1972, pp. 468-547.

Fishlow, Albert. "Comparative Consumption Patterns, the Extent of the Market, and Alternative Development Strategies," in Ayal (ed), *Micro Aspects of Development,* 1973, pp. 41-80.

Fishlow, Albert. "The New Economic History Revisited," *Journal of European Economic History,* 3(2), Fall 1974, pp. 453-68.

Fishlow, Albert. "Brazilian Development in Long-Term Perrspective," *American Economic Review,* Papers and Proceedings, 70(2), May 1980, pp. 102-8.

Fishlow, Albert and Fogel, Robert W. "Quantitative Economic History: An Interim Evaluation, Past Trends and Present Tendencies," *Journal of Economic History,* 31(1), March 1971, pp. 15-42.

Fitzharris, Joseph C. "Minnesota Agricultural Growth, 1880-1970," University of Minnesota Department of Agricultural and Applied Economics Staff Paper P76-4, June 1976.

Fitzharris, Joseph C. "Technology in Minnesota Agriculture, 1900-1940: Some Case Studies," University of Minnesota Department of Agricultural and Applied Economics Staff Paper Series.

Fitzharris, Joseph C. "The Development of Minnesota Agriculture, 1880-1970: A Study in Productivity Change," University of Minnesota Department of Agricultural and Applied Economics Staff Paper P74-2, October 1974.

FitzRandolph, Peter W. "The Rural Furnishing Merchant in the Postbellum United States: A Study in Spatial Economics," Ph.D. Dissertation, Tufts University, 1979.

Fleisig, Heywood. "Mechanizing the Cotton Harvest in the Nineteenth-Century South," (Summary of Doctoral Dissertation) *Journal of Economic History,* 25(4), December 1965, pp. 704-6.

Fleisig, Heywood. "The United States and the Non-European Periphery During the Early Years of the Great Depression," in Van der Wee (ed), *The Great Depression Revisited*, 1972, pp. 145-81.

Fleisig, Heywood. "The Union Pacific Railroad and the Railroad Land Grant Controversy," *Explorations in Economic History*, 11(2), Winter 1974, pp. 155-72.

Fleisig, Heywood. "Slavery and Technological Change: Comment on Aufhauser," *Journal of Economic History*, 34(1), March 1974, pp. 79-83.

Fleisig, Heywood. *Long Term Capital Flows and the Great Depression: The Role of the United States, 1927-1933*. New York: Arno Press, 1975.

Fleisig, Heywood. "The Central Pacific Railroad and the Railroad Land Grant Controversy," *Journal of Economic History*, 35(3), September 1975, pp. 552-66.

Fleisig, Heywood. "War-related Debts and the Great Depression," *American Economic Review*, Papers and Proceedings, 66(2), May 1976, pp. 52-8.

Fleisig, Heywood. "Slavery, the Supply of Agricultural Labor, and the Industrialization of the South," *Journal of Economic History*, 36(3), September 1976, pp. 572-97.

Flinn, M.W. "Trends in Real Wages, 1750-1850," *Economic History Review*, Second Series, 27(3), August 1974, pp. 395-413.

Flinn, M.W. "Real Wage Trends in Britain, 1750-1850: A Reply (to Gourvish)," *Economic History Review*, Second Series, 29(1), February 1976, pp. 143-5.

Floud, Roderick C. "Changes in the Productivity of Labour in the British Machine Tool Industry, 1856-1900," in McCloskey (ed), *Essays on a Mature Economy*, 1971, pp. 313-37.

Floud, Roderick C. *Essays in Quantitative Economic History*. Oxford: Clarendon Press for the Economic History Society, 1974.

Floud, Roderick C. "The Adolescence of American Engineering Competition, 1860-1900," *Economic History Review*, Second Series, 27(1), February 1974, pp. 57-71.

Floud, Roderick C. *The British Machine Tool Industry, 1850-1914*. Cambridge: Cambridge University Press, 1976.

Floud, Roderick C. "Britain, 1860-1914: A Survey," in Floud and McCloskey (eds), *The Economic History of Britain since 1700*, 1981.

Floud, Roderick C. "Technical Education and Economic Performance: Engineering in the Late 19th Century." [Working Paper]

Floud, Roderick C. and Craig, R.S. "The Evolution of Steam Shipping in Britain in the Nineteenth Century." [Working Paper]

Floud, Roderick C.; Fogel, Robert W.; Engerman, Stanley L.; Wimmer, Larry T.; Trussell, James and Pope, Clayne L. "The Economics of Mortality in North America, 1650-1910: A Description of a Research Project," *Historical Methods*, 11(2), June 1978, pp. 75-108.

Floud, Roderick C. and McCloskey, Donald N. "The Economic History of Britain since 1700: Editor's Introduction," in Floud and McCloskey (eds), *The Economic History of Britain since 1700*, 1981.

Floud, Roderick C. and McCloskey, Donald N., eds. *The Economic History of Britain since 1700* (2 volumes; vol. 1: 1700-1860; vol. 2: 1860 to the 1970s). Cambridge: Cambridge University Press, 1981.

Flueckiger, Gerald. "Observation and Measurement of Technical Change," *Explorations in Economic History*, 9(2), Winter 1971/72, pp. 145-77.

Flynn, Dennis O. "A New Perspective on the Spanish Price Revolution: The Monetary Approach to the Balance of Payments," *Explorations in Economic History*, 15(4), October 1978, pp. 388-406.

Flynn, Dennis O. "Silver and the Spanish Empire," in Soltow (ed), *Essays in Economic and Business History*, 1979, pp. 197-211.

Flynn, Dennis O. "Spanish-American Silver and World Markets in the Sixteenth Century," *Economic Forum*, 10(2), Winter 1979/80, pp. 46-72.

Flynn, Dennis O. "Sixteenth-Century Inflation from a Production Point of View," in Marcus (ed), *Inflation through the Ages*, 1981.

Fogel, Robert W. *The Union Pacific Railroad: A Case of Premature Enterprise*. Baltimore: Johns Hopkins University Press, 1960.

Fogel, Robert W. "A Quantitative Approach to the Study of Railroads in American Economic Growth: A Report of Some Preliminary Findings," reprinted in Swierenga, (ed), *Quantification in American History*, 1970, pp. 288-316. *Journal of Economic History*, 22(2), June 1962, pp. 163-97.

Fogel, Robert W. *Railroads and American Economic Growth: Essays in Econometric History* [Translated into Spanish (1972)]. Baltimore: Johns Hopkins University Press, 1964.

Fogel, Robert W. "A Provisional View of the 'New Economic History'," reprinted in Andreano (ed), *New Views*, 1965, pp. 201-8. *American Economic Review*, Papers and Proceedings, 54(3), May 1964, pp. 377-89.

Fogel, Robert W. "American Interregional Trade in the 19th Century," in Andreano (ed), *New Views*, 1965, pp. 213-24.

Fogel, Robert W. "Railroads and the Axiom of Indispensability," in Andreano (ed), *New Views*, 1965, pp. 225-41.

Fogel, Robert W. "The Reunification of Economic History With Economic Theory," *American Economic Review*, Papers and Proceedings, 55(2), May 1965, pp. 92-8.

Fogel, Robert W. "Railroads as an Analogy to the Space Effort: Some Economic Aspects," *Economic Journal*, 76(301), March 1966, pp. 16-43.

Fogel, Robert W. "The New Economic History: Its Findings and Methods," reprinted in Fogel and Engerman (eds), *The Reinterpretation of American Economic History*, 1971, pp. 1-12. *Economic History Review*, Second Series, 19(3), December 1966, pp. 642-56.

Fogel, Robert W. "The Specification Problem in Economic History." (A Correction for this article appears in this Journal, 28(1), March 1968, pp. 126) *Journal of Economic History*, 27(3), September 1967, pp. 283-308.

Fogel, Robert W. "Econometrics and Southern History: Comment on Conrad," *Explorations in Entrepreneurial History*, Second Series, 6(1), Fall 1968, pp. 54-8.

Fogel, Robert W. "Historiography and Retrospective Econometrics," *History and Theory*, 9(3), 1970, pp. 245-64.

Fogel, Robert W. "Railroads and American Economic Growth," in Fogel and Engerman (eds), *The Reinterpretation of American Economic History*, 1971, pp. 187-203.

Fogel, Robert W. "The Union Pacific Railroad: The Questions of Public Policy," in Fogel and Engerman (eds), *The Reinterpretation of American Economic History*, 1971, pp. 417-25.

Fogel, Robert W. "The Limits of Quantitative Methods in History,"

American Historical Review, 80(2), April 1975, pp. 329-51.

Fogel, Robert W. "Three Phases of Cliometric Research on Slavery and Its Aftermath," *American Economic Review,* Papers and Proceedings, 65(2), May 1975, pp. 37-46.

Fogel, Robert W. "From the Marxists to the Mormons: Thoughts on Cliometrics," *Times Literary Supplement,* 3823, June 13, 1975, pp. 667-70.

Fogel, Robert W. *Ten Lectures on the New Economic History* [In Japanese]. Tokyo: Nan-Un-Do, 1977.

Fogel, Robert W. "Cliometrics and Culture: Some Recent Developments in the Historiography of Slavery," *Journal of Social History,* 11(1), Fall 1977, pp. 34-51.

Fogel, Robert W. "Notes on the Social Saving Controversy," *Journal of Economic History,* 39(1), March 1979, pp. 1-54.

Fogel, Robert W. and Engerman, Stanley L. "A Model for the Explanation of Industrial Expansion During the Nineteenth Century: With an Application to the American Iron Industry," reprinted in Fogel and Engerman (eds), *The Reinterpretation of American Economic History,* 1971, pp. 148-62. *Journal of Political Economy,* 77(3), May/June 1969, pp. 306-28.

Fogel, Robert W. and Engerman, Stanley L. "The Economics of Slavery," in Fogel and Engerman (eds), *The Reinterpretation of American Economic History,* 1971, pp. 311-41.

Fogel, Robert W. and Engerman, Stanley L., eds. *The Reinterpretation of American Economic History.* New York: Harper & Row, 1971.

Fogel, Robert W. and Fishlow, Albert. "Quantitative Economic History: An Interim Evaluation, Past Trends and Present Tendencies," *Journal of Economic History,* 31(1), March 1971, pp. 15-42.

Fogel, Robert W. and Engerman, Stanley L. "The Relative Efficiency of Slavery: A Comparison of Northern and Southern Agriculture in 1860," *Explorations in Economic History,* 8(3), Spring 1971, pp. 353-67.

Fogel, Robert W. and Engerman, Stanley L. *Time on the Cross* (vol. 1: The Economics of American Negro Slavery; vol. 2: Evidence and Methods: A Supplement) [Translated into Spanish (1977), Italian (1977), Japanese (1978)]. Boston: Little, Brown, 1974.

Fogel, Robert W. and Engerman, Stanley L. "Philanthropy at Bargain Prices: Notes on the Economics of Gradual Emancipation," *Journal of Legal Studies,* 3(2), June 1974, pp. 377-401.

Fogel, Robert W. and Engerman, Stanley L. "A Comparison of the Relative Efficiency of Slave and Free Agriculture in the United States during 1860," in Van der Wee, Vinogradov, and Kotovsky (eds), *Fifth International Congress of Economic History,* 1976, pp. 141-6.

Fogel, Robert W. and Engerman, Stanley L. "Explaining the Relative Efficiency of Slave Agriculture in the Antebellum South," *American Economic Review,* 67(3), June 1977, pp. 275-96.

Fogel, Robert W.; Engerman, Stanley L.; Floud, Roderick C.; Wimmer, Larry T.; Trussell, James and Pope, Clayne L. "The Economics of Mortality in North America, 1650-1910: A Description of a Research Project," *Historical Methods,* 11(2), June 1978, pp. 75-108.

Fogel, Robert W. and Engerman, Stanley L. "Explaining the Relative Efficiency of Slave Agriculture in the Antebellum South: Reply (to David and Temin, Wright, and Schaefer and Schmitz)," *American*

Economic Review, 70(4), September 1980, pp. 672-90.

Fogel, Robert W. and Olson, John F. "Clock-Time vs. Real-Time: A Comparison of the Lengths of the Northern and the Southern Agricultural Work-Years." [Working Paper]

Fogel, Robert W. and Rutner, Jack L. "The Efficiency Effects of Federal Land Policy, 1850-1900: Some Provisional Findings," in Bogue, Aydelotte, and Fogel (eds), *The Dimensions of Quantitative Research in History,* 1972.

Fogel, Robert W. and Sokoloff, Kenneth. "The Economic and Demographic Significance of Secular Changes in Human Stature: The U.S., 1750-1960." [Working Paper]

Ford, A.G. "The Transfer of British Foreign Lending, 1870-1913," *Economic History Review,* Second Series, 11(2), 1958, pp. 302-8.

Ford, A.G. "Capital Exports and Growth for Argentina, 1880-1914," *Economic Journal,* 68(271), September 1958, pp. 589-93.

Ford, A.G. "Flexible Exchange Rates and Argentina, 1885-1900," *Oxford Economic Papers,* New Series, 10(3), October 1958, pp. 316-38.

Ford, A.G. "Notes on the Working of the Gold Standard Before 1914," *Oxford Economic Papers,* New Series, 12(1), February 1960, pp. 52-76.

Ford, A.G. "Capital Exports and Growth for Argentina: A Rejoinder (to Knapp)," *Economic Journal,* 70(279), September 1960, pp. 630-3.

Ford, A.G. *The Gold Standard, 1880-1914: Britain and Argentina* [Translated into Spanish (1966)]. Oxford: Oxford University Press, 1962.

Ford, A.G. "Notes on the Transfer of Overseas Lending and Grants," *Oxford Economic Papers,* New Series, 14(1), February 1962, pp. 94-102.

Ford, A.G. "Notes on the Role of Exports in British Economic Fluctuations, 1870-1914," *Economic History Review,* Second Series, 16(2), December 1963, pp. 328-37.

Ford, A.G. "Bank Rate, the British Balance of Payments and the Burdens of Adjustment, 1870-1914," *Oxford Economic Papers,* New Series, 16(1), March 1964, pp. 24-39.

Ford, A.G. "Overseas Lending and Internal Fluctuations: 1870-1914," reprinted in Hall (ed), *The Export of Capital from Britain,* 1968, pp. 84-102. *Yorkshire Bulletin of Economic and Social Research,* 17(1), May 1965, pp. 19-31.

Ford, A.G. "The Truth About Gold," *Lloyds Bank Review,* 71, July 1965, pp. 1-18.

Ford, A.G. "A Note on British Export Performance, 1899-1913," *Economic History Review,* Second Series, 22(1), April 1969, pp. 120-1.

Ford, A.G. "British Economic Fluctuations, 1870-1913," *Manchester School of Economic and Social Studies,* 37(2), June 1969, pp. 99-130.

Ford, A.G. "British Overseas Investment in Argentina and Long Swings, 1880-1914," reprinted in Floud (ed), *Essays in Quantitative Economic History,* 1974, pp. 216-27. *Journal of Economic History,* 31(3), September 1971, pp. 650-63.

Ford, A.G. "British Investment and Argentine Economic Development, 1880-1914," in Rock (ed), *Argentina in the Twentieth Century,* 1975, pp. 12-40.

Ford, A.G. "The Trade Cycle in Britain, 1860-1914," in Floud and McCloskey (eds), *The Economic History of Britain since 1700,* 1981.

Ford, A.G. "International Financial Policy and the Gold Standard, 1870-1914," in Mathias and Pollard (eds), *The Cambridge Economic History of Europe*, 1978.

Fordyce, Frederick E. and Rostow, W.W. "Growth Rates at Different Levels of Income and Stage of Growth: Reflections on Why the Poor Get Richer and the Rich Slow Down," in Uselding (ed), *Research in Economic History*, 1978, pp. 47-86.

Foreman-Peck, James S. "Tariff Protection and Economies of Scale: The British Motor Industry Before 1939," *Oxford Economic Papers*, New Series, 31(2), July 1979, pp. 237-57.

Foreman-Peck, James S. "Economies of Scale and the Development of the British Motor Industry Before 1939," Ph.D. Dissertation, London School of Economics, University of London, 1978.

Foreman-Peck, James S. "The Interdependence of the Manufacturing and Primary Product Sectors, 1881-1913," presented at the A.P.T.E. Conference, Plymouth, April 1979.

Forster, Colin. "Australian Manufacturing and the War of 1914-18," *Economic Record*, 29 November 1953, pp. 211-30.

Forster, Colin. *Industrial Development in Australia, 1920-1930*. Canberra: Australian National University Press, 1964.

Forster, Colin. "Australian Unemployment, 1900-1940," *Economic Record*, 41(95), September 1965, pp. 426-50.

Forster, Colin, ed. *Australian Economic Development in the Twentieth Century* [Reprinted in a Japanese Translation: Nijusseiki no Osutoraria Keizai (Tokyo: Kinokuniya Shoten, 1977)]. London: Allen & Unwin, 1970.

Forster, Colin. "Economies of Scale and Australian Manufacturing," in Forster (ed), *Australian Economic Development in the Twentieth Century*, 1970, pp. 123-68.

Forster, Colin. "Aspects of Australian Fertility, 1861-1901," *Australian Economic History Review*, 14(2), September 1974, pp. 105-22.

Forster, Colin. "Federation and the Tariff," *Australian Economic History Review*, 17(2), September 1977, pp. 95-116.

Forster, Colin. "Indexation and the Commonwealth Basic Wage, 1907-22," *Australian Economic History Review*, 20(2), September 1980, pp. 99-118.

Forster, Colin and Tucker, G.S.L. *Economic Opportunity and White American Fertility Ratios, 1800-1860*. New Haven: Yale University Press, 1972.

Foust, James D. "The Yeoman Farmer and Westward Expansion of U.S. Cotton Production," (Summary of Doctoral Dissertation) *Journal of Economic History*, 27(4), December 1967, pp. 611-4.

Foust, James D. *The Yeoman Farmer and Westward Expansion of U.S. Cotton Production*. New York: Arno Press, 1976.

Foust, James D.; Bateman, Fred and Weiss, Thomas J. "Large-Scale Manufacturing in the South and West, 1850-1860," *Business History Review*, 45(1), Spring 1971, pp. 18-34.

Foust, James D. and Bateman, Fred. "A Sample of Rural Households Selected from the 1860 Manuscript Censuses," *Agricultural History*, 48(1), January 1974, pp. 75-93.

Foust, James D.; Bateman, Fred and Weiss, Thomas J. "The Participation of Planters in Manufacturing in the Antebellum South," *Agricultural History*, 48(2), April 1974, pp. 277-97.

Foust, James D.; Bateman, Fred and Weiss, Thomas J. "Profitability in Southern Manufacturing: Estimates for 1860," *Explorations in Economic History*, 12(3), July 1975, pp. 211-32.

Foust, James D. and Swan, Dale E. "Productivity and Profitability of Antebellum Slave Labor: A Micro-Approach," in Parker (ed), *The Structure of the Cotton Economy of the Antebellum South*, 1970, pp. 39-62.

Fox-Genovese, Elizabeth. "Poor Richard at Work in the Cotton Fields: A Critique of the Psychological and Ideological Presuppositions of 'Time on the Cross'," *Review of Radical Political Economics*, 7(4), Fall 1975, pp. 67-83.

Fraas, Arthur. "The Second Bank of the United States: An Instrument for an Interregional Monetary Union," *Journal of Economic History*, 34(2), June 1974, pp. 447-67.

Frankel, S. Herbert. *Investment and the Return to Equity Capital in the South African Gold Mining Industry, 1887-1965: An International Comparison*. Cambridge: Harvard University Press, 1967.

Franks, Charles M. and McCormick, William W. "A Self-Generating Model of Long-Swings for the American Economy, 1860-1940," *Journal of Economic History*, 31(2), June 1971, pp. 295-343.

Fraundorf, Martha Norby. "Relative Earnings of Native- and Foreign-born Women," *Explorations in Economic History*, 15(2), April 1978, pp. 211-20.

Fremdling, Rainer. "Eisenbahnen und Deutsches Wirtschaftswachstum, 1840-1879. Ein Beitrag zur Entwicklungstheorie und zur Theorie der Infrastruktur (Untersuchungen zur Wirtschafts-, Sozial und Technikgeschichte, vol. 2)," [Railroads and German Economic Growth, 1840-1879: A Contribution to Development Theory and to the Theory of Infrastructure] *Gesellschaft fur Westfalische Wirtschaftgeschichte*, 1975.

Fremdling, Rainer. "Railroads and German Economic Growth: A Leading Sector Analysis with a Comparison to the United States and Great Britain," *Journal of Economic History*, 37(3), September 1977, pp. 583-604.

Fremdling, Rainer. "Modernisierung und Wachstum der Schwerindustrie in Deutschland, 1830-1860," [Modernization and Growth of Heavy Industry in Germany, 1830-1860] *Geschichte und Gesellschaft*, 5(2), 1979.

Fremdling, Rainer. "Freight Rates and State Budget: The Role of the National Prussian Railways, 1880-1913," *Journal of European Economic History*, 9(1), Spring 1980, pp. 21-40.

Fremdling, Rainer. "Die Rolle der Banken im Wachstumsprozess Deutschlands, 1850-1913," [The Role of Banks in the German Growth Process, 1850-1913] Ph.D. Dissertation, Universitat Munster, West Germany, 1969.

Fremdling, Rainer and Hohorst, Gerd. "Marktintegration der Preussischen Wirtschaft im 19. Jahrhundert: Skizze eines Forschungsansatzes zur Fluktuation der Roggenpreise zwischen 1821 und 1865," [Market Integration of the Prussian Economy in the 19th Century: Preliminary Findings on Fluctuations of Rye Prices Between 1821 and 1865] in Fremdling and Tilly (eds), *Industrialisierung und Raum*, 1979.

Fremdling, Rainer; Pierenkemper, Toni and Tilly, Richard H. "Regionale Differenzierung in Deutschland als Schwerpunkt

Wirtschaftshistorischer Forschung," [Regional Differentiation in
Germany as the Central Focus of Research in Economic History] in
Fremdling and Tilly (eds), *Industrialisierung und Raum*, 1979.

Fremdling, Rainer and Tilly, Richard H. "German Banks, German Growth,
and Econometric History: A Note on Neuberger and Stokes," *Journal
of Economic History*, 36(2), June 1976, pp. 416-24.

Fremdling, Rainer and Tilly, Richard H., eds. *Industrialisierung und
Raum, Studien zur Regionalen Differenzierung im Deutschland im 19.
Jahrhundert* [Industrialization and Spatial Relationships: Studies
on Regional Differentiation in Germany in the 19th Century]
(Historisch-Sozialwissenschaftliche Forschungen, vol. 7).
Stuttgart: Klett-Cotta, 1979.

Frenkel, Jacob A. "The Forward Exchange Rate, Expectations and the
Demand for Money: The German Hyperinflation," *American Economic
Review*, 67 September 1977, pp. 653-70.

Frenkel, Jacob A. "Purchasing Power Parity: Doctrinal Perspective and
Evidence from the 1920's," *Journal of International Economics*, 8,
May 1978, pp. 169-91.

Frenkel, Jacob A. "Exchange Rates, Prices, and Money: Lessons from the
1920's," *American Economic Review*, Papers and Proceedings, 70(2),
May 1980, pp. 235-42.

Freudenberger, Herman and Cummins, J. Gaylord. "Health, Work, and
Leisure before the Industrial Revolution," *Explorations in Economic
History*, 13(1), January 1976, pp. 1-12.

Freudenberger, Herman and Wolff, Klaus. "Transfer of Technology,"
(Summary of 1976 Research Workshop) *Journal of Economic History*,
37(1), March 1977, pp. 231-4.

Freund, W.M. and Shenton, R.W. "'Vent-for-Surplus' Theory and the
Economic History of West Africa," *Savanna*, 6(2), December 1977, pp.
191-6.

Friedman, Gerald. "Slave Heights: Trinidad and the United States."
[Working Paper]

Friedman, Gerald. "Slave Occupations in Trinidad and Eight Southern
States." [Working Paper]

Friedman, Gerald. "The Demography of Trinidad Slavery." [Working
Paper]

Friedman, Gerald. "The Registration of Slaves in Trinidad, 1813: More
Numbers for the Slavery Game." [Working Paper]

Friedman, Gerald and Medoff, James. "Slavery and the Termination of
Implicit Contracts." [Working Paper]

Friedman, Milton. "Monetary Data and National Income Estimates,"
Economic Development and Cultural Change, 9(3), April 1961, pp.
267-86.

Friedman, Milton. "Monetary Trends in the United States and United
Kingdom," *American Economist*, 16(1), Spring 1972, pp. 4-18.

Friedman, Milton. "Prices of Money and Goods Across Frontiers: The
Pound and the Dollar Over a Century," *The World Economy*, 2,
February 1980, pp. 497-511.

Friedman, Milton and Schwartz, Anna J. *A Monetary History of the
United States, 1867-1960*. Princeton: Princeton University Press
for the National Bureau of Economic Research, 1963.

Friedman, Milton and Schwartz, Anna J. "Money and Business Cycles,"
Review of Economics and Statistics, 45(1), Part 2 Supplement,
February 1963, pp. 32-78.

Friedman, Milton and Schwartz, Anna J. *Monetary Statistics of the United States: Estimates, Sources, Methods.* New York: Columbia University Press for the National Bureau of Economic Research, 1970.

Friedman, Philip. *The Impact of Trade Destruction Upon National Incomes: A Study of Europe, 1924-1938.* Gainsville: University of Florida Press, 1974.

Friedman, Philip. "The Welfare Costs of Bilateralism: German-Hungarian Trade, 1933-1938," *Explorations in Economic History,* 13(1), January 1976, pp. 113-25.

Friedman, Philip. "Traditionele en Nieuwe Economische Geschiedenis: Een Vergelijking Van Methoden," *Amsterdam/Streven,* November 1977, pp. 112-7.

Friedman, Philip. "An Econometric Model of National Income, Commercial Policy and the Level of International Trade: The Open Economies of Europe, 1924-1938," *Journal of Economic History,* 38(1), March 1978, pp. 148-80.

Friedman, Philip. "A Reconstructionist Production Function: Post Civil War South and the Optimal Path to Recovery," presented at the Meeting of the Western Economic Association, August 1973.

Friedman, Philip. "An Analysis of the International Transmission of Hyper-inflation: Central Europe, 1922-1925." [Working Paper]

Friedman, Philip. "Financial Intermediation and the Neutrality of Money: The Impact of Institutional Change Upon a Banker's Response, Post Civil War to the Great Depression." [Working Paper]

Friedman, Philip. "Inflation, Deflation, and Forward Markets: The Effects of Trade and Exchange Markets on the German Hyper-inflation." [Working Paper]

Fritsch, Winston. "Aspectos da Politica Economica no Brasil, 1906-1914," [Aspects of Economic Politics in Brazil, 1906-1914] in Neuhaus (ed), *A Economia Brasileira,* 1979.

Fua, Giorgio. *Lo sviluppo economico in Italia* (3 vols) 2nd ed. rev.: vol. 1 (1981); vol. 2 (1974); vol. 3 (1975). Milano: Franco Angeli, 1969.

Fua, Giorgio. *Formazione, distribuzione e impiego dal reddito del 1861: sintesi statistica* [Origin, Distribution, and Destination of National Income since 1861: Statistical Synthesis]. Roma: ISCO, 1972.

Fua, Giorgio. "La distribuzione del reddito in Italia, 1862-1970," [Income Distribution in Italy, 1862-1970] *Studi economici,* 1, 1973.

Fua, Giorgio. "Declino dell'agricoltura e legge di Engel nell'esperienza italiana, 1897-1967," [Agricultural Decline and Engel's Law in the Italian Experience, 1897-1967] *Moneta e credito,* 107, September 1974.

Fua, Giorgio. "Breve sintesi statistica dello sviluppo economico italiano 1861-1940," [Brief Statistical Synthesis of Italian Economic Development, 1861-1940] in Toniolo (ed), *L'economia italiana,* 1978, pp. 47-67.

Fujino, Shiro and Ono, Akira. "Textile Industry, 1890-1945," in Ohkawa and Hayami (eds), *Economic Growth,* 1973, pp. 154-64.

Furet, Francois. "L'Histoire Quantitative et la Construction du Fait Historique," [Quantitative History and the Construction of Historical Fact] *Annales: Economies, Societes, Civilisations,* 26(1), 1971, pp. 63-75.

Furet, Francois. "Quantitative History," in Gilbert and Graubard (eds), *Historical Studies Today*, 1974, pp. 45-61.

Furet, Francois; Bouvier, Jean and Gillet, Marcel, eds. *Le Mouvement du profit en France au XIXe siecle: Materiaux et Etudes* [The Movement of Profit in Nineteenth Century France]. Paris: Mouton, 1965.

Gagan, David P. "The Indivisibility of Land: A Microanalysis of the System of Inheritance in Nineteenth-Century Ontario," *Journal of Economic History*, 36(1), March 1976, pp. 126-41.

Gale, Bradley T. and Soper, John C. "Long Swings in British Economic Growth, 1700-1938," (Summary of Paper Presented at the Meetings of the Western Economic Association) *Western Economic Journal*, 9(3), September 1971, pp. 327.

Galenson, Alice C. *The Migration of the Cotton Textile Industry from New England to the South: 1880-1930*. Ithaca, N.Y.: Cornell University Press, 1975.

Galenson, David W. "The End of the Chisholm Trail," *Journal of Economic History*, 34(2), June 1974, pp. 350-64.

Galenson, David W. "Cattle Trailing in the Nineteenth Century: A Reply to Dennen," *Journal of Economic History*, 35(2), June 1975, pp. 461-6.

Galenson, David W. "Origins of the Long Drive," *Journal of the West*, 14(3), July 1975, pp. 3-14.

Galenson, David W. "Immigration and the Colonial Labor System: An Analysis of the Length of Indenture," *Explorations in Economic History*, 14(4), October 1977, pp. 360-77.

Galenson, David W. "The Profitability of the Long Drive," *Agricultural History*, 51(4), October 1977, pp. 737-58.

Galenson, David W. "British Servants and the Colonial Indenture System in the Eighteenth Century," *Journal of Southern History*, 44(1), February 1978, pp. 41-66.

Galenson, David W. "'Middling People' or 'Common Sort'?: The Social Origins of Some Early Americans Reexamined," *William and Mary Quarterly*, Third Series, 35(3), July 1978, pp. 499-524.

Galenson, David W. "The Social Origins of Some Early Americans: Rejoinder," *William and Mary Quarterly*, Third Series, 36(2), April 1979, pp. 264-77.

Galenson, David W. "Literacy and the Social Origins of Some Early Americans," *Historical Journal*, 22(1), May 1979, pp. 75-96.

Galenson, David W. "The Slave Trade to the English West Indies, 1673-1724: Evidence from Royal African Company Records," *Economic History Review*, Second Series, 32(2), May 1979, pp. 241-9.

Galenson, David W. "Demographic Aspects of White Servitude in Colonial British America," *Annales de Demographic Historique*, 1980, pp. 239-52.

Galenson, David W. *White Servitude in Colonial America: An Economic Analysis*. Cambridge and New York: Cambridge University Press, 1981.

Galenson, David W. and Menard, Russell R. "Approaches to the Analysis of Economic Growth in Colonial British America," *Historical*

Methods, 13(1), Winter 1980, pp. 3-18.

Gallaway, Lowell E. and Vedder, Richard K. "The Settlement Preferences of Scandinavian Emigrants to the United States, 1850-1960," *Scandinavian Economic History Review,* 18(2), 1970, pp. 159-76.

Gallaway, Lowell E. and Vedder, Richard K. "Internal Migration of Native-Born Ohioans: 1850-1960," *Bulletin of Business Research,* 15(6), June 1970, pp. 4-5.

Gallaway, Lowell E. and Vedder, Richard K. "Settlement Patterns of Canadian Emigrants to the United States, 1850-1960," *Canadian Journal of Economics,* 3(3), August 1970, pp. 476-86.

Gallaway, Lowell E. and Vedder, Richard K. "The Increasing Urbanization Thesis: Did 'New Immigrants' to the United States Have a Particular Fondness for Urban Life?," *Explorations in Economic History,* 8(3), Spring 1971, pp. 305-19.

Gallaway, Lowell E. and Vedder, Richard K. "Mobility of Native Americans," *Journal of Economic History,* 31(3), September 1971, pp. 613-49.

Gallaway, Lowell E. and Vedder, Richard K. "Emigration from the United Kingdom to the United States: 1860-1913," *Journal of Economic History,* 31(4), December 1971, pp. 885-97.

Gallaway, Lowell E. and Vedder, Richard K. "The Geographical Distribution of British and Irish Emigrants to the United States after 1800," *Scottish Journal of Political Economy,* 19(1), February 1972, pp. 19-36.

Gallaway, Lowell E.; Vedder, Richard K. and Shukla, Vishwa. "The Distribution of the Immigrant Population in the United States: An Economic Analysis," *Explorations in Economic History,* 11(3), Spring 1974, pp. 213-26.

Gallaway, Lowell E.; Vedder, Richard K. and Klingaman, David C. "The Ames-Rosenberg Hypothesis Revisited: A Note on Uselding," *Explorations in Economic History,* 11(3), Spring 1974, pp. 311-4.

Gallaway, Lowell E.; Vedder, Richard K. and Klingaman, David C. "The Profitability of Antebellum Agriculture in the Cotton Belt: Some New Evidence," *Atlantic Economic Journal,* 2(2), November 1974, pp. 30-47.

Gallaway, Lowell E. and Vedder, Richard K. "Migration and the Old Northwest," in Klingaman and Vedder (eds), *Essays in Nineteenth Century Economic History,* 1975, pp. 159-76.

Gallaway, Lowell E. and Vedder, Richard K. "Settlement Patterns of American Immigrants, 1850-1968," in Van der Wee, Vinogradov, and Kotovsky (eds), *Fifth International Congress of Economic History,* 1976, pp. 128-45.

Gallaway, Lowell E.; Vedder, Richard K.; Klingaman, David C. and Uselding, Paul. "Discrimination and Exploitation in Antebellum American Cotton Textile Manufacturing," in Uselding (ed), *Research in Economic History,* 1978, pp. 217-61.

Gallaway, Lowell E. and Vedder, Richard K. "The Profitability of Antebellum Manufacturing: Some New Estimates," *Business History Review,* 54(1), Spring 1980, pp. 92-103.

Gallaway, Lowell E. and Vedder, Richard K. "Population Transfers and the Postbellum Adjustments to Economic Dislocation, 1870-1920," *Journal of Economic History,* 40(1), March 1980, pp. 143-9.

Gallaway, Lowell E. and Vedder, Richard K. "A Nation of Movers: American Internal Migration in Historical Perspective." [Working

Paper]

Gallaway, Lowell E. and Vedder, Richard K. "The Great Depression: A Tale of Three Paradigms," Ohio University Economic History Research Paper no. F-47.

Gallaway, Lowell E.; Vedder, Richard K. and Lindley, Susan. "Some Quarterly Estimates of GNP, 1929-1940," Ohio University Economic History Research Paper no. F-48.

Gallman, Robert E. "Commodity Output, 1839-1899," in Parker (ed), *Trends in the American Economy in the Nineteenth Century*, 1960, pp. 13-67.

Gallman, Robert E. "Commodity Output, 1839-1899: Reply to Potter," in Parker (ed), *Trends in the American Economy in the Nineteenth Century*, 1960, pp. 69-71.

Gallman, Robert E. "Estimates of American National Product Made before the Civil War," reprinted in Andreano (ed), New Views on American Economic Development, 1965, pp. 168-186. *Economic Development and Cultural Change*, 9(3), April 1961, pp. 397-412.

Gallman, Robert E. "A Note on the Patent Office Crop Estimates, 1841-1848," *Journal of Economic History*, 23(2), June 1963, pp. 185-95.

Gallman, Robert E. *Developing the American Colonies, 1607-1783.* Chicago: Scott, Foresman, 1964.

Gallman, Robert E. "The Role of Economic History in the Education of the Economist," *American Economic Review*, Papers and Proceedings, 50(2), May 1965, pp. 109-11.

Gallman, Robert E. "Gross National Product in the United States, 1834-1909," in Brady (ed), *Output, Employment, and Productivity in the United States after 1800*, 1966, pp. 3-76.

Gallman, Robert E. "The Social Distribution of Wealth in the United States of America," in *Third International Conference of Economic History, Munich, 1965*, part 1. Paris and The Hague: Mouton, 1968, pp. 313-34.

Gallman, Robert E. "Trends in the Size Distribution of Wealth in the Nineteenth Century: Some Speculations," in Soltow (ed), *Six Papers on the Size Distribution of Wealth and Income*, 1969, pp. 1-25.

Gallman, Robert E. "Trends in the Size Distribution of Wealth in the Nineteenth Century: Reply to Soltow," in Soltow (ed), *Six Papers on the Size Distribution of Wealth and Income*, 1969, pp. 27-30.

Gallman, Robert E. "Self-Sufficiency in the Cotton Economy of the Antebellum South," reprinted in Parker (ed), The Structure of the Cotton Economy of the Antebellum South, 1970, pp. 5-23. *Agricultural History*, 44(1), January 1970, pp. 5-23.

Gallman, Robert E. "The Statistical Approach: Fundamental Concepts as Applied to History," in Taylor and Ellsworth (eds), *Approaches to American Economic History*, 1971, pp. 63-86.

Gallman, Robert E. "The Pace and Pattern of American Economic Growth," in Davis, Easterlin, and Parker (eds), *American Economic Growth*, 1972, pp. 15-60.

Gallman, Robert E. "Changes in Total U.S. Agricultural Factor Productivity in the Nineteenth Century," *Agricultural History*, 46(1), January 1972, pp. 191-210.

Gallman, Robert E. "The Agricultural Sector and the Pace of Economic Growth: U.S. Experience in the Nineteenth Century," in Klingaman and Vedder (eds), *Essays in Nineteenth Century Economic History*,

343

1975, pp. 35-76.

Gallman, Robert E. "Southern Antebellum Income Reconsidered: A Note (on Gunderson)," *Explorations in Economic History,* 12(1), January 1975, pp. 89-99.

Gallman, Robert E. "Human Capital in the First 80 Years of the Republic: How Much Did America Owe the Rest of the World?," *American Economic Review,* Papers and Proceedings, 67(1), February 1977, pp. 27-31.

Gallman, Robert E. "Slavery, the Supply of Agricultural Labor, and the Industrialization of the South: Comment on Fleisig," *Journal of Economic History,* 37(2), June 1977, pp. 473-4.

Gallman, Robert E. "Professor Pessen on 'The Egalitarian Myth'," *Social Science History,* 2(2), Winter 1978, pp. 194-207.

Gallman, Robert E. and Davis, Lance E. "Capital Formation in the United States during the 19th Century," in Mathias and Postan (eds), *The Cambridge Economic History of Europe,* 1978, pp. 1-69.

Gallman, Robert E. "Comment on Papers by Anderson, Haeger, Kulikoff, and Lindstrom Presented to the 38th Annual Meeting of the Economic History Association," *Journal of Economic History,* 39(1), March 1979, pp. 311-2.

Gallman, Robert E. "Slavery and Southern Economic Growth," *Southern Economic Journal,* 45(4), April 1979, pp. 1007-22.

Gallman, Robert E. "Economic Growth," in Porter (ed), *Encyclopedia of American Economic History,* 1980, pp. 133-50.

Gallman, Robert E. "Capital Formation and Capital Allocation." [Working Paper]

Gallman, Robert E. "Equality in the United States at the Time of Tocqueville." [Working Paper]

Gallman, Robert E. and Howle, E.S. "The U.S. Capital Stock in the 19th Century." [Working Paper]

Gallman, Robert E. and Anderson, Ralph V. "Slaves as Fixed Capital: Slave Labor and Southern Economic Development," *Journal of American History,* 64(1), June 1977, pp. 24-46.

Gallman, Robert E. and Davis, Lance E. "The Share of Savings and Investment in Gross National Product during the Nineteenth Century in the United States of America," in *Fourth International Conference of Economic History, Bloomington, 1968.* Paris and The Hague: Mouton, 1973, pp. 437-66.

Gallman, Robert E. and Howle, Edward S. "Trends in the Structure of the American Economy since 1840," in Fogel and Engerman (eds), *The Reinterpretation of American Economic History,* 1971, pp. 25-37.

Gallman, Robert E. and Weiss, Thomas J. "The Service Industries in the Nineteenth Century," in Fuchs (ed), *Production and Productivity in the Service Industries,* 1969, pp. 287-352.

Gallman, Robert E. and Weiss, Thomas J. "The Service Industries in the Nineteenth Century: Reply to Easterlin, Lebergott, Fabricant, and Firestone," in Fuchs (ed), *Production and Productivity in the Service Industries,* 1969, pp. 372-81.

Gallo, Giampaolo; Covino, Renato and Mantovani, Enrico. "L'industria dall'economia di guerra alla ricostruzione," [Industry from the War Economy to Reconstruction] in Ciocca and Toniolo (eds), *L'economia italiana nel periodo fascista,* 1976, pp. 171-270.

Gandolfi, Arthur E. "Stability of the Demand for Money during the Great Contraction, 1929-1933," *Journal of Political Economy,* 82(5),

September 1974, pp. 969-84.

Gandolfi, Arthur E. and Lothian, James R. "Review of 'Did Monetary Forces Cause the Great Depression?' by Peter Temin (New York: W.W. Norton, 1976)," *Journal of Money, Credit, and Banking,* 9(4), November 1977, pp. 679-90.

Garside, W.R. "Juvenile Unemployment and Public Policy between the Wars," *Economic History Review,* Second Series, 30(2), May 1977, pp. 322-39.

Garside, W.R. "Juvenile Unemployment between the Wars: A Rejoinder (to Benjamin and Kochin)," *Economic History Review,* Second Series, 32(4), November 1979, pp. 529-32.

Gatrell, V.A.C. "Labour, Power, and the Size of Firms in Lancashire Cotton in the Second Quarter of the Nineteenth Century," *Economic History Review,* Second Series, 30(1), February 1977, pp. 95-139.

Gaunt, David; Akerman, Sune and Johansen, Hans Chr., eds. *Chance and Change: Social and Economic Studies in Historical Demography in the Baltic Area.* Odense: Odense University Press, 1978.

Gayer, Arthur D.; Rostow, W.W. and Schwartz, Anna J. *The Growth and Fluctuation of the British Economy, 1790-1850* (Revised Second Edition, New York: Barnes & Noble, 1975). Oxford: Clarendon Press, 1953.

Gemery, Henry A. "Absorption of Population Pressure in Nineteenth Century Sweden," in Grebenik (ed), *Proceedings of the International Population Conference,* 1971, pp. 1688-702.

Gemery, Henry A. "Emigration from the British Isles to the New World, 1630-1700: Inferences from Colonial Populations," in Uselding (ed), *Research in Economic History,* 1980, pp. 179-232.

Gemery, Henry A. and Dunlevy, James A. "Settlement Patterns of 'Old' and 'New' Migrants: A Dynamic Appraisal," *Proceedings: American Statistical Association, Business and Economics Statistics Section (1976).* Washington, D.C.: American Statistical Association, 1976, pp. 282-5.

Gemery, Henry A. and Dunlevy, James A. "Some Additional Evidence on Settlements Patterns for Scandinavian Migrants to the United States: Dynamics and the Role of Family and Friends," *Scandinavian Economic History Review,* 24(2), 1976, pp. 143-52.

Gemery, Henry A. and Dunlevy, James A. "The Role of Migrant Stock and Lagged Migration in the Settlement Patterns of Nineteenth Century Immigrants," *Review of Economics and Statistics,* 59(2), May 1977, pp. 137-44.

Gemery, Henry A. and Dunlevy, James A. "British-Irish Settlement Patterns in the U.S.: The Role of Family and Friends," *Scottish Journal of Political Economy,* 24(3), November 1977, pp. 257-63.

Gemery, Henry A. and Dunlevy, James A. "Economic Opportunity and the Responses of 'Old' and 'New' Migrants to The United States," *Journal of Economic History,* 38(4), December 1978, pp. 901-17.

Gemery, Henry A. and Hogendorn, Jan S. "The Atlantic Slave Trade: A Tentative Economic Model," *Journal of African History,* 15(2), 1974, pp. 223-46.

Gemery, Henry A. and Hogendorn, Jan S. "Slave Labor Supply Elasticity and the Development of Slave Economies in the British Carribean: The 17th Century Experience," in Rubin and Tuden (ed), *Comparative Perspectives on Slavery in New World Plantation Societies,* 1977, pp. 72-83.

345

Gemery, Henry A. and Hogendorn, Jan S. "Technological Change, Slavery, and the Slave Trade," in Dewey and Hopkins (eds), *The Imperial Impact*, 1978, pp. 243-58.

Gemery, Henry A. and Hogendorn, Jan S. "Editor's Introduction," in Gemery and Hogendorn (eds), *The Uncommon Market*, 1979, pp. 1-19.

Gemery, Henry A. and Hogendorn, Jan S. "The Economic Costs of West African Participation in the Atlantic Slave Trade: A Preliminary Sampling for the Eighteenth Century," in Gemery and Hogendorn (eds), *The Uncommon Market*, 1979, pp. 143-61.

Gemery, Henry A. and Hogendorn, Jan S., eds. *The Uncommon Market: Essays in the Economic History of the Atlantic Slave Trade.* New York: Academic Press, 1979.

Gemery, Henry A. and Hogendorn, Jan S. "Comparative Disadvantage: The Case of Sugar Cultivation in West Africa," *Journal of Interdisciplinary History*, 9(3), Winter 1979, pp. 429-50.

Genovese, Eugene D. and Engerman, Stanley L., eds. *Race and Slavery in the Western Hemisphere: Quantitative Studies.* Princeton: Princeton University Press, 1975.

George, Peter J. "Rates of Return in Railway Investment and Implications for Government Subsidization of the Canadian Pacific Railway: Some Preliminary Results," *Canadian Journal of Economics*, 1(4), November 1968, pp. 740-62.

George, Peter J. "Rates of Return and Government Subsidization of the Canadian Pacific Railway: Some Further Remarks," *Canadian Journal of Economics*, 8(4), November 1975, pp. 591-600.

George, Peter J. *Government Subsidies and Railway Construction: The Building of the Canadian Pacific Railway, 1870-1896.* New York: Arno Press, 1980.

George, Peter J. and Oksanen, Ernest H. "Recent Methodological Developments in the Quantification of Economic History," *Histoire Sociale/Social History*, 2(3), April 1969, pp. 5-31.

George, Peter J. and Oksanen, Ernest H. "Recent Developments in the Quantification of Canadian Economic History," *Histoire Sociale/Social History*, 2(4), November 1969, pp. 76-95.

George, Peter J. and Oksanen, Ernest H. "Saturation in the Automobile Market in the Late Twenties: Some Further Results," *Explorations in Economic History*, 11(1), Fall 1973, pp. 73-86.

George, Peter J. and Oksanen, Ernest H. "An Index of Aggregate Economic Activity in Canada, 1896-1939: A Factor Analytic Approach," reprinted in Flinn (ed), *Proceedings of the Seventh International Economic History Congress*, 1978, pp. 87-95. *Explorations in Economic History*, 17(2), April 1980, pp. 165-75.

Gerber, Haim and Gross, Nachum T. "Inflation or Deflation in Nineteenth-Century Syria and Palestine: A Note (on Chevallier)," *Journal of Economic History*, 40(2), June 1980, pp. 351-7.

Gerschenkron, Alexander. "The Early Phases of Industrialization in Russia: Afterthoughts and Counterthoughts," in Rostow (ed), *The Economics of Take-off into Sustained Growth*, 1963, pp. 151-69.

Ghali, Moheb A. and Coelho, Philip R.P. "The End of the North-South Wage Differential," *American Economic Review*, 61(5), December 1971, pp. 932-7.

Ghali, Moheb A. and Coelho, Philip R.P. "The End of the North-South Wage Differential: Reply (to Ladenson)," *American Economic Review*, 63(4), September 1973, pp. 757-62.

346

Gilbert, Geoffrey N. "Baltimore's Flour Trade to the Carribean, 1750-1815," (Summary of Doctoral Dissertation) *Journal of Economic History*, 37(1), March 1977, pp. 249-51.

Gilbert, Geoffrey N. "The Role of Breadstuffs in American Trade, 1770-1790," *Explorations in Economic History*, 14(4), October 1977, pp. 378-87.

Ginzberg, Eli. "Slavery as an Obstacle to Economic Growth in the United States: A Panel Discussion of Conrad and Meyer," *Journal of Economic History*, 27(4), December 1967, pp. 538-40.

Gjolberg, Ole. "The Substitution of Steam for Sail in Norwegian Shipping, 1866-1914: A Study in the Economics of Diffusion," *Scandinavian Economic History Review*, 28(2), 1980, pp. 135-46.

Gjolberg, Ole. "Migration from Norway to the U.S., 1866-1914: A Comment." [Working Paper]

Glazier, I.A.; Wagner, J.R. and Tononelli, Pier Angelo. "Fiscal Policy, Public Sector and Economic Growth: The Case of Italy (1879-1913)," in *Seventh International Economic History Congress, Edinburgh, 1978*. Edinburgh: Edinburgh University Press, 1978.

Glynn, Sean and Lougheed, Alan L. "A Comment on United States Economic Policy and the. "Dollar Gap" of the 1920's," *Economic History Review*, Second Series, 26(4), November 1973, pp. 692-4.

Goldberg, Victor P. and Olmstead, Alan L. "Institutional Change and American Economic Growth: A Critique of Davis and North," *Explorations in Economic History*, 12(2), April 1975, pp. 193-210.

Goldberger, A.S. and Klein, L.R. *An Econometric Model of the United States, 1929-52*. Amsterdam: North-Holland, 1955.

Golden, James R. "Investment Behavior by United States Railroads: 1870-1914," (Summary of Doctoral Dissertation) *Journal of Economic History*, 32(1), March 1972, pp. 412-4.

Goldin, Claudia D. "The Economics of Emancipation," *Journal of Economic History*, 33(1), March 1973, pp. 66-85.

Goldin, Claudia D. "A Model to Explain the Relative Decline of Urban Slavery: Empirical Results," in Engerman and Genovese (eds), *Race and Slavery in the Western Hemisphere*, 1975, pp. 427-50.

Goldin, Claudia D. "Cities and Slavery: The Issue of Compatibility," in Schnore (ed), *The New Urban History*, 1975.

Goldin, Claudia D. *Urban Slavery in the American South, 1820-1860: A Quantitative History*. Chicago: University of Chicago Press, 1976.

Goldin, Claudia D. "Female Labor Force Participation: The Origin of Black and White Differences, 1870 and 1880," *Journal of Economic History*, 37(1), March 1977, pp. 87-108.

Goldin, Claudia D. "'N' Kinds of Freedom: An Introduction to the Issues," *Explorations in Economic History*, 16(1), January 1979, pp. 8-30.

Goldin, Claudia D. "Comments on Dissertations by Alston and Shlomovitz Presented to the 38th Annual Meeting of the Economic History Association," *Journal of Economic History*, 39(1), March 1979, pp. 336-8.

Goldin, Claudia D. "Household and Market Production of Families in a Late Nineteenth Century American City," *Explorations in Economic History*, 16(2), April 1979, pp. 111-31.

Goldin, Claudia D. "War," in Porter (ed), *Encyclopedia of American Economic History*, 1980, pp. 935-57.

Goldin, Claudia D. and Lewis, Frank D. "The Role of Exports in

American Economic Growth during the Napoleonic Wars, 1793 to 1807,"
Explorations in Economic History, 17(1), January 1980, pp. 6-25.

Goldin, Claudia D. "The Work and Wages of Single Women, 1870 to 1920,"
Journal of Economic History, 40(1), March 1980, pp. 81-8.

Goldin, Claudia D. "Family Strategies and the Family Economy in the
Late Nineteenth Century: The Role of Secondary Workers," in
Hershberg (ed), *Philadelphia,* 1981, pp. 240-76.

Goldin, Claudia D. and Lewis, Frank D. "The Economic Cost of the
American Civil War: Estimates and Implications," *Journal of
Economic History,* 35(2), June 1975, pp. 299-326.

Goldin, Claudia D. and Lewis, Frank D. "The Postbellum Recovery of the
South and the Cost of the Civil War: Comment on Temin," *Journal of
Economic History,* 38(2), June 1978, pp. 487-92.

Goldin, Claudia D. and Lewis, Frank D. "Growth and Exports, 1793 to
1807, and a Re-Examination of Growth before 1840." [Working Paper]

Goldsmith, Raymond W. *A Study of Saving in the United States, vol. 1:
Introduction; Tables of Annual Estimates of Saving, 1897 to 1949.*
Princeton: Princeton University Press, 1955.

Goldsmith, Raymond W. "National Balance Sheets and National Wealth
Statements, 1896 to 1949," in Goldsmith et al (eds), *A Study of
Saving in the United States,* 1957, pp. 3-138.

Goldsmith, Raymond W. "Experiments with the Saving Function," in
Goldsmith et al (eds), *A Study of Saving in the United States,*
1957, pp. 385-420.

Goldsmith, Raymond W. "Estimates of National Product, National Income,
and Personal Income, 1897 to 1949," in Goldsmith et al (eds), *A
Study of Saving in the United States,* 1957, pp. 421-46.

Goldsmith, Raymond W. *Financial Intermediaries in the American Economy
Since 1900.* Princeton: Princeton University Press, 1958.

Goldsmith, Raymond W. "The Economic Growth of Tsarist Russia,
1860-1913," *Economic Development and Cultural Change,* 9(3), April
1961, pp. 441-75.

Goldsmith, Raymond W. "Long Period Growth in Income and Product,
1839-1960," in Andreano (ed), *New Views,* 1965, pp. 337-61.

Goldsmith, Raymond W. "The Quantitative International Comparison of
Financial Structure and Development," *Journal of Economic History,*
35(1), March 1975, pp. 216-37.

Goldsmith, Raymond W. "A Synthetic Estimate of the National Wealth of
Japan, 1885-1973," *Review of Income and Wealth,* 21(2), June 1975,
pp. 125-52.

Goldsmith, Raymond W. "The Share of Financial Intermediaries in
National Wealth and National Assets, 1900-1949," National Bureau of
Economic Research, Occasional Paper no. 42, 1954.

Goldsmith, Raymond W.; Brady, Dorothy S. and Menderhausen, Horst. *A
Study of Saving in the United States, vol. 3: Special Studies.*
Princeton: Princeton University Press, 1957.

Gomez-Mendoza, Antonio. "Railways and Spanish Economic Growth,
1875-1914," Ph.D. Dissertation, St. Antony's College, Oxford, 1980.

Gommel, Rainer. *Wachstum und Konjunktur der Nurnberger Wirtschaft
(1815-1914)* [Growth and Business Cycles of the Nurembergian
Economy, 1815-1914]. Stuttgart: Klett-Cotta, 1978.

Gommel, Rainer. "The Development of a Growth Pole in the Nineteenth
Century illustrated by the Example of Nuremberg," in Bairoch and
Levy-Leboyer (eds), *Disparities in Economic Development since the*

Industrial Revolution, 1980.

Gommel, Rainer; Schneider, Jurgen and Kellenbenz, Hermann. *Wirtschaftliches Wachstum im Spiegel der Wirtschaftsgeschichte* [Economic Growth in Economic Historical Perspective]. Darmstadt: Wissenschaftliche Buchgesellschaft, 1978.

Good, David F. "Backwardness and the Role of Banking in Nineteenth-Century European Industrialization: A Note (on Gerschenkron)," *Journal of Economic History*, 33(4), December 1973, pp. 845-50.

Good, David F. "Stagnation and 'Take-Off' in Austria, 1873-1913," *Economic History Review*, Second Series, 27(1), February 1974, pp. 72-87.

Good, David F. "The Cost-of-Living in Austria, 1874-1913," *Journal of European Economic History*, 5(2), Fall 1976, pp. 391-400.

Good, David F. "National Bias in the Austrian Capital Market before World War I," *Explorations in Economic History*, 14(2), April 1977, pp. 141-66.

Good, David F. "Financial Integration in Late Nineteenth-Century Austria," *Journal of Economic History*, 37(4), December 1977, pp. 890-910.

Good, David F. "The Great Depression and Austrian Economic Growth after 1873: A Reply to Komlos," *Economic History Review*, Second Series, 31(2), May 1978, pp. 290-4.

Good, David F. "Discrimination in the Austrian Capital Market? A Reply to Komlos," *Explorations in Economic History*, 17(4), October 1980, pp. 428-33.

Good, David F. "Economic Integration and Regional Development in Austria-Hungary, 1867-1913," in Bairoch and Levy-Leboyer (eds), *Disparities in Economic Development since the Industrial Revolution*, 1981, pp. 137-50.

Goodhart, Charles A.E. "Profit on National Bank Notes, 1900-1913," *Journal of Political Economy*, 73(5), October 1965, pp. 516-22.

Goodhart, Charles A.E. *The New York Money Market and the Finance of Trade, 1900-1913*. Cambridge: Harvard University Press, 1969.

Goodhart, Charles A.E. *The Business of Banking, 1891-1914*. London: Weidenfeld & Nicholson, 1972.

Goodhart, Charles A.E. "The Determination of the volume of Bank Deposits 1891-1914," Ph.D. Dissertation, University of Cambridge, 1963.

Goodrich, Carter. "Recent Contributions to Economic History: The United States, 1789-1860," *Journal of Economic History*, 19(1), March 1959, pp. 25-43.

Goodrich, Carter. "Economic History: One Field or Two?," *Journal of Economic History*, 20(4), December 1960, pp. 531-8.

Goodrich, Carter, ed. *Canals and American Economic Development*. New York: Columbia University Press, 1961.

Goodrich, Carter. "Internal Improvements Reconsidered," *Journal of Economic History*, 30(2), June 1970, pp. 289-311.

Gordon, Donald F. and Chambers, Edward J. "Primary Products and Economic Growth: An Empirical Measurement," [Translated into Spanish in Journal of the Fundacion de Investigationes Economicas Lationoamericanas] *Journal of Political Economy*, 74(4), August 1966, pp. 315-32.

Gordon, Donald F. and Chambers, Edward J. "Primary Products and

Economic Growth: Rejoinder to Dales, McManus, and Watkins," *Journal of Political Economy*, 75(6), December 1967, pp. 881-5.

Gordon, Donald F. and Walton, Gary M. "A Theory of Regenerative Growth and the Experience of Post-World War II West Germany." [Working Paper]

Gordon, R.A. "Cyclical Experience in the Interwar Period: The Investment Boom of the Twenties," in Universities-National Bureau Conference for Economic Research, (ed), *Conference on Business Cycles*, 1951, pp. 163-214.

Gordon, Robert J. "A Consistent Characterization of a Near-Century of Price Behavior," *American Economic Review*, Papers and Proceedings, 70(2), May 1980, pp. 243-9.

Gordon, Robert J. and Wilcox, James A. "Monetarist Interpretations of the Great Depression: An Evaluation and Critique," in Brunner (ed), *The Great Depression Revisited*, 1981, pp. 49-107.

Gordon, Robert J. and Wilcox, James A. "Monetarist Interpretations of the Great Depression: A Rejoinder (to Comments by Lothian and Meltzer)," in Brunner (ed), *The Great Depression Revisited*, 1981, pp. 165-73.

Gottlieb, Manuel. "New Measures of Value of Nonfarm Building for the United States: Annually, 1850-1939," *Review of Economics and Statistics*, 47(4), November 1965, pp. 412-9.

Gottlieb, Manuel. "Building in Ohio Between 1837 and 1914," in Brady (ed), *Output, Employment, and Productivity in the United States After 1800*, 1966, pp. 243-80.

Gottlieb, Manuel. "Building in Ohio Between 1837 and 1914: Reply to David," in Brady (ed), *Output, Employment, and Productivity in the United States After 1800*, 1966, pp. 288-90.

Gould, J.M. *Output and Productivity in the Electric and Gas Utilities, 1899-1942* (General Series 47). New York: National Bureau of Economic Research, 1946.

Gould, John D. "Agricultural Fluctuations and the English Economy in the Eighteenth Century," *Journal of Economic History*, 22(3), September 1962, pp. 313-33.

Gould, John D. "A Case of Unbalanced Growth. Review Essay of 'Investment in Australian Economic Development, 1861-1900' by Noel G. Butlin (London: Cambridge University Press, 1964)," *Economic Record*, 42(98), June 1966, pp. 312-20.

Gould, John D. "Hypothetical History," *Economic History Review*, Second Series, 22(2), August 1969, pp. 195-207.

Gould, John D. "The 'Price Revolution': Comments on a Comment," *Australian Economic History Review*, 9(2), September 1969, pp. 179-81.

Gould, John D. *The Great Debasement: Currency and the Economy in Mid-Tudor Emgland*. Oxford: Clarendon Press, 1970.

Gould, John D. *Economic Growth in History: Survey and Analysis*. London: Methuen, 1972.

Gould, John D. "Currency and the Exchange Rate in Sixteenth-Century England," *Journal of European Economic History*, 2(1), Spring 1973, pp. 149-59.

Gould, John D. "The Landscape and the Machine: A Comment on David," *Economic History Review*, Second Series, 27(3), August 1974, pp. 455-60.

Gould, John D. "European Inter-Continental Emigration, 1815-1914:

Patterns and Causes," *Journal of European Economic History*, 8(3), Winter 1979, pp. 593-680.

Gould, John D. "European Inter-Continental Emigration. The Road Home: Return Migration from the U.S.A.," *Journal of European Economic History*, 9(1), Spring 1980, pp. 41-112.

Gould, John D. "European International Emigration: The Role of 'Diffusion' and 'Feedback'," *Journal of European Economic History*, 9(2), Fall 1980, pp. 267-316.

Gourvish, T.R. "Flinn and Real Wage Trends in Britain, 1750-1850: A Comment," *Economic History Review*, Second Series, 29(1), February 1976, pp. 136-42.

Gramm, William P. "The Real-Balance Effect in the Great Depression," *Journal of Economic History*, 32(2), June 1972, pp. 499-519.

Granger, C.W.J. and Elliott, C.M. "A Fresh Look at Wheat Prices and Markets in the Eighteenth Century," *Economic History Review*, Second Series, 20(2), August 1967, pp. 257-65.

Grant, Kenneth G. "The Rate of Settlement of Canadian Provinces, 1870-1911: A Comment on Norrie," *Journal of Economic History*, 38(2), June 1978, pp. 471-3.

Grantham, George W. "Scale and Organization in French Farming, 1840-1880," in Parker and Jones (eds), *European Peasants and Their Markets*, 1975, pp. 293-326.

Grantham, George W. "The Diffusion of the New Husbandry in Northern France, 1815-1840," *Journal of Economic History*, 38(2), June 1978, pp. 311-37.

Grantham, George W. "The Persistence of Open-Field Farming in Nineteenth-Century France," *Journal of Economic History*, 40(3), September 1980, pp. 515-31.

Gray, Lewis C. *History of Agriculture in the Southern United States to 1860* (Reprinted by Peter Smith, Gloucester, Mass., 1958). Washington, D.C.: Carnegie Institution of Washington, 1933.

Gray, Ralph and Peterson, John M. *Economic Development of the United States*. Homewood, Ill.: Richard D. Irwin, 1969.

Gray, Ralph and Wood, Betty. "The Transition from Indentured to Involuntary Servitude in Colonial Georgia," *Explorations in Economic History*, 13(4), October 1976, pp. 353-70.

Grebler, Leo; Blank, David M. and Winnick, Louis. *Capital Formation in Residential Real Estate: Trends and Prospects*. Princeton: Princeton University Press for the National Bureau of Economic Research, 1956.

Green, Alan G. "Regional Aspects of Canada's Economic Growth, 1890-1929," *Canadian Journal of Economics and Political Science*, 33(2), May 1967, pp. 232-45.

Green, Alan G. "Regional Inequality, Structural Change, and Economic Growth in Canada, 1890-1956," *Economic Development and Cultural Change*, 17(4), July 1969, pp. 567-83.

Green, Alan G. "Regional Inequality, Structural Change, and Economic Growth in Canada, 1890-1956," *Economic Development and Cultural Change*, 17(4), July 1969, pp. 567-83.

Green, Alan G. "Is Foreign Labour Complementary or Competitive (In Terms of Skill) with Native-Born Labour? The Canadian Case, 1911-1941," *International Migration*, 12(1-2), 1974, pp. 49-60.

Green, Alan G. and Urquhart, M.C. "Factor and Commodity Flows in the International Economy of 1870-1914: A Multi-Country View," *Journal of Economic History,* 26(1), March 1976, pp. 217-52.

Green, George D. "Banking and Finance in Antebellum Louisiana: Their Influence on the Course of Economic Development," (Summary of Doctoral Dissertation) *Journal of Economic History,* 26(4), December 1966, pp. 579-81.

Green, George D. "Potentialities and Pitfalls in Economic History: Comment on Redlich," *Explorations in Entrepreneurial History,* Second Series, 6(1), Fall 1968, pp. 109-15.

Green, George D. "The Louisiana Bank Act of 1842: Policy Making during Financial Crisis," *Explorations in Economic History,* 7(4), Summer 1970, pp. 399-412.

Green, George D. *Finance and Economic Development in the Old South: Louisiana Banking, 1804-1861.* Stanford: Stanford University Press, 1972.

Green, George D. "Louisiana, 1804-61," in Cameron (ed), *Banking and Economic Development,* 1972, pp. 199-231.

Green, George D. "The Economic Impact of the Stock Market Boom and Crash of 1929," in *Consumer Spending and Monetary Policy: The Linkages.* Boston: Federal Reserve Bank of Boston, 1972, pp. 189-220.

Green, George D. "Monetary Systems and Regional Economies: Comments on Papers by Rockoff and Bateman/Weiss," *Journal of Economic History,* 35(1), March 1975, pp. 212-5.

Green, George D. "Financial Intermediaries," in Porter (ed), *Encyclopedia of American Economic History,* 1980, pp. 707-26.

Green, J. "The Effect of the Iron Tariff in the United States," presented to the Cliometrics Conference, Madison, Wisconsin, 1970.

Greenwood, Michael J. and Thomas, Lloyd B. "Geographic Labor Mobility in Nineteenth Century England and Wales," *Annals of Regional Science,* 7(2), December 1973, pp. 90-105.

Gregory, Paul R. "1913 Russian National Income: Some Insights into Russian Economic Development," *Quarterly Journal of Economics,* 90, August 1976, pp. 445-59.

Gregory, Paul R. "The Russian Balance of Payments, the Gold Standard, and Monetary Policy: A Historical Example of Foreign Capital Movements," *Journal of Economic History,* 39(2), June 1979, pp. 379-99.

Gregory, Paul R. "Grain Marketings and Peasant Consumption, Russia, 1885-1913," *Explorations in Economic History,* 17(2), April 1980, pp. 135-64.

Gregory, Paul and Sailors, Joel W. "Russian Monetary Policy and Industrialization, 1861-1913," *Journal of Economic History,* 36(4), December 1976, pp. 836-51.

Griliches, Zvi. "Hybrid Corn and the Economics of Innovation," reprinted in Fogel and Engerman (eds), *The Reinterpretation of American Economic History,* 1971, pp. 207-13. *Science,* 132, July 29, 1960, pp. 275-80.

Gross, Nachum T. "Austrian Industrial Statistics 1880/85 and 1911/13," reprinted in Giersch and Sauermann (eds), *Quantitative Aspects of Economic History. Zeitschrift fur die gesamte Staatswissenschaft,* 124(1), February 1968, pp. 35-69.

Gross, Nachum T. "An Estimate of Industrial Product in Austria in 1841," *Journal of Economic History,* 28(1), March 1968, pp. 80-101.

Gross, Nachum T. "Economic Growth and the Consumption of Coal in

Austria and Hungary, 1831-1913," *Journal of Economic History,* 31(4), December 1971, pp. 898-916.

Gross, Nachum T. and Gerber, Haim. "Inflation or Deflation in Nineteenth-Century Syria and Palestine: A Note (on Chevallier)," *Journal of Economic History,* 40(2), June 1980, pp. 351-7.

Gross, Nachum T. and Metzer, Jacob. "Public Finance in the Jewish Economy in Interwar Palestine," Uselding (ed), *Research in Economic History,* 1978, pp. 87-159.

Grunig, Ferdinand. "An Estimate of the National Capital Account of the Federal German Republic," in Goldsmith and Saunders (eds), *The Measurement of National Wealth,* 1959.

Gulicher, Herbert; Hoffmann, Walther G. and Joksch, H.C., eds. *Studien zur wirtschaftlichen Verfahrensforschung.* Koln: Westdeutscher Verlag, 1964.

Gunderson, Gerald A. "Issues in the Measurement of Efficiency of American Dairy Farming, 1850-1910: A Comment on Bateman," *Journal of Economic History,* 29(3), September 1969, pp. 501-5.

Gunderson, Gerald A. "The Nature of Social Saving," *Economic History Review,* Second Series, 23(2), August 1970, pp. 207-19.

Gunderson, Gerald A. "Southern Antebellum Income Reconsidered," *Explorations in Economic History,* 10(2), Winter 1973, pp. 151-76.

Gunderson, Gerald A. "The Origin of the American Civil War," *Journal of Economic History,* 34(4), December 1974, pp. 915-50.

Gunderson, Gerald A. "Southern Income Reconsidered: A Reply to Gallman," *Explorations in Economic History,* 12(1), January 1975, pp. 101-2.

Gunderson, Gerald A. *A New Economic History of America.* New York: McGraw-Hill, 1976.

Gunderson, Gerald A. "Economic Change and the Demise of the Roman Empire," *Explorations in Economic History,* 13(1), January 1976, pp. 43-68.

Gunderson, Gerald A. "Real Incomes in the Late Middle Ages: A Test of the Common Case for Diminishing Returns," *Social Science History,* 2(1), Fall 1977, pp. 90-118.

Gunderson, Gerald A. "Slavery," in Porter (ed), *Encyclopedia of American Economic History,* 1980, pp. 552-61.

Gurley, John G. and Shaw, E.S. "The Growth of Debt and Money in the United States, 1800-1950: A Suggested Interpretation," *Review of Economics and Statistics,* 39(3), August 1957, pp. 250-62.

Gurley, John G. and Shaw, E.S. "Money," in Harris (ed), *American Economic History,* 1961, pp. 101-29.

Gutman, Herbert; David, Paul A.; Sutch, Richard C.; Temin, Peter and Wright, Gavin. *Reckoning with Slavery: A Critical Study in the Quantitative History of American Negro Slavery.* New York: Oxford University Press, 1976.

Gutman, Herbert G.; David, Paul A.; Sutch, Richard C.; Temin, Peter and Wright, Gavin. "Time on the Cross and the Burden of Quantitative History," in David et al (eds), *Reckoning with Slavery,* 1976, pp. 339-57.

Gutman, Herbert G. and Sutch, Richard C. "Sambo Makes Good, or Were Slaves Imbued with the Protestant Work Ethic?," in David et al (eds), *Reckoning with Slavery,* 1976, pp. 55-93.

Gutman, Herbert G. and Sutch, Richard C. "The Slave Family: Protected Agent of Capitalist Masters or Victim of the Slave Trade?," in

David et al (eds), *Reckoning with Slavery*, 1976, pp. 94-133.

Gutman, Herbert G. and Sutch, Richard C. "Victorians All? The Sexual Mores and Conduct of Slaves and Their Masters," in David et al (eds), *Reckoning with Slavery*, 1976, pp. 134-64.

Habakkuk, H.J. "Fluctuations in House-Building in Britain and the United States in the Nineteenth Century," *Journal of Economic History*, 22, 1962, pp. 198-230.

Habakkuk, H.J. *American and British Technology in the 19th Century: The Search for Labour-Saving Inventions*. Cambridge: Cambridge University Press, 1962.

Habakkuk, H.J. "Economic History and Economic Theory," in Gilbert and Graubard (eds), *Historical Studies Today*, 1972, pp. 27-44.

Habakkuk, H.J. and Deane, Phyllis. "The Take-Off in Britain," in Rostow (ed), *The Economics of Take-Off into Sustained Growth*, 1963, pp. 63-82.

Hacker, Louis H. "The New Revolution in Economic History. Review Essay of 'Railroads and Economic Growth: Essays in Econometric History' by Robert W. Fogel (Baltimore: Johns Hopkins University Press, 1964)," *Explorations in Entrepreneurial History*, 3(3), Spring 1966, pp. 159-75.

Haddad, Claudio L.S. "Crescimento do Produto Real Brasileiro, 1900-1947," [Growth of Brazilian Real Product, 1900-1947] *Revista Brasileira de Economia*, 29(1), January/March 1975, pp. 3-26.

Haddad, Claudio L.S. "Crescimento do Produto Real no Brasil, 1900-1947," [Growth of Brazilian Real Output, 1900-1947] Ph.D. Dissertation, University of Chicago, 1974.

Haddad, Claudio L.S. "Crescimento Economico do Brasil, 1900-76," [Economic Growth of Brazil, 1900-76] in Neuhaus (ed), *A Economia Brasileira*, 1979.

Haddad, Claudio L.S. and Contador, Claudio R. "Produto Real, Moeda e Precos: A Experiencia Brasileira no Periodo 1861-1970," [Real Product, Money and Prices: The Brazilian Experience in the Period 1861-1970] *Revista Brasileira de Estatistica*, 36(143), July/September 1975, pp. 407-40.

Haddock, David D. "An Empirical Study of the Regulation of the Rail Industry." [Working Paper]

Haddock, David D. "Determinants of Industrial Concentration in the United States Automobile Industry, 1907 to 1979." [Working Paper]

Haddock, David D. "The Advent of Federal Regulation of Railroads." [Working Paper]

Haddock, David D. "The Black Death, the Voyages of Columbus, and Other Timely Acts of God." [Working Paper]

Haddock, David D. "The Origins of Regulation: Competing Theories and Critical Tests." [Working Paper]

Haig, Brian D. "1938/39 National Income Estimates," *Australian Economic History Review*, 7(2), September 1967, pp. 172-86.

Haig, Brian D. "Manufacturing Output and Productivity, 1910 to 1948/9," *Australian Economic History Review*, 15(2), September 1975, pp. 136-61.

Haig, Brian D. *Expenditure and Living Standards, Australia 1920-1950* (vol. 1: Basic Estimates; vol. 2: Analysis and Sources). Canberra: Australian National University, 1980.

Haig, Brian D. *Capital Stock in Manufacturing, 1920 to 1978.* Australian National University Department of Economics/Research School of Social Sciences Series Monograph. Canberra: Australian National University Press, 1981.

Haig, Brian D. and Keating, M. "A Comment on the Butlin-Dowie Australian Work Force and Employment Estimates," *Australian Economic History Review,* 11(1), March 1971, pp. 59-62.

Haines, Michael R. "Economic-Demographic Interrelations in Developing Agricultural Regions: A Case Study of Prussian Upper Silesia, 1840-1914" (Summary of Doctoral Dissertation) *Journal of Economic History,* 33(10, March 1973, pp. 302-4.

Haines, Michael R. "Fertility and Occupation: Coal Mining Populations in the Nineteenth and Early Twentieth Centuries in Europe and America," (Summary), *Population Index,* 40(3), 1974, pp. 417-8.

Haines, Michael R. "Population and Economic Change in Nineteenth-Century Eastern Europe: Prussian Upper Silesia, 1840-1913," *Journal of Economic History,* 36(2), June 1976, pp. 334-58.

Haines, Michael R. "Fertility, Nuptiality, and Occupation: A Study of Coal Mining Populations and Regions in England and Wales in the Mid-Nineteenth Century," *Journal of Interdisciplinary History,* 8(2), Autumn 1977, pp. 245-80.

Haines, Michael R. "Fertility, Marriage and Occupation in the Pennsylvania Anthracite Region, 1850-1880," *Journal of Family History,* 2(1), Spring 1977, pp. 28-55.

Haines, Michael R. *Economic-Demographic Interrelations in Developing Agricultural Regions: A Case Study of Prussian Upper Silesia, 1840-1914.* New York: Arno Press, 1978.

Haines, Michael R. "Fertility Decline in Industrial America: An Analysis of the Pennsylvania Anthracite Region, 1850-1900, Using Own-Children Methods," *Population Studies,* 32(2), July 1978, pp. 327-54.

Haines, Michael R. *Fertility and Occupation: Population Patterns in Industrialization.* New York: Academic Press, 1979.

Haines, Michael R. "Industrial Work and the Family Life Cycle, 1889-1890," in Uselding (ed), *Research in Economic History,* 1979.

Haines, Michael R. "Fertility and Marriage in a Nineteenth-Century Industrial City: Philadelphia, 1850-1880," *Journal of Economic History,* 40(1), March 1980, pp. 151-8.

Haines, Michael R. "Poverty, Economic Stress, and the Family in a Late Nineteenth-Century American City: Whites in Philadelphia, 1880," in Hershberg (ed), *Philadelphia,* 1981, pp. 240-76.

Haines, Michael R. "Why Were Nineteenth Century U.S. Urban Black Fertility Rates So Low? (Evidence from Philadelphia, 1850-1880)," presented at the University of Chicago, Workshop in Economic History, no. 8081-4, October 1980.

Haines, Michael R. "The Role of Agriculture in Economic Development: A Regional Case Study of Prussian Upper Silesia, 1846-1913," *Journal of Economic History.*

Haites, Erik F.; Atack, Jeremy; Mak, James and Walton Gary M. "The Profitability of Steamboating on the Western Rivers: 1850,"

Business History Review, 49(3), Autumn 1975, pp. 346-54.

Haites, Erik F. and Mak, James. "Ohio and Mississippi River Transportation, 1810-1860," *Explorations in Economic History,* 8(2), Winter 1970/71, pp. 153-80.

Haites, Erik F. and Mak, James. "Steamboating on the Mississippi, 1810-1860: A Purely Competitive Industry," *Business History Review,* 45(1), Spring 1971, pp. 52-78.

Haites, Erik F. and Mak, James. "The Decline of Steamboating on the Antebellum Western Rivers: Some New Evidence and an Alternative Hypothesis," *Explorations in Economic History,* 11(1), Fall 1973, pp. 25-36.

Haites, Erik F.; Mak, James and Walton, Gary M. *Western River Transportation during the Era of Early Internal Improvements.* Baltimore: Johns Hopkins University Press, 1975.

Haites, Erik F. and Mak, James. "Economies of Scale in Western River Steamboating," *Journal of Economic History,* 36(3), September 1976, pp. 689-703.

Haites, Erik F. and Mak, James. "Economies of Scale in Western River Steamboating: A Reply to Atack," *Journal of Economic History,* 38(2), June 1978, pp. 467-70.

Haites, Erik F. and Mak, James. "Social Savings Due to Western River Steamboats," in Uselding (ed), *Research in Economic History,* 1978, pp. 263-303.

Hall, A.R. "A Note on the English Capital Market as a Source of Funds for Home Investment before 1914," *Economica,* 24(93), February 1957, pp. 59-66.

Hall, A.R. "The English Capital Market before 1914: A Reply to Cairncross," *Economica,* 25(100), November 1958, pp. 339-43.

Hall, A.R. "Long Waves in Building in the British Economy of the Nineteenth Century: A Comment on Cooney," *Economic History Review,* Second Series, 14(2), 1961, pp. 330-2.

Hall, A.R. *The London Capital Market and Australia, 1870-1914.* Canberra: Australian National University Press, 1963.

Hall, A.R. "Some Long Period Effects of the Kinked Age Distribution of the Population of Australia, 1861-1961," *Economic Record,* 39(85), March 1963, pp. 43-52.

Hall, A.R. "Capital Imports and the Composition of Investment in a Borrowing Country," in Hall (ed), *The Export of Capital from Britain,* 1968.

Hall, A.R. *The Export of Capital from Britain, 1870-1914.* London: Methuen, 1968.

Hall, A.R.; Butlin, S.J. and White, R.C. *Australian Banking and Monetary Statistics, 1817-1945.* Sydney: Reserve Bank of Australia, 1971.

Hallagan, William S. "Share Contracting for California Gold," *Explorations in Economic History,* 15(2), April 1978, pp. 196-210.

Hallagan, William S. "Labor Contracting in Turn-Of-The-Century California Agriculture," *Journal of Economic History,* 40(4), December 1980, pp. 757-76.

Hamberg, Eva M. *Studier i Internationell Migration* [Studies in International Migration] (Contains an English Summary). Stockholm: Almqvist & Wiksell, 1976.

Hamilton, Earl J. *American Treasure and the Price Revolution in Spain, 1501-1650.* Cambridge: Harvard University Press, 1934.

Hamilton, Earl J. *Money, Prices, and Wages in Valencia, Aragon, and Navarre, 1351-1500.* Cambridge: Harvard University Press, 1936.

Hamilton, Earl J. "Prices, Wages, and the Industrial Revolution," *Economics and Industrial Relations.* Philadelphia: University of Pennsylvania Press, 1941, pp. 99-112.

Hamilton, *Earl J. War and Prices in Spain, 1651-1800.* Cambridge: Harvard University Press, 1947.

Hamilton, Earl J. "Prices as a Factor in Business Growth: Prices and Progress," *Journal of Economic History,* 12(4), Fall 1952, pp. 325-49.

Hamilton, Earl J. "The History of Prices before 1750," *XIe Congres International des Sciences Historiques, Stockholm, 1960.* Stockholm: Almqvist & Wiksell, 1962, pp. 144-64.

Hamilton, Earl J. "Imports of American Gold and Silver into Spain, 1503-1660," *Quarterly Journal of Economics,* 43, May 1929, pp. 436-72.

Hamilton, Earl J. "American Treasure and the Rise of Capitalism (1500-1700)," *Economica,* 9(27), November 1929, pp. 338-57.

Hamilton, Earl J. "Use and Misuse of Price History," *Journal of Economic History,* 4, (Supplement), 1944, pp. 47-60.

Hamilton, Earl J. "American Treasure and Andalusian Prices, 1503-1660: A Study in the Spanish Price Revolution," in Ramsey (ed), *The Price Revolution in the Sixteenth Century,* 1971, pp. 147-81.

Hamilton, Earl J. "Price History," in Sills (ed), *International Encyclopedia of the Social Sciences,* 1968, pp. 471-7.

Hamilton, Earl J. "The Role of War in Modern Inflation," *Journal of Economic History,* 37(1), March 1977, pp. 13-36.

Handfield-Jones, Stephen J. and Phelps Brown, E.H. "The Climacteric of the 1890's: A Study in the Expanding Economy," *Oxford Economic Papers,* New Series, 4(3), October 1952, pp. 266-307.

Handfield-Jones, Stephen J. and Weber, Brian A. "Variations in the Rate of Economic Growth in the U.S.A., 1869-1939," *Oxford Economic Papers,* 6, June 1954, pp. 101-32.

Hanisch, Tore Jorgen. "The Economic Crisis in Norway in the 1930s: A Tentative Analysis of Its Causes," *Scandinavian Economic History Review,* 26(2), 1978, pp. 145-55.

Hanisch, Tore Jorgen. "Okonomiske Virkninger av Paripolitikken et Essay om Norsk Okonomi i 1920-Arene," [Economic Consequences of Restoring the Norwegian Krone to Gold Parity in the 1920s] *Norsk Historisk Tidsskrift,* 3, 1979.

Hanley, Susan B. and Yamamura, Kozo. "Population Trends and Economic Growth in Preindustrial Japan," in Glass and Revelle (eds), *Population and Social Change,* 1972.

Hanley, Susan B. and Yamamura, Kozo. "Quantitative Data for Japanese Economic History," in Lorwin and Price (eds), *The Dimensions of the Past,* 1972, pp. 503-30.

Hanley, Susan B. and Yamamura, Kozo. *Economic and Demographic Change in Preindustrial Japan, 1600-1868.* Princeton: Princeton University Press, 1977.

Hannah, Leslie. "Mergers in British Manufacturing Industry, 1880-1918," *Oxford Economic Papers,* New Series, 26(1), March 1974, pp. 1-20.

Hannah, Leslie. *The Rise of the Corporate Economy: The British Experience.* Baltimore: Johns Hopkins University Press, 1976.

357

Hannah, Leslie and Kay, J.A. *Concentration in Modern Industry: Theory Measurement and the U.K. Experience.* London: Macmillan, 1977.

Hannah, Leslie. "Mergers," in Porter (ed), *Encyclopedia of American Economic History*, 1980, pp. 639-51.

Hannah, Leslie. "Mergers, Cartels and Concentration: The U.S. and European Experience 1890-1914," in Horn and Kocka (eds), *Recht und Entwicklung der GroBunternehmen*, 1979, pp. 306-16.

Hannon, Joan Underhill. "The Economics of the Melting Pot: Discussion of Papers by Higgs, Kirk/Kirk, and Kahan Presented to the 37th Annual Meeting of the Economic History Association," *Journal of Economic History*, 38(1), March 1978, pp. 252-5.

Hannon, Joan Underhill. "The Immigrant Worker in the Promised Land: Human Capital and Ethnic Discrimination in the Michigan Labor Market, 1888-1891," (Summary of Doctoral Dissertation) *Journal of Economic History*, 38(1), March 1978, pp. 279-80.

Hannon, Joan Underhill. "The Immigrant Worker in the Promised Land: Human Capital and Ethnic Discrimination in the Michigan Labor Market, 1888-1890," Ph.D. Dissertation, University of Wisconsin-Madison, 1978.

Hansen, Bert and Lucas, Edward F. "Egyptian Foreign Trade, 1885-1961: A New Set of Trade Indices," *Journal of European Economic History*, 7(2-3), Fall/Winter 1978, pp. 429-60.

Hansen, Bent and Tourk, Khairy. "The Profitability of the Suez Canal as a Private Enterprise, 1859-1956," *Journal of Economic History*, 38(4), December 1978, pp. 938-58.

Hanson, II, John R. "Economic Consequences of Rapid Population Growth: A Comment on Enke," *Economic Journal*, 83(329), March 1973, pp. 217-9.

Hanson, II, John R. "The Nineteenth Century Exports of the Less Developed Countries," (Summary of Doctoral Dissertation) *Journal of Economic History*, 33(1), March 1973, pp. 305-8.

Hanson, II, John R. "Exchange-Rate Movements and Economic Development in the Late Nineteenth Century: A Critique," *Journal of Political Economy*, 83(4), August 1975, pp. 859-62.

Hanson, II, John R. "The Leff Conjecture: Some Contrary Evidence," *Journal of Political Economy*, 84(2), April 1976, pp. 401-5.

Hanson, II, John R. "Diversification and Concentration of LDC Exports: Victorian Trends," *Explorations in Economic History*, 14(1), January 1977, pp. 44-68.

Hanson, II, John R. "More on Trade as a Handmaiden of Growth," *Economic Journal*, 87(347), September 1977, pp. 554-7.

Hanson, II, John R. "Export Instability in Historical Perspective," *Explorations in Economic History*, 14(4), October 1977, pp. 293-310.

Hanson, II, John R. "Money in the Colonial American Economy: An Extension," *Economic Inquiry*, 17(2), April 1979, pp. 281-6.

Hanson, II, John R. "World Demand for Cotton during the Nineteenth Century: Wright's Estimates Re-examined," (see note in this Journal, 40(1), March 1980, for a Corrigenda concerning this article) *Journal of Economic History*, 39(4), December 1979, pp. 1015-21.

Hanson, II, John R. "Export Instability in Historical Perspective: Further Results," *Journal of Economic History*, 40(1), March 1980, pp. 17-23.

Hanson, II, John R. "Small Notes in the American Colonies,"

Explorations in Economic History, 17(4), October 1980, pp. 411-20.

Hareven, Tamara K.; Mason, Karen and Vinovskis, Maris A. "Determinants of Women's Labor Force Participation in Late Nineteenth-Century America," in Family Transitions and the Life Course in Historical Perspective. New York: Academic Press, 1978.

Harder, K. Peter. "The American Economy in 1776: Some Perspectives," in Soltow (ed), *Essays in Economic and Business History,* 1979, pp. 251-8.

Harley, C. Knick. "British Shipbuilding and Merchant Shipping: 1850-1890," (Summary of Doctoral Dissertation) *Journal of Economic History,* 30(1), March 1970, pp. 262-6.

Harley, C. Knick. "The Shift from Sailing Ships to Steamships, 1850-1890: A Study in Technological Change and Its Diffusion," in McCloskey (ed), *Essays on a Mature Economy,* 1971, pp. 215-34.

Harley, C. Knick. "On the Persistence of Old Techniques: The Case of North American Wooden Shipbuilding," *Journal of Economic History,* 33(2), June 1973, pp. 372-98.

Harley, C. Knick. "Skilled Labour and the Choice of Technique in Edwardian Industry," *Explorations in Economic History,* 11(4), Summer 1974, pp. 391-414.

Harley, C. Knick. "Goschen's Conversion of the National Debt and the Yield on Consols," *Economic History Review,* Second Series, 29(1), February 1976, pp. 101-6.

Harley, C. Knick. "The Interest Rate and Prices in Britain, 1873-1913: A Study of the Gibson Paradox," *Explorations in Economic History,* 14(1), January 1977, pp. 69-89.

Harley, C. Knick. "Comments on Dissertations Presented at the 37th Annual Meeting of the Economic History Association," *Journal of Economic History,* 38(1), March 1978, pp. 297-300.

Harley, C. Knick. "Western Settlement and the Price of Wheat, 1872-1913," *Journal of Economic History,* 38(4), December 1978, pp. 865-78.

Harley, C. Knick. "Transportation, the World Wheat Trade and the Kuznets Cycle, 1850-1913," *Explorations in Economic History,* 17(3), July 1980, pp. 218-50.

Harley, C. Knick. "World Demand and Transportation Cost: Determinants of Prices and Output of Wheat in Exporting and Importing Regions, 1850-1913," University of Western Ontario, Department of Economics Research Report #2901.

Harley, C. Knick and McCloskey, Donald N. "Foreign Trade, Competition and the Expanding International Economy," in Floud and McCloskey (eds), *The Economic History of Britain since 1700,* 1981.

Harnetty, Peter. "Cotton Exports and Indian Agriculture, 1861-1870," *Economic History Review,* Second Series, 24(3), August 1971, pp. 414-29.

Harris, Curtis C., Jr. and Olson, Mancur L. "Free Trade in 'Corn': A Statistical Study of the Prices and Production of Wheat in Great Britain from 1873 to 1914," reprinted in Floud (ed), *Essays in Quantitative Economic History,* 1974, pp. 196-215. *Quarterly Journal of Economics,* 73(1), February 1959, pp. 145-69.

Harris, John R. "Some Problems in Identifying the Role of Entrepreneurship in Economic Development: The Nigerian Case," *Explorations in Economic History,* 7(3), Spring 1970, pp. 347-70.

Hart, P.E. "Profits in Non-Manufacturing Industries in the United

Kingdom, 1920-1938," *Scottish Journal of Political Economy,* 10(2), June 1963, pp. 167-97.

Hart, P.E. "A Long-Run Analysis of the Rate of Return on Capital in Manufacturing Industry, United Kingdom, 1920-62," in Hart (ed), *Studies in Profit, Business Saving and Investment in the United Kingdom,* 1968, pp. 220-83.

Hart, P.E. "A Macroeconometric Analysis of the Appropriation of Profit in Manufacturing," in Hart (ed), *Studies in Profit, Business Saving and Investment in the United Kingdom,* 1968, pp. 109-43.

Hart, P.E., ed. *Studies in Profit, Business Saving and Investment in the United Kingdom 1920-1962* (2 vols) (vol 1, 1965; vol 2, 1968). London: Allen & Unwin, 1965, 1968.

Hart, P.E. "The Factor Distribution of Income in the United Kingdom, 1870-1963," in Hart (ed), *Studies in Profit, Business Saving and Investment in the United Kingdom,* 1968, pp. 17-72.

Hart, P.E. and Phelps Brown, E.H. "The Share of Wages in National Income," *Economic Journal,* 62(246), June 1952, pp. 253-77.

Hartland, Penelope. "Canadian Balance of Payments since 1868," in Parker (ed), *Trends in the American Economy in the Nineteenth Century,* 1960, pp. 717-53.

Hartley, W.B. "Estimation of the Incidence of Poverty in the United States, 1870 to 1914," Ph.D. Dissertation, University of Wisconsin-Madison, 1969.

Hartwell, R.M. "Is the New Economic History an Export Product? A Comment on J.R.T. Hughes," in McCloskey (ed), *Essays on a Mature Economy,* 1971, pp. 413-22.

Hartwell, R.M. "Good Old Economic History," *Journal of Economic History,* 33(1), March 1973, pp. 28-40.

Hartwell, R.M. "Slave Labour and Factory Labour," presented at the MSSB-University of Rochester Conference Time on the Cross: A First Appraisal, October 1974.

Hartwell, R.M. and Engerman, Stanley L. "Models of Immiseration: The Theoretical Basis of Pessimism," in Taylor (ed), *The Standard of Living in Britain in the Industrial Revolution,* 1975.

Hartwell, R.M. and North, Douglass C. "Law, Property Rights, Legal Institutions, and the Performance of Economies," in Flinn (ed), *Proceedings of the Seventh International Economic History Congress,* 1978.

Hatanaka, Michio. "Kuznets and Juglar Cycles during the Industrialization of 1874-1940: Comment on Shinohara," in Ohkawa and Hayami (eds), *Economic Growth,* 1973, pp. 265-8.

Hausman, William J. "Size and Profitability of English Colliers in the Eighteenth Century," *Business History Review,* 51(4), Winter 1977, pp. 460-73.

Hausman, William J. "Public Policy and the Supply of Coal to London, 1700-1770," (Summary of Doctoral Dissertation) *Journal of Economic History,* 37(1), March 1977, pp. 252-4.

Hausman, William J. *Public Policy and the Supply of Coal to London, 1700-1770.* New York: Arno Press, 1980.

Hausman, William J. "A Model of the London Coal Trade in the Eighteenth Century," *Quarterly Journal of Economics,* 94, February 1980, pp. 1-14.

Hausman, William J. and Watts, James M. "Structural Change in the 18th-Century British Economy: A Test Using Cubic Splines,"

Explorations in Economic History, 17, October 1980, pp. 400-10.

Hawke, Gary R. "Mr. Hunt's Study of the Fogel Thesis: A Comment," *History,* 53(177), February 1968, pp. 18-23.

Hawke, Gary R. "Economic Decisions and Political Ossification: New Zealand Retail Electricity Tariff," in Munz (ed), *The Feel of Truth,* 1969, pp. 219-33.

Hawke, Gary R. "Pricing Policy of Railways in England and Wales before 1881," in Reed (ed), *Railways in the Victorian Economy,* 1969, pp. 76-110.

Hawke, Gary R. *Railways and Economic Growth in England and Wales, 1840-1870.* Oxford: Clarendon Press, 1970.

Hawke, Gary R. *The Development of the British Economy, 1870-1914.* Auckland: Heinemann, 1970.

Hawke, Gary R. "Quantitative Economic History," in Social Science Research Council (ed), *Research in Economic and Social History,* 1971, pp. 19-25.

Hawke, Gary R. "Railway Passenger Traffic in 1865," in McCloskey (ed), *Essays on a Mature Economy,* 1971, pp. 367-84.

Hawke, Gary R. "New Zealand and the Return to Gold in 1925," *Australian Economic History Review,* 11(1), March 1971, pp. 48-58.

Hawke, Gary R. "D.C. Coleman on the Counterfactual History of the New Draperies," *Economic History Review,* Second Series, 24(2), May 1971, pp. 258-9.

Hawke, Gary R. *Between Governments and Banks: A History of the Reserve Bank of New Zealand.* Wellington: Government Printer, 1973.

Hawke, Gary R. "The Government and the Depression of the 1930s in New Zealand: An Essay towards a Revision," *Australian Economic History Review,* 13(1), March 1973, pp. 72-95.

Hawke, Gary R. "The United States Tariff and Industrial Protection in the Late Nineteenth Century," *Economic History Review,* Second Series, 28(1), February 1975, pp. 84-99.

Hawke, Gary R. "Income Estimation from Monetary Data: Further Explorations," *Review of Income and Wealth,* 21(3), September 1975, pp. 301-8.

Hawke, Gary R. *Evolution of the New Zealand Economy.* Auckland: Heinemann, 1977.

Hawke, Gary R. "Long-Term Trends in New Zealand Imports," *Australian Economic History Review,* 18(1), March 1978, pp. 1-28.

Hawke, Gary R. "Acquisitiveness and Equality in New Zealand's Economic Development," *Economic History Review,* Second Series, 32(3), August 1979, pp. 376-90.

Hawke, Gary R. "A Note on 'Some Economic Aspects of Railroad Development in Tsarist Russia' by Jacob Metzer." [Working Paper]

Hawke, Gary R. and Higgins, J.P.P. "Transport and Social Overhead Capital," in Floud and McCloskey (eds), *The Economic History of Britain since 1700,* 1981, pp. 226-51.

Hawke, Gary R. and Reed, M.C. "Railway Capital in the United Kingdom in the Nineteenth Century," *Economic History Review,* Second Series, 22(2), August 1969, pp. 269-86.

Hayami, Yujiro. "Elements of Induced Innovation: A Historical Perspective for the Green Revolution," *Explorations in Economic History,* 8(4), Summer 1971, pp. 445-72.

Hayami, Yujiro. "Conditions for the Diffusion of Agricultural Technology: An Asian Perspective," *Journal of Economic History,*

34(1), March 1974, pp. 131-48.

Hayami, Yujiro; Akino, Masakatsu; Shintani, Masahiko and Yamada, Saburo. *A Century of Agricultural Growth in Japan: Its Relevance to Asian Development.* Tokyo and Minneapolis: University of Tokyo Press and University of Minnesota Press, 1975.

Hayami, Yujiro and Kikuchi, Masao. "Agricultural Growth against a Land Resource Constraint: A Comparative History of Japan, Taiwan, Korea and the Philippines," *Journal of Economic History,* 38(4), December 1978, pp. 839-64.

Hayami, Yujiro and Nghiep, Le Thanh. "Mobilizing Slack Resources for Economic Development: The Summer-Fall Reaping Technology of Sericulture in Japan," *Explorations in Economic History,* 16(2), April 1979, pp. 163-81.

Heath, D.; O'Brien, Patrick K. and Keyder, Caglar. "Agriculture in Britain and France, 1815-1914," *Journal of European Economic History,* 6(2), Fall 1977, pp. 339-91.

Hayami, Yujiro and Ohkawa, Kazushi, eds. *Economic Growth: The Japanese Experience since the Meiji Era* (2 vols). Tokyo: Japan Economic Research Center, 1973.

Hayami, Yujiro and Ruttan, V.W. "Factor Prices and Technical Changes in Agricultural Development: The United States and Japan, 1880-1960," *Journal of Political Economy,* 78(5), September/October 1970, pp. 1115-41.

Hayami, Yujiro; Ruttan, Vernon W.; Binswanger, Hans P.; Wade, W.W. and Weber. "Factor Productivity and Growth: A Historical Interpretation," in Binswanger et al (ed), *Induced Innovation,* 1978.

Hayami, Yujiro and Yamada, Saburo. "Agriculture, 1880-1965," in Ohkawa and Hayami (eds), *Economic Growth,* 1973, pp. 7-25.

Hayami, Yujiro and Yamada, Saburo. "Agricultural Productivity at the Beginning of Industrialization," in Ohkawa, Johnston, and Kaneda (eds), *Agriculture and Economic Growth,* 1970, pp. 105-35.

Heavner, Robert O. "Indentured Servitude: The Philadelphia Market, 1771-1773," *Journal of Economic History,* 38(3), September 1978, pp. 701-13.

Heckscher, Eli. "A Plea for Theory in Economic History," *Economic Journal,* 39, Supplement, January 1929, pp. 525-34.

Heckscher, Eli. "Natural and Money Economy as Illustrated from Swedish History in the Sixteenth Century," *Journal of Economic and Business History,* 3(1), November 1930, pp. 1-29.

Heckscher, Eli. "The Aspects of Economic History," in *Economic Essays in Honour of Gustav Cassel.* London: Allen & Unwin, 1933, pp. 705-20.

Hekman, John S. "An Analysis of the Changing Location of Iron and Steel Production in the Twentieth Century," *American Economic Review,* 68(1), March 1978, pp. 123-33.

Hekman, John S. "The Product Cycle and New England Textiles in the Nineteenth Century." [Working Paper]

Hellie, Richard. "Time on the Cross from a Comparative Perspective of Early Modern Russian Slavery," presented at the MSSB-University of Rochester Conference Time on the Cross: A First Appraisal, October 1974.

Henning, Graydon R. and Trace, Keith. "Britain and the Motorship: A Case of the Delayed Adoption of New Technology?," *Journal of*

Economic History, 35(2), June 1975, pp. 353-85.

Henriksson, Rolf G.H. "An Interpretation of the Significance of Emigration for the Growth of Economic Welfare in Sweden 1860-1910," Ph.D. Dissertation, Northwestern University, 1969.

Herbst, Anthony F. and Wu, Joseph S.K. "Some Evidence of Subsidization: the U.S. Trucking Industry, 1900-1920," *Journal of Economic History,* 33(2), June 1973, pp. 417-33.

Herbst, Lawrence A. "Interregional Commodity Trade from the North to the South and American Economic Development in the Antebellum Period," (Summary of Doctoral Dissertation) *Journal of Economic History,* 35(1), March 1975, pp. 264-70.

Herbst, Lawrence A. *Interregional Commodity Trade from the North to the South and American Economic Development in the Antebellum Period.* New York: Arno Press, 1978.

Herbst, Lawrence A. "Patterns of American Interregional Commodity Trade North to South, 1824-1839," *American Economist,* 12(2), Fall 1978, pp. 61-6.

Herbst, Lawrence A. "Trade and Transportation in North America," (Summary of 1978 Research Workshop) *Journal of Economic History,* 39(1), March 1979, pp. 317-9.

Herbst, Lawrence A. "Antebellum Interregional Trade in Agricultural Goods: Discussion of Paper by Callahan and Hutchinson," *Journal of Economic History,* 40(1), March 1980, pp. 43-4.

Herfindahl, Orris C. "Development of the Major Metal Mining Industries in the United States from 1839 to 1909," in Brady (ed), *Output, Employment, and Productivity in the United States after 1800,* 1966, pp. 293-346.

Herlihy, David. "Quantification and the Middle Ages," in Lorwin and Price (eds), *The Dimensions of the Past,* 1972, pp. 13-51.

Heston, Alan W. "Official Yields Per Acre in India, 1886-1947: Some Questions of Interpretation," *Indian Economic and Social History Review,* 10(4), December 1973, pp. 303-32.

Heston, Alan W. and North, Douglass C. "The Estimation of Shipping Earnings in Historical Studies of the Balance of Payments," *Canadian Journal of Economics and Political Science,* 26(2), May 1960, pp. 265-76.

Heston, Alan W. and Summers, Robert. "Comparative Indian Economic Growth, 1870 to 1970," *American Economic Review,* Papers and Proceedings, 70(2), May 1980, pp. 96-101.

Hicks, Neville. "Demographic Transition in the Antipodes: Australian Population Structure and Growth, 1891-1911," *Australian Economic History Review,* 14(2), September 1974, pp. 123-42.

Higgins, J.P.P. and Hawke, Gary R. "Transport and Social Overhead Capital," in Floud and McCloskey (eds), *The Economic History of Britain since 1700,* 1981, pp. 226-51.

Higgins, J.P.P. and Pollard, Sidney, eds. *Aspects of Capital Investment in Great Britain, 1750-1850.* London: Methuen, 1971.

Higgs, Robert. "The Growth of Cities in a Midwestern Region, 1870-1900," *Journal of Regional Science,* 9(3), December 1969, pp. 369-75.

Higgs, Robert. "Railroad Rates and the Populist Uprising," *Agricultural History,* 44(3), July 1970, pp. 291-7.

Higgs, Robert. "Williamson and Swanson on City Growth: A Critique," *Explorations in Economic History,* 8(2), Winter 1970/71, pp. 203-11.

Higgs, Robert. "Regional Specialization and the Supply of Wheat in the United States, 1867-1914: A Comment on Fisher and Temin," *Review of Economics and Statistics*, 53(1), February 1971, pp. 101-2.

Higgs, Robert. "American Inventiveness, 1870-1920," *Journal of Political Economy*, 79(3), May/June 1971, pp. 661-7.

Higgs, Robert. "Race, Skills, and Earnings: American Immigrants in 1909," *Journal of Economic History*, 31(2), June 1971, pp. 420-8.

Higgs, Robert. "Cities and Yankee Ingenuity, 1870-1920," in Jackson and Schultz (eds), *Cities in American History*, 1972, pp. 16-22.

Higgs, Robert. "Did Southern Farmers Discriminate?," *Agricultural History*, 46(2), April 1972, pp. 325-8.

Higgs, Robert. "Property Rights and Resource Allocation under Alternative Land Tenure Forms: A Comment on Sau," *Oxford Economic Papers*, New Series, 24(3), November 1972, pp. 428-31.

Higgs, Robert. "Mortality in Rural America, 1870-1920: Estimates and Conjectures," *Explorations in Economic History*, 10(2), Winter 1973, pp. 177-95.

Higgs, Robert. "Race, Tenure, and Resource Allocation in Southern Agriculture, 1910," (see Editor's Notes this journal, 33(3), September 1973, pp. 668 for correction of a printer's error in this article) *Journal of Economic History*, 33(1), March 1973, pp. 149-69.

Higgs, Robert. "Patterns of Farm Rental in the Georgia Cotton Belt, 1880-1900," *Journal of Economic History*, 34(2), June 1974, pp. 468-82.

Higgs, Robert. "Urbanization and Inventiveness in the United States, 1870-1920," in Schnore (ed), *The New Urban History*, 1975, pp. 247-59.

Higgs, Robert. "Did Southern Farmers Discriminate?: Interpretive Problems and Further Evidence," *Agricultural History*, 49(2), April 1975, pp. 445-7.

Higgs, Robert. "Participation of Blacks and Immigrants in the American Merchant Class, 1890-1910: Some Demographic Relations," *Explorations in Economic History*, 13(2), April 1976, pp. 153-64.

Higgs, Robert. "The Boll Weevil, the Cotton Economy, and Black Migration, 1910-1930," *Agricultural History*, 50(2), April 1976, pp. 335-50.

Higgs, Robert. *Competition and Coercion: Blacks in the American Economy, 1865-1914*. New York: Cambridge University Press, 1977.

Higgs, Robert. "Firm-Specific Evidence on Racial Wage Differentials and Workforce Segregation," *American Economic Review*, 67(2), March 1977, pp. 236-45.

Higgs, Robert. "Race and Economy in the South, 1890-1950," in Haws (ed), *The Age of Segregation*, 1978.

Higgs, Robert. "Landless by Law: Japanese Immigrants in California Agriculture to 1941," *Journal of Economic History*, 38(1), March 1978, pp. 205-25.

Higgs, Robert. "Racial Wage Differentials in Agriculture: Evidence from North Carolina in 1887," *Agricultural History*, 52(2), April 1978, pp. 308-11.

Higgs, Robert. "The Wealth of Japanese Tenant Farmers in California, 1909," *Agricultural History*, 53(2), April 1979, pp. 488-93.

Higgs, Robert. "Urbanization and Invention in the Process of Economic Growth: Simultaneous Equations Estimates for the United States,

1880-1920," in Simon and Davanzo (eds), *Research in Population Economics*, 1980.

Higgs, Robert and Booth, David. "Mortality Differentials Within Large American Cities in 1890," *Human Ecology*, 7(4), December 1979, pp. 353-70.

Higgs, Robert and McGuire, Robert A. "Cotton, Corn and Risk in the Nineteenth Century: Another View," *Explorations in Economic History*, 14(2), April 1977, pp. 167-82.

Higgs, Robert and Stettler III, H. Louis. "Colonial New England Demography: A Sampling Approach," *William and Mary Quarterly*, Third Series, 27(2), April 1970, pp. 282-94.

Higonnet, Renc P. "Bank Deposits in the United Kingdom, 1870-1914," *Quarterly Journal of Economics*, 71(3), August 1957, pp. 329-67.

Hill, Marvin S.; Wimmer, Larry T. and Rooker, C. Keith. *The Kirtland Economy Revisited*. Provo, Utah: Brigham Young University Press, 1978.

Hill, Peter J. "The Economic Impact of Immigration into the United States," (Summary of Doctoral Dissertation) *Journal of Economic History*, 31(1), March 1971, pp. 260-3.

Hill, Peter J. *The Economic Impact of Immigration into the United States*. New York: Arno Press, 1975.

Hill, Peter J. "Relative Skill and Income Levels of Native and Foreign Born Workers in the United States," *Explorations in Economic History*, 12(1), January 1975, pp. 47-60.

Hill, Peter J. and Anderson, Terry L. "The Evolution of Property Rights: A Study of the American West," *Journal of Law and Economics*, 18(1), April 1975, pp. 163-80.

Hill, Peter J. and Anderson, Terry L. "The Role of Private Property in the History of American Agriculture, 1776-1976," *American Journal of Agricultural Economics*, 58(5), December 1976, pp. 937-45.

Hill, Peter J. and Anderson, Terry L. "From Free Grass to Fences: Transforming the Commons of the American West," in Hardin and Baden (eds), *Managing the Commons*, 1977, pp. 200-16.

Hill, Peter J. and Anderson, Terry L. "The Role of Private Property in the History of American Agriculture, 1776-1976: Reply (to Schmid)," *American Journal of Agricultural Economics*, 59(3), August 1977, pp. 590-1.

Hill, Peter J. and Anderson, Terry L. "An American Experiment in Anarcho-Capitalism: The Not So Wild, Wild West," *Journal of Libertarian Studies*, 3(1), 1979, pp. 9-29.

Hill, Peter J. and Anderson, Terry L. *The Birth of a Transfer Society*. Stanford: Hoover Institute Press, 1980.

Hilton, George W. "The British Truck System in the Nineteenth Century," *Journal of Political Economy*, 65(3), June 1957, pp. 237-56

Hinderliter, Roger H. and Rockoff, Hugh T. "The Management of Reserves by Banks in Antebellum Eastern Financial Centers," *Explorations in Economic History*, 11(1), Fall 1973, pp. 37-54.

Hinderliter, Roger H. and Rockoff, Hugh T. "Banking under the Gold Standard: An Analysis of Liquidity Management in the Leading Financial Centers," *Journal of Economic History*, 36(2), June 1976, pp. 379-8.

Hines, A.G. "Trade Unions and Wage Inflation in the United Kingdom, 1893-1961," *Review of Economic Studies*, 31, 1964, pp. 221-52.

Hines, A.G. "Unemployment and the Rate of Change of Money Wage Rates in the United Kingdom, 1862-1963: A Reappraisal," *Review of Economics and Statistics,* 50(1), February 1968, pp. 60-7.

Ho, Samuel Pao-San. "Agricultural Transformation Under Colonialism: The Case of Taiwan," *Journal of Economic History,* 28(3), September 1968, pp. 313-40.

Hoffman, Elizabeth. *The Sources of Mortality Changes in Italy since Unification.* Ann Arbor: University Microfilms, 1973.

Hoffman, Ronald and Earle, Carville V. "Staple Crops and Urban Development in the Eighteenth Century South," *Perspectives in American History,* 10, 1976, pp. 7-78.

Hoffmann, Walther G. *Stadien und Typen der Industrialisierung: ein Beitrag zur quantitativen Analyse historischer Wirtschaftsprozesse.* Jena: G. Fischer, 1931.

Hoffmann, Walther G. *British Industry, 1700-1950* (Translated by W.O. Henderson and W.H. Chaloner). Oxford: Blackwell, 1955.

Hoffmann, Walther G. *The Growth of Industrial Economies* (Translated by W.O. Henderson and W.H. Chaloner). Manchester: Manchester University Press, 1958.

Hoffmann, Walther G. *Das Deutsche volkseinkommen 1811-1957.* Tubingen: J.C.B. Mohr, 1959.

Hoffmann, Walther G. "The Take-Off in Germany," in Rostow (ed), *The Economics of Take-Off into Sustained Growth,* 1963, pp. 95-118.

Hoffmann, Walther G. "Der tertiare Sektor im Wachstumprozess," [The Service Sector in the Growth Process] (with English Summary) *Jahrbucher fur Nationalokonomie und Statistik,* 183(1), June 1969, pp. 1-29.

Hoffmann, Walther G. "Die 'Phillips-Kurve' in Deutschland," (with English Summary) *Kyklos,* 22(2), 1969, pp. 219-31.

Hoffmann, Walther G.; Grumbach, F. and Hesse, H. *Das Wachstum der Deutschen Wirtschaft seit der Mitte des 19. Jahrhunderts.* Berlin and New York: Springer-Verlag, 1965.

Hoffmann, Walther G.; Gulicher, Herbert and Joksch, H.C., eds. *Studien zur wirtschaftlichen Verfahrensforschung.* Koln: Westdeutscher Verlag, 1964.

Hogendorn, Jan S. "Economic Initiative and African Cash Farming: Precolonial Origins and Early Colonial Developments," in Duignan and Gann (eds), *Colonialism in Africa,* 1975.

Hogendorn, Jan S. "The Vent for Surplus Model and African Cash Agriculture to 1914," *Savanna,* 5(1), June 1976, pp. 15-28.

Hogendorn, Jan S. "The Economics of Slave Use on Two 'Plantations' in the Zaria Emirate of the Sokoto Caliphate," *International Journal of African Historical Studies,* 10(3), 1977, pp. 369-83.

Hogendorn, Jan S. "Vent-For Surplus Theory: A Reply to Freund and Shenton," *Savanna,* 6(2), December 1977, pp. 196-9.

Hogendorn, Jan S. *Nigerian Groundnut Exports: Origins and Early Development.* London and Zaria: Oxford University Press and Ahmadu Bello University Press, 1978.

Hogendorn, Jan S. "Slave Acquisition and Delivery in Precolonial Hausaland," in Schwartz, Jr. and Dumett (eds), *West African Culture Dynamics,* 1980, pp. 477-93.

Hogendorn, Jan S. and Brown, Wilson B. "Agricultural Export Growth and Myint's Model: Nigeria and Peru, 1900-1920," *Agricultural History,* 46(2), April 1972, pp. 313-24.

366

Hogendorn, Jan S. and Gemery, Henry A. "The Atlantic Slave Trade: A Tentative Economic Model," *Journal of African History*, 15(2), 1974, pp. 223-46.

Hogendorn, Jan S. and Gemery, Henry A. "Slave Labor Supply Elasticity and the Development of Slave Economies in the British Caribbean: The 17th Century Experience," in Rubin and Tuden (eds), *Comparative Perspectives on Slavery*, 1977.

Hogendorn, Jan S. and Gemery, Henry A. "Technological Change, Slavery, and the Slave Trade," in Dewey and Hopkins (eds), *The Imperial Impact*, 1978.

Hogendorn, Jan S. and Gemery, Henry A. "Editor's Introduction," in Gemery and Hogendorn (eds), *The Uncommon Market*, 1979, pp. 1-19.

Hogendorn, Jan S. and Gemery, Henry A. "The Economic Costs of West African Participation in the Atlantic Slave Trade: A Preliminary Sampling for the Eighteenth Century," in Gemery and Hogendorn (eds), *The Uncommon Market*, 1979, pp. 143-61.

Hogendorn, Jan S. and Gemery, Henry A., eds. *The Uncommon Market: Essays in the Economic History of the Atlantic Slave Trade.* New York: Academic Press, 1979.

Hogendorn, Jan S. and Gemery, Henry A. "Comparative Disadvantage: The Case of Sugar Cultivation in West Africa," *Journal of Interdisciplinary History*, 9(3), Winter 1979, pp. 429-50.

Hohenberg, Paul M. *Chemicals in Western Europe, 1850-1914: An Economic Study of Technical Change.* Amsterdam and Chicago: North-Holland and Rand-McNally, 1967.

Hohenberg, Paul M. "Comments on Dissertations Presented to the 33rd Annual Meeting of the Economic History Association," *Journal of Economic History*, 34(1), March 1974, pp. 308-12.

Hohenberg, Paul M. "Migrations et fluctuations demographiques dans la France rurale, 1836-1901," [Migration and Natural Population Change in Rural France, 1836-1901] *Annales: Economies, Societies, Civilisation,* 29(2), March/April 1974, pp. 461-97.

Hohorst, Gerd. "Bevolkerungsentwicklung und Wirtschaftswachstum als Historischer Entwicklungsprozess Demo-Okonomischer Systeme," [Population Expansion and Economic Growth as an Historical Development Process of Demographic-Economic Systems] in Mackensen and Wewer (eds), *Dynamik der Bevolkerungsentwicklung: Strukturen, Bedingungen, Folgen* [The Dynamics of Population Expansion]. Munchen: C. Hanser, 1972, pp. 91-118.

Hohorst, Gerd. "Historische Sozialstatistik und statistische Methoden in der Geschichtswissenschaft," [Historical Social Statistics and Statistical Methods in the Science of History] *Geschichte und Gesellschaft,* 3(1), 1977, pp. 109-24.

Hohorst, Gerd. *Wirtschaftswachstum und Bevolkerungsentwicklung in Preussen 1816 bis 1914* [Economic Growth and Population Expansion in Prussia, 1816 to 1914]. New York: Arno Press, 1977.

Hohorst, Gerd. "Demo-Okonomische Entwicklungsprozesse in Preussen im 19. Jahrhundert: Versuch eines Simulationstheoretischen Ansatzes," [Demographic-Economic Development Processes in Prussia in the 19th Century: A Hypothetical Simulation Experiment] [Working Paper]

Hohorst, Gerd and Fremdling, Rainer. "Marktintegration der Preussischen Wirtschaft im 19. Jahrhundert: Skizze eines Forschungsansatzes zur Fluktuation der Roggenpreise zwischen 1821 und 1865," [Market Integration of the Prussian Economy in the 19th

Century: Preliminary Findings on Fluctuations of Rye Prices Between 1821 and 1865] in Fremdling and Tilly (eds), *Industrialisierung und Raum*, 1979.

Hohorst, Gerd; Kocka, Jurgen and Ritter, Gerhard A. *Materialien zur Statistik des Kaiserreichs 1870-1914* [Statistical Material on the German Empire, 1870-1914] (Sozialgeschichtliches Arbeitsbuch, vol. 2). Munchen: Verlag C.H. Beck, 1975.

Holden, K. and Lund, P.J. "Study of Private Sector Gross Fixed Capital Formation in the United Kingdom, 1923-1938," *Oxford Economic Papers*, 20(1), March 1968, pp. 56-73.

Holt, Charles F. *The Role of State Government in the Nineteenth-Century American Economy, 1820-1902: A Quantitative Study*. New York: Arno Press, 1977.

Holt, Charles F. "Who Benefited from the Prosperity of the Twenties?," *Explorations in Economic History*, 14(3), July 1977, pp. 277-89.

Holtfrerich, Karl-Ludwig. *Quantitative Wirtschaftsgeschichte des Ruhrkohlenbergbaus im 19. Jahrhundert. Eine Fuhrungssektoranalyse* [Quantitative Economic History of the Ruhr Coal-Mining Industry in the 19th Century: A Leading-Sector Analysis]. Dortmund: Gesellschaft fur Westfalische Wirtschaftsgeschichte, 1973.

Holtfrerich, Karl-Ludwig. "Amerikanischer Kapitalexport und Wiederaufbau der Deutschen Wirtschaft 1919-23 im Vergleich zu 1924-29," [American Capital Export and the Reconstruction of the German Economy, 1919-23 in Comparison with 1924-29] reprinted in Sturmer, (ed), *Die Weimerer Republik*, 1980. *Vierteljahrschrift fur Sozial- und Wirtschaftsgeschichte*, 64(4), 1977, pp. 497-529.

Holtfrerich, Karl-Ludwig. "Internationale Verteilungsfolgen der Deutschen Inflation 1918-1923," [International Distributional Consequences of the German Inflation, 1918-1923] *Kyklos*, 30(2), August 1977, pp. 271-92.

Holtfrerich, Karl-Ludwig. "Reichsbankpolitik 1918-1923 zwischen Zahlungsbilanz- und Quantitats theorie," *Zeitschrift fur Wirtsschafts- und Sozialwissenschaften*, 1977, pp. 193-214.

Holtfrerich, Karl-Ludwig. "Die Diskontpolitik der Reichsbank wahrend der Inflation 1918 bis 1923: Ein Beurteilungsraster," [The Discount Policy of the Reichsbank during the Inflation, 1918 to 1923: A Framework for Judgement] in Henning, (ed), *Entwicklung und Aufgaben*, 1980, pp. 283-95.

Holtfrerich, Karl-Ludwig. *Die Deutsche Inflation 1914-1923: Ursachen und Folgen in Internationaler Perspektive* [The German Inflation, 1914-1923: Causes and Consequences in International Perspective]. Berlin: DeGruyter, 1980.

Holtfrerich, Karl-Ludwig. "Wachstum I: Volkswirtschaftliche Probleme," [Growth I: Economic Problems] *Handworterbuch der Wirtschaftswissenschaften*, 1979.

Holtfrerich, Karl-Ludwig. "Domestic and Foreign Expectations and the Demand for Money During the German Inflation 1920-1923." [Working Paper]

Holyfield, Jr., James and Poulson, Barry W. "A Note on European Migration: A Cross Spectral Anaylsis," *Explorations in Economic History*, 11(3), Spring 1974, pp. 299-310.

Hoover, Ethel D. "Retail Prices after 1850," in Parker (ed), *Trends in the American Economy in the Nineteenth Century*, 1960, pp. 141-86.

Hopkins, Mark M. "Emancipation: The Dominant Cause of Southern

Stagnation," Presented at the 18th Annual Cliometrics Conference, University of Chicago, May 1978.

Hopkins, Mark M. and Cardell, Nicholas S. "The Effect of Milk Intolerance on the Consumption of Milk by Slaves in 1860," *Journal of Interdisciplinary History*, 8(3), Winter 1978, pp. 507-14.

Hopkins, Sheila V. and Phelps Brown, E.H. "The Course of Wage-Rates in Five Countries, 1860-1939," *Oxford Economic Papers*, New Series, 2(2), June 1950, pp. 226-96.

Hopkins, Sheila V. and Phelps Brown, E.H. "Seven Centuries of Building Wages," *Economica*, 22(87), August 1955, pp. 195-206.

Hopkins, Sheila V. and Phelps Brown, E.H. "Seven Centuries of the Prices of Consumables, Compared with Builders' Wage Rates," reprinted in Ramsey (ed), *The Price Revolution in the Sixteenth Century*, 1971, pp. 18-41. *Economica*, 23(92), November 1956, pp. 296-314.

Hopkins, Sheila V. and Phelps Brown, E.H. "Wage-Rates and Prices: Evidence for Population Pressure in the Sixteenth Century," *Economica*, 24(96), November 1957, pp. 289-306.

Hopkins, Sheila V. and Phelps Brown, E.H. "Builders' Wage-Rates, Prices and Population: Some Further Evidence," *Economica*, 26(101), February 1959, pp. 18-38.

Hopkins, Sheila V. and Phelps Brown, E.H. "Seven Centuries of Wages and Prices: Some Earlier Estimates," *Economica*, 28(109), February 1961, pp. 30-6.

Hornby, Ove C. and Nilsson, Carl-Axel. "The Transition from Sail to Steam in the Danish Merchant Fleet, 1865-1910," *Scandinavian Economic History Review*, 28(2), 1980, pp. 109-34.

Horwich, George. "Effective Reserves, Credit, and Causality in the Banking System of the Thirties," in Hughes (ed), *Purdue Faculty Papers in Economic History*, 1967, pp. 269-89.

Hoselitz, Bert F. "Some Problems in the Quantitative Study of Industrialization," *Economic Development and Cultural Change*, 9(3), April 1961, pp. 537-50.

Howells, P.G. and Climo, T.A. "Cause and Counterfactuals," *Economic History Review*, Second Series, 27(3), August 1974, pp. 461-8.

Howle, Edward S. and Gallman, Robert E. "Trends in the Structure of the American Economy since 1840," in Fogel and Engerman (eds), *The Reinterpretation of American Economic History*, 1971, pp. 25-37.

Howle, E.S. and Gallman, Robert E. "The U.S. Capital Stock in the 19th Century." [Working Paper]

Howson, Susan. "The Origins of Dear Money, 1919-20," *Economic History Review*, Second Series, 27(1), February 1974, pp. 88-107.

Howson, Susan. *Domestic Monetary Management in Britain, 1919-38*. Cambridge: Cambridge University Press, 1975.

Howson, Susan. "The Managed Floating Pound, 1932-39," *Banker*, 126(601), March 1976, pp. 249-55.

Howson, Susan. "Slump and Unemployment," in Floud and McCloskey (eds), *The Economic History of Britain since 1700*, 1981.

Howson, Susan. "The Management of Sterling, 1932-1939," *Journal of Economic History*, 40(1), March 1980, pp. 53-60.

Huber, J. Richard. "The Effect on Prices of Japanese Entry into World Commerce after 1858," *Journal of Political Economy*, 79(3), May/June 1971, pp. 614-28.

Huber, Paul B. "Historische Verkehrsanalyse, 1830 bis 1913,"

[Historical Analysis of Transportation in Germany from 1820 to 1913] in Nuesser (ed), *Fernverkehrssysteme*, 1977, pp. 289-350.

Huber, Paul B. "Regionale Expansion und Entleerung in Deutschland des Neunzehnten Jahrhunderts: eine Folge der Eisenbahnentwicklung?," [Regional Expansion and Evacuation in 19th Century Germany: A Result of Railroad Development?] in Fremdling and Tilly (eds), *Industrialisierung und Raum*, 1979, pp. 27-53.

Hudgins, Jr., Maxwell W. and Whitaker, John K. "The Floating Pound Sterling of the Nineteen-thirties: An Econometric Study," *Southern Economic Journal*, 44(1), July 1977, pp. 1478-85.

Hueckel, Glenn. "The Napoleonic Wars and Their Impact on Factor Returns and Output Growth in England, 1793-1815," (Summary of Doctoral Dissertation) *Journal of Economic History*, 33(1), March 1973, pp. 309-11.

Hueckel, Glenn. "War and the British Economy, 1793-1815: A General Equilibrium Analysis," *Explorations in Economic History*, 10(4), Summer 1973, pp. 365-96.

Hueckel, Glenn. "English Farming Profits during the Napoleonic Wars, 1793-1815," *Explorations in Economic History*, 13(3), July 1976, pp. 331-46.

Hueckel, Glenn. "Relative Prices and Supply Response in English Agriculture during the Napoleonic Wars," *Economic History Review*, Second Series, 29(3), August 1976, pp. 401-14.

Hueckel, Glenn. "Agriculture during Industrialization," in Floud and McCloskey (eds), *The Economic History of Britain since 1700*, 1981, pp. 182-202.

Huertas, Thomas F. *Economic Growth and Economic Policy in a Multinational Setting: The Hapsburg Monarchy, 1841-1865.* New York: Arno Press, 1978.

Huertas, Thomas F. "Economic Growth and Economic Policy in a Multinational Setting: The Habsburg Monarchy, 1841-1865," (Summary of Doctoral Dissertation) *Journal of Economic History*, 38(1), March 1978, pp. 281-2.

Huertas, Thomas F. "Damnifying Growth in the Antebellum South," *Journal of Economic History*, 39(1), March 1979, pp. 87-100.

Huffman, Wallace and Lothian, James R. "Money in the United Kingdom, 1833-80," *Journal of Money, Credit and Banking*, 12, May 1980, pp. 155-74.

Hughes, Jonathan R.T. "The Commerical Crisis of 1857," reprinted in Hughes (ed), *Purdue Faculty Papers in Economic History*, 1967, pp. 207-34. *Oxford Economic Papers*, New Series, 8(2), June 1956, pp. 194-222.

Hughes, Jonathan R.T. "Ocean Freight Rates and Economic Development, 1750-1910: Discussion of North," *Journal of Economic History*, 18(4), December 1958, pp. 575-9.

Hughes, Jonathan R.T. "Foreign Trade and Balanced Growth: The Historical Framework," reprinted in Hughes (ed), *Purdue Faculty Papers in Economic History*, 1967, pp. 83-90. *American Economic Review*, Papers and Proceedings, 49(2), May 1959, pp. 330-7.

Hughes, Jonathan R.T. *Fluctuations in Trade, Industry and Finance: A Study of British Economic Development, 1850-1860.* Oxford: Clarendon Press, 1960.

Hughes, Jonathan R.T. "Measuring British Economic Growth: Review of Deane and Cole," reprinted in Hughes (ed), *Purdue Faculty Papers in*

Economic History, 1967, pp. 59-82. *Journal of Economic History,* 24(1), March 1964, pp. 60-82.

Hughes, Jonathan R.T. "Eight Tycoons: The Entrepreneur and American History," reprinted in Andreano (ed), *New Views,* 1965, pp. 261-76. *Explorations in Entrepreneurial History,* Second Series, 1(3), Spring/Summer 1964, pp. 213-31.

Hughes, Jonathan R.T. "A Note in Defense of Clio (A Reply to Burstein)," *Explorations in Entrepreneurial History,* Second Series, 2(2), Winter 1965, pp. 154.

Hughes, Jonathan R.T. "Fact and Theory in Economic History," reprinted in Hughes (ed), *Purdue Faculty Papers in Economic History,* 1967, pp. 35-57. *History,* Second Series, 3(2), Winter 1966, pp. 75-100.

Hughes, Jonathan R.T., ed. *Purdue Faculty Papers in Economic History, 1956-1966.* Homewood, Ill.: Richard D. Irwin, 1967.

Hughes, Jonathan R.T. "Economic Aspects of Industrialization," in Sills (ed), *International Encyclopedia of the Social Sciences,* 1968.

Hughes, Jonathan R.T. *Industrialization and Economic History: Theses and Conjectures.* New York: McGraw-Hill, 1970.

Hughes, Jonathan R.T. "Is the New Economic History an Export Product?," in McCloskey (ed), *Essays on a Mature Economy,* 1971, pp. 401-12.

Hughes, Jonathan R.T. "Economic Growth and Change: How and Why," *Journal of Interdisciplinary History,* 2(3), Winter 1972, pp. 263-80.

Hughes, Jonathan R.T. "The Colonial Origins of Modern Social Control," in Krooss (ed), *Proceedings of the Business History Conference, 1974,* 1975, pp. 67-95.

Hughes, Jonathan R.T. *Social Control in the Colonial Economy.* Charlottesville: University Press of Virginia, 1976.

Hughes, Jonathan R.T. "Transference and Development of Constraints Upon Economic Activity," in Uselding (ed), *Research in Economic History,* 1976.

Hughes, Jonathan R.T. *The Governmental Habit: Economic Control from Colonial Times to the Present.* New York: Basic Books, 1977.

Hughes, Jonathan R.T. "What Difference Did the Beginning Make?," *American Economic Review,* Papers and Proceedings, 67(1), February 1977, pp. 15-20.

Hughes, Jonathan R.T. "Entrepreneurship and the American Economy: A Sketch," in Uselding (ed), *Research in Economic History,* 1978, pp. 361-8.

Hughes, Jonathan R.T. "Roots of Regulation: The New Deal," in Walton (ed), *Regulatory Change in an Atmosphere of Crisis,* 1979, pp. 31-55.

Hughes, Jonathan R.T. "Entrepreneurship," in Porter (ed), *Encyclopedia of American Economic History,* 1980, pp. 214-28.

Hughes, Jonathan R.T. and Davis, Lance E. "A Dollar-Sterling Exchange, 1803-1895," reprinted in Hughes (ed), *Purdue Faculty Papers in Economic History,* 1967, pp. 235-68. *Economic History Review,* Second Series, 13(1), August 1960, pp. 52-78.

Hughes, Jonathan R.T.; Davis, Lance E. and Reiter, Stanley. "Aspects of Quantitative Research in Economic History," reprinted in Hughes (ed), *Purdue Faculty Papers in Economic History,* 1967, pp. 3-10. *Journal of Economic History,* 20(4), December 1960, pp.

539-47.

Hughes, Jonathan R.T.; Davis, Lance E. and McDougall, Duncan. *American Economic History: The Development of a National Economy*. Homewood, Ill.: Richard D. Irwin, 1961.

Hughes, Jonathan R.T. and Rosenberg, Nathan. "The United States Business Cycle before 1860: Some Problems of Interpretation," reprinted in Hughes (ed), *Purdue Faculty Papers in Economic History*, 1967, pp. 187-206. *Economic History Review*, Second Series, 15(3), April 1963, pp. 476-93.

Hum, Derek; Spencer, Barbara and Deprey, Paul. "Spectral Analysis and the Study of Seasonal Fluctuations in Historical Demography," *Journal of European Economic History*, 5(1), Spring 1976, pp. 171-90.

Hunt, E.H. "Railroad Social Saving in Nineteenth Century America: Comment on Fogel," *American Economic Review*, 57(4), September 1967, pp. 909-10.

Hunt, E.H. "The New Economic History: Professor Fogel's Study of American Railways," *History*, 53(177), February 1968, pp. 3-18.

Hunt, E.H. "The 'New' Economics of Slavery. Review Essay of 'Time on the Cross (2 Vols)' by Robert W. Fogel and Stanley L. Engerman (Boston: Little, Brown, 1974)," *Review of Social Economy*, 33(2), October 1975, pp. 166-73.

Hurd, II, John. "Railways and the Expansion of Markets in India, 1861-1921," (Symposium on Economic Change in Indian Agriculture. Edited by Morris D. Morris) *Explorations in Economic History*, 12(3), July 1975, pp. 263-88.

Hurt, J.S. "Professor West on Early Nineteenth-Century Education," *Economic History Review*, Second Series, 24(4), November 1971, pp. 624-32.

Hutchinson, William K., ed. *American Economic History: An Annotated Bibliography*. Detroit: Gale Research, 1979.

Hutchinson, William K. "Regional Exports to Foreign Countries, U.S. 1870-1910: A Structural Analysis." [Working Paper]

Hutchinson, William K. and Callahan, Colleen M. "Antebellum Interregional Trade in Agricultural Goods: Preliminary Results," *Journal of Economic History*, 40(1), March 1980, pp. 25-31.

Hutchinson, William K. and Williamson, Samual H. "The Self-Sufficiency of the Antebellum South: Estimates of the Food Supply," *Journal of Economic History*, 31(3), September 1971, pp. 591-612.

Huttenback, Robert A. and Davis, Lance E. "Public Expenditure and Private Profit: Budgetary Decision in the British Empire, 1860-1912," *American Economic Review*, Papers and Proceedings, 67(1), February 1977, pp. 282-7.

Huttenback, Robert A. and Davis, Lance E. "Aspects of Late-Nineteenth Century Imperialism," Presented at the Annual Meetings of the Organization of American Historians, New Orleans, April 1979.

Huttenback, Robert A. and Davis, Lance E. "British Imperialism and Military Expenditure," Presented at the Anglo-American Conference of Historians, London, July 1978.

Huttenback, Robert A. and Davis, Lance E. "Social Choice and Public Welfare: British and Colonial Expenditure in the Late Nineteenth Century," Presented at the 14th International Congress of Historical Societies, San Francisco, August 1975.

Hyde, Charles K. "Technological Change and the Development of the

British Iron Industry, 1700-1870," (Summary of Doctoral Dissertation) *Journal of Economic History,* 33(1), March 1973, pp. 312-3.

Hyde, Charles K. "The Adoption of the Hot Blast by the British Iron Industry: A Reinterpretation," *Explorations in Economic History,* 10(3), Spring 1973, pp. 281-94.

Hyde, Charles K. "The Adoption of Coke-Smelting by the British Iron Industry, 1709-1790," *Explorations in Economic History,* 10(4), Summer 1973, pp. 397-418.

Hyde, Charles K. "Technological Change in the British Wrought Iron Industry, 1750-1815: A Reinterpretation," *Economic History Review,* Second Series, 27(2), May 1974, pp. 190-206.

Hyde, Charles K. *Technological Change and the British Iron Industry, 1700-1870.* Princeton: Princeton University Press, 1977.

Hymer, Stephen H. "Economic Forms in Pre-Colonial Ghana," *Journal of Economic History,* 30(1), March 1970, pp. 33-50.

Imlah, Albert H. "British Balance of Payments and Export of Capital, 1816-1913," *Economic History Review,* Second Series, 5(2), 1952, pp. 208-39.

Imlah, A.H. *Economic Elements in the Pax Britannica.* Cambridge: Harvard University Press, 1958.

Ippolito, Richard A. "The Effect of the 'Agricultural Depression' on Industrial Demand in England: 1730-1750," *Economica,* 42(167), August 1975, pp. 298-312.

Ireland, N.J. and Crafts, N.F.R. "Family Limitation and the English Demographic Revolution: A Simulation Approach," *Journal of Economic History,* 36(3), September 1976, pp. 598-623.

Ishikawa, Tsuneo. "Conceptualization of Learning by Doing: A Note on Paul David's 'Learning by Doing and the Antebellum United States Textile Industry'," *Journal of Economic History,* 33(4), December 1973, pp. 851-61.

Ishiwata, Shigeru. "Capital Stocks, 1888-1937," in Ohkawa and Hayami (eds), *Economic Growth,* 1973, pp. 101-12.

Israelsen, L. Dwight. "The Determinants of Russian State Income, 1800-1914: An Econometric Analysis," Ph.D. Dissertation, Massachusetts Institute of Technology, 1979.

Itzcovich, Oscar. "I metodi matematici e statistici nella storiografia," [Mathematical and Statistical Methods in Historiography] in *Introduzione allo studio della storia,* vol. 2. Milano: Marzorati Editore, 1974, pp. 351-428.

Itzcovich, Oscar. "Un modello matematico dell'"Economia della riserva signorile' di W. Kula," [A Mathematical Model of W. Kula's 'Economics of the Lord's Reserve'] *Miscellanea storica ligure,* 10, 1978, pp. 67-93.

Itzcovitch, Oscar and Bulferetti, Luigi. *Orientamenti della storiografia quantitativa* [Trends in Quantitative Historiography]. Roma: Citta nuova editrice.

Jackson, R.V. "Owner-occupation of Houses in Sydney, 1871 to 1891," *Australian Economic History Review*, 10(2), September 1970, pp. 138-54.

Jackson, R.V. "House Building and the Age Structure of Population in New South Wales, 1861-1900," *Australian Economic History Review*, 14(2), September 1974, pp. 143-59.

Jaeger, Hans. "Nuovi metodi ed ipotesi nella storia economica tedesca," [New Methods and Hypotheses in German Economic History] *Quaderni Storici*, 31, April 1976, pp. 409-21.

James, John A. "The Evolution of the National Money Market, 1888-1911," (Summary of Doctoral Dissertation) *Journal of Economic History*, 36(1), March 1976, pp. 271-5.

James, John A. "The Conundrum of the Low Issue of National Bank Notes," *Journal of Political Economy*, 84(2), April 1976, pp. 359-67.

James, John A. "A Note on Interest Paid on New York Bankers' Balances in the Postbellum Period," *Business History Review*, 50(2), Summer 1976, pp. 198-202.

James, John A. "Banking Market Structure, Risk and the Pattern of Local Interest Rates in the United States, 1893-1911," *Review of Economics and Statistics*, 58(4), November 1976, pp. 453-62.

James, John A. "The Development of the National Money Market, 1893-1911," *Journal of Economic History*, 36(4), December 1976, pp. 878-97.

James, John A. *Money and Capital Markets in Postbellum America*. Princeton: Princeton University Press, 1978.

James, John A. "Cost Functions of Postbellum National Banks," *Explorations in Economic History*, 15(2), April 1978, pp. 184-95.

James, John A. "The Welfare Effects of the Antebellum Tariff: A General Equilibrium Analysis," *Explorations in Economic History*, 15(3), July 1978, pp. 231-56.

James, John A. "Some Evidence on Relative Labor Scarcity in Nineteenth-Century American Manufacturing." [Working Paper]

James, John A. and Sylla, Richard E. "The Changing Nature of American Public Debt, 1690-1835," in *La Dette Publique aux XVIIIe et XIXe Siecles*. Brussels: Credit Communal de Belgique, 1980.

Japanese Economic Planning Board. *National Income and National Economic Accounts of Japan, 1930-56*. Tokyo: Economic Planning Board, 1957.

Jefferys, James B. and Walters, Dorothy. *National Income and Expenditure of the United Kingdom* (Income and Wealth, Series 5). London: Bowes & Bowes," 1955.

Jennings, Frederic B., Jr. "Interdependence, Incentives, and Institutional Bias: An Organizational Perspective on the British Canals," Ph.D. Dissertation, Stanford University, 1982.

Jensen, Richard. "Quantitative American Studies: The State of the Art," *American Quarterly*, 26(3), August 1974, pp. 225-40.

Johansen, Hans Chr. *Dansk Okonomisk Politik I Arene efter 1784* [Danish Economic Policy after 1784] [Contains English Summary]. Aarhus: Universitetsforlaget, 1968.

Johansen, Hans Chr. "Kriser och Krispolitik I Norden under Mellankrigstiden," [Crises and Crisis-Policy in Scandinavia during the Inter-War Period] in Uppsala: Almqvist & Wiksell, 1974, pp. 13-26.

Johansen, Hans Chr. *Befolkningsudvikling og Familiestruktur I Det 18. Arhundrede* [Population Development and Family Structure in the 19th Century]. Odense: Odense University Press, 1975.

Johansen, Hans Chr. "Den Danske Skibsfart I Sidste Halvdel af Det 18. Arhundrede," [Eighteenth Century Danish Shipping] *Erhvervshistorisk Arbog*, 26, 1975, pp. 62-89.

Johansen, Hans Chr., ed. *Studier I Dansk Befolkningshistorie 1750-1890* [Studies in Danish Population History 1750-1890]. Odense: Odense University Press, 1976.

Johansen, Hans Chr. "Ostersohandelen og den Svensk-Russiske Krig 1788-90," [Baltic Trade and the Swedish-Russian War, 1788-90] *Erhvervshistorisk Arbog*, 27, 1976/77, pp. 35-54.

Johansen, Hans Chr.; Akerman, Sune and Gaunt, David, eds. *Chance and Change: Social and Economic Studies in Historical Demography in the Baltic Area*. Odense: Odense University Press, 1978.

Johansen, Hans Chr. "Shipping through the Sound, 1784-95." [Working Paper]

Johanson, Hans Chr. *Den okonomiske og sociale udvikling i Danmark, 1864-1901* [Danish Economic and Social Development, 1864-1901]. Copenhagen: Hojres Fond, 1962.

Johansen, Hans Chr. and Dybdahl, Vagn., eds. *Krise I Danmark: Strukturaendringer og Krisepolitik I 1930' Erne* [Crisis in Denmark]. Kobenhavn: Berlingske, 1975.

Johansson, O. *The Gross Domestic Product of Sweden and Its Composition*. Stockholm: Almquist & Wicksell, 1967.

Johnson, Arthur M. "The American Petroleum Industry: Comment on Williamson, Andreano, and Menezes," in Brady (ed), *Output, Employment, and Productivity in the United States After 1800*, 1966, pp. 403-4.

Johnson, H. Thomas. "Relation of Building Volume and Construction Inputs: A Note," *Explorations in Entrepreneurial History*, Second Series, 5(1), Fall 1967, pp. 108-10.

Johnson, Harry G. *Clearing Bank Holdings of Public Debt, 1930-50* (Reprint Series no. 54). Cambridge: Cambridge University Press, 1952.

Johnson, Harry G. "A Quantity Theorist's Monetary History of the United States. Review Essay of 'A Monetary History of the United States, 1867-1960' by Milton Friedman and Anna J. Schwartz (New York: National Bureau of Economic Research, 1963)," *Economic Journal*, 75(298), June 1965, pp. 388-96.

Johnson, Ronald N. and Libecap, Gary D. "Property Rights, Nineteenth-Century Federal Timber Policy, and the Conservation Movement," *Journal of Economic History*, 39(1), March 1979, pp. 129-42.

Johnson, Ronald N. and Libecap, Gary D. "Efficient Markets and Great Lakes Timber: A Conservation Issue Reexamined," *Explorations in Economic History*, 17(4), October 1980, pp. 372-85.

Johnson, Thomas H. "Postwar Optimism and the Rural Financial Crisis of the 1920's," *Explorations in Economic History*, 11(2), Winter 1974, pp. 173-91.

Johnston, Jack and Curran, Christopher. "The Antebellum Money Market and the Economic Impact of the Bank War: A Comment on Sushka," *Journal of Economic History*, 39(2), June 1979, pp. 461-6.

Johnston, J. and Murphy, G.W. "The Growth of Life Assurance in the

United Kingdom since 1880," *Manchester School of Economic and Social Studies*, 25, May 1957, pp. 107-82.

Joksch, H.C.; Hoffmann, Walther G. and Gulicher, Herbert, eds. *Studien zur wirtschaftlichen Verfahrensforschung.* Koln: Westdeutscher Verlag, 1964.

Jones, Andrew. "The Rise and Fall of the Manorial System: A Critical Comment (on North and Thomas)," *Journal of Economic History*, 32(4), December 1972, pp. 938-44.

Jones, Alice Hanson. "La Fortune Privee en Pennsylvanie, New Jersey, Delaware (1774)," [The Private Wealth in Pennsylvania, New Jersey, and Delaware (1774)] *Annales: Economies, Societes, Civilisations*, 24(2), March/April 1969, pp. 235-49.

Jones, Alice Hanson. "Wealth Estimates for the American Middle Colonies, 1774," *Economic Development and Cultural Change*, 18(4), Part 2, July 1970, pp. 1-172.

Jones, Alice Hanson. "Wealth Estimates for the New England Colonies about 1770," *Journal of Economic History*, 32(1), March 1972, pp. 98-127.

Jones, Alice Hanson. "Components of Private Wealth Per Free Capita for the Thirteen Colonies," in U.S. Bureau of the Census (ed), *Historical Statistics of the United States*, 1976, pp. 1175.

Jones, Alice Hanson, ed. *American Colonial Wealth: Documents and Methods.* New York: Arno Press, 1978.

Jones, Alice Hanson. "American Probate Inventories: A Source to Estimate Wealth in 1774 in Thirteen Colonies and Three Regions," *A.A.G. Bijdragen*, 23, 1980, pp. 239-56.

Jones, Alice Hanson. *Wealth of a Nation to Be: The American Colonies on the Eve of the Revolution.* New York: Columbia University Press, 1980.

Jones, Alice Hanson. "Wealth Distribution in the American Middle Colonies in the Third Quarter of the Eighteenth Century." [Working Paper]

Jones, Alice Hanson. "Wealth Estimates for the Southern Colonies about 1770," *Claremont Economic Papers*, 86, December 1973.

Jones, Donald W. "Emigration from the United Kingdom to the United States, 1875-1913." [Working Paper]

Jones, Donald W. "Land Use and Land Tenure: Theory and Empirical Analysis." [Working Paper]

Jones, Donald W. "Migration and Urban Unemployment in Dualistic Economic Development," University of Chicago, Department of Geography Research Series #165, 1975.

Jones, Donald W. "Prices, Gold and Interest Rates in Gold Rush California: An Inquiry into Domestic and International Economic Relations of California, 1850-1855," presented at the Meetings of the North American Economic Studies Association, Atlantic City, New Jersey, September 1976.

Jones, Donald W. "The Gold Standard in California during the Greenback Period and the Origins of the Specific Contract Act," presented at the 38th Annual Meeting of the Economic History Association, Toronto, Ontario, September 1978.

Jones, Eric L. "The Constraints on Economic Growth in Southern England, 1650-1850," *Third International Conference of Economic History, Munich, 1965*, part 5. Paris: Mouton, 1974, pp. 423-30.

Jones, Eric L. "Agriculture, 1700-80," in Floud and McCloskey (eds),

The Economic History of Britain since 1700, 1981, pp. 66-86.

Jones, Eric L. and Falkus, Malcolm E. "Urban Improvement and the English Economy in the Seventeenth and Eighteenth Centuries," in Uselding (ed), *Research in Economic History*, 1979.

Jones, Eric L. and Parker, William N., eds. *European Peasants and Their Markets: Essays in European Agrarian History*. Princeton: Princeton University Press, 1975.

Jones, Ethel B. "State Legislation and Hours of Work in Manufacturing," *Southern Economic Journal*, 41(4), April 1975, pp. 602-12.

Jones, H.G. and Mitchell, B.R., eds. *Second Abstract of British Historical Statistics*. Cambridge University Press, 1971.

Jones, Homer. "Banking Reforms in the 1930s," in Walton (ed), *Regulatory Change in an Atmosphere of Crisis*, 1979, pp. 79-92.

Jones, Lewis R. "The Mechanization of Reaping and Mowing in American Agriculture, 1833-1870: Comment (on Olmstead)," *Journal of Economic History*, 37(2), June 1977, pp. 451-5.

Jones, S.R.H. "Price Associations and Competition in the British Pin Industry, 1814-40," *Economic History Review*, Second Series, 26(2), May 1973, pp. 237-53.

Jones, S.R.H. "The Development of Needle Manufacturing in the West Midlands before 1750," *Economic History Review*, Second Series, 31(3), August 1978, pp. 354-68.

Jonson, P.D. "Money and Economic Activity in the Open Economy: The United Kingdom, 1880-1970," *Journal of Political Economy*, 84(5), October 1976, pp. 979-1012.

Jonson, Peter D. "Monetary and Economic Activity in the Open Economy: The United Kingdom, 1880-1970," *Journal of Political Economy*, 84, October 1976, pp. 979-1012.

Jonson, Peter D. "Inflation and Growth in the United Kingdom: A Longer Run Perspective," *Journal of Monetary Economics*, 3, January 1977, pp. 1-23.

Jonung, Lars. "Money and Prices in Sweden, 1732-1972," *Scandinavian Journal of Economics*, 78(1), 1976, pp. 40-58.

Jonung, Lars. "Sources of growth in the Swedish money stock, 1871-1971," *Scandinavian Journal of Economics*, 78(4), 1976, pp. 611-27.

Jonung, Lars. "The Legal Framework and the Economics of Private Bank Notes in Sweden, 1831-1902," in Skogh (ed), *Law and Economics*, 1978, pp. 185-201.

Jonung, Lars and Wadensjo, Eskil. "Wages and Prices in Sweden, 1912-1922: A Retrospective Test," *Scandinavian Journal of Economics*, 81(1), 1979, pp. 60-71.

Jonung, Lars. "The Depression in Sweden and the United States: A Comparison of Causes and Policies," in Brunner (ed), *The Great Depression Revisited*, 1981, pp. 286-315.

Jonung, Lars and Bordo, Michael D. "The Long Run Behavior of the Income Velocity of Money: A Cross Country Comparison of Five Advanced Countries, 1870-1975." [Working Paper]

Jonung, Lars and Wadensjo, Eskil. "A Model of the Determination of Wages and Prices in Sweden, 1922-1971," *Economy and History*, 21(2), 1978, pp. 104-13.

Jorberg, Lennart. *A History of Prices in Sweden, 1732-1914* (vol. 1: Sources, Methods, Tables; vol. 2: Description, Analysis). Lund:

University of Lund Press, 1972.

Jorberg, Lennart and Bengtsson, Tommy. "Market Integration in Sweden during the 18th and 19th Centuries: Spectral Analysis of Grain Prices," *Economy and History*, 18(2), 1975, pp. 93-106.

Jorberg, Lennart and Bengtsson, Tommy. "Regional Wages in Sweden during the 19th Century," in Bairoch and Levy-Leboyer (eds), *Disparities in Economic Development since the Industrial Revolution*, 1980.

Joskow, Paul L. and McFelvey, Edward F. "The Fogel-Engerman Iron Model: A Clarifying Note," *Journal of Political Economy*, 81(5), September/October 1973, pp. 1236-40.

Jostock, Paul. "The Long-Term Growth of National Income in Germany," in Kuznets, (ed), *Income and Wealth*, Series 5, 1955, pp. 79-122.

Juba, Bruce and Uselding, Paul J. "Biased Technical Progress in American Manufacturing, 1839-1899," *Explorations in Economic History*, 11(1), Fall 1973, pp. 55-72.

Judd, John and Olmstead, Alan L. "Saved from Sociology: The Frugal Scot and His Banking System." [Working Paper]

Juster, F. Thomas. *Household Capital Formation and Financing, 1897-1962* (General Series 83). New York: Columbia University Press for the National Bureau of Economic Research, 1966.

Kagel, John and Battalio, Raymond C. "The Structure of Antebellum Southern Agriculture: South Carolina, A Case Study," in Parker (ed), *The Structure of the Cotton Economy of the Antebellum South*, 1970, pp. 25-37.

Kahan, Arcadius. "Continuity in Economic Activity and Policy during the Post-Petrine Period in Russia," *Journal of Economic History*, 25(1), March 1965, pp. 61-85.

Kahan, Arcadius. "Quantitative Data for the Study of Russian History," in Lorwin and Price (eds), *The Dimensions of the Past*, 1972, pp. 361-430.

Kahan, Arcadius. "Notes on Serfdom in Western and Eastern Europe," *Journal of Economic History*, 33(1), March 1973, pp. 86-99.

Kahan, Arcadius. "Economic Opportunities and Some Pilgrims' Progress: Jewish Immigrants from Eastern Europe in the U.S., 1890-1914," *Journal of Economic History*, 38(1), March 1978, pp. 235-51.

Kahn, Charles. "The Use of Complicated Models as Explanations: A Re-examination of Williamson's Late Nineteenth Century America," presented at the Harvard University Workshop in Economic History 1980-1, June 1980.

Kammeyer, Kenneth C.W. and Skidmore, Arthur. "Demographic Transition: A Forcing Model?: Comment," *Demography*, 12(2), May 1975, pp. 343-50.

Kano, Tsuneo and Kelly, William J. "Crude Oil Production in the Russian Empire: 1818-1919," *Journal of European Economic History*, 6(2), Fall 1977, pp. 307-38.

Katz, Barbara G. "Purges and Production: Soviet Economic Growth, 1928-1940," *Journal of Economic History*, 35(3), September 1975, pp. 567-90.

378

Kau, James and Meeker, Edward F. "Racial Discrimination and Occupational Attainment at the Turn of the Century," *Explorations in Economic History*, 14(3), July 1977, pp. 250-76.

Kavanagh, N.J. and Walters, A.A. "The Demand for Money in the U.K., 1877-1961: Some Preliminary Findings," *Oxford Bulletin of Economics and Statistics*, 28), May 1966, pp. 98-116.

Kay, J.A. and Hannah, Leslie. *Concentration in Modern Industry: Theory Measurement and the U.K. Experience*. London: Macmillan, 1977.

Kearl, J.R.; Pope, Clayne L. and Wimmer, Larry T. "Household Wealth in a Settlement Economy: Utah, 1850-1870," *Journal of Economic History*, 40(3), September 1980, pp. 477-96.

Keat, Paul G. "Long-Run Changes in Occupational Wage Structure, 1900-1956," *Journal of Political Economy*, 68(6), December 1960, pp. 584-600.

Keating, M. and Haig, Brian D. "A Comment on the Butlin-Dowie Australian Work Force and Employment Estimates," *Australian Economic History Review*, 11(1), March 1971, pp. 59-62.

Keehn, Richard H. "Market Structure and Bank Performance: Wisconsin, 1870-1900," *Transactions of the Wisconsin Academy of Sciences, Arts and Letters*, 56, 1973, pp. 149-56.

Keehn, Richard H. "Federal Bank Policy, Bank Market Structure, and Bank Performance: Wisconsin, 1863-1914," *Business History Review*, 48(1), Spring 1974, pp. 1-27.

Keehn, Richard H. "Market Power and Bank Lending: Some Evidence from Wisconsin, 1870-1900," *Journal of Economic History*, 40(1), March 1980, pp. 45-52.

Keehn, Richard H. and Bowman, John D. "Agricultural Terms of Trade in Four Midwestern States, 1870-1900," *Journal of Economic History*, 34(3), September 1974, pp. 592-609.

Keehn, Richard H. and Smiley, Gene. "A Note on John A. James' Analysis of Interest Paid on Bankers' Balances in the Postbellum Period," *Business History Review*, 51(3), Autumn 1977, pp. 367-9.

Keehn, Richard H. and Smiley, Gene. "Mortgage Lending by National Banks, 1870-1914," *Business History Review*, 51(4), Winter 1977, pp. 474-91.

Keehn, Richard H. and Smiley, Gene. "Short Term Interest Rates in New York City and San Francisco, 1872-1898," Marquette University Department of Economics Working Paper, July 1978.

Keesing, Donald B. "Structural Change Early in Development: Mexico's Changing Industrial and Occupational Structure from 1895 to 1950," *Journal of Economic History*, 29(4), December 1969, pp. 716-38.

Kellenbenz, Hermann; Schneider, Jurgen and Gommel, Rainer. *Wirtschaftliches Wachstum im Spiegel der Wirtschaftsgeschichte* [Economic Growth in Economic Historical Perspective]. Darmstadt: Wissenschaftliche Buchgesellschaft, 1978.

Keller, Robert R. "Factor Income Distribution in the United States During the 1920's: A Reexamination of Fact and Theory," *Journal of Economic History*, 33(1), March 1973, pp. 252-73.

Keller, Robert R. "Estimates of National Income and Product, 1919-1941: The Best of all Possible Worlds," *Explorations in Economic History*, 11(1), Fall 1973, pp. 87-94.

Keller, Robert R. "Monopoly Capital and the Great Depression: Testing Baran and Sweezy's Hypothesis," *Review of Radical Political Economics*, 7(4), Winter 1975, pp. 65-75.

Keller, Robert R. "An Analysis of Relative Income Shares in the United States during the 1920's," Ph.D. Dissertation, University of Wisconsin-Madison, 1971.

Kelley, Allen C. "International Migration and Economic Growth: Australia, 1865-1935," *Journal of Economic History*, 25(3), September 1965, pp. 333-54.

Kelley, Allen C. "Demographic Change and Economic Growth: Australia, 1861-1911," *Explorations in Entrepreneurial History*, Second Series, 5(3), Spring/Summer 1968, pp. 207-77.

Kelley, Allen C. "Demographic Cycles and Economic Growth: The Long Swing Reconsidered," *Journal of Economic History*, 29(4), December 1969, pp. 633-56.

Kelley, Allen C. "Demographic Changes and American Economic Development: Past, Present, and Future," in Morse and Reed (eds), *Economic Aspects of Population Change*, 1972, pp. 9-48.

Kelley, Allen C. "Scale Economies, Inventive Activity, and the Economics of American Population Growth," *Explorations in Economic History*, 10(1), Fall 1972, pp. 35-52.

Kelley, Allen C.; Cheetham, Russell J. and Williamson, Jeffrey G. *Dualistic Economic Development: Theory and History.* Chicago: University of Chicago Press, 1972.

Kelley, Allen C. and Weisbrod, Burton A. "Disease and Economic Development: The Impact of Parasitic Disease in St. Lucia," *Journal of Social Economics*, Fall 1973.

Kelley, Allen C. and Williamson, Jeffrey G. "Writing History Backwards: Meiji Japan Revisited," *Journal of Economic History*, 31(4), December 1971, pp. 729-76.

Kelley, Allen C. and Williamson, Jeffrey G. "Simple Parables of Japanese Economic Progress: Report on Early Findings," in Ohkawa and Hayami (eds), *Nihon Keizai No Chokiteki Bunseki*, 1973.

Kelley, Allen C. and Williamson, Jeffrey G. "Modelling Economic Development and General Equilibrium Histories," *American Economic Review*, Papers and Proceedings, 63(2), May 1973, pp. 450-8.

Kelley, Allen C. and Williamson, Jeffrey G. "General Equilibrium Analysis of Agricultural Development: The Case of Meiji Japan," in Reynolds (ed), *Agricultural Development and Theory*, 1974.

Kelley, Allen C. and Williamson, Jeffrey G. *Lessons from Japanese Development: An Analytical Economic History.* Chicago: University of Chicago Press, 1974.

Kelley, Allen C. and Williamson, Jeffrey G. "Simple Parables of Japanese Economic Progress: Report on Early Findings," in Ohkawa and Hayami (eds), *Long-Term Analysis of the Japanese Economy*, 1974, pp. 141-85.

Kelly, William J. "Railroad Development and Market Integration in Tsarist Russia: Evidence on Oil Products and Grain: A Note on Metzer," *Journal of Economic History*, 36(4), December 1976, pp. 908-16.

Kelly, William J. and Kano, Tsuneo. "Crude Oil Production in the Russian Empire: 1818-1919," *Journal of European Economic History*, 6(2), Fall 1977, pp. 307-38.

Kelso, Charles. "Slavery as an Obstacle of Economic Growth in the United States: A Panel Discussion of Conrad and Meyer," *Journal of Economic History*, 27(4), December 1967, pp. 544-7.

Kendrick, John W. "Retail Prices after 1850: Comment on Hoover," in

380

Parker (ed), *Trends in the American Economy in the Nineteenth Century*, 1960, pp. 186-90.

Kendrick, John W. "Productivity," in Porter (ed), *Encyclopedia of American Economic History*, 1980, pp. 157-66.

Kendrick, John W.; Lethem, Yvonne and Rowley, Jennifer. *The Formation and Stocks of Total Capital* (National Bureau of Economic Research General Series(100). New York: Columbia University Press for the National Bureau of Economic Research, 1976.

Kendrick, John W. and Pech, Maude R. *Productivity Trends in the United States* (National Bureau of Economic Research General Series 71). Princeton: Princeton University Press for the National Bureau of Economic Research, 1961.

Kennedy, Charles J. "Railroad Investment Before the Civil War: Comment on Wicker," in Parker (ed), *Trends in the American Economy in the Nineteenth Century*, 1960, pp. 544-5.

Kennedy, William P., Jr. "Foreign Investment, Trade, and Growth in the United Kingdom, 1870-1913," *Explorations in Economic History,* 11(4), Summer 1974, pp. 415-44.

Kennedy, William P., Jr. "Institutional Response to Economic Growth: Capital Markets in Britain to 1914," in Hannah (ed), *Management Strategy and Business Development*, 1976, pp. 151-83.

Kennedy, William P., Jr. "Economic Growth and Structural Change in the U.K., 1870-1914." [Working Paper]

Kenwood, A.G. "Fixed Capital Formation on Merseyside, 1800-1913," *Economic History Review,* Second Series, 31(2), May 1978, pp. 214-37.

Kessel, Reuben A. and Alchian, Armen A. "Real Wages in the North During the Civil War: Mitchell's Data Reinterpreted," reprinted in Fogel and Engerman (eds), *The Reinterpretation of American Economic History*, 1971, pp. 459-67. *Journal of Law and Economics,* 2, October 1959, pp. 95-113.

Kesselman, Jonathan R. and Savin, N. Eugene. "Three-and-a-Half Million Workers Never Were Lost," *Economic Inquiry,* 16(2), April 1978, pp. 205-25.

Kessinger, Tom G. "The Peasant Farm in North India, 1848-1968," (Symposium on Economic Change in Indian Agriculture. Edited by Morris D. Morris) *Explorations in Economic History,* 12(3), July 1975, pp. 303-31.

Keyder, Caglar and O'Brien, Patrick K. "Niveles de vida en Gran Bretana y Francia entre 1780 y 1914," [The Standard of Living in Britain and France, 1780-1914] *Investigaciones Economicas,* 6, August 1978, pp. 5-41.

Keyder, Caglar; O'Brien, Patrick K. and Heath, D. "Agriculture in Britain and France, 1815-1914," *Journal of European Economic History,* 6(2), Fall 1977, pp. 339-91.

Keyder, Caglar and O'Brien, Patrick K. *Economic Growth in Britain and France, 1780-1914: Two Paths to the Twentieth Century.* London: Allen & Unwin, 1978.

Keyfitz, Nathan. "A Historical Perspective on Economic Aspects of the Population Explosion: Comment on Lee," in Easterlin (ed), *Population and Economic Change in Developing Countries*, 1980, pp. 557-9.

Khan, Mohsin S. "The Stability of the Demand-For-Money Function in the United States, 1901-1965," *Journal of Political Economy,* 82(6),

November/December 1974, pp. 1205-20.

Kikuchi, Masao and Hayami, Yujiro. "Agricultural Growth against a Land Resource Constraint: A Comparative History of Japan, Taiwan, Korea and the Philippines," *Journal of Economic History*, 38(4), December 1978, pp. 839-64.

Kikuchi, Shigeru. "The Settlement Patterns of Oriental Immigrants to the United States: An Economic Analysis of Immigrant Behavior," Ohio University Economic History Research Paper no. G-12.

Kindahl, James K. "Economic Factors in Specie Resumption: The United States, 1865-79," reprinted in Fogel and Engerman (eds), *The Reinterpretation of American Economic History*, 1971), pp. 468-79. *Journal of Political Economy*, 69(1), February 1961, pp. 30-48.

Kindleberger, Charles P.; Van der Tak, Herman G. and Vanek, Jaroslav. *The Terms of Trade: A European Case Study*. Cambridge, Mass. and New York: Technology Press of M.I.T. and Wiley, 1956.

Kindleberger, Charles P. *Economic Growth in France and Britain, 1851-1950*. Cambridge: Harvard University Press, 1964.

Kindleberger, Charles P. *The World in Depression, 1929-1939*. Berkeley: University of California Press, 1973.

Kindleberger, Charles P. "The Rise of Free Trade in Western Europe, 1820-1875," *Journal of Economic History*, 35(1), March 1975, pp. 20-55.

Kindleberger, Charles P. *Economic Response: Comparative Studies in Trade, Finance, and Growth*. Cambridge: Harvard University Press, 1978.

Kindleberger, Charles P. *Manias, Panics, and Crashes: A History of Financial Crises*. New York: Basic Books, 1978.

Kirchhain, Gunter. *Das Wachstum der Deutschen Baumwollindustrie im 19. Jahrhundert* [The Growth of the German Cotton Textile Industry in the 19th Century]. New York: Arno Press, 1977.

Kirchhain, Gunter. "Geldmenge, Zinssatze und Wachstum in Deutschland, 1870-1913," [Money Supply, Interest Rates and Economic Growth in Germany, 1870-1913] Diploma Thesis, Universitat Munster, 1968.

Kiyokawa, Yukihiko and Saxonhouse, Gary R. "The Supply and Demand for Quality Workers in the Cotton Textile Industries in Japan and India," in Ohkawa and Hayami (eds), *The Comparative Analysis of Japan and the Less Developed Countries*.

Klein, Benjamin. "Our New Monetary Standard: The Measurement and Effects of Price Uncertainty, 1800-1973," *Economic Inquiry*, 13(4), December 1975, pp. 461-83.

Klein, Herbert S. "Reflections on the Viability of Slavery and the Causes of Abolition in 19th Century Cuba," presented at the MSSB-University of Rochester Conference Time on the Cross: A First Appraisal, October 1974.

Klein, Herbert S. "The Cuban Slave Trade in a Period of Transition, 1790-1843," *Revue francaise d'histoire d'outre-mer*, 62(226-227), 1975, pp. 67-89.

Klein, John J. "German Money and Prices, 1932-44," in Friedman, (ed), *Studies in the Quantity Theory of Money*, 1956, pp. 121-59.

Klein, Judith V. "Farm-Making Costs in the 1850's: A Comment on Ankli," *Agricultural History*, 48(1), January 1974, pp. 71-4.

Klein, Judith L.V. and Parker, William N. "Productivity Growth in Grain Production in the United States, 1840-60 and 1900-10," in Brady (ed), *Output, Employment, and Productivity in the United*

States after 1800, 1966, pp. 523-80.

Klein, L.R. and Goldberger, A.S. *An Econometric Model of the United States, 1929-52.* Amsterdam: North-Holland, 1955.

Klein, Maury and Yamamura, Kozo. "The Growth Strategies of Southern Railroads, 1865-1893," *Business History Review*, 41(4), Winter 1967, pp. 358-77.

Klep, Paul M.M. *Groeidynamiek en Stagnatie in een Agrarisch Grensgebied, De Economische Ontwikkeling in de Noordantwerpse Kempen en de Baronie Van Breda, 1750-1850* [Growth and Stagnation in an Agrarian Borderland, The Economic Development in the Northantwerp Kempen (In Belgium) and the Barony of Breda (The Netherlands), 1750-1850]. Tilburg: Stichting Zuidelijk Historisch Contact, 1973.

Klep, Paul M.M. *Bevolking en Arbeid in Transformatie, Brabant 1700-1900: Een Analyse Van Ongelijktijdige Ontwikkelingen in een Maatschappij Opweg Naar Moderne Economische Groei* [Population and Labour in Transformation, Brabant 1700-1900: An Analysis of Uneven Development in a Society on Its Way to Modern Economic Growth] Nijmegen: Socialistiese Vitgeverij, 1981.

Klep, Paul M.M. and Daems, Herman. "The Effect of Population, Exports and Rents on the Employment Structure of Agrarian Economy," presented at the Workshop on Quantitative Economic History, Leuven, 1974.

Klepper, Robert. "The Economic Bases for Agrarian Protest Movements in the United States, 1870-1900," (Summary of Doctoral Dissertation) *Journal of Economic History*, 34(1), March 1974, pp. 283-5.

Klingaman, David C. "The Coastwise Trade of Virginia in the Late Colonial Period," *Virginia Magazine of History and Biography*, 77(1), January 1969, pp. 26-45.

Klingaman, David C. "The Significance of Grain in the Development of the Tobacco Colonies," *Journal of Economic History*, 29(2), June 1969, pp. 268-78.

Klingaman, David C. "Food Surpluses and Deficits in the American Colonies, 1768-1772," *Journal of Economic History*, 31(3), September 1971, pp. 553-69.

Klingaman, David C. "The Coastwise Trade of Colonial Massachusetts," *Essex Institute Historical Collections*, 108(3), July 1972, pp. 217-34.

Klingaman, David C. *Colonial Virginia's Coastwise and Grain Trade.* New York: Arno Press, 1975.

Klingaman, David C. "Individual Wealth in Ohio in 1860," in Klingaman and Vedder (eds), *Essays in Nineteenth Century Economic History*, 1975, pp. 177-90.

Klingaman, David C.; Vedder, Richard K. and Gallaway, Lowell E. "The Ames-Rosenberg Hypothesis Revisited: A Note on Uselding," *Explorations in Economic History*, 11(3), Spring 1974, pp. 311-4.

Klingaman, David C.; Vedder, Richard K. and Gallaway, Lowell E. "The Profitability of Antebellum Agriculture in the Cotton Belt: Some New Evidence," *Atlantic Economic Journal*, 2(2), November 1974, pp. 30-47.

Klingaman, David C. and Vedder, Richard K., eds. *Essays in Nineteenth Century Economic History: The Old Northwest.* Athens: Ohio University Press, 1975.

Klingaman, David C.; Vedder, Richard K.; Gallaway, Lowell E. and

Uselding, Paul. "Discrimination and Exploitation in Antebellum American Cotton Textile Manufacturing," in Uselding (ed), *Research in Economic History*, 1978, pp. 217-61.

Klotz, Benjamin P. and Neal, Larry D. "Spectral and Cross-Spectral Analysis of the Long Swing Hypothesis," *Review of Economics and Statistics*, 55(3), August 1973, pp. 291-8.

Klundert, Th. Van de and David, Paul A. "Biased Efficiency Growth and Capital-Labor Substitution in the U.S., 1899-1960," *American Economic Review*, 55(3), June 1965, pp. 357-94.

Kmenta, Jan and Williamson, Jeffrey G. "Determinants of Investment Behavior: United States Railroads, 1872-1941," *Review of Economics and Statistics*, 48(2), May 1966, pp. 172-81.

Knapp, J. "Capital Exports and Growth for Argentina: A Comment (on Ford)," *Economic Journal*, 69(275), September 1959, pp. 593-7.

Knauerhase, Ramon. "The Compound Steam Engine and Productivity in the German Merchant Marine Fleet, 1871-1887," *Journal of Economic History*, 28(3), September 1968, pp. 390-403.

Kochin, Levis A. "Unemployment and Dole: Evidence from Interwar Britain," in Brabel and Walker (eds), *Unemployment Insurance*, 1978.

Kochin, Levis A. and Benjamin, Daniel K. "Searching for an Explanation of Unemployment in Interwar Britain," *Journal of Political Economy*, 87(3), June 1979, pp. 441-78.

Kochin, Levis A. and Benjamin, Daniel K. "What Went Right with Juvenile Unemployment Policy between the Wars: A Comment (on Garside)," *Economic History Review*, Second Series, 32(4), November 1979, pp. 523-8.

Kochin, Levis A. and Benjamin, Daniel K. "The British National Debt." [Working Paper]

Kochin, Levis A. and Choudri, Ehsan. "The International Transmission of Business Cycles: Evidence from Spain and the Gold Standard Countries in the Great Depression." [Working Paper]

Kocka, Jurgen; Hohorst, Gerd and Ritter, Gerhard A. *Materialien zur Statistik des Kaiserreichs 1870-1914* [Statistical Material on the German Empire, 1870-1914] (Sozialgeschichtliches Arbeitsbuch, vol. 2). Munchen: Verlag C.H. Beck, 1975.

Koenker, Roger. "Was Bread Giffen? The Demand for Food in England Circa 1790," *Review of Economics and Statistics*, 59(2), May 1977, pp. 225-9.

Komlos, John. "Is the Depression in Austria after 1873 a 'Myth'? A Comment on Good," *Economic History Review*, Second Series, 31(2), May 1978, pp. 287-9.

Komlos, John. "German Banks and German Growth: Rejoinder to Neuberger and Stokes," *Journal of Economic History*, 8(2), June 1978, pp. 483-6.

Komlos, John. "The Kreditbanken and German Growth: A Postscript to Neuberger and Stokes," *Journal of Economic History*, 38(2), June 1978, pp. 476-9.

Komlos, John. "The Emancipation of the Hungarian Peasantry and Agricultural Development," in Volgyes (ed), *The East European Peasantry*, 1979, pp. 109-18.

Komlos, John. "Astro-Hungarian Agricultural Development, 1827-1877," *Journal of European Economic History*, 8(1), Spring 1979, pp. 37-60.

Komlos, John. "Discrimination in the Austrian Capital Market? Comment on Good," *Explorations in Economic History*, 17(4), October 1980,

pp. 421-7.

Komlos, John. "The Habsburg Monarchy as a Customs Union: Economic Development in Austria-Hungary in the Nineteenth Century," Ph.D. Dissertation, University of Chicago, 1978.

Korpelainen, Lauri. "Trends and Cyclical Movements in Industrial Employment in Finland, 1885-1952," *Scandinavian Economic History Review,* 5(1), 1957, pp. 26-48.

Kotlikoff, Laurence J. and Pinera, Sebastian E. "The Old South's Stake in the Inter-Regional Movement of Slaves, 1850-1860," *Journal of Economic History,* 37(2), June 1977, pp. 434-50.

Kotlikoff, Laurence J. "Towards a Quantitative Description of the New Orleans Slave Market," presented at the Annual Cliometrics Conference, University of Wisconsin-Madison, 1976.

Kotowitz, Yehuda. "Capital-Labour Substitution in Canadian Manufacturing, 1926-1939 and 1946-1961," *Canadian Journal of Economics,* 1(3), August 1968, pp. 619-32.

Kowalska-Glikman, Stefania. "Quantitative Methods in History: A Conference Report," *Journal of European Economic History,* 3(1), Spring 1974, pp. 189-201.

Krantz, Olle. *Studies in the Growth of Swedish Freight Transportation with Special Reference to the Expansion of Road Transportation after 1920.* Lund: University of Lund Press, 1972.

Krantz, Olle. "The Competition between Railways and Domestic Shipping in Sweden, 1870-1914," *Economy and History,* 15, 1972, pp. 19-40.

Kravis, Irving B. "Trade as a Handmaiden of Growth: Similarities between the Nineteenth and Twentieth Centuries," *Economic Journal,* 80(320), December 1970, pp. 850-72.

Kravis, Irving B. "The Role of Exports in Nineteenth-Century United States Growth," *Economic Development and Cultural Change,* 20(3), April 1972, pp. 387-405.

Kravis, Irving B. "Trade as a Handmaiden of Growth: A Reply to Crafts," *Economic Journal,* 83(329), March 1973, pp. 885-9.

Kravis, Irving B. "Trade as a Handmaiden of Growth: Reply to Adams," *Economic Journal,* 83(329), March 1973, pp. 212-17.

Krier, Donald F. and Loschky, David J. "Income and Family Size in Three Eighteenth Century Lancashire Parishes: A Reconstitution Study," *Journal of Economic History,* 29(3), September 1969, pp. 429-48.

Krishnamurty, J. "Some Aspects of the Distribution of the Working Force in the Indian States, 1911-1961," in Van der Wee, Vinogradov, and Kotovsky (eds), *Fifth International Congress of Economic History,* 1976, pp. 62-74.

Krogh, D.C. "The National Income and Expenditures of South-West Africa (1920-1956)," *South African Journal of Economics,* 28(1), March 1960, pp. 3-22.

Kuczynski, Thomas. "Mathematik und Gesellschaftswissenschaften," [Mathematics and the Social Sciences] *Jahrbuch fur Wirtschaftsgeschichte,* 2, 1969, pp. 379-82.

Kuczynski, Thomas. *Das Ende der Weltwirtschaftskrise in Deutschland 1932/33* [The End of the World Economic Crisis in Germany, 1932-33]. Berlin: Hochschule fur Okonomie, 1972.

Kuczynski, Thomas. "Wirtschaftsgeschichte und Mathematik: Einige Methodologische Uberlegungen," [Economic History and Mathematics: Some Methodological Considerations] *Gesellscaft und Umwelt.*

Berlin: Akademie-Verlag, 1976, pp. 76-9.

Kuczynski, Thomas. "Wirtschaftsgeschichte und Mathematik (Gesellschaftswissenschaftler beantworten Fragen unserer Zeit)," [Economic History and Mathematics (Scientists of History Answer Questions of Our Time)] *Spektrum*, 5, 1976, pp. 13-4.

Kuczynski, Thomas. "Kondratieff Cycles: Appearance or Reality?," *Proceedings of the Seventh International Economic History Congress, Edinburgh, 1978* (vol. 2). Edinburgh: Edinburgh University Press, 1978, pp. 79-86.

Kuczynski, Thomas. "Methodologische Uberlegungen zur Anwendbarkeit Mathematischer Methoden in der Wirtschaftsgeschichte," [Methodological Considerations on the Applicability of Mathematical Methods in Economic History] *Jahrbuch fur Wirtschaftsgeschichte*, 2, 1978, pp. 157-76.

Kuczynski, Thomas. "Burgerliche Gesellschaftsgeschichte und Mathematik: zumeist unnutze Theorie und nutzliche Empirie, aber auch 'verruckte Ideen'," [Bourgeois Social History and Mathematics: Mostly Unused Theory and Useful Empirical Results, but also 'Crazy Ideas'] *Jahrbuch fur Wirtschaftsgeschichte*, 1, 1979, pp. 159-73.

Kuczynski, Thomas. "Uberproduktion und Innovation," [Overproduction and Innovation] *Jahrbuch fur Wirtschaftsgeschichte*, 4, 1979, pp. 139-45.

Kuczynski, Thomas. *Zur Anwendbarkeit Mathematischer Methoden in der Wirtschaftsgeschichtsschreibung: Methodologische Uberlegungen und Praktische Versuche* [On the Applicability of Mathematical Methods in Economic History: Methodological Considerations and Practical Tests]. Berlin: Akademie Verlag, 1979.

Kuczynski, Thomas. "Have there been Differences between the Growth Rates in Different Periods of the Development of the Capitalist World Economy since 1850? An Application of Cluster Analysis in Time Series Analysis," *Historisch-Sozialwissenschaftliche Forschungen, vol. 5*. Stuttgart, 1980.

Kulikoff, Allan. "The Economic Growth of the Eighteenth-Century Chesapeake Colonies," *Journal of Economic History*, 39(1), March 1979, pp. 275-88.

Kumar, Dharma, ed. *A Cambridge Economic History of India*, vol. 2. Cambridge: Cambridge University Press, 1981.

Kumar, Dhumar. *Land and Caste in South India: Agricultural Labor in the Madras Presidency during the Nineteenth Century*. Cambridge: Cambridge University Press, 1965.

Kunreuther, Howard and Wright, Gavin. "Cotton, Corn, and Risk in the Nineteenth Century," *Journal of Economic History*, 35(3), September 1975, pp. 526-51.

Kunreuther, Howard and Wright, Gavin. "Cotton, Corn and Risk in the Nineteenth Century: A Reply to McGuire and Higgs," *Explorations in Economic History*, 14(2), April 1977, pp. 183-95.

Kunreuther, Howard and Wright, Gavin. "Safety-First, Gambling and the Subsistence Farmer," in Roumasset, Boussard, and Singh (ed), *Risk, Uncertainty and Agricultural Development*, 1979, pp. 213-46.

Kuznets, Simon S. *Secular Movements in Production and Prices: Their Nature and Bearing upon Cyclical Fluctuations*. New York: Houghton Mifflin, 1930.

Kuznets, Simon S. "Statistics and Economic History," *Journal of Economic History*, 1(1), May 1941, pp. 26-41.

Kuznets, Simon S., ed. *Problems in the Study of Economic Growth.* New York: National Bureau of Economic Research, 1949.

Kuznets, Simon S., ed. *Income and Wealth of the United States: Trends and Structure* (Income and Wealth, Series 2). London: Bowes & Bowes for the International Association for Research in Income and Wealth, 1952.

Kuznets, Simon S. "Long-Term Changes in the National Income of the United States of America Since 1870," in Kuznets (ed), *Income and Wealth of the United States,* 1952, pp. 29-41.

Kuznets, Simon S. "National Income Estimates for the Period prior to 1870," in Kuznets (ed), *Income and Wealth of the United States,* 1952, pp. 221-41.

Kuznets, Simon S. "National Income Estimates for the United States Prior to 1870," *Journal of Economic History,* 12(2), Spring 1952, pp. 115-30.

Kuznets, Simon S. *Economic Change: Selected Essays in Business Cycles, National Income, and Economic Growth.* New York: W.W. Norton, 1953.

Kuznets, Simon S. "Quantitative Aspects of the Economic Growth of Nations (Part 1): Level and Variability of Rates of Growth," *Economic Development and Cultural Change,* 5(1), Part 1, October 1956, pp. 5-94.

Kuznets, Simon S. "Quantitative Aspects of the Economic Growth of Nations (Part 2): Industrial Distribution of National Product and Labor Force," *Economic Development and Cultural Change,* 5(4), Part 2, July 1957, pp. 3-110.

Kuznets, Simon S. "The Integration of Economic Theory and History: Comments on Rostow and Meyer & Conrad," *Journal of Economic History,* 17(4), December 1957, pp. 545-53.

Kuznets, Simon S. "Long Swings in the Growth of Population and in Related Economic Variables," *Proceedings of the American Philosophical Society,* 102, February 1958, pp. 31-6.

Kuznets, Simon S. "Quantitative Aspects of the Economic Growth of Nations (Part 3): Industrial Distribution of Income and Labor Force by States, United States, 1919-1921 to 1955," *Economic Development and Cultural Change,* 6(4), Part 2, July 1958, pp. 1-128.

Kuznets, Simon S. "Quantitative Aspects of the Economic Growth of Nations (Part 4): Distribution of National Income by Factor Shares," *Economic Development and Cultural Change,* 7(3), Part 2, April 1959, pp. 1-106.

Kuznets, Simon S. *Six Lectures on Economic Growth.* Glencoe, Ill.: Free Press, 1960.

Kuznets, Simon S. "The Changing Distribution and Structure of Economic Activity," in Kuznets, Miller, and Easterlin (eds), *Population, Redistribution and Economic Growth,* 1960, pp. 205-87.

Kuznets, Simon S. "Quantitative Aspects of the Economic Growth of Nations (Part 6): Long-Term Trends in Capital Formation Proportions," *Economic Development and Cultural Change,* 9(4), Part 2, July 1961, pp. 1-124.

Kuznets, Simon S. "Quantitative Aspects of the Economic Growth of Nations (Part 7): The Share and Structure of Consumption," *Economic Development and Cultural Change,* 10(2), Part 2, January 1962, pp. 1-92.

Kuznets, Simon S. "Notes on the Take-off," in Rostow (ed), *The Economics of Take-off into Sustained Growth,* 1963, pp. 22-43.

Kuznets, Simon S. "Quantitative Aspects of the Economic Growth of Nations (Part 8): Distribution of Income by Size," *Economic Development and Cultural Change*, 11(2), Part 2, January 1963, pp. 1-80.

Kuznets, Simon S. *Economic Growth and Structure* (Second Edition published by Yale University Press, New Haven, 1970). New York: W.W. Norton, 1965.

Kuznets, Simon S. *Modern Economic Growth: Rate, Structure, and Spread* (Studies in Comparative Economics 7). New Haven: Yale University Press, 1966.

Kuznets, Simon S. "Quantitative Aspects of the Economic Growth of Nations (Part 10): Level and Structure of Foreign Trade: Long Term Trends," *Economic Development and Cultural Change*, 15(2), Part 2, January 1967, pp. 1-140.

Kuznets, Simon S. "Capital Formation in Modern Economic Growth (and some implications for the past)," *Third International Conference of Economic History, Munich, 1965*, part 1. Paris: Mouton, 1968, pp. 15-53.

Kuznets, Simon S. *Economic Growth of Nations: Total Output and Production Structure*. Cambridge, Mass.: Belknap Press, 1971.

Kuznets, Simon S. "Notes on the Pattern of U.S. Economic Growth," in Fogel and Engerman (eds), *The Reinterpretation of American Economic History*, 1971, pp. 17-24.

Kuznets, Simon S. "The Contribution of Immigration to the Growth of the Labor Force," in Fogel and Engerman (eds), *The Reinterpretation of American Economic History*, 1971, pp. 396-401.

Kuznets, Simon S. *Growth, Population, and Income Distribution: Selected Essays*. New York: W.W. Norton, 1979.

Kuznets, Simon S.; Epstein, Lillian and Jenks, Elizabeth. *National Product since 1869* (Reprinted by Arno Press, New York, 1975). New York: National Bureau of Economic Research, 1946.

Kuznets, Simon S. and Jenks, Elizabeth. *Capital in the American Economy: Its Formation and Financing Since 1870*. Princeton: Princeton University Press for the National Bureau of Economic Research, 1961.

Kuznets, Simon S.; Miller, Ann Ratner and Easterlin, Richard A. *Population, Redistribution and Economic Growth: United States, 1870-1950, vol. 2: Analyses of Economic Change* (Series edited by Simon S. Kuznets and Dorothy Swaine Thomas). Philadelphia: American Philosophical Society, 1960.

Kuznets, Simon S.; Moore, Wilbert E. and Spengler, Joseph J., eds. *Economic Growth: Brazil, India, Japan*. Durham, N.C.: Duke University Press, 1955.

Kuznets, Simon S. and Rubin, Ernest. *Immigration and the Foreign Born* (National Bureau of Economic Research Occasional Paper 46). New York: National Bureau of Economic Research, 1954.

La Tourette, J.E. "Potential Output and the Capital-Output Ratio in the United States Private Business Sector, 1909-1959," *Kyklos*, 18(2), 1965, pp. 316-31.

La Tourette, J.E. "Sources of Variation in the Capital-Output Ratio in

the United States Private Business Sector, 1909-1959," *Kyklos,*
18(4), 1965, pp. 635-50.

Ladenson, Mark L. "The End of the North-South Wage Differential:
Comment (on Coelho and Ghali)," *American Economic Review,* 63(4),
September 1973, pp. 754-6.

Lamoureaux, Naomi R. "Industrial Organization and Market Behavior: The
Great Merger Movement in American Industry," (Summary of Doctoral
Dissertation) *Journal of Economic History,* 40(1), March 1980, pp.
169-71.

Lampard, Eric E. "The United States Balance of Payments, 1861-1900:
Comment on Simon," in Parker (ed), *Trends in the American Economy
in the Nineteenth Century,* 1960, pp. 711-5.

Lampard, Eric E. "The Evolving System of Cities in the United States:
Urbanization and Economic Development," in Perloff and Wingo (eds),
Issues in Urban Economics, 1968, pp. 81-139.

Lampard, Eric E.; Perloff, Harvey and Muth, Richard F. *Regions,
Resources, and Economic Growth.* Baltimore: Johns Hopkins
University Press, 1960.

Lampe, John R. "Varieties of Unsuccessful Industrialization: The
Balkan States Before 1914," *Journal of Economic History,* 35(1),
March 1975, pp. 56-85.

Lampman, Robert J. "Changes in the Share of Wealth Held by Top
Wealth-Holders, 1922-1956," *Review of Economics and Statistics,*
41(4), November 1959, pp. 379-92.

Lampman, Robert J. *The Share of Top Wealth-Holders in National Wealth,
1922-56* (General Series 74). Princeton: Princeton University Press
for the National Bureau of Economic Research, 1962.

Landes, David S. "Feudal Incomes and Demand Elasticity for Bread in
Late 18th Century France: Reply to Mr. Daniere and Some Reflections
on the Significance of the Debate," *Journal of Economic History,*
18(3), September 1958, pp. 331-8.

Landes, David S. "Feudal Incomes and Demand Elasticity for Bread in
Late 18th Century France: A Second Reply to Daniere," *Journal of
Economic History,* 18(3), September 1958, pp. 342-4.

Landes, David S. "Statistics as a Source for the History of Economic
Development in Western Europe: The Protostatistical Era," in Lorwin
and Price (eds), *The Dimensions of the Past,* 1972, pp. 53-91.

Landes, David S. "On Avoiding Babel," *Journal of Economic History,*
38(1), March 1978, pp. 3-12.

Landes, William M. and Solmon, Lewis C. "Compulsory Schooling
Legislation: An Economic Analysis of Law and Social Change in the
Nineteenth Century," *Journal of Economic History,* 32(1), March
1972, pp. 54-91.

Lane, Frederic C. "The Role of Governments in Economic Growth in Early
Modern Times," *Journal of Economic History,* 35(1), March 1975, pp.
8-17.

Lang, Edith M. "The Effect of Net Interregional Migration on
Agricultural Income Growth: The United States, 1850-1860," (Summary
of Doctoral Dissertation) *Journal of Economic History,* 32(1), March
1972, pp. 393-5.

Lansberg, Hans and Olson, Mancur L. *The No Growth Society* (Also,
Published as the Fall 1973 Issue of Daedalus, in Japanese
Translation (Tokyo, 1974), and in a Separate British Edition
(Woborn Press, 1975)). New York: W.W. Norton, 1974.

Larna, K. *The Money Supply, Money Flows, and Domestic Product in Finland, 1910-1956*. Helsinki: Finnish Economic Association, 1959.

Latham, A.J.H. *The International Economy and the Undeveloped World, 1886-1914*. London: Croom Helm, 1978.

Latham, A.J.H. "Merchandise Trade Imbalances and Uneven Economic Development in India and China," *Journal of European Economic History*, 7(1), Spring 1978, pp. 33-60.

Latham, A.J.H. *The Depression and the Developing World, 1914-1939*. London and Totowa, N.J.: Croom Helm and Barnes & Noble, 1981.

Laurent, Jerome K. "Sources of Capital and Expenditures for Internal Improvements in a Developing Region: The Case of Wisconsin Lake Ports, 1836-1910," *Exploration in Economic History*, 13(2), April 1976, pp. 179-201.

Laurie, Bruce and Schmitz, Mark D. "Manufacture and Productivity: The Making of an Industrial Base," in Hershberg (ed), *Toward an Interdisciplinary History of the City*, 1978.

Layton, T. Brent. "New Zealand's Social Accounting Aggregates and Official Trade Statistics, 1859-1939," Victoria University of Wellington, Working Papers in Economic History (77/4), 1977.

Lazonick, William. "Factor Costs and the Diffusion of Ring Spinning in Britain Prior to World War I," *Quarterly Journal of Economics*, 96(1), February 1981, pp. 89-109.

Lazonick, William H. "Karl Marx and Enclosures in England," *Review of Radical Political Economics*, 6(2), Summer 1974, pp. 1-32.

Lazonick, William H. and Cannings, Kathleen. "The Development of the Nursing Labor Force in the United States: A Basic Analysis," *International Journal of Health Services*, 5(2), 1975, pp. 185-216.

Lazonick, William H. "Industrial Relations and Technical Change: The Case of the Self-Acting Mule," *Cambridge Journal of Economics*, 3(3), September 1979, pp. 231-62.

Lebergott, Stanley. "Earnings of Nonfarm Employees in the U.S., 1890-1946," *Journal of the American Statistical Association*, 43(241), March 1948, pp. 74-93.

Lebergott, Stanley. "Annual Estimates of Unemployment in the United States, 1900-1954," in Universities-National Bureau Committee for Economic Research (ed), *The Measurement and Behavior of Unemployment*, 1957.

Lebergott, Stanley. "Long Term Factors in Labor Mobility and Unemployment," *Monthly Labor Review*, 82(8), August 1959, pp. 876-81.

Lebergott, Stanley. "Wage Trends, 1800-1900," in Parker (ed), *Trends in the American Economy in the Nineteenth Century*, 1960, pp. 449-98.

Lebergott, Stanley. "The Pattern of Employment since 1800," in Harris (ed), *American Economic History*, 1961, pp. 281-310.

Lebergott, Stanley. "Factor Shares in the Long Term: Some Theoretical and Statistical Aspects," in *The Behavior of Income Shares* (Studies in Income and Wealth, Vol 27). Princeton: Princeton University Press for the National Bureau of Economic Research, 1964.

Lebergott, Stanley. *Manpower in Economic Growth: The American Record since 1800*. New York: McGraw-Hill, 1964.

Lebergott, Stanley. "Labor Force Mobility and Unemployment, 1800-1960," in Andreano (ed), *New Views*, 1965, pp. 362-76.

Lebergott, Stanley. "Long Term Factors in Labor Mobility and

Unemployment," in Andreano (ed), *New Views*, 1965.

Lebergott, Stanley. "Labor Force and Employment, 1800-1960," in Brady (ed), *Output, Employment and Productivity in the United States after 1800*, 1966, pp. 117-204.

Lebergott, Stanley. "United States Transport Advance and Externalities," *Journal of Economic History*, 26(4), December 1966, pp. 437-61.

Lebergott, Stanley. "United States Transport Advance and Externalities: A Reply to Weiss," *Journal of Economic History*, 28(4), December 1968, pp. 635.

Lebergott, Stanley. "The Service Industries in the Nineteenth Century: Comment on Gallman and Weiss," in Fuchs (ed), *Production and Productivity in the Service Industries*, 1969, pp. 365-8.

Lebergott, Stanley. "Migration in the United States, 1800-1960: Some New Estimates," *Journal of Economic History*, 30(4), December 1970, pp. 839-47.

Lebergott, Stanley. "Changes in Unemployment 1800-1960," in Fogel and Engerman (eds), *The Reinterpretation of American Economic History*, 1971, pp. 73-83.

Lebergott, Stanley. "The American Labor Force," in Davis, Easterlin, and Parker (eds), *American Economic Growth*, 1972, pp. 184-232.

Lebergott, Stanley. "Comments on Measuring Agricultural Change," *Agricultural History*, 46(1), January 1972, pp. 227-34.

Lebergott, Stanley. "A New Technique for Time Series: A Comment on Coen," *Review of Economics and Statistics*, 55(4), February 1973, pp. 525-7.

Lebergott, Stanley. *Wealth and Want*. Princeton: Princeton University Press, 1975.

Lebergott, Stanley. "Industrialization, Regional Change, and the Sectoral Distribution of the U.S. Labor Force, 1850-1880: A Reply to Vatter," *Economic Development and Cultural Change*, 23(4), July 1975, pp. 749-50.

Lebergott, Stanley. *The American Economy*. Princeton: Princeton University Press, 1976.

Lebergott, Stanley. "Are the Rich Getting Richer? Trends in U.S. Wealth Concentration," *Journal of Economic History*, 36(1), March 1976, pp. 147-62.

Lebergott, Stanley. "The Returns to U.S. Imperialism, 1890-1929," *Journal of Economic History*, 40(2), June 1980, pp. 229-52.

Lebergott, Stanley. "Confederate Cotton Exports." [Working Paper]

Lebergott, Stanley. "Estimates of PCE, by Detailed Item: U.S. Totals 1900-1928, Annually by State, 1970." [Working Paper]

Lee, Clive H. "The Effects of the Depression on Primary Producing Countries," *Journal of Contemporary History*, 4(4), October 1969, pp. 139-55.

Lee, Clive H. *Regional Economic Growth in the United Kingdom since the 1880's*. London: McGraw-Hill, 1971.

Lee, Clive H. *The Quantitative Approach to Economic History*. London: Martin Robertson, 1977.

Lee, Clive H. *British Regional Employment Statistics, 1841-1971*. Cambridge: Cambridge University Press, 1980.

Lee, Clive H. "Regional Structural Change in the Long Run: Great Britain, 1841-1971," in Pollard (ed), *Region und Industrialisierung*, 1980.

Lee, Clive H.   "The British Cotton Industry, 1825-75," in Church (ed), *Victorian Business*, 1980.

Lee, Everett S.   "Migration Estimates," in Lee, Miller, Brainerd, and Easterlin (eds), *Population, Redistribution and Economic Growth*, 1957, pp. 9-61.

Lee, Everett S.; Miller, Ann Ratner; Brainerd, Carol P. and Easterlin, Richard A.   *Population, Redistribution and Economic Growth: United States, 1870-1950, vol. 1: Methodological Considerations and Reference Tables* (Series edited by Simon S. Kuznets and Dorothy Swaine Thomas).   Philadelphia: American Philosophical Society, 1957.

Lee, Pong S.   "Unbalanced Growth: The Case of Japan 1878-1918," *Yale Economic Essays*, 6(2), Fall 1966, pp. 479-526.

Lee, Ronald D.   "An Historical Perspective on Economic Aspects of the Population Explosion: The Case of Preindustrial England," in Easterlin (ed), *Population and Economic Change in Less Developed Countries*, 1980, pp. 517-57.

Lee, Ronald D.   "Causes and Consequences of Age Structure Fluctuations: The Easterlin Hypothesis," presented at the IUSSP Economic Demography Conference, Helsinki, August 1978.

Lee, Ronald D. and Schofield, R.S.   "British Population in the Eighteenth Century," in Floud and McCloskey (eds), *The Economic History of Britain since 1700*, 1981, pp. 17-35.

Lee, Susan P. and Passell, Peter.   *A New Economic View of American History*.   New York: W.W. Norton, 1979.

Leet, Don R.   "Population Pressure and Human Fertility Response: Ohio, 1810-1860," (Summary of Doctoral Dissertation) *Journal of Economic History*, 34(1), March 1974, pp. 286-8.

Leet, Don R.   "Human Fertility and Agricultural Opportunities in Ohio Counties: from Frontier to Maturity, 1810-60," in Klingaman and Vedder (eds), *Essays in Nineteenth Century Economic History*, 1975, pp. 138-58.

Leet, Don R.   "The Determinants of the Fertility Transition in Antebellum Ohio," *Journal of Economic History*, 36(2), June 1976, pp. 359-78.

Leet, Don R.   "Interrelations of Population Density, Urbanization, Literacy, and Fertility," *Explorations in Economic History*, 14(4), October 1977, pp. 388-401.

Leet, Don R.   *Population Pressure and Human Fertility Response: Ohio, 1810-1860*.   New York: Arno Press, 1978.

Leet, Don R.   "Agricultural Opportunities in a Frontier Community: Ohio, 1810-1860," presented at the Annual Cliometrics Conference, University of Wisconsin-Madison, April 1973.

Leet, Don R. and Shaw, John A.   "French Economic Stagnation, 1700-1960: Old Economic History Revisited," *Journal of Interdisciplinary History*, 8(3), Winter 1978, pp. 531-44.

Leff, Nathaniel H.   "Export Stagnation and Autarkic Development in Brazil, 1947-1962," [Translated into Portugese in El Trimestre Economico, 1969] *Quarterly Journal of Economics*, 81(2), May 1967, pp. 286-301.

Leff, Nathaniel H.   *The Brazilian Capital Goods Industry, 1929-1964*.   Cambridge: Harvard University Press, 1968.

Leff, Nathaniel H.   "Long-Term Brazilian Economic Development," [Translated into Portuguese in El Trimestre Economico, 1970]

Journal of Economic History, 29(3), September 1969, pp. 473-93.

Leff, Nathaniel H. "Economic Development and Regional Inequality: Origins of the Brazilian Case," [Translated into Portuguese in *Revista Brasileira de Economia,* 1972] *Quarterly Journal of Economics,* 86(2), May 1972, pp. 243-62.

Leff, Nathaniel H. "Uma Perspectiva a Longo Prazo do Desenvolvimento e do Subdesenvolvimento Brasileiros," [A Long Term Perspective on the Development and Underdevelopment of Brazil] *Revista Brasileira de Economia,* 26(3), July/September 1972, pp. 147-68.

Leff, Nathaniel H. "Economic Retardation in Nineteenth-Century Brazil," *Economic History Review,* Second Series, 25(3), August 1972, pp. 489-507.

Leff, Nathaniel H. "A Technique for Estimating Income Trends from Currency Data and an Application to Nineteenth-Century Brazil," [Translated into Portuguese in Revista Brasileira de Economia, 1972] *Review of Income and Wealth,* 18(4), December 1972, pp. 355-68.

Leff, Nathaniel H. "Tropical Trade and Development in the Nineteenth Century: The Brazilian Experience," *Journal of Political Economy,* 81(3), May/June 1973, pp. 678-96.

Leff, Nathaniel H. "Long-Term Viability of Slavery in a Backward Closed Economy," *Journal of Interdisciplinary History,* 5(1), Summer 1974, pp. 103-8.

Leff, Nathaniel H. "Entrepreneurship and Economic Development: The Problem Revisited," *Journal of Economic Literature,* 17(1), March 1979, pp. 46-64.

Legler, John B. "Regional Distribution of Federal Receipts and Expenditures in the Nineteenth Century," *Regional Science Association,* Papers and Proceedings, 19, 1967, pp. 141-60.

Legler, John and Davis, Lance E. "The Government in the American Economy, 1815-1902: A Quantitative Study," *Journal of Economic History,* 26(4), December 1966, pp. 514-52.

Legler, John B. and Davis, Lance E. "The Regional Impact of the Federal Budget, 1815-1900: A Preliminary Survey (Summary)," *Third International Conference of Economic History, Munich, 1965,* part 1. Paris and The Hague: Mouton, 1968, pp. 753-9.

Legler, John B. and Davis, Lance E. "The Regional Impact of the Federal Budget, 1815-1900," presented at the Third International Economic History Conference, Munich, 1965.

Leiman, M. "A Note on Slave Profitability and Economic Growth: An Examination of the Conrad-Meyer Thesis," *Social and Economic Studies,* 16(2), June 1967, pp. 211-5.

Leontief, Wassily. *The Structure of the American Economy, 1919-1939.* New York: Oxford University Press, 1951.

Leontief, Wassily. "When Should History Be Written Backwards?," *Economic History Review,* Second Series, 16(1), August 1963, pp. 1-8.

Lerner, Eugene M. "Inflation in the Confederacy, 1861-65," in Friedman, (ed), *Studies in the Quantity Theory of Money,* 1956, pp. 163-75.

Lester, Richard. "Currency Issues to Overcome Depressions in Pennsylvania," in Andreano (ed), *New Views,* 1965, pp. 73-118.

Levy-Leboyer, Maurice. "La Croissance Economique en France au XIXe Siecle: Resultats Preliminaires," [Economic Growth in France in the

Nineteenth Century: Preliminary Results] *Annales: Economies, Societes, Civilisations,* 23(4), July/August 1968, pp. 788-807.

Levy-Leboyer, Maurice. "La New Economic History," [The New Economic History] *Annales: Economies, Societies, Civilisations,* 24(5), September/October 1969, pp. 1035-69.

Levy-Leboyer, Maurice. "L'heritage de Simiand: prix, profit et termes d'echange au XXXe siecle," *Revue Historique,* 493, January/March 1970, pp. 77-120.

Levy-Leboyer, Maurice. "La Deceleration de L'Economie Francaise dans la Seconde Moitie Du XIXe Siecle," [The French Economic Slowdown in the Second Half of the Nineteenth Century] *Revue D'Histoire Economique et Sociale,* 49(4), 1971, pp. 485-507.

Levy-Leboyer, Maurice. "Productivite et croissance economique en France," in Van der Wee, Vinogradov, and Kotovsky (eds), *Fifth International Congress of Economic History,* 1976, pp. 169-91.

Levy-Leboyer, Maurice. "Capital Investment and Economic Growth in France, 1820-1930," Mathias and Postan (eds), *The Cambridge Economic History of Europe,* 1978, pp. 231-95.

Levy-Leboyer, Maurice. "Les Inegalites Regionales de Croissance dans L'Agriculture Francaise, 1823-1939," [Regional Inequalities of Growth in French Agriculture, 1823-1939] in Bairoch and Levy-Leboyer (eds), *Disparities in Economic Development since the Industrial Revolution,* 1980.

Lewis, Frank D. "The Canadian Wheat Boom and Per Capita Income: New Estimates," *Journal of Political Economy,* 83(6), December 1975, pp. 1249-57.

Lewis, Frank D. "Explaining the Shift of Labor from Agriculture to Industry in the United States: 1869 to 1899," *Journal of Economic History,* 39(3), September 1979, pp. 681-98.

Lewis, Frank D. and Goldin, Claudia D. "The Economic Cost of the American Civil War: Estimates and Implications," *Journal of Economic History,* 35(2), June 1975, pp. 299-326.

Lewis, Frank D. and Goldin, Claudia D. "The Postbellum Recovery of the South and the Cost of the Civil War: Comment on Temin," *Journal of Economic History,* 38(2), June 1978, pp. 487-92.

Lewis, Frank D. and Goldin, Claudia D. "The Role of Exports in American Economic Growth during the Napoleonic Wars, 1793 to 1807," *Explorations in Economic History,* 17(1), January 1980, pp. 6-25.

Lewis, Frank D. and Goldin, Claudia D. "Growth and Exports, 1793 to 1807, and a Re-Examination of Growth before 1840." [Working Paper]

Lewis, Frank D. and McInnis, R. Marvin. "The Efficiency of the French-Canadian Farmer in the Nineteenth Century," *Journal of Economic History,* 40(3), September 1980, pp. 497-514.

Lewis, J. Parry. "Indices of House-Building in the Manchester Conurbation, South Wales and Great Britain, 1851-1913," *Scottish Journal of Political Economy,* 8(2), June 1961, pp. 148-56.

Lewis, J. Parry and Weber, Brian A. "New Industrial Building in Great Britain, 1923-1938," *Scottish Journal of Political Economy,* 8(1), February 1961, pp. 57-64.

Lewis, Kenneth A. and Yamamura, Kozo. "Industrialization and Interregional Interest Rate Structure, The Japanese Case: 1889-1925," *Explorations in Economic History,* 8(4), Summer 1971, pp. 473-99.

Lewis, W. Arthur. *Economic Survey, 1919-1939* (Reprinted by Harper &

Row, New York, 1969). London: Allen & Unwin, 1949.

Lewis, W. Arthur. "International Competition in Manufactures," *American Economic Review*, Papers and Proceedings, 47(2), May 1957, pp. 578-87.

Lewis, W. Arthur. *The Deceleration of British Growth, 1873-1913.* Princeton: Princeton University Development Research Project, 1967.

Lewis, W. Arthur. *Aspects of Tropical Trade, 1883-1965.* Stockholm: Almquist, 1969.

Lewis, W. Arthur, ed. *Tropical Development, 1883-1913.* London and Evanston, Ill.: Allen & Unwin and Northwestern University Press, 1970.

Lewis, W. Arthur. *Growth and Fluctuations, 1870-1913.* London: Allen & Unwin, 1978.

Lewis, W. Arthur. *The Evolution of the International Economic Order.* Princeton: Princeton University Press, 1978.

Lewis, W. Arthur. "The Slowing Down of the Engine of Growth," *American Economic Review*, 70(3), September 1980, pp. 555-64.

LeVeen, E. Phillip. "British Slave Trade Suppression Policies, 1821-1865: Impact and Implications," (Summary of Doctoral Dissertation) *Journal of Economic History*, 32(1), March 1972, pp. 415-6.

LeVeen, E. Phillip. "The African Slave Supply Response," *African Studies Review*, 18, 1975, pp. 9-28.

LeVeen, E. Phillip. "A Quantitative Analysis of the Impact of British Suppression Policies on the Volume of the Nineteenth Century Atlantic Slave Trade," in Engerman and Genovese (eds), *Race and Slavery in the Western Hemisphere*, 1975, pp. 51-81.

Libecap, Gary D. "Aspects of Modern Growth: A Report of the Economic History Association Meetings," *Journal of European Economic History*, 5(1), Spring 1976, pp. 191-7.

Libecap, Gary D. *The Evolution of Private Mining Rights: Nevada's Comstock Lode.* New York: Arno Press, 1978.

Libecap, Gary D. "Economic Variables and the Development of the Law: The Case of Western Mineral Rights," *Journal of Economic History*, 38(2), June 1978, pp. 338-62.

Libecap, Gary D. "Government Support of Private Claims to Public Minerals: Western Mineral Rights," *Business History Review*, 53(3), Autumn 1979, pp. 364-85.

Libecap, Gary D. and Johnson, Ronald N. "Property Rights, Nineteenth-Century Federal Timber Policy, and the Conservation Movement," *Journal of Economic History*, 39(1), March 1979, pp. 129-42.

Libecap, Gary D. and Johnson, Ronald N. "Efficient Markets and Great Lakes Timber: A Conservation Issue Reexamined," *Explorations in Economic History*, 17(4), October 1980, pp. 372-85.

Lindert, Peter H. *Key Currencies and Gold, 1900-1913.* Princeton: Princeton University Press, 1969.

Lindert, Peter H. and Trace, Keith. "Yardsticks for Victorian Entrepreneurs," in McCloskey (ed), *Essays on a Mature Economy*, 1971, pp. 239-74.

Lindert, Peter H. "Land Scarcity and American Growth," *Journal of Economic History*, 34(4), December 1974, pp. 851-84.

Lindert, Peter H. "A Century of International Monetary Evolution," in Van der Wee, Vinogradov, and Kotovsky (eds), *Fifth International*

Congress of Economic History, pp. 167-77.

Lindert, Peter H. "American Fertility Patterns since the Civil War," in Lee (ed), *Population Patterns in the Past*, 1977, pp. 229-76.

Lindert, Peter H. *Fertility and Scarcity in America.* Princeton: Princeton University Press, 1978.

Lindert, Peter H. "Child Costs and Economic Development," in Easterlin (ed), *Population and Economic Change in Developing Countries*, 1980, pp. 5-69.

Lindert, Peter H. "Discussion of Dissertations Presented to the 39th Annual Meeting of the Economic History Association," *Journal of Economic History*, 40(1), March 1980, pp. 181-3.

Lindert, Peter H. "English Occupations, 1670-1811," *Journal of Economic History*, 40(4), December 1980, pp. 685-712.

Lindert, Peter H. "Understanding 1929-1933: Comment on Schwartz," in Brunner (ed), *The Great Depression Revisited*, 1981, pp. 125-33.

Lindert, Peter H. and Williamson, Jeffrey G. "Three Centuries of American Inequality," Uselding (ed), *Research in Economic History*, 1976, pp. 69-123.

Lindert, Peter H. and Williamson, Jeffrey G. *American Inequality: A Macroeconomic History.* New York: Academic Press, 1980.

Lindert, Peter H. and Williamson, Jeffrey G. "Long Term Trends in American Wealth Inequality," in Smith (ed), *Modeling the Distribution*, 1980, pp. 9-93.

Lindert, Peter H. and Williamson, Jeffrey G. "English Experience with the Distribution of Wealth and Income Since the Late 17th Century and Their Determinants: A Companion Volume to 'A Macroeconomic History of American Inequality'." [Working Paper]

Lindley, Susan; Vedder, Richard K. and Gallaway, Lowell E. "Some Quarterly Estimates of GNP, 1929-1940," Ohio University Economic History Research Paper no. F-48.

Lindstrom, Diane. "Another Look at Industry and Agricultural Wage Differentials, 1800-1830," in Cain (ed), *Proceedings of the Business History Conference, 1972*, 1973, pp. 111-4.

Lindstrom, Diane. "Domestic Trade and Regional Specialization," in Porter (ed), *Encyclopedia of American Economic History*, 1980, pp. 264-80.

Lindstrom, Diane L. "Southern Dependence upon Interregional Grain Supplies: A Review of the Trade Flows, 1840-1860," in Parker (ed), *The Structure of the Cotton Economy of the Antebellum South.* Washington, D.C., 1970, pp. 101-13.

Lindstrom, Diane L. "Demand, Markets, and Eastern Economic Development: Philadelphia, 1815-1840," (Summary of Doctoral Dissertation) *Journal of Economic History*, 35(1), March 1975, pp. 271-3.

Lindstrom, Diane L. "American Economic Growth before 1840: New Evidence and New Directions," *Journal of Economic History*, 39(1), March 1979, pp. 289-301.

Lindstrom, Diane and Sharpless, John. "Urban Growth and Economic Structure in Antebellum America," in Uselding (ed), *Research in Economic History*, 1978, pp. 161-216.

Lineham, B.T. "New Zealand's Gross Domestic Product 1918-38," *New Zealand Economic Papers*, 2, 1968, pp. 15-26.

Linneman, Peter D. "An Econometric Examination of the English Parlimentary Enclosure Movement," *Explorations in Economic History*,

15(2), April 1978, pp. 221-8.

Lipsey, Richard G. "The Relation between Unemployment and the Rate of Change of Money Wage Rates in the United Kingdom, 1862-1957: A Further Analysis," *Economica*, 27(105), February 1960, pp. 1-31.

Lipsey, Robert E. *Price and Quantity Trends in the Foreign Trade Sector of the United States.* Princeton: Princeton University Press, 1963.

Lipsey, Robert E. "Foreign Trade," in Davis, Easterlin, and Parker (eds), *American Economic Growth*, 1972, pp. 548-81.

Litt, R.M. and Ankli, Robert E. "The Growth of Prairie Agriculture: Economic Considerations," *Canadian Papers in Rural History*, 1, 1978, pp. 35-64.

Liu, Ts'ui-Jung and Fei, John C.H. "An Analysis of the Land Tax Burden in China, 1650-1865," *Journal of Economic History*, 37(2), June 1977, pp. 359-81.

Livesay, Harold C. and Porter, Glenn. "The Financial Role of Merchants in the Development of U.S. Manufacturing, 1815-1860," *Explorations in Economic History*, 9(1), Fall 1971, pp. 63-87.

Livesay, Harold C. and Porter, Patrick G. "Oligopoly in Small Manufacturing Industries," *Explorations in Economic History*, 7(3), Spring 1970, pp. 371-9.

Lobdell, Richard A. "Patterns of Investment and Sources of Credit in the British West Indian Sugar Industry, 1838-97," *Journal of Caribbean History*, 4, May 1972, pp. 31-53.

Long, Clarence D. *Wages and Earnings in the United States, 1860-1890* (General Series 67). Princeton: Princeton University Press for the National Bureau of Economic Research, 1960.

Lorwin, Val R. and Price, Jacob M. *The Dimensions of the Past: Materials, Problems, and Opportunities for Quantitative Work in History.* New Haven and London: Yale University Press, 1972.

Loschky, David J. "The Usefulness of England's Parish Registers," *Review of Economics and Statistics*, 49(4), November 1967, pp. 471-9.

Loschky, David J. "Urbanization and England's Eighteenth Century Crude Death and Birth Rates," *Journal of European Economic History*, 1(3), Winter 1972, pp. 697-712.

Loschky, David J. "Counterfactuals in Logically Formed Economic Analyses," *Journal of European Economic History*, 2(2), Fall 1973, pp. 421-37.

Loschky, David J. "Studies of the Navigation Acts: New Economic Non-History?" *Economic History Review*, Second Series, 26(4), November 1973, pp. 689-91.

Loschky, David J. "What's Happening in the New Economic History," *Journal of European Economic History*, 3(3), Winter 1974, pp. 747-58.

Loschky, David J. "Are Counterfactuals Necessary to 'The Discipline and They'?" *Journal of European Economic History*, 4(2), Fall 1975, pp. 481-5.

Loschky, David J. and Krier, Donald F. "Income and Family Size in Three Eighteenth Century Lancashire Parishes: A Reconstitution Study," *Journal of Economic History*, 29(3), September 1969, pp. 429-48.

Loschky, David J. and Wilcox, William C. "Demographic Transition: A Forcing Model?," *Demography*, 11(2), May 1974, pp. 215-25.

Loschky, David J. and Wilcox, William C. "Demographic Transition: A Forcing Model?: Reply to Kammeyer and Skidmore," *Demography*, 12(2), May 1975, pp. 351-60.

Lothian, James R. and Gandolfi, Arthur E. "Review of 'Did Monetary Forces Cause the Great Depression?' by Peter Temin (New York: W.W. Norton, 1976)," *Journal of Money, Credit, and Banking*, 9(4), November 1977, pp. 679-90.

Lothian, James R. and Huffman, Wallace. "Money in the United Kingdom, 1833-80," *Journal of Money, Credit and Banking*, 12, May 1980, pp. 155-74.

Lothian, James R. "Monetarist Interpretations of the Great Depression: Comment on Gordon and Wilcox," in Brunner (ed), *The Great Depression Revisited*, 1981, pp. 134-47.

Lougheed, Alan L. and Glynn, Sean. "A Comment on United States Economic Policy and the 'Dollar Gap' of the 1920's," *Economic History Review*, Second Series, 26(4), November 1973, pp. 692-4.

Lowe, Adolph. "Cyclical Experience in the Interwar Period: The Investment Boom of the Twenties (Comment on Gordon)," Universities-National Bureau Committee for Economic Research, (ed), *Conference on Business Cycles*, 1951, pp. 222-3.

Lucas, Edward F. and Hansen, Bert. "Egyptian Foreign Trade, 1885-1961: A New Set of Trade Indices," *Journal of European Economic History*, 7,(2-3), Fall/Winter 1978, pp. 429-60.

Lucas, Robert E., Jr. and Rapping, Leonard A. "Unemloyment in the Great Depression: Is There a Full Explanation?," *Journal of Political Economy*, 80(1), January/February 1972, pp. 186-91.

Lund, P.J. and Holden, K. "Study of Private Sector Gross Fixed Capital Formation in the United Kingdom, 1923-1938," *Oxford Economic Papers*, 20(1), March 1968, pp. 56-73.

Lundgreen, Peter. "Technicians and the Labour Market in Prussia, 1810-1850," *Annales Cisalpines d'Histoire Sociale*, 1(2), 1971, pp. 9-29.

Lundgreen, Peter. *Bildung und Wirtschaftswachstum im Industrialisierungsprozess des 19. Jahrhunderts. Methodische Ansatze, Empirische Studien und Internationale Vergleiche* [Education and Economic Growth in the Industrialization Process of the 19th Century: Methodology, Empirical Studies and International Comparisons] (Historische und Padagogische Studien, vol. 5). Berlin: Colloqium-Verlag, 1973.

Lundgreen, Peter. "Quantifizierung in der Sozialgeschichte der Bildung," [Quantification in the Social History of Education] *Vierteljahrschrift fur Sozial-und Wirtschaftsgeschichte*, 63(4), 1976, pp. 433-53.

Lundgreen, Peter. "Wissenschaft und Wirtschaft: Methodische Ansatze und Empirische Ergebnisse (unter besonderer Berucksichtigung Deutschlands im 19. Jahrhundert)," [Science and the Economy: Methods and Empirical Results] *Technikgeschichte*, 44, 1977, pp. 302-14.

Lundgreen, Peter and Thirlwall, A.P. "Educational Expansion and Economic Growth in Nineteenth Century Germany: A Quantitative Study," in Stone (ed), *Schooling and Society*, 1976, pp. 20-66.

Luraghi, Raimondo. "Wage Labor in the 'Rice Belt' of Northern Italy and Slave Labor in the American South: A First Approach," presented at the MSSB-University of Rochester Conference Time on the Cross: A

Lyons, John S. "The Lancashire Cotton Industry and the Introduction of the Powerloom, 1815-1850," (Summary of Doctoral Dissertation) *Journal of Economic History*, 38(1), March 1978, pp. 283-4.

Lyons, John S. "The Lancashire Cotton Industry and the Introduction of the Powerloom, 1815-1850," Ph.D. Dissertation, University of California-Berkeley, 1977.

Lyons, John; Sutch, Richard C.; Roehl, Richard and Boskins, Michael. "Urban Migration in the Process of Industrialization: Britain and the United States in the Nineteenth Century," University of California-Berkeley, Center for Research in Management Science, Working Papers in Economic Theory and Econometrics no. 162, August 1970.

Macesich, George. "Sources of Monetary Disturbances in the United States, 1834-1845," *Journal of Economic History*, 20(3), September 1960, pp. 407-34.

Macesich, George. "International Trade and United States Economic Development Revisited: Reply to Williamson," reprinted in Coben and Hill (eds), *American Economic History*, 1966, pp. 256-8. *Journal of Economic History*, 21(3), September 1961, pp. 384-5.

Macesich, George. "The Quantity Theory and the Income Expenditure Theory in an Open Economy: Canada, 1926-1958," *Canadian Journal of Economics and Political Science*, 30(3), August 1964, pp. 368-90.

Macesich, George. "Empirical Testing and the Income Expenditure Theory (Reply to Barber)," *Canadian Journal of Economics and Political Science*, 32(3), August 1966, pp. 377-9.

MacAvoy, P.W. *The Economic Effects of Regulation*. Cambridge, Mass.: M.I.T. Press, 1965.

MacKay, Robert J. and Reid, Joseph D., Jr. "On Understanding the Birth and Evolution of the Securities and Exchange Commission: Where Are We in the Theory of Regulation?," in Walton (ed), *Regulatory Change in an Atmosphere of Crisis*, 1979, pp. 101-21.

Main, Gloria L. "Personal Wealth in Colonial America: Explorations in the Use of Probate Records from Maryland and Massachusetts, 1650 to 1720," (Summary of Doctoral Dissertation) *Journal of Economic History*, 34(1), March 1974, pp. 289-94.

Main, Gloria L. "Inequality in Early America: The Evidence from Probate Records of Massachusetts and Maryland," *Journal of Interdisciplinary History*, 7(4), Spring 1977, pp. 559-81.

Main, Jackson T. "Trends in Wealth Concentration Before 1860: A Note," *Journal of Economic History*, 31(2), June 1971, pp. 445-7.

Maizels, Alfred. *Industrial Growth and World Trade* (Second Edition, with corrections, published 1969). Cambridge: Cambridge University Press, 1965.

Mak, James; Atack, Jeremy; Haites, Erik F. and Walton, Gary M. "The Profitability of Steamboating on Western Rivers: 1850," *Business History Review*, 49(3), Autumn 1975, pp. 346-54.

Mak, James and Haites, Erik F. "Ohio and Mississippi River Transportation, 1810-1860," *Explorations in Economic History*, 8(2), Winter 1970/71, pp. 153-80.

Mak, James and Haites, Erik F. "Steamboating on the Mississippi: A

Purely Competitive Industry," *Business History Review,* 45(1), Spring 1971, pp. 52-78.

Mak, James and Haites, Erik F. "The Decline of Steamboating on the Antebellum Western Rivers: Some New Evidence and an Alternative Hypothesis," *Explorations in Economic History,* 11(1), Fall 1973, pp. 25-36.

Mak, James; Haites, Erik F. and Walton, Gary M. *Western River Transportation during the Era of Early Internal Improvements.* Baltimore: Johns Hopkins University Press, 1975.

Mak, James and Haites, Erik F. "Economies of Scale in Western River Steamboating," *Journal of Economic History,* 36(3), September 1976, pp. 689-703.

Mak, James and Haites, Erik F. "Economies of Scale in Western River Steamboating: A Reply to Atack," *Journal of Economic History,* 38(2), June 1978, pp. 467-70.

Mak, James and Haites, Erik F. "Social Savings Due to Western River Steamboats," in Uselding (ed), *Research in Economic History,* 1978, pp. 263-303.

Mak, James and Matsuba, S. "A Concise Economic History of the Hawaiian Islands." [Working Paper]

Mak, James and Walton, Gary M. "Steamboats and the Great Productivity Surge in River Transportation," *Journal of Economic History,* 32(3), September 1972, pp. 619-40.

Mak, James and Walton, Gary M. "On the Persistence of Old Technologies: The Case of Flatboats," *Journal of Economic History,* 33(2), June 1973, pp. 444-51.

Mamalakis, Markos J., ed. *Historical Statistics of Chile.* Westport, Conn.: Greenwood Press, 1978.

Mancke, R.B. "American Trade Union Growth, 1900-1960: A Comment on Ashenfelter and Pencavel," *Quarterly Journal of Economics,* 85(1), February 1971, pp. 187-93.

Mandle, Jay R. "The Reestablishment of the Plantation Economy in the South, 1865-1970," *Review of Black Political Economy,* 3(2), Winter 1973, pp. 68-88.

Mandle, Jay R. "Strength and Growth in the Plantation Economy: An Appraisal of Time on the Cross," presented at the MSSB-University of Rochester Conference Time on the Cross: A First Appraisal, October 1974.

Mandle, Jay R. "The Plantation States as a Sub-Region of the Postbellum South: A Note," *Journal of Economic History,* 34(3), September 1974, pp. 732-8.

Mann, R. and Best, H. *Quantitative Methoden in der Historisch-Sozialwissenschaftlichen Forschung* [Quantitative Methods in Historical and Sociological Research]. Stuttgart: Klett-Cotta, 1977.

Mantovani, Enrico; Covino, Renato and Gallo, Giampaolo. "L'industria dall'economia di guerra alla ricostruzione," [Industry from the War Economy to Reconstruction] in Ciocca and Toniolo, (eds), *L'economia italiana nel periodo fascista,* 1976, pp. 171-270.

Marburg, Theodore F. "Income Originating in Trade, 1799-1869," in Parker (ed), *Trends in the American Economy in the Nineteenth Century,* 1960, pp. 317-26.

Marczewski, Jean. "The Take-Off Hypothesis and the French Experience," in Rostow (ed), *The Economics of Take-Off into Sustained Growth,*

1963, pp. 119-38.

Marczewski, Jean. "Le Produit Physique de L'Economie Francaise de 1789 a 1913 (Comparaison Avec la Grande-Bretagne)," [The Physical Product of the French Economy, 1789-1913 (Comparison with Great Britain)] in *Cahiers de L'Institut de Science Economique Appliquee*, 1965.

Margo, Robert A. "Civilian Occupation of Ex-Slaves in the Union Army, 1862-1865," in Fogel and Engerman (eds), *Without Consent or Contract*.

Margo, Robert A. and Steckel, Richard. "Height, Health, and Nutrition: Analysis of Evidence for U.S. Slaves," *Social Science History*.

Margo, Robert A. "School Finance and the Economics of Segregated Schools in the U.S. South, 1890-1920." [Working Paper]

Margo, Robert A.; Sokoloff, Kenneth and Villaflor, Georgia. "The Economic and Demographic Significance of Secular Changes in Human Stature: The U.S., 1750-1960," *NBER Reporter*, Winter 1979, pp. 6-8.

Mariger, Randall. "Predatory Price Cutting: The Standard Oil of New Jersey Case Revisited," *Explorations in Economic History*, 15(4), October 1978, pp. 341-67.

Markovitch, Tihomir J. *L'industrie francaise de 1789 a 1964* (4 Vols) [French Industry, 1789-1964] in *Cahiers de l'Institute de Science Economique Appliquee*, 1966.

Markovitch, Tihomir J. "Les secteurs dominants de L'industrie francaise," [The Dominant Sectors in French Industry] *Analyse et Prevision*, 1(3), March 1966, pp. 161-75.

Markovitch, Tihomir J. *Salaires et profits industriels en France* [Wages and Industrial Profits in France] in *Cahiers de l'Institute de Science Economique Appliquee*, 1967.

Markovitch, Tihomir J. *L'industrie lainiere francaise au debut du XVIIIe siecle* [The French Woolen Industry at the Beginning of the Eighteenth Century] in *Cahiers de l'Institute de Science Economique Appliquee*, 1968.

Markovitch, Tihomir J. "La Revolution industrielle: le cas de la France," [The Industrial Revolution: The Case of France] *Revue d'Histoire economique et sociale*, 1(1), 1974, pp. 115-25.

Markovitch, Tihomir J. *Les industries lainieres de Colbert a la Revolution* [The Woolen Industry From Colbert to the Revolution]. Geneva: Editions Droz, 1976.

Markovitch, Tihomir J. "La croissance industrielle sous l'Ancien Regime," [Industrial Growth During the Ancien Regime] *Annales: Economies, Societes, Civilisations*, 31(3), May/June 1976, pp. 648-55.

Marr, William L. "The Expanding Role of Government and Wars: A Further Elaboration," *Public Finance*, 29(3-4), 1974, pp. 416-21.

Marr, William L. "The Economics of Lincoln's Proposal for Compensated Emancipation: Comment on Weintraub," *American Journal of Economics and Sociology*, 35(1), January 1976, pp. 105-7.

Marr, William L. "United Kingdom's International Migration in the Interwar Period: Theoretical Considerations and Empirical Testing," *Population Studies*, 31(3), November 1977, pp. 571-80.

Marr, William L. and Paterson, Donald G. *Canada, An Economic History*. Toronto: Macmillan of Canada, 1980.

Marr, William L. and Percy, Michael B. "The Government and the Rate of

Canadian Prairie Settlement (Comment on Norrie)," *Canadian Journal of Economics,* 11(4), November 1978, pp. 757-67.

Martin, David A. "Bimetallism in the United States before 1850," *Journal of Political Economy,* 76(3), May/June 1968, pp. 428-42.

Martin, David A. "Did the 'Crime of 1873' Really Occur in 1853?," *Papers and Proceedings of the New York State Economics Association,* December 1968, pp. 43-76.

Martin, David A. "Economics Is Not History: A Comment on the Current State of Economic History," *Agora,* 1(2), Spring 1970, pp. 67-85.

Martin, David A. "1853: The End of Bimetallism in the United States," *Journal of Economic History,* 33(4), December 1973, pp. 825-44.

Martin, David A. "Metallism, Small Notes, and Jackson's War with the B.U.S.," *Explorations in Economic History,* 11(3), Spring 1974, pp. 227-48.

Martin, David A. "United States Gold Production Prior to the California Gold Rush," *Explorations in Economic History,* 13(4), October 1976, pp. 437-50.

Martin, David A. "The Impact of Mid-Nineteenth Century Gold Depreciation upon Western Monetary Standards," *Journal of European Economic History,* 6(3), Winter 1977, pp. 641-58.

Martin, David A. "The Changing Role of Foreign Money in the United States, 1782-1857," *Journal of Economic History,* 37(4), December 1977, pp. 1009-27.

Marvel, Howard P. "Factory Regulation: A Reinterpretation of Early English Experience," *Journal of Law and Economics,* 20(2), October 1977, pp. 379-402.

Mason, Karen; Vinovskis, Maris A. and Hareven, Tamara K. "Determinants of Women's Labor Force Participation in Late Nineteenth-Century America," *Family Transitions and the Life Course in Historical Perspective.* New York: Academic Press, 1978.

Mathias, Peter and O'Brien, Patrick. "Taxation in Britain and France, 1715-1810: A Comparison of the Social and Economic Incidence of Taxes Collected for the Central Governments," *Journal of European Economic History,* 5(3), Winter 1976, pp. 601-50.

Mathias, Peter and O'Brien, Patrick K. "The Incidence of Taxes and the Burden of Proof: Reply to McCloskey," *Journal of European Economic History,* 7(1), Spring 1978, pp. 211-3.

Matis, Herbert. "The Pattern of Austrian Industrial Growth from the Eighteenth to the Early Twentieth Century: Comment on Rudolph," *Austrian History Yearbook,* 11, 1975, pp. 33-6.

Matsuba, S. and Mak, James. "A Concise Economic History of the Hawaiian Islands." [Working Paper]

Matteuzzi, Massimo. *Aspetti dell'economia italiana dal 1861 al 1967* (da una lezione di Giorgia Fua) [Aspects of the Italian Economy from 1861 to 1967 (from a lesson by Giorgia Fua)]. Bologna: Consorzio provinciale pubblica lettura, 1976.

Matthews, M. Scott; DeCanio, Stephen J. and Cooley, Thomas F. "Atics: An Agricultural Time Series-Cross Section Dataset," National Bureau of Economic Research, no. 197, August 1977.

Matthews, R.C.O. *A Study in Trade Cycle History: Economic Fluctuations in Great Britain, 1833-1842.* Cambridge: Cambridge University Press, 1954.

Matthews, R.C.O. "Duesenberry on Growth and Fluctuations. Review Essay of 'Business Cycles and Economic Growth' by J.S. Duesenberry

(New York: McGraw-Hill, 1958)," *Economic Journal,* 69(276), December 1959, pp. 749-65.

Matthews, R.C.O. "Some Aspects of Postwar Growth in the British Economy in Relation to Historical Experience," reprinted in Floud (ed), Essays in Quantitative Economic History, 1974, pp. 228-47. *Transactions of the Manchester Statistical Society,* Session 1964-65, pp. 1-25.

Matthews, R.C.O. "The New Economic History in Britain: A Comment on the Papers by Hughes, Hartwell and Supple," in McCloskey (ed), *Essays on a Mature Economy,* 1971, pp. 431-4.

Mauro, F. "Towards an 'Intercontinental Model': European Overseas Expansion between 1500 and 1800," *Economic History Review,* Second Series, 14(1), 1961, pp. 1-17.

Maxwell, Thomas. "The Long Run Demand for Money in South Africa, 1918-1960: Some Preliminary Findings," *South African Journal of Economics,* 39(1), March 1971, pp. 18-30.

May, Dean L. and Soltow, Lee C. "Accumulation and Discrimination in the Postbellum South," *Explorations in Economic History,* 16(2), April 1979, pp. 151-62.

Mayer, Thomas. "Money and the Great Depression: A Critique of Professor Temin's Thesis," *Explorations in Economic History,* 15(2), April 1978, pp. 127-45.

Maywald, K. "Income and Investment in the United Kingdom, 1856-1914: A Note (on Feinstein)," *Economic Journal,* 71(284), December 1961, pp. 856-7.

Mazlish, Bruce, ed. *The Railroad and the Space Program: An Exploration in Historical Analogy.* Cambridge, Mass.: M.I.T. Press, 1965.

Mazur, Michael P. "The Dispersion of Holdings in the Open Fields: An Interpretation in Terms of Property Rights," *Journal of European Economic History,* 6(2), Fall 1977, pp. 461-71.

Mazur, Michael P. "Scattering in Open Fields: Reply to McCloskey," *Journal of European Economic History,* 9(1), Spring 1980, pp. 215-8.

McAlpin, Michelle Burge. "Comments on Dissertations by Almquist and Kussmaul Presented to the 38th Annual Meeting of the Economic History Association," *Journal of Economic History,* 39(1), March 1979, pp. 338-9.

McAlpin, Michelle Burge. "Railroads, Prices, and Peasant Rationality: India, 1860-1900," *Journal of Economic History,* 34(3), September 1974, pp. 662-84.

McAlpin, Michelle Burge. "Railroads, Cultivation Patterns, and Foodgrain Availability: India, 1860-1900," *Indian Economic and Social History Review,* 12(1), January/March, 1975, pp. 43-60.

McAlpin, Michelle Burge. "The Effects of Expansion of Markets on Rural Income Distribution in Nineteenth Century India," (Symposium on Economic Change in Indian Agriculture. Edited by Morris D. Morris) *Explorations in Economic History,* 12(3), July 1975, pp. 289-301.

McAlpin, Michelle Burge. "Dearth, Famine, and Risk: The Changing Impact of Crop Failures in Western India, 1870-1920," *Journal of Economic History,* 39(1), March 1979, pp. 143-57.

McAlpin, Michelle Burge. "The Impact of Trade on Agricultural Development: Bombay Presidency, 1855-1920," *Explorations in Economic History,* 17(1), January 1980, pp. 26-47.

McAlpin, Michelle Burge. "Price Movements and Fluctuations in Economic Activity, 1860-1947," in Kumar and Desai (ed), *The Cambridge*

Economic History of India, 1982, pp. 878-904.

McAlpin, Michelle Burge. "Death, Famine and Changes in Risk: A Preliminary Exploration of the Changing Impact of Crop Failures in Bombay Presidency," presented at the Workshop on 'The Effects of Risk and Uncertainty on Economic and Social Processes in South Asia' of the ACLS-SSRC Joint Committee on South Asia and the University of Pennsylvania, November 1977.

McAlpin, Michelle Burge. "Notes on Sources of Agricultural and Demographic Data for South Asia," presented at the Workshop on the Generation of Quantifiable Historical Indicators for Asian History of the International Studies Association and the Social Science History Association, February 1976.

McAlpin, Michelle Burge. "Speculations on the Social and Economic Consequences of British Famine Policy in Bombay Presidency, 1870-1920," presented at the Meetings of the Association for Asian Studies, Toronto, Canada, March 1976.

McAlpin, Michelle Burge. "The Demographic Effects of Famines in Bombay Presidency, 1871-1931: Some Preliminary Findings," presented at the Annual Cliometrics Conference, University of Wisconsin-Madison, April 1976.

McCalla, Douglas. "The Wheat Staple and Upper Canadian Development," *Canadian Historical Association: Historical Papers,* 1978, pp. 34-46.

McClelland, Peter D. "The New Brunswick Economy in the Nineteenth Century," (Summary of Doctoral Dissertation) *Journal of Economic History,* 25(4), December 1965, pp. 686-90.

McClelland, Peter D. "Railroads, American Growth, and the New Economic History: A Critique of Fogel and Fishlow," *Journal of Economic History,* 27(1), March 1968, pp. 102-23.

McClelland, Peter D. "New Perspectives on the Disposal of Western Lands in Nineteenth Century America," *Business History Review,* 43(1), Spring 1969, pp. 77-83.

McClelland, Peter D. "The Cost to America of British Imperial Policy," *American Economic Review,* Papers and Proceedings, 59(2), May 1969, pp. 370-81.

McClelland, Peter D. "On Navigating the Navigation Acts with Peter McClelland: Reply to Reid," *American Economic Review,* 60(5), December 1970, pp. 956-8.

McClelland, Peter D. "Comments on Dissertations Presented at the 31st Annual Meeting of the Economic History Association," *Journal of Economic History,* 32(1), March 1972, pp. 423-7.

McClelland, Peter D. "Social Rates of Return on American Railroads in the Nineteenth Century," *Economic History Review,* Second Series, 25(3), August 1972, pp. 471-88.

McClelland, Peter D. "Model Building in the New Economic History," *American Behavioral Scientist,* 16(5), May/June 1973, pp. 631-51.

McClelland, Peter D. "The New Economic History and the Burdens of the Navigation Acts: A Comment on Walton," *Economic History Review,* Second Series, 26(4), November 1973, pp. 679-86.

McClelland, Peter D. *Causal Explanation and Model Building in History, Economics, and the New Economic History.* Ithaca: Cornell University Press, 1975.

McClelland, Peter D. "Cliometrics Versus Institutional History," in Uselding (ed), *Research in Economic History,* 1978, pp. 369-78.

McClelland, Peter D. "Transportation," in Porter (ed), *Encyclopedia of American Economic History*, 1980, pp. 309-34.

McClelland, Peter D. "The Demographic Dimensions of the New Republic: American Interregional Migration, Vital Statistics, and Manumissions, 1800-1860." [Working Paper]

McCloskey, Donald N. "Productivity Change in British Pig Iron, 1870-1939," *Quarterly Journal of Economics*, 82(2), May 1968, pp. 281-96.

McCloskey, Donald N. "The British Iron and Steel Industry, 1870-1914: A Study of the Climacteric in Productivity," (Summary of Doctoral Dissertation) *Journal of Economic History*, 29(1), March 1969, pp. 173-5.

McCloskey, Donald N. "Did Victorian Britain Fail?," *Economic History Review*, Second Series, 23(3), December 1970, pp. 446-59.

McCloskey, Donald N., ed. *Essays on a Mature Economy: Britain after 1840. Proceedings of the MSSB Conference on the New Economic History of Britain, 1840-1930.* London and Princeton: Methuen and Princeton University Press, 1971.

McCloskey, Donald N. "International Differences in Productivity? Coal and Steel in America and Britain before World War I," in McCloskey (ed), *Essays on a Mature Economy*, 1971, pp. 285-304.

McCloskey, Donald N. "Britain's Loss from Foreign Industrialization: A Provisional Estimate," *Explorations in Economic History*, 8(2), Winter 1970/71, pp. 141-52.

McCloskey, Donald N. "The New Economic History: An Introduction," [In Spanish] *Revista Espanola de Economia*, May/August 1971.

McCloskey, Donald N. "The Enclosure of Open Fields: Preface to a Study of Its Impact on the Efficiency of English Agriculture in the Eighteenth Century," *Journal of Economic History*, 32(1), March 1972, pp. 15-35.

McCloskey, Donald N. *Economic Maturity and Entrepreneurial Decline: British Iron and Steel, 1870-1913.* Cambridge: Harvard University Press, 1973.

McCloskey, Donald N. "New Perspectives on the Old Poor Law," *Explorations in Economic History*, 10(4), Summer 1973, pp. 419-36.

McCloskey, Donald N. "Victorian Growth: A Rejoinder (to Aldcroft)," *Economic History Review*, Second Series, 27(2), May 1974, pp. 275-7.

McCloskey, Donald N. "The Economics of Enclosure: A Market Analysis," in Parker and Jones (eds), *European Peasants and Their Markets*, 1975, pp. 123-60.

McCloskey, Donald N. "The Persistence of English Common Fields," in Parker and Jones (eds), *European Peasants and Their Markets*, 1975, pp. 73-119.

McCloskey, Donald N. "La nuova storia economica nella Gran Bretagna," [The New Economic History of Britain] *Quaderni Storici*, 31, April 1975, pp. 401-9.

McCloskey, Donald N. "English Open Fields as Behavior toward Risk," Uselding (ed), *Research in Economic History*, 1976.

McCloskey, Donald N. "Does the Past Have Useful Economics?," *Journal of Economic Literature*, 14(2), June 1976, pp. 434-61.

McCloskey, Donald N. "Fenoaltea on Open Fields: A Comment," *Explorations in Economic History*, 14(4), October 1977, pp. 402-4.

McCloskey, Donald N. "The Achievements of the Cliometric School," *Journal of Economic History*, 38(1), March 1978, pp. 13-28.

McCloskey, Donald N. "A Mismeasurement of the Incidence of Taxation in Britain and France, 1715-1810: Comment on O'Brien and Mathias," *Journal of European Economic History*, 7(1), Spring 1978, pp. 209-10.

McCloskey, Donald N. "Explaining Open Fields: A Reply to Professor Charles Wilson," *Journal of European Economic History*, 8(1), Spring 1979, pp. 193-202.

McCloskey, Donald N. "Another Way of Observing Open Fields: A Reply to A.R.H. Baker," *Journal of Historical Geography*, 5(4), October 1979, pp. 426-9.

McCloskey, Donald N. "No It Did Not: A Reply to Crafts," *Economic History Review*, Second Series, 32(4), November 1979, pp. 538-41.

McCloskey, Donald N. "The Industrial Revolution, 1780-1860: A Survey," in Floud and McCloskey (eds), *The Economic History of Britain since 1700*, 1981, pp. 103-27.

McCloskey, Donald N. "Scattering in Open Fields: A Comment on Mazur," *Journal of European Economic History*, 9(1), Spring 1980, pp. 209-14.

McCloskey, Donald N. "Magnanimous Albion: Free Trade and British National Income, 1841-1881," *Explorations in Economic History*, 17(3), July 1980, pp. 303-20.

McCloskey, Donald N. "A Dialogue between William P. Kennedy and McCloskey on Late Victorian Failure or the Lack of It," in McCloskey (ed), *Trade and Enterprise in Victorian Britain*, 1981.

McCloskey, Donald N. "A Working Bibliography on English Open Fields and Enclosure." [Working Paper]

McCloskey, Donald N. "Markets Abroad and British Economic Growth, 1820-1913." [Working Paper]

McCloskey, Donald N. "The Mathematics of the Fisheries Case Applied to Open Fields." [Working Paper]

McCloskey, Donald N. and Floud, Roderick C. "The Economic History of Britain since 1700: Editor's Introduction," in Floud and McCloskey (eds), *The Economic History of Britain since 1700*, 1981.

McCloskey, Donald N. and Floud, Roderick C., eds. *The Economic History of Britain since 1700* (2 Volumes; vol. 1: 1700-1860; vol. 2: 1860 to the 1970s). Cambridge: Cambridge University Press, 1981.

McCloskey, Donald N. and Harley, C. "Foreign Trade, Competition and the Expanding International Economy," in Floud and McCloskey (eds), *The Economic History of Britain since 1700*, 1981.

McCloskey, Donald N. and Sandberg, Lars G. "From Damnation to Redemption: Judgements on the Late Victorian Entrepreneur," *Explorations in Economic History*, 9(1), Fall 1971, pp. 89-108.

McCloskey, Donald N. and Thomas, Robert P. "Overseas Trade and Empire, 1700-1860," in Floud and McCloskey (eds), *The Economic History of Britain since 1700*, 1981, pp. 87-102.

McCloskey, Donald N. and Zecher, J. Richard. "How the Gold Standard Worked, 1880-1914," in Frenkel and Johnson (eds), *The Monetary Approach to the Balance of Payments*, 1975.

McCormick, William W. and Franks, Charles M. "A Self-Generating Model of Long-Swings for the American Economy, 1860-1940," *Journal of Economic History*, 31(2), June 1971, pp. 295-343.

McDougall, Duncan M. "Development of Canada's Economy, 1850-1900: Comment on Firestone," in Parker (ed), *Trends in the American Economy in the Nineteenth Century*, 1960, pp. 248-9.

McDougall, Duncan M. "Machine Tool Ouput, 1861-1910," in Brady (ed), *Employment, and Productivity in the United States After 1800*, 1966, pp. 497-517.

McDougall, Duncan M. "Canadian Manufactured Commodity Output, 1870-1915," *Canadian Journal of Economics*, 4(1), February 1971, pp. 21-36.

McDougall, Duncan M. "The Domestic Availability of Manufactured Commodity Output: Canada, 1870-1915," *Canadian Journal of Economics*, 6(2), May 1973, pp. 189-206.

McDougall, Duncan M. "Immigration into Canada, 1851-1920," reprinted in Hughes (ed), *Purdue Faculty Papers in Economic History*, 1967, pp. 103-18. *Canadian Journal of Economics and Political Science*, 27, pp. 162-75.

McDougall, Duncan; Davis, Lance E. and Hughes, Jonathan R.T. *American Economic History: The Development of a National Economy.* Homewood, Ill.: Richard D. Irwin, 1961.

McFelvey, Edward F. and Joskow, Paul L. "The Fogel-Engerman Iron Model: A Clarifying Note," *Journal of Political Economy*, 81(5), September/October 1973, pp. 1236-40.

McGann, Paul W. "Development of the Major Metal Mining Industries in the United States from 1839 to 1909: Comment on Herfindahl," in Brady (ed), *Output, Employment, and Productivity in the United States After 1800*, 1966, pp. 347-8.

McGann, Paul W. "Some Aspects of Development in the Coal Mining Industry, 1839-1918: Comment on Eliasberg," in Brady (ed), *Output, Employment, and Productivity in the United States After 1800*, 1966, pp. 436-7.

McGouldrick, Paul F. "The New England Textile Industry, 1825-60: Comment on Davis and Stettler," in Brady (ed), *Output, Employment, and Productivity in the United States After 1800*, 1966, pp. 239-40.

McGouldrick, Paul F. *New England Textiles in the Nineteenth Century: Profits and Investment.* Cambridge: Harvard University Press, 1968.

McGouldrick, Paul F. and Tannen, Michael B. "Did American Manufacturers Discriminate against Immigrants before 1914?," *Journal of Economic History*, 37(3), September 1977, pp. 723-46.

McGouldrick, Paul F. and Tannen. "The Increasing Pay Gap for Women in the Textile and Clothing Industries, 1910 to 1970," *Journal of Economic History*, 40(4), December 1980, pp. 799-814.

McGouldrick, Paul and Tannen, Michael B. "Further Results on Male and Female Pay Differentials, 1910 to 1970." [Working Paper]

McGreevey, William Paul. "Quantitative Research in Latin American History of the Nineteenth and Twentieth Centuries," in Lorwin and Price (eds), *The Dimensions of the Past*, 1972, pp. 477-501.

McGuire, Robert A. "A Portfolio Analysis of Crop Diversification and Risk in the Cotton South," *Explorations in Economic History*, 17(4), October 1980, pp. 342-71.

McGuire, Robert A. and Higgs. "Cotton, Corn and Risk in the Nineteenth Century: Another View," *Explorations in Economic History*, 14(2), April 1977, pp. 167-82.

McGuire, William J. and Allison, Chris. "Wage Discrimination and Economies of Scale in the American Manufacturing Sector, 1820-1920," Ohio University Economic History Research Paper no. G-6.

McGuire, William J. and Vedder, Richard K. "Bank Failures, 1929-1933:

An Empirical Analysis," *Ohio University Economic History Research Paper* no. F-37.

McIlwraith, Thomas F. "Freight Capacity and Utilization of the Erie and Great Lakes Canals before 1850," *Journal of Economic History,* 36(4), December 1976, pp. 852-77.

McInnis, R. Marvin. "Regional Income Differentials in Canada, 1911-1961," (Summary of Doctoral Dissertation) *Journal of Economic History,* 26(4), December 1966, pp. 586-8.

McInnis, R. Marvin. "The Trend of Regional Income Differentials in Canada," *Canadian Journal of Economics,* 1(2), May 1968, pp. 440-70.

McInnis, R. Marvin. "Long-Run Changes in the Industrial Structure of the Canadian Work Force," *Canadian Journal of Economics,* 4(3), August 1971, pp. 353-61.

McInnis, R. Marvin. "Long-Term Changes in Industrial Composition with Particular Attention to Canada, 1911 and 1961," in Van der Wee, Vinogradov, and Kotovsky (eds), *Fifth International Congress of Economic History,* 1976, pp. 9-27.

McInnis, R. Marvin. "The Indivisibility of Land: A Microanalysis of the System of Inheritance in Nineteenth-Century Ontario (A Comment on Gagan)," *Journal of Economic History,* 36(1), March 1976, pp. 142-6.

McInnis, R. Marvin. "Childbearing and Availability: Some Evidence from Individual Household Data," in Lee (ed), *Population Patterns in the Past,* 1977, pp. 201-27.

McInnis, R. Marvin. "The Demographic Focus in Economic History," (Summary of 1976 Research Workshop) *Journal of Economic History,* 37(1), March 1977, pp. 234-5.

McInnis, R. Marvin and Lewis, Frank D. "The Efficiency of the French-Canadian Farmer in the Nineteenth Century," *Journal of Economic History,* 40(3), September 1980, pp. 497-514.

McInnis, R. Marvin and Urquhart, Mac C. "Estimation of Historical Series of Farm Income for Canada." [Working Paper]

McKenna, Edward E. "Age, Region, and Marriage in Post-Famine Ireland: An Empirical Examination," *Economic History Review,* Second Series, 31(2), May 1978, pp. 238-56.

McLean, Ian W. "The Australian Balance of Payments on Current Account, 1901 to 1964-65," *Australian Economic Papers,* 7(10), June 1968, pp. 77-90.

McLean, Ian W. "The Adoption of Harvest Machinery in Victoria in the Late Nineteenth Century," *Australian Economic History Review,* 13(1), March 1973, pp. 41-56.

McLean, Ian W. "Growth and Technological Change in Agriculture: Victoria, 1870-1910," *Economic Record,* 49(128), December 1973, pp. 560-74.

McLean, Ian W. "Growth and Technological Change in Agriculture: A Reply (to Powell)," *Economic Record,* 50(132), December 1974, pp. 620-2.

McLean, Ian W. "Anglo-American Engineering Competition, 1870-1914: Some Third-Market Evidence," *Economic History Review,* Second Series, 29(3), August 1976, pp. 452-64.

McLean, Ian W. "Rural Output, Inputs, and Mechanisation in Victoria, 1870-1910," Ph.D. Dissertation, Australian National University, 1971.

McMahon, Marshall; Bolch, Ben and Fels, Rendig. "Housing Surplus in the 1920's?," *Explorations in Economic History*, 8(3), Spring 1971, pp. 259-84.

McManus, John C. "An Economic Analysis of Indian Behavior in the North American Fur Trade," *Journal of Economic History*, 32(1), March 1972, pp. 36-53.

McManus, John C.; Dales, John H. and Watkins, Melville H. "Primary Products and Economic Growth: A Comment on Chambers and Gordon," *Journal of Political Economy*, 75(6), December 1967, pp. 876-80.

McMullen, Neil J. and Uselding, Paul J. "The Changing Basis of American Prosperity," *Economia Internazionale*, 29(3-4), August/November 1977, pp. 446-61.

McRandle, James H. and Quirk, James P. "An Interpretation of the German Risk Fleet Concept, 1899-1914," in Hughes (ed), *Purdue Faculty Papers in Economic History*, 1967, pp. 484-537.

Medoff, James and Friedman, Gerald. "Slavery and the Termination of Implicit Contracts." [Working Paper]

Meeker, Edward F. "The Improving Health of the United States, 1850-1915," *Explorations in Economic History*, 9(4), Summer 1972, pp. 353-74.

Meeker, Edward F. "The Social Rate of Return on Investment in Public Health, 1880-1910," *Journal of Economic History*, 34(2), June 1974, pp. 392-421.

Meeker, Edward F. "Mortality Trends of Southern Blacks, 1850-1910: Some Preliminary Findings," *Explorations in Economic History*, 13(1), January 1976, pp. 13-42.

Meeker, Edward F. "Freedom, Economic Opportunity, and Fertility: Black Americans, 1860-1910," *Economic Inquiry*, 15(3), July 1977, pp. 397-412.

Meeker, Edward F. and Kau. "Racial Discrimination and Occupational Attainment at the Turn of the Century," *Explorations in Economic History*, 14(3), July 1977, pp. 250-76.

Meerman, Jacob P. "The Climax of the Bank War: Biddle's Contraction, 1833-1834," *Journal of Political Economy*, 71(4), August 1963, pp. 378-88.

Mellman, Robert "A Reinterpretation of the Economic History of the Post-Reconstruction South, 1877-1919," Ph.D. Dissertation, Massachusetts Institute of Technology, 1975.

Meltzer, Allan H. "Monetarist Interpretations of the Great Depression: Comment on Gordon and Wilcox," in Brunner (ed), *The Great Depression Revisited*, 1981, pp. 148-64.

Menard, Russell R. "Agricultural Productivity Change in Eighteenth-Century Pennsylvania: Comment on Ball and Walton," *Journal of Economic History*, 36(1), March 1976, pp. 118-25.

Menard, Russell R. and Galenson, David W. "Approaches to the Analysis of Economic Growth in Colonial British America," *Historical Methods*, 13(1), Winter 1980, pp. 3-18.

Mendels, Franklin F. "Proto-Industrialization: The First Phase of the Industrialization Process," *Journal of Economic History*, 32(1), March 1972, pp. 241-61.

Mendels, Franklin F. "Agriculture and Peasant Industry in Eighteenth-Century Flanders," in Parker and Jones (eds), *European Peasants and Their Markets*, 1975, pp. 179-204.

Mendels, Franklin F. "La Composition du Menage Paysan en France au XIXe Siecle: Une Analyse Economique du Mode de Production

Domestique," [The Makeup of the French Country Household in the 19th Century: an Economic Analysis along the Line of Domestic Production] *Annales: Economies, Societes, Civilisations,* 33(4), July/August 1978, pp. 780-802.

Mendels, Franklin F. "Industrialization and Population Pressure in Eighteenth-Century Flanders," (Summary of Doctoral Dissertation) *Journal of Economic History,* 31(1), March 1971, pp. 269-71.

Menderhausen, Horst; Goldsmith, Raymond W. and Brady, Dorothy S. *A Study of Saving in the United States, vol. 3: Special Studies.* Princeton: Princeton University Press, 1957.

Menezes, Carmen; Andreano, Ralph L. and Williamson, Harold F. "The American Petroleum Industry," in Brady (ed), *Output, Employment, and Productivity in the United States After 1800,* 1966, pp. 349-403.

Mercer, Lloyd J. "Land Grants to American Railroads: Social Cost or Social Benefits?," *Business History Review,* 43(2), Summer 1969, pp. 134-51.

Mercer, Lloyd J. "Rates of Return for Land-Grant Railroads: The Central Pacific System," *Journal of Economic History,* 30(3), September 1970, pp. 602-26.

Mercer, Lloyd J. "Taxpayers or Investors: Who Paid for the Land-Grant Railroads?," *Business History Review,* 46(3), Autumn 1972, pp. 279-94.

Mercer, Lloyd J. "Rates of Return and Government Subsidization of the Canadian Pacific Railway: An Alternate View," *Canadian Journal of Economics,* 6(3), August 1973, pp. 428-37.

Mercer, Lloyd J. "Building Ahead of Demand: Some Evidence for the Land Grant Railroads," *Journal of Economic History,* 34(2), June 1974, pp. 492-500.

Mercer, Lloyd J. and Morgan, W. "Alternative Interpretations of Market Saturation: Evaluation for the Automobile Market in the Late Twenties," *Explorations in Economic History,* 9(3), Spring 1972, pp. 269-90.

Mercer, Lloyd J. and Morgan, W. "Internal Funds and Automobile Investment: An Evaluation of the Seltzer Hypothesis," *Journal of Economic History,* 32(3), September 1972, pp. 682-90.

Mercer, Lloyd J. and Morgan, W. "The American Automobile Industry: Investment Demand, Capacity and Capacity Utilization, 1921-1940," *Journal of Political Economy,* 80(6), November/December 1972, pp. 1214-31.

Mercer, Lloyd J. and Morgan, W. "Housing Surplus in the 1920s? Another Evaluation," *Explorations in Economic History,* 10(3), Spring 1973, pp. 295-303.

Merrill, Robert S.; Strassman, W. Paul; Wilkening, E.A. and Parker, William N. *The Diffusion of Technical Knowledge as an Instrument of Economic Development* (Symposia Studies Series no. 13). National Institute of Social and Behavioral Science, 1962.

Metzer, Jacob. "Some Economic Aspects of Railroad Development in Tsarist Russia," (Summary of Doctoral Dissertation) *Journal of Economic History,* 33(1), March 1973, pp. 314-6.

Metzer, Jacob. "Railroad Development and Market Integration: The Case of Tsarist Russia," (see the Editor's Note this Journal, 35(2), June 1975, pp. 467 for an Erratum statement concerning this article). *Journal of Economic History,* 34(3), September 1974, pp.

529-50.

Metzer, Jacob. "Rational Management, Modern Business Practices, and Economies of Scale in the Antebellum Southern Plantations," *Explorations in Economic History,* 12(2), April 1975, pp. 123-50.

Metzer, Jacob. "Institutional Change and Economic Analysis: Some Issues Related to American Slavery," *Louisiana Studies,* 15(4), Winter 1976, pp. 321-43.

Metzer, Jacob. "Railroads in Tsarist Russia: Direct Gains and Implications," *Explorations in Economic History,* 13(1), January 1976, pp. 85-112.

Metzer, Jacob. "Railroad Development and Market Integration in Tsarist Russia: A Rejoinder to Kelly," *Journal of Economic History,* 36(4), December 1976, pp. 917-8.

Metzer, Jacob. *Some Economic Aspects of Railroad Development in Tsarist Russia.* New York: Arno Press, 1977.

Metzer, Jacob. *National Capital for a National Home: The Formation of the Zionist Public Sector in the Early Mandate Period.* Jerusalem: Ben Zvi Press, 1979.

Metzer, Jacob and Gross, Nachum T. "Public Finance in the Jewish Economy in Interwar Palestine," in Uselding (ed), *Research in Economic History,* 1978, pp. 87-159.

Meyer, John R. "An Input-Output Approach to Evaluating the Influence of Exports on British Industrial Production in the Late 19th Century," *Explorations in Entrepreneurial History,* 8(1), October 1955, pp. 12-34.

Meyer, John R. "Slavery as an Obstacle to Economic Growth in the United States: A Panel Discussion of Conrad and Meyer," *Journal of Economic History,* 27(4), December 1967, pp. 549-51.

Meyer, John R. "Comment on Papers by Engerman, Goldin, and Kahan presented to the 32nd Annual Meeting of the Economic History Association," *Journal of Economic History,* 33(1), March 1973, pp. 100-5.

Meyer, John R. and Conrad, Alfred H. "Economic Theory, Statistical Inference, and Economic History," reprinted in Conrad and Meyer (eds), *The Economics of Slavery,* 1964, pp. 3-30. *Journal of Economic History,* 17(4), December 1957, pp. 524-44.

Meyer, John R. and Conrad, Alfred H. "The Economics of Slavery in the Antebellum South," reprinted in Fogel and Engerman (eds), *The Reinterpretation of American Economic History,* 1971, pp. 342-361. *Journal of Political Economy,* 66(2), April 1958, pp. 95-130.

Meyer, John R. and Conrad, Alfred H. "The Economics of Slavery in the Antebellum South: A Reply to Dowd," *Journal of Political Economy,* 66(5), October 1958, pp. 442-3.

Meyer, John R. and Conrad, Alfred H. "The Economics of Slavery in the Antebellum South: Reply to Moes," *Journal of Political Economy,* 68(2), April 1960, pp. 187-9.

Meyer, John R. and Conrad, Alfred H. *The Economics of Slavery and Other Essays on the Quantitative Study of Economic History.* Chicago: Aldine Press, 1964.

Meyer, John R. and Conrad, Alfred H. "Slavery as an Obstacle to Economic Growth in the United States: A Panel Discussion of Conrad and Meyer," reprinted in Aitken (ed), *Did Slavery Pay?,* 1971, pp. 270-287. *Journal of Economic History,* 27(4), December 1967, pp. 518-31.

411

Millar, James. "The Birth and Death of Taxes: Comment (on Ames and Rapp)," *Journal of Economic History,* 37(1), March 1977, pp. 179-81.

Miller, Ann Ratner. "Labor Force Trends and Differentials in Kuznets, Miller, and Easterlin (eds), *Population, Redistribution and Economic Growth,* 1960, pp. 7-101.

Miller, Ann Ratner and Brainerd, Carol P. "Labor Force Estimates," in Lee et al (eds), *Population, Redistribution and Economic Growth,* 1957, pp. 363-633.

Miller, Ann Ratner; Kuznets, Simon S. and Easterlin, Richard A. *Population, Redistribution and Economic Growth: United States, 1870-1950, vol. 2: Analyses of Economic Change* (Series edited by Simon S. Kuznets and Dorothy Swaine Thomas). Philadelphia: American Philosophical Society, 1960.

Miller, Edward. "England in the Twelfth and Thirteenth Centuries: An Economic Contrast?," *Economic History Review,* Second Series, 24(1), February 1971, pp. 1-14.

Miller, Edward. "Farming of Manors and Direct Management: Rejoinder (to Reed and Anderson)," *Economic History Review,* Second Series, 26(1), February 1973, pp. 138-40.

Miller, Roger Leroy and Walton, Gary M. *Economic Issues in American History.* New York: Harper & Row, 1978.

Miller, William L. "Slavery and the Population of the South," *Southern Economic Journal,* 28, July 1961, pp. 46-54.

Miller, William L. "A Note on the Importance of the Interstate Slave Trade of the Antebellum South," *Journal of Political Economy,* 73(2), April 1965, pp. 181-7.

Mills, T.; Nishimura, Shizuya and Wood, G.E. "The Estimates of Bank Deposits in the U.K., 1870-1913." [Working Paper]

Minami, Ryoshin. "Railroads and Electric Utilities, 1872-1960," in Ohkawa and Hayami (eds), *Economic Growth,* 1973, pp. 38-50.

Minami, Ryoshin. "Sources of Agricultural Growth in Japan, 1880-1965: Comment on Akino and Hayami," in Ohkawa and Hayami (eds), *Econom Growth,* 1973, pp. 219-31.

Minami, Ryoshin. "Mechanical Power in the Industrialization of Japan," *Journal of Economic History,* 37(4), December 1977, pp. 935-58.

Mintz, Ilse. *Cyclical Flucuations in the Exports of the United States since 1879.* New York: Columbia University Press for the National Bureau of Economic Research, 1967.

Mirowski, Philip. "The Birth of the Business Cycle," (Summary of Doctoral Dissertation) *Journal of Economic History,* 40(1), March 1980, pp. 171-4.

Mirowski, Philip. "The Rise (and Retreat) of a Market: English Joint Stocks in the Eighteenth Century," *Journal of Economic History,* 41(3), September 1981.

Mirowski, Philip "The Birth of the Business Cycle." [Working Paper]

Mishkin, Frederic S. "The Household Balance Sheet and the Great Depression," *Journal of Economic History,* 38(4), December 1978, pp. 918-37.

Mitch, David F. "Historical Dimensions of Social and Political Economy: A Report on the 1976 Meetings of the Economic History Association," *Journal of European Economic History,* 6(2), Fall 1977, pp. 481-6.

Mitch, David F. "Education as Consumption and Investment in Britain during the Nineteenth Century." [Working Paper]

Mitchell, B.R. "The Coming of the Railway and United Kingdom Economic Growth," *Journal of Economic History,* 24(3), September 1964, pp. 315-36.

Mitchell, B.R. *European Historical Statistics, 1750-1970* (Abridged Edition, 1978). London and New York: Macmillan and Columbia University Press, 1975.

Mitchell, B.R. and Deane, Phyllis, eds. *Abstract of British Historical Statistics* (Reprinted in a revised 2nd edition, 1970). Cambridge: Cambridge University Press, 1962.

Mitchell, B.R. and Jones, H.G.G., eds. *Second Abstract of British Historical Statistics.* Cambridge University Press, 1971.

Miyamoto, Mataji; Sakudo, Yotaro and Yasuba, Yasukichi. "Economic Development in Preindustrial Japan, 1859-1894," *Journal of Economic History,* 25(4), December 1965, pp. 541-64.

Mizruchi, M.S. and Bunting. "The Transfer of Control in Large Corporations: 1912-1919 (Summary)," in Uselding (ed), *Business and Economic History,* 1980, pp. 120-3.

Moe, Thorvald. "Some Economic Aspects of Norwegian Population Movements, 1740-1940: An Econometric Study," (Summary of Doctoral Dissertation) *Journal of Economic History,* 30(1), March 1970, pp. 267-70.

Moes, John E. "The Economics of Slavery in the Antebellum South: Another Comment on Conrad and Meyer," *Journal of Political Economy,* 68(2), April 1960, pp. 183-7.

Moggridge, Donald E. *The Return to Gold, 1925: The Formulation of Economic Policy and Its Critics.* Cambridge: Cambridge University Press, 1969.

Moggridge, Donald E. "The Norman Conquest of $4.86: Britain and the Return to Gold, 1925," *Annales D'Etudes Internationales,* 1, 1970, pp. 115-29.

Moggridge, Donald E. "British Controls on Long Term Capital Movements, 1924-1931," in McCloskey (ed), *Essays on a Mature Economy,* 1971, pp. 113-38.

Moggridge, Donald E. "The Bank of England and the Management of the Inter-War Gold Standard," *International Currency Review,* 3(3), August 1971, pp. 17-25.

Moggridge, Donald E. "Bank of England Foreign Exchange Operations 1924-1931," *International Review of the History of Banking,* 5, 1972, pp. 1-23.

Moggridge, Donald E. *British Monetary Policy, 1924-1931: The Norman Conquest of $4.86.* London: Cambridge University Press, 1972.

Moggridge, Donald E. "Comments on Papers by Friedman and Vandagna Presented to the 37th Annual Meeting of the Economic History Association," *Journal of Economic History,* 38(1), March 1978, pp. 202-4.

Moggridge, Donald E. "The Gold Standard and National Economic Policies, 1919-1939," in Mathias and Pollard (eds), *The Cambridge Economic History of Europe.*

Mokyr, Joel. "The Industrial Revolution in the Low Countries in the First Half of the Nineteenth Century: A Comparative Case Study," *Journal of Economic History,* 34(2), June 1974, pp. 365-91.

Mokyr, Joel. "Capital, Labor and the Delay of the Industrial Revolution in the Netherlands," *Yearbook of Economic History,* 38, 1975, pp. 280-99.

413

Mokyr, Joel. *Industrialization in the Low Countries, 1795-1850.* New Haven: Yale University Press, 1976.

Mokyr, Joel. "Government Finance, Taxation, and Economic Policy in Old Regime Europe," (Summary of the 1975 Research Workshop) *Journal of Economic History,* 36(1), March 1976, pp. 28-9.

Mokyr, Joel. "Industrial Growth and Stagnation in the Low Countries," (Summary of Doctoral Dissertation) *Journal of Economic History,* 36(1), March 1976, pp. 276-8.

Mokyr, Joel. "Growing-Up and the Industrial Revolution in Europe," *Explorations in Economic History,* 13(4), October 1976, pp. 371-96.

Mokyr, Joel. "Demand vs. Supply in the Industrial Revolution," *Journal of Economic History,* 37(4), December 1977, pp. 981-1008.

Mokyr, Joel. "The Deadly Fungus: An Econometric Investigation into the Short-Term Demographic Impact of the Irish Famine, 1846-1851," in Simon and Davanzo (eds), *Research in Population Economics,* 1980.

Mokyr, Joel. "Industrialization and Poverty in Ireland and the Netherlands," *Journal of Interdisciplinary History,* 10(3), Winter 1980, pp. 429-58.

Mokyr, Joel. "Malthusian Models and Irish History," *Journal of Economic History,* 40(1), March 1980, pp. 159-66.

Mokyr, Joel and DeCanio, Stephen J. "Inflation and the Wage Lag during the American Civil War," *Explorations in Economic History,* 14(4), October 1977, pp. 311-36.

Mokyr, Joel and Savin, N. Eugene. "Stagflation in Historical Perspective: The Napoleonic Wars Revisited," Uselding (ed), *Research in Economic History,* 1976, pp. 198-259.

Mokyr, Joel and Savin, N. Eugene. "Some Econometric Problems in the Standard of Living Controversy," *Journal of European Economic History,* 7(2-3), Fall/Winter 1978, pp. 517-25.

Moliner, Jean-Claude. "Les calculs d'agregat en France anterieurement a 1850," *Revue d'economie politique,* 67(4), 1957, pp. 875-987.

Mooney, Peter J. and Orsagh, Thomas J. "A Model for the Dispersion of the Migrant Labor Force and Some Results for the United States, 1880-1920," *Review of Economics and Statistics,* 52(3), August 1970, pp. 306-12.

Moore, Geoffrey H. "Business Cycles, Panics, and Depressions," in Porter (ed), *Encyclopedia of American Economic History,* 1980, pp. 151-6.

Moore, Wilbert E.; Kuznets, Simon S. and Spengler, Joseph J., eds. *Economic Growth: Brazil, India, Japan.* Durham, N.C.: Duke University Press, 1955.

Morgan, Theodore. "The Decline of Rural Industry Under Export Expansion: A Comparison among Burma, Philippines, and Thailand, 1870-1938 and Economic Forms in Pre-Colonial Ghana: Comments (on Resnick and Hymer)," *Journal of Economic History,* 30(2), June 1970, pp. 442-5.

Morgan, W. Douglas. "Investment Behavior by American Railroads, 1897-1914: A Comment on Neal," *Review of Economics and Statistics,* 53(3), August 1971, pp. 294-8.

Morgan, W. Douglas and Mercer, Lloyd J. "Alternative Interpretations of Market Saturation: Evaluation for the Automobile Market in the Late Twenties," *Explorations in Economic History,* 9(3), Spring 1972, pp. 269-90.

Morgan, W. Douglas and Mercer, Lloyd J. "Internal Funds and Automobile

Investment: An Evaluation of the Seltzer Hypothesis," *Journal of Economic History*, 32(3), September 1972, pp. 682-90.

Morgan, W. Douglas and Mercer, Lloyd J. "The American Automobile Industry: Investment Demand, Capacity and Capacity Utilization, 1921-1940," *Journal of Political Economy*, 80(6), November/December 1972, pp. 1214-31.

Morgan, W. Douglas and Mercer, Lloyd J. "Housing Surplus in the 1920s? Another Evaluation," *Explorations in Economic History*, 10(3), Spring 1973, pp. 295-303.

Morineau, Michel. "The Agricultural Revolution in Nineteenth-Century France: Comment on Newell," *Journal of Economic History*, 36(2), June 1976, pp. 436-7.

Morley, S. and Williamson, Jeffrey G. "Class Pay Differentials, Wage Stretching and Early Capitalist Development," in Nash (ed), *Essays on Economic Development and Cultural Change*, 1977, pp. 407-27.

Morris, Cynthia Taft. "Productivity Change and Grain Farm Practice on the Canadian Prairie, 1900-1930: A Discussion of Dick," *Journal of Economic History*, 40(1), March 1980, pp. 121-2.

Morris, Cynthia Taft and Adelman, Irma. *Economic Growth and Social Equity in Developing Countries*. Stanford: Stanford University Press, 1973.

Morris, Cynthia Taft and Adelman, Irma. "An Inquiry into the Course of Poverty in the Ninteenth and Early Twentieth Centuries," in Matthews (ed), *Measurement, History, and Factors of Economic Growth*, 1978.

Morris, Cynthia Taft and Adelman, Irma. "Patterns of Market Expansion in the Nineteenth Century: A Quantitative Study," in Dalton (ed), *Research in Economic Anthropology*, 1978.

Morris, Cynthia Taft and Adelman, Irma. "The Role of Institutional Influences in Patterns of Agricultural Development in the Nineteenth and Early Twentieth Centuries: A Cross-Section Quantitative Study," *Journal of Economic History*, 39(1), March 1979, pp. 159-76.

Morris, Cynthia Taft and Adelman, Irma. "Patterns of Industrialization in the Nineteenth and Early Twentieth Centuries: A Cross-Sectional Quantitative Study," in Uselding (ed), *Research in Economic History*, 1980.

Morris, Morris D. "The Problem of the Peasant Agriculturist in Meiji Japan, 1873-1885," *Far Eastern Quarterly*, 15(3), May 1956, pp. 357-70.

Morris, Morris D. "Two Classic Cases of Industrialization Reconsidered: A Comment on Kisch and Krause," *Journal of Economic History*, 19(4), December 1959, pp. 565-9.

Morris, Morris D. "The Recruitment of an Industrial Labor Force in Asia, with British and American Comparisons," *Comparative Studies in Society and History*, 2(3), April 1960, pp. 305-28.

Morris, Morris D. *The Emergence of an Industrial Labor Force in India: A Study of the Bombay Cotton Mills, 1854-1947*. Berkeley and Los Angeles: University of California Press, 1965.

Morris, Morris D. "Economic Change and Agriculture in 19th Century India," *Indian Economic and Social History Review*, 3(2), June 1966, pp. 185-209.

Morris, Morris D. "Some Comments on the State of Economic History," in Dasgupta (ed), *Methodology of Economic Research*, 1968, pp. 110-6.

Morris, Morris D. "Trends and Tendencies in Indian Economic History," *Indian Economic and Social History Review*, 5(4), December 1968, pp. 319-88.

Morris, Morris D. "The Economist as Economic Historian,"*Transactions, India Institute of Advanced Studies, vol. 3: Social and Economic History of India.* Calcutta: India Institute of Advanced Studies, 1971.

Morris, Morris D. "Quantitative Resources for the Study of Indian History," in Lorwin and Price (eds), *The Dimensions of the Past*, 1972, pp. 531-49.

Morris, Morris D. "Private Industrial Investment on the Indian Subcontinent, 1900-1939: Some Methodological Considerations. Review Essay of 'Private Investment in India, 1900-1939' by Amiya K. Bagchi (Cambridge: Cambridge University Press, 1972)," *Modern Asian Studies*, 8(4), October 1974, pp. 535-55.

Morris, Morris D. "Introduction to a Symposium on Economic Change in Indian Agriculture," *Explorations in Economic History*, 12(3), July 1975, pp. 253-61.

Morris, Morris D. "Industrialization in South Asia, 1800-1947," in Kumar and Desai (eds), *Cambridge Economic History of India*, 1982, pp. 553-676.

Morris, Morris D. and Dudley, Clyde B. "Selected Railway Statistics for the Indian Subcontinent, 1853-1946/47," *Artha Vijnana*, 17(3), September 1975, pp. 187-298.

Morris, Morris D. and Stein, Burton. "The Economic History of India: A Bibliographic Essay," *Journal of Economic History*, 21(2), June 1961, pp. 179-207.

Morrissey, M.J. and Burt, R. "A Theory of Mineral Discovery: A Note on Blainey," *Economic History Review*, Second Series, 26(3), August 1973, pp. 497-505.

Morrow, Richard B. "Family Limitation in Pre-Industrial England: A Reappraisal of Wrigley," *Economic History Review*, Second Series, 31(3), August 1978, pp. 419-28.

Mosk, Carl A. "Demographic Transition in Japan," *Journal of Economic History*, 37(3), September 1977, pp. 655-74.

Mosk, Carl A. "Demographic Transition in Japan, 1920-1960," *Journal of Economic History*, 38(1), March 1978, pp. 285-6.

Mosk, Carl A. "Fecundity, Infanticide and Food Consumption in Japan," *Explorations in Economic History*, 15(3), July 1978, pp. 269-89.

Mosk, Carl A. "The Decline of Marital Fertility in Japan," *Population Studies*, 33(1), March 1979, pp. 19-38.

Mueller, Eva. "Child Costs and Economic Development: Comment on Lindert," in Easterlin (ed), *Population and Economic Change in Developing Countries*, 1980, pp. 69-74.

Mukerjee, Moni. *The National Income of India: Trends and Structure.* Calcutta: Statistical Pub. Society, 1969.

Munoz, Oscar E. "An Essay on the Progress of Industrialization in Chile since 1914," *Yale Economic Essays*, 8(2), Fall 1968, pp. 137-84.

Munroe, Tapan. "The Theory of Economic Drain: Britain in India in the Nineteenth Century (Abstract)," *Western Economic Journal*, 7(3), September 1969, pp. 255.

Munroe, Tapan. "A Critique of Theories of Imperialism," in Pfaff (ed), *Frontiers in Social Thought*, 1976.

Munroe, Tapan and Boulding, Kenneth E. "Unprofitable Empire: Britain in India, 1800-1967: A Critique of the Hobson-Lenin Thesis on Imperialism," *Peace Research Society Papers*, 16, 1970.

Munroe, Tapan and Boulding, Kenneth E., eds. *Economic Imperialism.* Ann Arbor: University of Michigan Press, 1972.

Munroe, Tapan and Fennel, Lee. "The Myth of the Dependency Paradigm: A Study in Grants Economics," *International Studies Association,* 48, 1975.

Munyon, Paul G. "A Critical Review of Estimates of Net Income from Agriculture for 1880 and 1900: New Hampshire, a Case Study," *Journal of Economic History,* 37(3), September 1977, pp. 634-54.

Munyon, Paul G. "Agricultural Income Statistics Since the Civil War," (Summary of 1977 Research Workshop) *Journal of Economic History,* 38(1), March 1978, pp. 265-7.

Murphy, Earl F. "Comment on Papers by McCloskey, McManus, and Landes and Solmon Presented to the 31st Annual Meeting of the Economic History Association," *Journal of Economic History,* 32(1), March 1972, pp. 95-7.

Murphy, G.S. "On Counterfactual Propositions," *History and Theory,* 8, (Beiheft 9), 1969.

Murphy, G.S. "On the Costs and Benefits of the American Civil War (Abstract)," *Western Economic Journal,* 3(3), September 1970, pp. 277.

Murphy, G.W. and Johnston, J. "The Growth of Life Assurance in the United Kingdom since 1880," *Manchester School of Economic and Social Studies,* 25, May 1957, pp. 107-82.

Musoke, Moses S. "Technical Change in Cotton Production in the United States, 1925-1960," (Summary of Doctoral Dissertation) *Journal of Economic History,* 37(1), March 1977, pp. 258-60.

Muth, Richard F.; Perloff, Harvey S. and Lampard, Eric E. *Regions, Resources, and Economic Growth.* Baltimore: Johns Hopkins University Press, 1960.

Myers, Ramon H. and Dittrich, Scott R. "Resource Allocation in Traditional Agriculture: Republican China, 1937-1940," *Journal of Political Economy,* 79(4), July/August 1971, pp. 887-96.

Myrdal, Gunnar. "The Theories of 'Stages of Growth'," *Scandinavian Economic History Review,* 15(1 & 2), 1967, pp. 1-12.

Nardinelli, Clark. "Child Labor and the Factory Acts," *Journal of Economic History,* 40(4), December 1980, pp. 739-55.

Nardinelli, Clark. "An Economic History of the Factory Acts," Unpublished Ph.D. Dissertation, University of Chicago, 1979.

National Bureau of Economic Research. *Corporate Bond Statistics, 1900-1938.* New York: National Bureau of Economic Research, 1941.

National Bureau of Economic Research. *The Behavior of Income Shares: Selected Theoretical and Empirical Issues* (Studies in Income and Wealth, vol. 27). Princeton: Princeton University Press, 1964.

Neal, Larry D. "Investment Behavior by American Railroads, 1897-1914," *Review of Economics and Statistics,* 51(2), May 1969, pp. 126-35.

Neal, Larry D. "Investment Behavior by American Railroads, 1897-1914: A Reply to Morgan," *Review of Economics and Statistics,* 53(3),

August 1971, pp. 299-300.

Neal, Larry D. "Deane and Cole on Industrialization and Population Change in the Eighteenth Century: Comment," *Economic History Review*, Second Series, 24(4), November 1971, pp. 643-7.

Neal, Larry D. "Structural Breaks, Shifting Harmonics, or Random Effects? The Spectral Results of the Passing of the Kuznets Cycle," *Proceedings of the Business and Economics Section of the American Statistical Association*. American Statistical Association, 1974, pp. 34-43.

Neal, Larry D. "Cross Spectral Analysis of Atlantic Migration," in Uselding (ed), *Research in Economic History*, 1976, pp. 260-97.

Neal, Larry D. "Interpreting Power and Profit in Economic History: A Case Study of the Seven Years War," *Journal of Economic History*, 27(1), March 1977, pp. 20-35.

Neal, Larry D. "The Cost of Impressment during the Seven Years War," *Mariner's Mirror*, 64(1), February 1978, pp. 45-56.

Neal, Larry D. "The Economics and Finance of Bilateral Clearing Agreements: Germany, 1934-8," *Economic History Review*, Second Series, 32(3), August 1979, pp. 391-404.

Neal, Larry D. and Klotz, Benjamin P. "Spectral and Cross-Spectral Analysis of the Long Swing Hypothesis," *Review of Economics and Statistics*, 55(3), August 1973, pp. 291-8.

Neal, Larry D. and Simon, Julian. "A Calculation of the Black Reparations Bill," *Review of Black Political Economy*, 4(2), Winter 1974, pp. 75-86.

Neal, Larry D. and Uselding, Paul J. "Immigration: A Neglected Source of American Economic Growth, 1790 to 1912," *Oxford Economic Papers*, New Series, 24(1), March 1972, pp. 68-88.

Neill, R.F. "The Nature and Measurement of Canada's Reliance on Primary Product Exports," Carleton University Economic Working Paper no. 79-15, July 1979.

Neisser, Hans. "Cyclical Experience in the Interwar Period: The Investment Boom of the Twenties (Comment on Gordon)," in Universities-National Bureau Committee for Economic Research (ed), *Conference on Business Cycles*, 1951, pp. 215-22.

Nelson, Ralph. *Merger Movements in American Industry* (National Bureau of Economic Research General Series 66). Princeton: Princeton University Press for the National Bureau of Economic Research, 1959.

Nerlove, Marc. "Railroads and American Economic Growth. Review Essay of 'Railroads and American Economic Growth: Essays in Econometric History' by Robert W. Fogel (Baltimore: Johns Hopkins University Press, 1964)," *Journal of Economic History*, 26(1), March 1966, pp. 107-15.

Nerlove, Mark. "A Historical Perspective on Economic Aspects of the Population Explosion: Comment on Lee," in Easterlin (ed), *Population and Economic Change in Developing Countries*, 1980, pp. 559-63.

Neuberger, Hugh M. *German Banks and German Economic Growth from Unification to World War I*. New York: Arno Press, 1977.

Neuberger, Hugh M. and Stokes, Houston H. "German Banking and Japanese Banking: A Comparative Analysis," *Journal of Economic History*, 35(1), March 1975, pp. 238-52.

Neuberger, Hugh M. and Stokes, Houston H. "German Banks and German

Growth: Reply to Fremdling and Tilly," *Journal of Economic History,* 36(2), June 1976, pp. 425-7.

Neuberger, Hugh M. and Stokes, Houston H. "German Banks and German Growth: Reply to Komlos," *Journal of Economic History,* 38(2), June 1978, pp. 480-2.

Neuberger, Hugh M. and Stokes, Houston H. "The Effect of Monetary Changes on the Interest Rates during the National Banking Period, 1875-1907: A Box-Jenkins Approach," presented at the Seminar on Economic History, Columbia University, May 1976.

Neuburger, Hugh M. and Stokes, Houston H. "German Banks and German Growth, 1883-1913: an Empirical View," *Journal of Economic History,* 34(3), September 1974, pp. 710-31.

Neuhaus, Paulo. "A Doutrina do Credito Legitimo e o Primeiro Banco Central Brasileiro," [The Real Bills Doctrine and the First Brazilian Central Bank] *Revista Brasileira de Mercado de Capitais,* 1(1), 1974.

Neuhaus, Paulo. *Historia Monetaria do Brasil, 1900-1945* [The Monetary History of Brazil, 1900-1945]. Rio de Janeiro: IBMEC, 1975.

Neuhaus, Paulo. "Trinta Anos de Historia Economica na Revista Brasileira de Economia," [Thirty Years of Economic History in the Revista Brasileira de Economia] *Revista Brasileira de Economia,* 31(4), October/December 1977, pp. 587-606.

Neuhaus, Paulo, ed. *A Economia Brasileira: Uma Visao Historica* [The Brazilian Economy: An Historical View]. Rio de Janeiro: Editora Campus, 1979.

Newell, William H. "The Agricultural Revolution in Nineteenth-Century France," *Journal of Economic History,* 33(4), December 1973, pp. 697-731.

Newell, William H. "The Agricultural Revolution in Nineteenth-Century France: Reply to Morineau," *Journal of Economic History,* 36(2), June 1976, pp. 438.

Newell, William H. *Population Change and Agricultural Development in Nineteenth Century France.* New York: Arno Press, 1977.

Nghiep, Le Thanh and Hayami, Yujiro. "Mobilizing Slack Resources for Economic Development: The Summer-Fall Reaping Technology of Sericulture in Japan," *Explorations in Economic History,* 16(2), April 1979, pp. 163-81.

Nicholas, Stephen J. "The American Export Invasion of Britain: The Case of the Engineering Industry, 1870-1914," *Technology and Culture,* 21(4), October 1980, pp. 570-88.

Nicholas, Stephen J. "Measurement of Productivity, Climacterics and Technical Change in the 1870-1939 British Economy," University of New South Wales Working Paper in Economic History, 1976.

Nicholas, Stephen J. "Technical Change, Returns to Scale and Imperfect Markets in the British Inter-War Economy," University of New South Wales Working Paper in Economic History, 1978.

Nicholas, Stephen J. "The Staple Theory of Economic Development: An Economic Criticism," University of New South Wales Working Paper in Economic History, 1976.

Nicholas, Stephen J. "The Theory and Measurement of Technological Change in the British Inter-War Economy, 1920-1938," University of New South Wales Working Paper in Economic History, 1977.

Nicholas, Stephen J. and Dziegielewski, M. "Supply Elasticities, Rationality and Structural Change in Irish Agriculture, 1850-1925:

Comment on O'Grada," *Economic History Review,* Second Series, 33(3), August 1980, pp. 411-4.

Nicholas, Stephen J. and Purcell, W. "Returns to Scale and Imperfect Markets in Australian Manufacturing 1908-1975," University of New South Wales Working Paper in Economic History, 1978.

Nickless, Pamela J. "Changing Labor Productivity and the Utilization of Native Women Workers in the American Cotton Textile Industry, 1825-1860," (Summary of Doctoral Dissertations) *Journal of Economic History,* 38(1), March 1978, pp. 287-8.

Nickless, Pamela J. "A New Look at Productivity in the New England Cotton Textile Industry, 1835-1860," *Journal of Economic History,* 39(4), December 1979, pp. 889-910.

Nickless, Pamela J. "The Work and Wages of Single Women, 1870 to 1920: A Discussion of Goldin," *Journal of Economic History,* 40(1), March 1980, pp. 96-7.

Nickless, Pamela J. "Learning-By-Doing Revisited: The Case of Cotton Textiles." [Working Paper]

Niemi, Albert W., Jr. "Some Aspects of the Relative Decline of the British Steel Industry, 1870-1913," *American Economist,* 13(2), Fall 1969, pp. 40-9.

Niemi, Albert W., Jr. "A Further Look at Interregional Canals and Economic Specialization: 1820-1840," *Explorations in Economic History,* 7(4), Summer 1970, pp. 499-520.

Niemi, Albert W., Jr. "The Development of Industrial Structure in Southern New England: A Note," *Journal of Economic History,* 30(3), September 1970, pp. 657-62.

Niemi, Albert W., Jr. "Structural Shifts in Southern Manufacturing, 1849-1899," *Business History Review,* 45(1), Spring 1971, pp. 79-84.

Niemi, Albert W., Jr. "The Role of Immigration in United States Commodity Production, 1869-1929," *Social Science Quarterly,* 52(1), June 1971, pp. 190-6.

Niemi, Albert W., Jr. "Structural and Labor Productivity Patterns in United States Manufacturing, 1849-1899," *Business History Review,* 46(1), Spring 1972, pp. 67-84.

Niemi, Albert W., Jr. "A Closer Look at Canals and Western Manufacturing in the Canal Era: A Reply to Ransom," *Explorations in Economic History,* 9(4), Summer 1972, pp. 423-4.

Niemi, Albert W., Jr. "Empirical Tests of the Heckscher-Ohlin Hypothesis for New England and Southern Manufacturing, 1860-1958," *Review of Regional Studies,* 4, (Supplement), 1974, pp. 87-94.

Niemi, Albert W., Jr. "Interregional Canals and Manufacturing Development in the West before 1840," *International Review of the History of Banking,* 9, 1974, pp. 192-212.

Niemi, Albert W., Jr. *State and Regional Patterns in American Manufacturing, 1860-1900.* Westport, Conn.: Greenwood Press, 1974.

Niemi, Albert W., Jr. *U.S. Economic History: A Survey of the Major Issues.* Chicago: Rand McNally, 1975.

Niemi, Albert W., Jr. "Inequality in the Distribution of Slave Wealth: The Cotton South and Other Southern Agricultural Regions," *Journal of Economic History,* 37(3), September 1977, pp. 747-54.

Nilsson, Carl-Axel and Hornby, Ove C. "The Transition from Sail to Steam in the Danish Merchant Fleet, 1865-1910," *Scandinavian Economic History Review,* 28(2), 1980, pp. 109-34.

Nishikawa, Shunsaku. "Productivity, Subsistence, and By-Employment in the Mid-Nineteenth Century Choshu," (Erratum: a correction for this article appears in vol. 15(3), July 1978, pp. 338 of this journal) *Explorations in Economic History,* 15(1), January 1978, pp. 69-83.

Nishimura, Shizuya. *The Decline of Inland Bills of Exchange in the London Money Market, 1855-1913.* Cambridge: Cambridge University Press, 1971.

Nishimura, Shizuya. "A Study of the International Gold Standard, 1870-1914." [Working Paper]

Nishimura, Shizuya; Wood, G.E. and Mills, T. "The Estimates of Bank Deposits in the U.K., 1870-1913." [Working Paper]

Noda, Tsutomu. "Commodity Prices and Wages, 1880-1965," in Ohkawa and Hayami (eds), *Economic Growth,* 1973, pp. 113-32.

Norrie, Kenneth H. "Agricultural Implement Tariffs, the National Policy, and Income Distribution in the Wheat Economy," *Canadian Journal of Economics,* 7(3), August 1974, pp. 449-62.

Norrie, Kenneth H. "The Rate of Settlement of the Canadian Prairies, 1870-1911," *Journal of Economic History,* 35(2), June 1975, pp. 410-27.

Norrie, Kenneth H. "Dry Farming and the Economics of Risk Bearing: The Canadian Prairies, 1870-1930," *Agricultural History,* 51(1), January 1977, pp. 134-48.

Norrie, Kenneth H. "The National Policy and Prairie Economic Discrimination in Canada, 1870-1930," *Canadian Papers in Rural History,* 1, 1978, pp. 13-32.

Norrie, Kenneth H. "The Rate of Settlement of the Canadian Prairies, 1870-1911: A Reply to Grant," *Journal of Economic History,* 38(2), June 1978, pp. 474-5.

Norrie, Kenneth H. "Cultivation Techniques as a Response to Risk in Early Canadian Prairie Agriculture," *Explorations in Economic History,* 17(4), October 1980, pp. 386-99.

Norrie, Kenneth H. "Canadian Pacific Railroad Land Sale: A Model of the Sale and Pricing of the Canadian Pacific Railroad Land Grant." [Working Paper]

North, Douglass C. "Location Theory and Regional Economic Growth," *Journal of Political Economy,* 63(3), June 1955, pp. 243-58.

North, Douglass C. "The Spatial and Interregional Framework of the United States Economy: An Historical Perspective," Carrothers (ed), *Papers and Proceedings of the Regional Science Association,* 1956, pp. 201-9.

North, Douglass C. "International Capital Flows and the Development of the American West," *Journal of Economic History,* 16(4), December 1956, pp. 493-505.

North, Douglass C. "A Note on Professor Rostow's Take-Off into Self-Sustained Growth," *Manchester School of Economic and Social Studies,* 26(1), January 1958, pp. 68-75.

North, Douglass C. "Ocean Freight Rates and Economic Development, 1750-1910," *Journal of Economic History,* 18(4), December 1958, pp. 537-55.

North, Douglass C. "Agriculture in Regional Economic Growth," reprinted in Coben and Hill (eds), *American Economic History,* 1966, pp. 258-67. *Journal of Farm Economics,* 41(5), December 1959, pp. 943-51.

North, Douglass C. "Canadian Balance of Payments Since 1868: Comment on Hartland," in Parker (ed), *Trends in the American Economy in the*

Nineteenth Century, 1960, pp. 754-5.

North, Douglass C. "The United States Balance of Payments, 1790-1860," in Parker (ed), *Trends in the American Economy in the Nineteenth Century*, 1960, pp. 573-627.

North, Douglass C. *The Economic Growth of the United States, 1790-1860*. Englewood Cliffs, N.J.: Prentice-Hall, 1961.

North, Douglass C. "The United States in the International Economy, 1790-1950," in Harris (ed), *American Economic History*, 1961, pp. 181-206.

North, Douglass C. "Early National Income Estimates of the U.S.," *Economic Development and Cultural Change*, 9(3), April 1961, pp. 387-96.

North, Douglass C. "International Capital Movements in Historical Perspective," in Mikesell (ed), *U.S. Private and Government Investment Abroad*, 1962.

North, Douglass C. "Industrialization in the United States (1815-60)," in Rostow (ed), *The Economics of Take-Off into Sustained Growth*, 1963, pp. 44-62.

North, Douglass C. "Quantitative Research in American Economic History," reprinted in Andreano (ed), *New Views*, 1965), pp. 9-12. *American Economic Review*, 53(1), (Part 1), March 1963, pp. 128-30.

North, Douglass C. "Douglass C. North on American Economic Growth: Comments on Stuart Bruchey's Paper," *Explorations in Entrepreneurial History*, Second Series, 1(2), Winter 1964, pp. 159-63.

North, Douglass C. "Capital Formation in the United States during the Early Period of Industrialization: A Reexamination of the Issues," *Second International Conference of Economic History, Aix-en-Provence, 1962, vol. 2*. Paris and The Hague: Mouton, 1965, pp. 643-56.

North, Douglass C. "Industrialization in the United States," in Habakkuk and Postan (eds), *The Cambridge Economic History of Europe*, 1965, pp. 673-705.

North, Douglass C. "The State of Economic History," *American Economic Review*, Papers and Proceedings, 55(2), May 1965, pp. 86-91.

North, Douglass C. *Growth and Welfare in the American Past: A New Economic History* (Second Edition Printed in 1974). Englewood Cliffs, N.J.: Prentice-Hall, 1966.

North, Douglass C. "A New Economic History for Europe," in Giersch (ed), *Festschrift in Honor of Walther Hoffmann*, 1968, pp. 139-47.

North, Douglass C. "Economic History," in Sills (ed), *International Encyclopedia of the Social Sciences*, 1968, pp. 468-74.

North, Douglass C. "Sources of Productivity Change in Ocean Shipping, 1600-1850," reprinted in Fogel and Engerman (eds), *The Reinterpretation of American Economic History*, 1971, pp. 163-74. *Journal of Political Economy*, 76(5), September/October 1968, pp. 953-70.

North, Douglass C. "Institutional Change and Economic Growth," *Journal of Economic History*, 31(1), March 1971, pp. 118-25.

North, Douglass C. "Government and the American Economy," in Davis, Easterlin, and Parker (eds), *American Economic Growth*. New York: Harper & Row, 1972, pp. 636-64.

North, Douglass C. "Innovation and the Diffusion of Technology (a Theoretical Framework)," *Fourth International Conference of*

Economic History, Bloomington, 1968. Paris and The Hague: Mouton, 1973, pp. 221-31.

North, Douglass C. "Beyond the New Economic History," *Journal of Economic History,* 34(1), March 1974, pp. 1-7.

North, Douglass C. "The Achievements of Economic History: Comments on Papers by McCloskey, Cohen, and Forster," *Journal of Economic History,* 38(1), March 1978, pp. 77-80.

North, Douglass C. "The Role of Transportation in the Economic Development of North America." [Working Paper]

North, Douglass C.; Caves, Richard E. and Price, Jacob M. "Introduction: Exports and Economic Growth," *Explorations in Economic History,* 17(1), January 1980, pp. 1-5.

North, Douglass C. and Davis, Lance E. *Institutional Change and American Economic Growth.* Cambridge: Cambridge University Press, 1971.

North, Douglass C. and Hartwell, R.M. "Law, Property Rights, Legal Institutions, and the Performance of Economies," in Flinn (ed), *Proceedings of the Seventh International Economic History Congress, Edinburgh,* 1978.

North, Douglass C. and Heston, Alan. "The Estimation of Shipping Earnings in Historical Studies of the Balance of Payments," *Canadian Journal of Economics and Political Science,* 26(2), May 1960, pp. 265-76.

North, Douglass C. and Thomas, Robert P. *A Documentary History of American Economic Growth, 1607-1860.* New York: Harper & Row, 1968.

North, Douglass C. and Thomas, Robert P. "An Economic Theory of the Growth of the Western World," *Economic History Review,* Second Series, 23(1), April 1970, pp. 1-17.

North, Douglass C. and Thomas, Robert P. "The Rise and Fall of the Manorial System: A Theoretical Model," *Journal of Economic History,* 31(4), December 1971, pp. 777-803.

North, Douglass C. and Thomas, Robert P. "European Economic Growth: Reply to Professor D. Ringose," *Economic History Review,* Second Series, 26(2), May 1973, pp. 293-4.

North, Douglass C. and Thomas, Robert P. *The Rise of the Western World: A New Economic History* [Translated into Italian, Spanish, and French]. Cambridge: Cambridge University Press, 1975.

North, Douglass C. and Thomas, Robert P. "The Role of Governments in Economic Growth in Early Modern Times: Comment on Lane," *Journal of Economic History,* 35(1), March 1975, pp. 18-9.

North, Douglass C. and Thomas, Robert P. "The First Economic Revolution," *Economic History Review,* Second Series, 30(2), May 1977, pp. 229-41.

Novak, David E. and Perlman, Richard. "The Structure of Wages in the American Iron and Steel Industry, 1860-1890," *Journal of Economic History,* 22(3), September 1962, pp. 334-47.

Novak, David E. and Simon, Matthew. "Some Dimensions of the American Commercial Invasion of Europe, 1871-1914: An Introductory Essay," *Journal of Economic History,* 24(4), December 1964, pp. 591-605.

Nugent, Jeffrey B. "Exchange-Rate Movements and Economic Development in the Late Nineteenth Century," *Journal of Political Economy,* 81(5), September/October 1973, pp. 1110-35.

Nutter, G. Warren; Boronstein, Israel and Kaufman, Adam. *Growth of Industrial Production in the Soviet Union* (General Series 45).

Princeton: Princeton University Press for the National Bureau of Economic Research, 1962.

Nwani, Okonkwo A. "The Quantity Theory in the Early Monetary System of West Africa with Particular Emphasis on Nigeria, 1850-1895," *Journal of Political Economy,* 83(1), February 1975, pp. 185-94.

Nye, William W. *The Old Lady Shows Her Metals: The British Money Market in the 1860's.*

O'Brien, Patrick K. "British Incomes and Property in the Early Nineteenth Century," *Economic History Review,* Second Series, 12(2), 1959, pp. 255-67.

O'Brien, Patrick K. "Turning Points in the Economic History of Egypt," in Sinor (ed), *Proceedings of the 27th World Congress of Orientalists,* 1967.

O'Brien, Patrick K. "The Long-Term Growth of Agricultural Production in Egypt, 1821-1962," in Holt (ed), *Political and Social Change in Modern Egypt,* 1968.

O'Brien, Patrick K. "Structural Changes in the Egyptian Economy, 1937-1965," in Cook (ed), *Studies in the Economic History of the Middle East from the Rise of Islam to the Present Day,* 1970.

O'Brien, Patrick K. *The New Economic History of Railways: A Critique.* London: Croom Helm, 1977.

O'Brien, Patrick K. "Agriculture and the Industrial Revolution: An Essay in Bibliography and Criticism," *Economic History Review,* Second Series, 30(1), February 1977, pp. 166-81.

O'Brien, Patrick K. "Economic Growth in Britain and France from the End of the 17th Century to Present Day," in Bedarida, Crouzet, and Johnson, (eds), *Dix siecles d'histoire Franco-britannique De Guillaume le conquerant au Marche commun,* 1979.

O'Brien, Patrick K. "British Public Finances in the Wars against France, 1793-1815," Ph.D. Dissertation, Oxford University, 1966.

O'Brien, Patrick K. "Productivity in the Economies of Europe, 1780-1914." [Working Paper]

O'Brien, Patrick K. "Russian Backwardness in European Perspective." [Working Paper]

O'Brien, Patrick K. "The Intersectoral Terms of Trade in European Industrialization, 1660-1820." [Working Paper]

O'Brien, Patrick K. "Theories of Economic Change for Historians." [Working Paper]

O'Brien, Patrick K. and Engerman, Stanley L. "Changes in Income and Its Distribution during the Industrial Revolution," in Floud and McCloskey (eds), *The Economic History of Britain since 1700,* 1981, pp. 164-81.

O'Brien, Patrick K.; Heath, D. and Keyder, Caglar. "Agriculture in Britain and France, 1815-1914," *Journal of European Economic History,* 6(2), Fall 1977, pp. 339-91.

O'Brien, Patrick K. and Keyder, Caglar. *Economic Growth in Britain and France, 1780-1914: Two Paths to the Twentieth Century.* London: Allen & Unwin, 1978.

O'Brien, Patrick K. and Keyder, Caglar. "Niveles de vida en Gran Bretana y Francia entre 1780 y 1914," [The Standard of Living in

Britain and France, 1780-1914] *Investigaciones Economicas,* 6, August 1978, pp. 5-41.

O'Brien, Patrick and Mathias, Peter. "Taxation in Britain and France, 1715-1810: A Comparison of the Social and Economic Incidence of Taxes Collected for the Central Governments," *Journal of European Economic History,* 5(3), Winter 1976, pp. 601-50.

O'Brien, Patrick K. and Mathias, Peter. "The Incidence of Taxes and the Burden of Proof: Reply to McCloskey," *Journal of European Economic History,* 7(1), Spring 1978, pp. 211-3.

O'Grada, Cormac. "Supply Responsiveness in Irish Agriculture during the Nineteenth Century," *Economic History Review,* Second Series, 28(2), May 1975, pp. 312-7.

O'Grada, Cormac. "The Beginnings of the Irish Creamery System, 1880-1914," *Economic History Review,* Second Series, 30(2), May 1977, pp. 284-305.

O'Grada, Cormac. "The Landlord and Agricultural Transformation, 1870-1900: A Comment on Richard Perren's Hypothesis," *Agricultural History Review,* 27(1), 1979, pp. 40-2.

O'Grada, Cormac. "Agricultural Decline, 1860-1914," in Floud and McCloskey (eds), *The Economic History of Britain since 1700,* 1981.

O'Grada, Cormac. "Supply Elasticities in Irish Agriculture: A Reply to Nicholas and Dziegielewski," *Economic History Review,* Second Series, 33(3), August 1980, pp. 415-6.

O'Grada, Cormac. "Demographic Adjustment and Seasonal Migration in Nineteenth-Century Ireland," in Cullen and Furet (eds), *Ireland and France in the 17th-20th Centuries,* 1981, pp. 181-93.

O'Grada, Cormac. "Productivity Growth in Irish Agriculture, 1845-1926." [Working Paper]

O'Grada, Cormac and Edelstein, Michael. "Property Rights and History: A Report of the Meetings of the Economic History Association," *Journal of European Economic History,* 2(2), Fall 1973, pp. 439-46.

O'Hara, Maureen and Easley, David. "The Postal Savings System in the Depression," *Journal of Economic History,* 39(3), September 1979, pp. 741-53.

O'Leary, Paul M. "The Scene of the Crime of 1873 Revisited: A Note," *Journal of Political Economy,* 68(4), August 1960, pp. 388-92.

Oates, Mary J. "The Role of the Cotton Textile Industry in the Economic Development of the American Southeast: 1900-1940," (Summary of Doctoral Dissertation) *Journal of Economic History,* 31(1), March 1971, pp. 281-4.

Oden, Birgitta. "Historical Statistics in the Nordic Countries," in Lorwin and Price (eds), *The Dimensions of the Past,* 1972, pp. 263-99.

Offer, Avner. "Ricardo's Paradox and the Movement of Rent, c. 1870-1910," *Economic History Review,* Second Series, 33(2), May 1980, pp. 236-52.

Officer, Lawrence H. and Smith, Lawrence B. "The Canadian-American Reciprocity Treaty of 1855 to 1866," *Journal of Economic History,* 28(4), December 1968, pp. 598-623.

Officer, Lawrence H. and Smith, Lawrence B. "Canadian-American Reciprocity: A Reply (to Ankli)," *Journal of Economic History,* 30(2), June 1970, pp. 432-4.

Ohkawa, Kazushi. "National Product and Expenditure, 1885-1969," in Ohkawa and Hayami (eds), *Economic Growth,* 1973, pp. 133-53.

Ohkawa, Kazushi and Hayami, Yujiro, eds. *Economic Growth: The Japanese Experience since the Meiji Era (2 vols)*. Tokyo: Japan Economic Research Center, 1973.

Ohkawa, Kazushi and Rosovsky, Henry. *Japanese Economic Growth: Trend Acceleration in the Twentieth Century* [Japanese Edition Appears in Japanese]. Stanford and Tokyo: Stanford University Press and Toyo Keizai Shimpo-Sha, 1973.

Ohkawa, Kazushi and Shinohara, Miyohei, eds. *The Growth Rate of the Japanese Economy since 1878*. Tokyo: Kinokuniya, 1957.

Ohkawa, Kazushi; Shinohara, Miyohei and Umemura, Mataji, eds. *Estimates of Long Term Economic Statistics of Japan since 1868*. Tokyo: Toyo Keizai Shinpo Sha, 1965.

Ohkura, Takehiko and Shimbo, Hiroshi. "The Tokugawa Monetary Policy in the Eighteenth and Nineteenth Centuries," *Explorations in Economic History*, 15(1), January 1978, pp. 101-24.

Ohlin, G. "No Safety in Numbers: Some Pitfalls of Historical Statistics," in Floud (ed), *Essays in Quantitative Economic History*, 1974, pp. 59-78.

Ohlsson, Rolf. *Invandrarna pa Arbetsmarknadan* [Immigrants on the Labour Market] [Contains an English Summary]. Lund: University of Lund Press, 1975.

Ohlsson, Rolf. *Ekonomisk Strukturforendring och Invendring* [Economic Structural Change and Immigration] [Contains an English Summary]. Lund: University of Lund Press, 1978.

Ohlsson, Rolf and Bengtsson, Tommy. "Population and Economic Fluctuations in Sweden, 1749-1914: Spectral Analysis on National Data." [Working Paper]

Oksanen, Ernest H. and George, Peter J. "Recent Methodological Developments in the Quantification of Economic History," *Histoire Sociale/Social History*, 2(3), April 1969, pp. 5-31.

Oksanen, Ernest H. and George, Peter J. "Recent Developments in the Quantification of Canadian Economic History," *Histoire Sociale/Social History*, 2(4), November 1969, pp. 76-95.

Oksanen, Ernest H. and George, Peter J. "Saturation in the Automobile Market in the Late Twenties: Some Further Results," *Explorations in Economic History*, 11(1), Fall 1973, pp. 73-86.

Oksanen, Ernest H. and George, Peter J. "An Index of Aggregate Economic Activity in Canada, 1896-1939: A Factor Analytic Approach," reprinted in Flinn (ed), *Proceedings of the Seventh International Economic History Congress*, 1978, pp. 87-95. *Explorations in Economic History*, 17(2), April 1980, pp. 165-75.

Olmstead, Alan L. "New York City Mutual Savings Banks in the Antebellum Years," (Summary of Doctoral Dissertation) *Journal of Economic History*, 31(1), March 1971, pp. 272-5.

Olmstead, Alan L. "Investment Constraints and New York City Mutual Savings Bank Financing of Antebellum Development," *Journal of Economic History*, 32(4), December 1972, pp. 811-40.

Olmstead, Alan L. "Davis vs. Bigelow Revisited: Antebellum American Interest Rates," *Journal of Economic History*, 34(2), June 1974, pp. 483-91.

Olmstead, Alan L. "New York City Mutual Savings Bank Portfolio Management and Trustee Objectives," *Journal of Economic History*, 34(4), December 1974, pp. 815-34.

Olmstead, Alan L. "Mutual Savings Bank Depositors in New York,"

Business History Review, 49(3), Autumn 1975, pp. 287-311.

Olmstead, Alan L. and Goldberg, Victor P. "Institutional Change and American Economic Growth: A Critique of Davis and North," *Explorations in Economic History,* 12(2), April 1975, pp. 193-210.

Olmstead, Alan L. "The Mechanization of Reaping and Mowing in American Agriculture, 1833-1870," *Journal of Economic History,* 35(2), June 1975, pp. 327-52.

Olmstead, Alan L. *New York City Mutual Savings Banks, 1819-1861.* Chapel Hill: University of North Carolina Press, 1976.

Olmstead, Alan L. "The Civil War as a Catalyst of Technological Change in Agriculture," Uselding (ed), *Business and Economic History,* 1976, pp. 36-50.

Olmstead, Alan L. "The Diffusion of the Reaper: One More Time! (Reply to Jones)," *Journal of Economic History,* 39(2), June 1979, pp. 475-6.

Olmstead, Alan L. "The Cost of Economic Growth," in Porter (ed), *Encyclopedia of American Economic History,* 1980, pp. 863-81.

Olmstead, Alan L. "Discussion of Dissertations Presented at the 39th Annual Meeting of the Economic History Association," *Journal of Economic History,* 40(1), March 1980, pp. 183-6.

Olmstead, Alan L. "The Civil War, Farm Mechanization, and the Agricultural Machinery Industry." [Working Paper]

Olmstead, Alan L. and Ankli, Robert E. "The Adoption of the Reaper: The State of the Debate." [Working Paper]

Olmstead, Alan L. and Judd, John. "Saved from Sociology: The Frugal Scot and His Banking System." [Working Paper]

Olmstead, Alan L. and Smolensky, Eugene. *The Urbanization of the United States.* Morristown, N.J.: General Learning, 1973.

Olsen, Bernard M. "Measurement of 18th and 19th century agricultural productivity in Sweden." [Working Paper]

Olson, John F. and Fogel, Robert W. "Clock-Time vs. Real-Time: A Comparison of the Lengths of the Northern and the Southern Agricultural Work-Years." [Working Paper]

Olson, John F. "The Occupational Structure and Characteristics of Skilled Slave Labor in the Late Antebellum Plantation Economy," Ph.D. Dissertation, University of Rochester.

Olson, Mancur L. *The Economics of the Wartime Shortage: A History of British Food Shortages in the Napoleonic War and World Wars I and II.* Durham: Duke University Press, 1963.

Olson, Mancur L. "The Economic Growth of the Chesapeake and the European Market, 1697-1775: Discussion of Price," *Journal of Economic History,* 24(4), December 1964, pp. 512-6.

Olson, Mancur L. "The United Kingdom and the World Market in Wheat, 1870-1914," *Explorations in Economic History,* 11(4), Summer 1974, pp. 325-55.

Olson, Mancur L. "The Causes and Quality of Southern Growth," in Liner and Lynch (eds), *The Economics of Southern Growth,* 1977, pp. 107-30.

Olson, Mancur L. "Reports of 'Shortages of Money' in Medieval Europe." [Working Paper]

Olson, Mancur L. "Some Historic Variations in Property Institutions." [Working Paper]

Olson, Mancur L. and Harris, Curtis C., Jr. "Free Trade in 'Corn': A Statistical Study of the Prices and Production of Wheat in Great

Britain from 1873 to 1914," reprinted in Floud (ed), *Essays in Quantitative Economic History*, 1974, pp. 196-215. *Quarterly Journal of Economics*, 73(1), February 1959, pp. 145-69.

Olson, Mancur L. and Lansberg, Hans. *The No Growth Society* (Also, Published as the Fall 1973 Issue of Daedalus, in Japanese Translation (Tokyo, 1974), and in a Separate British Edition (Woborn Press, 1975)). New York: W.W. Norton, 1974.

Olsson, Carl-Axel. "Swedish Agriculture during the Interwar Years," *Economy and History*, 11, 1968, pp. 67-107.

Olsson, Carl-Axel. "Estimates of the Aggregate Swedish Farm Supply Function, 1935-1950: Some Preliminary Results," *Economy and History*, 17, 1974, pp. 3-19.

Olsson, Carl-Axel. *Om Jordbrukssektorns Ekonomi Med Sarskild Hansyn Till Sverige Under Det Andra Varldskriget*. Lund: University of Lund Press, 1974.

Ono, Akira and Fujino, Shiro. "Textile Industry, 1890-1945," in Ohkawa and Hayami (eds), *Economic Growth*, 1973, pp. 154-64.

Orsagh, Thomas J. and Mooney, Peter J. "A Model for the Dispersion of the Migrant Labor Force and Some Results for the United States, 1880-1920," *Review of Economics and Statistics*, 52(3), August 1970, pp. 306-12.

Overton, Mark. "Estimating Crop Yields from Probate Inventories: An Example from East Anglia, 1585-1735," *Journal of Economic History*, 39(2), June 1979, pp. 363-78.

Page, Walter P. "A Study of the Fixed Coefficients Model of Production for Agriculture in a Selected Region of the Great Plains, 1899-1903: Some Tentative Results," *Mississippi Valley Journal of Business and Statistics*, 5(1), Fall 1969, pp. 34-42.

Paquet, Gilles. "L'emigration des Canadiens francais vers la Nouvelle-Angleterre, 1870-1910: prises de vue quantitatives," *Recherches Sociographiques*, 5(3), September/December 1964, pp. 319-70.

Paquet, Gilles. "La demographie historique au Canada," *Recherches Sociographiques*, 8(2), 1967, pp. 214-7.

Paquet, Gilles and Faucher, Albert. "L'experience economique du Quebec et la Confederation," *Journal of Canadian Studies*, 1, November 1966, pp. 16-30.

Paquet, Gilles and Wallot, Jean-Pierre. "Apercu sur le commerce international et les prix domestique dans le Bas Canada, 1793-1812," *Revue d'Histoire de l'Amerique Francaise*, 21(3), December 1967, pp. 447-73.

Paquet, Gilles and Wallot, Jean-Pierre. "Canada, 1760-1850: anamorphoses et prospective," *Cahiers de l'Universite de Quebec*, 1-2, September 1969, pp. 255-300.

Paquet, Gilles and Wallot, Jean-Pierre. "Le Bas Canada au debut du XIXe siecle: une hypothese," *Revue d'Histoire de l'Amerique Francaise*, 25(1), June 1971, pp. 39-61.

Paquet, Gilles and Wallot, Jean-Pierre. "Crise agricole et tensions socio-techniques dans le Bas Canada au tournant du XIXe siecle," *Revue d'Histoire de l'Amerique Francaise*, 26(2), September 1972,

pp. 185-237.

Paquet, Gilles and Wallot, Jean-Pierre. "International Circumstances of Lower Canada, 1786-1810: Prolegomena," *Canadian Historical Review*, 53(4), December 1972, pp. 371-401.

Paquet, Gilles and Wallot, Jean-Pierre. "The Agricultural Crisis in Lower Canada, 1802-1812: mise au point," *Canadian Historical Review*, 56(2), June 1975, pp. 133-61.

Paquet, Gilles and Wallot, Jean-Pierre. "Rentes foncieres, dimes et revenus paysans: le cas canadien," in Ladurie and Goy (eds), *Prestations paysannes*.

Paradisi, Mariangela. "Il commercio estero e la struttura industriale," [Foreign Trade and Industrial Structure] in Ciocca and Toniolo (eds), *L'economia italiana nel periodo fascista* [The Italian Economy during the Fascist Era]. Bologna: il Mulino, 1976, pp. 271-328.

Parker, William N. "Entrepreneurship, Industrial Organization, and Economic Growth: A German Example," *Journal of Economic History*, 14(4), December 1954, pp. 380-400.

Parker, William N. "Coal and Steel Output Movements in Western Europe, 1880-1956," *Explorations in Entrepreneurial History*, 9(4), April 1957, pp. 213-30.

Parker, William N. "Nation States and National Development: French and German Ore Mining in the Late Nineteenth Century," Aitken (ed), *The State and Economic Growth*, 1959, pp. 201-12.

Parker, William N., ed. *Trends in the American Economy in the Nineteenth Century* (Studies in Income and Wealth, vol. 24). Princeton: Princeton University Press for the National Bureau of Economic Research, 1960.

Parker, William N. "Economic Development in Historical Perspective," *Economic Development and Cultural Change*, 10(1), October 1961, pp. 1-7.

Parker, William N. *Commerce, Cotton, and Westward Expansion, 1820-1860*. Chicago: Scott, Foresman, 1964.

Parker, William N. "The International Market for Agricultural Commodities, 1850-1873: Comment on Rothstein," in Gilchrist and Lewis (eds), *Economic Change in the Civil War Era*, 1965, pp. 73-6.

Parker, William N. "Economic History and National Accounts. Review Essay of 'Modern Economic Growth: Rate, Structure, and Spread' by Simon S. Kuznets (New Haven and London: Yale University Press, 1966)," *Review of Income and Wealth*, 13(2), June 1967, pp. 199-204.

Parker, William N. "Sources of Agricultural Productivity in the Nineteenth Century," *Journal of Farm Economics*, 49(5), December 1967, pp. 1455-68.

Parker, William N. "American Economic Growth: Its Historiography in the Twentieth Century," *Ventures*, 8(2), Fall 1968, pp. 71-82.

Parker, William N. "Measurement of Productivity in American Agriculture, 1840-1910," *Third International Conference of Economic History, Munich, 1965, part 3*. Paris and The Hague: Mouton, 1969, pp. 37-43.

Parker, William N. "The Slave Plantation in American Agriculture," in Coats and Robertson (eds), *Essays in American Economic History*, 1969.

Parker, William N., ed. *The Structure of the Cotton Economy of the Antebellum South* (Originally Published as an Issue of *Agricultural*

History, 44(1), January 1970). Washington, D.C.: Agricultural History Society, 1970.

Parker, William N. "Slavery and Southern Economic Development: An Hypothesis and Some Evidence," reprinted in Parker (ed), *The Structure of the Cotton Economy of the Antebellum South*, 1970. *Agricultural History*, 44(1), January 1970, pp. 115-25.

Parker, William N. "Problemi e prospettive di storia americana: l'agricoltura negli Stati Uniti del Nord," [Problems and Perspectives of American History: Agriculture in the Northern United States] *Quaderni Storici*, 14, August 1970, pp. 393-415.

Parker, William N. "Productivity Growth in American Grain Farming: An Analysis of Its 19th Century Sources," in Fogel and Engerman (eds), *The Reinterpretation of American Economic History*, 1971, pp. 175-86.

Parker, William N. "From Old to New to Old in Economic History," *Journal of Economic History*, 31(1), March 1971, pp. 3-14.

Parker, William N. "Agriculture," in Davis, Easterlin, and Parker (eds), *American Economic Growth*, 1972, pp. 369-417.

Parker, William N. "Technology, Resources and Economic Change in the West," in Youngson (ed), *Economic Development in the Long Run*, 1972, pp. 62-78.

Parker, William N. "The Land, Minerals, Water, and Forests," in Davis, Easterlin, and Parker (eds), *American Economic Growth*, 1972, pp. 93-120.

Parker, William N. "On a Certain Parallelism in Form between Two Historical Processes of Productivity Growth," *Agricultural History*, 50(1), January 1976, pp. 101-16.

Parker, William N. "Labor Productivity in Cotton Farming: The History of a Research," *Agricultural History*, 53(1), January 1979, pp. 228-44.

Parker, William N. "Comment on Papers by McAlpin, Libecap and Johnson, and Adelman and Morris Presented to the 38th Annual Meeting of the Economic History Association," *Journal of Economic History*, 39(1), March 1979, pp. 177-9.

Parker, William N. "Historiography of American Economic History," in Porter (ed), *Encyclopedia of American Economic History*, 1980, pp. 3-16.

Parker, William N.; Davis, Lance E. and Easterlin, Richard A., eds. *American Economic Growth: An Economist's History of the United States*. New York: Harper & Row, 1972.

Parker, William N. and DeCanio, Stephen. "Agricultural Output and Productivity," (Summary of 1976 Research Workshop) *Journal of Economic History*, 37(1), March 1977, pp. 230-1.

Parker, William N. and DeCanio, Stephen J. "Two Hidden Sources of Productivity Growth in American Agriculture, 1860-1930," presented at the International Economic History Congress, Edinburgh, August 1978.

Parker, William N. and Jones, Eric L., eds. *European Peasants and Their Markets: Essays in European Agrarian History*. Princeton: Princeton University Press, 1975.

Parker, William N. and Klein, Judith L.V. "Productivity Growth in Grain Production in the United States, 1840-60 and 1900-10," in Brady (ed), *Output, Employment, and Productivity in the United States after 1800*, 1966, pp. 523-80.

Parker, William N. and Pounds, J.G. *Coal and Steel in Western Europe.*
Bloomington: Indiana University Press, 1957.

Parker, William N.; Strassman, W. Paul; Wilkening, E.A. and Merrill,
Robert S. *The Diffusion of Technical Knowledge as an Instrument of
Economic Development* (Symposia Studies Series no. 13). National
Institute of Social and Behavioral Science, 1962.

Parker, William N. and Whartenby, Franklee. "The Growth of Output
Before 1840," in Parker (ed), *Trends in the American Economy in the
Nineteenth Century*, 1960, pp. 191-212.

Parks, Richard W. "Price Responsiveness of Factor Utilization in
Swedish Manufacturing, 1870-1950," *Review of Economics and
Statistics,* 53(2), May 1971, pp. 129-39.

Paskoff, Paul F. "Labor Productivity and Managerial Efficiency against
a Static Technology: The Pennsylvania Iron Industry, 1750-1800,"
Journal of Economic History, 40(1), March 1980, pp. 129-35.

Passell, Peter. "The Impact of Cotton Land Distribution on the
Antebellum Economy," *Journal of Economic History,* 31(4), December
1971, pp. 917-37.

Passell, Peter. *Essays in the Economics of 19th Century Land Policy.*
New York: Arno Press, 1975.

Passell, Peter and Lee, Susan P. *A New Economic View of American
History.* New York: W.W. Norton, 1979.

Passell, Peter and Schmundt, Maria. "Pre-Civil War Policy and the
Growth of Manufacturing," *Explorations in Economic History,* 9(1),
Fall 1971, pp. 35-48.

Passell, Peter and Wright, Gavin. "The Effects of Pre-Civil War
Territorial Expansion on the Price of Slaves," *Journal of Political
Economy,* 80(6), November/December 1972, pp. 1188-202.

Patel, Surendra J. "Rates of Industrial Growth in the Last Century,
1860-1958," *Economic Development and Cultural Change,* 9(3), April
1961, pp. 316-30.

Paterson, Donald G. "The Failure of British Business in Canada,
1890-1914," in Krooss (ed), *Proceedings of the Business History
Conference*, 1975, pp. 14-31.

Paterson, Donald G. *British Direct Investment in Canada, 1890-1914:
Estimates and Determinants.* Toronto and Buffalo: University of
Toronto Press, 1976.

Paterson, Donald G. "The North Pacific Seal Hunt, 1886-1910: Rights
and Regulations," *Explorations in Economic History,* 14(2), April
1977, pp. 97-119.

Paterson, Donald G.; Blain, L. and Rae, J.D. "The Regional Impact of
Economic Fluctuations during the Inter-War Period: The Case of
British Columbia," *Canadian Journal of Economics,* 7(3), August
1974, pp. 381-401.

Paterson, Donald G. and Cain, Louis P. "Factor Biases and Technical
Change in Manufacturing: The American System, 1850-1919." [Working
Paper]

Paterson, Donald G. and Wilen, J. "Depletion and Diplomacy: The North
Pacific Seal Hunt, 1886-1910," in Uselding (ed), *Research in
Economic History,* 1977, pp. 81-139.

Patrick, Hugh T. "External Equilibrium and Internal Convertibility:
Financial Policy in Meiji Japan," *Journal of Economic History,*
25(2), June 1965, pp. 187-213.

Patrick, Hugh T. "Japan, 1868-1914," in Cameron et al (ed), *Banking in*

   the Early Stages of Industrialization, 1967, pp. 239-89.
Patrick, Hugh T. "The Government Sector in Japan's Development and Growth: Comment," in Ohkawa and Hayami (eds), *Economic Growth,* 1973, pp. 389-96.
Patrick, Hugh T. *Japanese Industrialization and Its Social Consequences.* Berkeley and Los Angeles: University of California Press, 1976.
Patrick, Hugh T. "A Dynamic Model of Japanese Economic Development, 1887-1915: A Review Article," *Journal of Asian Studies,* 35(3), May 1976, pp. 475-82.
Patrick, Hugh T.; Cameron, Rondo E.; Crisp, Olga and Tilly, Richard. *Banking in the Early Stages of Industrialization: A Study in Comparative Economic History.* London and New York: Oxford University Press, 1967.
Patterson, C.C. "Silver Stocks and Losses in Ancient and Medieval Times," *Economic History Review,* Second Series, 25(2), May 1972, pp. 205-35.
Pavese, Claudio; Toninelli, Pier Angelo and Violante, Sante. *Fiscalita e finanza pubblica in Italia (1861-1913)* [Taxation and Public Budgets in Italy, 1861-1913]. Milano: Unicopli Universitaria, 1979.
Payne, Peter L. and Davis, Lance E. "From Benevolence to Business: The Story of Two Savings Banks," reprinted in Hughes (ed), *Purdue Faculty Papers in Economic History,* 1967, pp. 643-62. *Business History Review,* 32(4), Winter 1958, pp. 386-406.
Peet, Richard. "Von Thunen Theory and the Dynamics of Agricultural Expansion," *Explorations in Economic History,* 8(2), Winter 1970/71, pp. 181-202.
Peklar, Conrad. "Wealth in Colonial Connecticut, 1650-1760," Ohio University Economic History Research Paper no. G-10.
Pelaez, Carlos M. "As Consequencias Economicas da Ortodoxia Monetaria, Cambial e Fiscal no Brasil entre 1889 e 1945," [The Economic Consequences of Monetary, Exchange and Fiscal Orthodoxy in Brasil, 1889-1945] *Revista Brasileira de Economia,* 25(3), July/September 1971, pp. 5-82.
Pelaez, Carlos M. "Analise Economica do Programa Brasileiro de Sustentacao do Cafe, 1906-1945: Teoria, Politica e Medicao," [An Economic Analysis of the Brazilian Coffee Support Program, 1906-1945: Theory, Policy and Measurement] *Revista Brasileira de Economia,* 25(4), October/December 1971, pp. 5-212.
Pelaez, Carlos M. "An Economic Analysis of the Brazilian Coffee Support Program, 1906-1945," in Pelaez (ed), *Essays on Coffee and Economic Development,* 1973, pp. 181-249.
Pelaez, Carlos M. "A Comparison of Long-Term Monetary Behaviour and Institutions in Brazil, Europe, and the United States," *Journal of European Economic History,* 5(2), Fall 1976, pp. 439-50.
Pelaez, Carlos M. "World War I and the Economy of Brazil: Some Evidence from Monetary Statistics," *Journal of Interdisciplinary History,* 7(4), Spring 1977, pp. 683-9.
Pelaez, Carlos M. "Unbalance in Demand and Supply, and Input-Provision Capital Formation: Brazil, 1920-1951," (Summary of Doctoral Dissertation) *Journal of Economic History,* 25(4), December 1965, pp. 700-3.
Pelaez, Carlos M. "The Theory and Reality of Imperialism in the Coffee

Economy of Nineteenth-Century Brazil," *Economic History Review*,
Second Series, 29(2), May 1976, pp. 276-90.

Pelaez, Carlos M. and Suzigan, Wilson. *Historia Monetaria do Brasil:
Analise da Politica, Comportamento e Instituicoes Monetarias*
[Monetary History of Brasil: Analysis of Policy Behavior and
Monetary Institutions] (IPEA Serie Monografica no. 23). Rio de
Janeiro: Instituto de Planejamento Economico e Social, 1976.

Pelaez, Carlos M. and Suzigan, Wilson. "Comportamento e Instituicoes
Monetarias no Brasil, 1852-1972," [Monetary Institutions and their
Behavior in Brazil, 1852-1872] in Neuhaus (ed), *A Economia
Brasileira*, 1979, pp. 161-90.

Pelaez, Carlos M. and Suzigan, Wilson. *Historia Economica do Brasil*
[Economic History of Brazil]. Sao Paulo: Editora Atlas, 1979.

Pencavel, John H. and Ashenfelter, Orley. "American Trade Union
Growth: 1900-1960," *Quarterly Journal of Economics*, 83(3), August
1964, pp. 434-48.

Peppers, Larry. "Full-Employment Surplus Analysis and Structural
Change: The 1930's," *Explorations in Economic History*, 10(2),
Winter 1973, pp. 197-210.

Percy, Michael B. "The Impact of American Immigration Legislation of
the 1920's on the Rate of Canadian Emigration to the United
States." [Working Paper]

Percy, Michael B. and Bertram, Gordon W. "Real Wage Trends in Canada,
1900-1926: Some Provisional Estimates," *Canadian Journal of
Economics*, 12(2), May 1979, pp. 299-312.

Percy, Michael B. and Marr, William L. "The Government and the Rate of
Canadian Prairie Settlement (Comment on Norrie)," *Canadian Journal
of Economics*, 11(4), November 1978, pp. 757-67.

Perkins, Dwight H. *Agricultural Development in China, 1368-1968*.
Chicago: Aldine Press, 1969.

Perkins, Dwight H. "The Economic Performance of China and Japan,
1842-1970," H.I.E.R. Paper no. 177.

Perkins, Edwin J. "The Emergence of a Futures Market for Foreign
Exchange in the United States," *Explorations in Economic History*,
11(3), Spring 1974, pp. 193-212.

Perkins, Edwin J. "Foreign Interest Rates in American Financial
Markets: A Revised Series of Dollar-Sterling Exchange Rates,
1835-1900," *Journal of Economic History*, 38(2), June 1978, pp.
392-417.

Perlman, Richard and Novak, David E. "The Structure of Wages in the
American Iron and Steel Industry, 1860-1890," *Journal of Economic
History*, 22(3), September 1962, pp. 334-47.

Perloff, Harvey S.; Muth, Richard F. and Lampard, Eric E. *Regions,
Resources, and Economic Growth*. Baltimore: Johns Hopkins
University Press, 1960.

Perren, Richard. "The Landlord and Agricultural Transformation,
1870-1900," *Agricultural History Review*, 18(1), 1970, pp. 36-51.

Perren, Richard. "The Landlord and Agricultural Transformation,
1870-1900: A Rejoinder (to O'Grada)," *Agricultural History Review*,
27(1), 1979, pp. 43-7.

Persky, Joseph. "The Dominance of the Rural-Industrial South,
1900-1930," *Journal of Regional Science*, 13(3), December 1973, pp.
409-19.

Peterson, John M. and Gray, Ralph. *Economic Development of the United*

States. Homewood, Ill.: Richard D. Irwin, 1969.

Pettengill, John S. "The Impact of Military Technology on European Income Distribution," *Journal of Interdisciplinary History*, 10(2), Autumn 1979, pp. 201-25.

Phelps Brown, E.H. "The Long Term Movement in Real Wages," in Dunlop (ed), *The Theory of Wage Determination*, 1957.

Phelps Brown, E.H. "Levels and Movements of Industrial Productivity and Real Wages Internationally Compared, 1860-1970," *Economic Journal*, 83(329), March 1973, pp. 58-71.

Phelps-Brown, E.H. *A Century of Pay*. London: Macmillan, 1968.

Phelps Brown, E.H. and Hart, P.E. "The Share of Wages in National Income," *Economic Journal*, 62(246), June 1952, pp. 253-77.

Phelps Brown, E.H. and Handfield-Jones, Stephen J. "The Climacteric of the 1890's: A Study in the Expanding Economy," *Oxford Economic Papers*, New Series, 4(3), October 1952, pp. 266-307.

Phelps Brown, E.H. and Hopkins, Sheila V. "The Course of Wage-Rates in Five Countries, 1860-1939," *Oxford Economic Papers*, New Series, 2(2), June 1950, pp. 226-96.

Phelps Brown, E.H. and Hopkins, Sheila V. "Seven Centuries of Building Wages," *Economica*, 22(87), August 1955, pp. 195-206.

Phelps Brown, E.H. and Hopkins, Sheila V. "Seven Centuries of the Prices of Consumables, Compared with Builders' Wage Rates," reprinted in Ramsey (ed), *The Price Revolution in the Sixteenth Century*, 1971, pp. 18-41. *Economica*, 23(92), November 1956, pp. 296-314.

Phelps Brown, E.H. and Hopkins, Sheila V. "Wage-Rates and Prices: Evidence for Population Pressure in the Sixteenth Century," *Economica*, 24(96), November 1957, pp. 289-306.

Phelps Brown, E.H. and Hopkins, Sheila V. "Builders' Wage-Rates, Prices and Population: Some Further Evidence," *Economica*, 26(101), February 1959, pp. 18-38.

Phelps Brown, E.H. and Hopkins, Sheila V. "Seven Centuries of Wages and Prices: Some Earlier Estimates," *Economica*, 28(109), February 1961, pp. 30-6.

Phelps Brown, E.H. and Weber, Brian A. "Accumulation, Productivity and Distribution in the British Economy, 1870-1938," *Economic Journal*, 63(250), June 1953, pp. 263-88.

Phillips, A.W. "The Relation between Unemployment and the Rate of Change of Money Wage Rates in the United Kingdom, 1861-1957," *Economica*, 25(100), November 1958, pp. 283-99.

Philpot, Gordon. "Enclosure and Population Growth in Eighteenth-Century England," *Explorations in Economic History*, 12(1), January 1975, pp. 29-46.

Philpot, Gordon. "Parliamentary Enclosure and Population Change in England, 1750-1830: A Reply to Turner," *Explorations in Economic History*, 13(4), October 1976, pp. 469-71.

Pickersgill, Joyce E. "Hyperinflation and Monetary Reform in the Soviet Union, 1921-1926," *Journal of Political Economy*, 76(5), September/October 1968, pp. 1037-48.

Pierenkemper, Toni; Fremdling, Rainer and Tilly, Richard H. "Regionale Differenzierung in Deutschland als Schwerpunkt Wirtschaftshistorischer Forschung," [Regional Differentiation in Germany as the Central Focus of Research in Economic History] in Fremdling and Tilly (eds), *Industrialisierung und Raum*, 1979.

Pilgrim, John D. "The Upper Turning Point of 1920: A Reappraisal," *Explorations in Economic History*, 11(3), Spring 1974, pp. 271-98.

Pilgrim, John D. and Bolch, Ben W. "A Reappraisal of Some Factors Associated with Fluctuations in the United States in the Interwar Period," *Southern Economic Journal*, 39(3), January 1973, pp. 327-44.

Pincus, Jonathan J. "A Positive Theory of Tariff Formation Applied to Nineteenth Century United States," (Summary of Doctoral Dissertation) *Journal of Economic History*, 34(1), March 1974, pp. 273-4.

Pincus, Jonathan J. "Pressure Groups and the Pattern of Tariffs," *Journal of Political Economy*, 83(4), August 1975, pp. 757-78.

Pincus, Jonathan J. *Pressure Groups and Politics in Antebellum Tariffs*. New York: Columbia University Press, 1977.

Pincus, Jonathan J. "Tariffs," in Porter (ed), *Encyclopedia of American Economic History*, 1980, pp. 439-50.

Pincus, Jonathan J.; Barnard, A. and Butlin, Noel G. "Public and Private Sector Employment in Australia, 1901-1974," *Australian Economic Review*, 10(37), 1st Quarter 1977, pp. 43-52.

Pincus, Jonathan J.; Barnard, A. and Butlin, Noel G. "Big Government in Australia, 1901-1978." [Working Paper]

Pinera, Sebastian E. and Kotlikoff, Laurence J. "The Old South's Stake in the Inter-Regional Movement of Slaves, 1850-1860," *Journal of Economic History*, 37(2), June 1977, pp. 434-50.

Pippenger, John E. "Speculation in the Flexible Exchange Re-Revisited: Comment (on Aliber)," *Kyklos*, 26(3), 1973, pp. 613-8.

Pollack, Martin and Uselding, Paul J. "Data, 'Evidence' and Interpretation in Economic History," *Economic Inquiry*, 12(3), September 1974, pp. 406-14.

Pollard, Sidney. "The Growth and Distribution of Capital in Great Britain, c. 1770-1870," *Third International Conference of Economic History, Munich, 1965*, part 1. Paris and The Hague: Mouton, 1968, pp. 335-65.

Pollard, Sidney and Higgins, J.P.P., eds. *Aspects of Capital Investment in Great Britain, 1750-1850*. London: Methuen, 1971.

Pomfret, Richard W.T. "The Mechanization of Reaping in Nineteenth Century Ontario: A Case Study of the Pace and Causes of the Diffusion of Embodied Technical Change," *Journal of Economic History*, 36(2), June 1976, pp. 399-415.

Pomfret, Richard W.T. *The Introduction of the Mechanical Reaper in Canada, 1850-1870*. New York: Arno Press, 1979.

Pomfret, Richard W.T. "Capital Formation in Canada 1870-1900," Concordia University Working Paper no. 77-1, January 1977.

Pomfret, Richard W.T. "The Staple Theory and Canadian Economic Development," Concordia University Working Paper no. 77-08, October 1977.

Pope, Clayne L. "The Impact of the Antebellum Tariff on Income Distribution," (Summary of Doctoral Dissertation) *Journal of Economic History*, 31(1), March 1971, pp. 276-8.

Pope, Clayne L. "The Impact of the Antebellum Tariff on Income Distribution," *Explorations in Economic History*, 9(4), Summer 1972, pp. 375-422.

Pope, Clayne L. *The Impact of the Antebellum Tariff on Income Distribution*. New York: Arno Press, 1975.

Pope, Clayne L. "Measurement and Analysis of Distributions of Income and Wealth," (Summary of 1978 Research Workshop) *Journal of Economic History,* 39(1), March 1979, pp. 319-21.

Pope, Clayne L.; Engerman, Stanley L.; Floud, Roderick C.; Wimmer, Larry T.; Trussell, James and Fogel, Robert W. "The Economics of Mortality in North America, 1650-1910: A Description of a Research Project," *Historical Methods,* 11(2), June 1978, pp. 75-108.

Pope, Clayne L.; Kearl, J.R. and Wimmer, Larry T. "Household Wealth in a Settlement Economy: Utah, 1850-1870," *Journal of Economic History,* 40(3), September 1980, pp. 477-96.

Pope, Clayne L. and Wimmer, Larry T. "The Genealogical Society of Salt Lake City: A Source of Data for Economic and Social Historians," *Historical Methods,* 8(2), March 1975, pp. 51-8.

Pope, David H. "Empire Migration to Canada, Australia and New Zealand, 1910-1929," *Australian Economic Papers,* 7(11), December 1968, pp. 167-88.

Pope, David H. "Viticulture and Phylloxera in North-East Victoria, 1880-1910," *Australian Economic History Review,* 11(1), March 1971, pp. 21-38.

Pope, David H. "An Index of Melbourne Building Activity, 1896-1939," *Australian Economic Papers,* 11(18), June 1972, pp. 103-11.

Pope, David H. "Economic History and Scientific Inference," *Australian Economic History Review,* 13(1), March 1973, pp. 1-15.

Pope, David H. "The Push-Pull Model of Australian Migration," *Australian Economic History Review,* 16(2), September 1976, pp. 144-52.

Pope, David H. "The Contribution of United Kingdom Migrants to Australia's Population, Employment and Economic Growth: Federation to the Depression," *Australian Economic Papers,* 16(29), December 1977, pp. 194-210.

Pope, David H. "Some Aspects of the Australian Labour Market and the Standard of Living, 1900-30." [Working Paper]

Pope, David H. "The Peopling of Australia, 1900-1930," presented at the Eighth Conference of Economists, La Trobe University, 1979.

Pope, David H. "The Peopling of Australia: United Kingdom Immigration into Australia, Federation to the Depression," Ph.D. Dissertation, Australian National University, 1977.

Porter, Glenn, ed. *Encyclopedia of American Economic History: Studies of the Principal Movements and Ideas* (3 vols). New York: Charles Scribner's Sons, 1980.

Porter, Glenn and Livesay, Harold C. "The Financial Role of Merchants in the Development of U.S. Manufacturing, 1815-1860," *Explorations in Economic History,* 9(1), Fall 1971, pp. 63-87.

Porter, Patrick G. and Livesay, Harold C. "Oligopoly in Small Manufacturing Industries," *Explorations in Economic History,* 7(3), Spring 1970, pp. 371-9.

Postma, Johannes. "The Dutch Slave Trade: A Quantitative Assessment," *Revue Francaise D'Histoire D'Outre-Mer,* 62(226-227), 1975, pp. 232-44.

Potter, Neal. "Commodity Output, 1839-1899: Comment on Gallman," in Parker (ed), *Trends in the American Economy in the Nineteenth Century,* 1960, pp. 67-9.

Poulson, Barry W. "Quantitative Aspects of Technological Innovation in American Industry before the Civil War," *Rocky Mountain Social*

Science Journal, 4(1), April 1967, pp. 1-11.

Poulson, Barry W. "Estimates of the Value of Manufacturing Output in the Early Nineteenth Century," *Journal of Economic History*, 29(3), September 1969, pp. 521-5.

Poulson, Barry W. *Value Added in Manufacturing, Mining, and Agriculture in the American Economy 1809 to 1839.* New York: Arno Press, 1975.

Poulson, Barry W. "The Dynamic Properties of a Macro Economic Model of U.S. Economic Growth, 1855-1965," Cambridge University Faculty of Economics and Politics Working Paper, December 1975.

Poulson, Barry W. and Dowling, J. Malcolm. "Background Conditions and the Spectral Analytic Test of the Long Swings Hypothesis," *Explorations in Economic History*, 8(3), Spring 1971, pp. 343-52.

Poulson, Barry W. and Dowling, J. Malcolm. "The Climacteric in U.S. Economic Growth," *Oxford Economic Papers*, New Series, 25(3), November 1973, pp. 420-34.

Poulson, Barry W. and Dowling, J. Malcolm. "Long Swings in the U.S. Economy: A Spectral Analysis of 19th and 20th Century Data," *Southern Economic Journal*, 40(3), January 1974, pp. 473-80.

Poulson, Barry W. and Dowling, J. Malcolm. "Long Swings in Factor Flows between Great Britain and the United States," *Papers and Proceedings of the American Statistical Association*, August 1974, pp. 44-54.

Poulson, Barry W. and Holyfield, James, Jr. "A Note on European Migration: A Cross Spectral Anaylsis," *Explorations in Economic History*, 11(3), Spring 1974, pp. 299-310.

Pounds, J.G. and Parker, William N. *Coal and Steel in Western Europe.* Bloomington: Indiana University Press, 1957.

Powell, R.A. "Growth and Technological Change in Agriculture: A Comment (on McLean)," *Economic Record*, 50(132), December 1974, pp. 616-9.

Prest, A.R. "National Income of the United Kingdom, 1870-1946," *Economic Journal*, 58, March 1948, pp. 31-62.

Prest, A.R. and Adams, A.A. *Consumers' Expenditure in the United Kingdom, 1900-1919.* Cambridge: Cambridge University Press, 1954.

Price, Jacob M. "A Note on the Value of Colonial Exports of Shipping," *Journal of Economic History*, 36(3), September 1976, pp. 704-24.

Price, Jacob M.; Caves, Richard E. and North, Douglass C. "Introduction: Exports and Economic Growth," *Explorations in Economic History*, 17(1), January 1980, pp. 1-5.

Price, Jacob M. and Lorwin, Val R. *The Dimensions of the Past: Materials, Problems, and Opportunities for Quantitative Work in History.* New Haven and London: Yale University Press, 1972.

Primack, Martin L. "Land Clearing Under Nineteenth-Century Techniques: Some Preliminary Calculations," *Journal of Economic History*, 22(4), December 1962, pp. 484-97.

Primack, Martin L. "Farm Construction as a Use of Farm Labor in the United States, 1850-1910," *Journal of Economic History*, 25(1), March 1965, pp. 114-25.

Primack, Martin L. "Farm Capital Formation as a Use of Farm Labor, 1850-1910," *Journal of Economic History*, 26(3), September 1966, pp. 348-62.

Pryor, Frederic L.; Pryor, Zora P.; Stadnik, Milos and Staller, George J. "Czechoslovak Aggregate Production in the Interwar Period,"

Review of Income and Wealth, 17(1), March 1971, pp. 35-60.

Pryor, Zora P. "Czechoslovak Fiscal Policies in the Great Depression," *Economic History Review,* Second Series, 32(2), May 1979, pp. 228-40.

Pryor, Zora P.; Pryor, Frederick L.; Stadnik, Milos and Staller, George J. "Czechoslovak Aggregate Production in the Interwar Period," *Review of Income and Wealth,* 17(1), March 1971, pp. 35-60.

Purcell, W. and Nicholas, Stephen J. "Returns to Scale and Imperfect Markets in Australian Manufacturing 1908-1975," University of New South Wales Working Paper in Economic History, 1978.

Purdum, Jack J. "Profitability and Timing of Parliamentary Land Enclosures," *Explorations in Economic History,* 15(3), July 1978, pp. 313-26.

Purdum, Jack J. "Ranking Graduate Schools in Economic History." [Working Paper]

Puskas, J. and Eddie, Scott M. "Landownership Structure in Hungary," Hungarian Academy of Sciences Historical Institute Working Paper.

Quigley, J.M. "An Economic Model of Swedish Emigration," *Quarterly Journal of Economics,* 86, February 1972, pp. 111-26.

Quirk, James P. and McRandle, James H. "An Interpretation of the German Risk Fleet Concept, 1899-1914," in Hughes (ed), *Purdue Faculty Papers in Economic History,* 1967, pp. 484-537.

Rae, J.D.; Paterson, Donald G. and Blain, L. "The Regional Impact of Economic Fluctuations during the Inter-War Period: The Case of British Columbia," *Canadian Journal of Economics,* 7(3), August 1974, pp. 381-401.

Ranis, Gustav and Saxonhouse, Gary R. "Technology Choice, Adaptation and the Quality Dimension in the Japanese Cotton Textile Industry," in Okhawa and Hayami (eds), *The Comparative Analysis of Japan and Less Developed Countries.*

Ransom, Roger L. "Canals and Economic Development: A Discussion of the Issues," *American Economic Review,* Papers and Proceedings, 54(3), May 1964, pp. 365-76.

Ransom, Roger L. "Interregional Canals and Economic Specialization in the Antebellum United States," *Explorations in Entrepreneurial History,* Second Series, 5(1), Fall 1967, pp. 12-35.

Ransom, Roger L. "British Policy and Colonial Growth: Some Implications of the Burden of the Navigation Acts," *Journal of Economic History,* 28(3), September 1968, pp. 427-35.

Ransom, Roger L. "Social Returns from Public Transport Investment: A Case Study of the Ohio Canal," *Journal of Political Economy,* 78(5), September/October 1970, pp. 1041-60.

Ransom, Roger L. "A Closer Look at Western Manufacturing in the Canal Era: A Comment on Niemi," *Explorations in Economic History,* 8(4), Summer 1971, pp. 501-8.

Ransom, Roger L. "A Closer Look at Canals and Western Manufacturing in the Canal Era: A Rebuttal to Niemi," *Explorations in Economic History*, 9(4), Summer 1972, pp. 425-6.

Ransom, Roger L. "Public Canal Investment and the Opening of the Old Northwest," in Klingaman and Vedder (eds), *Essays in Nineteenth Century Economic History*, 1975, pp. 246-68.

Ransom, Roger L. and Sutch, Richard C. "Debt Peonage in the Cotton South after the Civil War," *Journal of Economic History*, 32(3), September 1972, pp. 641-69.

Ransom, Roger L. and Sutch, Richard C. "The Ex-Slave in the Postbellum South: A Study of the Economic Impact of Racism in a Market Environment," *Journal of Economic History*, 33(1), March 1973, pp. 131-47.

Ransom, Roger L. and Sutch, Richard C. "The Impact of the Civil War and of Emancipation on Southern Agriculture," *Explorations in Economic History*, 12(1), January 1975, pp. 1-28.

Ransom, Roger L. and Sutch, Richard C. "The 'Lock-In' Mechanism and Overproduction of Cotton in the Postbellum South," *Agricultural History*, 49(2), April 1975, pp. 405-25.

Ransom, Roger L. and Sutch, Richard C. *One Kind of Freedom: The Economic Consequences of Emancipation.* New York: Cambridge University Press, 1977.

Ransom, Roger L. and Sutch, Richard C. "Sharecropping: Market Response or Mechanism of Race Control?," in Sansing (ed), *What Was Freedom's Price?*, 1978, pp. 51-69.

Ransom, Roger L. and Sutch, Richard C. "Credit Merchandising in the Post-Emancipation South: Structure, Conduct, and Performance," *Explorations in Economic History*, 16(1), January 1979, pp. 64-89.

Ransom, Roger L. and Sutch, Richard C. "Growth and Welfare in the American South of the Nineteenth Century," *Explorations in Economic History*, 16(2), April 1979, pp. 207-36.

Ransom, Roger L. and Sutch, Richard C. "Economic Dimensions of Reconstruction: An Overview." [Working Paper]

Rapp, Richard T. and Clough, Shepard B. *European Economic History: The Economic Development of Western Civilization.* New York: McGraw-Hill, 1975.

Rapp, Richard T. "The Unmaking of the Mediterranean Trade Hegemony: International Trade Rivalry and the Commercial Revolution," *Journal of Economic History*, 35(3), September 1975, pp. 499-525.

Rapp, Richard T. *Industry and Economic Decline in Seventeenth-Century Venice.* Cambridge: Harvard University Press, 1976.

Rapp, Richard T. "A Theory of Premodern Economic Growth. Review Essay of 'The Rise of the Western World: A New Economic History' by Douglass C. North and Robert Paul Thomas (Cambridge: Cambridge University Press, 1975)," *Reviews in European History*, 2(2), June 1976, pp. 181-8.

Rapp, Richard T. "Real Estate and Rational Investment in Early Modern Venice," *Journal of European Economic History*, 8(2), Fall 1979, pp. 269-90.

Rapp, Richard T. and Ames, Edward. "The Birth and Death of Taxes: A Hypothesis," *Journal of Economic History*, 37(1), March 1977, pp. 161-78.

Rapp, Richard T. and Ames, Edward. "Capital Transfers and Foreign Indebtedness: The Long-Term Experience." [Working Paper]

Rapp, Richard T. and Edelstein, Michael. "Comparative Economic

History: Promises and Problems. A Report of the Meetings of the
Economic History Association," *Journal of European Economic
History*, 4(1), Spring 1975, pp. 209-14.

Rapp, William V. "A Theory of Changing Trade Patterns under Economic
Growth: Tested for Japan," *Yale Economic Essays*, 7(2), Fall 1967,
pp. 69-138.

Rapping, Leonard A. and Lucas, Robert E., Jr. "Unemloyment in the
Great Depression: Is There a Full Explanation?," *Journal of
Political Economy*, 80(1), January/February 1972, pp. 186-91.

Rasmussen, Wayne D. "The Impact of Technological Change on American
Agriculture, 1862-1962," *Journal of Economic History*, 22(4),
December 1962, pp. 578-91.

Rasmussen, Wayne D. and Towne, Marvin W. "Farm Gross Product and Gross
Investment in the Nineteenth Century," in Parker (ed), *Trends in
the American Economy in the Nineteenth Century*, 1960, pp. 255-312.

Rastatter, Edward H. "Nineteenth Century Public Land Policy: The Case
for the Speculator," in Klingaman and Vedder (eds), *Essays in
Nineteenth Century Economic History*, 1975, pp. 118-37.

Ratner, Sidney. "Taxation," in Porter (ed), *Encyclopedia of American
Economic History*, 1980, pp. 451-67.

Ratner, Sidney; Soltow, James H. and Sylla, Richard E. *The Evolution
of the American Economy: Growth, Welfare and Decision Making*. New
York: Basic Books, 1979.

Rawski, Thomas G. "The Growth of Producer Industries, 1900-1971," in
Perkins (ed), *China's Modern Economy in Historical Perspective*,
1975, pp. 203-34.

Rawski, Thomas G. "China's Republican Economy: An Introduction."
[Working Paper]

Ray, Edward J. and Baack, Bennett D. "Tariff Policy and Comparative
Advantage in the Iron and Steel Industry, 1870-1929," *Explorations
in Economic History*, 11(1), Fall 1973, pp. 3-24.

Ray, Edward J. and Baack, Bennett D. "Tariff Policy and Income
Distribution: The Case of the U.S., 1830-1860," *Explorations in
Economic History*, 11(2), Winter 1974, pp. 103-22.

Reder, Melvyn W. and David, Paul A., eds. *Nations and Households in
Economic Growth: Essays in Honor of Moses Abramovitz*. New York:
Academic Press, 1974.

Redlich, Fritz. "'New' and Traditional Approaches to Economic History
and Their Interdependence," *Journal of Economic History*, 25(4),
December 1965, pp. 480-95.

Redlich, Fritz. "Potentialities and Pitfalls in Economic History,"
reprinted in Andreano (ed), *The New Economic History*, 1970, pp.
85-99. *Explorations in Entrepreneurial History*, Second Series,
6(1), Fall 1968, pp. 93-108.

Redlich, Fritz. "American Banking and Growth in the Nineteenth
Century: Epistemological Reflections (Comment on Sylla),"
Explorations in Economic History, 10(3), Spring 1973, pp. 305-14.

Redmond, John. "An Indicator of the Effective Exchange Rate of the
Pound in the Nineteen-Thirties," *Economic History Review*, Second
Series, 33(1), February 1980, pp. 83-91.

Reed, Clyde G. "Transactions Costs and Differential Growth in
Seventeenth Century Western Europe," *Journal of Economic History*,
33(1), March 1973, pp. 178-90.

Reed, Clyde G. "The Profits of Cultivation in England during the Later

Middle Ages," *Agricultural History*, 50(4), October 1976, pp. 645-8.

Reed, Clyde G. "Price Movements, Balance of Payments, Bullion Flows, and Unemployment in the Fourteenth and Fifteenth Centuries," *Journal of European Economic History*, 8(2), Fall 1979, pp. 479-86.

Reed, Clyde G. and Anderson, Terry L. "An Economic Explanation of English Agricultural Organization in the Twelfth and Thirteenth Centuries: Comment (on Miller)," *Economic History Review*, Second Series, 26(1), February 1973, pp. 134-7.

Reed, Clyde G. and Devoretz, Donald. "Evidence from the Skilled-Unskilled Canadian Wage Index: 1930-1972." [Working Paper]

Reed, M.C., ed. *Railways in the Victorian Economy: Studies in Finance and Economic Growth.* Newton Abbot: David & Charles, 1969.

Reed, M.C. *Investment in Railways in Britain, 1820-1844: A Study in the Development of the Capital Market.* Oxford: Oxford University Press, 1975.

Reed, M.C. and Hawke, Gary R. "Railway Capital in the United Kingdom in the Nineteenth Century," *Economic History Review*, Second Series, 22(2), August 1969, pp. 269-86.

Rees, Albert. "Wage Trends, 1800-1900: Comment on Lebergott," in Parker (ed), *Trends in the American Economy in the NIneteenth Century*, 1960, pp. 498-9.

Rees, Albert and Jacobs, Donald P. *Real Wages in Manufacturing, 1890-1914* (General Series 70). Princeton: Princeton University Press for the National Bureau of Economic Research, 1961.

Reid, Joseph D.,Jr. "On Navigating the Navigation Acts with Peter D. McClelland: Comment," *American Economic Review*, 60(5), December 1970, pp. 949-55.

Reid, Joseph D.,Jr. "Sharecropping as an Understandable Market Response: The Postbellum South," *Journal of Economic History*, 33(1), March 1973, pp. 106-30.

Reid, Joseph D.,Jr. "Sharecropping in History and Theory," *Agricultural History*, 49(2), April 1975, pp. 426-40.

Reid, Joseph D.,Jr. "Progress on Agricultural Credit: Comment on Bogue and Parker," *Agricultural History*, 50(1), January 1976, pp. 117-24.

Reid, Joseph D.,Jr. "Antebellum Southern Rental Contracts," *Explorations in Economic History*, 13(1), January 1976, pp. 69-84.

Reid, Joseph D.,Jr. "Sharecropping and Agricultural Uncertainty," *Economic Development and Cultural Change*, 24(3), April 1976, pp. 549-76.

Reid, Joseph D.,Jr. "The Economic Costs of War: Comment on Papers by Neal and Hamilton," *Journal of Economic History*, 37(1), March 1977, pp. 52-5.

Reid, Joseph D.,Jr. "Understanding Political Events in the New Economic History," *Journal of Economic History*, 37(2), June 1977, pp. 302-28.

Reid, Joseph D.,Jr. "Economic Burden: Spark to the American Revolution?," *Journal of Economic History*, 38(1), March 1978, pp. 81-100.

Reid, Joseph D.,Jr. "Tenancy in American History," in Roumasset, Boussard, and Singh (eds), *Risk, Uncertainty and Agricultural Development*, 1979.

Reid, Joseph D.,Jr. "The Evaluations and Implications of Southern Tenancy," *Agricultural History*, 53(1), January 1979, pp. 153-69.

Reid, Joseph D.,Jr. "White Land, Black Labor, and Agricultural Stagnation: The Causes and Effects of Sharecropping in the Postbellum South," *Explorations in Economic History*, 16(1), January 1979, pp. 31-55.

Reid, Joseph D.,Jr. "Government Regulatory Institutions: Origin and Evolution," (Summary of 1978 Research Workshop) *Journal of Economic History*, 39(1), March 1979, pp. 321-2.

Reid, Joseph D.,Jr. and Baack, Bennett D. "Land Tenure Patterns and Property Rights in Agriculture," (Summary of 1975 Research Workshop) *Journal of Economic History*, 36(1), March 1976, pp. 29-32.

Reid, Joseph D.,Jr. and MacKay, Robert J. "On Understanding the Birth and Evolution of the Securities and Exchange Commission: Where Are We in the Theory of Regulation?," in Walton (ed), *Regulatory Change in an Atmosphere of Crisis*, 1979, pp. 101-21.

Reiter, Stanley; Davis, Lance E. and Hughes, Jonathan R.T. "Aspects of Quantitative Research in Economic History," reprinted in Hughes (ed), *Purdue Faculty Papers in Economic History*, 1967, pp. 3-10. *Journal of Economic History*, 20(4), December 1960, pp. 539-47.

Reiter, Stanley and Hughes, Jonathan R.T. "The First 1,945 British Steamships," reprinted in Hughes (ed), *Purdue Faculty Papers in Economic History*, 1967, pp. 453-83. *Journal of the American Statistical Association*, 53(282), June 1958, pp. 360-81.

Resnick, Stephen A. "The Decline of Rural Industry under Export Expansion: A Comparison among Burma, Philippines, and Thailand, 1870-1938," *Journal of Economic History*, 30(1), March 1970, pp. 51-73.

Resnick, Stephen A. and Birnberg, Thomas. *Colonial Development: An Econometric Study*. New Haven: Yale University Press, 1975.

Rey, Guido M. "Una sintesi dell'economia italiana durante il fascismo," [A Synthesis of the Italian Economy under Fascism] in Toniolo, (ed), *L'economia italiana*, 1978, pp. 269-312.

Rey, Guido M.; Filosa, Renato and Sitzia, Bruno. "Uno schema di analisi quantitativa del'economia italiana durante il fascismo," [Outline of a Quantitative Analysis of the Italian Economy under Fascism] in Ciocca and Toniolo (eds), *L'economia italiana nel periodo fascista*, 1976, pp. 51-102.

Reynolds, Morgan O. and Brown, William W. "Debt Peonage Re-examined: A Note (on Ransom and Sutch)," *Journal of Economic History*, 33(4), December 1973, pp. 862-71.

Rezneck, Samuel. "The Growth of Output Before 1840: Comment on Parker and Whartenby," in Parker (ed), *Trends in the American Economy in the Nineteenth Century*, 1960, pp. 212-6.

Rice, Richard. "Success Illgotten? The Role of Meiji Militarism in Japan's Technological Progress: Comment (on Yamamura)," *Journal of Economic History*, 37(1), March 1977, pp. 136-8.

Rich, Georg. "The Cross of Gold, Money and the Canadian Business Cycle 1867-1913." [Working Paper]

Richards, Alan R. "Accumulation, Distribution and Technical Change in Egyptian Agriculture: 1800-1940," (Summary of Doctoral Dissertation) *Journal of Economic History*, 36(1), March 1976, pp. 279-82.

Richards, Alan R. "Primitive Accumulation in Egypt, 1798-1882," *Review*, 1(2), Fall 1977, pp. 3-49.

Richards, Alan R. "Technical and Social Change in Egyptian Agriculture, 1890-1914," *Economic Development and Cultural Change,* 26(4), July 1978, pp. 725-45.

Richards, Alan R. "Land and Labor on Egyptian Cotton Farms: 1882-1940," *Agricultural History,* 52(4), October 1978, pp. 503-18.

Richards, C.S. "Investment and the Return to Equity Capital in the South African Gold Mining Industry, 1887-1965," *South African Journal of Economics,* 36(4), December 1968, pp. 330-7.

Richards, G.M. "Wages and the Wage Share: Australian Manufacturing in the 1920s," *Australian Economic History Review,* 20(2), September 1980, pp. 119-35.

Richardson, H.W. "Retardation in Britain's Industrial Growth, 1870-1913," *Scottish Journal of Political Economy,* 12(2), June 1965, pp. 125-49.

Richardson, H.W. "British Emigration and Overseas Investment, 1870-1914," *Economic History Review,* Second Series, 25(1), February 1972, pp. 99-113.

Riefler, Roger F. "Nineteenth-Century Urbanization Patterns in the United States," *Journal of Economic History,* 39(4), December 1979, pp. 961-74.

Ringrose, D.R. "European Economic Growth: Comments on the North-Thomas Theory," *Economic History Review,* Second Series, 26(2), May 1973, pp. 285-92.

Riskin, Carl. "Surplus and Stagnation in Modern China," in Perkins (ed), *China's Modern Economy in Historical Perspective,* 1975, pp. 49-84.

Ritter, Gerhard A.; Kocka, Jurgen and Hohorst, Gerd. *Materialien zur Statistik des Kaiserreichs 1870-1914* [Statistical Material on the German Empire, 1870-1914] (Sozialgeschichtliches Arbeitsbuch, vol. 2). Munchen: Verlag C.H. Beck, 1975.

Roberts, Charles A. "Interregional Per Capita Income Differentials and Convergence: 1880-1950," *Journal of Economic History,* 39(1), March 1979, pp. 101-12.

Robertson, Ross M. "Changing Production of Metalworking Machinery, 1860-1920," in Brady (ed), *Output, Employment, and Productivity in the United States After 1800,* 1966, pp. 479-96.

Robertson, Ross M. and Walton, Gary M. *History of the American Economy (Fourth Edition).* New York: Harcourt, Brace, Jovanovich, 1978.

Rockoff, Hugh T. "Money, Prices, and Banks in the Jacksonian Era," in Fogel and Engerman (eds), *The Reinterpretation of American Economic History* 1971, pp. 448-58.

Rockoff, Hugh T. "American Free Banking before the Civil War: A Re-Examination," (Summary of Doctoral Dissertation) *Journal of Economic History,* 32(1), March 1972, pp. 417-20.

Rockoff, Hugh T. "The Free Banking Era: A Re-Examinaton," *Journal of Money, Credit and Banking,* 6(2), May 1974, pp. 141-67.

Rockoff, Hugh T. *The Free Banking Era: A Re-Examination.* New York: Arno Press, 1975.

Rockoff, Hugh T. "Varieties of Banking and Regional Economic Development in the United States, 1840-1860," *Journal of Economic History,* 35(1), March 1975, pp. 160-81.

Rockoff, Hugh T. "Regional Interest Rates and Bank Failures, 1870-1914," *Explorations in Economic History,* 14(1), January 1977, pp. 90-5.

Rockoff, Hugh T. "Banking in the South," in Twyman and Roller (eds), *Encyclopedia of Southern History,* 1979.

Rockoff, Hugh T. "Money Supply," in Porter (ed), *Encyclopedia of American Economic History,* 1980, pp. 424-38.

Rockoff, Hugh T. "History of Price Controls in the United States." [Working Paper]

Rockoff, Hugh T. and Hinderliter, Roger H. "The Management of Reserves by Banks in Antebellum Eastern Financial Centers," *Explorations in Economic History,* 11(1), Fall 1973, pp. 37-54.

Rockoff, Hugh T. and Hinderliter, Roger H. "Banking under the Gold Standard: An Analysis of Liquidity Management in the Leading Financial Centers," *Journal of Economic History,* 36(2), June 1976, pp. 379-98.

Roehl, Richard. "Plan and Reality in a Medieval Monastic Economy: The Cistercians," (Summary of Doctoral Dissertation) *Journal of Economic History,* 29(1), March 1969, pp. 180-2.

Roehl, Richard. "Patterns and Structure of Demand, 1000-1500," in Cipolla (ed), *The Fontana Economic History of Europe,* 1970.

Roehl, Richard. "Plan and Reality in a Medieval Monastic Economy: The Cistercians," in Adelson (ed), *Studies in Medieval and Renaissance History,* 1972.

Roehl, Richard. "Comment on Papers by Reed and Bean Presented to the 32nd Annual Meeting of the Economic History Association," *Journal of Economic History,* 33(1), March 1973, pp. 228-31.

Roehl, Richard. "L'Industrialisation Francaise: Une Remise en Cause," [French Industrialization: A Reconsideration] *Revue D'Histoire Economique et Sociale,* 54(3), 1976, pp. 406-27.

Roehl, Richard. "French Industrialization: A Reconsideration," *Explorations in Economic History,* 13(3), July 1976, pp. 233-82.

Roehl, Richard. "Comments on Dissertations Presented to the 36th Annual Meeting of the Economic History Association," *Journal of Economic History,* 37(1), March 1977, pp. 272-5.

Roehl, Richard; Sutch, Richard C.; Lyons, John and Boskins, Michael. "Urban Migration in the Process of Industrialization: Britain and the United States in the Nineteenth Century," University of California-Berkeley, Center for Research in Management Science, Working Papers in Economic Theory and Econometrics no. 162, August 1970.

Roll, Richard. "Interest Rates and Price Expectations During the Civil War," *Journal of Economic History,* 32(2), June 1972, pp. 476-98.

Romano, R. "Conveniencias y peligros de aplicar los metodos de la 'nueva historia economica'," [Opportunities and Dangers in Applying the 'New Economic History' Methods] in *La historia economica en America Latina, vol. 1: Situaciones y metodos.* Mexico City: Ed. SepSetentas, 1972, pp. 237-52.

Rooker, C. Keith; Wimmer, Larry T. and Hill, Marvin S. *The Kirtland Economy Revisited.* Provo, Utah: Brigham Young University Press, 1978.

Rosenberg, Nathan. "Technological Change in the Machine Tool Industry, 1840-1910," reprinted in Hughes (ed), *Purdue Faculty Papers in Economic History,* 1967, pp. 405-30. *Journal of Economic History,* 23(4), December 1963, pp. 414-43.

Rosenberg, Nathan. "Anglo-American Wage Differences in the 1820's," *Journal of Economic History,* 27(2), June 1967, pp. 221-9.

Rosenberg, Nathan. *The American System of Manufactures: The Report of the Committee on the Machinery of the United States 1855, and the Special Reports of George Wallis and Joseph Whitworth 1854.* Edinburgh: University of Edinburgh Press, 1969.

Rosenberg, Nathan. "The Direction of Technological Change: Inducement Mechanisms and Focusing Devices," *Economic Development and Cultural Change,* 18(1), (Part 1), October 1969, pp. 1-24.

Rosenberg, Nathan. "Economic Development and the Transfer of Technology: Some Historical Perspectives," *Technology and Culture,* 11(4), October 1970, pp. 550-75.

Rosenberg, Nathan. "Technological Change," in Davis, Easterlin, and Parker (eds), *American Economic Growth,* 1972, pp. 233-79.

Rosenberg, Nathan. *Technology and American Economic Growth.* New York: Harper & Row, 1972.

Rosenberg, Nathan. "Factors Affecting the Diffusion of Technology," *Explorations in Economic History,* 10(1), Fall 1972, pp. 3-34.

Rosenberg, Nathan. "Innovative Responses to Materials Shortages," *American Economic Review,* Papers and Proceedings, 63(2), May 1973, pp. 111-8.

Rosenberg, Nathan. "Science, Invention and Economic Growth," *Economic Journal,* 84(333), March 1974, pp. 90-108.

Rosenberg, Nathan. "America's Rise to Woodworking Leadership," in Hindle (ed), *America's Wooden Age,* 1975.

Rosenberg, Nathan. "Machine Tools," Adams (ed), *Dictionary of American History,* 1976.

Rosenberg, Nathan. *Perspectives on Technology.* New York: Cambridge University Press, 1976.

Rosenberg, Nathan. "American Technology: Imported or Indigenous?," *American Economic Review,* Papers and Proceedings, 67(1), February 1977, pp. 21-6.

Rosenberg, Nathan. "The Role of Science and Technology in the National Development of the U.S.," in Beranek, Jr. and Ranis (eds), *Science, Technology and Economic Development,* 1978.

Rosenberg, Nathan and Ames, Edward. "The Enfield Arsenal in Theory and History," *Economic Journal,* 78(312), December 1968, pp. 827-42.

Rosenberg, Nathan and Hughes, Jonathan R.T. "The United States Business Cycle before 1860: Some Problems of Interpretation," reprinted in Hughes (ed), *Purdue Faculty Papers in Economic History,* 1967, pp. 187-206. *Economic History Review,* Second Series, 15(3), April 1963, pp. 476-93.

Rosenberg, W. "Capital Imports and Growth - The Case of New Zealand: Foreign Investment in New Zealand, 1840-58," *Economic Journal,* 71(281), March 1961, pp. 93-114.

Rosenberg, W. "Mr. Rosenberg on Capital Imports and Growth: A Rejoinder to Delivanis," *Economic Journal,* 71(284), December 1961, pp. 855-6.

Rosovsky, Henry. "The Statistical Measurement of Japanese Economic Growth. Review Essay of 'The Growth Rate of the Japanese Economy since 1878' by Kazushi Ohkawa, ed (Tokyo: Institute of Economic Research, Hitotsubashi University, 1957)," *Economic Development and Cultural Change,* 7(1), October 1958, pp. 75-84.

Rosovsky, Henry. "Japanese Capital Formation: The Role of the Public Sector," *Journal of Economic History,* 19(3), September 1959, pp. 350-75.

Rosovsky, Henry. "L'iniziativa dello stato nell'industriallizzazione giapponese," [State Initiative in Japanese Industrialization] *Mercurio,* June 1960.

Rosovsky, Henry. *Nihon no Shihon Keisei to Seifu no Yakuwari* [The Role of the State in Japanese Capital Formation]. Tokyo: Japan Economic Planning Agency, June 1960.

Rosovsky, Henry. "Senzen Nihon no Shihon Keisei," [Capital Formation in Prewar Japan] *Shakai Keizai-Shi Gaku,* February 1963.

Rosovsky, Henry. "The Take-Off into Sustained Controversy. Review Essay of 'The Economics of Take-Off into Sustained Growth' by W.W. Rostow, ed (London: Macmillan, 1963)," *Journal of Economic History,* 25(2), June 1965, pp. 271-5.

Rosovsky, Henry. "The Economic Position of Japan: Past, Present, and Future," in U.S. Commission on International Trade and Investment Policy (ed), *United States International Economic Policy in an Interdependent World,* 1971.

Rosovsky, Henry. "What Are the 'Lessons' of Japanese Economic History," in Youngson (ed), *Economic Development in the Long Run,* 1972, pp. 229-53.

Rosovsky, Henry. "Meiji-Ki Nihon no Keizei Hattan to Gendai," [Early Japanese Economic Development and Its Modern Implications] *Nichi-Bei Foramu,* August 1972.

Rosovsky, Henry. *The Modernization of Japan and Russia.* New York: Free Press, 1975.

Rosovsky, Henry and Emi, Koichi. "Seifu Kensetsu toshi no Sokutei, 1868-1940," [The Measurement of Japanese Government Investment in Constructon, 1868-1940] *Keizai Kenkyu,* 9(1), January 1958, pp. 52-60.

Rosovsky, Henry and Emi, Koichi. "Nihon no Shihon Keisei to Shite no Kensetsu," [Construction as a Part of Japanese Capital Formation] *Nikon Tokei Gakkai Kaiho,* April 1958.

Rosovsky, Henry and Ohkawa, K. *Japanese Economic Growth: Trend Acceleration in the Twentieth Century* [Japanese Edition Appears in Japanese]. Stanford and Tokyo: Stanford University Press and Toyo Keizai Shimpo-Sha, 1973.

Rosovsky, Henry and Yamamura, Kozo. "Entrepreneurial Studies in Japan: An Introduction," *Business History Review,* 44(1), Spring 1970, pp. 1-12.

Rostow, W.W., ed. *British Economy of the Nineteenth Century: Essays.* Oxford: Clarendon Press, 1948.

Rostow, W.W. *The Process of Economic Growth.* New York: W.W. Norton, 1952.

Rostow, W.W. "Some Reflections on Capital Formation and Economic Growth," Universities-National Bureau Conference Series, no 6: *Capital Formation and Economic Growth.* New York: Arno Press, 1955, pp. 635-67.

Rostow, W.W. "The Interrelation of Theory and Economic History," *Journal of Economic History,* 17(4), December 1957, pp. 509-23.

Rostow, W.W. "The Stages of Economic Growth," *Economic History Review,* Second Series, 12(1), 1959, pp. 1-16.

Rostow, W.W. *The Stages of Economic Growth: A Non-Communist Manifesto.* Cambridge: Cambridge University Press, 1960.

Rostow, W.W., ed. *The Economics of Take-Off into Sustained Growth: Proceedings of a Conference Held by the International Economic*

Association. New York: St. Martin's Press, 1963.

Rostow, W.W. *Politics and the Stages of Growth.* Cambridge: Cambridge University Press, 1971.

Rostow, W.W. "The Strategic Role of Theory: A Commentary," *Journal of Economic History,* 31(1), March 1971, pp. 76-86.

Rostow, W.W. *How It All Began: Origins of the Modern Economy.* New York: McGraw-Hill, 1975.

Rostow, W.W. "Kondratieff, Schumpeter, and Kuznets: Trend Periods Revisited," *Journal of Economic History,* 35(4), December 1975, pp. 719-53.

Rostow, W.W. *Getting from Here to There.* New York: McGraw-Hill, 1978.

Rostow, W.W. *The World Economy: History & Prospect.* Austin: University of Texas Press, 1978.

Rostow, W.W. "No Random Walk: A Comment on 'Why Was England First?'," *Economic History Review,* Second Series, 31(4), November 1978, pp. 610-2.

Rostow, W.W. "Leading Sectors and the Take-off," in Rostow (ed), *The Economics of Take-off into Sustained Growth,* 1963, pp. 1-21.

Rostow, W.W. and Fordyce, Frederick E. "Growth Rates at Different Levels of Income and Stage of Growth: Reflections on Why the Poor Get Richer and the Rich Slow Down," in Uselding (ed), *Research in Economic History,* 1978, pp. 47-86.

Rostow, W.W.; Gayer, Arthur D. and Schwartz, Anna J. *The Growth and Fluctuation of the British Economy, 1790-1850* (Revised Second Edition, New York: Barnes & Noble, 1975). Oxford: Clarendon Press, 1953.

Rotella, Elyce J. "Women's Labor Force Participation and the Growth of Clerical Employment in the United States, 1870-1930," (Summary of Doctoral Dissertation) *Journal of Economic History,* 39(1), March 1979, pp. 331-3.

Rotella, Elyce J. "Women's Labor Force Participation and the Decline of the Family Economy in the United States," *Explorations in Economic History,* 17(2), April 1980, pp. 95-117.

Rotella, Elyce J. "The Expansion of the Clerical Sector in the United States, 1870-1930." [Working Paper]

Rotella, Elyce J. "Women's Labor Force Participation and the Growth of Clerical Employment in the United States, 1870-1930," Ph.D. Dissertation, University of Pennsylvania, 1977.

Rotella, Elyce J. "Women's Participation in the U.S. Labor Force, 1870-1930: The Decline of the Family Economy and the Rise of the Clerical Sector," presented at the Annual Meetings of the Social Science History Association, 1977.

Rothenberg, Winifred B. "A Price Index for Rural Massachusetts, 1750-1855," (see note in this Journal, 40(1), March 1980, for a Corregenda concerning this article) *Journal of Economic History,* 39(4), December 1979, pp. 975-1001.

Rothstein, Morton. "The International Market for Agricultural Commodities, 1850-1873," in Gilchrist and Lewis (eds), *Economic Change in the Civil War Era,* 1965, pp. 62-72.

Rothstein, Morton. "The Cotton Frontier of the Antebellum South: A Methodological Battleground," in Parker (ed), *The Structure of the Cotton Economy of the Antebellum South,* 1970, pp. 149-65.

Rothstein, Morton. "Comments on Dissertations Presented to the 32nd Annual Meeting of the Economic History Association," *Journal of*

Economic History, 33(1), March 1973, pp. 333-5.

Rothstein, Morton. "Measurement Calculus and Direction: Prometheus in the Antebellum Southland," presented at the MSSB-University of Rochester Conference Time on the Cross: A First Appraisal, October 1974.

Rothstein, Morton. "Foreign Trade," in Porter (ed), *Encylopedia of American Economic History*, 1980, pp. 247-63.

Rowe, D.A. and Stone, J.R.F. *The Measurement of Consumers' Expenditure and Behaviour in the United Kingdom, 1920-1938 (2 vols).* Cambridge: Cambridge University Press, 1954.

Royd, J. Hayden and Walton, Gary M. "The Social Savings from Nineteenth-Century Rail Passenger Services," *Explorations in Economic History*, 9(3), Spring 1972, pp. 233-54.

Rozenberg, Yakov and Silber, Jacques. "The Monetary Approach to the Balance of Payments of Palestine," [In Hebrew] *Quarterly Banking Review*, 18(69), November 1978, pp. 32-51.

Rozenberg, Yakov and Silber, Jacques. "Adaptation Process of the Balance of Payments of Palestine: 1922-1935," *Topics in Economics: Proceedings of the Israeli Economic Association*, April 1979, pp. 201-18.

Rozenberg, Yakov and Silber, Jacques. "The Balance of Payments of Palestine under the British Mandate: A Monetary Approach." [Working Paper]

Rubin, Ernest and Kuznets, Simon S. *Immigration and the Foreign Born* (National Bureau of Economic Research Occasional Paper 46). New York: National Bureau of Economic Research, 1954.

Rubin, Julius and Fischbaum, Marvin. "Slavery and the Economic Development of the American South: Comment on Engerman," reprinted in Aitken (ed), *Did Slavery Pay?*, 1971, pp. 327-41. *Explorations in Entrepreneurial History*, Second Series, 6(1), Fall 1968, pp. 116-27.

Rudolph, Richard L. "Austria, 1800-1914," in Cameron (ed), *Banking and Economic Development*, 1972.

Rudolph, Richard L. "Austrian Industrialization: A Case Study in Leisurely Economic Growth," in *Sozialismus, Geschichte und Wirtschaft: Festschrift fur Eduard Marz*. Vienna: Europaverlag, 1973.

Rudolph, Richard L. "Quantitative Aspekte der Industrialisierung in Cisleithanien," in Wandruszka and Urbanitsch (eds), *Die Habsburgermonarchie*, 1973.

Rudolph, Richard L. "The New Versus the Old in Austrian Economic History," *Austrian History Yearbook*, 11, 1975, pp. 37-43.

Rudolph, Richard L. "The Pattern of Austrian Industrial Growth from the Eighteenth to the Early Twentieth Century," *Austrian History Yearbook*, 11, 1975, pp. 3-25.

Rudolph, Richard L. *Banking and Industrialization in Austria-Hungary.* Cambridge: Cambridge University Press, 1976.

Rudolph, Richard L. "Social Structure and the Beginning of Austrian Economic Growth," *East Central Europe/L'Europe de Centre-Est*, 7(2), 1980, pp. 207-24.

Rudolph, Richard L. "Family Structure and Proto-Industrialization in Russia," *Journal of Economic History*, 40(1), March 1980, pp. 111-8.

Rudolph, Richard L. "Agricultural Structure and Proto-Industrialization in Russia: Economic Development with Serf Labor,"

448

in Deyon and Mendels (eds), *Protoindustrialization*, 1982.

Rudolph, Richard L. "Economic Revolution in Austria? The Meaning of 1848 in Austrian Economic History," in Komlos (ed), *Essays on the Habsburg Economy*.

Rutner, Jack L. and Fogel, Robert W. "The Efficiency Effects of Federal Land Policy, 1850-1900: Some Provisional Findings," in Bogue, Aydelotte, and Fogel (eds), *The Dimensions of Quantitative Research in History*, 1972.

Ruttan, Vernon W. and Hayami, Yujiro. "Factor Prices and Technical Changes in Agricultural Development: The United States and Japan, 1880-1960," *Journal of Political Economy*, 78(5), September/October 1970, pp. 1115-41.

Ruttan, Vernon W. "Structural Retardation and the Modernization of French Agriculture: A Skeptical View," *Journal of Economic History*, 38(3), September 1978, pp. 714-28.

Ruttan, Vernon W.; Hayami, Yujiro; Binswanger, Hans P.; Wade, W.W. and Weber, A. "Factor Productivity and Growth: A Historical Interpretation," in Binswanger et al (ed), *Induced Innovation: Technology, Institutions, and Development*, 1978.

Rutten, Andrew. "But It Will Never Be Science, Either," *Journal of Economic History*, 40(1), March 1980, pp. 137-42.

Ryan, Terrance C.I. "The Economics of Trading in Slaves," (Summary of Doctoral Dissertation) *African Economic History*, 1, Spring 1976, pp. 40-1.

Ryan, Terrance C.I. "The Economics of Trading in Slaves," Ph.D. Dissertation, Massachusetts Institute of Technology, 1975.

Sachs, Jeffrey. "The Changing Cyclical Behavior of Wages and Prices: 1890-1976," *American Economic Review*, 70(1), March 1980, pp. 78-90.

Sailors, Joel W. and Gregory, Paul. "Russian Monetary Policy and Industrialization, 1861-1913," *Journal of Economic History*, 36(4), December 1976, pp. 836-51.

Saito, Osamu. "The Labor Market in Tokugawa Japan: Wage Differentials and the Real Wage Level, 1727-1830," *Explorations in Economic History*, 15(1), January 1978, pp. 84-100.

Sakudo, Yotaro; Miyamoto, Mataji and Yasuba, Yasukichi. "Economic Development in Preindustrial Japan, 1859-1894," *Journal of Economic History*, 25(4), December 1965, pp. 541-64.

Salsbury, Stephen. "Comment on Papers by McCloskey, McManus, and Landes and Solmon Presented to the 31st Annual Meeting of the Economic History Association," *Journal of Economic History*, 32(1), March 1972, pp. 92-4.

Sanchez-Albornoz, Nicolas. "Congruence Among Spanish Economic Regions in the Nineteenth Century," *Journal of European Economic History*, 3(3), Winter 1974, pp. 725-45.

Sandberg, Lars G. "Movements in the Quality of British Cotton Textile Exports, 1815-1913," *Journal of Economic History*, 28(1), March 1968, pp. 1-27.

Sandberg, Lars G. "The Draper Loom in New England Textiles: Comment on Feller," *Journal of Economic History*, 28(4), December 1968, pp. 624-7.

Sandberg, Lars G. "American Rings and English Mules: The Role of Economic Rationality," reprinted in Floud (ed), *Essays in Quantitative Economic History*, 1974, pp. 181-95. *Quarterly Journal of Economics*, 83(1), February 1969, pp. 25-43.

Sandberg, Lars G. "Monetary Policy and Politics in Mid-Eighteenth Century Sweden: A Comment on Eagly," *Journal of Economic History*, 30(3), September 1970, pp. 653-4.

Sandberg, Lars G. "A Note on British Cotton Cloth Exports to the United States: 1815-1860 (Comment on Zevin)," *Explorations in Economic History*, 9(4), Summer 1972, pp. 427-8.

Sandberg, Lars G. *Lancashire in Decline: A Study in Entrepreneurship, Technology and International Trade*. Columbus: Ohio State University Press, 1974.

Sandberg, Lars G. "La 'New Economic History' negli Stati Uniti: rassegna del risultati," [The New Economic History in the United States: A Survey of Results] *Quaderni Storici*, 31, April 1976, pp. 382-401.

Sandberg, Lars G. "Banking and Economic Growth in Sweden before World War I," *Journal of Economic History*, 38(3), September 1978, pp. 650-80.

Sandberg, Lars G. "The Case of the Impoverished Sophisticate: Human Capital and Swedish Economic Growth before World War I," *Journal of Economic History*, 39(1), March 1979, pp. 225-41.

Sandberg, Lars G. "The Entrepreneur and Technological Change," in Floud and McCloskey (eds), *The Economic History of Britain since 1700*, 1981.

Sandberg, Lars G. and McCloskey, Donald N. "From Damnation to Redemption: Judgements on the Late Victorian Entrepreneur," *Explorations in Economic History*, 9(1), Fall 1971, pp. 89-108.

Sanderson, Allen R. "Child-Labor Legislation and the Labor Force Participation of Children," (Summary of Doctoral Dissertation) *Journal of Economic History*, 34(1), March 1974, pp. 297-9.

Sanderson, Warren C. "The Fertility of American Women since 1920," (Summary of Doctoral Dissertation) *Journal of Economic History*, 30(1), March 1970, pp. 271-2.

Sanderson, Warren C. "On Two Schools of the Economics of Fertility," *Population and Development Review*, 2(3-4), September/December 1976, pp. 469-78.

Sanderson, Warren C. "Quantitative Aspects of Marriage, Fertility and Family Limitation in Nineteenth Century America: Another Application of the Coale Specifications," *Demography*, 16(3), August 1979, pp. 339-58.

Sanderson, Warren C. "Herbert G. Gutman's The Black Family in Slavery and Freedom, 1750-1925: A Cliometric Reconsideration," *Social Science History*, 3(3-4), October 1979, pp. 66-85.

Sanderson, Warren C. *The Fertility of American Women, 1800-1975*. New York: Academic Press, 1980.

Sanderson, Warren C. and David, Paul A. "The Effectiveness of Nineteenth Century Contraceptive Practices: An Application of Microdemographic Modelling Approaches," in International Economic History Association (eds), *Proceedings of the Seventh International Economic History Congress*, 1978, pp. 60-70.

Sanderson, Warren C. and David, Paul A. "Contraceptive Technology and Family Limiting Behavior: Towards a Quantitative History of the

Diffusion of Contraceptive Practices in America, 1850-1920."
[Working Paper]

Sanderson, Warren C. and David, Paul A. "How Did They Do It?:
Strategies of Marital Fertility Control among the Urban Middle
Class in Victorian America," Stanford Project on the History of
Fertility Control Working Paper no. 6, November 1979.

Sands, Saul S. "Changes in Scale of Production in U.S. Manufacturing
Industry, 1904-1947," *Review of Economics and Statistics*, 43(4),
November 1961, pp. 365-8.

Sapsford, D. "A Time Series Analysis of U.K. Industrial Disputes,"
Industrial Relations, 14(2), May 1975, pp. 242-9.

Saraydar, Edward. "A Note on the Profitability of Antebellum Slavery,"
reprinted in Aitken (ed), *Did Slavery Pay?*, 1971, pp. 209-20.
Southern Economic Journal, 30(4), April 1964, pp. 325-32.

Saraydar, Edward. "The Profitability of Antebellum Slavery: A Reply to
Sutch," reprinted in Aitken (ed), *Did Slavery Pay?*, 1971, pp.
242-50. *Southern Economic Journal*, 31(4), April 1965, pp. 377-83.

Sau, R.K. "Land Tenancy, Rent, and the Optimal Terms of Trade between
Industry and Agriculture," *Oxford Economic Papers*, New Series,
23(3), November 1971.

Saul, S.B. "Some Thoughts on the Papers and Discussion on the
Performance of the Late Victorian Economy," in McCloskey (ed),
Essays on a Mature Economy, 1971, pp. 393-400.

Savin, N. Eugene and Mokyr, Joel. "Stagflation in Historical
Perspective: The Napoleonic Wars Revisited," Uselding (ed),
Research in Economic History, 1976, pp. 198-259.

Savin, N. Eugene and Kesselman, Jonathan R. "Three-and-a-Half Million
Workers Never Were Lost," *Economic Inquiry*, 16(2), April 1978, pp.
205-25.

Savin, N. Eugene and Mokyr, Joel. "Some Econometric Problems in the
Standard of Living Controversy," *Journal of European Economic
History*, 7(2-3), Fall/Winter 1978, pp. 517-25.

Savin, N. Eugene and Von Tunzelmann, G. Nicholas. "The Standard of
Living Debate and Optimal Economic Growth." [Working Paper]

Saxonhouse, Gary R. "A Tale of Technological Diffusion in the Meiji
Period," *Journal of Economic History*, 36(1), March 1974, pp.
149-65.

Saxonhouse, Gary R. "Country Girls and Communication among Competitors
in the Japanese Cotton Spinning Industry," in Patrick (ed),
Japanese Industrialization and Its Social Consequences, 1976, pp.
97-125.

Saxonhouse, Gary R. "Concetti e metodi della scienza economica nelle
ricerche di storia giapponese," [Economic Concepts and Methods in
Japanese Historical Research] *Quaderni Storici*, 31, April 1976, pp.
421-44.

Saxonhouse, Gary R. "Productivity Change and Labor Absorption in
Japanese Cotton Spinning, 1891-1935," *Quarterly Journal of
Economics*, 91(2), May 1977, pp. 195-219.

Saxonhouse, Gary R. "The Supply of Quality Workers and the Demand for
Quality in Jobs in Japan's Early Industrialization," *Explorations
in Economic History*, 15(1), January 1978, pp. 40-68.

Saxonhouse, Gary R. "The Colonial Labor Force and Korean Economic
Development," in Sato (ed), *The Japan Economy in the Interwar
Years*.

Saxonhouse, Gary R. and Kiyokawa, Yukihiko. "The Supply and Demand for Quality Workers in the Cotton Textile Industries in Japan and India," in Ohkawa and Hayami (eds), *The Comparative Analysis of Japan and the Less Developed Countries.*

Saxonhouse, Gary R. and Ranis, Gustav. "Technology Choice, Adaptation and the Quality Dimension in the Japanese Cotton Textile Industry," in Okhawa and Hayami (eds), *The Comparative Analysis of Japan and Less Developed Countries.*

Sayers, Richard S. "The Springs of Technical Progress, 1919-39," *Economic Journal,* 60(238), June 1950, pp. 275-91.

Sayers, Richard S. *Central Banking after Bagehot.* Oxford: Oxford University Press, 1957.

Sayers, Richard S. *The Bank of England, 1891-1944* (3 vols). Cambridge: Cambridge University Press, 1976.

Sayers, Richard S. and Ashton, T.S. *Papers in English Monetary History.* Oxford: Oxford University Press, 1953.

Schaeffer, Donald F. "Productivity in the Antebellum South: The Western Tobacco Region," in Uselding (ed), *Research in Economic History,* 1978.

Schaeffer, Donald F. "Yeoman Farmers and Economic Democracy: A Study of Wealth and Economic Mobility in the Western Tobacco Region, 1850 to 1860," *Explorations in Economic History,* 15(4), October 1978, pp. 421-37.

Schaeffer, Donald F. and Schmitz, Mark D. "Slavery, Freedom, and the Elasticity of Substitution," *Explorations in Economic History,* 15(3), July 1978, pp. 327-37.

Schaeffer, Donald F. and Schmitz, Mark D. "The Relative Efficiency of Slave Agriculture: A Comment on Fogel and Engerman," *American Economic Review,* 69(1), March 1979, pp. 208-12.

Schaeffer, Donald F. and Weiss, Thomas J. "The Use of Simulation Techniques in Historical Analysis: Railroads Versus Canals," *Journal of Economic History,* 31(4), December 1971, pp. 854-84.

Scheiber, Harry N. "The Role of the Railroads in United States Economic Growth: Discussion of Cootner," *Journal of Economic History,* 23(4), December 1963, pp. 525-8.

Scheiber, Harry N. "On the New Economic History and Its Limitations: A Review Essay," *Agricultural History,* 41(4), October 1967, pp. 383-95.

Scheiber, Harry N. "Slavery as an Obstacle to Economic Growth in the United States: A Panel Discussion of Conrad and Meyer," *Journal of Economic History,* 27(4), December 1967, pp. 547-9.

Scheiber, Harry N. *Ohio Canal Era: A Case Study of Government and the Economy, 1820-1861.* Athens: Ohio University Press, 1969.

Scheiber, Harry N. "Black Is Computable: An Essay on 'Time on the Cross' and Its Critics," *American Scholar,* 44(4), Autumn 1975, pp. 656-73.

Scheiber, Harry N. "Poetry, Proasism, and Analysis in American Agricultural History: A Review Article," *Journal of Economic History,* 36(4), December 1976, pp. 919-27.

Schlote, Werner. *British Overseas Trade from 1700 to the 1930s* translated by W.O. Henderson and W.H. Chaloner. Oxford: Basil Blackwell, 1952.

Schmid, A. Allan. "The Role of Private Property in the History of American Agriculture, 1776-1976: Comment (on Anderson and Hill),"

American Journal of Agricultural Economics, 59(3), August 1977, pp. 590-1.

Schmitz, Mark D. "Postbellum Developments in the Louisiana Cane Sugar Industry," in Uselding (ed), *Business and Economic History*, 1976, pp. 88-101.

Schmitz, Mark D. *Economic Analysis of Antebellum Sugar Plantations in Louisiana*. New York: Arno Press, 1977.

Schmitz, Mark D. "Economies of Scale and Farm Size in the Antebellum Sugar Sector," *Journal of Economic History*, 37(4), December 1977, pp. 959-80.

Schmitz, Mark D. "Farm Interdependence in the Antebellum Sugar Sector," *Agricultural History*, 52(1), January 1978, pp. 93-103.

Schmitz, Mark D. "The Transformation of the Southern Cane Sugar Sector, 1860-1930," *Agricultural History*, 53(1), January 1979, pp. 270-85.

Schmitz, Mark D. "Agricultural Uncertainty and Discontent in the Populist Era." [Working Paper]

Schmitz, Mark D. and Laurie, Bruce. "Manufacture and Productivity: The Making of an Industrial Base," in Hershberg (ed), *Toward an Interdisciplinary History of the City*, 1978.

Schmitz, Mark D. and Schaeffer, Donald F. "Slavery, Freedom, and the Elasticity of Substitution," *Explorations in Economic History*, 15(3), July 1978, pp. 327-37.

Schmitz, Mark D. and Schaeffer, Donald F. "The Relative Efficiency of Slave Agriculture: A Comment on Fogel and Engerman," *American Economic Review*, 69(1), March 1979, pp. 208-12.

Schmookler, Jacob. "Economic Sources of Inventive Activity," *Journal of Economic History*, 22(1), March 1962, pp. 1-20.

Schmookler, Jacob. *Invention and Economic Growth*. Cambridge: Harvard University Press, 1966.

Schmundt, Maria and Passell, Peter. "Pre-Civil War Policy and the Growth of Manufacturing," *Explorations in Economic History*, 9(1), Fall 1971, pp. 35-48.

Schneider, Jurgen; Kellenbenz, Hermann and Gommel, Rainer. *Wirtschaftliches Wachstum im Spiegel der Wirtschaftsgeschichte* [Economic Growth in Economic Historical Perspective]. Darmstadt: Wissenschaftliche Buchgesellschaft, 1978.

Schofield, R.S. and Lee, Ronald D. "British Population in the Eighteenth Century," in Floud and McCloskey (eds), *The Economic History of Britain since 1700*, 1981, pp. 17-35.

Schremmer, Eckart. "Agrareinkommen und Kapitalbildung im 19. Jahrhundert in Sudwestdeutschland," [Agricultural Income and Capital Formation in Southwest Germany in the 19th Century] *Jahrbucher fur Nationalokonomie und Statistik*, 176(3), June 1964, pp. 196-240.

Schremmer, Eckart. "Standortausweitung der Warenproduktion im Langfristigen Wirtschaftswachstum. Zur Stadt-Land-Arbeitsteilung im Gewerbe des 18. Jahrhunderts," [Locational Diffusion of Goods Production in Long-Run Economic Growth: About the Division of Labor in the City and in the Country in the Trade of the 18th Century] *Vierteljahrschrift fur Sozial-und Wirtschaftsgeschichte*, 59(1), 1972, pp. 1-40.

Schremmer, Eckart. "Wie Gross war der 'Technische Fortschritt' wahrend der Industriellen Revolution in Deutschland, 1850-1913,"

[How Large was the Technical Progress during the Industrial Revolution in Germany, 1850-1913?] *Vierteljahrschrift fur Sozial-und Wirtschaftsgeschichte,* 60(4), 1973, pp. 433-58.

Schremmer, Eckart. "Zusammenhange Zwischen Katastersteuersystem, Wirtschaftswachstum und Wirtschaftsstruktur im 19. Jahrhundert; das Beispiel Wurttemberg; 1821-1877/1903," [Relationships between the Kataster Tax System, Economic Growth and Economic Structure in the 19th Century: The Case of Wurttemberg, 1821-1877/1903] in Bog, Franz, Kaufhold, Kellenbenz, and Zorn (eds), *Wirtschaftliche und soziale Strukturen im sakularen Wandel,* 1974, pp. 679-706.

Schremmer, Eckart. "Industrielle Ruckstandigkeit und Strukturstabilisierender Fortschritt. Uber den Einsatz von Produktionsfaktoren in der Deutschen (Land-)Wirtschaft zwischen 1850 und 1913," [Industrial Backwardness and Structure-stabilizing Progress: On the Input of Factors of Production in German Agriculture Between 1850 and 1913] in Kellenbenz (ed), *Wirtschaftswachstum,* 1978, pp. 205-33.

Schremmer, Eckart. "Value-Judgement and Measurement in Quantitative History," *Studia Historiae Oeconomicae.*

Schultz, Theodore W. "Capital Formation by Education," reprinted in Fogel and Engerman (eds), *The Reinterpretation of American Economic History,* 1971, pp. 257-64. *Journal of Political Economy,* 68(6), December 1960, pp. 571-83.

Schulze, David and Denslow, David, Jr. "Optimal Replacement of Capital Goods in Early New England and British Textile Firms: A Comment (on Williamson)," *Journal of Political Economy,* 82(3), May/June 1974, pp. 631-7.

Schur, Leon M. "The Second Bank of the United States and the Inflation after the War of 1812," *Journal of Political Economy,* 68(2), April 1960, pp. 118-34.

Schwartz, Anna J. "The Beginning of Competitive Banking in Philadelphia, 1782-1809," *Journal of Political Economy,* 55(5), October 1947, pp. 417-31.

Schwartz, Anna J. "Gross Dividend and Interest Payments by Corporations at Selected Dates in the 19th Century," in Parker (ed), *Trends in the American Economy in the Nineteenth Century,* 1960, pp. 407-45.

Schwartz, Anna J. "Secular Price Change in Historical Perspective," *Journal of Money, Credit and Banking,* 5(1), (Part 2), February 1973, pp. 243-69.

Schwartz, Anna J. "Monetary Trends in the United States and the United Kingdom, 1878-1970: Selected Findings," *Journal of Economic History,* 35(1), March 1975, pp. 138-59.

Schwartz, Anna J. "The Banking Reforms of the 1930s: Discussion (of Jones)," in Walton (ed), *Regulatory Change in an Atmosphere of Crisis,* 1979, pp. 93-9.

Schwartz, Anna J. "Understanding 1929-1933," in Brunner (ed), *The Great Depression Revisited,* 1981, pp. 5-48.

Schwartz, Anna J. "Keynesians vs. Monetarists on 1929-1933," in Harik (ed), *Monetarists and Keynesians.*

Schwartz, Anna J. and Bordo, Michael D. "Issues in Monetary Economics and Their Impact on Research in Economic History," in Gallman (ed), *Recent Developments in the Study of Economic and Business History,* 1977, pp. 81-129.

Schwartz, Anna J. and Bordo, Michael D. "Money and Prices in the Nineteenth Century: An Old Debate Rejoined," *Journal of Economic History,* 40(1), March 1980, pp. 61-7.

Schwartz, Anna J. and Bordo, Michael D. "Money and Prices in the Nineteenth Century: Was Thomas Tooke Right?," UCLA Discussion Paper, 1980.

Schwartz, Anna J.; Gayer, Arthur D. and Rostow, W.W. *The Growth and Fluctuation of the British Economy, 1790-1850* (Revised Second Edition, New York: Barnes & Noble, 1975). Oxford: Clarendon Press, 1953.

Schwartz, Anna J. and Friedman, Milton. *A Monetary History of the United States, 1867-1960.* Princeton: Princeton University Press for the National Bureau of Economic Research, 1963.

Schwartz, Anna J. and Friedman, Milton. "Money and Business Cycles," *Review of Economics and Statistics,* 45(1), (Part 2 Supplement), February 1963, pp. 32-78.

Schwartz, Anna J. and Friedman, Milton. *Monetary Statistics of the United States: Estimates, Sources, Methods.* New York: Columbia University Press for the National Bureau of Economic Research, 1970.

Schweitzer, Mary McKinney. "Economic Regulation and the Colonial Economy: The Maryland Tobacco Inspection Act of 1747," *Journal of Economic History,* 40(3), September 1980, pp. 551-69.

Scott, Robert H. "A 'Liquidity' Factor Contributing to Those Downward Sloping Yield Curves, 1900-1916," *Review of Economics and Statistics,* 45(3), August 1963, pp. 328-9.

Scott, Ira O., Jr. "Gold and the Great Depression," in Van der Wee, Vinogradov, and Kotovsky (eds), *Fifth International Congress of Economic History,* 1976, pp. 203-11.

Scully, Gerald W. "The North-South Manufacturing Wage Differential, 1869-1919," *Journal of Regional Science,* 11(2), August 1971, pp. 235-52.

Seagrave, Charles E. "The Southern Negro Agricultural Worker: 1850-1870," (Summary of Doctoral Dissertation) *Journal of Economic History,* 31(1), March 1971, pp. 279-80.

Segal, Harvey H. "Canal Investment, 1815-1860: Comment on Cranmer," in Parker (ed), *Trends in the American Economy in the Nineteenth Century,* 1960, pp. 565-70.

Severson, Robert F. "The American Manufacturing Frontier, 1870-1940," *Business History Review,* 34(3), Autumn 1960, pp. 356-72.

Severson, Robert F. "The American Manufacturing Frontier, 1870-1914: Reply to Andreano," *Business History Review,* 35(1), Spring 1961, pp. 109-13.

Shapiro, Seymour. *Capital and the Cotton Industry in the Industrial Revolution.* Ithaca: Cornell University Press, 1967.

Sharpless, John and Lindstrom, Diane. "Urban Growth and Economic Structure in Antebellum America," in Uselding (ed), *Research in Economic History,* 1978, pp. 161-216.

Shaw, E.S. and Gurley, John G. "The Growth of Debt and Money in the United States, 1800-1950: A Suggested Interpretation," *Review of Economics and Statistics,* 39(3), August 1957, pp. 250-62.

Shaw, E.S. and Gurley, John G. "Money," in Harris (ed), *American Economic History,* 1961, pp. 101-29.

Shaw, John A. "Railroads, Irrigation, and Economic Growth: The San

Joaquin Valley of California," *Explorations in Economic History,*
10(2), Winter 1973, pp. 211-28.

Shaw, John A. and Leet, Don R. "French Economic Stagnation, 1700-1960:
Old Economic History Revisited," *Journal of Interdisciplinary
History,* 8(3), Winter 1978, pp. 531-44.

Shaw, W.H. *Value of Commodity Output since 1869* (General Series 48).
New York: National Bureau of Economic Research, 1947.

Shearer, Ronald A. and Clark, Carolyn. "Statistics of Canada's
International Gold Flows, 1920-1934," presented at the Eighth
Conference on Quantitative Methods in Canadian Economic History,
Hamilton, Ontario, October 1976.

Shearer, Ronald A. and Clark, Carolyn. "The Suspension of the Gold
Standard, 1928-1931," University of British Columbia, Department of
Economics Discussion Paper no. 79-36, 1979.

Shenton, R.W. and Freund, W.M. "'Vent-for-Surplus' Theory and the
Economic History of West Africa," *Savanna,* 6(2), December 1977, pp.
191-6.

Shepherd, James F. "A Balance of Payments for the Thirteen Colonies,
1768-1772: A Summary," (Summary of Doctoral Dissertation) *Journal
of Economic History,* 25(4), December 1965, pp. 691-5.

Shepherd, James F. "Commodity Exports from the British North American
Colonies to Overseas Areas, 1768-1772: Magnitudes and Patterns of
Trade," *Explorations in Economic History,* 8(1), Fall 1970, pp.
5-76.

Shepherd, James F. "The Development of Wheat Production in the Pacific
Northwest," *Agricultural History,* 49(1), January 1975, pp. 258-71.

Shepherd, James F. "The Economy from Revolution to 1815," in Porter
(ed), *Encyclopedia of American Economic History,* 1980, pp. 51-65.

Shepherd, James F. "The Development of New Wheat Varieties in the
Pacific Northwest," *Agricultural History,* 54(1), January 1980, pp.
52-63.

Shepherd, James F. "Newfoundland and the Staple Theory: Export-Led
Growth or Decline?," presented at the Ninth Conference on the
Application of Economic Theory and Quantitative Methods to Canadian
Economic History, University of Western Ontario, London, Ontario,
March 1978.

Shepherd, James F. and Coelho, Philip R.P. "Differences in Regional
Prices: The United States, 1851-1880," *Journal of Economic History,*
34(3), September 1974, pp. 551-91.

Shepherd, James F. and Coelho, Philip R.P. "Regional Differences in
Real Wages: The United States, 1851-1880," *Explorations in Economic
History,* 13(2), April 1976, pp. 203-30.

Shepherd, James F. and Coelho, Philip R.P. "The Impact of Regional
Differences in Prices and Wages on Economic Growth: The United
States in 1890," *Journal of Economic History,* 39(1), March 1979,
pp. 69-85.

Shepherd, James F. and Walton, Gary M. "Estimates of 'Invisible'
Earnings in the Balance of Payments of the British North American
Colonies, 1768-1772," *Journal of Economic History,* 29(2), June
1969, pp. 230-63.

Shepherd, James F. and Walton, Gary M. *Shipping, Maritime Trade, and
the Economic Development of Colonial North America.* London:
Cambridge University Press, 1972.

Shepherd, James F. and Walton, Gary M. "Trade, Distribution and

Economic Growth in Colonial America," *Journal of Economic History,* 32(1), March 1972, pp. 128-45.

Shepherd, James F. and Walton, Gary M. "The Effects of the American Revolution on American Maritime Trade and Shipping," *The American Revolution and the Sea: Proceedings of the 14th Conference of the International Commission for Maritime History at Greenwich, London, England.* London: National Maritime Museum, 1974, pp. 58-69.

Shepherd, James F. and Walton, Gary M. "Economic Change after the Revolution: Pre- and Post-War Comparisons of Maritime Shipping and Trade," *Explorations in Economic History,* 13(4), October 1976, pp. 397-422.

Shepherd, James F. and Walton, Gary M. *The Economic Rise of Early America.* Cambridge: Cambridge University Press, 1979.

Shepherd, James F. and Walton, Gary M., eds. *Market Institutions and Economic Progress in the New South, 1865-1900.* New York: Academic Press, 1980.

Shepherd, James F. and Williamson, Samuel H. "The Coastal Trade of the British North American Colonies, 1768-1772," *Journal of Economic History,* 32(4), December 1972, pp. 783-810.

Sheppard, David K. *The Growth and Role of U.K. Financial Institutions, 1880-1962.* London: Methuen, 1971.

Shergold, Peter R. "The Walker Thesis Revisited: Immigration and White American Fertility, 1800-60," *Australian Economic History Review,* 14(2), September 1974, pp. 168-89.

Shergold, Peter R. "Relative Skill and Income Levels of Native and Foreign Born Workers: A Reexamination," *Explorations in Economic History,* 13(4), October 1976, pp. 451-62.

Shetler, Douglass D. and Thomas, Robert P. "Railroad Social Saving: A Comment on Hunt," *American Economic Review,* 58(1), March 1968, pp. 186-9.

Shimbo, Hiroshi and Ohkura, Takehiko. "The Tokugawa Monetary Policy in the Eighteenth and Nineteenth Centuries," *Explorations in Economic History,* 15(1), January 1978, pp. 101-24.

Shinohara, Miyohei. "Kuznets and Juglar Cycles during the Industrialization of 1874-1940 - by Growth Cycle Approach," in Ohkawa and Hayami (eds), *Economic Growth,* 1973, pp. 237-52.

Shinohara, Miyohei. "Manufacturing, 1874-1940," in Ohkawa and Hayami (eds), *Economic Growth,* 1973, pp. 26-37.

Shinohara, Miyohei. "Personal Consumption Expenditures, 1874-1940," in Ohkawa and Hayami (eds), *Economic Growth,* 1973, pp. 51-66.

Shinohara, Miyohei and Ohkawa, Kazushi, eds. *The Growth Rate of the Japanese Economy since 1878.* Tokyo: Kinokuniya, 1957.

Shinohara, Miyohei; Ohkawa, Kazushi and Umemura, Mataji, eds. *Estimates of Long Term Economic Statistics of Japan since 1868.* Tokyo: Toyo Keizai Shinpo Sha, 1965.

Shlomovitz, Ralph. "The Transition from Slave to Freedman Labor Arrangements in Southern Agriculture, 1865-1870," (Summary of Doctoral Dissertation) *Journal of Economic History,* 39(1), March 1979, pp. 333-6.

Shlomowitz, Ralph. "New and Old Views on the Rural Economy of the Postbellum American South: A Review." [Working Paper]

Shukla, Vishwa; Gallaway, Lowell E. and Vedder, Richard K. "The Distribution of the Immigrant Population in the United States: An Economic Analysis," *Explorations in Economic History,* 11(3), Spring

1974, pp. 213-26.

Siengenthaler, Jurg K. "A Scale Analysis of Nineteenth-Century Industrialization," *Explorations in Economic History*, 10(1), Fall 1972, pp. 75-108.

Silber, Jacques. "Some Demographic Characteristics of the Jewish Population in Russia at the End of the Nineteenth Century," *Jewish Social Studies*, 42(3-4), Summer/Fall 1980, pp. 269-80.

Silber, Jacques and Rozenberg, Yakov. "The Monetary Approach to the Balance of Payments of Palestine," [In Hebrew] *Quarterly Banking Review*, 18(69), November 1978, pp. 32-51.

Silber, Jacques and Rozenberg, Yakov. "Adaptation Process of the Balance of Payments of Palestine: 1922-1935," *Topics in Economics: Proceedings of the Israeli Economic Association*, April 1979, pp. 201-18.

Silber, Jacques and Rozenberg, Yakov. "The Balance of Payments of Palestine under the British Mandate: A Monetary Approach." [Working Paper]

Simon, Julian and Neal, Larry D. "A Calculation of the Black Reparations Bill," *Review of Black Political Economy*, 4(2), Winter 1974, pp. 75-86.

Simon, Matthew. "The United States Balance of Payments, 1861-1900," in Parker (ed), *Trends in the American Economy in the Nineteenth Century*, 1960, pp. 629-711.

Simon, Matthew. "The Role of the Railroads in United States Economic Growth: Discussion of Cootner," *Journal of Economic History*, 23(4), December 1963, pp. 522-4.

Simon, Matthew. "The Pattern of New British Portfolio Foreign Investment, 1865-1914," in Hall (ed), *The Export of Capital from Britain*, 1968, pp. 15-44.

Simon, Matthew and Novak, David E. "Some Dimensions of the American Commercial Invasion of Europe, 1871-1914: An Introductory Essay," *Journal of Economic History*, 24(4), December 1964, pp. 591-605.

Sinclair, Al. "Internal Migration in Canada, 1871-1951," Ph.D. Dissertation, Harvard University, 1966.

Sinclair, William A. "The Tariff and Manufacturing Employment in Victoria, 1860-1900: A Note," *Economic Record*, 31(60), May 1955, pp. 100-4.

Sinclair, William A. "Public Capital Formation in Australia: 1919-20 to 1929-30: A Note," *Economic Record*, 31(61), November 1955, pp. 299-310.

Sinclair, William A. *Economic Recovery in Victoria 1894-1899.* Canberra: Australian National University, 1956.

Sinclair, William A. "Aspects of Economic Growth 1900-1920," in Boxer (ed), *Aspects of the Australian Economy*, 1965.

Sinclair, William A. "The Depressions of the 1890's and the 1930's in Australia: A Comparison," in Doran and Day (ed), *Readings in Australian Economics*, 1965.

Sinclair, William A. "Capital Formation," in Forster (ed), *Australian Economic Development in the Twentieth Century*, 1970.

Sinclair, William A. "The Tariff and Economic Growth in Pre-Federation Victoria," *Economic Record*, 47(117), March 1971, pp. 77-92.

Sinclair, William A. "Was Labour Scarce in the 1830's?," *Australian Economic History Review*, 11(2), September 1971, pp. 115-32.

Sinclair, William A. "Economic Growth and Well-Being: Melbourne,

1870-1914," *Economic Record,* 51(134), June 1975, pp. 153-73.

Sinclair, William A. "Economic Development and Fluctuation in Australia in the 1920s: Comment (on Boehm)," *Economic Record,* 51(135), September 1975, pp. 409-13.

Sinclair, William A. *The Process of Economic Development in Australia.* Melbourne: Cheshire, 1976.

Sinclair, William A. *Australian Economic Development: Old Model and New Model.* Nedlands, W.A.: University of Western Australia Press, 1977.

Singer, H.W. "Quantitative Aspects of the Economic Growth of Nations: A Footnote to Professor Kuznets," *Economic Development and Cultural Change,* 7(1), October 1958, pp. 73-4.

Sitzia, Bruno; Filosa, Renato and Rey, Guido M. "Uno schema di analisi quantitativa del'economia italiana durante il fascismo," [Outline of a Quantitative Analysis of the Italian Economy under Fascism] in Ciocca and Toniolo (eds), *L'economia italiana nel periodo fascista,* 1976, pp. 51-102.

Skidmore, Arthur and Kammeyer, Kenneth C.W. "Demographic Transition: A Forcing Model?: Comment," *Demography,* 12(2), May 1975, pp. 343-50.

Slenes, Robert W. and De Mello, Pedro C. "Analise Economica da Escravidao no Brasil," [Economic Analysis of Slavery in Brazil] in Neuhaus (ed), *A Economia Brasileira,* 1979, pp. 89-122.

Smiley, Gene. "Interest Rate Movement in the United States, 1888-1913," *Journal of Economic History,* 35(3), September 1975, pp. 591-620.

Smiley, Gene. "The 1898-1902 Expansion of the Securities Market," *Journal of Economics,* 4, 1978, pp. 193-6.

Smiley, Gene. "Regional Cost Differences among Country National Banks, 1888-1913," Marquette University Department of Economics Working Paper, August 1978.

Smiley, Gene. "Revised Estimates of Short Term Interest Rates of National Banks for States and Reserve Cities, 1888-1913," Marquette University Department of Economics Working Paper, October 1976.

Smiley, Gene. "Risk, Market Structure, and Transactions Costs in the Development of the National Short Term Capital Market, 1888-1913," Marquette University Department of Economics Working Paper, August 1978.

Smiley, Gene and Britton, Charles R. "Interregional Resource Allocation: Mid-South Resource Flows during the 1880-1913 Period," *Annals of the Midsouth Academy of Economists,* 3, 1975, pp. 175-96.

Smiley, Gene and Keehn, Richard H. "A Note on Interest Paid on New York Bankers' Balances in the Postbellum Period: A Note on James," *Business History Review,* 51(3), Autumn 1977, pp. 367-9.

Smiley, Gene and Keehn, Richard H. "Mortgage Lending by National Banks," *Business History Review,* 51(4), Winter 1977, pp. 474-91.

Smiley, Gene and Keehn, Richard H. "Short Term Interest Rates in New York City and San Francisco, 1872-1898," Marquette University Department of Economics Working Paper, July 1978.

Smith, David. "A Monetary Model of the British Economy 1880-1975," *National Westminster Bank Quarterly Review,* February 1977, pp. 18-32.

Smith, James D. and Soltow, Lee C. "The Wealth, Income, and Social Class of Men in Large Nothern Cities of the United States in 1860," in Smith (ed), *The Personal Distribution of Income and Wealth,*

1975.

Smith, Kenneth R.; Williamson, Jeffrey G. and Swanson, Joseph A. "The Size Distribution of Cities and Optimal City Size," *Journal of Urban Economics,* 1(4), October 1974, pp. 395-409.

Smith, Lawrence B. and Officer, Lawrence H. "The Canadian-American Reciprocity Treaty of 1855 to 1866," *Journal of Economic History,* 28(4), December 1968, pp. 598-623.

Smith, Lawrence B. and Officer, Lawrence H. "Canadian-American Reciprocity: A Reply (to Ankli)," *Journal of Economic History,* 30(2), June 1970, pp. 432-4.

Smith, V. Kerry. "The Ames-Rosenberg Hypothesis and the Role of Natural Resources in the Production Technology," *Explorations in Economic History,* 15(3), July 1978, pp. 257-68.

Smith, V. Kerry and Eagly, Robert V. "Domestic and International Integration of the London Money Market, 1731-1789," *Journal of Economic History,* 36(1), March 1976, pp. 198-212.

Smith, Vernon L. "The Primitive Hunter Culture, Pleistocene Extinction, and the Rise of Agriculture," *Journal of Political Economy,* 83(4), August 1975, pp. 727-56.

Smolensky, Eugene. "The Composition of Iron and Steel Products, 1869-1909: Discussion of Temin," *Journal of Economic History,* 23(4), December 1963, pp. 472-6.

Smolensky, Eugene. *Adjustments to Depressions and War, 1930-1945.* Chicago: Scott Foresman, 1964.

Smolensky, Eugene. "The Past and Present Poor," in Fogel and Engerman (eds), *The Reinterpretation of American Economic History,* 1971, pp. 84-96.

Smolensky, Eugene. "Industrial Location and Urban Growth," in Davis, Easterlin, and Parker (eds), *American Economic Growth,* 1972, pp. 582-610.

Smolensky, Eugene. "The Management of Urban Agglomeration," in Davis, Easterlin, and Parker (eds), *American Economic Growth,* 1972, pp. 611-35.

Smolensky, Eugene and Olmstead, Alan L. *The Urbanization of the United States.* Morristown, N.J.: General Learning, 1973.

Smolensky, Eugene and Weinstein, Michael M. "Poverty," in Porter (ed), *Encyclopedia of American Economic History,* 1978, pp. 1136-54.

Snooks, G.D. "Regional Estimates of Gross Domestic Product and Capital Formation: Western Australia, 1923/24-1938/39," *Economic Record,* 48(124), December 1972, pp. 536-53.

Snooks, G.D. "Depression and Recovery in Western Australia 1928-29 to 1938-39: A Deviation from the Norm," *Economic Record,* 49(127), September 1973, pp. 420-39.

Snooks, G.D. *Depression and Recovery in Western Australia, 1928/29 to 1938/39: A Study in Cyclical and Structural Change.* Nedlands, W.A.: University of Western Australia Press, 1974.

Snooks, G.D. "Orthodox and Radical Interpretations of the Development of Australian Capitalism," *Labour History,* 28, May 1975, pp. 1-11.

Snooks, G.D. "The Radical View of Australian Capitalism: A Reply," *Labour History,* 28, May 1975, pp. 18-21.

Snooks, G.D. "Development in Adversity, (Western Australia) 1913 to 1946," in Appleyard, Bolton, de Garis, Stannage (eds), *New History of Western Australia,* 1979.

Snooks, G.D. "The Arithmetic of Regional Growth: Western Australia,

1912/13 to 1957/58," *Australian Economic History Review,* 19(1), March 1979, pp. 63-74.

Sokoloff, Kenneth. "Capital Markets and Industrialization in Early America." [Working Paper]

Sokoloff, Kenneth. "Industrialization and the Growth of Manufacturing in Early America: Evidence from the 1820 Census." [Working Paper]

Sokoloff, Kenneth and Fogel, Robert W. "The Economic and Demographic Significance of Secular Changes in Human Stature: The U.S., 1750-1960." [Working Paper]

Sokoloff, Kenneth; Margo, Robert A. and Villaflor, Georgia. "The Economic and Demographic Significance of Secular Changes in Human Stature: The U.S., 1750-1960," *NBER Reporter,* Winter 1979, pp. 6-8.

Sokoloff, Kenneth and Villaflor, Georgia. "Colonial and Revolutionary Muster Rolls: Some New Evidence on Nutrition and Migration in Early America," National Bureau of Economic Research Working Paper No. 374, July 1979.

Solar, Peter and David, Paul A. "A Bicentenary Contribution to the History of the Cost of Living in America," Uselding (ed), *Research in Economic History,* 1977, pp. 1-80.

Solmon, Lewis C. "Capital Formation by Expenditures on Formal Education, 1880 and 1890," (Summary of Doctoral Dissertation) *Journal of Economic History,* 29(1), March 1969, pp. 167-72.

Solmon, Lewis C. "Estimates of the Costs of Schooling in 1880 and 1890," *Explorations in Economic History,* 7(4), (Supplement), Summer 1970, pp. 531-81.

Solmon, Lewis C. "Opportunity Costs and Models of Schooling in the Nineteenth Century," *Southern Economic Journal,* 37(1), July 1970, pp. 66-83.

Solmon, Lewis C. and Landes, William M. "Compulsory Schooling Legislation: An Economic Analysis of Law and Social Change in the Nineteenth Century," *Journal of Economic History,* 32(1), March 1972, pp. 54-91.

Solmon, Lewis C. and Tierney, Michael. "Education," in Porter (ed), *Encyclopedia of American Economic History,* 1980, pp. 1012-27.

Solow, Barbara Lewis. "The Irish Land Question After 1870," (Summary of Doctoral Dissertation). *Journal of Economic History,* 27(4), December 1967, pp. 618-20.

Solow, Barbara Lewis. *The Land Question and the Irish Economy, 1870-1903.* Cambridge: Harvard University Press, 1971.

Solow, Robert M. and Temin, Peter. "Introduction: The Inputs for Growth," in Mathias and Postan (eds), *The Cambridge Economic History of Europe,* 1978, pp. 1-27.

Soltow, James H. "The Entrepreneur in Economic History," *American Economic Review,* 58(2), May 1968, pp. 84-92.

Soltow, James H. "Recent Literature in American Economic History," *American Studies International,* 17(1), Autumn 1978, pp. 5-33.

Soltow, James H., ed. *Essays in Economic and Business History* (Michigan State University Business Studies). East Lansing: Michigan State University Press, 1979.

Soltow, James H.; Ratner, Sidney and Sylia, Richard E. *The Evolution of the American Economy: Growth, Welfare and Decision Making.* New York: Basic Books, 1979.

Soltow, Lee C. "Income Equality in a Factory Payroll," *Southern Economic Journal,* 25(3), January 1959, pp. 343-8.

Soltow, Lee C. "Long-Run Changes in British Income Inequality,"
reprinted in Floud (ed), *Essays in Quantitative Economic History*,
1974, pp. 152-65. *Economic History Review*, Second Series, 21(1),
April 1968, pp. 17-29.

Soltow, Lee C., ed. *Six Papers on the Size Distribution of Wealth and
Income* (Studies in Income and Wealth, vol. 33). New York: Columbia
University Press for the National Bureau of Economic Research,
1969.

Soltow, Lee C. "Trends in the Size Distribution of Wealth in the
Nineteenth Century: A Comment on Gallman," in Soltow (ed), *Six
Papers on the Size Distribution of Wealth and Income*, 1969, pp.
25-7.

Soltow, Lee C. "Evidence on Income Inequality in the United States,
1866-1965," *Journal of Economic History*, 29(2), June 1969, pp.
279-86.

Soltow, Lee C. *Patterns of Wealthholding in Wisconsin since 1850*.
Madison: University of Wisconsin Press, 1971.

Soltow, Lee C. "An Index of the Poor and Rich of Scotland, 1861-1961,"
Scottish Journal of Political Economy, 18(1), February 1971, pp.
49-67.

Soltow, Lee C. "Economic Inequality in the United States in the Period
from 1790 to 1860," *Journal of Economic History*, 31(4), December
1971, pp. 822-39.

Soltow, Lee C. "A Century of Personal Wealth Accumulation," in Vatter
and Palm (eds), *The Economics of Black America*, 1972.

Soltow, Lee C. "The Censuses of Wealth of Men in Australia in 1915 and
in the United States in 1860 and 1870," *Australian Economic History
Review*, 12(2), September 1972, pp. 125-41.

Soltow, Lee C. *Men and Wealth in the United States, 1850-1870*. New
Haven: Yale University Press, 1975.

Soltow, Lee C. "The Growth of Wealth in Ohio, 1800-1969," in Klingaman
and Vedder (eds), *Essays in Nineteenth Century Economic History*,
1975, pp. 191-207.

Soltow, Lee C. "The Economic Heritage of an Iowa County," *Annals of
Iowa*, Third Series, 43(1), Summer 1975, pp. 24-38.

Soltow, Lee C. "Are the Rich Getting Richer? Trends in U.S. Wealth
Concentration: Comment on Lebergott," *Journal of Economic History*,
36(1), March 1976, pp. 163-5.

Soltow, Lee C. "Wealth Distribution in Denmark in 1789," *Scandinavian
Economic History Review*, 27(2), 1979, pp. 121-38.

Soltow, Lee C. "Distribution of Income and Wealth," in Porter (ed),
Encyclopedia of American Economic History, 1980, pp. 1087-119.

Soltow, Lee C. and May, Dean L. "Accumulation and Discrimination in
the Postbellum South," *Explorations in Economic History*, 16(2),
April 1979, pp. 151-62.

Soltow, Lee C. and Smith, James D. "The Wealth, Income, and Social
Class of Men in Large Nothern Cities of the United States in 1860,"
in James D. Smith (ed), *The Personal Distribution of Income and
Wealth*, 1975.

Soltow, Lee C. and Stevens, Edward. "Economic Aspects of School
Participation in Mid-Nineteenth Century United States," *Journal of
Interdisciplinary History*, 8(2), Autumn 1977, pp. 221-43.

Sonnemann, Rolf. *Die Auswirkungen des Schutzzolls auf die
Monopolisierung der Deutschen Eisen- und Stahl-Industrie, 1879-1892*

[The Effects of Protective Tariffs on the Monopolization of the German Iron and Steel Industry, 1879-1892]. Berlin: Akademie Verlag, 1960.

Soper, John C. and Gale, Bradley T. "Long Swings in British Economic Growth, 1700-1938," (Summary of Paper Presented at the Meetings of the Western Economic Association) *Western Economic Journal*, 9(3), September 1971, pp. 327.

Soper, John C. "Myth and Reality in Economic Time Series: The Long Swing Revisited," *Southern Economic Journal*, 41(4), April 1975, pp. 570-9.

Soper, John C. *The Long Swing in Historical Perspective: An Interpretive Study*. New York: Arno Press, 1978.

Spechler, Martin C. "The Regional Concentration of Industry in Imperial Russia, 1854-1917," *Journal of European Economic History*, 9(2), Fall 1980, pp. 401-30.

Spencer, Austin H. "An Examination of the Relative Downward Industrial Price Flexibility, 1870-1921," (Summary of Doctoral Dissertation) *Journal of Economic History*, 34(1), March 1974, pp. 300-3.

Spencer, Austin H. "Relative Downward Industrial Price Flexibility, 1870-1921," *Explorations in Economic History*, 14(1), January 1977, pp. 1-19.

Spencer, Austin H. *Relative Downward Price Flexibility, 1870-1921*. New York: Arno Press, 1978.

Spencer, Barbara; Hum, Derek and Deprey, Paul. "Spectral Analysis and the Study of Seasonal Fluctuations in Historical Demography," *Journal of European Economic History*, 5(1), Spring 1976, pp. 171-90.

Spengler, Joseph J.; Moore, Wilbert E. and Kuznets, Simon S., eds. *Economic Growth: Brazil, India, Japan*. Durham, N.C.: Duke University Press, 1955.

Spree, Reinhard. *Die Wachstumszyklen der Deutschen Wirtschaft von 1840 bis 1880* [Growth Cycles of the German Economy from 1840 to 1880]. Berlin: Duncker & Humblot, 1977.

Spree, Reinhard. "Zur Quantitativ-Historischen Analyse okonomischer Zeitreihen: Trends und Zyklen in der Deutschen Volkswirtschaft von 1820 bis 1913," [On the Quantitative-Historical Analysis of Economic Time Series: Trends and Cycles in the German Economy from 1820 to 1913] in Best and Mann (eds), *Quantitative Methoden in der Historisch-Sozialwissenschaftlichen Forschung*, 1977.

Spree, Reinhard. "Zur Theoriebedurftigkeit Quantitativer Wirtschaftsgeschichte (am Beispiel der Historischen Konjunkturforschung und ihrer Validitatsprobleme)," [On the Theoretical Shortcomings of Quantitative Economic History (as seen in the Historical Trade Cycle Research and its Validation Problems)] in Kocka (ed), *Theorien in der Praxis des Historikers*, 1977.

Spree, Reinhard. *Wachstumtrends und Konjunkturzyklen in der Deutschen Wirtschaft von 1820 bis 1913 - Quantitiver Rahmen fur eine Konjunkturgeschichte des 19. Jahrhunderts* [Growth Trends and Business Cycles in the German Economy from 1820 to 1913 - A Quantitative Framework for a Business Cycle History of the 19th Century]. Gottingen: Vandenhoeck & Ruprecht, 1978.

Spree, Reinhard. "Veranderungen der Muster zyklischen Wachstums Patternen Wirtschaft von der Fruh- zur Hochindustrialisierung,"

[Changes in the Character of Cyclical Growth in the German Economy from Early to Late Industrialization] *Geschichte und Gesellschaft,* 5(2), 1979.

Spree, Reinhard. *Wachstumszyklen der Deutschen Wirtschaft im 19. und 20. Jahrhundert - Ergebnisse, Methoden, Erklarungsansatze* [Growth Cycles of the German Economy in the 19th and 20th Centuries - Results, Methods, Explanations]. Stuttgart: Klett-Cotta, 1980.

Spree, Reinhard. "Probleme der Messung des Technischen Fortschritts im Wachstum der Deutschen Volkswirtschaft seit 1850 mit Hilfe Makrookonomischer Produktionsfunktionen," [Problems of Measuring Technical Progress in the Growth of the German Economy since 1850 with the Help of Macroeconomic Production Functions] Ph.D. Dissertation, Freie Universitat Berlin, 1969.

Spree, Reinhard and Bergmann, J. "Die konjunkturelle Entwicklung der Deutschen Wirtschaft 1840 bis 1864," [The Cyclical (Business) Process in the German Economy, 1840 to 1864] in Wehler (ed), *Sozialgeschichte Heute,* 1974.

Stadler, J.J. "The Gross Domestic Product of South Africa, 1911-1959," *South African Journal of Economics,* 31(3), September 1963, pp. 185-208.

Stampp, Kenneth M. "Introduction: A Humanistic Perspective," in David et al (eds), *Reckoning with Slavery,* 1976, pp. 1-30.

Steckel, Richard H. *The Economics of U.S. Slave and Southern White Fertility.* New York: Arno Press, 1977.

Steckel, Richard H. "The Economics of U.S. Slave and Southern White Fertility," (Summary of Doctoral Dissertation) *Journal of Economic History,* 38(1), March 1978, pp. 289-91.

Steckel, Richard H. "Antebellum Southern White Fertility: A Demographic and Economic Analysis," *Journal of Economic History,* 40(2), June 1980, pp. 331-50.

Steckel, Richard H. and Trussell, James. "The Age of Slaves at Menarche and Their First Birth," *Journal of Interdisciplinary History,* 8(3), Winter 1978, pp. 477-505.

Stadnik, Milos; Pryor, Frederic L.; Pryor, Zora P. and Staller, George J. "Czechoslovak Aggregate Production in the Interwar Period," *Review of Income and Wealth,* 17(1), March 1971, pp. 35-60.

Staller, George J.; Pryor, Zora P.; Stadnik, Milos and Pryor, Frederic L. "Czechoslovak Aggregate Production in the Interwar Period," *Review of Income and Wealth,* 17(1), March 1971, pp. 35-60.

Steckel, Richard and Margo, Robert A. "Height, Health, and Nutrition: Analysis of Evidence for U.S. Slaves," *Social Science History.*

Stein, Burton and Morris, Morris D. "The Economic History of India: A Bibliographic Essay," *Journal of Economic History,* 21(2), June 1961, pp. 179-207.

Stettler, III, H. Louis and Davis, Lance E. "The New England Textile Industry, 1825-60: Reply to McGouldrick," in Brady (ed), *Output, Employment, and Productivity in the United States After 1800,* 1966, pp. 240-2.

Stettler III, H. Louis and Higgs, Robert. "Colonial New England Demography: A Sampling Approach," *William and Mary Quarterly,* Third Series, 27(2), April 1970, pp. 282-94.

Stevens, Edward J. "Composition of the Money Stock Prior to the Civil War," *Journal of Money, Credit and Banking,* 3(1), February 1971, pp. 84-101.

Stevens, Edward J. and Soltow, Lee C. "Economic Aspects of School Participation in Mid-Nineteenth Century United States," *Journal of Interdisciplinary History*, 8(2), Autumn 1977, pp. 221-43.

Stigler, George J. *Capital and Rates of Return in Manufacturing Industries* (General Series 78). Princeton: Princeton University Press for the National Bureau of Economic Research, 1963.

Stockdale, David E. and Vedder, Richard K. "The Profitability of Slavery Revisited: A Different Approach," *Agricultural History*, 49(2), April 1975, pp. 392-404.

Stokes, Houston H. and Neuberger, Hugh M. "German Banks and German Growth, 1883-1913: an Empirical View," *Journal of Economic History*, 34(3), September 1974, pp. 710-31.

Stokes, Houston H. and Neuberger, Hugh M. "German Banking and Japanese Banking: A Comparative Analysis," *Journal of Economic History*, 35(1), March 1975, pp. 238-52.

Stokes, Houston H. and Neuberger, Hugh M. "German Banks and German Growth: Reply to Fremdling and Tilly," *Journal of Economic History*, 36(2), June 1976, pp. 425-7.

Stokes, Houston H. and Neuberger, Hugh M. "German Banks and German Growth: Reply to Komlos," *Journal of Economic History*, 38(2), June 1978, pp. 480-2.

Stokes, Houston H. and Neuberger, Hugh M. "The Effect of Monetary Changes on the Interest Rates during the National Banking Period, 1875-1907: A Box-Jenkins Approach." presented at the Seminar on Economic History, Columbia University, May 1976.

Stone, Irving. "British Long-Term Investment in Latin America, 1865-1913," *Business History Review*, 42(3), Autumn 1968, pp. 311-39.

Stone, Irving. "La distribuzione geografica degli investimenti inglesi nell'America Latina (1825-1913)," [The Geographic Distribution of British Investment in Latin America, 1825-1913] *Storia contemporanea*, 2(3), 1971, pp. 495-518.

Stone, Irving. "British Investment in Argentina: A Note on Ford," *Journal of Economic History*, 32(2), June 1972, pp. 546-7.

Stone, Irving. "British Direct and Portfolio Investment in Latin America before 1914," *Journal of Economic History*, 37(3), September 1977, pp. 690-722.

Stone, Irving. "Global Export of Capital from Great Britain, 1865-1914." [Working Paper]

Stone, Irving. "The (Annual) Export of Capital from Great Britain to Latin America, 1865-1914." presented at the Seventh International Congress on Economic History at Edinburgh, Scotland, August, 1978.

Stone, J.R.F. and Rowe, D.A. *The Measurement of Consumers' Expenditure and Behaviour in the United Kingdom, 1920-1938* (2 vols). Cambridge: Cambridge University Press, 1954.

Stone, James M. "Financial Panics: Their Implications for the Mix of Domestic and Foreign Investments in Britain, 1880-1913," *Quarterly Journal of Economics*, 85(2), May 1971, pp. 304-26.

Stout, Harry S. and Swierenga, Robert P. "Dutch Immigration in the Nineteenth Century, 1820-1877: A Quantitative Overview," *Indiana Social Studies Quarterly*, 28(2), Autumn 1975, pp. 7-34.

Stout, Harry S. and Swierenga, Robert P. "Socio-Economic Patterns of Migration from the Netherlands to the U.S. in the Nineteenth Century," in Uselding (ed), *Research in Economic History*, 1976, pp.

298-333.

Strassmann, W. Paul. "Technological Change in the Machine Tool Industry, 1840-1910: Discussion of Rosenberg," *Journal of Economic History*, 23(4), December 1963, pp. 444-6.

Strassman, W. Paul; Parker, William N.; Wilkening, E.A. and Merrill, Robert S. *The Diffusion of Technical Knowledge as an Instrument of Economic Development* (Symposia Studies Series no. 13). National Institute of Social and Behavioral Science, 1962.

Strober, Myra H. and Best, Laura. "Female-Male Salary Differential in Public Schools: Some Lessons from San Francisco, 1879," *Economic Inquiry*, 17(2), April 1979, pp. 218-36.

Summers, Robert and Heston, Alan W. "Comparative Indian Economic Growth, 1870 to 1970," *American Economic Review, Papers and Proceedings, 70(2), May 1980, pp. 96-101.*

Sundarajan, V. *"The Impact of the Tariff on Some Selected Products of the U.S. Iron and Steel Industry, 1870-1914,"* Quarterly Journal of Economics, 84(4), November 1970, pp. 590-610.

Supple, Barry. "Economic History and Economic Growth," *Journal of Economic History,* 20(4), December 1960, pp. 548-56.

Supple, Barry. "Can the New Economic History Become an Import Substitute?," in McCloskey (ed), *Essays on a Mature Economy*, 1971, pp. 423-30.

Supple, Barry. "Thinking About Economic Development," in Youngson (ed), *Economic Development in the Long Run*, 1972, pp. 19-35.

Supple, Barry E. "Income and Demand, 1860-1914," in Floud and McCloskey (eds), *The Economic History of Britain since 1700,* 1981.

Sushka, Marie E. "An Economic Model of the Money Market in the United States, 1823-1859," (Summary of Doctoral Dissertation) *Journal of Economic History*, 35(1), March 1975, pp. 280-5.

Sushka, Marie E. "The Antebellum Money Market and the Economic Impact of the Bank War," *Journal of Economic History,* 36(4), December 1976, pp. 809-35.

Sushka, Marie E. "The Antebellum Money Market and the Economic Impact of the Bank War: A Reply to Curran and Johnston," *Journal of Economic History*, 39(2), June 1979, pp. 467-74.

Sutch, Richard C. "The Profitability of Antebellum Slavery: Revisited (Comment on Saraydar)," reprinted in Aitken (ed), *Did Slavery Pay?*, 1971, pp. 221-41. *Southern Economic Journal,* 31(4), April 1965, pp. 365-77.

Sutch, Richard C. "Slavery as an Obstacle to Economic Growth in the United States: A Panel Discussion of Conrad and Meyer," *Journal of Economic History,* 27(4), December 1967, pp. 540-1.

Sutch, Richard C. "Comments on Papers by Smith and Vinovskis Presented to the 31st Annual Meeting of the Economic History Association," *Journal of Economic History*, 32(1), March 1972, pp. 216-8.

Sutch, Richard C. "The Breeding of Slaves for Sale and the Westward Expansion of Slavery, 1850-1860," in Engerman and Genovese (eds), *Race and Slavery in the Western Hemisphere*, 1975, pp. 173-210.

Sutch, Richard C. "The Treatment Received by American Slaves: A Critical Review of Evidence Presented in Time on the Cross," (Symposium on Time on the Cross. Edited by Gary M. Walton) *Explorations in Economic History,* 12(4), October 1975, pp. 335-438.

Sutch, Richard C. "The Care and Feeding of Slaves," in David et al (eds), *Reckoning with Slavery*, 1976, pp. 231-301.

466

Sutch, Richard C. The Frontiers of Quantitative Economic History, Circa 1975," in Intrilligator (ed), *Frontiers of Quantitative Economics,* 1977, pp. 399-416.

Sutch, Richard C.; David, Paul A.; Gutman, Herbert; Temin, Peter and Wright, Gavin. *Reckoning with Slavery: A Critical Study in the Quantitative History of American Negro Slavery.* New York: Oxford University Press, 1976.

Sutch, Richard C.; David, Paul A.; Gutman, Herbert; Temin, Peter and Wright, Gavin. "'Time on the Cross' and the Burden of Quantitative History," in David et al (eds), *Reckoning with Slavery,* 1976, pp. 339-82.

Sutch, Richard C. and Gutman, Herbert. "Sambo Makes Good, or Were Slaves Imbued with the Protestant Work Ethic?," in David et al (eds), *Reckoning with Slavery,* 1976, pp. 55-93.

Sutch, Richard C. and Gutman, Herbert. "The Slave Family: Protected Agent of Capitalist Masters or Victim of the Slave Trade?," in David et al (eds), *Reckoning with Slavery,* 1976, pp. 94-133.

Sutch, Richard C. and Gutman, Herbert. "Victorians All? The Sexual Mores and Conduct of Slaves and Their Masters," in David et al (eds), *Reckoning with Slavery,* 1976, pp. 134-64.

Sutch, Richard C. and Ransom, Roger L. "Debt Peonage in the Cotton South after the Civil War," *Journal of Economic History,* 32(3), September 1972, pp. 641-69.

Sutch, Richard C. and Ransom, Roger L. "The Ex-Slave in the Postbellum South: A Study of the Economic Impact of Racism in a Market Environment," *Journal of Economic History,* 33(1), March 1973, pp. 131-47.

Sutch, Richard C. and Ransom, Roger L. "The Impact of the Civil War and of Emancipation on Southern Agriculture," *Explorations in Economic History,* 12(1), January 1975, pp. 1-28.

Sutch, Richard C. and Ransom, Roger L. "The 'Lock-In' Mechanism and Overproduction of Cotton in the Postbellum South," *Agricultural History,* 49(2), April 1975, pp. 405-25.

Sutch, Richard C. and Ransom, Roger L. "Sharecropping: Market Response or Mechanism of Race Control?," in Sansing (ed), *What Was Freedom's Price?,* 1978, pp. 51-69.

Sutch, Richard C. and Ransom, Roger L. "Credit Merchandising in the Post-Emancipation South: Structure, Conduct, and Performance," *Explorations in Economic History,* 16(1), January 1979, pp. 64-89.

Sutch, Richard C. and Ransom, Roger L. "Growth and Welfare in the American South of the Nineteenth Century," *Explorations in Economic History,* 16(2), April 1979, pp. 207-36.

Sutch, Richard C. and Ransom, Roger L. "Economic Dimensions of Reconstruction: An Overview." [Working Paper]

Sutch, Richard C. and Ransom, Roger L. *One Kind of Freedom: The Economic Consequences of Emancipation.* New York: Cambridge University Press, 1977.

Sutch, Richard C.; Roehl, Richard; Lyons, John and Boskins, Michael. "Urban Migration in the Process of Industrialization: Britain and the United States in the Nineteenth Century," University of California-Berkeley, Center for Research in Management Science, Working Papers in Economic Theory and Econometrics no. 162, August 1970.

Sutch, Richard C. and Roehl, Richard. "Urban Migration during the

Process of Industrialization: The United States and England in the Nineteenth Century," presented at the International Econometric Society Meetings, September 1970.

Suzigan, Wilson. "A Politica Cambial Brasileira, 1889-1946," [Analysis of Brazilian Exchange Rate Policy, 1889-1946] *Revista Brasileira de Economia*, 25(3), July/September 1971, pp. 93-111.

Suzigan, Wilson. "Industrializacao e Politica Economica: Uma Interpretacao em Perspectiva Historica," [An Interpretation of Brazilian Industrialization and Economic Policy in Historical Perspective] *Pesquisa e Planejamento Economico*, 5(2), December 1975, pp. 433-74.

Suzigan, Wilson. "Industrialization and Economic Policy in Historical Perspective," *Brazilian Economic Studies*, 2, 1976, pp. 5-33.

Suzigan, Wilson and Pelaez, Carlos M. "Bases para a Interpretacao Monetaria da Historia Economica Brasileira," [Basis for a Monetary Interpretation of Brazilian Economic History] *Revista Brasileira de Economia*, 26(4), October/December 1972, pp. 57-94.

Suzigan, Wilson and Pelaez, Carlos M. *Historia Monetaria do Brasil: Analise da Politica, Comportamento e Instituicoes Monetarias* [Monetary History of Brasil: Analysis of Policy Behavior and Monetary Institutions] (IPEA Serie Monografica no. 23). Rio de Janeiro: Instituto de Planejamento Economico e Social, 1976.

Suzigan, Wilson and Pelaez, Carlos M. "Comportamento e Instituicoes Monetarias no Brasil, 1852-1972," [Monetary Institutions and their Behavior in Brazil, 1852-1872] in Neuhaus (ed), *A Economia Brasileira*, 1979, pp. 161-90.

Suzigan, Wilson and Pelaez, Carlos M. *Historia Economica do Brasil* [Economic History of Brazil]. Sao Paulo: Editora Atlas, 1979.

Suzigan, Wilson and Villela, Annibal V. *Politica do Governo e Crescimento da Economia Brasileira, 1889-1945* [Government Policy and the Economic Growth of Brazil, 1889-1945]. Rio de Janeiro: I.P.E.A., 1973.

Suzuki, M. "A Spectral Analysis of Japanese Economic Time Series since the 1880's," *Kyklos*, 18(2), 1965, pp. 227-58.

Swan, Dale E. "The Structure and Profitability of the Antebellum Rice Industry: 1859," (Summary of Doctoral Dissertation) *Journal of Economic History*, 33(1), March 1973, pp. 321-5.

Swan, Dale E. and Foust, James D. "Productivity and Profitability of Antebellum Slave Labor: A Micro-Approach," in Parker (ed), *The Structure of the Cotton Economy of the Antebellum South*, 1970, pp. 39-62.

Swan, Peter L. "Optimum Replacement of Capital Goods with Labor-Saving Technical Progress: A Comparison of the Early New England and British Textile Firm," *Journal of Political Economy*, 84(6), December 1976, pp. 1293-304.

Swanson, Joseph A. and Curran, Christopher. "The Fiscal Behavior of Municipal Governments: 1905-1930," *Journal of Urban Economics*, 3(4), October 1976, pp. 344-56.

Swanson, Joseph A.: Smith, Kenneth R. and Williamson, Jeffrey G. "The Size Distribution of Cities and Optimal City Size," *Journal of Urban Economics*, 1(4), October 1974, pp. 395-409.

Swanson, Joseph A. and Williamson, Jeffrey G. "The Growth of Cities in the American Northeast, 1820-1870," *Explorations in Entrepreneurial History*, Second Series, 4(1), (Supplement), Fall 1966, pp. 1-101.

468

Swanson, Joseph A. and Williamson, Jeffrey G. "A Model of Urban
Capital Formation and the Growth of Cities in History,"
Explorations in Economic History, 8(2), Winter 1970/71, pp. 213-22.
Swanson, Joseph A. and Williamson, Jeffrey G. "Explanations and
Issues: A Prospectus for Quantitative Economic History," *Journal of
Economic History*, 31(1), March 1971, pp. 43-57.
Swanson, Joseph A. and Williamson, Jeffrey G. "Firm Location and
Optimal City Size in American History," in Schnore (ed), *The New
Urban History*, 1975, pp. 260-73.
Swanson, Joseph A. and Williamson, Samuel H. "Estimates of National
Product and Income for the United States Economy, 1919-1941,"
Explorations in Economic History, 10(1), Fall 1972, pp. 53-74.
Sweden Statistika Centralbyran. *Historisk Statistik for Sverige, Del.
1: Befolkning, 1720-1967* [Historical Statistics of Sweden, part 1:
Population, 1720-1967]. Stockholm: National Central Bureau of
Statistics.
Sweden Statistika Centralbyran. *Historisk statistik for Sverige, Del.
2: Vaderlek, lantmateri, jordbruk, skogsbruk, fiske tom ar*
[Historical Statistics of Sweden, part 2: Climate, Land Surveying,
Agriculture, Forestry, Fisheries]. Stockholm: National Central
Bureau of Statistics, 1955.
Sweden Statistika Centralbyran. *Historisk Statistik for Sverige, Del.
3: Utrikeshandel, 1732-1970* [Historical Statistics of Sweden, part
3: Foreign Trade, 1732-1970]. Stockholm: National Central Bureau
of Statistics, 1972.
Swierenga, Robert P. "Land Speculator 'Profits' Reconsidered: Central
Iowa as a Test Case," reprinted in Swierenga (ed), *Quantification
in American History*, 1970, pp. 317-40. *Journal of Economic
History*, 26(1), March 1966, pp. 1-28.
Swierenga, Robert P. *Pioneers and Profits: Land Speculation on the
Iowa Frontier*. Ames: Iowa State University Press, 1968.
Swierenga, Robert P. "The Tax Buyer as a Frontier Investor Type,"
Explorations in Economic History, 7(3), Spring 1970, pp. 257-92.
Swierenga, Robert P. "Land Speculation and Frontier Tax Assessments,"
Agricultural History, 44(3), July 1970, pp. 253-66.
Swierenga, Robert P. "The Equity Effects of Public Land Speculation in
Iowa: Large versus Small Speculators," *Journal of Economic History*,
34(4), December 1974, pp. 1008-20.
Swierenga, Robert P. "Land Speculation and Its Impact on American
Economic Growth and Welfare: An Historiographical Review," *Western
Historical Quarterly*, 8, July 1977, pp. 283-302.
Swierenga, Robert P. "Dutch Immigrant Demography, 1820-1880," *Journal
of Family History*, 5, Winter 1980, pp. 390-405.
Swierenga, Robert P. and Stout, Harry S. "Dutch Immigration in the
Nineteenth Century, 1820-1877: A Quantitative Overview," *Indiana
Social Studies Quarterly*, 28(2), Autumn 1975, pp. 7-34.
Swierenga, Robert P. and Stout, Harry S. "Socio-Economic Patterns of
Migration from the Netherlands to the U.S. in the Nineteenth
Century," in Uselding (ed), *Research in Economic History*, 1976, pp.
298-333.
Sylla, Richard E. "Finance and Capital in the United States,
1850-1900," (Summary of Doctoral Dissertation) *Journal of Economic
History*, 27(4), December 1967, pp. 621-4.
Sylla, Richard E. "Federal Policy, Banking Market Structure, and

Capital Mobilization in the United States, 1863-1913," *Journal of Economic History,* 29(4), December 1969, pp. 657-86.

Sylla, Richard E. "The United States, 1863-1913," in Cameron (ed), *Banking and Economic Development,* 1972, pp. 232-62.

Sylla, Richard E. "American Banking and Growth in the Nineteenth Century: A Partial View of the Terrain," *Explorations in Economic History,* 9(2), Winter 1971/72, pp. 197-227.

Sylla, Richard E. "Economic History 'von unten nach oben' and 'von oben nach unten': A Reply to Fritz Redlich," *Explorations in Economic History,* 10(3), Spring 1973, pp. 315-8.

Sylla, Richard E. *The American Capital Market, 1846-1914.* New York: Arno Press, 1975.

Sylla, Richard E. "The Denigration of Cotton and Other Dissertations: A Discussion," *Journal of Economic History,* 35(1), March 1975, pp. 291-5.

Sylla, Richard E. "Forgotten Men of Money: Private Bankers in Early U.S. History," *Journal of Economic History,* 36(1), March 1976, pp. 173-88.

Sylla, Richard E. "Financial Intermediaries in Economic History: Quantitative Research on the Seminal Hypotheses of Lance Davis and Alexander Gerschenkron," in Gallman (ed), *Recent Developments in the Study of Business and Economic History,* 1977.

Sylla, Richard E. "Small-Business Banking in the United States, 1780-1920," in Bruchey (ed), *Small Business in American Life,* 1980, pp. 240-62.

Sylla, Richard E. "Money: A Discussion of Papers by Keehn, Howson, and Bordo/Schwartz Presented to the 39th Annual Meeting of the Economic History Association," *Journal of Economic History,* 40(1), March 1980, pp. 70-2.

Sylla, Richard E. "The Concept of the Corporation in Early British and American Banking." [Working Paper]

Sylla, Richard E. "The Public Sector and the Price Level in America, 1720-1977." [Working Paper]

Sylla, Richard E. and James, John A. "The Changing Nature of American Public Debt, 1690-1835," in *La Dette Publique aux XVIIIe et XIXe Siecles.* Brussels: Credit Communal de Belgique, 1980.

Sylla, Richard E.; Soltow, James H. and Ratner, Sidney. *The Evolution of the American Economy: Growth, Welfare and Decision Making.* New York: Basic Books, 1979.

Sylla, Richard E. and Toniolo, Gianni. "La 'New Economic History' -- metodi, obiettivi, limiti," [The New Economic History: Methods, Objects, Limits] reprinted in Toniolo (ed), *Lo sviluppo economico italiano,* 1973. pp. 41-70. *Quaderni Storici,* 11, 1969, pp. 229-64.

Synnott, III, Thomas W. "Investment Policies, Growth, and Profitability in the New England Cotton Textile Industry, 1830-1914," *Yale Economic Essays,* 11(1 & 2), Spring/Fall 1971, pp. 97-144.

Taira, Koji. "Growth, Trends, and Swings in Japanese Agriculture and Industry. Review Essay of 'Agriculture and Economic Growth: Japan's Experience'," *Economic Development and Cultural Change,* 24(2),

January 1976, pp. 423-36.

Tannen, Michael B. and McGouldrick, Paul F. "Did American Manufacturers Discriminate against Immigrants before 1914?," *Journal of Economic History,* 37(3), September 1977, pp. 723-46.

Tannen, Michael B. and McGouldrick, Paul F. "The Increasing Pay Gap for Women in the Textile and Clothing Industries, 1910 to 1970," *Journal of Economic History,* 40(4), December 1980, pp. 799-814.

Tannen, Michael B. and McGouldrick, Paul. "Further Results on Male and Female Pay Differentials, 1910 to 1970." [Working Paper]

Tanner, J. Ernest and Bonomo, Vittorio. "Gold, Capital Flows and Long Swings in American Business Activity," *Journal of Political Economy,* 76(1), January/February 1968, pp. 44-52.

Tattara, Giuseppe. "Cerealicultura e politica agraria durante il fascismo," [Cereal Production and Agricultural Policy under Fascism] in Toniolo (ed), *Lo sviluppo economico italiano,* 1973, pp. 373-405. Reprinted in Toniolo (ed), *L'economia italiana,* 1978.

Tattara, Giuseppe and Toniolo, Gianni. "L'industria manifatturiera: cicli, politiche e mutamenti di struttura (1921-37)," [Industrial Manufacturing: Cycles, Policies, and Structural Change (1921-37)] in Ciocca and Toniolo (ed), *L'economia italiana nel periodo fascista,* 1976.

Taylor, George Rogers. "Railroad Investment Before the Civil War: Comment on Wicker," in Parker (ed), *Trends in the American Economy in the Nineteenth Century,* 1960, pp. 524-44.

Taylor, George Rogers. "American Economic Growth Before 1840: An Exploratory Essay," in Andreano (ed), *New Views,* 1965, pp. 57-72.

Teijl, J. "National Inkomen van Nederland in de periode 1850-1900," *Economisch-en-Sociaal-Historisch Jaarboek,* 34), 1971, pp. 232-62.

Temin, Peter. "The Composition of Iron and Steel Products, 1869-1909," *Journal of Economic History,* 23(4), December 1963, pp. 447-71.

Temin, Peter. *Iron and Steel in Nineteenth Century America: An Economic Inquiry.* Cambridge: M.I.T. Press, 1964.

Temin, Peter. "A New Look at Hunter's Hypothesis about the Antebellum Iron Industry," reprinted in Fogel and Engerman (eds), *The Reinterpretation of American Economic History,* 1971, pp. 116-21. *American Economic Review,* Papers and Proceedings, 54(3), May 1964, pp. 344-51.

Temin, Peter. "The Relative Decline of the British Steel Industry, 1880-1913," in Rosovsky (ed), *Industrialization in Two Systems,* 1966.

Temin, Peter. "Steam and Waterpower in the Early Nineteenth Century," reprinted in Fogel and Engerman (eds), *The Reinterpretation of American Economic History,* 1971, pp. 228-37. *Journal of Economic History,* 26(2), June 1966, pp. 187-205.

Temin, Peter. "In Pursuit of the Exact," *Times Literary Supplement,* 65(3361), July 28, 1966, pp. 652-3.

Temin, Peter. "Labor Scarcity and the Problem of American Industrial Efficiency in the 1850's," *Journal of Economic History,* 26(3), September 1966, pp. 277-98.

Temin, Peter. "A Time-Series Test of Patterns of Industrial Growth," *Economic Development and Cultural Change,* 15(2), (Part 1), January 1967, pp. 174-82.

Temin, Peter. "The Causes of Cotton-Price Fluctuations in the 1830's," *Review of Economics and Statistics,* 46(4), November 1967, pp.

463-70.

Temin, Peter. "Labor Scarcity and the Problem of American Industrial Efficiency in the 1850's: A Reply to Drummond," *Journal of Economic History*, 28(1), March 1968, pp. 124-5.

Temin, Peter. "The Economic Consequences of the Bank War," *Journal of Political Economy*, 76(2), March/April 1968, pp. 257-74.

Temin, Peter. "Labor Scarcity in America," *Journal of Interdisciplinary History*, 1(2), Winter 1971, pp. 251-64.

Temin, Peter. "General Equilibrium Models in Economic History," *Journal of Economic History*, 31(1), March 1971, pp. 58-75.

Temin, Peter. "The Beginning of the Depression in Germany," *Economic History Review*, Second Series, 24(2), May 1971, pp. 240-8.

Temin, Peter. "Manufacturing," in Davis, Parker, and Easterlin (eds), *American Economic Growth*, 1972, pp. 418-67.

Temin, Peter, ed. *The New Economic History: Selected Readings.* Harmondsworth: Penguin Books, 1973.

Temin, Peter. "The Anglo-American Business Cycle, 1820-60," *Economic History Review*, Second Series, 27(2), May 1974, pp. 207-21.

Temin, Peter. "Methodology and Evidence in Economic History," *Economic Inquiry*, 12(3), September 1974, pp. 415-8.

Temin, Peter. *Causal Factors in American Economic Growth in the Nineteenth Century.* London: Macmillan, 1975.

Temin, Peter. "The Panic of 1857," *Inter-Mountain Economic Review*, 6(1), Spring 1975, pp. 1-12.

Temin, Peter. *Did Monetary Forces Cause the Great Depression?* New York: W.W. Norton, 1976.

Temin, Peter. "Lessons for the Present from the Great Depression," *American Economic Review*, Papers and Proceedings, 66(2), May 1976, pp. 40-5.

Temin, Peter. "The Postbellum Recovery of the South and the Cost of the Civil War," *Journal of Economic History*, 36(4), December 1976, pp. 898-907.

Temin, Peter. "The German Business Cycle in the 1920's: A Comment on Balderston and Reply to Falkus," *Economic History Review*, Second Series, 30(1), February 1977, pp. 162-4.

Temin, Peter. "Money, Money Everywhere: A Retrospective. Review Essay of 'The Monetary History of the United States, 1867-1960' by Milton Friedman and Anna J. Schwartz," *Reviews in American History*, 5(2), June 1977, pp. 151-9.

Temin, Peter. "The Postbellum Recovery of the South and the Cost of the Civil War: A Reply to Goldin and Lewis," *Journal of Economic History*, 38(2), June 1978, pp. 493.

Temin, Peter. "Roots of Regulation: The New Deal (Discussion of Hughes)," in Walton (ed), *Regulatory Change in an Atmosphere of Crisis*, 1979, pp. 57-62.

Temin, Peter. "Freedom and Coercion: Notes on the Analysis of Debt Peonage in 'One Kind of Freedom'," *Explorations in Economic History*, 16(1), January 1979, pp. 56-63.

Temin, Peter. "The Origin of Compulsory Drug Prescriptions," *Journal of Law and Economics*, 22(1), April 1979, pp. 91-106.

Temin, Peter. "Notes on the Causes of the Great Depression," in Brunner (ed), *The Great Depression Revisited*, 1981, pp. 108-24.

Temin, Peter and David, Paul A. "Slavery: The Progressive Institution? Review Essay of 'Time on the Cross (2 vols)' by Robert W. Fogel and

Stanley L. Engerman (Boston: Little, Brown, 1974)," reprinted in David et al (eds), *Reckoning with Slavery*, 1976, pp. 165-230. *Journal of Economic History*, 34(3), September 1974, pp. 739-83.

Temin, Peter and David, Paul A. "Capitalist Masters, Bourgeois Slaves. Review Essay of 'Time on the Cross (2 vols)' by Robert W. Fogel and Stanley L. Engerman (Boston: Little, Brown, 1974)," reprinted in David et al (eds), *Reckoning with Slavery*, 1976, pp. 33-54. *Journal of Interdisciplinary History*, 5(3), Winter 1975, pp. 445-57.

Temin, Peter and David, Paul A. "Explaining the Relative Efficiency of Slave Agriculture in the Antebellum South: A Comment (on Fogel and Engerman)," *American Economic Review*, 69(1), March 1979, pp. 213-8.

Temin, Peter and Fisher, Franklin M. "Regional Specialization and the Supply of Wheat in the United States, 1867-1914," *Review of Economics and Statistics*, 52(2), May 1970, pp. 134-49.

Temin, Peter and Fisher, Franklin M. "Regional Specialization and the Supply of Wheat in the United States, 1867-1914: A Reply to Higgs," *Review of Economics and Statistics*, 53(1), February 1971, pp. 102-3.

Temin, Peter and Fisher, Franklin M. "Returns to Scale in Research and Development: What does the Schumpeterian Hypothesis Imply?," *Journal of Political Economy*, 81(1), January/February 1973, pp. 56-70.

Temin, Peter; Gutman, Herbert; Sutch, Richard C.; David, Paul A. and Wright, Gavin. *Reckoning with Slavery: A Critical Study in the Quantitative History of American Negro Slavery*. New York: Oxford University Press, 1976.

Temin, Peter; Gutman, Herbert; Sutch, Richard C.; David, Paul A. and Wright, Gavin. "Time on the Cross and the Burden of Quantitative History," in David et al (eds), *Reckoning with Slavery*, 1976, pp. 339-57.

Temin, Peter and Solow, Robert M. "Introduction: The Inputs for Growth," in Mathias and Postan (eds), *The Cambridge Economic History of Europe*, 1978, pp. 1-27.

TePaske, John J. "Quantification in Latin American Colonial History," in Lorwin and Price (eds), *The Dimensions of the Past*, 1972, pp. 431-76.

Thirlwall, A.P. and Lundgreen, Peter. "Educational Expansion and Economic Growth in Nineteenth Century Germany: A Quantitative Study," in Stone (ed), *Schooling and Society*, 1976, pp. 20-66.

Thomas, Brinley. "Migration and the Rhythm of Economic Growth, 1830-1913," *Manchester School of Economic and Social Studies*, 19(3), September 1951, pp. 215-71.

Thomas, Brinley. "The Changing Pattern of Internal Migration in the United Kingdom, 1920-50," *World Population Congress, 1st, Rome, 1954: Proceedings*. New York: United Nations Department of Economic and Social Affairs, 1955.

Thomas, Brinley. "The Rhythm of Growth in the Atlantic Economy," in Hegeland (ed), *Money, Growth and Methodology*, 1961, pp. 39-48.

Thomas, Brinley. "International Factor Movements and Unequal Rates of Growth," *Manchester School of Economic and Social Studies*, 29(1), January 1961, pp. 1-21.

Thomas, Brinley, ed. *The Welsh Economy: Studies in Expansion*. Cardiff: University of Wales Press, 1962.

Thomas, Brinley. "Long Swings in Internal Migration and Capital Formation," *Bulletin of the International Statistical Institute, Proceedings of the 34th Session.* Toronto: International Statistical Institute, 40, 1964, pp. 398-412.

Thomas, Brinley. "The Dimensions of British Economic Growth, 1688-1959. Review Essay of 'British Economic Growth, 1688-1959: Trends and Structure' by Phyllis Deane and W.A. Cole (Cambridge: Cambridge University Press, 1964)," *Journal of the Royal Statistical Society,* 127, Series A (General), (Part 1), 1964, pp. 111-23.

Thomas, Brinley. "Consumption, Investment and Employment: General Comment," in Brady (ed), *Output, Employment, and Productivity in the United States after 1800,* 1966, pp. 205-10.

Thomas, Brinley. "Intra-Commonwealth Flows of Capital and Skills," in Hamilton, Robinson, and Goodwin (eds), *a Decade of the Commonwealth,* 1966, pp. 407-27.

Thomas, Brinley. *The Changing Pattern of Anglo-Danish Trade, 1913-1963.* Aarhus, Denmark: Erhvervshistorisk Arbog, 1966.

Thomas, Brinley. "The Historical Record of International Capital Movements to 1913," in Adler (ed), *Capital Movements and Economic Development,* 1967, pp. 3-32.

Thomas, Brinley. "Migration and International Investment," in Hall (ed), *The Export of Capital from Britain,* 1968, pp. 45-54.

Thomas, Brinley. "The Migration of Labour into Glamorganshire Coalfield, 1861-1911," in Minchinton (ed), *Industrial South Wales,* pp. 37-56.

Thomas, Brinley. "Demographic Determinants of British and American Building Cycles, 1870-1913," in McCloskey (ed), *Essays on a Mature Economy,* 1971, pp. 39-74.

Thomas, Brinley. *Migration and Urban Development: A Reappraisal of British and American Long Cycles.* London: Methuen, 1972.

Thomas, Brinley. "Long Swings and the Atlantic Economy: A Reappraisal," in David and Reder (eds), *Nations and Households in Economic Growth,* 1974, pp. 383-406.

Thomas, Brinley. *The Drive to Industrial Maturity: The U.S. Economy 1860-1940.* Westport, Conn.: Greenwood Press, 1975.

Thomas, Brinley. "The Rhythm of Growth in the Atlantic Economy of the Eighteenth Century," in Uselding (ed), *Research in Economic History,* 1978, pp. 1-46.

Thomas, Brinley. "Towards an Energy Interpretation of the Industrial Revolution," *Atlantic Economic Journal,* 8(1), March 1980, pp. 1-15.

Thomas, Dorothy Swaine. "Temporal and Spatial Interrelations between Migration and Economic Opportunities," in Eldridge and Thomas (eds), *Population, Redistribution and Economic Growth,* 1964, pp. 319-68.

Thomas, Dorothy Swaine and Eldridge, Hope T., eds. *Population Redistribution and Economic Growth, United States, 1870-1950, vol. 3: Demographic Analyses and Interrelations* (Series edited by Simon S. Kuznets and Dorothy Swaine Thomas). Philadelphia: American Philosophical Society, 1964.

Thomas, Lloyd B. "Behavior of Flexible Exchange Rates: Additional Tests from the Post-World War I Episode," *Southern Economic Journal,* 40(2), October 1973, pp. 167-82.

Thomas, Lloyd B. and Greenwood, Michael J. "Geographic Labor Mobility in Nineteenth Century England and Wales," *Annals of Regional Science*, 7(2), December 1973, pp. 90-105.

Thomas, Robert P. "Business Failure in the Early Automobile Industry, 1895-1910," in Fenstermaker (ed), *Business History Conference*, 1962.

Thomas, Robert P. "A Quantitative Approach to the Study of the Effects of British Imperial Policy upon Colonial Welfare: Some Preliminary Findings," *Journal of Economic History*, 25(4), December 1965, pp. 615-38.

Thomas, Robert P. "The Sugar Colonies of the Old Empire: Profit or Loss for Great Britain?," *Economic History Review*, Second Series, 21(1), April 1968, pp. 30-45.

Thomas, Robert P. "British Imperial Policy and the Economic Interpretation of the American Revolution: Reply to Ransom," *Journal of Economic History*, 28(3), September 1968, pp. 436-40.

Thomas, Robert P. "The Automobile Industry and Its Tycoon," *Explorations in Entrepreneurial History*, Second Series, 6(2), Winter 1969, pp. 139-57.

Thomas, Robert P. "Style Change and the Automobile Industry during the Roaring Twenties," in Cain and Uselding (eds), *Business Enterprise and Economic Change*, 1973, pp. 118-38.

Thomas, Robert P. *An Analysis of the Pattern of Growth of the Automobile Industry*. New York: Arno Press, 1977.

Thomas, Robert P. and Anderson, Terry L. "White Population, Labor Force and Extensive Growth of the New England Economy in the Seventeenth Century," *Journal of Economic History*, 33(3), September 1973, pp. 634-67.

Thomas, Robert P. and Anderson, Terry L. "The Growth of Population and Labor Force in the 17th-Century Chesapeake," *Explorations in Economic History*, 15(3), July 1978, pp. 290-312.

Thomas, Robert P.; Anderson, Terry L. and Bean, Richard N. "Economic Growth in the Seventeenth Century American Colonies: Applications of an Export-Led Growth Model." [Working Paper]

Thomas, Robert P. and Baack, Bennett D. "The Enclosure Movement and the Supply of Labor During the Industrial Revolution," *Journal of European Economic History*, 3(2), Fall 1974, pp. 401-23.

Thomas, Robert P. and Bean, Richard N. "The Fishers of Men: The Profits of the Slave Trade," *Journal of Economic History*, 34(4), December 1974, pp. 885-914.

Thomas, Robert P. and Bean, Richard N. "The Adoption of Slave Labor in British America," in Gemery and Hogendorn (eds), *The Uncommon Market*, 1979, pp. 377-98.

Thomas, Robert P. and McCloskey, Donald N. "Overseas Trade and Empire, 1700-1860," in Floud and McCloskey (eds), *The Economic History of Britain since 1700*, 1981, pp. 87-102.

Thomas, Robert P. and North, Douglass C. *A Documentary History of American Economic Growth, 1607-1860*. New York: Harper & Row, 1968.

Thomas, Robert P. and North, Douglass C. "An Economic Theory of the Growth of the Western World," *Economic History Review*, Second Series, 23(1), April 1970, pp. 1-17.

Thomas, Robert P. and North, Douglass C. "The Rise and Fall of the Manorial System: A Theoretical Model," *Journal of Economic History*, 31(4), December 1971, pp. 777-803.

Thomas, Robert P. and North, Douglass C. "European Economic Growth:

Reply to Professor D. Ringose," *Economic History Review,* Second Series, 26(2), May 1973, pp. 293-4.

Thomas, Robert P. and North, Douglass C. *The Rise of the Western World: A New Economic History* [Translated into Italian, Spanish, and French]. Cambridge: Cambridge University Press, 1975.

Thomas, Robert P. and North, Douglass C. "The Role of Governments in Economic Growth in Early Modern Times: Comment on Lane," *Journal of Economic History,* 35(1), March 1975, pp. 18-9.

Thomas, Robert P. and North, Douglass C. "The First Economic Revolution," *Economic History Review,* Second Series, 30(2), May 1977, pp. 229-41.

Thomas, Robert P. and Shetler, Douglass D. "Railroad Social Saving: A Comment on Hunt," *American Economic Review,* 58(1), March 1968, pp. 186-9.

Thomas, T. "Aggregate Demand in the United Kingdom, 1918-45," in Floud and McCloskey (eds), *The Economic History of Britain since 1700,* 1981.

Thompson, Alexander M. *Technology, Labor, and Industrial Structure in the U.S. Coal Industry.* New York: Garland Press, 1979.

Thompson, Alexander M. "Technological Change and the Control of Work." [Working Paper]

Thompson, Alexander M. "Workers' Control and the Fracturing of Miners' Skills in Appalachian Coal Mining." [Working Paper]

Thornton, Judith G. "The Index Number Problem in the Measurement of Soviet National Income: A Review Article. Review Essay of 'The Real National Income of Soviet Russia Since 1928' by Abram Bergson (Cambridge: Harvard University Press, 1961)," *Journal of Economic History,* 22(3), September 1962, pp. 379-89.

Tice, Helen Stone. "Depreciation, Obsolescence, and the Measurement of the Aggregate Capital Stock of the United States, 1900-1962," *Review of Income and Wealth,* 13(2), June 1967, pp. 119-54.

Tierney, Michael and Solmon, Lewis C. "Education," in Porter (ed), *Encyclopedia of American Economic History,* 1980, pp. 1012-27.

Tilly, Charles and Tilly, Louise A. "A Selected Bibliography of Quantitative Sources for French History and French Sources for Quantitative History since 1789," in Lorwin and Price (eds), *The Dimensions of the Past,* 1972, pp. 157-75.

Tilly, Louise A. "Materials of the Quantitative History of France since 1789," in Lorwin and Price (eds), *The Dimensions of the Past,* 1972, pp. 127-55.

Tilly, Louise A. and Tilly, Charles. "A Selected Bibliography of Quantitative Sources for French History and French Sources for Quantitative History since 1789," in Lorwin and Price (eds), *The Dimensions of the Past,* 1972, pp. 157-75.

Tilly, Richard H. "Germany, 1815-1870," in Cameron (ed), *Banking in the Early Stages of Industrialization,* 1967, pp. 151-82.

Tilly, Richard H. "Zur Entwicklung des Kapitalmarktes und Industrialisierung im 19. Jahrhundert unter Besonderer Berucksichtigung Deutschlands," [The Development of the Capital Market and Industrialization in the 19th Century: the Case of Germany] reprinted in Kellenbenz, Schneider, and Gommel (eds), *Wirtschaftliches Wachstum im Spiegel der Wirtschaftsgeschichte,* 1978. *Vierteljahrschrift fur Sozial- und Wirtschaftsgeschichte,* 60(2), 1973, pp. 145-65.

476

Tilly, Richard H. "Zeitreihen zum Geldumlauf in Deutschland, 1870-1913," [Time Series on the Money Circulation in Germany, 1870-1913] *Jahrbucher fur Nationalokonomie und Statistik,* 187(4), May 1973, pp. 330-63.

Tilly, Richard H. "Capital Formation in Germany in the Nineteenth Century," in Mathias and Postan (eds), *The Cambridge Economic History of Europe,* 1978, pp. 382-441.

Tilly, Richard H. "Das Wachstum Industrieller Grossunternehmen in Deutschland, 1870-1913," [The Growth of Large Industrial Firms in Germany, 1870-1913] in Kellenbenz (ed), *Wirtschaftliches Wachstum, Energie und Verkehr,* 1981.

Tilly, Richard H.; Crisp, Olga; Patrick, Hugh T. and Cameron, Rondo E. *Banking in the Early Stages of Industrialization: A Study in Comparative Economic History.* London and New York: Oxford University Press, 1967.

Tilly, Richard H. and Fremdling, Rainer. "German Banks, German Growth, and Econometric History: A Note on Neuberger and Stokes," *Journal of Economic History,* 36(2), June 1976, pp. 416-24.

Tilly, Richard H. and Fremdling, Rainer, eds. *Industrialisierung und Raum, Studien zur Regionalen Differenzierung im Deutschland im 19. Jahrhundert* [Industrialization and Spatial Relationships: Studies on Regional Differentiation in Germany in the 19th Century] (Historisch-Sozialwissenschaftliche Forschungen, vol. 7). Stuttgart: Klett-Cotta, 1979.

Tilly, Richard H.; Fremdling, Rainer and Pierenkemper, Toni. "Regionale Differenzierung in Deutschland als Schwerpunkt Wirtschaftshistorischer Forschung," [Regional Differentiation in Germany as the Central Focus of Research in Economic History] in Fremdling and Tilly (eds), *Industrialisierung und Raum,* 1979.

Timberlake, Richard H., Jr. "Denominational Factors in Nineteenth-Century Currency Experience," *Journal of Economic History,* 34(4), December 1974, pp. 835-50.

Timberlake, Richard H., Jr. "The Specie Circular and the Distribution of the Surplus," *Journal of Policital Economy,* 68(2), April 1960, pp. 109-17.

Timberlake, Richard H., Jr. "The Independent Treasury and Monetary Policy before the Civil War," *Southern Economic Journal,* 27(2), October 1960, pp. 92-103.

Timberlake, Richard H., Jr. "Mr. Shaw and His Critics: Monetary Policy in the Golden Era Reviewed," *Quarterly Journal of Economics,* 77(1), February 1963, pp. 40-54.

Timberlake, Richard H., Jr. "Ideological Factors in Specie Resumption and Treasury Policy," *Journal of Economic History,* 24(1), March 1964, pp. 29-52.

Timberlake, Richard H., Jr. "The Resumption Act and the Money Supply," *Journal of Monetary Economics,* 1(3), July 1975, pp. 343-54.

Timberlake, Richard H., Jr. "Repeal of Silver Monetization in the Late Nineteenth Century," *Journal of Money, Credit, and Banking,* 10(1), February 1978, pp. 27-45.

Tinbergen, Jan. *Statistical Testing of Business-cycle Theories.* New York: Agathon Press, 1968.

Tipton, Frank B., Jr. "Farm Labor and Power Politics: Germany, 1850-1914," *Journal of Economic History,* 34(4), December 1974, pp. 951-79.

Tobin, James. "The Monetary Interpretation of History: A Review Article," *American Economic Review*, 55(3), June 1965, pp. 464-85.

Toda, Yasushi. "An Intercountry Comparison of the Consumption Levels of Industrial Workers' Families: Russia 1913-United States of America 1901," *Fourth International Conference of Economic History, Bloomington, 1968*. Paris: Mouton, 1973, pp. 477-84.

Tomaske, John A. "International Migration and Economic Growth: The Swedish Experience," (Summary of Doctoral Dissertation) *Journal of Economic History*, 25(4), December 1965, pp. 696-9.

Tomaske, John A. "Enclosures and Population Movement in England, 1700-1830: A Methodological Comment (on White)," *Explorations in Economic History*, 8(2), Winter 1970/71, pp. 223-8.

Tomaske, John A. "The Determinants of Intercountry Differences in European Emigration: 1881-1900," *Journal of Economic History*, 31(4), December 1971, pp. 840-53.

Tomaske, John A. and Canarella, Giorgio. "The Optimal Utilization of Slaves," *Journal of Economic History*, 35(3), September 1975, pp. 621-9.

Toms, M. *Outline of National Income Development During 1937-1948 in Czechoslovakia*. Prague: Economic Institute of the Czechoslovak Academy of Sciences, 1966.

Toninelli, Pier Angelo. "Innovazioni tecniche, mutamenti strutturali e accumulazione capitalistica nelle campagne cremonesi (1861-1914)," [Technical Innovation, Structural Change, and Capitalistic Accumulation in the Cremonan Countryside, 1861-1914] *Rivista di storia dell'agricoltura*, 2, August 1973.

Toninelli, Pier Angelo; Pavese, Claudio and Violante, Sante. *Fiscalita e finanza pubblica in Italia (1861-1913)* [Taxation and Public Budgets in Italy, 1861-1913]. Milano: Unicopli Universitaria, 1979.

Toninelli, Pier Angelo; Wagner, J.R. and Glazier, I.A. "Fiscal Policy, Public Sector and Economic Growth: The Case of Italy (1879-1913)," in *Seventh International Economic History Congress, Edinburgh, 1978*. Edinburgh: Edinburgh University Press, 1978.

Toniolo, Gianni. "Patterns of Industrial Growth and Italy's Industrialization from 1894 to 1913," *Rendiconti*, 1, 1969, pp. 259-83.

Toniolo, Gianni. "Cause dello sviluppo economico europeo del dopoguerra: una riconsiderazione," [Origins of Post-War European Economic Development: A Reconsideration] *Quaderni Storici*, 16, 1971, pp. 174-200.

Toniolo, Gianni. "Cento anni di economia portuale a Venezia," [One Hundred Years of Harbour Economy in Venice] *Coses Informazioni*, 3, 1972, pp. 33-73.

Toniolo, Gianni. "Alcune tendenze dello sviluppo economico italiano 1861-1940," [Some Tendencies in Italian Economic Development, 1861-1940] in Toniolo (ed), *Lo sviluppo economico italiano*, 1973, pp. 1-37. Reprinted in Toniolo (ed), *L'economia italiana*, 1978, pp. 3-46.

Toniolo, Gianni, ed. *Lo sviluppo economico italiano 1861-1940* [Italian Economic Development, 1861-1940]. Bari: Laterza, 1973.

Toniolo, Gianni. "Alcune considerazioni sull'uso della teoria nella storia economica," [Some Comments on the Use of Theory in Economic History] *Annali della Fondazione Luigi Einaudi*, 8, 1974, pp.

143-50.

Toniolo, Gianni. "La 'New Economic History'," *Quaderni Storici*, 31, 1976, pp. 380-461.

Toniolo, Gianni. "Politica economica fascista e industrializzazione del Mezzogiorno: alcune considerazioni," [Fascist Economic Policy and the Industrialization of the South: Some Comments] *Ricerche economiche*, 31, 1977, pp. 177-89.

Toniolo, Gianni. "Effective Protection and Industrial Growth: The Case of Italian Engineering, 1898-1913," *Journal of European Economic History*, 6(3), Winter 1977, pp. 659-73.

Toniolo, Gianni. "Ricerche recenti e problemi aperti sull'economia italiana durante la 'grande crisi'," [Recent Research and Unresolved Problems of the Italian Economy during the Great Depression] in Toniolo (ed), *Industria e banca nella grande crisi*, 1978, pp. 18-32.

Toniolo, Gianni, ed. *Industria e banca nella grande crisi (1929-34)* [Banks and Industry in the Great Depression]. Milano: Etas Libri, 1978.

Toniolo, Gianni, ed. *L'economia italiana 1861-1940*. Bari: Laterza, 1978.

Toniolo, Gianni. *L'economia dell'Italia Fascista* [The Economy of Fascist Italy]. Bari: Laterza, 1980.

Toniolo, Gianni and Ciocca, Pierluigi, eds. *L'economia italiana nel periodo fascista* [The Italian Economy during the Fascist Era]. Bologna: il Mulino, 1976.

Toniolo, Gianni and Sylla, Richard E. "La 'New Economic History' - metodi, obiettivi, limiti," [The New Economic History: Methods, Objects, Limits] reprinted in Toniolo (ed), *Lo sviluppo economico italiano*, 1973, pp. 41-70. *Quaderni Storici*, 11, 1969, pp. 229-64.

Toniolo, Gianni and Tattara, Giuseppe. "L'industria manifatturiera: cicli, politiche e mutamenti di struttura (1921-37)," [Industrial Manufacturing: Cycles, Policies, and Structural Change (1921-37)] in Ciocca and Toniolo (ed), *L'economia italiana nel periodo fascista*, 1976.

Tortella Casares, Gabriel. "El desarrollo de la industria azucarera y la guerra de Cuba," [The Development of the Sugar Industry and the Cuban War] *Moneda y Credito*, 91, December 1964, pp. 131-63.

Tortella Casares, Gabriel. "El principio de responsabilidad limitada y el desarrollo industrial de Espana: 1829-1869," [The Principal of Limited Liability and the Industrial Development of Spain, 1829-1869] *Moneda y Credito*, 104, March 1968, pp. 69-84.

Tortella Casares, Gabriel. "Banking and Industry in Spain, 1829-1874," (Summary of Doctoral Dissertation) *Journal of Economic History*, 29(1), March 1969, pp. 163-6.

Tortella Casares, Gabriel. "La evolution del sistema financiero espanol de 1856 a 1868," [The Evolution of the Spanish Financial System from 1856 to 1868] in Giron (ed), *Ensayos sobre la economia espanola a mediados del siglo XIX*, 1970, pp. 17-146.

Tortella Casares, Gabriel. *Los origenes del capitalismo en Espana* [The Origins of Capitalism in Spain]. Madrid: Tecnos, 1973.

Tortella Casares, Gabriel. "El profesor Hicks y la historia economica," [Professor Hicks and Economic History] *Sistema, Revista de Ciencias Sociales*, 1(3), October 1973.

479

Tortella Casares, Gabriel. *La Banca espanola en la Restauracion* (vol. 1: Politica y Finanzas; vol. 2: Datos para una historia economica) [The Spanish Banking System during the Restoration Period]. Madrid: Banco de Espana, 1974.

Tortella Casares, Gabriel. *Banks, Railroads, and Industry in Spain, 1829-1874*. New York: Arno Press, 1977.

Tortella Casares, Gabriel. "Las balanzas del comercio exterior espanol: un experimento historico-estadistico," [The Spanish Foreign Trade Balances: a Statistical-Historical Experiment] in Segura and Delgado (eds), *Realidad Social y Analisis Economico*, 1978.

Tortella Casares, Gabriel and Bustelo, Francisco. "Monetary Inflation in Spain, 1800-1970," *Journal of European Economic History*, 5(1), Spring 1976, pp. 141-50.

Tostlebe, Alvin S. *Capital in Agriculture: Its Formation and Financing since 1870*. Princeton: Princeton University Press for the National Bureau of Economic Research, 1957.

Tostlebe, Alvin S. "The Growth of Physical Capital in Agriculture, 1870-1950," National Bureau of Economic Research, Occasional Paper no. 44, 1954.

Tourk, Khairy and Hansen, Bent. "The Profitability of the Suez Canal as a Private Enterprise, 1859-1956," *Journal of Economic History*, 38(4), December 1978, pp. 938-58.

Toutain, Jean-Claude. "Le produit de L'Agriculture Francaise de 1700 a 1958," [French Agricultural Product, 1700-1958] *Cahiers de L'Institut de Science Economique Appliquee*, 1961, pp. 288-96.

Toutain, Jean-Claude. "La population de la France de 1700 a 1959," [The Population of France, 1700-1959] *Cahiers de L'Institut de Science Economique Appliquee*, 1963.

Toutain, Jean-Claude. "Les transports en France de 1830 a 1965," [The Transportation Sector in the French Economy, 1830-1965] *Cahiers de L'Institut de Science Economique Appliquee*, 1968.

Toutain, Jean-Claude. "La consommation alimentaire de la France de 1789 a 1964," [Food Consumption in France, 1789-1964] *Cahiers de L'Institut de Science Economique Appliquee*, 1971.

Toutain, Jean-Claude. "Les structures du commerce exterieur de la France, 1789-1970," [The Structure of French Foreign Commerce, 1789-1970] in Levy-Leboyer (ed), *La Position Internationale de la France*, 1977.

Toutain, Jean-Claude. *Le produit interieur brut de la France de 1889 a 1970*.

Towne, Marvin W. and Rasmussen, Wayne D. "Farm Gross Product and Gross Investment in the Nineteenth Century," in Parker (ed), *Trends in the American Economy in the Nineteenth Century*, 1960, pp. 255-312.

Trace, Keith. "The New Deal: Some Trends in Re-interpretation," *Proceedings of the Australian and New Zealand Society for the Advancement of American Studies*, 1965, pp. 60-71.

Trace, Keith, ed. "The Chemical Industry," in Roderick and Stephens (eds), *Industry, Education and the Economy in Victorian England*, 1980.

Trace, Keith and Henning, Graydon R. "Britain and the Motorship: A Case of the Delayed Adoption of New Technology?," *Journal of Economic History*, 35(2), June 1975, pp. 353-85.

Trace, Keith and Lindert, Peter H. "Yardsticks for Victorian

Entrepreneurs," in McCloskey (ed), *Essays on a Mature Economy*, 1971, pp. 239-74.

Tracy, Michael. "Agriculture in the Great Depression: World Market Developments and European Protectionism," in Van der Wee (ed), *The Great Depression Revisited*, 1972, pp. 91-119.

Tranter, N.L. "The Labour Supply, 1780-1860," in Floud and McCloskey (eds), *The Economic History of Britain since 1700*, 1981, pp. 203-25.

Tremblay, Rodrique. "L'Equilibre de la Balance des Paiements et L'Integration des Marches de Capitaux le Cas du Canada, 1923-1930," [The Equilibrium of the Balance of Payments and the Integration of Capital Markets: the Case of Canada, 1923-1930] *Canadian Journal of Economics*, 1(4), November 1968, pp. 805-15.

Trescott, Paul B. "The United States Government and National Income, 1790-1860," in Parker (ed), *Trends in the American Economy in the Nineteenth Century*, 1960, pp. 337-61.

Trescott, Paul B. "Civil War Finance in the United States: An Appraisal of the Economic Impact of the Monetary and Fiscal Policies of the Federal Government, 1861-1867," *Third International Conference of Economic History, Munich, 1965, part 1*. Paris: Mouton, 1968, pp. 763-70.

Triffin, Robert. *The Evolution of the International Monetary System: Historical Reappraisal and Future Perspectives* (Princeton Studies in International Finance (12)). Princeton, N.J.: Princeton University, Department of Economics, 1964.

Trojanowski, Joseph and DeCanio, Stephen J. "Kanatics: A Kansas Agricultural Time Series-Cross Section Dataset," Inter-University Consortium for Political and Social Research, Ann Arbor, Paper no. 41, November 1977.

Trussell, James; Engerman, Stanley L.; Floud, Roderick C.; Wimmer, Larry T.; Fogel, Robert W. and Pope, Clayne L. "The Economics of Mortality in North America, 1650-1910: A Description of a Research Project," *Historical Methods*, 11(2), June 1978, pp. 75-108.

Trussell, James and Steckel, Richard H. "The Age of Slaves at Menarche and Their First Birth," *Journal of Interdisciplinary History*, 8(3), Winter 1978, pp. 477-505.

Tsuru, Shigeto. "The Take-off in Japan (1868-1900)," in Rostow (ed), *The Economics of Take-off into Sustained Growth*, 1963, pp. 139-50.

Tucker, G.S.L. "A Note on the Reliability of Fertility Ratios," *Australian Economic History Review*, 14(2), September 1974, pp. 160-7.

Tucker, G.S.L. "The Old Poor Law Revisited," *Explorations in Economic History*, 12(3), July 1975, pp. 233-52.

Tucker, G.S.L. and Butlin, Noel G. "The Quantitative Study of British Economic Growth: A Review. Review Essay of 'British Economic Growth, 1688-1959' by Phyllis Deane and W.A. Cole (Cambridge: Cambridge University Press, 1968)," *Economic Record*, 40(91), September 1964, pp. 455-60.

Tucker, G.S.L. and Forster, Colin. *Economic Opportunity and White American Fertility Ratios, 1800-1860*. New Haven: Yale University Press, 1972.

Tucker, K.A. and Capie, Forrest. "British and New Zealand Trading Relationships, 1841-1852," *Economic History Review, Second Series*, 25(2), May 1972, pp. 293-302.

Tuma, Elias H. *European Economic History: Tenth Century to the Present; Theory and History of Economic Change.* New York: Harper & Row, 1971.

Tuma, Elias H. "New Approaches in Economic History and Related Social Sciences," *Journal of European Economic History,* 3(1), Spring 1974, pp. 169-88.

Turner, Michael. "Parliamentary Enclosure and Population Change in England, 1750-1830: A Comment on Philpot," *Explorations in Economic History,* 13(4), October 1976, pp. 463-8.

Tussing, Arlon. "The Labor Force in Meiji Economic Growth: A Quantitative Study of Yamanashi Prefecture," reprinted in Ohkawa, Johnston, and Kaneda (eds), *Agriculture and Economic Growth,* 1970, pp. 198-221. *Journal of Economic History,* 26(1), March 1966, pp. 59-92.

U.S. Bureau of the Census, ed. *Historical Statistics of the United States, colonial times to 1957.* Washington, D.C.: Government Printing Office, 1960.

U.S. Bureau of the Census, ed. *Historical Statistics of the United States, Colonial Times to 1970* (2 vols). Washington, D.C.: U.S. Government Printing Office, 1975.

Ulen, Thomas S. "Cartels and Regulation: Late Nineteenth-Century Railroad Collusion and the Creation of the Interstate Commerce Commission," (Summary of Doctoral Dissertation) *Journal of Economic History,* 40(1), March 1980, pp. 179-81.

Ulen, Thomas S. "The Market for Regulation: The ICC from 1887 to 1920," *American Economic Review,* Papers and Proceedings, 70(2), May 1980, pp. 306-10.

Ulen, Thomas S. "Voting Behavior for the Interstate Commerce Act: 1879-1886." [Working Paper]

Ulen, Thomas S. "Was the ICC Necessary as a Cartel Manager?," presented at the Cliometrics Conference, University of Wisconsin-Madison, May 1977.

Ulmer, Melville J. *Capital in Transportation, Communications, and Public Utilities: Its Formation and Financing.* Princeton: Princeton University Press for the National Bureau of Economic Research, 1960.

Ulmer, Melville J. "Trends and Cycles in Capital Formation by United States Railroads, 1870-1950," National Bureau of Economic Research, Occasional Paper no. 43, 1954.

Umbeck, John. "The California Gold Rush: a Study of Emerging Property Rights," *Explorations in Economic History,* 14(3), July 1977, pp. 197-226.

Umemura, Mataji; Shinohara, Miyohei and Ohkawa, Kazushi, eds. *Estimates of Long Term Economic Statistics of Japan since 1868.* Tokyo: Toyo Keizai Shinpo Sha, 1965.

Umemura, Mataji. "Gainful Workers, 1870-1940," in Ohkawa and Hayami (eds), *Economic Growth,* 1973, pp. 95-100.

Umemura, Mataji. "Note on Economic Development in Agriculture in the Tokugawa Period," in Ohkawa and Hayami (eds), *Economic Growth,* 1973, pp. 175-83.

Unger, Richard W. "Dutch Herring, Technology, and International Trade in the Seventeenth Century," *Journal of Economic History,* 40(2), June 1980, pp. 253-79.

Updike, Helen Hill. *The National Banks and American Economic Development, 1870-1900.* New York: Arno Press, 1977.

Urquhart, M.C. and Buckley, K.A.H., eds. *Historical Statistics of Canada.* Toronto: Macmillan, 1965.

Urquhart, M.C. and Green, Alan G. "Factor and Commodity Flows in the International Economy of 1870-1914: A Multi-Country View," *Journal of Economic History,* 26(1), March 1976, pp. 217-52.

Urquhart, M.C. and McInnis, R. Marvin. "Estimation of Historical Series of Farm Income for Canada." [Working Paper]

Uselding, Paul J. "Studies in the Technological Development of the American Economy during the First Half of the Nineteenth Century," (Summary of Doctoral Dissertation) *Journal of Economic History,* 31(1), March 1971, pp. 264-5.

Uselding, Paul J. "Conjectural Estmates of Gross Human Capital Inflows to the American Economy: 1790-1860," *Explorations in Economic History,* 9(1), Fall 1971, pp. 49-61.

Uselding, Paul J. "Technical Progress at the Springfield Armory, 1820-1850," *Explorations in Economic History,* 9(3), Spring 1972, pp. 291-316.

Uselding, Paul J. "Factor Substitution and Labor Productivity Growth in American Manufacturing, 1839-1899," *Journal of Economic History,* 32(3), September 1972, pp. 670-81.

Uselding, Paul J. "The Ames-Rosenberg Hypothesis Revisited: A Rejoinder to Klingaman, Vedder, and Gallaway," *Explorations in Economic History,* 11(3), Spring 1974, pp. 315-6.

Uselding, Paul J. *Studies in the Technological Development of the American Economy during the First Half of the Nineteenth Century.* New York: Arno Press, 1975.

Uselding, Paul J. "Wages and Capital Consumption Levels in England and on the Continent in the 1830's," *Journal of European Economic History,* 4(2), Fall 1975, pp. 501-13.

Uselding, Paul J. "Occupational Mortality in the United States: 1890-1910," in Uselding (ed), *Research in Economic History,* 1976, pp. 334-71.

Uselding, Paul J. "A Note on the Inter-Regional Trade in Manufactures in 1840," *Journal of Economic History,* 36(2), June 1976, pp. 428-35.

Uselding, Paul J. "Studies of Technology in Economic History," in Gallman (ed), *Recent Developments in the Study of Business and Economic History,* 1977, pp. 159-220.

Uselding, Paul J. "Manufacturing," in Porter (ed), *Encyclopedia of American Economic History,* 1980, pp. 397-412.

Uselding, Paul J. "Britain's Industrial Marathon," *Reviews in European History.*

Uselding, Paul J. "Accurate Size Measurement and Precision in the 'Making' and 'Manufacturing' Systems of the 19th Century," in Mayr (ed), *The American System of Manufacturing.*

Ussing, Niels and Bjerke, Kjeld. *Studier over Danmarks Nationalprodukt 1870-1950.* Kobenhavn: Universitits Okonomiske Institut, 1958.

Uselding, Paul J. and McMullen, Neil J. "The Changing Basis of American Prosperity," *Economia Internazionale,* 29(3-4),

August/November 1977, pp. 446-61.

Uselding, Paul J. and Neal, Larry D. "Immigration: A Neglected Source of American Economic Growth, 1790 to 1912," *Oxford Economic Papers,* New Series, 24(1), March 1972, pp. 68-88.

Uselding, Paul J. and Juba, Bruce. "Biased Technical Progress in American Manufacturing, 1839-1899," *Explorations in Economic History,* 11(1), Fall 1973, pp. 55-72.

Uselding, Paul J. and Pollack, Martin. "Data, 'Evidence' and Interpretation in Economic History," *Economic Inquiry,* 12(3), September 1974, pp. 406-14.

Vaillancourt, Francois and Ferron, Jean-Olivier. "Qui Perd Sa Langue, Perd Sa Foi," [He Who Loses His Language Loses Faith] *Revue D'Histoire de L'Amerique Francaise,* 33(2), September 1979, pp. 263-5.

Vamplew, Wray. "The Railways and the Iron Industry: A Study of Their Relationship in Scotland," in Reed (ed), *Railways in the Victorian Economy,* 1969, pp. 33-75.

Vamplew, Wray. "Sources of Scottish Railway Share Capital before 1860," *Scottish Journal of Political Economy,* 17(3), November 1970, pp. 425-39.

Vamplew, Wray. "Nihilistic Impressions of British Railway History," in McCloskey (ed), *Essays on a Mature Economy,* 1971, pp. 345-66.

Vamplew, Wray. "Railways and the Transformation of the Scottish Economy," *Economic History Review,* Second Series, 24(1), February 1971, pp. 37-54.

Vamplew, Wray. "The Financing of Scottish Railways before 1860: A Reply to Gourvish and Reed," *Scottish Journal of Political Economy,* 18(2), June 1971, pp. 221-3.

Vamplew, Wray. "The Protection of English Cereal Producers: The Corn Laws Reassessed," *Economic History Review,* Second Series, 33(3), Augustt 1980, pp. 382-95.

Van der Wee, Herman, ed. *The Great Depression Revisited: Essays on the Economics of the Thirties.* The Hague: Martinus Nijhoff, 1972.

Van der Wee, Herman. "Real Wage Income during the Ancien Regime in the Light of Economic Growth," *Fourth International Conference of Economic History, Bloomington, 1968.* Paris: Mouton, 1973, pp. 467-73.

Van der Wee, Herman. "European Historical Statisics and Economic Growth," *Explorations in Economic History,* 13(3), July 1976, pp. 347-51.

Vanek, Jaroslav. "The Natural Resource Content of Foreign Trade, 1870-1955, and the Relative Abundance of Natural Resources in the United States," *Review of Economics and Statistics,* 41(1), February 1959, pp. 146-53.

Vatter, Barbara. "Industrial Borrowing by the New England Textile Mills, 1840-1860: A Comment on Davis," *Journal of Economic History,* 21(2), June 1961, pp. 216-21.

Vatter, Harold G. "The Closure of Entry in the American Automobile Industry," *Oxford Economic Papers,* New Series, 4(3), October 1952, pp. 213-34.

Vatter, Harold G. "Has There Been a Twentieth-Century Consumer Durables Revolution?," *Journal of Economic History*, 27(1), March 1967, pp. 1-16.

Vatter, Harold G. "An Estimate of Import Substitution for Manufactured Products in the U.S. Economy, 1859 and 1899," *Economic Development and Cultural Change*, 18(1), (Part 1), October 1969, pp. 40-3.

Vatter, Harold G. "Industrialization, Regional Change, and the Sectoral Distribution of the U.S. Labor Force, 1850-1880," *Economic Development and Cultural Change*, 23(3), April 1975, pp. 739-47.

Vatter, Harold G. "Industrialization, Regional Change, and the Sectoral Distribution of the U.S. Labor Force, 1850-1880 (Comment on Lebergott)," *Economic Development and Cultural Change*, 23(4), July 1975, pp. 739-47.

Vatter, Harold G. "U.S. Economic Development and the Sectoral Distribution of the Labor Force, 1850-1880," in Van der Wee, Vinogradov, and Kotovsky (eds), *Fifth International Congress of Economic History*, 1976, pp. 28-49.

Vedder, Richard K. "The Slave Exploitation (Expropriation) Rate," (Symposium on Time on the Cross. Edited by Gary M. Walton) *Explorations in Economic History*, 12(4), October 1975, pp. 453-8.

Vedder, Richard K. "Some Evidence on the Scale of the Antebellum Farm Implement Industry," in Uselding (ed), *Proceedings of the Twenty-Third Annual Meeting of the Business History Conference*, 1976.

Vedder, Richard K. *The American Economy in Historical Perspective.* Belmont, California: Wadsworth, 1976.

Vedder, Richard K. and Cebula, Richard J. "An Empirical Analysis of Income Expectations and Interstate Migration," *Review of Regional Studies*, 5(1), Spring 1975, pp. 19-28.

Vedder, Richard K. and Cooper, David C. "Nineteenth Century English and Welsh Geographic Labor Mobility: Some Further Evidence," *Annals of Regional Science*, 8(2), June 1974, pp. 131-9.

Vedder, Richard K. and Gallaway, Lowell E. "The Settlement Preferences of Scandinavian Emigrants to the United States, 1850-1960," *Scandinavian Economic History Review*, 18(2), 1970, pp. 159-76.

Vedder, Richard K. and Gallaway, Lowell E. "Internal Migration of Native-Born Ohioans: 1850-1960," *Bulletin of Business Research*, 15(6), June 1970, pp. 4-5.

Vedder, Richard K. and Gallaway, Lowell E. "Settlement Patterns of Canadian Emigrants to the United States, 1850-1960," *Canadian Journal of Economics*, 3(3), August 1970, pp. 476-86.

Vedder, Richard K. and Gallaway, Lowell E. "Internal Migration Patterns in the Midwest, 1850-1960," *Regional Science Perspectives*, 1(1), Spring 1971, pp. 65-82.

Vedder, Richard K. and Gallaway, Lowell E. "Mobility of Native Americans," *Journal of Economic History*, 31(3), September 1971, pp. 613-49.

Vedder, Richard K. and Gallaway, Lowell E. "Emigration from the United Kingdom to the United States: 1860-1913," *Journal of Economic History*, 31(4), December 1971, pp. 885-97.

Vedder, Richard K. and Gallaway, Lowell E. "The Geographic Distribution of British and Irish Emigrants to the United States after 1800," *Scottish Journal of Political Economy*, 19(1), February 1972, pp. 19-36.

Vedder, Richard K.; Gallaway, Lowell E. and Shukla, Vishwa. "The Distribution of the Immigrant Population in the United States: An Economic Analysis," *Explorations in Economic History*, 11(3), Spring 1974, pp. 213-26.

Vedder, Richard K.; Gallaway, Lowell E. and Klingman, David C. "The Profitability of Antebellum Agriculture in the Cotton Belt: Some New Evidence," *Atlantic Economic Journal*, 2(2), November 1974, pp. 30-47.

Vedder, Richard K. and Gallaway, Lowell E. "Settlement Patterns of American Immigrants, 1850-1968," in Van der Wee, Vinogradov, and Kotovsky (eds), *Fifth International Congress of Economic History*, 1976, pp. 128-45.

Vedder, Richard K. and Gallaway, Lowell E. "Population Transfers and the Postbellum Adjustments to Economic Dislocation, 1870-1920," *Journal of Economic History*, 40(1), March 1980, pp. 143-9.

Vedder, Richard K. and Gallaway, Lowell E. "The Profitability of Antebellum Manufacturing: Some New Estimates," *Business History Review*, 54(1), Spring 1980, pp. 92-103.

Vedder, Richard K. and Gallaway, Lowell E. "A Nation of Movers: American Internal Migration in Historical Perspective." [Working Paper]

Vedder, Richard K. and Gallaway, Lowell E. "The Great Depression: A Tale of Three Paradigms," Ohio University Economic History Research Paper no. F-47.

Vedder, Richard K. and Gallaway, Lowell E. "Migration and the Old Northwest," in Klingaman and Vedder (eds), *Essays in Nineteenth Century Economic History*, 1975, pp. 159-76.

Vedder, Richard K.; Klingaman, David C. and Gallaway, Lowell E. "The Ames-Rosenberg Hypothesis Revisited: A Note (on Uselding)," *Explorations in Economic History*, 11(3), Spring 1974, pp. 311-4.

Vedder, Richard K. and Klingaman, David C., eds. *Essays in Nineteenth Century Economic History: The Old Northwest.* Athens: Ohio University Press, 1975.

Vedder, Richard K.; Klingaman, David C.; Gallaway, Lowell E. and Uselding, Paul. "Discrimination and Exploitation in Antebellum American Cotton Textile Manufacturing," in Uselding (ed), *Research in Economic History*, 1978, pp. 217-61.

Vedder, Richard K.; Lindley, Susan and Gallaway, Lowell E. "Some Quarterly Estimates of GNP, 1929-1940," Ohio University Economic History Research Paper no. F-48.

Vedder, Richard K. and McGuire, William J. "Bank Failures, 1929-1933: An Empirical Analysis," Ohio University Economic History Research Paper no. F-37.

Vedder, Richard K. and Stockdale, David E. "The Profitability of Slavery Revisited: A Different Approach," *Agricultural History*, 49(2), April 1975, pp. 392-404.

Versiani, Flavio Rabelo. "Industrial Investment in an 'Export' Economy: The Brazilian Experience Before 1914," *Journal of Development Economics*, 7(3), September 1980, pp. 307-29.

Veverka, J. "The Growth of Government Expenditure in the United Kingdom since 1790," *Scottish Journal of Political Economy*, 10(1), February 1963, pp. 111-27.

Vicziany, Antonia Markka. "The Cotton Trade and the Commercial Development of Bombay 1855-1875," (Unpublished Ph.D. Dissertation,

University of London, 1975).

Villaflor, Georgia; Sokoloff, Kenneth and Margo, Robert A. "The Economic and Demographic Significance of Secular Changes in Human Stature: The U.S., 1750-1960," *NBER Reporter*, Winter 1979, pp. 6-8.

Villaflor, Georgia and Sokoloff, Kenneth. "Colonial and Revolutionary Muster Rolls: Some New Evidence on Nutrition and Migration in Early America," National Bureau of Economic Research Working Paper no. 374, July 1979.

Villela, Annibal V. and Suzigan, Wilson. *Politica do Governo e Crescimento da Economia Brasileira, 1889-1945* [Government Policy and the Economic Growth of Brazil, 1889-1945]. Rio de Janeiro: I.P.E.A., 1973.

Vinovskis, Maris A. "The Demography of the Slave Population in Antebellum America: A Critique of 'Time on the Cross'," *Journal of Interdisciplinary History*, 5(3), Winter 1975, pp. 459-67.

Vinovskis, Maris A.; Mason, Karen and Hareven, Tamara K. "Determinants of Women's Labor Force Participation in Late Nineteenth-Century America," in *Family Transitions and the Life Course in Historical Perspective*. New York: Academic Press, 1978.

Vinski, Ivo. "National Product and Fixed Assets in the Territory of Yugoslavia, 1909-59," Deane (ed), *Studies in Social and Financial Accounting*, 1961, pp. 206-33.

Violante, Sante; Pavese, Claudio and Toninelli, Pier Angelo. *Fiscalita e finanza pubblica in Italia (1861-1913)* [Taxation and Public Budgets in Italy, 1861-1913]. Milano: Unicopli Universitaria, 1979.

Von Tunzelmann, G. Nicholas. "Inverse Relations of the Australian and New Zealand Economies, 1871-1900: An Hypothesis Re-Examined," *Australian Economic Papers*, 5(3), June 1967, pp. 124-7.

Von Tunzelmann, G. Nicholas. "On a Thesis by Matthews. Comment on 'A Study in Trade-Cycle History: Economic Fluctuations in Great Britain, 1833-42' by R.C.O. Matthews (Cambridge: Cambridge University Press, 1954)," *Economic History Review*, Second Series, 20(3), December 1967, pp. 548-54.

Von Tunzelmann, G. Nicholas. "The New Economic History: An Econometric Appraisal," *Explorations in Entrepreneurial History*, Second Series, 5(2), Winter 1968, pp. 175-200.

Von Tunzelmann, G. Nicholas. "Technological Diffusion during the Industrial Revolution: The Case of the Cornish Pumping Engine," in Hartwell (ed), *The Industrial Revolution*, 1970, pp. 77-98.

Von Tunzelmann, G. Nicholas. *Steam Power and British Industrialization to 1860*. New York and London: Oxford University Press, 1978.

Von Tunzelmann, G. Nicholas. "Trends in Real Wages, 1750-1850, Revisited," *Economic History Review*, Second Series, 32(1), February 1979, pp. 33-49.

Von Tunzelmann, G. Nicholas. "Britain, 1900-45: A Survey," in Floud and McCloskey (eds), *The Economic History of Britain since 1700*, 1981.

Von Tunzelmann, G. Nicholas. "Technical Progress during the Industrial Revolution," in Floud and McCloskey (eds), *The Economic History of Britain since 1700*, 1981, pp. 143-63.

Von Tunzelmann, G. Nicholas. "The Cliometric Conference at Warwick (G.B.), 1978," *Journal of European Economic History*, 9(1), Spring 1980, pp. 219-32.

Von Tunzelmann, G. Nicholas. *Analytical Approaches and Interdisciplinarity in History*. Paris: UNESCO.

Von Tunzelmann, G. Nicholas. "Britain's New Industries between the Wars: A New 'Development Block'?," presented at the Cliometrics Conference, Warwick, 1978.

Von Tunzelmann, G. Nicholas. "Steam Power and Smoke Pollution in English Cities to 1870." [Working Paper]

Von Tunzelmann, G. Nicholas and Savin, N. Eugene. "The Standard of Living Debate and Optimal Economic Growth." [Working Paper]

Wade, W.W.; Ruttan, Vernon W.; Binswanger, Hans P.; Hayami, Yujiro and Weber, A. "Factor Productivity and Growth: A Historical Interpretation," in Binswanger et al (ed), *Induced Innovation*, 1978.

Wadensjo, Eskil and Jonung, Lars. "A Model of the Determination of Wages and Prices in Sweden, 1922-1971," *Economy and History*, 21(2), 1978, pp. 104-13.

Wadensjo, Eskil and Jonung, Lars. *"Wages and Prices in Sweden, 1912-1922: A Retrospective Test,"* Scandinavian Journal of Economics, 81(1), 1979, pp. 60-71.

Wagner, J.R.; Toninelli, Pier Angelo and Glazier, I.A. "Fiscal Policy, Public Sector and Economic Growth: The Case of Italy (1879-1913)," in *Seventh International Economic History Congress, Edinburgh, 1978*. Edinburgh: Edinburgh University Press, 1978.

Wallot, Jean-Pierre and Paquet, Gilles. "Apercu sur le commerce international et les prix domestique dans le Bas Canada, 1793-1812," *Revue d'Histoire de l'Amerique Francaise*, 21(3), December 1967, pp. 447-73.

Wallot, Jean-Pierre and Paquet, Gilles. "Canada, 1760-1850: anamorphoses et prospective," *Cahiers de l'Universite de Quebec*, 1-2, September 1969, pp. 255-300.

Wallot, Jean-Pierre and Paquet, Gilles. "Le Bas Canada au debut du XIXe siecle: une hypothese," *Revue d'Histoire de l'Amerique Francaise*, 25(1), June 1971, pp. 39-61.

Wallot, Jean-Pierre and Paquet, Gilles. "Crise agricole et tensions socio-techniques dans le Bas Canada au tournant du XIXe siecle," *Revue d'Histoire de l'Amerique Francaise*, 26(2), September 1972, pp. 185-237.

Wallot, Jean-Pierre and Paquet, Gilles. "International Circumstances of Lower Canada, 1786-1810: Prolegomena," *Canadian Historical Review*, 53(4), December 1972, pp. 371-401.

Wallot, Jean-Pierre and Paquet, Gilles. "The Agricultural Crisis in Lower Canada, 1802-1812: mise au point," *Canadian Historical Review*, 56(2), June 1975, pp. 133-61.

Wallot, Jean-Pierre and Paquet, Gilles. "Rentes foncieres, dimes et revenus paysans: le cas canadien," in Roy Ladurie and Goy (eds), *Prestations paysannes*.

Walsh, William D. "The Diffusion of Technological Change in the Pennsylvania Pig Iron Industry, 1850-1870: A Summary," (Summary of Doctoral Dissertation) *Journal of Economic History*, 26(4), December 1966, pp. 591-4.

Walsh, William D. "New Technology in the Mid-Nineteenth Century Pennsylvania Pig Iron Industry," *Yale Economic Essays*, 11(1 & 2), Spring/Fall 1971, pp. 3-52.

Walters, A.A. "Money Multipliers in the United Kingdom, 1880-1962," *Oxford Economic Papers*, 18(3), November 1966, pp. 270-83.

Walters, A.A. and Barrett, C.R. "The Stability of Keynesian and Monetary Multipliers in the United Kingdom," *Review of Economics and Statistics*, 38, November 1966, pp. 395-405.

Walters, A.A. and Kavanagh, N.J. "The Demand for Money in the U.K., 1877-1961: Some Preliminary Findings," *Oxford Bulletin of Economics and Statistics*, 28, May 1966, pp. 98-116.

Walters, Dorothy and Jefferys, James B. *National Income and Expenditure of the United Kingdom* (Income and Wealth, Series 5). London:Bowes & Bowes, 1955.

Walton, Gary M. "A Quantitative Study of American Colonial Shipping: A Summary," (Summary of Doctoral Dissertation) *Journal of Economic History*, 26(4), December 1966, pp. 595-8.

Walton, Gary M. "Sources of Productivity Change in American Colonial Shipping, 1675-1775," *Economic History Review*, Second Series, 20(1), April 1967, pp. 67-78.

Walton, Gary M. "Colonial Tonnage Measurement: A Comment on McCusker," *Journal of Economic History*, 27(3), September 1967, pp. 392-7.

Walton, Gary M. "A Measure of Productivity Change in American Colonial Shipping," (See 24(4), November 1971, pp. 682, for Erratum Statement concerning this article) *Economic History Review*, Second Series, 21(2), August 1968, pp. 268-82.

Walton, Gary M. "New Evidence on Colonial Commerce," *Journal of Economic History*, 28(3), September 1968, pp. 363-89.

Walton, Gary M. "Trade Routes, Ownership Proportions, and American Colonial Shipping Characteristics," *Las Rutas Del Atlantico*. Sevilla: Trabajos del Noveno Coloquio International de Historia Martima, 1969, pp. 471-502.

Walton, Gary M. "Productivity Change in Ocean Shipping after 1870: A Comment on Knauerhase," *Journal of Economic History*, 30(2), June 1970, pp. 435-41.

Walton, Gary M. "Obstacles to Technical Diffusion in Ocean Shipping, 1675-1775," *Explorations in Economic History*, 8(2), Winter 1970/71, pp. 123-40.

Walton, Gary M. "The New Economic History and the Burdens of the Navigation Acts," *Economic History Review*, Second Series, 24(4), November 1971, pp. 533-42.

Walton, Gary M. "Comments on Dissertations Presented to the 32nd Annual Meeting of the Economic History Association," *Journal of Economic History*, 33(1), March 1973, pp. 326-32.

Walton, Gary M. "The Burdens of the Navigation Acts: A Reply to Broeze and McClelland," *Economic History Review*, Second Series, 26(4), November 1973, pp. 687-8.

Walton, Gary M. "Monetary Crisis and Government Reliance in Modern Times," in Walton (ed), *Regulatory Change in an Atmosphere of Crisis*, 1979, pp. 1-11.

Walton, Gary M., ed. *Regulatory Change in an Atmosphere of Crisis: Current Implications of the Roosevelt Years*. New York: Academic Press, 1979.

Walton, Gary M. "Regenerative Failings of the New South: An

Introduction," in Shepherd and Walton (eds), *Market Institutions and Economic Progress in the New South*, 1980.

Walton, Gary M. "The Colonial Economy," in Porter (ed), *Encyclopedia of American Economic History*, 1980, pp. 34-50.

Walton, Gary M.; Atack, Jeremy; Haites, Erik F. and Mak, James. "Profitability of Steamboating on Western Rivers: 1850," *Business History Review*, 49(3), Autumn 1975, pp. 346-54.

Walton, Gary M. and Ball, Duane E. "Agricultural Productivity Change in Eighteenth-Century Pennsylvania," *Journal of Economic History*, 36(1), March 1976, pp. 102-17.

Walton, Gary M. and Gordon, Donald F. "A Theory of Regenerative Growth and the Experience of Post-World War II West Germany." [Working Paper]

Walton, Gary M.; Haites, Erik F. and Mak, James. *Western River Transportation during the Era of Early Internal Improvements.* Baltimore: Johns Hopkins University Press, 1975.

Walton, Gary M. and Mak, James. "Steamboats and the Great Productivity Surge in River Transportation," *Journal of Economic History*, 32(3), September 1972, pp. 619-40.

Walton, Gary M. and Mak, James. "On the Persistence of Old Technologies: The Case of Flatboats," *Journal of Economic History*, 33(2), June 1973, pp. 444-51.

Walton, Gary M. and Miller, Roger Leroy. *Economic Issues in American History.* New York: Harper & Row, 1978.

Walton, Gary M. and Robertson, Ross M. *History of the American Economy* (Fourth Edition). New York: Harcourt, Brace, Jovanovich, 1978.

Walton, Gary M. and Royd, J. Hayden. "The Social Savings from Nineteenth-Century Rail Passenger Services," *Explorations in Economic History*, 9(3), Spring 1972, pp. 233-54.

Walton, Gary M. and Shepherd, James F. *Shipping, Maritime Trade, and the Economic Development of Colonial North America.* London: Cambridge University Press, 1972.

Walton, Gary M. and Shepherd, James F. "Estimates of 'Invisible' Earnings in the Balance of Payments of the British North American Colonies, 1768-1772," *Journal of Economic History*, 29(2), June 1969, pp. 230-63.

Walton, Gary M. and Shepherd, James F. "Trade, Distribution and Economic Growth in Colonial America," *Journal of Economic History*, 32(1), March 1972, pp. 128-45.

Walton, Gary M. and Shepherd, James F. "The Effects of the American Revolution on American Maritime Trade and Shipping," *The American Revolution and the Sea: Proceedings of the 14th Conference of the International Commission for Maritime History at Greenwich, London, England.* London: National Maritime Museum, 1974, pp. 58-69.

Walton, Gary M. and Shepherd, James F. "Economic Change after the Revolution: Pre- and Post-War Comparisons of Maritime Shipping and Trade," *Explorations in Economic History*, 13(4), October 1976, pp. 397-422.

Walton, Gary M. and Shepherd, James F. *The Economic Rise of Early America.* Cambridge: Cambridge University Press, 1979.

Walton, Gary M. and Shepherd, James F., eds. *Market Institutions and Economic Progress in the New South, 1865-1900.* New York: Academic Press, 1980.

Warburton, Clark. "Variations in Economic Growth and Banking

Developments in the United States from 1835 to 1885," *Journal of Economic History*, 18(3), September 1958, pp. 283-97.

Watkins, Melville H.; Dales, John H. and McManus, John C. "Primary Products and Economic Growth: A Comment on Chambers and Gordon," *Journal of Political Economy*, 75(6), December 1967, pp. 876-80.

Watts, James M. and Hausman, William J. "Structural Change in the 18th-Century British Economy: A Test Using Cubic Splines," *Explorations in Economic History*, 17, October 1980, pp. 400-10.

Webb, Steven B. "Tariff Protection for the Iron Industry, Cotton Textiles and Agriculture in Germany, 1879-1914," [Appears in German] *Jahrbucher fur Nationalokonomie und Statistik*, 192(3-4), November 1977, pp. 336-57.

Webb, Steven B. "Tariffs, Cartels, Technology, and Growth in the German Steel Industry, 1879 to 1914," *Journal of Economic History*, 40(2), June 1980, pp. 309-29.

Webb, Steven B. "Motives for Emancipation: A Statistical Analysis of the British Parliament of 1834." [Working Paper]

Webb, Steven B. "The Economic Effects of Protective Tarrifs in Imperial Germany, 1879-1914," Ph.D. Dissertation, University of Chicago, 1978.

Weber, A.; Ruttan, Vernon W.; Binswanger, Hans P.; Wade, W.W. and Hayami, Yujiro. "Factor Productivity and Growth: A Historical Interpretation," in Binswanger et al (ed), *Induced Innovation: Technology, Institutions, and Development*, 1978.

Weber, Brain A. "A New Index of House Rents for Great Britain, 1874-1913," *Scottish Journal of Political Economy*, 7(3), November 1960, pp. 232-7.

Weber, Brian A. and Cairncross, Alec K. "Fluctuations in Building in Great Britain, 1785-1849," *Economic History Review*, Second Series, 9(2), 1956, pp. 283-97.

Weber, Brain A. and Handfield-Jones, Stephen J. "Variations in the Rate of Economic Growth in the U.S.A., 1869-1939," *Oxford Economic Papers*, 6, June 1954, pp. 101-32.

Weber, Brain A. and Lewis, J. Parry. "New Industrial Building in Great Britain, 1923-1938," *Scottish Journal of Political Economy*, 8(1), February 1961, pp. 57-64.

Weber, Brian A. and Phelps Brown, E.H. "Accumulation, Productivity and Distribution in the British Economy, 1870-1938," *Economic Journal*, 63(250), June 1953, pp. 263-88.

Weiher, Kenneth. "Slavery and Southern Urbanization: A Reformulation of the Argument," in Soltow (ed), *Essays in Economic and Business History*, 1979, pp. 259-67.

Weinstein, Michael M. *Recovery and Redistribution under the NIRA.* Amsterdam: North-Holland, 1980.

Weinstein, Michael M. "Some Macroeconomic Impacts of the National Industrial Recovery Act, 1933-1935," in Brunner (ed), *The Great Depression Revisited*, 1981, pp. 262-81.

Weinstein, Michael M. and Smolensky, Eugene. "Poverty," in Porter (ed), *Encyclopedia of American Economic History*, 1978, pp. 1136-54.

Weinstein, Paul A. "Occupational Convergence and the Role of the Military in Economic Development," *Explorations in Economic History*, 7(3), Spring 1970, pp. 325-46.

Weintraub, Andrew. "Economics of Lincoln's Proposal for Compensated Emancipation," *American Journal of Economics and Sociology*, 35(2),

April 1973, pp. 171-8.

Weisbrod, Burton A. and Kelley, Allen C. "Disease and Economic Development: The Impact of Parasitic Disease in St. Lucia," *Journal of Social Economics,* Fall 1973.

Weiss, Roger W. "The Issue of Paper Money in the American Colonies, 1720-1774," *Journal of Economic History,* 30(4), December 1970, pp. 770-84.

Weiss, Roger W. "Comment on Papers by Jones, Shepherd and Walton, and McCusker Presented to the 31st Annual Meeting of the Economic History Association," *Journal of Economic History,* 32(1), March 1972, pp. 163-4.

Weiss, Roger W. "The Colonial Monetary Standard of Massachusetts," *Economic History Review,* Second Series, 27(4), November 1974, pp. 577-92.

Weiss, Thomas J. "The Service Sector in the United States, 1839 to 1899," (Summary of Doctoral Dissertation) *Journal of Economic History,* 27(4), December 1967, pp. 625-8.

Weiss, Thomas J. "United States Transport Advance and Externalities: A Comment on Lebergott," *Journal of Economic History,* 28(4), December 1968, pp. 631-4.

Weiss, Thomas J. "Urbanization and the Growth of the Service Workforce," *Explorations in Economic History,* 8(3), Spring 1971, pp. 241-59.

Weiss, Thomas J. "The Industrial Distribution of the Urban and Rural Workforces: Estimates for the United States, 1870-1910," *Journal of Economic History,* 32(4), December 1972, pp. 919-37.

Weiss, Thomas J. *The Service Sector in the United States, 1839 through 1899.* New York: Arno Press, 1975.

Weiss, Thomas J. "Economies of Scale in Nineteenth-Century Economic Growth," (Summary of 1975 Research Workshop) *Journal of Economic History,* 36(1), March 1976, pp. 39-41.

Weiss, Thomas J.; Atack, Jeremy and Bateman, Fred. "Risk, the Rate of Return and the Pattern of Investment in 19th Century American Industrialization." [Working Paper]

Weiss, Thomas J.; Atack, Jeremy and Bateman, Fred. "The Manuscript Census as a Nineteenth Century Data Source." [Working Paper]

Weiss, Thomas J.; Bateman, Fred and Foust, James D. "Large Scale Manufacturing in the South and West, 1850 and 1860," *Business History Review,* 45(1), Spring 1971, pp. 18-34.

Weiss, Thomas J. and Bateman, Fred. "Comparative Regional Development in Antebellum Manufacturing," *Journal of Economic History,* 35(1), March 1975, pp. 182-208.

Weiss, Thomas J. and Bateman, Fred. "Market Structure before the Age of Big Business: Concentration and Profit in Early Southern Manufacturing," *Business History Review,* 49(3), Autumn 1975, pp. 312-36.

Weiss, Thomas J. and Bateman, Fred. "Manufacturing in the Antebellum South," in Uselding (ed), *Research in Economic History,* 1976.

Weiss, Thomas J.; Bateman, Fred and Foust, James D. "The Participation of Planters in Manufacturing in the Antebellum South," *Agricultural History,* 48(2), April 1974, pp. 277-97.

Weiss, Thomas J.; Bateman, Fred and Atack, Jeremy. "The Regional Diffusion and Adoption of the Steam Engine in American Manufacturing," *Journal of Economic History,* 40(2), June 1980, pp.

492

281-308.

Weiss, Thomas J. and Bateman, Fred. "A Sample of Industrial Firms from the Manuscripts of the U.S. Censuses of Manufacturing, 1850-1870." [Working Paper]

Weiss, Thomas J. and Bateman, Fred. "Industrialization in the Slave Economy." [Working Paper]

Weiss, Thomas J. and Ermisch, John. "The Impact of the Rural Market on the Growth of the Urban Workforce: U.S., 1870-1900," *Explorations in Economic History*, 11(2), Winter 1974, pp. 137-54.

Weiss, Thomas J.; Foust, James and Bateman, Fred. "Profitability in Southern Manufacturing: Estimates for 1860," *Explorations in Economic History*, 12(3), July 1975, pp. 211-32.

Weiss, Thomas J. and Gallman, Robert E. "The Service Industries in the Nineteenth Century," in Fuchs (ed), *Production and Productivity in the Service Industries*, 1969, pp. 287-352.

Weiss, Thomas J. and Gallman, Robert E. "The Service Industries in the Nineteenth Century: Reply to Easterlin, Lebergott, Fabricant, and Firestone," in Fuchs (ed), *Production and Productivity in the Service Industries*, 1969, pp. 372-81.

Weiss, Thomas J. and Schaeffer, Donald F. "The Use of Simulation Techniques in Historical Analysis: Railroads Versus Canals," *Journal of Economic History*, 31(4), December 1971, pp. 854-84.

Weisskoff, Richard and Wolff, Edward. "Development and Trade Dependence: The Case of Puerto Rico, 1848-1963," *Review of Economics and Statistics*, 57(4), November 1975, pp. 470-7.

Weitzman, Martin L. and Cohen, Jon S. "A Mathematical Model of Enclosures," in Los and Los (eds), *Mathematical Models in Economics*, 1974.

Weitzman, Martin L. and Cohen, Jon S. "Enclosures and Depopulation: A Marxian Analysis," in Parker and Jones (eds), *European Peasants and Their Markets*, 1975, pp. 161-76.

Weitzman, Martin L. and Cohen, Jon S. "A Marxian Model of Enclosures," *Journal of Development Economics*, 1(4), February 1975, pp. 287-336.

Weitzman, Martin L. and Cohen, Jon S. "A Marxian Model of Enclosures: Reply to Fenoaltea," *Journal of Development Economics*, 3(2), July 1976, pp. 199-200.

West, E.G. "Tom Paine's Voucher Scheme for Education," *Southern Economic Journal*, 33(3), January 1967, pp. 378-82.

West, E.G. "Social Legislation and the Demand for Children: A Comment on Branson," *Western Economic Journal*, 6(5), December 1968, pp. 419-24.

West, E.G. "Resource Allocation and Growth in Early Nineteenth-Century British Education," *Economic History Review*, Second Series, 23(1), April 1970, pp. 68-95.

West, E.G. "The Interpretation of Early Nineteenth-Century Education Statistics: Reply to Hurt," *Economic History Review*, Second Series, 24(4), November 1971, pp. 633-42.

West, E.G. *Education and the Industrial Revolution*. London: Batsford's, 1975.

West, E.G. "Educational Slowdown and Public Intervention in Nineteenth Century Britain: A Study in the Economics of Bureaucracy," *Explorations in Economic History*, 12(1), January 1975, pp. 61-88.

West, E.G. "The Political Economy of American Public School Legislation," *Journal of Law and Economics*, 19(1), April 1976, pp.

101-28.

West, E.G. "Literacy and the Industrial Revolution," *Economic History Review,* Second Series, 31(3), August 1978, pp. 369-83.

West, Robert C. and Adams, John. "Money, Prices, and Economic Development in India, 1861-1895," *Journal of Economic History,* 39(1), March 1979, pp. 55-68.

Whartenby, Franklee and Parker, William N. "The Growth of Output Before 1840," in Parker (ed), *Trends in the American Economy in the Nineteenth Century,* 1960, pp. 191-212.

Whitaker, John K. and Hudgins, Maxwell W., Jr. "The Floating Pound Sterling of the Nineteen-thirties: An Econometric Study," *Southern Economic Journal,* 44(1), July 1977, pp. 1478-85.

White, Colin M. "The Concept of Social Saving in Theory and Practice," *Economic History Review,* Second Series, 29(1), February 1976, pp. 82-100.

White, Eugene N. "State Deposit Insurance before the FDIC." [Working Paper]

White, Lawrence J. "Enclosures and Population Movement in England, 1700-1830," *Explorations in Entrepreneurial History,* Second Series, 6(2), Winter 1969, pp. 175-86.

Whitney, W.G. "The Structure of the American Economy in the Late Nineteenth Century," Ph.D. Dissertation, Harvard University, 1968.

Whitten, David O. "Tariff and Profit in the Antebellum Louisiana Sugar Industry," (Abstract Appears in the *Journal of Economic Literature,* 9(1), March 1971, pp. 306) *Business History Review,* 44(2), Summer 1970, pp. 226-33.

Whitten, David O. "A Black Entrepreneur in Antebellum Louisiana," *Business History Review,* 45(2), Summer 1971, pp. 201-19.

Whitten, David O. "Sugar Slavery: A Profitability Model of Slave Investments in the Antebellum Louisiana Sugar Industry," *Louisiana Studies,* 12(2), Summer 1973, pp. 423-42.

Whitten, David O. "An Economic Inquiry into the Whisky Rebellion of 1794," *Agricultural History,* 49(3), Summer 1975, pp. 491-504.

Whitten, David O. "Medical Care of Slaves: Louisiana Sugar Region and South Carolina Rice District," *Southern Studies: An Interdisciplinary Journal of the South,* 16(2), Summer 1977, pp. 153-80.

Wicker, Elmus R. "Railroad Investment Before the Civil War," in Parker (ed), *Trends in the American Economy in the Nineteenth Century,* 1960, pp. 503-24.

Wicker, Elmus R. "Federal Reserve Monetary Policy, 1922-1933: A Reinterpretation," *Journal of Political Economy,* 73(4), August 1965, pp. 325-43.

Wicker, Elmus R. "A Reconsideration of the Causes of the Banking Panic of 1930," *Journal of Economic History,* 40(3), September 1980, pp. 571-83.

Wilcox, James A. and Gordon, Robert J. "Monetarist Interpretations of the Great Depression: An Evaluation and Critique," in Brunner (ed), *The Great Depression Revisited,* 1981, pp. 49-107.

Wilcox, James A. and Gordon, Robert J. "Monetarist Interpretations of the Great Depression: A Rejoinder (to Comments by Lothian and Meltzer)," in Brunner (ed), *The Great Depression Revisited,* 1981, pp. 165-73.

Wilcox, William C. and Loschky, David J. "Demographic Transition: A

Forcing Model?," *Demography,* 11(2), May 1974, pp. 215-25.

Wilcox, William C. and Loschky, David J. "Demographic Transition: A Forcing Model?: Reply to Kammeyer and Skidmore," *Demography,* 12(2), May 1975, pp. 351-60.

Wilen, J. and Paterson, Donald G. "Depletion and Diplomacy: The North Pacific Seal Hunt, 1886-1910," in Uselding (ed), *Research in Economic History,* 1977, pp. 81-139.

Wilkening, E.A.; Strassman, W. Paul; Parker, William N. and Merrill, Robert S. *The Diffusion of Technical Knowledge as an Instrument of Economic Development* (Symposia Studies Series no. 13). National Institute of Social and Behavioral Science, 1962.

Wilkinson, Maurice. "Evidences of Long Swings in the Growth of Swedish Population and Related Economic Variables, 1860-1965," *Journal of Economic History,* 27(1), March 1967, pp. 17-38.

Wilkinson, Maurice. "European Migration to the United States: An Econometric Analysis of Aggregate Labor Supply and Demand," *Review of Economics and Statistics,* 52(3), August 1970, pp. 272-9.

Willett, Thomas D. "International Specie Flows and American Monetary Stability, 1834-1860," *Journal of Economic History,* 28(1), March 1968, pp. 28-50.

Williams, J.E. "The British Standard of Living, 1750-1850," in Kellenbenz, Schneider, and Gommel (eds), *Wirtschaftliches Wachstum im Speigel der Wirtschaftsgeschichte,* 1978.

Williams, L.J. and Boyns, T. "Occupation in Wales, 1851-1971," *Bulletin of Economic Research,* 29(2), November 1977, pp. 71-83.

Williamson, Harold F. and Andreano, Ralph L. "Integration and Competition in the Oil Industry: A Review Article," *Journal of Political Economy,* 69(4), August 1961, pp. 381-5.

Williamson, Jeffrey G. "International Trade and United States Economic Development, 1827-1843: Comment on Macesich," reprinted in Cohen and Hill (eds), *American Economic History,* 1966, pp. 245-56. *Journal of Economic History,* 21(3), September 1961, pp. 372-83.

Williamson, Jeffrey G. "The Long Swing: Comparisons and Interactions between British and American Balance of Payments, 1820-1913," reprinted in Hall (eds), *The Export of Capital from Britain,* 1968, pp. 55-83. *Journal of Economic History,* 22(1), March 1962, pp. 21-46.

Williamson, Jeffrey G. "Real Growth, Monetary Disturbances and the Transfer Process: The United States, 1879-1900," *Southern Economic Journal,* 29(3), January 1963, pp. 167-80.

Williamson, Jeffrey G. "Dollar Scarcity and Surplus in Historical Perspective," *American Economic Review,* 53(2), May 1963, pp. 519-29.

Williamson, Jeffrey G. *American Growth and the Balance of Payments, 1820-1913: A Study of the Long Swing.* Chapel Hill: University of North Carolina Press, 1964.

Williamson, Jeffrey G. "Growth and Trade: Some Hypotheses About Long-Term Trade: Discussion of Cooper," *Journal of Economic History,* 24(4), December 1964, pp. 629-33.

Williamson, Jeffrey G. "Regional Inequality and the Process of National Development: A Description of Patterns," reprinted in Needleman (ed), *Regional Analysis,* 1968, pp. 99-158. *Economic Development and Cultural Change,* 13(4), (Part 2), July 1965, pp. 1-84.

495

Williamson, Jeffrey G. "Antebellum Urbanization in the American Northeast," reprinted in Fogel and Engerman (eds), *The Reinterpretation of American Economic History*, 1971, pp. 426-36. *Journal of Economic History*, 25(4), December 1965, pp. 592-608.

Williamson, Jeffrey G. "Consumer Behavior in the Nineteenth Century: Carroll D. Wright's Massachusetts Workers in 1875," *Explorations in Entrepreneurial History*, Second Series, 4(2), Winter 1967, pp. 98-135.

Williamson, Jeffrey G. "Optimal Replacement of Capital Goods: The Early New England and British Textile Firm," *Journal of Political Economy*, 79(6), November/December 1971, pp. 1320-34.

Williamson, Jeffrey G. "Embodiment, Disembodiment, Learning by Doing, and Returns to Scale in Nineteenth Century Cotton Textiles: A Comment on David," *Journal of Economic History*, 32(3), September 1972, pp. 691-705.

Williamson, Jeffrey G. "Late Nineteenth Century Retardation: A Neoclassical Analysis," (See the Editor's Note this Journal, 34(2), June 1974, pp. 501, for an Errata Statement on this article) *Journal of Economic History*, 33(3), September 1973, pp. 581-607.

Williamson, Jeffrey G. "Optimal Replacement of Capital Goods in Early New England and British Textile Firms: Reply to Denslow and Schulze," *Journal of Political Economy*, 82(3), May/June 1974, pp. 638-40.

Williamson, Jeffrey G. "Migration to the New World: Long Term Influences and Impact," *Explorations in Economic History*, 11(4), Summer 1974, pp. 357-89.

Williamson, Jeffrey G. "Watersheds and Turning Points: Conjectures on the Long-Term Impact of Civil War Financing," *Journal of Economic History*, 34(3), September 1974, pp. 636-61.

Williamson, Jeffrey G. "The Railroads and Midwestern Development, 1870-90: A General Equilibrium History," in Klingaman and Vedder (eds), *Essays in Nineteenth Century Economic History*, 1975, pp. 269-352.

Williamson, Jeffrey G. "American Prices and Urban Inequality Since 1820," *Journal of Economic History*, 36(2), June 1976, pp. 303-33.

Williamson, Jeffrey G. "Technology, Growth, History," *Journal of Political Economy*, 84(4), (Part 1), August 1976, pp. 809-20.

Williamson, Jeffrey G. "The Sources of American Inequality, 1896-1948," *Review of Economics and Statistics*, 58(4), November 1976, pp. 387-97.

Williamson, Jeffrey G. "'Strategic' Wage Goods, Prices and Inequality," *American Economic Review*, 67(2), March 1977, pp. 29-41.

Williamson, Jeffrey G. "Inequality, Accumulation, and Technological Imbalance: A Growth-Equity Conflict in American History?," *Economic Development and Cultural Change*, 27(2), January 1979, pp. 231-54.

Williamson, Jeffrey G. "Unbalanced Growth, Inequality and Regional Development: Some Lessons from American History," in Arnold (ed), *Alternatives to Confrontation*, 1980, pp. 3-62.

Williamson, Jeffrey G. "Greasing the Wheels of Sputtering Export Engines: Midwestern Grains and American Growth," *Explorations in Economic History*, 17(3), July 1980, pp. 189-217.

Williamson, Jeffrey G. "Earnings Inequality in Nineteenth-Century Britain," *Journal of Economic History*, 40(3), September 1980, pp.

457-75.

Williamson, Jeffrey G. "Immigrant-Inequality Trade-Offs in the Promised Land: American Growth, Distribution and Immigration Prior to the Quotas," in Chiswick (ed), *The Gateway*, 1981.

Williamson, Jeffrey G. "Inequality and Regional Development: The View from America," in Bairoch and Levy-Leboyer (eds), *Disparities in Economic Development Since the Industrial Revolution*, 1981, pp. 373-91.

Williamson, Jeffrey G. "Urban Disamenities, Dark Satanic Mills and the British Standard of Living Debate," *Journal of Economic History*, 41(1), March 1981, pp. 75-84.

Williamson, Jeffrey G. "What Should the Civil War Tariffs Have Done Anyway?," presented at the Social System Research Institute Workshop, Madison, Wisconsin, October 1973.

Williamson, Jeffrey G. and Brito, D.L. "Skilled Labor and Nineteenth-Century Anglo-American Managerial Behavior," *Explorations in Economic History*, 10(3), Spring 1973, pp. 235-52.

Williamson, Jeffrey G. and De Bever, Leo J. "Saving, Accumulation and Modern Economic Growth: The Contemporary Relevance of Japanese History," *Journal of Japanese Studies*, 4(1), Winter 1978, pp. 125-67.

Williamson, Jeffrey G. and Kelley, Allen C. "Writing History Backwards: Meiji Japan Revisited," *Journal of Economic History*, 31(4), December 1971, pp. 729-76.

Williamson, Jeffrey G.; Kelley, Allen C. and Cheetham, Russell J. *Dualistic Economic Development: Theory and History*. Chicago: University of Chicago Press, 1972.

Williamson, Jeffrey G. and Kelley, Allen C. "Simple Parables of Japanese Economic Progress: Report on Early Findings," in Ohkawa and Hayami (eds), *Nihon Keizai No Chokiteki Bunseki*, 1973.

Williamson, Jeffrey G. and Kelley, Allen C. "Modelling Economic Development and General Equilibrium Histories," *American Economic Review*, Papers and Proceedings, 63(2), May 1973, pp. 450-8.

Williamson, Jeffrey G. and Kelley, Allen C. "General Equilibrium Analysis of Agricultural Development: The Case of Meiji Japan," in Reynolds (ed), *Agricultural Development and Theory*, 1974.

Williamson, Jeffrey G. and Kelley, Allen C. *Lessons from Japanese Development: An Analytical Economic History*. Chicago: University of Chicago Press, 1974.

Williamson, Jeffrey G. and Kelley, Allen C. "Simple Parables of Japanese Economic Progress: Report on Early Findings," in Ohkawa and Hayami (eds), *Long-Term Analysis of the Japanese Economy*, 1974, pp. 141-85.

Williamson, Jeffrey G. and Kmenta, Jan. "Determinants of Investment Behavior: United States Railroads, 1872-1941," *Review of Economics and Statistics*, 48(2), May 1966, pp. 172-81.

Williamson, Jeffrey G. and Lindert, Peter H. "Three Centuries of American Inequality," in Uselding (ed), *Research in Economic History*, 1976, pp. 69-123.

Williamson, Jeffrey G. and Lindert, Peter H. *American Inequality: A Macroeconomic History*. New York: Academic Press, 1980.

Williamson, Jeffrey G. and Lindert, Peter H. "Long Term Trends in American Wealth Inequality," in Smith (ed), *Modeling the Distribution and Intergenerational Transmission of Wealth*, 1980,

497

pp. 9-93.

Williamson, Jeffrey G. and Lindert, Peter H. "English Experience with the Distribution of Wealth and Income Since the Late 17th Century and Their Determinants: A Companion Volume to 'A Macroeconomic History of American Inequality'." [Working Paper]

Williamson, Jeffrey G. and Morley, S. "Class Pay Differentials, Wage Stretching and Early Capitalist Development," in Nash (ed), *Essays on Economic Development and Cultural Change*, 1977, pp. 407-27.

Williamson, Jeffrey G.; Smith, Kenneth R. and Swanson, Joseph A. "The Size Distribution of Cities and Optimal City Size," *Journal of Urban Economics*, 1(4), October 1974, pp. 395-409.

Williamson, Jeffrey G. and Swanson, Joseph A. "The Growth of Cities in the American Northeast, 1820-1870," *Explorations in Entrepreneurial History*, Second Series, 4(1), (Supplement), Fall 1966, pp. 1-101.

Williamson, Jeffrey G. and Swanson, Joseph A. "A Model of Urban Capital Formation and the Growth of Cities in History," *Explorations in Economic History*, 8(2), Winter 1970/71, pp. 213-22.

Williamson, Jeffrey G. and Swanson, Joseph A. "Explanations and Issues: A Prospectus for Quantitative Economic History," *Journal of Economic History*, 31(1), March 1971, pp. 43-57.

Williamson, Jeffrey G. and Swanson, Joseph A. "Firm Location and Optimal City Size in American History," in Schnore (ed), *The New Urban History*, 1975, pp. 260-73.

Williamson, Samuel H. "The Growth of the Great Lakes as a Major Transportation Resource, 1870-1911," in Uselding (ed), *Research in Economic History*, 1977.

Williamson, Samuel H. and Hutchinson, William K. "The Self-Sufficiency of the Antebellum South: Estimates of the Food Supply," *Journal of Economic History*, 31(3), September 1971, pp. 591-612.

Williamson, Samuel H. and Shepherd, James F. "The Coastal Trade of the British North American Colonies, 1768-1772," *Journal of Economic History*, 32(4), December 1972, pp. 783-810.

Williamson, Harold F. and Andreano, Ralph L. "A Reappraisal of the Competitive Structure of the American Petroleum Industry Before 1911," in Andreano (ed), *New Views on American Economic Development*, 1960, pp. 307-16.

Williamson, Harold F. and Andreano, Ralph L. *A History of the American Petroleum Industry* (Two Volumes: vol. 1, 1959; vol. 2, 1963). Evanston: Northwestern University Press, 1959, 1963.

Williamson, Harold F.; Andreano, Ralph L. and Menezes, Carmen. "The American Petroleum Industry," in Brady (ed), *Output, Employment, and Productivity in the United States After 1800*, 1966, pp. 349-403.

Wilson, Charles. "Explaining Open Fields: A Letter to Professor McCloskey," *Journal of European Economic History*, 8(1), Spring 1979, pp. 193-202.

Wimmer, Larry T. "The Gold Crisis of 1869: Stabilizing or Destabilizing Speculation under Floating Exchange Rates?," *Explorations in Economic History* , 12(2), April 1975, pp. 105-22.

Wimmer, Larry T. "Changing Economic Structure and the Rise of Inequality in Early Utah: 1850-1870." [Working Paper]

Wimmer, Larry T. "Income and Wealth in the Nineteenth Century: The Utah Experience." [Working Paper]

Wimmer, Larry T. "Relative Mobility through Nineteenth Century Wealth

Distributions." [Working Paper]

Wimmer, Larry T. "The Gold Crisis of 1869," Ph.D. Dissertation, University of Chicago, 1968.

Wimmer, Larry T. "Utah Heads of Households: Index of the 1850, 1860, and 1870 Censuses." [Working Paper]

Wimmer, Larry T.; Engerman, Stanley L.; Floud, Roderick C.; Fogel, Robert W.; Trussell, James and Pope, Clayne L. "The Economics of Mortality in North America, 1650-1910: A Description of a Research Project," *Historical Methods*, 11(2), June 1978, pp. 75-108.

Wimmer, Larry T.; Hill, Marvin S. and Rooker, C. Keith. *The Kirtland Economy Revisited*. Provo, Utah: Brigham Young University Press, 1978.

Wimmer, Larry T.; Kearl, J.R. and Pope, Clayne L. "Household Wealth in a Settlement Economy: Utah, 1850-1870," *Journal of Economic History*, 40(3), September 1980, pp. 477-96.

Wimmer, Larry T. and Pope, Clayne L. "The Genealogical Society of Salt Lake City: A Source of Data for Economic and Social Historians," *Historical Methods*, 8(2), March 1975, pp. 51-8.

Winnick, Louis; Grebler, Leo and Blank, David M. *Capital Formation in Residential Real Estate: Trends and Prospects*. Princeton: Princeton University Press for the National Bureau of Economic Research, 1956.

Winters, Donald L. "Tenant Farming in Iowa, 1860-1900: A Study of the Terms of Rental Leases," *Agricultural History*, 48(1), January 1974, pp. 130-50.

Winters, Donald L. "Tenancy as an Economic Institution: The Growth and Distribution of Agricultural Tenancy in Iowa, 1850-1900," *Journal of Economic History*, 37(2), June 1977, pp. 382-408.

Winters, Donald L. *Farmers Without Farms: Agricultural Tenancy in Nineteenth Century Iowa*. Westport, Conn.: Greenwood Press, 1978.

Wogin, Gillian. "The Land Settlement and Freight Rate Policies of the Canadian Pacific Railway: a case study in wealth-maximizing behaviour," Ph.D. Dissertation, Carleton University, Ottawa.

Wolff, Edward and Weisskoff, Richard. "Development and Trade Dependence: The Case of Puerto Rico, 1848-1963," *Review of Economics and Statistics*, 57(4), November 1975, pp. 470-7.

Wolff, Klaus and Freudenberger, Herman. "Transfer of Technology," (Summary of 1976 Research Workshop) *Journal of Economic History*, 37(1), March 1977, pp. 231-4.

Wolpin, Kenneth I. "An Economic Analysis of Crime and Punishment in England and Wales, 1894-1967," *Journal of Political Economy*, 84(6), December 1976.

Wood, Betty and Gray, Ralph. "The Transition from Indentured to Involuntary Servitude in Colonial Georgia," *Explorations in Economic History*, 13(4), October 1976, pp. 353-70.

Wood, G.E.; Nishimura, Shizuya and Mills, T. "The Estimates of Bank Deposits in the U.K., 1870-1913." [Working Paper]

Woodman, Harold D. "The Profitability of Slavery: A Historical Perennial," reprinted in Aitken (ed), *Did Slavery Pay?*, 1971, pp. 1-25. *Journal of Southern History*, 29, August 1963, pp. 303-25.

Woodman, Harold D. "Economic History and Economic Theory: The New Economic History in America," *Journal of Interdisciplinary History*, 3, Autumn 1972, pp. 323-50.

Woodman, Harold D. "Economics and Scientific History," *Journal of*

Interdisciplinary History, 5, Autumn 1974, pp. 295-301.

Woodman, Harold D. "The Old South and the New History," presented at the MSSB-University of Rochester Conference Time on the Cross: A First Appraisal, October 1974.

Woodman, Harold D. "A Model to Explain the Relative Decline of Urban Slavery: Comment on Goldin," in Engerman and Genovese (eds), *Race and Slavery in the Western Hemisphere,* 1975.

Woodman, Harold D. "The Slave and Free Person of Color in an Urban Environment: General Comment," in Engerman and Genovese (eds), *Race and Slavery in the Western Hemisphere,* 1975.

Woodman, Harold D. "New Perspectives on Southern Economic Development: A Comment on Engerman and Rubin," *Agricultural History,* 49(2), April 1975, pp. 374-80.

Woodman, Harold D. "A Cliometric Key for a Historical Lock," *Reviews in American History,* 4, June 1976, pp. 230-6.

Woodman, Harold D. "Female Labor Force Participation: The Origin of Black and White Differences, 1870 and 1880: Comment on Paper by Goldin," *Journal of Economic History,* 37(1), March 1977, pp. 109-12.

Worland, Stephen T. "The 'New' Economic History: Historical and Philosophical Antecedents." [Working Paper]

Woroby, Tamara. "An Examination of Wage Inequality Changes in Canada, 1901-1921," Ph.D. Dissertation, Queen's University, Kingston, Ontario.

Wright, Gavin. "Note on the Manuscript Census Samples," in Parker (ed), *The Structure of the Cotton Economy of the Antebellum South,* 1970, pp. 95-9.

Wright, Gavin. "'Economic Democracy' and the Concentration of Agricultural Wealth in the Cotton South, 1850-1860," reprinted in Parker (ed), *The Structure of the Cotton Economy in the Antebellum South,* 1970. *Agricultural History,* 44(1), January 1970, pp. 63-94.

Wright, Gavin. "Econometric Studies of History," in Intriligator (ed), *Frontiers of Quantitative Economics,* 1971.

Wright, Gavin. "An Econometric Study of Cotton Production and Trade, 1830-1860," *Review of Economics and Statistics,* 53(2), May 1971, pp. 111-20.

Wright, Gavin. "Comments on Papers by Reid, Ransom/Sutch, and Higgs on the Postbellum South Presented to the 32nd Annual Meeting of the Economic History Association," *Journal of Economic History,* 33(1), March 1973, pp. 170-6.

Wright, Gavin. "New and Old Views on the Economics of Slavery: A Review Article," *Journal of Economic History,* 33(2), June 1973, pp. 452-66.

Wright, Gavin. "The Political Economy of New Deal Spending: An Econometric Analysis," *Review of Economics and Statistics,* 56(1), February 1974, pp. 30-8.

Wright, Gavin. "Comments on Dissertations Presented to the 33rd Annual Meeting of the Economic History Association," *Journal of Economic History,* 34(1), March 1974, pp. 304-7.

Wright, Gavin. "Cotton Competition and the Postbellum Recovery of the American South," *Journal of Economic History,* 34(3), September 1974, pp. 610-35.

Wright, Gavin. "The Economic Analysis of Time on the Cross," presented at the MSSB-University of Rochester Conference Time on the Cross: A

First Appraisal, October 1974.

Wright, Gavin. "Slavery and the Cotton Boom," (Symposium on Time on the Cross. Edited by Gary M. Walton) *Explorations in Economic History*, 12(4), October 1975, pp. 439-52.

Wright, Gavin. "Prosperity, Progress, and American Slavery," in David et al (eds), *Reckoning with Slavery*, 1976, pp. 302-38.

Wright, Gavin. *The Political Economy of the Cotton South: Households, Markets, and Wealth in the Nineteenth Century*. New York: W.W. Norton, 1978.

Wright, Gavin. "Freedom and the Southern Economy," *Explorations in Economic History*, 16(1), January 1979, pp. 90-108.

Wright, Gavin. "The Efficiency of Slavery: Another Interpretation," *American Economic Review*, 69(1), March 1979, pp. 219-26.

Wright, Gavin. "Cheap Labor and Southern Textiles before 1880," *Journal of Economic History*, 39(3), September 1979, pp. 655-80.

Wright, Gavin. "World Demand for Cotton during the Nineteenth Century: Reply to Hanson," *Journal of Economic History*, 39(4), December 1979, pp. 1023-4.

Wright, Gavin. "Agriculture in the South," in Porter (ed), *Encyclopedia of American Economic History*, 1980, pp. 371-85.

Wright, Gavin. "Cheap Labor and Southern Progress, 1880-1940," presented to Meetings of Southern Economics Association, November 1977.

Wright, Gavin. "Cheap Labor and Southern Textiles before 1880," presented to the Berkeley-Stanford Economic History Colloquium, June 1978.

Wright, Gavin; Gutman, Herbert; Sutch, Richard C.; Temin, Peter and David, Paul A. *Reckoning with Slavery: A Critical Study in the Quantitative History of American Negro Slavery*. New York: Oxford University Press, 1976.

Wright, Gavin; Gutman, Herbert G.; Sutch, Richard C.; Temin, Peter and David, Paul A. "Time on the Cross and the Burden of Quantitative History," in David, et al (eds), *Reckoning with Slavery*, 1976, pp. 339-57.

Wright, Gavin and Kunreuther, Howard. "Cotton, Corn, and Risk in the Nineteenth Century," *Journal of Economic History*, 35(3), September 1975, pp. 526-51.

Wright, Gavin and Kunreuther, Howard. "Cotton, Corn and Risk in the Nineteenth Century: A Reply to McGuire and Higgs," *Explorations in Economic History*, 14(2), April 1977, pp. 183-95.

Wright, Gavin and Kunreuther, Howard. "Safety-First, Gambling and the Subsistence Farmer," in Roumasset, Boussard, and Singh (ed), *Risk, Uncertainty and Agricultural Development*, 1979, pp. 213-46.

Wright, Gavin and Passell, Peter. "The Effects of Pre-Civil War Territorial Expansion on the Price of Slaves," *Journal of Political Economy*, 80(6), November/December 1972, pp. 1188-202.

Wrigley, E.A. "Family Limitation in Pre-Industrial England.," *Economic History Review*, Second Series, 19(1), April 1966, pp. 82-109.

Wrigley, E.A. "Marital Fertility in Seventeenth-Century Colyton: A Note on Morrow," *Economic History Review*, Second Series, 31(3), August 1978, pp. 429-36.

Wu, Joseph S.K. and Herbst, Anthony F. "Some Evidence of Subsidization: the U.S. Trucking Industry, 1900-1920," *Journal of Economic History*, 33(2), June 1973, pp. 417-33.

Yamada, Saburo and Hayami, Yujiro. "Agricultural Productivity at the Beginning of Industrialization," in Ohkawa, Johnston, and Kaneda (eds), *Agriculture and Economic Growth*, 1970, pp. 105-35.

Yamamura, Kozo. "The Role of the Samurai in the Development of Modern Banking in Japan," *Journal of Economic History*, 27(2), June 1967, pp. 198-220.

Yamamura, Kozo. "A Reexamination of Entrepreneurship in Meiji Japan (1868-1912)," *Economic History Review*, Second Series, 21(1), April 1968, pp. 144-58.

Yamamura, Kozo. "The Role of the Merchant Class as Entrepreneurs and Capitalists in Meiji Japan," *Sozial und Wirtschaftsgeschichte*, June 1969.

Yamamura, Kozo. "Evolution of a Unified Capital Market in Japan, 1889-1925: A Statistical Analysis," [in Japanese] *Shakai Keizai Shigaku (Tokyo University)*, 35(2), Spring 1970.

Yamamura, Kozo. "Agenda for Asian Economic History," *Journal of Economic History*, 31(1), March 1971, pp. 199-207.

Yamamura, Kozo. "The Increasing Poverty of the Samurai in Tokugawa Japan, 1600-1868," *Journal of Economic History*, 31(2), June 1971, pp. 378-406.

Yamamura, Kozo. "Japan, 1868-1912: A Revised View," in Cameron (ed), *Banking and Economic Development*, 1972.

Yamamura, Kozo. "The Role of Banking in Japan's Industrialization," in Cameron (ed), *Banking and Economic Development*, 1972.

Yamamura, Kozo. "Economic Responsiveness in Japanese Industrialization," in Cain and Uselding (eds), *Business Enterprise and Economic Change*, 1973, pp. 173-97.

Yamamura, Kozo. "The Development of Za in Medieval Japan," *Business History Review*, 47(4), Winter 1973, pp. 438-65.

Yamamura, Kozo. "Toward an Economic Analysis of the Sogoshosha," *Japan Business History Review (Keieishi)*, 10(1), Spring 1973.

Yamamura, Kozo. "Toward a Reexamination of the Economic History of Tokugawa Japan, 1600-1867," *Journal of Economic History*, 33(3), September 1973, pp. 509-46.

Yamamura, Kozo. *A Study of Samurai Income and Entrepreneurship.* Cambridge: Harvard University Press, 1974.

Yamamura, Kozo. "The Decline of the Ritsuryo System: Hypotheses on Economic and Institutional Change," *Journal of Japanese Studies*, 1(1), Autumn 1974, pp. 3-38.

Yamamura, Kozo. "General Trading Companies in Japan: Their Origins and Growth," in Patrick (ed), *Industrial Growth and Consequences in Japanese Economic Development*, 1976.

Yamamura, Kozo. "Recent Research in Japanese Economic History, 1600-1945," in Gallman (ed), *Recent Developments in the Study of Economic and Business History*, 1977, pp. 221-45.

Yamamura, Kozo. "Success Illgotten?: The Role of Meiji Militarism in Japan's Technological Change," *Journal of Economic History*, 37(1), March 1977, pp. 113-38.

Yamamura, Kozo. "A Comparative Analysis of Changes in Preindustrial Landholding Patterns and Systems in Japan and in England," in Craig (ed), *The Japanese Experience*, 1978.

Yamamura, Kozo. "Entrepreneurship, Ownership and Management in Japan," in Mathias and Postan (eds), *The Cambridge Economic History of Europe*, 1978, pp. 215-64.

Yamamura, Kozo. "The Agricultural and Commercial Revolution in Japan," in Uselding (ed), *Research in Economic History*, 1980.

Yamamura, Kozo and Crawcour, E.S. "The Tokugawa Monetary System: 1787-1868," *Economic Development and Cultural Change*, 18(4), (Part 1), July 1970, pp. 489-518.

Yamamura, Kozo and Duffy, William J. "Monetization and Integration of Markets in Tokugawa Japan: A Spectral Analysis," *Explorations in Economic History*, 8(4), Summer 1971, pp. 395-423.

Yamamura, Kozo and Hanley, Susan B. "A Quiet Transformation in Tokugawa Economic History," *Journal of Asian Studies*, 30(2), February 1971, pp. 373-84.

Yamamura, Kozo and Hanley, Susan B. "Population Trends and Economic Growth in Preindustrial Japan," in Glass and Revelle (eds), *Population and Social Change*, 1972.

Yamamura, Kozo and Hanley, Susan B. "Quantitative Data for Japanese Economic History," in Lorwin and Price (eds), *The Dimensions of the Past*, 1972, pp. 503-30.

Yamamura, Kozo and Hanley, Susan B. *Economic and Demographic Change in Preindustrial Japan, 1600-1868*. Princeton: Princeton University Press, 1977.

Yamada, Saburo and Hayami, Yujiro. "Agriculture, 1880-1965," in Ohkawa and Hayami (eds), *Economic Growth*, 1973, pp. 7-25.

Yamamura, Kozo and Klein, Maury. "The Growth Strategies of Southern Railroads, 1865-1893," *Business History Review*, 41(4), Winter 1967, pp. 358-77.

Yamamura, Kozo and Lewis, Kenneth A. "Industrialization and Interregional Interest Rate Structure, The Japanese Case: 1889-1925," *Explorations in Economic History*, 8(4), Summer 1971, pp. 473-99.

Yamamura, Kozo and Rosovsky, Henry. "Entrepreneurial Studies in Japan: An Introduction," *Business History Review*, 44(1), Spring 1970, pp. 1-12.

Yasuba, Yasukichi. "The Profitability and Viability of Plantation Slavery in the United States," reprinted in Fogel and Engerman (eds), *The Reinterpretation of American Economic History*, 1971, pp. 362-8. *Economic Studies Quarterly*, 12(1), September 1961, pp. 60-7.

Yasuba, Yasukichi. *Birth Rates of the White Population in the United States, 1800-1860: An Economic Study*. Baltimore: Johns Hopkins University Press, 1962.

Yasuba, Yasukichi; Sakudo, Yotaro and Miyamoto, Mataji. "Economic Development in Preindustrial Japan, 1859-1894," *Journal of Economic History*, 25(4), December 1965, pp. 541-64.

Yasuba, Yasukichi. "A Revised Index of Industrial Production for Japan, 1905-1935," *Osaka Economic Papers*, 19(34), March 1971, pp. 19-41.

Yasuba, Yasukichi. "General Comments on Statistical Estimates," in Ohkawa and Hayami (eds), *Economic Growth*, 1973, pp. 165-72.

Yasuba, Yasukichi. "The Evolution of Dualistic Wage Structure," in Patrick (ed), *Japanese Industrialization and its Social*

Consequences, 1976.

Yasuba, Yasukichi. "Freight Rates and Productivity in Ocean Transportation for Japan, 1875-1943," *Explorations in Economic History,* 15(1), January 1978, pp. 11-39.

Yeager, Leland B. "Fluctuating Exchange Rates in the Nineteenth Century: The Experiences of Austria and Russia," in Mundell and Swoboda (eds), *Monetary Problems and the International Economy,* 1969, pp. 61-89.

Yeager, LeLand B. *International Monetary Relations: Theory, History and Policy* (Second Edition). New York: Harper & Row, 1976.

Yeager, Mary. "Comment on Dissertations by Rotella and Easton Presented to the 38th Annual Meeting of the Economic History Association," *Journal of Economic History,* 39(1), March 1979, pp. 339-40.

Yeates, Maurice H. "Some Factors Affecting the Spatial Distribution of Chicago Land Values, 1910-1960," *Economic Geography,* 41(1), January 1965, pp. 57-70.

Yoshihara, Kunio. "Productivity Change in the Manufacturing Sector, 1906-65," in Ohkawa and Hayami (eds), *Economic Growth,* 1973, pp. 269-85.

Zabler, Jeffrey F. "Another Look at Industry and Agricultural Wage Differentials, 1800-1830," in Cain (ed), *Proceedings of the Business History Conference,* 1973, pp. 98-110.

Zabler, Jeffrey F. "More on the Wage Rates in the Iron Industry: A Reply to Adams," *Explorations in Economic History,* 11(1), Fall 1973, pp. 95-102.

Zahn, Frank. "Sectorial Labor Migration and Sustained Industrialization in the Japanese Development Experience," *Review of Economics and Statistics,* 53(3), August 1971, pp. 283-7.

Zamagni, Vera. "Istruzione e sviluppo economico: Il caso italiano 1861-1913," [Education and Economic Development: The Case of Italy, 1861-1913] in Toniolo (ed), *Lo sviluppo economico italiano,* 1973, pp. 187-240. Reprinted in Gianni Toniolo (ed), *L'economia italiana,* 1978. pp. 157-78.

Zamagni, Vera. "Le radici agricole del dualismo italiano," [The Agricultural Roots of Italian Dualism] *Nuova rivista storica,* 59(1-2), January-April 1975, pp. 55-99.

Zamagni, Vera. "La dinamica dei salari nel settore industriale," [Wage Movements in the Industrial Sector] in Ciocca and Toniolo (eds), *L'economia italiana nel periodo fascista,* 1976, pp. 329-78.

Zamagni, Vera. *Industrializzazione e squilibri regionali in Italia. Bilancio dell'eta giolittiana* [Industrialization and Regional Imbalance in Italy: An Evaluation of the Giolitti Years]. Bologna: il Mulino, 1978.

Zamagni, Vera. "The Rich in a Late Industrializer: The Case of Italy (1800-1945)," in Rubinstein (ed), *Wealth and the Wealthy in Modern Europe,* 1980.

Zecher, J. Richard and McCloskey, Donald N. "How the Gold Standard Worked, 1880-1914," in Frenkel and Johnson (eds), *The Monetary Approach to the Balance of Payments,* 1975.

Zepp, Thomas M. "On Returns to Scale and Input Substitutability in Slave Agriculture," *Explorations in Economic History,* 13(2), April 1976, pp. 165-78.

Zevin, Robert B. "The Growth of Manufacturing in Early Nineteenth Century New England," (Summary of Doctoral Dissertation) *Journal of Economic History,* 25(4), December 1965, pp. 680-2.

Zevin, Robert B. "The Growth of Cotton Textile Production after 1815," in Fogel and Engerman (eds), *The Reinterpretation of American Economic History*, 1971, pp. 122-47.

Zevin, Robert B. "An Interpretation of American Imperialism," *Journal of Economic History,* 32(1), March 1972, pp. 316-60.

Zevin, Robert B. *The Growth of Manufacturing in Early Nineteenth Century New England.* New York: Arno Press, 1975.

Zevin, Robert B. "The Economics of Normalcy." [Working Paper]